RESTORATION
PLAYS

MODERN LIBRARY COLLEGE EDITIONS

RESTORATION PLAYS

With an Introduction by

BRICE HARRIS

Arizona State University

THE MODERN LIBRARY · *New York*

Distributed by McGRAW-HILL, INC.

CONTENTS

INTRODUCTION

By Brice Harris

Not infrequently these days *Restoration Drama* has come erroneously to denote those comedies of manners which flourished between the appearance of George Etherege's *Comical Revenge* (1664) and William Congreve's *Way of the World* (1700). This popular error, easy to make and to perpetrate, is almost justifiable. Indeed, no plays in Restoration England came anywhere so near reflecting certain aspects of social London and ,the Court of Westminster as did those of Wycherley, Farquhar, Vanbrugh, Etherege, and Congreve. Other plays on the billboards reflected the current scene hardly at all except perhaps in indicating the taste of its audiences.

Thus Shakespeare, Ben Jonson, and Beaumont and Fletcher were popular during this forty-year period, but their plays, revived, adapted, or transmuted to satisfy the requirements of French classicism, were scarcely localized or timely. The blank-verse tragedies of Dryden, Otway, Nat Lee, and lesser writers were historical, or romantic, or "Elizabethan," and only occasionally topical. Despite its overwhelming popularity with London audiences, the *heroic drama* of Dryden and Orrery, and less exactly of Davenant and Howard, featured faraway places and remote times. *The Rehearsal* (1671), that delightful extravaganza which helped to terminate the rage of *heroic drama,* and the Jonsonian plays of Thomas Shadwell were, to be sure, closer to the London scene. Hence, it is understandable when twentieth-century readers think first of the Lord Foppingtons, the Dorimants, the Millamants, and the Miss Hoydens, their wit and their foibles and their indiscretions, as the sole constituents of Restoration drama. Actually, Restoration drama must be regarded as beginning with the formal reopening of the theaters shortly after the return of Charles II in 1660 and continuing to some vague date centering, say, around 1700.

Of these various types, none was more popular for a decade after .664 than the heroic plays of John Dryden, written alone or in collaboration with Sir Robert Howard, his brother-in-law. Sometimes inappropriately called heroic tragedies, these plays were reminiscent of the French prose romances of Calprenède and Mlle. de Scudéry. Male and female characters were dominated almost completely by the passions of love and honor, characteristics that were evident in the decadent drama before 1642. In Dryden's Conquest of Granada (1670), the warrior Almanzor found himself defending his chivalric honor at every turn while the heroine Almahide wept fervent, faithful tears at his feet. The dialogue was bombastic and unreal; the action was noisy and confusing, digressing frequently into songs and dances; the scenery fanciful and operatic. The line was the rhymed couplet, which Dryden defended vigorously as most appropriate for plays until eventually his cause was lost. Tyrannic Love (1669), The Conquest of Granada (1670), and Aureng-Zebe (1675) were the best known of Dryden's heroic plays.

The Rehearsal is best understood and appreciated after one has read an heroic drama, preferably The Conquest of Granada. Conceived as early as 1663 by Villiers, Second Duke of Buckingham, and his witty friends, Thomas Sprat of the Royal Society and the clergy, Martin Clifford, and perhaps even Samuel Butler, The Rehearsal shifted its target twice before selecting Dryden for the bull's-eye. It was aimed first at William Davenant, whose flattened nose still bobs up twice in the play, and then at Sir Robert Howard. Finally Dryden became the Mr. Bayes, poet of mode, who invited Smith and Johnson to witness the rehearsal of his new play. As Bayes screams directions and simpers foolishly to his guests, the poor players stumble through their parts: Thunder, whispering and restrained, and Lightning, slow and halting, render a burlesque prologue; four soldiers advance and give the countersign, are at once killed by four other soldiers whom they in turn kill, and all eight are revived at the sound of a musical note; Prince Pretty-man, rapturously and impatiently awaiting the arrival of his love, Cloris, lies down and falls asleep as she approaches; Drawcansir, obviously Dryden's Almanzor, huffs and puffs across the stage in burlesque heroics that conclude with a monstrous carnival of murder in which his mere appearance frightens to death two armies, one of foot soldiers, one of cavalry riding hobby-horses. Long ere this, Johnson and Smith have sneaked away, and the players are ready for mutiny. Thus, with ridiculous actions and scenes and abundant parody of actual lines from *The Conquest of Granada* and other heroic plays, Buckingham and his fellow wits helped to drive heroic drama from the stage. Read with imagination today, *The Rehearsal* can be almost as rollicking, merry, clever, sharp, and unforgettable as it was in 1671.

Dryden had fought valiantly for rhymed drama by providing several examples of it as well as by defending it in critical essays. Toward the end of his *Essay of Dramatic Poesy* (1668) he stated at length his preference for rhyme, and for a period of years argued the point with his brother-in-law, Sir Robert Howard, a controversy which he himself summarized at the conclusion of his *Defence of an Essay*. But steadily his convictions in the matter were changing. By 1675 in the prologue to *Aureng-Zebe* he confessed a truth: he was growing "weary of his long-lov'd mistress, Rhyme." He was ready for Shakespeare's medium, blank verse, and for Shakespeare's tragic subjects, for example, the story of Antony and Cleopatra.

All for Love (1678) was not Dryden's first adaptation of
Shakespeare, but it was his best as well as his greatest tragedy.
Here he eschewed rhetoric as well as rhyme and confined himself
to the neo-classical principles of the unities, which Crites had so
carefully explained in the *Essay of Dramatic Poesy*. Where
Shakespeare's Antony took twelve years to fret his way across
the stage, Dryden's appeared for one day only, his last. Thus, the
unity of time. In *Antony and Cleopatra,* action shifted at will between Alexandria, Rome, Athens, Messina, Actium, and various
other parts of the Roman Empire, whereas in *All for Love,* the
setting was solely Alexandria. Thus the unity of place. Dryden
cut the cast of characters from thirty-odd to a round dozen, and
restricting the narrative closely to the last affairs of Antony and
Cleopatra, emphasized the unity of action. For Enobarbus, clownish and human and realistic, he found no place, but for Ventidius
he created a place second only to the protagonists. Dryden's Cleopatra, too, lacked the "infinite variety" of Shakespeare's Cleopatra. She and Antony played the game of Love and Honor with
the simple emotions of Almahide and Almanzor. The story itself
needs no summarizing, but the first scene between Ventidius and
Antony, Dryden's favorite, and the dramatic meeting of Octavia
and Cleopatra in Act III are memorable.

Venice Preserved (1682), Thomas Otway's masterpiece and the
outstanding blank-verse tragedy of the Restoration, relates the
poignant story of a sensitive but irresolute young Venetian named
Jaffeir, his courageous friend, Pierre, and his tender and devoted
wife, Belvidera. Mistreated by his father-in-law, the senator
Priuli, Jaffeir listens readily to Pierre's plot to destroy the state.
During a series of night scenes he moves for a time in the sordid
world of anxious conspirators and an attractive harlot, Aquilina.
Then Jaffeir tells Belvidera of the plot. She encourages him to tell
the Senate all that he knows and request a pardon for the conspirators. Instead, the conspirators are condemned, and though

Belvidera secures a belated pardon for them through Priuli, Jaffeir stabs himself and Pierre at the scaffold. As the ghosts of Pierre and Jaffeir rise and sink before her, Belvidera goes mad and dies of a broken heart.

The comic underplot of the tragedy, variously admired and despised by readers, ridicules Anthony Ashley Cooper, Earl of Shaftesbury, as the Venetian senator Antonio. In name, appearance, age (each is sixty-one), and ambitions the comparison is exact. The conspiracy in Venice clearly reminds Otway of the recent "Popish Plot" in England. Belvidera, not present in St. Réal's *La Conjuration,* Otway's source, is his greatest character—tender, sensitive, Shakespearean. *Venice Preserved,* in fact, is Elizabethan rather than classical despite the fact that the unities of time and place are not forgotten. Romantic poetry is here, pity and sympathy and compassion are here, and so are those personal conflicts of love and friendship so peculiar to Shakespeare. Finally, this play is close to being a tragedy of the hearth, a domestic tragedy, of the type which Nicholas Rowe composed so successfully a generation later.

Otway, Dryden, and Nat Lee dominated blank-verse tragedy of the Restoration although Lee's plays have seldom become anthology pieces in the twentieth century. *The Rival Queens* (1677), his most popular play in his time and for a century after, is still the best known today. It recounts the story of Roxana and Statira, the two wives of Alexander the Great, who vie with each other to retain or regain his favor. Characterized by rant, melodrama, and artifice, *The Rival Queens* has bequeathed a much-used phrase to posterity: "When Greeks joined Greeks, then was the tug of war" (IV, ii, 419), although posterity seldom knows the source of the quotation and almost universally misquotes it. A more impressive blank-verse tragedy than any of Lee's was Otway's *The Orphan* (1680), the absorbing and emotional story of Polydore and Castalio, twin brothers who were in love with the same girl, the orphaned Monimia. With the exception of *All for Love,* Dryden's tragedies were not in the same class with Otway's two well-known tragedies.

The comedies of manners obviously did not encompass all of Restoration drama nor did they spring full grown from Restoration soil. Their rise was not independent or spontaneous, flaring up overnight after Restoration society discovered that it liked to see its image on the stage. The comedies of Molière influenced the English comedies of manners materially, but certain native tendencies and directions were more important. A courtly mode of conduct had found favor in Cavalier society before the Puritan ascendancy. Quite naturally it had become conventionalized and by the time Etherege began to write, its comic aspects were obvious. This social mode of life, where gallantry, wit, and artificiality were dominant, provided the chief materials of Restoration comedy. Indeed, the gay couples in these plays, the Harriets and the Dorimants who amused themselves with the game of love, have been successfully traced from Shakespeare through Fletcher and Suckling and Killigrew down to Etherege.

The conventionalized pattern which the social mode of Restoration life demanded of its followers was not basically different in intent from that of many other manners groups. It was simply more rigid. Its code was drawn with hair lines. Its fashionable gentlemen and ladies must meet the requirements if they wished to avoid the scorn and the ridicule that would inevitably follow if they erred or fell short. Those who professed the code and did not abide by it were even more amusing than the unfortunates who made no attempt to follow it. Thus country people, clergymen, scholars and poets, merchants and tradesmen, in fact anybody who worked for his living, had no time to engage in such activities. But dancing across the stage was an entire generation of fops and dunces, coquettes and mistresses, pseudo-wits and social enthusiasts of various orders that rocked the theater audiences with laughter. It is supremely easy for a modern reader to fall into step with this sophisticated and artificial brilliance and to enjoy it thoroughly. The steady barrage of wit, the cruelty of youth to crabbed age, the emptiness of an artificial social world, the sadistic abandonment to limbo of those who do not live as someone else thinks they should—all these may grow wearisome, may surfeit a reader at a distance of nearly three hundred years. However that may be, let us hope that he will not weary of the five representative plays here included: two from the early period by Etherege and Wycherley, three from the later period by Congreve, Vanbrugh, and Farquhar. These plays will span the thirty-two years from 1675 to 1707.

The Man of Mode (1676) was the last in point of time of three plays by Sir George Etherege, the other two being *The Comical Revenge* (1664) and *She Would if She Could* (1668). The story is negligible. One may not be chided for forgetting what happens in this play, but one can scarcely forget the animated scenes: Dorimant and Foggy Nan, the Orange-Woman; or Sir Fopling fresh from Paris, perfumed and overdressed and lisping, laughed at and mimicked by the wits; or Old Bellair shouting his pet expression "A-dod," paying suit to his son's lover, and otherwise amusing youth at the expense of crabbed age; or Dorimant passing himself off to Lady Woodvill as plain Mr. Courtage and affecting to love things old fashioned; or Bellinda paying an unexpected visit to Dorimant's mistress because the chairman assumed that she was the usual woman retreating from Dorimant's backstairs. Nor can one forget the duel of wits between the gay lovers, Harriet and Dorimant. Each is determined not to appear unfashionably in love, not to be the first to admit his love. From the moment that Dorimant first appears, repeating Edmund Waller's verses, to the concluding scene where Harriet is telling Dorimant about her melancholy country life, the dialogue abounds with epigram and simile, cleverness and innuendo. It was supposed in that day that Dorimant was a likeness of Lord Rochester, Medley was Sir Charles Sedley, Sir Fopling was Beau Hewitt. Enjoyment of the play does not turn on such topical interpretation. Dorimant shared his typical qualities with many of the courtiers of Charles II.

The Country Wife (1675), the third of William Wycherley's four plays, is a true comedy of manners, relatively free from the scorn, disillusion, and pessimism of *The Plain-Dealer,* his last play. By the very nature of his trickery Horner exhibits a certain scorn of mankind, but it is hardly noticeable compared to Manly's, which, combined with the sarcastic dedication to Madam B., places him well within the ranks of Butler and Swift. But Horner is still the courtier, the ideal gentleman of the social mode. Borrowing an idea from Terence's eunuch, he announces his impotency and thus unsuspected enjoys the favors of the Lady Fidget while the fops and pseudo-wits ridicule him. When Pinchwife, worn-out beau and jealous benedict, brings his wife Margery to London, Horner sees her at a play and pays his suit to her. Disguising her as a boy only aids and abets Horner's schemes. Now Pinchwife dictates a strong letter for her to sign and is duped by Margery into carrying a substitute letter to Horner in which she declares her regards. Conveyed by her own husband, who thinks the disguised girl is his sister Alithea, to Horner's apartment, Margery returns denying the reports about Horner. Pinchwife is assured by his sister and his erstwhile friend, Horner, that Margery is innocent, and apparently believes them. Pinchwife's jealousy is cleverly contrasted with the quite different attitudes of two other men on the same subject. The fop Sparkish poses as completely free from jealousy, so free that he encourages Harcourt to make love to Alithea before his very eyes. Sir Jasper Fidget, on the other hand, is so convinced of Horner's impotency that he laughs himself sick in one room while Lady Fidget and

Horner close the door in the next room to examine china—the famous china scene.

The Relapse (1696), first of a sizable number of plays by Sir John Vanbrugh, was a sequel to a play which is almost forgotten except by the learned—Colley Cibber's *Love's Last Shift,* produced early in 1696. Cibber at the time was a hanger-on at the Theatre Royal, an occasional actor who aspired to write. Either he was lucky or he recognized keenly the straws in the winds of public taste, for his *Love's Last Shift* was the first of the sentimental comedies that were to absorb the minds of early eighteenth-century audiences. The story of Cibber's play can be told in one sentence: Loveless, who deserted Amanda eight years ago, comes back to London, so completely fails to recognize her that he chooses her for his mistress, and then turns into a tender and repentant spouse when she convinces him of her identity. But John Vanbrugh saw the play and was not convinced by Loveless's repentance. *The Relapse* was his answer. Cibber himself was apparently not overcome by the dignity and seriousness of his play, in which he had taken the part of Sir Novelty Fashion, the coxcomb. He was delighted to act the part of Lord Foppington in Vanbrugh's play.

Loveless and Amanda are transferred to the cast of characters in *The Relapse,* and Sir Novelty is dubbed with a title, Lord Foppington. Vanbrugh changes the rest of the cast, it must be confessed, much to the improvement of personalities and of narrative. Sir Tunbelly Clumsey, country gentleman, and his flippant and irresponsible daughter, Miss Hoyden, both of whom break the social code at every turn, are as amusing a pair of characters as one could find in any comedy of the day. To revert to the main plot, Loveless assures Amanda that he will suffer no *relapse* into past indiscretions when he returns to London. But becoming enamored of a young widow named Berinthia, Loveless proceeds to disprove to Vanbrugh's entire satisfaction those qualities of repentance with which Cibber had endowed him in *Love's Last Shift*.

Two years after Vanbrugh's *Relapse* and two years before Congreve's *Way of the World*, Jeremy Collier blasted plays, players, and playgoers with his *Short View of the Immorality and Profaneness of the English Stage*. Various societies for reforming manners had sprung up during the 1690's, Dryden had earlier declaimed against the "steaming ordures of the stage" in those "lubric and adult'rate" times, and Cibber had wittingly or unwittingly hit upon a formula for writing clean plays. But it remained for Collier to supply the blow that actually destroyed them. The divine had read and digested a great many more plays than one would expect from the cloth. Furthermore, he had copiously extracted passages which he published, some of them proving his point, some of them proving nothing. But public opinion was largely on his side, and in the pamphlet warfare that followed, the controversy that bears his name, he won most of the battles.

The Way of the World (1700) was the last of four deservedly famous comedies which Congreve wrote, the other three being *The Old Batchelor* (1693), *The Double Dealer* (1693), and *Love for Love* (1695). Congreve, like Vanbrugh, was accused in Collier's *Short View*. It would seem that *The Way of the World* was his best answer to Collier, despite the fact that the public only mildly approved it. Here again the story is of small moment. The importance lies in the brilliance, the sparkle of the dialogue, the ridicule of false wit of which Witwoud and Petulant were guilty, and the exhibition of true wit in the word combats of Millamant and Mirabell. Here in one closely woven fabric are the ideal gentleman and lady who live scrupulously by the code, and here are the numerous defaulters. Lady Wishfort is the antiquated coquette who uses too much rouge and flutters painfully at middle age over the appearance of a budding love—Restoration dramatists and poets chronicled her type as gleefully as Horace did. Sir Wilfull is a drunkard and a rustic, therefore amusing. Mrs. Marwood and Mrs. Fainall have fallen unfashionably in love. Thus every character is pegged into a rigid position, and his character is carefully defined in the code of the day. The brilliance and the cruelty of the play are overwhelming and somewhat wearisome. But few readers will deny that *The Way of the World* is the ultimate in the Restoration comedy of manners. Whether they find it greater than more recent comedies of manners, say those of Oscar Wilde or Noel Coward, will depend on their own critical taste.

The Beaux' Stratagem (1707), George Farquhar's last play, has always been included with the best of the Restoration comedies of manners, despite the fact that in point of time it is out of line. It may be called a transition piece. Like Farquhar's early plays, which began to appear in 1698, it has some though not so much of the Restoration temper. But it also adheres to many of the principles of sentimental comedy. Aimwell, whose very name connotes the moral change, falls unfashionably in love with Dorinda and, romantically repentant, approaches the altar. The story of the stratagem of the two penniless beaus is also important and well told, 'an ingredient seldom found in the strict comedy of manners. Escaping to the country in search of adventures that will fill their flat purses, Aimwell and Archer meet Lady Bountiful's daughter, Dorinda, and her son's wife, Mrs. Sullen. After several mad and merry episodes, Aimwell receives his reward and Archer is well on the way to fortune and a wife, albeit a divorcée. Farquhar successfully fuses plot, situation, and character. He connects dialogue with plot and character, largely eschewing mere verbal brilliance. He leaves the refined circles in London rendezvous—their walks, their parks, their drawing-rooms—and hastens to Lichfield where he introduces one to real bourgeois life. Cherry and Boniface from the local inn are there, and Bagshot, the highwayman, and his companions are there. These people breathe. Blood flows in their veins. They remind one of characters in Fielding's or Smollett's novels. There is naturalness and fidelity to life. The comedy of manners is well on its way to the superb art form best expressed by Goldsmith and Sheridan in their comedies of the 1760's and 1770's.

SELECTED BIBLIOGRAPHY

GENERAL

Alleman, Gellert S., *Matrimonial Law and the Materials of Restoration Comedy*. Wallingford, Pennsylvania, 1942.

Barber, C. L., *The Idea of Honour in the English Drama, 1591-1700*. Stockholm, 1957.

Berkeley, David S., "*Préciosité* and the Restoration Comedy of Manners," *Huntington Library Quarterly*, XVIII (1955), 109-128.

Berkeley, David S., "The Art of 'Whining' Love," *Studies in Philology*, LII (1955), 478-496.

Dobrée, Bonamy, *Restoration Comedy, 1660-1720*. Oxford, 1924.

Dobrée, Bonamy, *Restoration Tragedy, 1660-1720*. Oxford, 1929.

Fujimura, Thomas H., *The Restoration Comedy of Wit*. Princeton, 1952.

Holland, Norman N., *The First Modern Comedies: The Significance of Etherege, Wycherley, and Congreve*. Cambridge, 1959.

Hughes, Leo, *A Century of English Farce*. Princeton, 1956.

Krutch, Joseph Wood, *Comedy and Conscience after the Restoration*. New Haven, 1925.

Lynch, Kathleen M., *The Social Mode of Restoration Comedy*. New York, 1926.

Mignon, Elisabeth, *Crabbed Age and Youth*. Durham, North Carolina, 1947.

Nicoll, Allardyce, *A History of Restoration Drama, 1660-1700*. Cambridge, England, 1923.

Palmer, John, *The Comedy of Manners*. London, 1913.

Perry, Henry Ten Eyck, *The Comic Spirit in Restoration Drama*. New Haven, 1925.

Restoration and 18th Century Theatre Research, ed. Carl J. Stratman and David G. Spencer. Loyola University, Chicago, annually since 1962.

Smith, John Harrington, *The Gay Couple in Restoration Comedy.* Cambridge, 1948.

Wain, John, "Restoration Comedy and its Modern Critics," *Essays in Criticism,* VI (1956), 367-385.

Woodward, G. L. and J. G. McManaway, *A Check List of English Plays, 1641-1700.* Chicago, 1945. Supplement by F. T. Bowers, Charlottesville, 1949.

INDIVIDUAL AUTHORS

Congreve, *Complete Works,* ed. Montague Summers. London, 1923, 4 vols.

Hodges, John C., *William Congreve, the Man.* New York, 1941.

Mueschke, Paul and Miriam, *A New View of Congreve's "Way of the World."* Ann Arbor, 1958.

Taylor, D. Crane, *William Congreve.* London, 1931.

Dryden, *Dramatic Works,* ed. Montague Summers. London, 1931-2, 6 vols.

Fujimura, Thomas H., "The Appeal of Dryden's Heroic Plays," *Publications of the Mod. Lang. Ass'n,* LXXV (1960), 37-45.

Gagen, Jean, "Love and Honor in Dryden's Heroic Plays," *Publications of the Mod. Lang. Ass'n,* LXXVII (1963), 208-220.

Osborn, Scott C., "Heroical Love in Dryden's Heroic Drama," *Publications of the Mod. Lang. Ass'n,* LXXIII (1958), 165-167.

Etherege, *Works,* ed. H. F. B. Brett-Smith. Oxford, 1927, 2 vols.

Underwood, Dale, *Etherege and the Seventeenth Century Comedy of Manners.* New Haven, 1957.

Farquhar, *Complete Works,* ed. Charles Stonehill. London, 1930, 2 vols.

Lee, *Works*, ed. Thomas B. Stroup and Arthur L. Cooke. New Brunswick, 1954, 2 vols.

Otway, *Works*, ed. J. C. Ghosh. Oxford, 1932, 2 vols.

  Ham, Roswell G., *Otway and Lee*. New Haven, 1931.

  Hauser, David R., "Otway Preserved; Theme and Form in *Venice Preserv'd*," *Studies in Philology*, LV (1958), 481-493.

  McBurney, William H., "Otway's Tragic Muse Debauch'd: Sensuality in *Venice Preserv'd*," *Jour. Engl. and Ger. Philology*, LVIII (1959), 380-399.

Vanbrugh, *Complete Works*, ed. Bonamy Dobrée and Geoffrey Webb. London, 1927-8, 4 vols.

  Whistler, Lawrence, *Sir John Vanbrugh, Architect and Dramatist*. London, 1938.

Wycherley, *Complete Works*, ed. Montague Summers. London, 1924, 4 vols.

  Connely, Willard, *Brawny Wycherley*. New York and London, 1930.

  Craik, T. W., "Some Aspects of Satire in Wycherley's Plays," *English Studies*, XLI (1960), 168-179.

  Rogers, K. M., "Fatal Inconsistency: Wycherley and *The Plain Dealer*," *Jour. of Engl. Literary Hist.*, XXVIII (1961), 148-162.

RESTORATION PLAYS

The Rehearsal

By GEORGE VILLIERS

Duke of Buckingham

(AND OTHERS)

PROLOGUE

We might well call this short mock-play of ours
A posy made of weeds instead of flowers;
Yet such have been presented to your noses,
And there are such, I fear, who thought 'em roses.
Would some of 'em were here, to see, this night,
What stuff it is in which they took delight.
Here, brisk, insipid rogues, for wit, let fall
Sometimes dull sense; but oft'ner, none at all:
There, strutting heroes, with a grim-fac'd train,
Shall brave the gods, in King Cambyses' vein.
For (changing rules, of late, as if men writ
In spite of reason, nature, art, and wit)
Our poets make us laugh at tragedy,
And with their comedies they make us cry.
Now, critics, do your worst, that here are met;
For, like a rook, I have hedg'd in my bet.
If you approve, I shall assume the state
Of those high-flyers whom I imitate:
And justly too, for I will teach you more
Than ever they would let you know before:
I will not only show the feats they do,

3

> But give you all their reasons for 'em too.
> Some honour may to me from hence arise.
> But if, by my endeavours, you grow wise,
> And what you once so prais'd shall now despise,
> Then I'll cry out, swell'd with poetic rage,
> 'Tis I, John Lacy, have reform'd your stage.

THE ACTORS' NAMES

MEN:

BAYES	TOM THIMBLE
JOHNSON	FISHERMAN
SMITH	SUN
TWO KINGS OF BRENTFORD	THUNDER
PRINCE PRETTY-MAN	PLAYERS
PRINCE VOLSCIUS	SOLDIERS
GENTLEMAN USHER	TWO HERALDS
PHYSICIAN	FOUR CARDINALS
DRAWCANSIR	MAYOR
GENERAL	JUDGES
LIEUTENANT-GENERAL	SERGEANTS AT ARMS
CORDELIO	

⎱MUTES (bracketing FOUR CARDINALS, MAYOR, JUDGES, SERGEANTS AT ARMS)

WOMEN:

AMARYLLIS
CLORIS
PARTHENOPE
PALLAS
LIGHTNING
MOON
EARTH

Attendants of Men and Women

SCENE: *Brentford*

THE REHEARSAL

ACT I

JOHNSON *and* SMITH

JOHNSON. Honest Frank! I'm glad to see thee with all my heart: how long hast thou been in town?

SMITH. Faith, not above an hour: and, if I had not met you here, I had gone to look you out; for I long to talk with you freely, of all the strange new things we have heard in the country.

JOHNSON. And, by my troth, I have longed as much to laugh with you, at all the impertinent, dull, fantastical things we are tired out with here.

SMITH. Dull and fantastical! that's an excellent composition. Pray, what are our men of business doing?

JOHNSON. I ne'er enquire after 'em. Thou knowest my humour lies another way. I love to please myself as much, and to trouble others as little as I can: and therefore do naturally avoid the company of those solemn fops who, being incapable of reason, and insensible of wit and pleasure, are always looking grave, and troubling one another, in hopes to be thought men of business.

SMITH. Indeed, I have ever observed that your grave lookers are the dullest of men.

JOHNSON. Aye, and of birds, and beasts too: your gravest bird is an owl, and your gravest beast is an ass.

SMITH. Well; but how dost thou pass thy time?

JOHNSON. Why, as I use to do; eat and drink as well as I can, have a she-friend to be private with in the afternoon, and sometimes see a play; where there are such things, Frank—such hideous, monstrous things—that it has almost made me forswear the stage and resolve to apply myself to the solid nonsense of your men of business, as the more ingenious pastime.

SMITH. I have heard, indeed, you have had lately many new plays; and our country wits commend 'em.

JOHNSON. Aye, so do some of our city wits, too; but they are of the new kind of wits.

SMITH. New kind! what kind is that?

JOHNSON. Why, your virtuosi, your civil persons, your drolls:

5

fellows that scorn to imitate nature, but are given altogether to elevate and surprise.

SMITH. Elevate and surprise? Prithee, make me understand the meaning of that.

JOHNSON. Nay, by my troth, that's a hard matter: I don't understand that myself. 'Tis a phrase they have got among them, to express their no-meaning by. I'll tell you, as near as I can, what it is. Let me see; 'tis fighting, loving, sleeping, rhyming, dying, dancing, singing, crying; and everything but thinking and sense.

MR. BAYES *passes o'er the stage*

BAYES. Your most obsequious, and most observant, very servant, Sir.

JOHNSON. Godso, this is an author! I'll fetch him to you.

SMITH. No, prithee, let him alone.

JOHNSON. Nay, by the Lord, I'll have him. (*goes after him*) Here he is. I have caught him.—— Pray, Sir, now for my sake, will you do a favour to this friend of mine?

BAYES. Sir, it is not within my small capacity to do favours, but receive 'em, especially from a person that does wear the honourable title you are pleased to impose, Sir, upon this.—— Sweet Sir, your servant.

SMITH. Your humble servant, Sir.

JOHNSON. But wilt thou do me a favour, now?

BAYES. Aye, Sir. What is't?

JOHNSON. Why, to tell him the meaning of thy last play.

BAYES. How, Sir, the meaning? Do you mean the plot?

JOHNSON. Aye, aye; anything.

BAYES. Faith, Sir, the intrigo's now quite out of my head; but I have a new one in my pocket, that I may say is a virgin; 't has never yet been blown upon. I must tell you one thing, 'tis all new wit; and though I say it, a better than my last: and you know well enough how that took. In fine, it shall read, and write, and act, and plot, and show—aye, and pit, box and gallery, I gad, with any play in Europe. This morning is its last rehearsal, in their habits, and all that, as it is to be acted; and if you and your friend will do it but the honour to see it in its virgin attire, though, perhaps, it may blush, I shall not be ashamed to discover its nakedness unto you. (*puts his hand in his pocket*) I think it is in this pocket.

JOHNSON. Sir, I confess I am not able to answer you in this new way; but if you please to lead, I shall be glad to follow you; and I hope my friend will do so too.

SMITH. Sir, I have no business so considerable as should keep me from your company.

BAYES. Yes, here it is.—No, cry you mercy! this is my book of *Drama Commonplaces*, the mother of many other plays.

JOHNSON. *Drama Commonplaces!* pray, what's that?

BAYES. Why, Sir, some certain helps that we men of art have found it convenient to make use of.

SMITH. How, Sir, helps for wit?

BAYES. Aye, Sir, that's my position. And I do here aver that no man yet the sun e'er shone upon has parts sufficient to furnish out a stage, except it were by the help of these my rules.

JOHNSON. What are those rules, I pray?

BAYES. Why, Sir, my first rule is the rule of transversion, or *regula duplex:* changing verse into prose, or prose into verse, *alternative* as you please.

SMITH. Well; but how is this done by a rule, Sir?

BAYES. Why, thus, Sir; nothing so easy when understood. I take a book in my hand, either at home or elsewhere, for that's all one —if there be any wit in't, as there is no book but has some, I transverse it: that is, if it be prose, put it into verse (but that takes up some time), and if it be verse, put it into prose.

JOHNSON. Methinks, Mr. Bayes, that putting verse into prose should be called transprosing.

BAYES. By my troth, Sir, 'tis a very good notion, and hereafter it shall be so.

SMITH. Well, Sir, and what d'ye do with it then?

BAYES. Make it my own. 'Tis so changed that no man can know it. My next rule is the rule of record, by way of table book. Pray, observe.

JOHNSON. We hear you, Sir: go on.

BAYES. As thus. I come into a coffee-house, or some other place where witty men resort. I make as if I minded nothing (do you mark?), but as soon as any one speaks, pop! I slap it down, and make that, too, my own.

JOHNSON. But, Mr. Bayes, are you not sometimes in danger of their making you restore, by force, what you have gotten thus by art?

BAYES. No, Sir; the world's unmindful; they never take notice of these things.

SMITH. But pray, Mr. Bayes, among all your other rules, have you no one rule for invention?

BAYES. Yes, Sir, that's my third rule that I have here in my pocket.

SMITH. What rule can that be, I wonder?

BAYES. Why, Sir, when I have anything to invent, I never trouble my head about it, as other men do; but presently turn over this book, and there I have, at one view, all that Perseus, Montaigne, Seneca's tragedies, Horace, Juvenal, Claudian, Pliny, Plutarch's *Lives,* and the rest, have ever thought upon this subject; and so, in a trice, by leaving out a few words or putting in others of my own, the business is done.

JOHNSON. Indeed, Mr. Bayes, this is as sure and compendious a way of wit as ever I heard of.

BAYES. Sirs, if you make the least scruple of the efficacy of these my rules, do but come to the playhouse and you shall judge of 'em by the effects.

SMITH. We'll follow you, Sir.   (*Exeunt.*)

Enter three Players upon the stage

1ST PLAYER. Have you your part perfect?

2D PLAYER. Yes, I have it without book; but I don't understand how it is to be spoken.

3D PLAYER. And mine is such a one as I can't guess for my life what humour I'm to be in—whether angry, melancholy, merry, or in love. I don't know what to make on't.

1ST PLAYER. Phoo! the author will be here presently and he'll tell us all. You must know, this is the new way of writing; and these hard things please forty times better than the old plain way. For, look you, Sir, the grand design upon the stage is to keep the auditors in suspense; for to guess presently at the plot and the sense, tires 'em before the end of the first act. Now, here, every line surprises you and brings in new matter. And, then, for scenes, clothes, and dances, we put 'em quite down, all that ever went before us; and those are the things, you know, that are essential to a play.

2D PLAYER. Well, I am not of thy mind; but, so it gets us money, 'tis no great matter.

Enter BAYES, JOHNSON, *and* SMITH

BAYES. Come, come in, gentlemen. Y'are very welcome, Mr.—a—. Ha' you your part ready?

1ST PLAYER. Yes, Sir.

BAYES. But do you understand the true humour of it?

1ST PLAYER. Aye, Sir, pretty well.

BAYES. And Amaryllis, how does she do? Does not her armour become her?

3D PLAYER. Oh, admirably!

BAYES. I'll tell you, now, a pretty conceit. What do you think I'll make 'em call her anon, in this play?

SMITH. What, I pray?

BAYES. Why, I'll make 'em call her Armaryllis, because of her armour—ha, ha, ha!

JOHNSON. That will be very well, indeed.

BAYES. Aye, it's a pretty little rogue; I knew her face would set off armour extremely, and, to tell you true, I writ that part only for her. You must know she is my mistress.

JOHNSON. Then I know another thing, little Bayes, that thou hast had her, I gad.

BAYES. No, I gad, not yet; but I'm sure I shall, for I have talked bawdy to her already.

JOHNSON. Hast thou, faith? Prithee, how was that?

BAYES. Why, Sir, there is, in the French tongue, a certain criticism which, by the variation of the masculine adjective instead of the feminine, makes a quite different signification of the word: as, for example, *Ma vie* is my life; but if before *vie* you put *Mon* instead of *Ma*, you make it bawdy.

JOHNSON. Very true.

BAYES. Now, Sir, I, having observed this, set a trap for her the other day in the tiring-room; for this said I: *Adieu, bel esperansa de ma vie* (which, I gad, is very pretty); to which she answered, I vow, almost as prettily every jot. For, said she, *Songes à ma vie, Mounsieur;* whereupon I presently snapped this upon her: *Non, non, Madam—songes vous à mon,* by gad, and named the thing directly to her.

SMITH. This is one of the richest stories, Mr. Bayes, that ever I heard of.

BAYES. Aye, let me alone, I gad, when I get to 'em; I'll nick 'em, I warrant you. But I'm a little nice; for you must know, at this time I am kept by another woman in the city.

SMITH. How kept? for what?

BAYES. Why, for a *beau gerson*. I am, i'fackins.

SMITH. Nay, then, we shall never have done.

BAYES. And the rogue is so fond of me, Mr. Johnson, that I vow to gad, I know not what to do with myself.

JOHNSON. Do with thyself! No; I wonder how thou canst make a shift to hold out at this rate.

BAYES. O devil, I can toil like a horse; only sometimes it makes me melancholy; and then, I vow to gad, for a whole day together I am not able to say you one good thing if it were to save my life.

SMITH. That we do verily believe, Mr. Bayes.

BAYES. And that's the only thing, I gad, which mads me in my amours; for I'll tell you, as a friend, Mr. Johnson, my acquaintances, I hear, begin to give it out that I am dull. Now I am the farthest from it in the whole world, I gad; but only, forsooth, they think I am so, because I can say nothing.

JOHNSON. Phoo! Pox! That's ill-naturedly done of 'em.

BAYES. Aye, gad, there's no trusting o' these rogues; but—a—come, let's sit down. Look you, Sirs, the chief hinge of this play, upon which the whole plot moves and turns, and that causes the variety of all the several accidents, which, you know, are the things in nature that make up the grand refinement of a play, is that I suppose two kings to be of the same place—as, for example, at Brentford, for I love to write familiarly. Now the people having the same relations to 'em both, the same affections, the same duty, the same obedience, and all that, are divided among themselves in point of *devoir* and interest, how to behave themselves equally between 'em: these kings differing sometimes in particular, though in the main they agree. (I know not whether I make myself well understood.)

JOHNSON. I did not observe you, Sir; pray, say that again.

BAYES. Why, look you, Sir (nay, I beseech you, be a little curious in taking notice of this, or else you'll never understand my notion of the thing), the people being embarrassed by their equal ties to both, and the sovereigns concerned in a reciprocal regard, as well to their own interest as the good of the people, may make a certain kind of a—you understand me—upon which there does arise several disputes, turmoils, heart-burnings, and all that. In fine, you'll apprehend it better when you see it.

(*Exit, to call the Players.*)

SMITH. I find the author will be very much obliged to the players, if they can make any sense out of this.

Enter BAYES

BAYES. Now, gentlemen, I would fain ask your opinion of one thing. I have made a prologue and an epilogue which may both serve for either (that is, the prologue for the epilogue, or the epilogue for the prologue)—do you mark? Nay, they may both serve too, I gad, for any other play as well as this.

SMITH. Very well. That's indeed artificial.

BAYES. And I would fain ask your judgments now which of them would do best for the prologue. For you must know there is, in nature, but two ways of making very good prologues. The one is by civility, by insinuation, good language, and all that, to—a—in a manner, steal your plaudit from the courtesy of the auditors: the other, by making use of some certain personal things, which may keep a hank upon such censuring persons as cannot otherways, a gad, in nature, be hindered from being too free with their tongues. To which end my first prologue is, that I come out in a long black veil, and a great, huge hangman behind me, with a furred cap and his sword drawn; and there tell 'em plainly that if, out of good nature, they will not like my play, I gad, I'll e'en kneel down, and he shall cut my head off. Whereupon they all clapping—a——

SMITH. Aye, but suppose they don't.

BAYES. Suppose! Sir, you may suppose what you please, I have nothing to do with your suppose, Sir; nor am not at all mortified at it—not at all, Sir; I gad, not one jot, Sir. "Suppose," quoth a!—ha, ha, ha!   (*walks away*)

JOHNSON. Phoo! prithee, Bayes, don't mind what he says. He is a fellow newly come out of the country; he knows nothing of what's the relish, here, of the town.

BAYES. If I writ, Sir, to please the country, I should have followed the old plain way; but I write for some persons of quality and peculiar friends of mine that understand what flame and power in writing is; and they do me the right, Sir, to approve of what I do.

JOHNSON. Aye, aye, they will clap, I warrant you; never fear it.

BAYES. I'm sure the design's good: that cannot be denied. And then, for language, I gad, I defy 'em all, in nature, to mend it. Besides, Sir, I have printed above a hundred sheets of paper to insinuate the plot into the boxes: and, withal, have appointed two or three dozen of my friends to be ready in the pit, who, I'm sure, will clap, and so the rest, you know, must follow; and then pray, Sir, what becomes of your "suppose"? ha, ha, ha!

JOHNSON. Nay, if the business be so well laid, it cannot miss.

BAYES. I think so, Sir, and therefore would choose this to be the prologue. For, if I could engage 'em to clap before they see the play, you know 'twould be so much the better, because then they were engaged: for let a man write never so well, there are, now-a-days, a sort of persons they call critics, that, I gad, have no more wit in them than so many hobby-horses; but they'll laugh you, Sir, and find fault, and censure things that, I gad, I'm sure they are not able to do themselves, a sort of envious persons that emulate the glories of persons of parts, and think to build their fame by calumniating of persons that, I gad, to my knowledge, of all persons in the world are, in nature, the persons that do as much despise all that as—a—— In fine, I'll say no more of 'em.

JOHNSON. Nay, you have said enough of 'em, in all conscience— I'm sure more than they'll e'er be able to answer.

BAYES. Why, I'll tell you, Sir, sincerely, and *bona fide;* were it not for the sake of some ingenious persons and choice female spirits that have a value for me, I would see 'em all hanged, I gad, before I would e'er more set pen to paper; but let 'em live in ignorance like ingrates.

JOHNSON. Aye, marry! that were a way to be revenged of 'em, indeed; and, if I were in your place, now, I would do so.

BAYES. No, Sir; there are certain ties upon me that I cannot be disengaged from; otherwise, I would. But pray, Sir, how do you like my hangman?

SMITH. By my troth, Sir, I should like him very well.

BAYES. But how do you like it, Sir? (for, I see, you can judge, Would you have it for the prologue, or the epilogue?

JOHNSON. Faith, Sir, 'tis so good, let it e'en serve for both.

BAYES. No, no! that won't do. Besides, I have made anothe

JOHNSON. What other, Sir?

BAYES. Why, Sir, my other is Thunder and Lightning.

JOHNSON. That's greater. I'd rather stick to that.

BAYES. Do you think so? I'll tell you then; though there have
been many witty prologues written of late, yet I think you'll say
this is a *non pareillo*. I'm sure nobody has hit upon it yet. For
here, Sir, I make my prologue to be dialogue; and as, in my first,
you see I strive to oblige the auditors by civility, by good nature,
good language, and all that, so, in this, by the other way, *in
terrorem*, I choose for the persons Thunder and Lightning. Do
you apprehend the conceit?

JOHNSON. Phoo, pox! then you have it cocksure. They'll be
hanged before they'll dare to affront an author that has 'em at
that lock.

BAYES. I have made, too, one of the most delicate, dainty
similes in the whole world, I gad, if I knew but how to apply it.

SMITH. Let's hear it, I pray you.

BAYES. 'Tis an allusion to love.

> So boar and sow, when any storm is nigh,
> Snuff up, and smell it gath'ring in the sky;
> Boar beckons sow to trot in chestnut groves,
> And there consummate their unfinish'd loves:
> Pensive, in mud, they wallow all alone,
> And snort and gruntle to each other's moan.

How do you like it now, ha?

JOHNSON. Faith, 'tis extraordinary fine; and very applicable to
Thunder and Lightning, methinks, because it speaks of a storm.

BAYES. I gad, and so it does, now I think on't. Mr. Johnson,
I thank you, and I'll put it in *profecto*. Come out, Thunder and
Lightning.

Enter Thunder and Lightning

THUNDER. I am the bold Thunder.

BAYES. Mr. Cartwright, prithee, speak that a little louder, and
with a hoarse voice. "I am the bold Thunder!" Pshaw! speak it
to me in a voice that thunders it out indeed: "I am the bold
Thunder!"

THUNDER. I am the bold Thunder.

LIGHTNING. The brisk Lightning, I.

BAYES. Nay, you must be quick and nimble.—"The brisk Lightning, I."—That's my meaning.

THUNDER. I am the bravest Hector of the sky.

LIGHTNING. And I, fair Helen, that made Hector die.

THUNDER. I strike men down.

LIGHTNING. I fire the town.

THUNDER. Let the critics take heed how they grumble,
For then begin I for to rumble.

LIGHTNING. Let the ladies allow us their graces,
Or I'll blast all the paint on their faces,
And dry up their peter to soot.

THUNDER. Let the critics look to't.

LIGHTNING. Let the ladies look to't.

THUNDER. For Thunder will do't.

LIGHTNING. For Lightning will shoot.

THUNDER. I'll give you dash for dash.

LIGHTNING. I'll give you flash for flash.
Gallants, I'll singe your feather.

THUNDER. I'll thunder you together.

BOTH. Look to't, look to't; we'll do't, we'll do't; look to't, we'll do't.
         (*twice or thrice repeated*)   (*Exeunt ambo.*)

BAYES. There's no more. 'Tis but a flash of a prologue—a droll.

SMITH. Yes, 'tis short, indeed, but very terrible.

BAYES. Aye, when the *simile's* in, it will do to a miracle, I gad.
Come, come, begin the play.

Enter FIRST PLAYER

1ST PLAYER. Sir, Mr. Ivory is not come yet, but he'll be here
presently; he's but two doors off.

BAYES. Come then, gentlemen, let's go out and take a pipe of
tobacco.   (*Exeunt.*)

ACT II

SCENE I

BAYES, JOHNSON, *and* SMITH

BAYES. Now, Sir, because I'll do nothing here that ever was
done before, instead of beginning with a scene that discovers
something of the plot, I begin this play with a whisper.

SMITH. Umph! very new, indeed.

BAYES. Come, take your seats. Begin, Sirs.

Enter Gentleman Usher and Physician

PHYSICIAN. Sir, by your habit, I should guess you to be the gentleman usher of this sumptuous place.

USHER. And by your gait and fashion I should almost suspect you rule the healths of both our noble kings, under the notion of physician.

PHYSICIAN. You hit my function right.

USHER. And you, mine.

PHYSICIAN. Then let's embrace.

USHER. Come.

PHYSICIAN. Come.

JOHNSON. Pray, Sir, who are those so very civil persons?

BAYES. Why, Sir, the gentleman usher and physician of the two kings of Brentford.

JOHNSON. But, pray then, how comes it to pass that they know one another no better?

BAYES. Phoo! that's for the better carrying on of the plot.

JOHNSON. Very well.

PHYSICIAN. Sir, to conclude——

SMITH. What, before he begins?

BAYES. No, Sir; you must know they had been talking of this a pretty while without.

SMITH. Where? In the tiring-room?

BAYES. Why, aye, Sir.—He's so dull!—Come, speak again.

PHYSICIAN. Sir, to conclude, the place you fill has more than amply exacted the talents of a wary pilot, and all these threatening storms which, like impregnate clouds, hover o'er our heads, will (when they once are grasped but by the eye of reason) melt into fruitful showers of blessings on the people.

BAYES. Pray, mark that allegory. Is not that good?

JOHNSON. Yes; that grasping of a storm with the eye is admirable.

PHYSICIAN. But yet some rumours great are stirring; and if Lorenzo should prove false (which none but the great gods can tell), you then perhaps would find that——   (*whispers*)

BAYES. Now he whispers.

USHER. Alone, do you say?

PHYSICIAN. No; attended with the noble——   (*whispers*)

BAYES. Again.

USHER. Who—he in grey?

PHYSICIAN. Yes; and at the head of——   (*whispers*)

BAYES. Pray, mark.

USHER. Then, Sir, most certain, 'twill in time appear. These are the reasons that have mov'd him to't: First, he—— (*whispers*)

BAYES. Now the other whispers.

USHER. Secondly, they—— (*whispers*)

BAYES. At it still.

USHER. Thirdly, and lastly, both he and they—— (*whispers*)

BAYES. Now they both whisper. (*Exeunt whispering.*)

Now, gentlemen, pray tell me true, and without flattery, is not this a very odd beginning of a play?

JOHNSON. In troth, I think it is, Sir. But why two kings of the same place?

BAYES. Why? because it's new, and that's it I aim at. I despise your Jonson and Beaumont, that borrowed all they writ from nature. I am for fetching it purely out of my own fancy, I.

SMITH. But what think you, Sir, of Sir John Suckling?

BAYES. By gad, I am a better poet than he.

SMITH. Well, Sir; but pray, why all this whispering?

BAYES. Why, Sir (besides that it is new, as I told you before), because they are supposed to be politicians; and matters of state ought not to be divulged.

SMITH. But then, Sir, why——

BAYES. Sir, if you'll but respite your curiosity till the end of the fifth act, you'll find it a piece of patience not ill recompensed.

(*goes to the door*)

JOHNSON. How dost thou like this, Frank? Is it not just as I told thee?

SMITH. Why, I did never, before this, see anything in nature, and all that (as Mr. Bayes says) so foolish but I could give some guess at what moved the fop to do it; but this, I confess, does go beyond my reach.

JOHNSON. It is all alike. Mr. Wintershul has informed me of this play already. And I'll tell thee, Frank, thou shalt not see one scene here worth one farthing, or like anything thou canst imagine has ever been the practice of the world. And then, when he comes to what he calls "good language," it is, as I told thee, very fantastical, most abominably dull, and not one word to the purpose.

SMITH. It does surprise me, I'm sure, very much.

JOHNSON. Aye, but it won't do so long: by that time thou hast seen a play or two that I'll show thee, thou wilt be pretty well acquainted with this new kind of foppery.

SMITH. Pox on't, but there's no pleasure in him: he's too gross a fool to be laughed at.

Enter BAYES

JOHNSON. I'll swear, Mr. Bayes, you have done this scene most admirably; though, I must tell you, Sir, it is a very difficult matter to pen a whisper well.

BAYES. Aye, gentlemen, when you come to write yourselves, o' my word, you'll find it so.

JOHNSON. Have a care of what you say, Mr. Bayes, for Mr. Smith there, I assure you, has written a great many fine things already.

BAYES. Has he, i'fackins? Why, then, pray, Sir, how do you do when you write?

SMITH. Faith, Sir, for the most part, I am in pretty good health.

BAYES. Aye, but I mean, what do you do, when you write?

SMITH. I take pen, ink, and paper, and sit down.

BAYES. Now I write standing; that's one thing: and then, another thing is, with what do you prepare yourself?

SMITH. Prepare myself! what the devil does the fool mean?

BAYES. Why, I'll tell you, now, what I do. If I am to write familiar things, as sonnets to Armida, and the like, I make use of stewed prunes only; but, when I have a grand design in hand, I ever take physic, and let blood, for, when you would have pure swiftness of thought and fiery flights of fancy, you must have a care of the pensive part. In fine, you must purge the belly.

SMITH. By my troth, Sir, this is a most admirable receipt for writing.

BAYES. Aye, 'tis my secret; and, in good earnest, I think, one of the best I have.

SMITH. In good faith, Sir, and that may very well be.

BAYES. May be, Sir? I gad, I'm sure on't: *experto crede Roberto*. But I must give you this caution by the way—be sure you never take snuff, when you write.

SMITH. Why so, Sir?

BAYES. Why, it spoiled me once, I gad, one of the sparkishest plays in all England. But a friend of mine, at Gresham College, has promised to help me to some spirit of brains, and, I gad, that shall do my business.

SCENE II

Enter the two Kings, hand in hand

BAYES. Oh, these now are the two kings of Brentford. Take notice of their style: 'twas never yet upon the stage; but, if you like it, I could make a shift, perhaps, to show you a whole play, writ all just so.

1ST KING. Did you observe their whisper, brother king?

2D KING. I did; and heard besides a grave bird sing
That they intend, sweetheart, to play us pranks.

BAYES. This is now familiar, because they are both persons of the same quality.

SMITH. 'Sdeath, this would make a man spew.

1ST KING. If that design appears,
I'll lug 'em by the ears
Until I make 'em crack.

2D KING. And so will I, i'fack.

1ST KING. You must begin, *mon foy.*

2D KING. Sweet Sir, *pardonnes moy.*

BAYES. Mark that: I makes 'em both speak French to show their breeding.

JOHNSON. Oh, 'tis extraordinary fine.

2D KING. Then, spite of Fate, we'll thus combined stand;
And, like true brothers, walk still hand in hand.   (*Exeunt Reges.*)

JOHNSON. This is a very majestic scene indeed.

BAYES. Aye, 'tis a crust, a lasting crust for your rogue critics I gad: I would fain see the proudest of 'em all but dare to nibble at this; I gad, if they do, this shall rub their gums for 'em, I promise you. It was I, you must know, that have written a whole play just in this very same style; but 'twas never acted yet.

JOHNSON. How so?

BAYES. I gad, I can hardly tell you for laughing (ha, ha, ha!). It is so pleasant a story—ha, ha, ha!

SMITH. What is't?

BAYES. I gad, the players refused to act it. Ha, ha, ha!

SMITH. That's impossible.

BAYES. I gad, they did it, Sir, point blank refused it, I gad.—
Ha, ha, ha!

JOHNSON. Fie, that was rude.

BAYES. Rude! Aye, I gad, they are the rudest, uncivilest persons, and all that, in the whole world, I gad: I gad, there's no
living with 'em. I have written, Mr. Johnson, I do verily believe,
a whole cart-load of things every whit as good as this; and yet,
I vow to gad, these insolent rascals have turned 'em all back upon
my hands again.

JOHNSON. Strange fellows, indeed.

SMITH. But pray, Mr. Bayes, how came these two kings to
know of this whisper? for, as I remember, they were not present
at it.

BAYES. No, but that's the actors' fault, and not mine; for the
two kings should (a pox take 'em) have popped both their heads
in at the door, just as the other went off.

SMITH. That, indeed, would ha' done it.

BAYES. Done it! Aye, I gad, these fellows are able to spoil the
best things in Christendom. I'll tell you, Mr. Johnson, I vow to
gad, I have been so highly disobliged by the peremptoriness of
these fellows, that I'm resolved hereafter to bend my thoughts
wholly for the service of the Nursery, and mump your proud
players, I gad. So; now Prince Pretty-man comes in, and falls
asleep making love to his mistress, which, you know, was a grand
intrigue in a late play written by a very honest gentleman, a
knight.

SCENE III

Enter PRINCE PRETTY-MAN

PRETTY-MAN. How strange a captive am I grown of late!
Shall I accuse my love, or blame my fate?
My love, I cannot; that is too divine:
And against Fate what mortal dares repine?

Enter CLORIS

—But here she comes.
Sure 'tis some blazing comet, is it not?   (*lies down*)

BAYES. Blazing comet! mark that. I gad, very fine.

PRETTY-MAN. But I am so surprised with sleep I cannot speak the rest. *(sleeps)*

BAYES. Does not that, now, surprise you, to fall asleep in the nick? His spirits exhale with the heat of his passion, and all that, and—swop! falls asleep, as you see. Now, here, she must make a *simile*.

SMITH. Where's the necessity of that, Mr. Bayes?

BAYES. Because she's surprised. That's a general rule—you must ever make a *simile* when you are surprised, 'tis the new way of writing.

CLORIS. As some tall pine, which we, on Ætna, find
T'have stood the rage of many a boist'rous wind,
Feeling without, that flames within do play
Which would consume his root and sap away,
He spreads his worsted arms unto the skies,
Silently grieves, all pale, repines and dies:
So, shrouded up, your bright eye disappears.
Break forth, bright scorching sun, and dry my tears.

(Exit.)

JOHNSON. Mr. Bayes, methinks this *simile* wants a little application, too.

BAYES. No, faith; for it alludes to passion, to consuming, to dying, and all that; which, you know, are the natural effects of an amour. But I'm afraid this scene has made you sad; for, I must confess, when I writ it, I wept myself.

SMITH. No, truly, Sir, my spirits are almost exhaled too, and I am likelier to fall asleep.

(PRINCE PRETTY-MAN starts up, and says)

PRETTY-MAN. It is resolved. *(Exit.)*

BAYES. That's all.

SMITH. Mr. Bayes, may one be so bold as to ask you a question now, and you not be angry?

BAYES. O Lord, Sir, you may ask me anything—what you please. I vow to gad, you do me a great deal of honour: you do not know me if you say that, Sir.

SMITH. Then, pray, Sir, what is it that this prince here has resolved in his sleep?

BAYES. Why, I must confess, that question is well enough asked for one that is not acquainted with this new way of writing. But you must know, Sir, that, to outdo all my fellow-writers, whereas they keep their *intrigo* secret till the very last scene before the dance, I now, Sir (do you mark me) a——

SMITH. Begin the play and end it, without ever opening the plot at all?

BAYES. I do so; that's the very plain troth on't. Ha, ha, ha! I do, I gad. If they cannot find it out themselves, e'en let 'em alone for Bayes, I warrant you. But here, now, is a scene of business. Pray observe it, for I dare say you'll think it no unwise discourse this, nor ill argued. To tell you true, 'tis a discourse I overheard once betwixt two grand, sober, governing persons.

SCENE IV

Enter Gentleman Usher and Physician

USHER. Come, Sir; let's state the matter of fact, and lay our heads together.

PHYSICIAN. Right! lay our heads together. I love to be merry sometimes; but when a knotty point comes, I lay my head close to it, with a snuff-box in my hand, and then I fegue it away, i'faith.

BAYES. I do just so, I gad, always.

USHER. The grand question is, whether they heard us whisper; which I divide thus——

PHYSICIAN. Yes, it must be divided so indeed.

SMITH. That's very complaisant, I swear, Mr. Bayes, to be of another man's opinion before he knows what it is.

BAYES. Nay, I bring in none here but well-bred persons, I assure you.

USHER. I divided the question into when they heard, what they heard, and whether they heard or no.

JOHNSON. Most admirably divided, I swear.

USHER. As to the when; you say, just now: so that is answered. Then, as for what; why, what answers itself; for what could they hear but what we talked of? So that naturally, and of necessity, we come to the last question, *videlicet*, whether they heard or no.

SMITH. This is a very wise scene, Mr. Bayes.

BAYES. Aye, you have it right: they are both politicians.

USHER. Pray, then, to proceed in method, let me ask you that question.

PHYSICIAN. No, you'll answer better; pray let me ask it you.

USHER. Your will must be a law.

PHYSICIAN. Come then, what is it I must ask?

SMITH. This politician, I perceive, Mr. Bayes, has somewhat a short memory.

BAYES. Why, Sir, you must know that t'other is the main politician, and this is but his pupil.

USHER. You must ask me whether they heard us whisper.

PHYSICIAN. Well, I do so.

USHER. Say it then.

SMITH. Hey day! here's the bravest work that ever I saw.

JOHNSON. This is mighty methodical!

BAYES. Aye, Sir; that's the way: 'tis the way of art; there is no other way, I gad, in business.

PHYSICIAN. Did they hear us whisper?

USHER. Why, truly I can't tell; there's much to be said upon the word *whisper*. To whisper, in Latin, is *susurrare*, which is as much as to say, to speak softly; now, if so they heard us speak softly, they heard us whisper: but then comes in the *quomodo*, the how: how did they hear us whisper? Why, as to that, there are two ways; the one, by chance or accident: the other, on purpose—that is, with design to hear us whisper.

PHYSICIAN. Nay, if they heard us that way, I'll never give 'em physic more.

USHER. Nor I e'er more will walk abroad before 'em.

BAYES. Pray mark this; for a great deal depends upon it, towards the latter end of the play.

SMITH. I suppose that's the reason why you brought in this scene, Mr. Bayes?

BAYES. Partly it was, Sir; but, I confess, I was not unwilling, besides, to show the world a pattern here how men should talk of business.

JOHNSON. You have done it exceeding well indeed.

BAYES. Yes, I think this will do.

PHYSICIAN. Well, if they heard us whisper, they'll turn us out, and nobody else will take us.

SMITH. Not for politicians, I dare answer for it.

PHYSICIAN. Let's then no more ourselves in vain bemoan;
We are not safe until we them unthrone.

USHER. 'Tis right.
And, since occasion now seems debonair,
I'll seize on this, and you shall take that chair.

(*They draw their swords, and sit down in the two great chairs upon the stage.*)

BAYES. There's now an odd surprise; the whole state's turn'd quite topsy-turvy, without any puther or stir in the whole world, I gad.

JOHNSON. A very silent change of a government, truly, as ever I heard of.

BAYES. It is so. And yet you shall see me bring 'em in again, by and by, in as odd a way every jot.

(*The Usurpers march out flourishing their swords.*)

Enter SHIRLEY

SHIRLEY. Hey ho, hey ho! what a change is here! Hey day, hey day! I know not what to do, nor what to say.   (*Exit.*)

JOHNSON. Mr. Bayes, in my opinion now, that gentleman might have said a little more upon this occasion.

BAYES. No, Sir, not at all; for I under-writ his part on purpose to set off the rest.

JOHNSON. Cry you mercy, Sir.

SMITH. But pray, Sir, how came they to depose the kings so easily?

BAYES. Why, Sir, you must know, they long had a design to do it before; but never could put it in practice till now; and, to tell you true, that's one reason why I made 'em whisper so at first.

SMITH. Oh, very well: now I'm fully satisfied.

BAYES. And then, to show you, Sir, it was not done so very easily neither, in this next scene you shall see some fighting.

SMITH. Oh, ho! so then you make the struggle to be after the business is done?

BAYES. Aye.

SMITH. Oh, I conceive you. That, I swear, is very natural.

SCENE V

Enter four men at one door, and four at another, with their swords drawn

1ST SOLDIER. Stand! Who goes there?

2D SOLDIER. A friend.

1ST SOLDIER. What friend?

2D SOLDIER. A friend to the house.

1ST SOLDIER. Fall on!   (*They all kill one another. Music strikes.*)

BAYES. (*to the music*) Hold, hold! (*It ceaseth.*) Now, here's an odd surprise: all these dead men you shall see rise up presently, at a certain note that I have made, in *Effaut flat*, and fall a-dancing. Do you hear, dead men? Remember your note in *Effaut flat*. (*to the music*) Play on. Now, now, now.

(*The music play his note, and the dead men rise; but cannot get in order.*)

O Lord, O Lord! Out, out, out!—Did ever men spoil a good thing so? no figure, no ear, no time, nothing! Udzookers, you dance worse than the angels in *Harry the Eight*, or the fat spirits in *The Tempest*, I gad.

1ST SOLDIER. Why, Sir, 'tis impossible to do anything in time to this tune.

BAYES. O Lord, O Lord! Impossible? why, gentlemen, if there be any faith in a person that's a Christian, I sate up two whole nights in composing this air and apting it for the business. For, if you observe, there are two several designs in this tune; it begins swift, and ends slow. You talk of time, and time; you shall see me do't. Look you now. (*Lies down flat on his face.*) Here I am dead. Now mark my note *Effaut flat.*—— Strike up music. Now.   (*As he rises up hastily, he falls down again.*) Ah, gadsookers! I have broke my nose.

JOHNSON. By my troth, Mr. Bayes, this is a very unfortunate note of yours, in *Effaut*.

BAYES. A plague of this damned stage, with your nails and your tenter-hooks, that a gentleman cannot come to teach you to act but he must break his nose, and his face, and the devil and all. Pray, Sir, can you help me to a wet piece of brown paper?

SMITH. No indeed, Sir; I don't usually carry any about me.

2D SOLDIER. Sir, I'll go get you some within presently.

BAYES. Go, go then; I follow you. Pray, dance out the dance, and I'll be with you in a moment. Remember you dance like horsemen.   (*Exit* BAYES.)

SMITH. Like horsemen! What a plague can that be?

(*They dance the dance, but can make nothing of it.*)

1ST SOLDIER. A devil! let's try this no longer. Play my dance that Mr. Bayes found fault with so.   (*Dance, and exeunt.*)

SMITH. What can this fool be doing all this while about his nose?

JOHNSON. Prithee, let's go see.   (*Exeunt.*)

ACT III

SCENE I

BAYES *with a paper on his nose, and the two Gentlemen*

BAYES. Now, Sirs, this I do because my fancy, in this play, is to end every act with a dance.

SMITH. Faith, that fancy is very good, but I should hardly have broke my nose for it, though.

JOHNSON. That fancy, I suppose, is new, too.

BAYES. Sir, all my fancies are so. I tread upon no man's heels, but make my flight upon my own wings, I assure you. Now, here comes in a scene of sheer wit, without any mixture in the whole world, I gad, between Prince Pretty-man and his tailor. It might properly enough be called a prize of wit; for you shall see 'em come in upon one another snip snap, hit for hit, as fast as can be. First one speaks, then presently t'other's upon him slap, with a repartee; then he at him again, dash! with a new conceit, and so eternally, eternally, I gad, till they go quite off the stage.   (*goes to call the Players*)

SMITH. What a plague does this fop mean by his snip snap, hit for hit, and dash?

JOHNSON. Mean? why, he never meant anything in's life. What dost talk of meaning for?

Enter BAYES

BAYES. Why don't you come in?

Enter PRINCE PRETTY-MAN *and* TOM THIMBLE

This scene will make you die with laughing, if it be well acted; for 'tis as full of drollery as ever it can hold: 'tis like an orange stuffed with cloves, as for conceit.

PRETTY-MAN. But prithee, Tom Thimble, why wilt thou needs marry? If nine tailors make but one man, and one woman cannot be satisfied with nine men, what work art thou cutting out here for thyself, trow?

BAYES. Good!

THIMBLE. Why, an't please your Highness, if I can't make up all the work I cut out, I shan't want journeymen to help me, I warrant you.

BAYES. Good again.

PRETTY-MAN. I am afraid thy journeymen, though, Tom, won't work by the day, but by the night.

BAYES. Good still.

THIMBLE. However, if my wife sits but cross-legged, as I do, there will be no great danger—not half so much as when I trusted you, Sir, for your coronation suit.

BAYES. Very good, i'faith.

PRETTY-MAN. Why, the times then lived upon trust; it was the fashion. You would not be out of time, at such a time as that, sure. A tailor, you know, must never be out of fashion.

BAYES. Right.

THIMBLE. I'm sure, Sir, I made your clothes in the Court fashion, for you never paid me yet.

BAYES. There's a bob for the Court.

PRETTY-MAN. Why, Tom, thou art a sharp rogue when thou art angry, I see; thou pay'st me now, methinks.

BAYES. There's pay upon pay! as good as ever was written, I gad!

THIMBLE. Aye, Sir, in your own coin: you give me nothing but words.

BAYES. Admirable, before gad!

PRETTY-MAN. Well, Tom, I hope shortly I shall have another coin for thee; for now the wars are coming on, I shall grow to be a man of mettle.

BAYES. Oh, you did not do that half enough.

JOHNSON. Methinks he does it admirably.

BAYES. Aye, pretty well; but he does not hit me in't. He does not top his part.

THIMBLE. That's the way to be stamped yourself, Sir. I shall see you come home, like an angel for the king's evil, with a hole bored through you. (*Exeunt.*)

BAYES. Ha, there he has hit it up to the hilts, I gad. How do you like it now, gentlemen? Is not this pure wit?

SMITH. 'Tis snip snap, Sir, as you say; but methinks, not pleasant nor to the purpose, for the play does not go on.

BAYES. Play does not go on? I don't know what you mean; why, is not this part of the play?

SMITH. Yes, but the plot stands still.

BAYES. Plot stand still! why, what a devil is the plot good for but to bring in fine things?

SMITH. Oh, I did not know that before.

BAYES. No, I think you did not, nor many things more that I am master of. Now, Sir, I gad, this is the bane of all us writers: let us soar but never so little above the common pitch, I gad, all's spoiled; for the vulgar never understand it. They can never conceive you, Sir, the excellency of these things.

JOHNSON. 'Tis a sad fate, I must confess. But you write on still, for all that?

BAYES. Write on? Aye, I gad, I warrant you. 'Tis not their talk shall stop me: if they catch me at that lock, I'll give 'em leave to hang me. As long as I know my things are good, what care I what they say?—What, are they gone without singing my last new song? 'Sbud, would it were in their bellies! I'll tell you, Mr. Johnson, if I have any skill in these matters, I vow to gad, this song is peremptorily the very best that ever yet was written. You must know it was made by Tom Thimble's first wife after she was dead.

SMITH. How, Sir? After she was dead?

BAYES. Aye, Sir, after she was dead. Why, what have you to say to that?

JOHNSON. Say? Why, nothing: he were a devil that had anything to say to that!

BAYES. Right.

SMITH. How did she come to die, pray, Sir?

BAYES. Phoo! that's no matter; by a fall. But here's the conceit—that upon his knowing she was killed by an accident, he supposes, with a sigh, that she died for love of him.

JOHNSON. Aye, aye, that's well enough. Let's hear it, Mr. Bayes.

BAYES. 'Tis to the tune of Farewell, fair Armida, On seas and in battles, in bullets, and all that.

Song

In swords, pikes, and bullets, 'tis safer to be
Than in a strong castle, remoted from thee:
My death's bruise pray think you gave me, though a fall
Did give it me more, from the top of a wall;
For then, if the moat on her mud would first lay,
And after, before you my body convey,
The blue on my breast when you happen to see,
You'll say, with a sigh, there's a true-blue for me.

Ha, rogues! when I am merry, I write these things as fast as
hops, I gad; for, you must know, I am as pleasant a debauchee
as ever you saw—I am, i'faith.

SMITH. But, Mr. Bayes, how comes this song in here? for, methinks, there is no great occasion for it.

BAYES. Alack, Sir, you know nothing. You must ever interlard
your plays with songs, ghosts, and dances if you mean to—a——

JOHNSON. Pit, box, and gallery, Mr. Bayes.

BAYES. I gad and you have nicked it. Hark you, Mr. Johnson,
you know I don't flatter; a gad, you have a great deal of wit.

JOHNSON. O Lord, Sir, you do me too much honour.

BAYES. Nay, nay, come, come, Mr. Johnson, i' faith this must
not be said, amongst us that have it. I know you have wit by
the judgment you make of this play, for that's the measure I
go by: my play is my touchstone. When a man tells me such
a one is a person of parts, "Is he so?" say I. What do I do but
bring him presently to see this play. If he likes it, I know what
to think of him; if not, your most humble servant, Sir, I'll no
more of him upon my word; I thank you. I am *clara voyant*, I
gad. Now here we go on to our business.

SCENE II

Enter the two Usurpers, hand in hand

USHER. But what's become of Volscius the great?
His presence has not grac'd our courts of late.

PHYSICIAN. I fear some ill, from emulation sprung,
Has from us that illustrious hero wrung.

BAYES. Is not that majestical?

SMITH. Yes, but who a devil is that Volscius?

BAYES. Why, that's a prince I make in love with Parthenope.

SMITH. I thank you, Sir.

Enter CORDELIO

CORDELIO. My lieges, news from Volscius the Prince.
USHER. His news is welcome, whatsoe'er it be.

SMITH. How, Sir, do you mean—whether it be good or bad?
BAYES. Nay, pray, Sir, have a little patience! Godsookers, you'll
spoil all my play! Why, Sir, 'tis impossible to answer every impertinent question you ask.
SMITH. Cry you mercy, Sir.

CORDELIO. His Highness, Sirs, commanded me to tell you
That the fair person whom you both do know,
Despairing of forgiveness for her fault,
In a deep sorrow, twice she did attempt
Upon her precious life; but, by the care
Of standers-by, prevented was.

SMITH. 'Sheart, what stuff's here!

CORDELIO.   At last,
Volscius the great this dire resolve embrac'd:
His servants he into the country sent,
And he himself to Peccadille went;
Where he's inform'd, by letters, that she's dead!
USHER. Dead! Is that possible? Dead!
PHYSICIAN.   O ye gods!   (*Exeunt.*)

BAYES. There's a smart expression of a passion—"O ye gods!"
That's one of my bold strokes, I gad.
SMITH. Yes, but who is the fair person that's dead?
BAYES. That you shall know anon, Sir.
SMITH. Nay, if we know it at all, 'tis well enough.
BAYES. Perhaps you may find too, by and by, for all this, that
she's not dead neither.
SMITH. Marry, that's good news indeed. I am glad of that with
all my heart.
BAYES. Now, here's the man brought in that is supposed to
have killed her.   (*a great shout within*)

SCENE III

Enter AMARYLLIS *with a book in her hand; and Attendants*
AMARYLLIS. What shout triumphant's that?

Enter a Soldier

SOLDIER. Shy maid, upon the river brink,
Near Twick'nam Town, the false assassinate
Is ta'en.
AMARYLLIS. Thanks to the powers above, for this deliverance!
I hope its slow beginning will portend
A forward exit to all future end.

BAYES. Pish, there you are out! "To all *future* end?" No, no—
"to all future *end*": you must lay the accent upon "end," or
else you lose the conceit.

SMITH. I see you are very perfect in these matters.

BAYES. Aye, Sir; I have been long enough at it, one would
think, to know something.

Enter Soldiers dragging in an old Fisherman

AMARYLLIS. Villain, what monster did corrupt thy mind
T'attack the noblest soul of human kind?
Tell me who set thee on.
FISHERMAN. Prince Pretty-man.
AMARYLLIS. To kill whom?
FISHERMAN. Prince Pretty-man.
AMARYLLIS. What, did Prince Pretty-man hire you to kill Prince
Pretty-man?
FISHERMAN. No; Prince Volscius.
AMARYLLIS. To kill whom?
FISHERMAN. Prince Volscius.
AMARYLLIS. What, did Prince Volscius hire you to kill Prince Vol-
scius?
FISHERMAN. No; Prince Pretty-man.
AMARYLLIS. So!—drag him hence,
Till torture of the rack produce his sense.   (*Exeunt.*)

BAYES. Mark how I make the horror of his guilt confound his
intellects, for he's out at one and t'other; and that's the design
of this scene.

SMITH. I see, Sir, you have a several design for every scene.

BAYES. Aye, that's my way of writing, and so, Sir, I can dispatch you a whole play before another man, I gad, can make
an end of his plot.

SCENE IV

BAYES. So, now enter Prince Pretty-man in a rage.—— Where the devil is he? Why, Pretty-man! Why, when, I say? Oh, fie, fie, fie, fie! all's marred, I vow to gad, quite marred.

Enter PRETTY-MAN

Phoo, pox! you are come too late, Sir; now you may go out again, if you please. I vow to gad, Mr.—a—I would not give a button for my play, now you have done this.

PRETTY-MAN. What, Sir?

BAYES. What, Sir! 'Slife, Sir, you should have come out in choler, rous upon the stage, just as the other went off. Must a man be eternally telling you of these things?

JOHNSON. Sure, this must be some very notable matter that he's so angry at.

SMITH. I am not of your opinion.

BAYES. Pish! come, let's hear your part, Sir.

PRETTY-MAN. Bring in my father; why d'ye keep him from me?
Although a fisherman, he is my father!
Was ever son yet brought to this distress,
To be, for being a son, made fatherless?
Ah, you just gods, rob me not of a father:
The being of a son take from me rather.   (*Exit.*)

SMITH. Well, Ned, what think you now?

JOHNSON. A devil! this is worst of all.—— Mr. Bayes, pray what's the meaning of this scene?

BAYES. O, cry you mercy, Sir; I purtest I had forgot to tell you. Why, Sir, you must know that, long before the beginning of this play, this prince was taken by a fisherman.

SMITH. How, Sir—taken prisoner?

BAYES. Taken prisoner! O Lord, what a question's there! did ever any man ask such a question? Godsookers, he has put the plot quite out of my head with this damned question. What was I going to say?

JOHNSON. Nay, the Lord knows; I cannot imagine.

BAYES. Stay, let me see——taken. Oh, 'tis true. Why, Sir, as I was going to say, his Highness here, the Prince, was taken in a cradle by a fisherman and brought up as his child.

SMITH. Indeed?

BAYES. Nay, prithee, hold thy peace.— And so, Sir, this murder being committed by the riverside, the fisherman, upon suspicion, was seized; and thereupon the prince grew angry.

SMITH. So, so; now 'tis very plain.

JOHNSON. But, Mr. Bayes, is not this some disparagement to a prince to pass for a fisherman's son? Have a care of that, I pray.

BAYES. No, no, not at all; for 'tis but for a while: I shall fetch him off again presently, you shall see.

Enter PRETTY-MAN and THIMBLE

PRETTY-MAN. By all the gods, I'll set the world on fire
Rather than let 'em ravish hence my sire.

THIMBLE. Brave Pretty-man, it is at length reveal'd
That he is not thy sire who thee conceal'd.

BAYES. Lo, you now; there he's off again.

JOHNSON. Admirably done, i' faith.

BAYES. Aye, now the plot thickens very much upon us.

PRETTY-MAN. What oracle this darkness can evince?
Sometimes a fisher's son, sometimes a prince.
It is a secret, great as is the world,
In which I, like the soul, am toss'd and hurl'd.
The blackest ink of fate, sure, was my lot,
And, when she writ my name, she made a blot.

                                                                    (*Exit.*)

BAYES. There's a blustering verse for you now.

SMITH. Yes, Sir, but why is he so mightily troubled to find he is not a fisherman's son?

BAYES. Phoo! that is not because he has a mind to be his son, but for fear he should be thought to be nobody's son at all.

SMITH. Nay, that would trouble a man, indeed.

BAYES. So; let me see.

SCENE V

BAYES (*reads*). "Enter Prince Volscius going out of town."

SMITH. I though he had been gone to Peccadille.

BAYES. Yes, he gave it out so; but that was only to cover his design.

JOHNSON. What design?

BAYES. Why, to head the army that lies concealed for him in Knightsbridge.

JOHNSON. I see here's a great deal of plot, Mr. Bayes.

BAYES. Yes, now it begins to break; but we shall have a world of more busines anon.

Enter PRINCE VOLSCIUS, CLORIS, AMARYLLIS, and HARRY
with a riding-cloak and boots

AMARYLLIS. Sir, you are cruel, thus to leave the town
And to retire to country solitude.

CLORIS. We hop'd this summer that we should at least
Have held the honour of your company.

BAYES. "Held the honour of your company!" prettily expressed!
—"Held the honour of your company!" Godsookers, these fellows will never take notice of anything.

JOHNSON. I assure you, Sir, I admire it extremely; I don't know what he does.

BAYES. Aye, aye, he's a little envious; but 'tis no great matter.
—— Come!

AMARYLLIS. Pray, let us two this single boon obtain,
That you will here with poor us still remain.
Before your horses come, pronounce our fate;
For then, alas, I fear 'twill be too late.

BAYES. Sad!

VOLSCIUS. Harry, my boots; for I'll go rage among
My blades encamp'd, and quit this urban throng.

SMITH. But pray, Mr. Bayes, is not this a little difficult, that you were saying e'en now, to keep an army thus concealed in Knightsbridge?

BAYES. In Knightsbridge?—— stay.

JOHNSON. No, not if the innkeepers be his friends.

BAYES. His friends! Aye, Sir, his intimate acquaintance; or else, indeed, I grant it could not be.

SMITH. Yes, faith, so it might be very easy.

BAYES. Nay, if I do not make all things easy, I gad, I'll give you leave to hang me. Now you would think that he is going out of town, but you shall see how prettily I have contrived to stop him presently.

SMITH. By my troth, Sir, you have so amazed me that I know not what to think.

Enter PARTHENOPE

VOLSCIUS. Bless me! how frail are all my best resolves!
How, in a moment, is my purpose chang'd!
Too soon I thought myself secure from love.
Fair Madam, give me leave to ask her name
Who does so gently rob me of my fame:
For I should meet the army out of town,
And, if I fail, must hazard my renown.

PARTHENOPE. My mother, Sir, sells ale by the town walls,
And me her dear Parthenope she calls.

BAYES. Now that's the Parthenope I told you of.

JOHNSON. Aye, aye; I gad, you are very right.

VOLSCIUS. Can vulgar vestment high-born beauty shroud?
Thou bring'st the morning pictur'd in a cloud.

BAYES. "The morning pictured in a cloud!" A, gadsookers,
what a conceit is there!

PARTHENOPE. Give you good ev'n, Sir.   (*Exit.*)

VOLSCIUS. O inauspicious stars! that I was born
To sudden love and to more sudden scorn!

AMARYLLIS. ⎱ —How! Prince Volscius in love?
CLORIS.   ⎰ Ha, ha, ha!   (*Exeunt laughing.*)

SMITH. Sure, Mr. Bayes, we have lost some jest here that they
laugh at so.

BAYES. Why did you not observe? He first resolves to go out
of town, and then, as he is pulling on his boots, falls in love with
her. Ha, ha, ha!

SMITH. Well, and where lies the jest of that?

BAYES. Ha?   (*turns to* JOHNSON)

JOHNSON. Why, in the boots: where should the jest lie?

BAYES. I gad, you are in the right: it does (*turns to* SMITH)
lie in the boots. Your friend and I know where a good jest lies,
though you don't, Sir.

SMITH. Much good do't you, Sir.

BAYES. Here, now, Mr. Johnson, you shall see a combat betwixt love and honour. An ancient author has made a whole play
on't, but I have dispatched it all in this scene.

          (VOLSCIUS *sits down to pull on his boots;* BAYES *stands
              by and over acts the part as he speaks it.*)

VOLSCIUS. How has my passion made me Cupid's scoff!
This hasty boot is on, the other off,

And sullen lies, with amorous design
To quit loud fame and make that beauty mine.

SMITH. Prithee, mark what pains Mr. Bayes takes to act this speech himself!

JOHNSON. Yes, the fool, I see, is mightily transported with it.

VOLSCIUS. My legs, the emblem of my various thought,
Show to what sad distraction I am brought.
Sometimes with stubborn honour, like this boot,
My mind is guarded, and resolv'd to do't:
Sometimes, again, that very mind, by love
Disarmed, like this other leg does prove.
Shall I to Honour or to Love give way?
"Go on," cries Honour; tender Love says, "Nay,"
Honour aloud commands, "Pluck both boots on";
But softer Love does whisper, "Put on none."
What shall I do? what conduct shall I find
To lead me through this twilight of my mind?
For as bright day with black approach of night
Contending, makes a doubtful, puzzling light,
So does my honour and my love together
Puzzle me so, I can resolve for neither.
                (goes out hopping with one boot on, and the other off)

JOHNSON. By my troth, Sir, this is as difficult a combat as ever I saw, and as equal; for 'tis determined on neither side.

BAYES. Aye, is't not now, I gad, ha? For to go off hip hop, hip hop, upon this occasion, is a thousand times better than any conclusion in the world, I gad.

JOHNSON. Indeed, Mr. Bayes, that hip hop in this place, as you say, does a very great deal.

BAYES. Oh, all in all, Sir; they are these little things that mar or set you off a play; as I remember once, in a play of mine, I set off a scene, I gad, beyond expectation, only with a petticoat and the belly-ache.

SMITH. Pray, how was that, Sir?

BAYES. Why, Sir, I contrived a petticoat to be brought in upon a chair (nobody knew how) into a prince's chamber, whose father was not to see it, that came in by chance.

JOHNSON. God's my life, that was a notable contrivance, indeed.

SMITH. Aye; but, Mr. Bayes, how could you contrive the belly-ache?

BAYES. The easiest i'th' world, I gad: I'll tell you how: I made the prince sit down upon the petticoat, no more than so, and pretended to his father that he had just then got the belly-ache; whereupon his father went out to call a physician, and his man ran away with the petticoat.

SMITH. Well, and what followed upon that?

BAYES. Nothing, no earthly thing, I vow to gad.

JOHNSON. O' my word, Mr. Bayes, there you hit it.

BAYES. Yes, it gave a world of content. And then I paid 'em away besides, for I made 'em all talk bawdy—ha, ha, ha!— beastly, downright bawdry upon the stage, I gad—ha, ha, ha! —but with an infinite deal of wit, that I must say.

JOHNSON. That, aye that, we know well enough, can never fail you.

BAYES. No, I gad, can't it. Come, bring in the dance.

(Exit to call 'em.)

SMITH. Now, the devil take thee for a silly, confident, unnatural, fulsome rogue!

Enter BAYES and Players

BAYES. Pray dance well, before these gentlemen. You are commonly so lazy, but you should be light and easy, tah, tah, tah.

(All the while they dance, Bayes puts 'em out with teaching 'em.)

Well, gentlemen, you'll see this dance, if I am not deceived, take very well upon the stage, when they are perfect in their motions, and all that.

SMITH. I don't know how 'twill take, Sir, but I am sure you sweat hard for't.

BAYES. Aye, Sir, it costs me more pains and trouble to do these things than almost the things are worth.

SMITH. By my troth, I think so, Sir.

BAYES. Not for the things themselves, for I could write you, Sir, forty of 'em in a day; but, I gad, these players are such dull persons that, if a man be not by 'em upon every point and at every turn, I gad, they'll mistake you, Sir, and spoil all.

Enter a Player

What, is the funeral ready?

PLAYER. Yes, Sir.

BAYES. And is the lance filled with wine?

PLAYER. Sir, 'tis just now a-doing.

BAYES. Stay, then, I'll do it myself.

SMITH. Come, let's go with him.

BAYES. A match! But, Mr. Johnson, I gad, I am not like other persons; they care not what becomes of their things, so they can but get money for 'em. Now, I gad, when I write, if it be not just as it should be in every circumstance, to every particular, I gad, I am no more able to endure it; I am not myself, I'm out of my wits, and all that; I'm the strangest person in the whole world. For what care I for money? I write for reputation.

(Exeunt.)

ACT IV

SCENE I

BAYES *and the two Gentlemen*

BAYES. Gentlemen, because I would not have any two things alike in this play, the last act beginning with a witty scene of mirth, I make this to begin with a funeral.

SMITH. And is that all your reason for it, Mr. Bayes?

BAYES. No, Sir, I have a precedent for it besides. A person of honour, and a scholar, brought in his funeral just so; and he was one (let me tell you) that knew as well what belonged to a funeral as any man in England, I gad.

JOHNSON. Nay, if that be so, you are safe.

BAYES. I gad, but I have another device—a frolic, which I think yet better than all this; not for the plot or characters (for in my heroic plays, I make no difference as to these matters), but for another contrivance.

SMITH. What is that, I pray?

BAYES. Why, I have designed a conquest that cannot possibly, I gad, be acted in less than a whole week; and I'll speak a bold word, it shall drum, trumpet, shout, and battle, I gad, with any the most warlike tragedy we have, either ancient or modern.

JOHNSON. Aye, marry, Sir, there you say something.

SMITH. And pray, Sir, how have you ordered this same frolic of yours?

BAYES. Faith, Sir, by the rule of romance. For example: they divided their things into three, four, five, six, seven, eight, or as many tomes as they please: now I would very fain know what should hinder me from doing the same with my things, if I please?

JOHNSON. Nay, if you should not be master of your own works, 'tis very hard.

BAYES. That is my sense. And then, Sir, this contrivance of mine has something of the reason of a play in it, too; for as every one makes you five acts to one play, what do me I but make five plays to one plot, by which means the auditors have every day a new thing.

JOHNSON. Most admirably good, i'faith! and must certainly take, because it is not tedious.

BAYES. Aye, Sir, I know that; there's the main point. And then, upon Saturday, to make a close of all (for I ever begin upon a Monday), I make you, Sir, a sixth play, that sums up the whole matter to 'em, and all that, for fear they should have forgot it.

JOHNSON. That consideration, Mr. Bayes, indeed, I think, will be very necessary.

SMITH. And when comes in your share, pray, Sir?

BAYES. The third week.

JOHNSON. I vow, you'll get a world of money.

BAYES. Why, faith, a man must live; and if you don't thus pitch upon some new device, I gad, you'll never do it; for this age (take it o' my word) is somewhat hard to please. But there's one pretty odd passage, in the last of these plays, which may be executed two several ways, wherein I'd have your opinion, gentlemen.

JOHNSON. What is't, Sir?

BAYES. Why, Sir, I make a male person to be in love with a female.

SMITH. Do you mean that, Mr. Bayes, for a new thing?

BAYES. Yes, Sir, as I have ordered it. You shall hear. He having passionately loved her through my five whole plays, finding at last that she consents to his love, just after that his mother had appeared to him like a ghost, he kills himself. That's one way. The other is, that she coming at last to love him with as violent a passion as he loved her, she kills herself. Now my question is, which of these two persons should suffer upon this occasion?

JOHNSON. By my troth, it is a very hard case to decide.

BAYES. The hardest in the world, I gad; and has puzzled this pate very much. What say you, Mr. Smith?

SMITH. Why, truly, Mr. Bayes, if it might stand with your justice now, I would spare 'em both.

BAYES. I gad, and I think—ha—why then, I'll make him hinder her from killing herself. Aye, it shall be so.—— Come, come, bring in the funeral.

Enter a Funeral, with the two Usurpers and Attendants

Lay it down there—no, no, here, Sir.—— So; now speak.

KING USHER. Set down the funeral pile, and let our grief
Receive from its embraces some relief.

KING PHYSICIAN. Was't not unjust to ravish hence her breath,
And, in life's stead, to leave us nought but death?
The world discovers now its emptiness,
And by her loss demonstrates we have less.

BAYES. Is not this good language, now? is not that elevate? 'Tis my *non ultra*, I gad. You must know they were both in love with her.

SMITH. With her?—with whom?

BAYES. Why, this is Lardella's funeral.

SMITH. Lardella! Aye, who is she?

BAYES. Why, Sir, the sister of Drawcansir—a lady that was drowned at sea and had a wave for her winding-sheet.

KING USHER. Lardella, O Lardella, from above
Behold the tragic issues of our love.
Pity us sinking under grief and pain,
For thy being cast away upon the main.

BAYES. Look you now, you see I told you true.

SMITH. Aye, Sir, and I thank you for it, very kindly.

BAYES. Aye, I gad, but you will not have patience; honest Mr. —a—you will not have patience.

JOHNSON. Pray, Mr. Bayes, who is that Drawcansir?

BAYES. Why, Sir, a fierce hero, that frights his mistress, snubs up kings, baffles armies, and does what he will, without regard to numbers, good manners, or justice.

JOHNSON. A very pretty character.

SMITH. But, Mr. Bayes, I thought your heroes had ever been men of great humanity and justice.

BAYES. Yes, they have been so; but, for my part, I prefer that one quality of singly beating of whole armies above all your moral virtues put together, I gad. You shall see him come in presently. (*to the Players*) Zookers, why don't you read the paper?

KING PHYSICIAN. Oh, cry you mercy.

(*goes to take the paper*)

BAYES. Pish!—nay, you are such a fumbler. Come, I'll read it myself. (*takes a paper from off the coffin*)—Stay, it's an ill hand; I must use my spectacles. This, now, is a copy of verses which I make Lardella compose just as she is dying, with design to have it pinned upon her coffin, and so read by one of the usurpers, who is her cousin.

SMITH. A very shrewd design that, upon my word, Mr. Bayes.

BAYES. And what do you think now I fancy her to make love like, here, in the paper?

SMITH. Like a woman. What should she make love like?

BAYES. O' my word you are out though, Sir; I gad, you are.

SMITH. What then? like a man?

BAYES. No, sir, like a humble-bee.

SMITH. I confess, that I should not have fancied.

BAYES. It may be so, Sir. But it is, though, in order to the opinion of some of your ancient philosophers who held the transmigration of the soul.

SMITH. Very fine.

BAYES. I'll read the title: "To my dear Couz, King Phys."

SMITH. That's a little too familiar with a king though, Sir, by your favour, for a humble-bee.

BAYES. Mr. Smith, in other things I grant your knowledge may be above me; but as for poetry, give me leave to say, I understand that better: it has been longer my practice; it has indeed, Sir.

SMITH. Your servant, Sir.

BAYES. Pray, mark it.   (*reads*)

> "Since death my earthly part will thus remove,
> I'll come a humble-bee to your chaste love.
> With silent wings I'll follow you, dear couz;
> Or else, before you, in the sun-beams buzz.
> And when to melancholy groves you come,
> An airy ghost, you'll know me by my hum;
> For sound, being air, a ghost does well become." }

SMITH (*after a pause*). Admirable!

BAYES. "At night into your bosom I will creep,
   And buzz but softly if you chance to sleep:
   Yet in your dreams I will pass sweeping by,
   And then both hum and buzz before your eye."

JOHNSON. By my troth, that's a very great promise.

SMITH. Yes, and a most extraordinary comfort to boot.

BAYES. "Your bed of love from dangers I will free;
   But most, from love of any future bee.
   And when with pity your heart-strings shall crack,
   With empty arms I'll bear you on my back."

SMITH. A pick-a-pack, a pick-a-pack.

BAYES. Aye, I gad, but is not that *tuant* now, ha? is it not *tuant?* Here's the end:

"Then, at your birth of immortality, ⎫
   Like any winged archer, hence I'll fly,   ⎬
   And teach you your first flutt'ring in the sky." ⎭

JOHNSON. Oh, rare! This is the most natural, refined fancy that ever I heard, I'll swear.

BAYES. Yes, I think, for a dead person, it is a good enough way of making love; for being divested of her terrestrial part, and all that, she is only capable of these little, pretty, amorous designs that are innocent, and yet passionate.——— Come, draw your swords.

KING PHYSICIAN. Come, sword, come sheathe thyself within this
   breast,
Which only in Lardella's tomb can rest.

KING USHER. Come, dagger, come, and penetrate this heart,
Which cannot from Lardella's love depart.

Enter PALLAS

PALLAS. Hold! stop your murd'ring hands
At Pallas's commands!
For the supposed dead, O kings,
Forbear to act such deadly things.
Lardella lives: I did but try
If princes for their loves could die.
Such celestial constancy
Shall, by the gods, rewarded be:
And from these funeral obsequies
A nuptial banquet shall arise.
             (*The coffin opens, and a banquet is discovered.*)

BAYES. So, take away the coffin. Now it's out. This is the very funeral of the fair person which Volscius sent word was dead, and Pallas, you see, has turned it into a banquet.

SMITH. Well, but where is this banquet?

BAYES. Nay, look you, Sir, we must first have a dance, for joy that Lardella is not dead. Pray, Sir, give me leave to bring in my things properly at least.

SMITH. That, indeed, I had forgot. I ask your pardon.

BAYES. O, d'ye so, Sir? I am glad you will confess yourself once in an error, Mr. Smith.

(dance)

KING USHER. Resplendent Pallas, we in thee do find
The fiercest beauty and a fiercer mind;
And since to thee Lardella's life we owe,
We'll supple statues in thy temple grow.

KING PHYSICIAN. Well, since alive Lardella's found,
Let, in full bowls, her health go round.
        (The two Usurpers take each of them a bowl in their hands.)
KING USHER. But where's the wine?
PALLAS. That shall be mine.
Lo, from this conquering lance,
Does flow the purest wine of France;
        (fills the bowls out of her lance)
And, to appease your hunger, I
Have, in my helmet, brought a pie:
Lastly to bear a part with these,
Behold a buckler made of cheese.   *(Vanish PALLAS.)*

BAYES. There's the banquet. Are you satisfied now, Sir?

JOHNSON. By my troth, now, that is new, and more than I expected.

BAYES. Yes, I knew this would please you: for the chief art in poetry is to elevate your expectation, and then bring you off some extraordinary way.

Enter DRAWCANSIR

KING PHYSICIAN. What man is this that dares disturb our feast?
DRAWCANSIR. He that dares drink, and for that drink dares die,
And, knowing this, dares yet drink on, am I.

JOHNSON. That is, Mr. Bayes, as much as to say that, though

he would rather die than not drink, yet he would fain drink for all that, too.

BAYES. Right; that's the conceit on't.

JOHNSON. 'Tis a marvellous good one, I swear.

BAYES. Now there are some critics that have advised me to put out the second *dare,* and print *must* in the place on't; but, I gad, I think 'tis better thus a great deal.

JOHNSON. Whoo! a thousand times!

BAYES. Go on, then.

KING USHER. Sir, if you please, we should be glad to know
How long you here will stay, how soon you'll go.

BAYES. Is not that now like a well-bred person, I gad? So modest, so gent!

SMITH. Oh, very like.

DRAWCANSIR. You shall not know how long I here will stay;
But you shall know I'll take your bowls away.
  (*snatches the bowls out of the Kings' hands and drinks 'em off*)

SMITH. But, Mr. Bayes, is that, too, modest and gent?

BAYES. No, I gad, Sir, but it's great.

KING USHER. Though Brother, this grum stranger be a clown,
He'll leave us, sure, a little to gulp down.

DRAWCANSIR. Whoe'er to gulp one drop of this dares think,
I'll stare away his very pow'r to drink.
    (*The two Kings sneak off the stage, with their Attendants.*)
I drink, I huff, I strut, look big and stare;
And all this I can do, because I dare. (*Exit.*)

SMITH. I suppose, Mr. Bayes, this is the fierce hero you spoke of.

BAYES. Yes, but this is nothing: you shall see him, in the last act, win above a dozen battles, one after another, I gad, as fast as they can possibly come upon the stage.

JOHNSON. That will be a sight worth the seeing, indeed.

SMITH. But pray, Mr. Bayes, why do you make the kings let him use 'em so scurvily?

BAYES. Phoo! that is to raise the character of Drawcansir.

JOHNSON. O' my word, that was well thought on.

BAYES. Now, Sirs, I'll show you a scene indeed; or rather, indeed, the scene of scenes. 'Tis an heroic scene.

SMITH. And pray, Sir, what's your design in this scene?

BAYES. Why, Sir, my design is gilded truncheons, forced conceit, smooth verse, and a rant: in fine, if this scene do not take, I gad, I'll write no more. Come, come in, Mr.—a—nay, come in as many as you can. Gentlemen, I must desire you to remove a little, for I must fill the stage.

SMITH. Why fill the stage?

BAYES. Oh, Sir, because your herioc verse never sounds well but when the stage is full.

SCENE II

Enter PRINCE PRETTY-MAN and PRINCE VOLSCIUS

BAYES. Nay, hold, hold! pray, by your leave a little.—— Look you, Sir, the drift of this scene is somewhat more than ordinary; for I make 'em both fall out because they are not in love with the same woman.

SMITH. Not in love? You mean, I suppose, because they are in love, Mr. Bayes?

BAYES. No, Sir; I say not in love. There's a new conceit for you. Now, speak.

PRETTY-MAN. Since fate, Prince Volscius, now has found the way
For our so long'd-for meeting here this day,
Lend thy attention to my grand concern.

VOLSCIUS. I gladly would that story from thee learn;
But thou to love dost, Pretty-man, incline:
Yet love in thy breast is not love in mine?

BAYES. *Antithesis!*—thine and mine.

PRETTY-MAN. Since love itself's the same, why should it be
Diff'ring in you from what it is in me?

BAYES. Reasoning! I gad, I love reasoning in verse.

VOLSCIUS. Love takes, chameleon-like, a various dye
From every plant on which itself does lie.

BAYES. *Simile!*

PRETTY-MAN. Let not thy love the course of nature fright:
Nature does most in harmony delight.

VOLSCIUS. How weak a deity would nature prove
Contending with the pow'rful god of love?

BAYES. There's a great verse!

VOLSCIUS. If incense thou wilt offer at the shrine
Of mighty love, burn it to none but mine.

Her rosy lips eternal sweets exhale;
And her bright flames make all flames else look pale.

BAYES. I gad, that is right.

PRETTY-MAN. Perhaps dull incense may thy love suffice;
But mine must be ador'd with sacrifice.
All hearts turn ashes which her eyes control:
The body they consume as well as soul.

VOLSCIUS. My love has yet a power more divine;
Victims her altars burn not, but refine:
Amidst the flames they ne'er give up the ghost,
But, with her looks, revive still as they roast.
In spite of pain and death, they're kept alive:
Her fiery eyes makes 'em in fire survive.

BAYES. That is as well, I gad, as I can do.

VOLSCIUS. Let my Parthenope at length prevail.

BAYES. Civil, I gad.

PRETTY-MAN. I'll sooner have a passion for a whale,
In whose vast bulk, though store of oil doth lie,
We find more shape, more beauty, in a fly.

SMITH. That's uncivil, I gad.

BAYES. Yes; but as far a fetched fancy though, I gad, as e'er
you saw.

VOLSCIUS. Soft, Pretty-man, let not thy vain pretence
Of perfect love defame love's excellence.
Parthenope is sure as far above
All other loves as above all is love.

BAYES. Ah! I gad, that strikes me.

PRETTY-MAN. To blame my Cloris, gods would not pretend.

BAYES. Now mark.

VOLSCIUS. Were all gods join'd, they could not hope to mend
My better choice, for fair Parthenope
Gods would, themselves, un-god themselves to see.

BAYES. Now the rant's a-coming.

PRETTY-MAN. Durst any of the gods be so uncivil,
I'd make that god subscribe himself a devil.

BAYES. Ah, godsookers, that's well writ!

(*Scratching his head, his peruke falls off.*)

VOLSCIUS. Couldst thou that god from heav'n to earth translate,
He could not fear to want a heav'nly state.
Parthenope, on earth, can heav'n create.

PRETTY-MAN. Cloris does heav'n itself so far excel,
She can transcend the joys of heav'n in hell.

BAYES. There's a bold flight for you now!—— 'Sdeath, I have
lost my peruke!—— Well, gentlemen, this is that I never yet
saw anyone could write but myself. Here's true spirit and flame
all through, I gad. So, so; pray clear the stage.

(*He puts 'em off the stage.*)

JOHNSON. I wonder how the coxcomb has got the knack of
writing smooth verse thus.

SMITH. Why, there's no need of brain for this; 'tis but scan-
ning; the labour's in the finger. But where's the sense of it?

JOHNSON. Oh, for that, he desires to be excused; he is too
proud a man to creep servilely after sense, I assure you.——
But pray, Mr. Bayes, why is this scene all in verse?

BAYES. O Sir, the subject is too great for prose.

SMITH. Well said, i'faith. I'll give thee a pot of ale for that
answer; 'tis well worth it.

BAYES. Come, with all my heart.
"I'll make that god subscribe himself a devil." That single line,
I gad, is worth all that my brother poets ever writ. Let down
the curtain. (*Exeunt.*)

ACT V

BAYES *and the two Gentlemen*

BAYES. Now, gentlemen, I will be bold to say, I'll show you
the greatest scene that ever England saw: I mean not for words,
for those I do not value, but for state, show, and magnificence.
In fine, I'll justify it to be as grand to the eye every whit, I gad,
as that great scene in *Harry the Eight*—and grander too, I gad;
for, instead of two bishops, I bring in here four cardinals.

*The Curtain is drawn up; the two usurping Kings appear in state,
with the four Cardinals,* PRINCE PRETTY-MAN, PRINCE VOL-
SCIUS, AMARYLLIS, CLORIS, PARTHENOPE, &c.; *before them,
Heralds and Sergeants at Arms with maces*

SMITH. Mr. Bayes, pray what is the reason that two of the
cardinals are in hats and the other in caps?

BAYES. Why, Sir, because—by gad, I won't tell you.—— Your country friend, Sir, grows so troublesome.

KING USHER. Now, Sir, to the business of the day.

KING PHYSICIAN. Speak, Volscius.

VOLSCIUS. Dread sovereign Lords, my zeal to you must not invade my duty to your son. Let me intreat that great Prince Pretty-man first do speak, whose high pre-eminence, in all things that do bear the name of good, may justly claim that privilege.

BAYES. Here it begins to unfold. You may perceive, now, that he is his son.

JOHNSON. Yes, Sir; and we are very much beholding to you for that discovery.

PRETTY-MAN. Royal Father, upon my knees I beg
That the illustrious Volscius first be heard.

VOLSCIUS. That preference is only due to Amaryllis, Sir.

BAYES. I'll make her speak very well, by and by; you shall see.

AMARYLLIS. Invincible sovereigns——   (*soft music*)

KING USHER. But stay, what sound is this invades our ears?

KING PHYSICIAN. Sure 'tis the music of the moving spheres.

PRETTY-MAN. Behold, with wonder! yonder comes from far,
A god-like cloud and a triumphant car,
In which our two right kings sit one by one,
With virgins' vests, and laurel garlands on.

KING USHER. Then, Brother Phys', 'tis time we
should be gone.

(*The two Usurpers steal out of the throne and go away.*)

BAYES. Look you now, did not I tell you that this would be as easy a change as the other?

SMITH. Yes, faith, you did so; though I confess, I could not believe you; but you have brought it about, I see.

(*The two right Kings of Brentford descend in the clouds, singing in white garments; and three fiddlers sitting before them, in green.*)

BAYES. Now, because the two right kings descend from above, I make 'em sing to the tune and style of our modern spirits.

1ST KING. Haste, Brother king, we are sent from above.

2D KING. Let us move, let us move——
Move to remove the fate
Of Brentford's long united state.

1ST KING. Tara, tan tara, full east and by south,

2D KING. We sail with thunder in our mouth,
In scorching noon-day, whilst the traveller stays,
Busy, busy, busy, busy, we bustle along.
Mounted upon warm Phœbus his rays,
                Through the heavenly throng,
                    Hasting to those
Who will feast us, at night, with a pig's pettitoes.
    1ST KING. And we'll fall with our pate
                    In an *olio* of hate.
    2D KING. But now supper's done, the servitors try,
Like soldiers, to storm a whole half-moon pie.
    1ST KING. They gather, they gather hot custard in spoons;
But alas, I must leave these half-moons,
And repair to my trusty dragoons.
    2D KING. Oh, stay, for you need not as yet go astray;
The tide, like a friend, has brought ships in our way,
And on their high ropes we will play.
Like maggots in filberts, we'll snug in our shell,
                We'll frisk in our shell,
                We'll firk in our shell,
                And farewell.
    1ST KING. But the ladies have all inclination to dance,
And the green frogs croak out a coranto of France.

    BAYES. Is not that pretty, now? The fiddlers are all in green.
    SMITH. Aye, but they play no coranto.
    JOHNSON. No, but they play a tune, that's a great deal better.
    BAYES. "No coranto," quoth a!—that's a good one, with all my
heart.—— Come, sing on.

    2D KING. Now mortals that hear
                How we tilt and career,
                With wonder will fear
The event of such things as shall never appear.
    1ST KING. Stay you to fulfil what the gods have decreed.
    2D KING. Then call me to help you if there shall be need.
    1ST KING. So firmly resolv'd is a true Brentford king
To save the distressed and help to 'em bring,
That ere a full pot of good ale you can swallow,
He's here with a whoop, and gone with a holla.

                    (BAYES *fillips his finger, and sings after 'em.*)
    BAYES. "He's here with a whoop, and gone with a holla." This,
Sir, you must know, I thought once to have brought in with a
conjurer.

    JOHNSON. Aye, that would have been better.

BAYES. No, faith, not when you consider it; for thus 'tis more compendious and does the thing every whit as well.

SMITH. Thing!—what thing?

BAYES. Why, bring 'em down again into the throne, Sir. What thing would you have?

SMITH. Well; but methinks the sense of this song is not very plain.

BAYES. Plain? why, did you ever hear any people in clouds speak plain? They must be all for flight of fancy, at its full range, without the least check or control upon it. When once you tie up spirits and people in clouds to speak plain, you spoil al..

SMITH. Bless me, what a monster's this!

(*The two Kings light out of the clouds and step into the throne.*)

1ST KING. Come, now to serious counsel we'll advance.
2D KING. I do agree; but first let's have a dance.

BAYES. Right. You did that very well, Mr. Cartwright. "But first, let's have a dance." Pray, remember that; be sure you do it always just so, for it must be done as if it were the effect of thought and premeditation.—"But first, let's have a dance." Pray, remember that.

SMITH. Well, I can hold no longer; I must gag this rogue; there's no enduring of him.

JOHNSON. No, prithee make use of thy patience a little longer; let's see the end of him now.

(*dance a grand dance*)

BAYES. This, now, is an ancient dance, of right belonging to the Kings of Brentford, but since derived, with a little alteration, to the Inns of Court.

An Alarm. Enter two Heralds

1ST KING. What saucy groom molests our privacies?
1ST HERALD. The army's at the door, and, in disguise,
Desires a word with both your Majesties:
2D HERALD. Having, from Knightsbridge, hither marched by stealth.
2D KING. Bid 'em attend a while and drink our health.

SMITH. How, Mr. Bayes—the army in disguise?

BAYES. Aye, Sir, for fear the usurpers might discover them, that went out but just now.

SMITH. Why, what if they had discovered them?

BAYES. Why, then they had broke the design.

1ST KING. Here, take five guineas for those warlike men.
2D KING. And here's five more; that makes the sum just
ten.
1ST HERALD. We have not seen so much the Lord knows
when.   (*Exeunt Heralds.*)
1ST KING. Speak on, brave Amaryllis.

AMARYLLIS. Invincible sovereigns, blame not my modesty
If at this grand conjuncture——

(*drum beat behind the stage*)
1ST KING. What dreadful noise is this that comes and goes?

Enter a Soldier with his sword drawn

SOLDIER. Haste hence, great Sirs, your royal persons save,
For the event of war no mortal knows!
The army, wrangling for the gold you gave,
First fell to words, and then to handy-blows.   (*Exit.*)

BAYES. Is not that now a pretty kind of a stanza, and a handsome come off?

2D KING. O dangerous estate of sovereign pow'r!
Obnoxious to the change of every hour.
1ST KING. Let us for shelter in our cabinet stay:
Perhaps these threat'ning storms may pass away.

(*Exeunt.*)

JOHNSON. But, Mr. Bayes, did not you promise us, just now, to
make Amaryllis speak very well?

BAYES. Aye, and so she would have done but that they hindered
her.

SMITH. How, Sir, whether you would or no?

BAYES. Aye, Sir; the plot lay so that, I vow to gad, it was not to
be avoided.

SMITH. Marry, that was hard.

JOHNSON. But, pray, who hindered her?

BAYES. Why, the battle, Sir, that's just coming in at door. And
I'll tell you now a strange thing—though I don't pretend to do
more than other men, I gad, I'll give you both a whole week to
guess how I'll represent this battle.

SMITH. I had rather be bound to fight your battle, I assure you,
Sir.

BAYES. Whoo! there's it now. Fight a battle? there's the common error. I knew presently where I should have you. Why, pray,

Sir, do but tell me this one thing: can you think it a decent thing, in a battle before ladies, to have men run their swords through one another, and all that?

JOHNSON. No, faith, 'tis not civil.

BAYES. Right! On the other side—to have a long relation of squadrons here, and squadrons there—what is it but dull prolixity?

JOHNSON. Excellently reasoned, by my troth!

BAYES. Wherefore, Sir, to avoid both those indecorums, I sum up my whole battle in the representation of two persons only—no more—and yet so lively that, I vow to gad, you would swear ten thousand men were at it, really engaged. Do you mark me?

SMITH. Yes, Sir; but I think I should hardly swear, though, for all that.

BAYES. By my troth, Sir, but you would, though, when you see it; for I make 'em both come out in armour, *cap-a-pie*, with their swords drawn, and hung with a scarlet ribbon at their wrists (which, you know, represents fighting enough).

JOHNSON. Aye, aye; so much that, if I were in your place, I would make 'em go out again without ever speaking one word.

BAYES. No; there you are out; for I make each of 'em hold a lute in his hand.

SMITH. How, Sir—instead of a buckler?

BAYES. O Lord, O Lord!—instead of a buckler? Pray, Sir, do you ask no more questions. I make 'em, Sir, play the battle in *recitativo*. And here's the conceit: just at the very same instant that one sings, the other, Sir, recovers you his sword, and puts himself in a warlike posture, so that you have at once your ear entertained with music and good language, and your eye satisfied with the garb and accoutrements of war.

SMITH. I confess, Sir, you stupefy me.

BAYES. You shall see.

JOHNSON. But, Mr. Bayes, might not we have a little fighting? for I love those plays where they cut and slash one another, upon the stage, for a whole hour together.

BAYES. Why, then, to tell you true, I have contrived it both ways. But you shall have my *recitativo* first.

JOHNSON. Aye, now you are right; there is nothing then can be objected against it.

BAYES. True; and so, I gad, I'll make it, too, a tragedy in a trice.

Enter, at several doors, the General and Lieutenant-General,
armed cap-a-pie, *with each of them a lute in his hand, and*
his sword drawn, and hung with a scarlet ribbon at his wrist

LIEUTENANT-GENERAL. Villain, thou liest!

GENERAL. Arm, arm, Gonsalvo, arm! What ho!
The lie no flesh can brook, I trow.

LIEUTENANT-GENERAL. Advance, from Acton, with the musketeers.

GENERAL. Draw down the Chelsea cuirassiers.

LIEUTENANT-GENERAL. The band you boast of, Chelsea cuirassiers,
Shall, in my Putney pikes, now meet their peers.

GENERAL. Chiswickians aged, and renown'd in fight,
Join with the Hammersmith brigade.

LIEUTENANT-GENERAL. You'll find my Mortlake boys will do them
            right,
Unless by Fulham numbers overlaid.

GENERAL. Let the left wing of Twick'nam foot advance
And line that eastern hedge.

LIEUTENANT-GENERAL. The horse I rais'd in Petty-France
Shall try their chance,
And scour the meadows, overgrown with sedge.

GENERAL. Stand! give the word.

LIEUTENANT-GENERAL. Bright sword.

GENERAL. That may be thine,
            But 'tis not mine.

LIEUTENANT-GENERAL. Give fire, give fire, at once give fire,
And let those recreant troops perceive mine ire.

GENERAL. Pursue, pursue! They fly
            That first did give the lie.   (*Exeunt.*)

BAYES. This, now, is not improper, I think, because the specta-
tors know all these towns, and may easily conceive them to be
within the dominions of the two kings of Brentford.

JOHNSON. Most exceeding well designed!

BAYES. How do you think I have contrived to give a stop to
this battle?

SMITH. How?

BAYES. By an eclipse—which, let me tell you, is a kind of fancy
that was yet never so much as thought of but by myself and one
person more that shall be nameless.

Enter Lieutenant-General

LIEUTENANT-GENERAL. What midnight darkness does invade the day,
And snatch the victor from his conquer'd prey?

Is the Sun weary of this bloody sight,
And winks upon us with his eye of light?
'Tis an eclipse. This was unkind, O Moon,
To clap between me and the Sun so soon.
Foolish eclipse! thou this in vain hast done;
My brighter honour had eclips'd the Sun.
But now behold eclipses two in one.   (*Exit.*)

JOHNSON. This is as admirable representation of a battle as ever
I saw.

BAYES. Aye, Sir. But how would you fancy now to represent an
eclipse?

SMITH. Why, that's to be supposed.

BAYES. Supposed! Aye, you are ever at your "suppose"—ha, ha,
ha! Why, you may as well suppose the whole play. No, it must
come in upon the stage, that's certain; but in some odd way that
may delight, amuse, and all that. I have a conceit for't that I am
sure is new and, I believe, to the purpose.

JOHNSON. How's that?

BAYES. Why, the truth is, I took the first hint of this out of a
dialogue between Phœbus and Aurora, in *The Slighted Maid,*
which, by my troth, was very pretty, but I think you'll confess this
is a little better.

JOHNSON. No doubt on't, Mr. Bayes. A great deal better.

(BAYES *hugs* JOHNSON, *then turns to* SMITH.)

BAYES. Ah, dear rogue! But—a—Sir, you have heard, I suppose, that your eclipse of the moon is nothing else but an inter-
position of the earth between the sun and moon: as likewise your
eclipse of the sun is caused by an interlocation of the moon betwixt the earth and sun?

SMITH. I have heard some such thing, indeed.

BAYES. Well, Sir, then what do me I but make the earth, sun,
and moon come out upon the stage, and dance the Hay?—hum!
And, of necessity, by the very nature of this dance, the earth must
be sometimes between the sun and the moon, and the moon between the earth and sun; and there you have both your eclipses,
by demonstration.

JOHNSON. That must needs be very fine, truly.

BAYES. Yes, it has fancy in't. And then, Sir, that there may be
something in't, too, of a joke, I bring 'em in all singing, and make
the moon sell the earth a bargain.—— Come, come out, eclipse,
to the tune of *Tom Tyler.*

Enter LUNA

LUNA. Orbis, O Orbis!
Come to me, thou little rogue Orbis.

Enter the EARTH

ORBIS. Who calls Terra Firma, pray?
LUNA. Luna that ne'er shines by day.
ORBIS. What means Luna in a veil?
LUNA. Luna means to show her tail.

BAYES. There's the bargain.

Enter SOL, *to the tune of* Robin Hood

SOL. Fie, sister, fie! thou mak'st me muse,
              Derry, derry down,
       To see thee Orb abuse.
LUNA. I hope his anger 'twill not move;
Since I show'd it out of love.
       Hey down, derry down.
ORBIS. Where shall I thy true love know,
              Thou pretty, pretty Moon?
LUNA. To-morrow soon, ere it be noon—
              On Mount Vesuvio.   (*bis*)
SOL. Then I will shine.

                                      (*to the tune of* Trenchmore)

ORBIS. And I will be fine.
LUNA. And we will drink nothing but Lipari wine.
OMNES. And we, etc.

                              (*As they dance the Hay,* BAYES *speaks.*)
BAYES. Now the earth's before the moon; now the moon's before the sun; there's the eclipse again.

SMITH. He's mightily taken with this, I see.

JOHNSON. Aye, 'tis so extraordinary, how can he choose?

BAYES. So, now, vanish eclipse, and enter t'other battle, and
fight. Here now, if I am not mistaken, you will see fighting
enough.

(*A battle is fought between foot and great hobby-horses. At last,*
    DRAWCANSIR *comes in, and kills 'em all on both sides. All this*
    while the battle is fighting, BAYES *is telling them when to shout,*
    and shouts with 'em.)

DRAWCANSIR. Others may boast a single man to kill;
But I the blood of thousands daily spill.

Let petty kings the names of parties know:
Where'er I come, I slay both friend and foe.
The swiftest horsemen my swift rage controls,
And from their bodies drives their trembling souls.
If they had wings and to the gods could fly,
I would pursue, and beat 'em through the sky:
And make proud Jove, with all his thunder, see
This single arm more dreadful is than he.   (*Exit.*)

BAYES. There's a brave fellow for you now, Sirs. You may talk
of your Hector, and Achilles, and I know not who; but I defy all
your histories, and your romances, too, to show me one such conqueror as this Drawcansir.

JOHNSON. I swear, I think you may.

SMITH. But, Mr. Bayes, how shall all these dead men go off?
for I see none alive to help 'em.

BAYES. Go off! why, as they came on—upon their legs. How
should they go off? Why, do you think the people here don't
know they are not dead? He is mighty ignorant, poor man; your
friend here is very silly, Mr. Johnson, I gad, he is—ha, ha, ha!
Come, Sir, I'll show you how they shall go off.—— Rise, rise, Sirs,
and go about your business. There's "go off" for you now—ha,
ha, ha! Mr. Ivory, a word.—— Gentlemen, I'll be with you
presently.   (*Exit.*)

JOHNSON. Will you so? then we'll be gone.

SMITH. Aye, prithee, let's go, that we may preserve our hearing. One battle more will take mine quite away.   (*Exeunt.*)

Enter BAYES *and Players*

BAYES. Where are the gentlemen?

1ST PLAYER. They are gone, Sir.

BAYES. Gone! 'Sdeath, this last act is best of all. I'll go fetch
'em again.   (*Exit.*)

1ST PLAYER. What shall we do, now he is gone away?

2D PLAYER. Why, so much the better. Then let's go to dinner.

3D PLAYER. Stay, here's a foul piece of paper of his. Let's see
what 'tis.

3D OR 4TH PLAYER. Aye, aye, come, let's hear it.

3D PLAYER (*reads: The Argument of the Fifth Act*):

"Cloris, at length, being sensible of Prince Pretty-man's passion,
consents to marry him; but just as they are going to church, Prince
Pretty-man meeting, by chance, with old Joan the chandler's widow,

and remembering it was she that first brought him acquainted with Cloris, out of a high point of honour breaks off his match with Cloris and marries old Joan. Upon which, Cloris, in despair, drowns herself: and Prince Pretty-man, discontentedly, walks by the river side."

This will never do; 'tis just like the rest. Come, let's be gone.

MOST OF THE PLAYERS. Aye, pox on't, let's go away.

(*Exeunt.*)

Enter BAYES

BAYES. A plague on 'em both for me! they have made me sweat, to run after 'em. A couple of senseless rascals that had rather go to dinner than see this play out, with a pox to 'em! What comfort has a man to write for such dull rogues?—(*calls*) Come Mr.—a—Where are you, Sir? Come away quick—quick!

Enter Stage-keeper

STAGE-KEEPER. Sir, they are gone to dinner.

BAYES. Yes, I know the gentlemen are gone; but I ask for the players.

STAGE-KEEPER. Why, an't please your Worship, Sir, the players are gone to dinner, too.

BAYES. How! are the players gone to dinner? 'Tis impossible: the players gone to dinner! I gad, if they are, I'll make 'em know what it is to injure a person that does 'em the honour to write for 'em, and all that. A company of proud, conceited, humourous, cross-grained persons, and all that. I gad, I'll make 'em the most contemptible, despicable, inconsiderable persons, and all that, in the whole world for this trick. I gad, I'll be revenged on 'em; I'll sell this play to the other house.

STAGE-KEEPER. Nay, good Sir, don't take away the book; you'll disappoint the company that comes to see it acted here this afternoon.

BAYES. That's all one. I must reserve this comfort to myself: my play and I shall go together; we will not part, indeed, Sir.

STAGE-KEEPER. But what will the town say, Sir?

BAYES. The town! Why, what care I for the town? I gad, the town has used me as scurvily as the players have done. But I'll be revenged on them too; for I'll lampoon 'em all. And since they will not admit of my plays, they shall know what a satirist I am. And so farewell to this stage, I gad, forever. (*Exit.*)

Enter Players

1ST PLAYER. Come, then, let's set up bills for another play.

2D PLAYER. Aye, aye; we shall lose nothing by this, I warrant you.

1ST PLAYER. I am of your opinion. But before we go, let's see Haynes and Shirley practise the last dance; for that may serve us another time.

2D PLAYER. I'll call 'em in; I think they are but in the tiring-room. (*the dance done*)

1ST PLAYER. Come, come; let's go away to dinner.

(*Exeunt omnes.*)

EPILOGUE

The play is at an end, but where's the plot?
That circumstance our poet Bayes forgot,
And we can boast, though 'tis a plotting age,
No place is freer from it than the stage.
The ancients plotted, though, and strove to please
With sense that might be understood with ease;
They every scene with so much wit did store
That who brought any in, went out with more:
But this new way of wit does so surprise,
Men lose their wits in wond'ring where it lies.
If it be true that monstrous births presage
The following mischiefs that afflict the age,
And sad disasters to the state proclaim,
Plays without head or tail may do the same.
Wherefore, for ours, and for the kingdom's peace,
May this prodigious way of writing cease.
Let's have, at least, once in our lives, a time
When we may hear some reason, not all rhyme:
We have these ten years felt its influence;
Pray let this prove a year of prose and sense.

The Country Wife

A COMEDY

By WILLIAM WYCHERLEY

Indignior quicquam reprehendi, non quia crassè
Compositum illepidéve putetur, sed quia nuper:
Nec veniam Antiquis, sed honorem & præmia posci.

HORAT.[1]

PROLOGUE

Spoken by MR. HORNER

Poets, like cudgell'd bullies, never do
At first or second blow submit to you;
But will provoke you still, and ne'er have done,
Till you are weary first with laying on.
The late so baffled scribbler of this day,
Though he stands trembling, bids me boldly say,

[1] I hate to see something criticized not on the grounds that it is clumsy and inelegant, but simply because it is modern. I hate to see people demand not merely indulgence for the older writers, but the actual prerogative of idolatry.—Horace, *Epistles*, 1,1, 76-78.

What we before most plays are us'd to do,
For poets out of fear first draw on you;
In a fierce prologue the still pit defy,
And, ere you speak, like Castril give the lie.
But though our Bayes's battles oft I've fought,
And with bruis'd knuckles their dear conquests bought;
Nay, never yet fear'd odds upon the stage,
In prologue dare not hector with the age,
But would take quarter from your saving hands,
Though Bayes within all yielding countermands,
Says you confed'rate wits no quarter give,
Therefore his play shan't ask your leave to live.
Well, let the vain rash fop, by huffing so,
Think to obtain the better terms of you;
But we, the actors, humbly will submit,
Now, and at any time, to a full pit;
Nay, often we anticipate your rage,
And murder poets for you on our stage:
We set no guards upon our tiring-room,
But when with flying colours there you come,
We patiently, you see, give up to you
Our poets, virgins, nay, our matrons too.

THE PERSONS

MR. HORNER	MRS. MARGERY PINCHWIFE
MR. HARCOURT	MRS. ALITHEA
MR. DORILANT	LADY FIDGET
MR. PINCHWIFE	MRS. DAINTY FIDGET
MR. SPARKISH	MRS. SQUEAMISH
SIR JASPER FIDGET	OLD LADY SQUEAMISH
A Boy	LUCY, *Alithea's Maid*
A Quack	*Waiters, Servants, and Attendants*

SCENE: *London*

THE COUNTRY WIFE

ACT I

Enter HORNER, *and* QUACK *following him at a distance*

HORN. (*aside*) A quack is as fit for a pimp as a midwife for a bawd; they are still but in their way, both helpers of nature.— (*aloud*) Well, my dear Doctor, hast thou done what I desired?

QUACK. I have undone you for ever with the women, and reported you throughout the whole town as bad as an eunuch, with as much trouble as if I had made you one in earnest.

HORN. But have you told all the midwives you know, the orange wenches at the playhouses, the city husbands, and old fumbling keepers of this end of the town, for they'll be the readiest to report it?

QUACK. I have told all the chambermaids, waiting-women, tire-women, and old women of my acquaintance; nay, and whispered it as a secret to 'em, and to the whisperers of Whitehall; so that you need not doubt 'twill spread, and you will be as odious to the handsome young women as——

HORN. As the small-pox. Well——

QUACK. And to the married women of this end of the town, as——

HORN. As the great ones; nay, as their own husbands.

QUACK. And to the city dames, as aniseed Robin, of filthy and contemptible memory; and they will frighten their children with your name, especially their females.

HORN. And cry, Horner's coming to carry you away. I am only afraid 'twill not be believed. You told 'em 'twas by an English-French disaster, and an English-French chirurgeon, who has given me at once not only a cure, but an antidote for the future against that damned malady, and that worse distemper, love, and all other women's evils?

QUACK. Your late journey into France has made it the more credible, and your being here a fortnight before you appeared in public looks as if you apprehended the shame, which I wonder you do not. Well, I have been hired by young gallants to belie 'em t'other way, but you are the first would be thought a man unfit for women.

HORN. Dear Mr. Doctor, let vain rogues be contented only to be thought abler men than they are; generally 'tis all the pleasure they have, but mine lies another way.

QUACK. You take, methinks, a very preposterous way to it, and as ridiculous as if we operators in physic should put forth bills to disparage our medicaments, with hopes to gain customers.

HORN. Doctor, there are quacks in love as well as physic, who get but the fewer and worse patients for their boasting; a good name is seldom got by giving it one's self; and women no more than honour are compassed by bragging. Come, come, Doctor, the wisest lawyer never discovers the merits of his cause till the trial; the wealthiest man conceals his riches, and the cunning gamester his play. Shy husbands and keepers, like old rooks, are not to be cheated but by a new unpractised trick: false friendship will pass now no more than false dice upon 'em; no, not in the city.

Enter Boy

BOY. There are two ladies and a gentleman coming up.

(*Exit.*)

HORN. A pox! some unbelieving sisters of my former acquaintance, who, I am afraid, expect their sense should be satisfied of the falsity of the report. No—this formal fool and women!

Enter SIR JASPER FIDGET, LADY FIDGET, *and* MRS. DAINTY FIDGET

QUACK. His wife and sister.

SIR JASP. My coach breaking just now before your door, Sir, I look upon as an occasional reprimand to me, Sir, for not kissing your hands, Sir, since your coming out of France, Sir; and so my disaster, Sir, has been my good fortune, Sir; and this is my wife and sister, Sir.

HORN. What then, Sir?

SIR JASP. My lady, and sister, Sir.—Wife, this is Master Horner.

LADY FID. Master Horner, husband!

SIR JASP. My lady, my Lady Fidget, Sir.

HORN. So, Sir.

SIR JASP. Won't you be acquainted with her, Sir?—(*aside*) So, the report is true, I find, by his coldness or aversion to the sex;

but I'll play the wag with him.—Pray salute my wife, my lady,
Sir.

HORN. I will kiss no man's wife, Sir, for him, Sir; I have taken
my eternal leave, Sir, of the sex already, Sir.

SIR JASP. (*aside*) Ha! ha! ha! I'll plague him yet.——Not know
my wife, Sir?

HORN. I do not know your wife, Sir; she's a woman, Sir, and
consequently a monster, Sir, a greater monster than a husband,
Sir.

SIR JASP. A husband! how, Sir?

HORN. So, Sir; but I make no more cuckolds, Sir.

(*makes horns*)

SIR JASP. Ha! ha! ha! Mercury! Mercury!

LADY FID. Pray, Sir Jasper, let us be gone from this rude fellow.

MRS. DAIN. Who, by his breeding, would think he had ever
been in France?

LADY FID. Foh! he's but too much a French fellow, such as hate
women of quality and virtue for their love to their husbands, Sir
Jasper; a woman is hated by 'em as much for loving her husband
as for loving their money. But pray, let's be gone.

HORN. You do well, Madam, for I have nothing that you came
for: I have brought over not so much as a bawdy picture, no new
postures, nor the second part of the *Escole des Filles;* nor——

QUACK. (*apart to* HORNER) Hold, for shame, Sir! what d'ye
mean? You will ruin yourself for ever with the sex——

SIR JASP. Ha! ha! ha! he hates women perfectly, I find.

MRS. DAIN. What pity 'tis he should!

LADY FID. Ay, he's a base rude fellow for't. But affectation
makes not a woman more odious to them than virtue.

HORN. Because your virtue is your greatest affectation, Madam.

LADY FID. How, you saucy fellow! would you wrong my honour?

HORN. If I could.

LADY FID. How d'ye mean, Sir?

SIR JASP. Ha! ha! ha! no, he can't wrong your Ladyship's honour, upon my honour; he, poor man—hark you in your ear—a
mere eunuch.

LADY FID. O filthy French beast! foh! foh! why do we stay? let's
be gone: I can't endure the sight of him.

SIR JASP. Stay but till the chairs come; they'll be here presently.

LADY FID. No, no.

SIR JASP. Nor can I stay longer. 'Tis—let me see, a quarter and a half quarter of a minute past eleven. The council will be sat; I must away. Business must be preferred always before love and ceremony with the wise, Mr. Horner.

HORN. And the impotent, Sir Jasper.

SIR JASP. Ay, ay, the impotent, Master Horner; ha! ha! ha!

LADY FID. What, leave us with a filthy man alone in his lodgings?

SIR JASP. He's an innocent man now, you know. Pray stay, I'll hasten the chairs to you.—— Mr. Horner, your servant; I should be glad to see you at my house. Pray come and dine with me, and play at cards with my wife after dinner; you are fit for women at that game yet, ha! ha!—(*aside*) 'Tis as much a husband's prudence to provide innocent diversion for a wife as to hinder her unlawful pleasures; and he had better employ her than let her employ herself.——Farewell.

HORN. Your servant, Sir Jasper.   (*Exit* SIR JASPER.)

LADY FID. I will not stay with him, foh!——

HORN. Nay, Madam, I beseech you stay, if it be but to see I can be as civil to ladies yet as they would desire.

LADY FID. No, no, foh! you cannot be civil to ladies.

MRS. DAIN. You as civil as ladies would desire?

LADY FID. No, no, no, foh! foh! foh!

(*Exeunt* LADY FIDGET *and* MRS. DAINTY FIDGET.)

QUACK. Now, I think, I, or you yourself, rather, have done your business with the women.

HORN. Thou art an ass. Don't you see already, upon the report and my carriage, this grave man of business leaves his wife in my lodgings, invites me to his house and wife, who before would not be acquainted with me out of jealousy?

QUACK. Nay, by this means you may be the more acquainted with the husbands, but the less with the wives.

HORN. Let me alone; if I can but abuse the husbands, I'll soon disabuse the wives. Stay—I'll reckon you up the advantages I am like to have by my stratagem. First, I shall be rid of all my old acquaintances, the most insatiable sorts of duns, that invade our lodgings in a morning; and next to the pleasure of making a new mistress is that of being rid of an old one, and of all old debts. Love, when it comes to be so, is paid the most unwillingly.

QUACK. Well, you may be so rid of your old acquaintances; but how will you get any new ones?

HORN. Doctor, thou wilt never make a good chemist, thou art so incredulous and impatient. Ask but all the young fellows of the town if they do not lose more time, like huntsmen, in starting the game, than in running it down. One knows not where to find 'em, who will or will not. Women of quality are so civil you can hardly distinguish love from good breeding, and a man is often mistaken: but now I can be sure she that shows an aversion to me loves the sport, as those women that are gone, whom I warrant to be right. And then the next thing is, your women of honour, as you call 'em, are only chary of their reputations, not their persons; and 'tis scandal they would avoid, not men. Now may I have, by the reputation of an eunuch, the privileges of one, and be seen in a lady's chamber in a morning as early as her husband; kiss virgins before their parents or lovers; and maybe, in short, the *passe-partout* of the town. Now, Doctor.

QUACK. Nay, now you shall be the doctor, and your process is so new that we do not know but it may succeed.

HORN. Not so new neither; *probatum est,* Doctor.

QUACK. Well, I wish you luck, and many patients, whilst I go to mine. (*Exit.*)

Enter HARCOURT *and* DORILANT *to* HORNER

HAR. Come, your appearance at the play yesterday has, I hope, hardened you for the future against the women's contempt and the men's raillery; and now you'll abroad as you were wont

HORN. Did I not bear it bravely?

DOR. With a most theatrical impudence, nay, more than the orange-wenches show there, or a drunken vizard-mask, or a great-bellied actress; nay, or the most impudent of creatures, an ill poet; or what is yet more impudent, a second-hand critic.

HORN. But what say the ladies? have they no pity?

HAR. What ladies? The vizard-masks, you know, never pity a man when all's gone, though in their service.

DOR. And for the women in the boxes, you'd never pity them when 'twas in your power.

HAR. They say 'tis pity but all that deal with common women should be served so.

DOR. Nay, I dare swear they won't admit you to play at cards with them, go to plays with 'em, or do the little duties which other shadows of men are wont to do for 'em.

HORN. What do you call shadows of men?

DOR. Half-men.

HORN. What, boys?

DOR. Ay, your old boys, old *beaux garçons,* who, like super-annuated stallions, are suffered to run, feed, and whinny with the mares as long as they live, though they can do nothing else.

HORN. Well, a pox on love and wenching! Women serve but to keep a man from better company. Though I can't enjoy them, I shall you the more. Good fellowship and friendship are lasting, rational, and manly pleasures.

HAR. For all that, give me some of those pleasures you call effeminate too; they help to relish one another.

HORN. They disturb one another.

HAR. No, mistresses are like books. If you pore upon them too much, they doze you, and make you unfit for company; but if used discreetly, you are the fitter for conversation by 'em.

DOR. A mistress should be like a little country retreat near the town; not to dwell in constantly, but only for a night and away, to taste the town the better when a man returns.

HORN. I tell you, 'tis as hard to be a good fellow, a good friend, and a lover of women, as 'tis to be a good fellow, a good friend, and a lover of money. You cannot follow both, then choose your side. Wine gives you liberty, love takes it away.

DOR. Gad, he's in the right on't.

HORN. Wine gives you joy; love, grief and tortures, besides the chirurgeon's. Wine makes us witty; love, only sots. Wine makes us sleep; love breaks it.

DOR. By the world, he has reason, Harcourt.

HORN. Wine makes——

DOR. Ay, wine makes us—makes us princes; love makes us beggars, poor rogues, egad—and wine——

HORN. So, there's one converted.—No, no, love and wine, oil and vinegar.

HAR. I grant it; love will still be uppermost.

HORN. Come, for my part, I will have only those glorious manly pleasures of being very drunk and very slovenly.

Enter Boy

BOY. Mr. Sparkish is below, Sir. (*Exit.*)

HAR. What, my dear friend! a rogue that is fond of me, only I think, for abusing him.

DOR. No, he can no more think the men laugh at him than that women jilt him, his opinion of himself is so good.

HORN. Well, there's another pleasure by drinking I thought not of—I shall lose his acquaintance, because he cannot drink: and you know 'tis a very hard thing to be rid of him, for he's one of those nauseous offerers at wit, who, like the worst fiddlers, run themselves into all companies.

HAR. One that, by being in the company of men of sense, would pass for one.

HORN. And may so to the short-sighted world, as a false jewel amongst true ones is not discerned at a distance. His company is as troublesome to us as a cuckold's when you have a mind to his wife's.

HAR. No, the rogue will not let us enjoy one another, but ravishes our conversation, though he signifies no more to't than Sir Martin Mar-all's gaping, and awkward thrumming upon the lute, does to his man's voice and music.

DOR. And to pass for a wit in town shows himself a fool every night to us, that are guilty of the plot.

HORN. Such wits as he are, to a company of reasonable men, like rooks to the gamesters, who only fill a room at the table, but are so far from contributing to the play, that they only serve to spoil the fancy of those that do.

DOR. Nay, they are used like rooks too, snubbed, checked, and abused; yet the rogues will hang on.

HORN. A pox on em, and all that force nature, and would be still what she forbids 'em! Affectation is her greatest monster.

HAR. Most men are the contraries to that they would seem. Your bully, you see, is a coward with a long sword; the little humbly fawning physician, with his ebony cane, is he that destroys men.

DOR. The usurer, a poor rogue, possessed of mouldy bonds and mortgages; and we they call spendthrifts are only wealthy who lay out his money upon daily new purchases of pleasure.

HORN. Ay, your arrantest cheat is your trustee or executor, your jealous man, the greatest cuckold, your churchman the greatest atheist, and your noisy pert rogue of a wit, the greatest fop, dullest ass, and worst company, as you shall see; for here he comes.

Enter SPARKISH

SPARK. How is't, sparks? how is't? Well, faith, Harry, I must rally thee a little, ha! ha! ha! upon the report in town of thee, ha! ha! ha! I can't hold i'faith; shall I speak?

HORN. Yes; but you'll be so bitter then.

SPARK. Honest Dick and Frank here shall answer for me, I will not be extreme bitter, by the universe.

HAR. We will be bound in a ten-thousand-pound bond, he shall not be bitter at all.

DOR. Nor sharp, nor sweet.

HORN. What, not downright insipid?

SPARK. Nay then, since you are so brisk, and provoke me, take what follows. You must know, I was discoursing and rallying with some ladies yesterday, and they happened to talk of the fine new signs in town.

HORN. Very fine ladies, I believe.

SPARK. Said I, I know where the best new sign is.—Where? says one of the ladies.—In Covent Garden, I replied.—Said another, In what street?—In Russel Street, answered I.—Lord, says another, I'm sure there was ne'er a fine new sign there yesterday.—Yes, but there was, said I again, and it came out of France, and has been there a fortnight.

DOR. A pox! I can hear no more, prithee.

HORN. No, hear him out; let him tune his crowd a while.

HAR. The worst music, the greatest preparation.

SPARK. Nay, faith, I'll make you laugh.—It cannot be, says a third lady.—Yes, yes, quoth I again.—Says a fourth lady——

HORN. Look to't, we'll have no more ladies.

SPARK. No—then mark, mark, now. Said I to the fourth, Did you never see Mr. Horner? he lodges in Russel Street, and he's a sign of a man, you know, since he came out of France; ha! ha! ha!

HORN. But the devil take me if thine be the sign of a jest.

SPARK. With that they all fell a-laughing, till they bepissed themselves. What, but it does not move you, methinks? Well, I see one had as good go to law without a witness, as break a jest without a laugher on one's side.——Come, come, sparks, but where do we dine? I have left at Whitehall an earl to dine with you.

DOR. Why, I thought thou hadst loved a man with a title better than a suit with a French trimming to't.

HAR. Go to him again.

SPARK. No, Sir, a wit to me is the greatest title in the world.

HORN. But go dine with your earl, Sir; he may be exceptious. We are your friends, and will not take it ill to be left, I do assure you.

HAR. Nay, faith, he shall go to him.

SPARK. Nay, pray, gentlemen.

DOR. We'll thrust you out, if you won't; what, disappoint anybody for us?

SPARK. Nay, dear gentlemen, hear me.

HORN. No, no, Sir, by no means; pray go, Sir.

SPARK. Why, dear rogues——

DOR. No, no.   (*They all thrust him out of the room.*)

ALL. Ha! ha! ha!

SPARKISH *returns*

SPARK. But, sparks, pray hear me. What, d'ye think I'll eat then with gay shallow fops and silent coxcombs? I think wit as necessary at dinner as a glass of good wine, and that's the reason I never have any stomach when I eat alone.—Come, but where do we dine?

HORN. Even where you will.

SPARK. At Chateline's?

DOR. Yes, if you will.

SPARK. Or at the Cock?

DOR. Yes, if you please.

SPARK. Or at the Dog and Partridge?

HORN. Ay, if you have a mind to't; for we shall dine at neither.

SPARK. Pshaw! with your fooling we shall lose the new play; and I would no more miss seeing a new play the first day, than I would miss sitting in the wits' row. Therefore I'll go fetch my mistress, and away.   (*Exit.*)

Manent HORNER, HARCOURT, DORILANT: *enter to them*
MR. PINCHWIFE

HORN. Who have we here? Pinchwife?

PINCH. Gentlemen, your humble servant.

HORN. Well, Jack, by thy long absence from the town, the grumness of thy countenance, and the slovenliness of thy habit, I should give thee joy, should I not, of marriage?

PINCH. (*aside*) Death! does he know I'm married too? I thought to have concealed it from him at least.——My long stay in the country will excuse my dress; and I have a suit of law that brings me up to town, that puts me out of humour. Besides, I must give Sparkish to-morrow five thousand pound to lie with my sister.

HORN. Nay, you country gentlemen, rather than not purchase, will buy anything; and he is a cracked title, if we may quibble. Well, but am I to give thee joy? I heard thou wert married.

PINCH. What then?

HORN. Why, the next thing that is to be heard is, thou'rt a cuckold.

PINCH. (*aside*) Insupportable name!

HORN. But I did not expect marriage from such a whoremaster as you, one that knew the town so much, and women so well.

PINCH. Why, I have married no London wife.

HORN. Pshaw! that's all one. That grave circumspection in marrying a country wife, is like refusing a deceitful pampered Smithfield jade, to go and be cheated by a friend in the country.

PINCH. (*aside*) A pox on him and his simile!——At least we are a little surer of the breed there, know what her keeping has been, whether foiled or unsound.

HORN. Come, come, I have known a clap gotten in Wales; and there are cuzens, justices' clerks, and chaplains in the country, I won't say coachmen. But she's handsome and young?

PINCH. (*aside*) I'll answer as I should do.——No, no; she has no beauty but her youth, no attraction but her modesty: wholesome, homely, and huswifely; that's all.

DOR. He talks as like a grazier as he looks.

PINCH. She's too awkward, ill-favoured, and silly to bring to town.

HAR. Then methinks you should bring her to be taught breeding.

PINCH. To be taught! no, Sir, I thank you. Good wives and private soldiers should be ignorant—I'll keep her from your instructions, I warrant you.

HAR. (*aside*) The rogue is as jealous as if his wife were not ignorant.

HORN. Why, if she be ill-favoured, there will be less danger here for you than by leaving her in the country. We have such variety of dainties that we are seldom hungry.

DOR. But they have always coarse, constant, swingeing stomachs in the country.

HAR. Foul feeders indeed!

DOR. And your hospitality is great there.

HAR. Open house; every man's welcome.

PINCH. So, so, gentlemen.

HORN. But prithee, why wouldst thou marry her? If she be ugly, ill-bred, and silly, she must be rich then.

PINCH. As rich as if she brought me twenty thousand pound out of this town; for she'll be as sure not to spend her moderate portion as a London baggage would be to spend hers, let it be what it would: so 'tis all one. Then, because she's ugly, she's the likelier to be my own; and being ill-bred, she'll hate conversation; and since silly and innocent, will not know the difference betwixt a man of one-and-twenty and one of forty.

HORN. Nine—to my knowledge. But if she be silly, she'll expect as much from a man of forty-nine, as from him of one-and-twenty. But methinks wit is more necessary than beauty; and I think no young woman ugly that has it, and no handsome woman agreeable without it.

PINCH. 'Tis my maxim, he's a fool that marries; but he's a greater that does not marry a fool. What is wit in a wife good for, but to make a man a cuckold?

HORN. Yes, to keep it from his knowledge.

PINCH. A fool cannot contrive to make her husband a cuckold.

HORN. No; but she'll club with a man that can: and what is worse, if she cannot make her husband a cuckold, she'll make him jealous, and pass for one: and then 'tis all one.

PINCH. Well, well, I'll take care for one. My wife shall make me no cuckold, though she had your help, Mr. Horner. I understand the town, Sir.

DOR. (*aside*) His help!

HAR. (*aside*) He's come newly to town, it seems, and has not heard how things are with him.

HORN. But tell me, has marriage cured thee of whoring, which it seldom does?

HAR. 'Tis more than age can do.

HORN. No, the word is, I'll marry and live honest: but a marriage vow is like a penitent gamester's oath, and entering into bonds and penalties to stint himself to such a particular small sum at play for the future, which makes him but the more eager; and not being able to hold out, loses his money again, and his forfeit to boot.

DOR. Ay, ay, a gamester will be a gamester whilst his money lasts, and a whoremaster whilst his vigour.

HAR. Nay, I have known 'em, when they are broke, and can lose no more, keep a-fumbling with the box in their hands to fool with only, and hinder other gamesters.

DOR. That had wherewithal to make lusty stakes.

PINCH. Well, gentlemen, you may laugh at me; but you shall never lie with my wife: I know the town.

HORN. But prithee, was not the way you were in better? is not keeping better than marriage?

PINCH. A pox on't! the jades would jilt me, I could never keep a whore to myself.

HORN. So, then you only married to keep a whore to yourself. Well, but let me tell you, women, as you say, are like soldiers, made constant and loyal by good pay, rather than by oaths and covenants. Therefore I'd advise my friends to keep rather than marry, since too I find, by your example, it does not serve one's turn; for I saw you yesterday in the eighteen-penny place with a pretty country wench.

PINCH. (*aside*) How the devil! did he see my wife then? I sat there that she might not be seen. But she shall never go to a play again.

HORN. What! dost thou blush at nine-and-forty for having been seen with a wench?

DOR. No, faith, I warrant 'twas his wife, which he seated there out of sight; for he's a cunning rogue, and understands the town.

HAR. He blushes. Then 'twas his wife; for men are now more ashamed to be seen with them in public than with a wench.

PINCH. (*aside*) Hell and damnation! I'm undone, since Horner has seen her, and they know 'twas she.

HORN. But prithee, was it thy wife? She was exceedingly pretty: I was in love with her at that distance.

PINCH. You are like never to be nearer to her. Your servant, gentlemen.   (*offers to go*)

HORN. Nay, prithee stay.

PINCH. I cannot; I will not.

HORN. Come, you shall dine with us.

PINCH. I have dined already.

HORN. Come, I know thou hast not: I'll treat thee, dear rogue; thou shalt spend none of thy Hampshire money to-day.

PINCH. (*aside*) Treat me! So, he uses me already like his cuckold.

HORN. Nay, you shall not go.

PINCH. I must; I have business at home.   (*Exit.*)

HAR. To beat his wife. He's as jealous of her as a Cheapside husband of a Covent Garden wife.

HORN. Why, 'tis as hard to find an old whoremaster without jealousy and the gout, as a young one without fear or the pox.

    As gout in age from pox in youth proceeds,

    So wenching past, then jealousy succeeds:

    The worst disease that love and wenching breeds.

                        (*Exeunt.*)

ACT II

MRS. MARGERY PINCHWIFE *and* ALITHEA.
PINCHWIFE *peeping behind at the door*

MRS. PINCH. Pray, Sister, where are the best fields and woods to walk in, in London?

ALITH. A pretty question! Why, Sister, Mulberry Garden and St. James's Park; and, for close walks, the New Exchange.

MRS. PINCH. Pray, Sister, tell me why my husband looks so grum here in town, and keeps me up so close, and will not let me go a-walking, nor let me wear my best gown yesterday.

ALITH. Oh, he's jealous, Sister.

MRS. PINCH. Jealous! what's that?

ALITH. He's afraid you should love another man.

MRS. PINCH. How should he be afraid of my loving another man, when he will not let me see any but himself?

ALITH. Did he not carry you yesterday to a play?

MRS. PINCH. Ay; but we sat amongst ugly people. He would not let me come near the gentry, who sat under us, so that I could not see 'em. He told me none but naughty women sat there, whom they toused and moused. But I would have ventured, for all that.

ALITH. But how did you like the play?

MRS. PINCH. Indeed I was aweary of the play, but I liked hugeously the actors. They are the goodliest, properest men, Sister!

ALITH. Oh, but you must not like the actors, Sister.

MRS. PINCH. Ay, how should I help it, Sister? Pray, Sister, when my husband comes in, will you ask leave for me to go a-walking?

ALITH. (aside) A-walking! ha! ha! Lord, a country-gentlewoman's leisure is the drudgery of a footpost; and she requires as much airing as her husband's horses.——But here comes your husband: I'll ask, though I'm sure he'll not grant it.

MRS. PINCH. He says he won't let me go abroad for fear of catching the pox.

ALITH. Fy! the small-pox you should say.

Enter PINCHWIFE *to them*

MRS. PINCH. O my dear, dear bud, welcome home! Why dost thou look so fropish? who has nangered thee?

PINCH. You're a fool.

(MRS. PINCHWIFE *goes aside, and cries.*)

ALITH. Faith, so she is, for crying for no fault, poor tender creature!

PINCH. What, you would have her as impudent as yourself, as arrant a jillflirt, a gadder, a magpie; and to say all, a mere notorious town-woman?

ALITH. Brother, you are my only censurer; and the honour of your family shall sooner suffer in your wife there than in me, though I take the innocent liberty of the town.

PINCH. Hark you, mistress, do not talk so before my wife.—— The innocent liberty of the town!

ALITH. Why, pray, who boasts of any intrigue with me? what lampoon has made my name notorious? what ill women frequent my lodgings? I keep no company with any women of scandalous reputations.

PINCH. No, you keep the men of scandalous reputations company.

ALITH. Where? would you not have me civil? answer 'em in a box at the plays, in the drawing-room at Whitehall, in St. James's Park, Mulberry Garden, or——

PINCH. Hold, hold! Do not teach my wife where the men are to be found: I believe she's the worse for your town-documents already. I bid you keep her in ignorance, as I do.

MRS. PINCH. Indeed, be not angry with her, bud, she will tell me nothing of the town, though I ask her a thousand times a day.

PINCH. Then you are very inquisitive to know, I find?

MRS. PINCH. Not I indeed, dear; I hate London. Our place-house in the country is worth a thousand of't: would I were there again!

PINCH. So you shall, I warrant. But were you not talking of plays and players when I came in?——You are her encourager in such discourses.

MRS. PINCH. No, indeed, dear; she chid me just now for liking the playermen.

PINCH. (aside) Nay, if she be so innocent as to own to me her liking them, there is no hurt in't.——Come, my poor rogue, but thou lik'st none better than me?

MRS. PINCH. Yes, indeed, but I do. The playermen are finer folks.

PINCH. But you love none better than me?

MRS. PINCH. You are mine own dear bud, and I know you. I hate a stranger.

PINCH. Ay, my dear, you must love me only, and not be like the naughty town-women, who only hate their husbands, and love every man else; love plays, visits, fine coaches, fine clothes, fiddles, balls, treats, and so lead a wicked town-life.

MRS. PINCH. Nay, if to enjoy all these things be a town-life, London is not so bad a place, dear.

PINCH. How! if you love me, you must hate London.

ALITH. (aside) The fool has forbid me discovering to her the pleasures of the town, and he is now setting her agog upon them himself.

MRS. PINCH. But, husband, do the town-women love the playermen too?

PINCH. Yes, I warrant you.

MRS. PINCH. Ay, I warrant you.

PINCH. Why, you do not, I hope?

MRS. PINCH. No, no, bud. But why have we no playermen in the country?

PINCH. Ha!—Mrs. Minx, ask me no more to go to a play.

MRS. PINCH. Nay, why love? I did not care for going: but when you forbid me, you make me, as 'twere, desire it.

ALITH. (*aside*) So 'twill be in other things, I warrant.

MRS. PINCH. Pray let me go to a play, dear.

PINCH. Hold your peace, I wo' not.

MRS. PINCH. Why, love?

PINCH. Why, I'll tell you.

ALITH. (*aside*) Nay, if he tell her, she'll give him more cause to forbid her that place.

MRS. PINCH. Pray why, dear?

PINCH. First, you like the actors; and the gallants may like you.

MRS. PINCH. What, a homely country girl! No, bud, nobody will like me.

PINCH. I tell you yes, they may.

MRS. PINCH. No, no, you jest—I won't believe you: I will go.

PINCH. I tell you then, that one of the lewdest fellows in town, who saw you there, told me he was in love with you.

MRS. PINCH. Indeed! who, who, pray who was't?

PINCH. (*aside*) I've gone too far, and slipped before I was aware; how overjoyed she is!

MRS. PINCH. Was it any Hampshire gallant, any of our neighbours? I promise you, I am beholden to him.

PINCH. I promise you, you lie; for he would but ruin you, as he has done hundreds. He has no other love for women but that; such as he look upon women, like basilisks, but to destroy 'em.

MRS. PINCH. Ay, but if he loves me, why should he ruin me? answer me to that. Methinks he should not, I would do him no harm.

ALITH. Ha! ha! ha!

PINCH. 'Tis very well; but I'll keep him from doing you any harm, or me either. But here comes company; get you in, get you in.

MRS. PINCH. But, pray, husband, is he a pretty gentleman that loves me?

PINCH. In, baggage, in.   (*thrusts her in, shuts the door*)

Enter SPARKISH *and* HARCOURT

What, all the lewd libertines of the town brought to my lodging by this easy coxcomb! 'Sdeath, I'll not suffer it.

SPARK. Here, Harcourt, do you approve my choice?——Dear little rogue, I told you I'd bring you acquainted with all my friends, the wits and——   (HARCOURT *salutes her.*)

PINCH. Ay, they shall know her, as well as you yourself will, I warrant you.

SPARK. This is one of those, my pretty rogue, that are to dance at your wedding to-morrow; and him you must bid welcome ever, to what you and I have.

PINCH. (*aside*) Monstrous!

SPARK. Harcourt, how dost thou like her, faith? Nay, dear, do not look down; I should hate to have a wife of mine out of countenance at anything.

PINCH. (*aside*) Wonderful!

SPARK. Tell me, I say, Harcourt, how dost thou like her? Thou hast stared upon her enough to resolve me.

HAR. So infinitely well, that I could wish I had a mistress too, that might differ from her in nothing but her love and engagement to you.

ALITH. Sir, Master Sparkish has often told me that his acquaintance were all wits and railleurs, and now I find it.

SPARK. No, by the universe, Madam, he does not rally now; you may believe him. I do assure you, he is the honestest, worthiest, true-hearted gentleman—a man of such perfect honour, he would say nothing to a lady he does not mean.

PINCH. (*aside*) Praising another man to his mistress!

HAR. Sir, you are so beyond expectation obliging, that——

SPARK. Nay, egad, I am sure you do admire her extremely; I see't in your eyes.——He does admire you, Madam.——By the world, don't you?

HAR. Yes, above the world, or the most glorious part of it, her whole sex: and till now I never thought I should have envied you, or any man about to marry, but you have the best excuse for marriage I ever knew.

ALITH. Nay, now, Sir, I'm satisfied you are of the society of the wits and railleurs, since you cannot spare your friend, even when he is but too civil to you; but the surest sign is, since you are an

enemy to marriage, for that I hear you hate as much as business
or bad wine.

HAR. Truly, Madam, I never was an enemy to marriage till
now, because marriage was never an enemy to me before.

ALITH. But why, Sir, is marriage an enemy to you now? Because it robs you of your friend here? for you look upon a friend
married as one gone into a monastery, that is, dead to the world.

HAR. 'Tis indeed, because you marry him; I see, Madam, you
can guess my meaning. I do confess heartily and openly I wish it
were in my power to break the match; by Heavens I would.

SPARK. Poor Frank!

ALITH. Would you be so unkind to me?

HAR. No, no, 'tis not because I would be unkind to you.

SPARK. Poor Frank! no gad, 'tis only his kindness to me.

PINCH. (aside) Great kindness to you indeed! Insensible fop,
let a man make love to his wife to his face!

SPARK. Come, dear Frank, for all my wife there, that shall be,
thou shalt enjoy me sometimes, dear rogue. By my honour, we
men of wit condole for our deceased brother in marriage, as much
as for one dead in earnest: I think that was prettily said of me,
ha, Harcourt?——But come, Frank, be not melancholy for me.

HAR. No, I assure you, I am not melancholy for you.

SPARK. Prithee, Frank, dost think my wife that shall be there,
a fine person?

HAR. I could gaze upon her till I became as blind as you are.

SPARK. How as I am? how?

HAR. Because you are a lover, and true lovers are blind, stock
blind.

SPARK. True, true; but by the world she has wit too, as well as
beauty: go, go with her into a corner, and try if she has wit; talk
to her anything; she's bashful before me.

HAR. Indeed if a woman wants wit in a corner, she has it nowhere.

ALITH. (aside to SPARKISH) Sir, you dispose of me a little before
your time——

SPARK. Nay, nay, Madam, let me have an earnest of your obedience, or—go, go, Madam——

                              (HARCOURT courts ALITHEA aside.)

PINCH. How, Sir! if you are not concerned for the honour of a wife, I am for that of a sister; he shall not debauch her. Be a pander to your own wife! bring men to her! let 'em make love before your face! thrust 'em into a corner together, then leave 'em in private! is this your town wit and conduct?

SPARK. Ha! ha! ha! a silly wise rogue would make one laugh more than a stark fool, ha! ha! I shall burst. Nay, you shall not disturb 'em; I'll vex thee, by the world.

> (*struggles with* PINCHWIFE *to keep him from* HARCOURT *and* ALITHEA)

ALITH. The writings are drawn, Sir, settlements made; 'tis too late, Sir, and past all revocation.

HAR. Then so is my death.

ALITH. I would not be unjust to him.

HAR. Then why to me so?

ALITH. I have no obligation to you.

HAR. My love.

ALITH. I had his before.

HAR. You never had it; he wants, you see, jealousy, the only infallible sign of it.

ALITH. Love proceeds from esteem; he cannot distrust my virtue: besides, he loves me, or he would not marry me.

HAR. Marrying you is no more sign of his love than bribing your woman, that he may marry you, is a sign of his generosity. Marriage is rather a sign of interest than love; and he that marries a fortune covets a mistress, not loves her. But if you take marriage for a sign of love, take it from me immediately.

ALITH. No, now you have put a scruple in my head; but in short, Sir, to end our dispute, I must marry him; my reputation would suffer in the world else.

HAR. No; if you do marry him, with your pardon, Madam, your reputation suffers in the world, and you would be thought in necessity for a cloak.

ALITH. Nay, now you are rude, Sir.——Mr. Sparkish, pray come hither, your friend here is very troublesome, and very loving.

HAR. (*aside to* ALITHEA) Hold! hold!——

PINCH. D'ye hear that?

SPARK. Why, d'ye think I'll seem to be jealous, like a country bumpkin?

PINCH. No, rather be a cuckold, like a credulous cit.

HAR. Madam, you would not have been so little generous as to have told him.

ALITH. Yes, since you could be so little generous as to wrong him.

HAR. Wrong him! no man can do't, he's beneath an injury: a bubble, a coward, a senseless idiot, a wretch so contemptible to all the world but you, that——

ALITH. Hold, do not rail at him, for since he is like to be my husband, I am resolved to like him: nay, I think I am obliged to tell him you are not his friend.——Master Sparkish, Master Sparkish!

SPARK. What, what?——Now, dear rogue, has not she wit?

HAR. Not so much as I thought, and hoped she had.

(speaks surlily)

ALITH. Mr. Sparkish, do you bring people to rail at you?

HAR. Madam——

SPARK. How! no; but if he does rail at me, 'tis but in jest, I warrant: what we wits do for one another, and never take any notice of it.

ALITH. He spoke so scurrilously of you, I had no patience to hear him; besides, he has been making love to me.

HAR. *(aside)* True, damned tell-tale woman!

SPARK. Pshaw! to show his parts—we wits rail and make love often, but to show our parts: as we have no affections, so we have no malice, we——

ALITH. He said you were a wretch below an injury——

SPARK. Pshaw!

HAR. *(aside)* Damned, senseless, impudent, virtuous jade! Well, since she won't let me have her, she'll do as good, she'll make me hate her.

ALITH. A common bubble——

SPARK. Pshaw!

ALITH. A coward——

SPARK. Pshaw, pshaw!

ALITH. A senseless, drivelling idiot——

SPARK. How! did he disparage my parts? Nay, then, my honour's concerned, I can't put up that, Sir, by the world—brother, help me to kill him.—*(aside)* I may draw now, since we have the odds of him—'tis a good occasion, too, before my mistress——

(offers to draw)

ALITH. Hold, hold!

SPARK. What, what?

ALITH. (*aside*) I must not let 'em kill the gentleman neither, for his kindness to me: I am so far from hating him, that I wish my gallant had his person and understanding. Nay, if my honour——

SPARK. I'll be thy death.

ALITH. Hold, hold! Indeed, to tell the truth, the gentleman said after all, that what he spoke was but out of friendship to you.

SPARK. How! say, I am—I am a fool, that is no wit, out of friendship to me?

ALITH. Yes, to try whether I was concerned enough for you; and made love to me only to be satisfied of my virtue, for your sake.

HAR. (*aside*) Kind, however.

SPARK. Nay, if it were so, my dear rogue, I ask thee pardon; but why would not you tell me so, faith?

HAR. Because I did not think on't, faith.

SPARK. Come, Horner does not come; Harcourt, let's be gone to the new play.—Come, Madam.

ALITH. I will not go, if you intend to leave me alone in the box and run into the pit, as you use to do.

SPARK. Pshaw! I'll leave Harcourt with you in the box to entertain you, and that's as good; if I sat in the box, I should be thought no judge but of trimmings.—Come away, Harcourt, lead her down. (*Exeunt* SPARKISH, HARCOURT, *and* ALITHEA)

PINCH. Well, go thy ways, for the flower of the true town fops, such as spend their estates before they come to 'em, and are cuckolds before they're married. But let me go look to my own freehold.—How!

Enter MY LADY FIDGET, MRS. DAINTY FIDGET, *and* MRS. SQUEAMISH

LADY FID. Your servant, Sir: where is your lady? We are come to wait upon her to the new play.

PINCH. New play!

LADY FID. And my husband will wait upon you presently.

PINCH. (*aside*) Damn your civility.——Madam, by no means; I will not see Sir Jasper here till I have waited upon him at home; nor shall my wife see you till she has waited upon your ladyship at your lodgings.

LADY FID. Now we are here, Sir?

PINCH. No, Madam.

MRS. DAIN. Pray, let us see her.

MRS. SQUEAM. We will not stir till we see her.

PINCH. (*aside*) A pox on you all!—(*goes to the door, and returns*) She has locked the door, and is gone abroad.

LADY FID. No, you have locked the door, and she's within.

MRS. DAIN. They told us below she was here.

PINCH. (*aside*) Will nothing do?——Well, it must out then. To tell you the truth, ladies, which I was afraid to let you know before, lest it might endanger your lives, my wife has just now the small-pox come out upon her; do not be frightened, but pray be gone, ladies; you shall not stay here in danger of your lives; pray get you gone, ladies.

LADY FID. No, no, we have all had 'em.

MRS. SQUEAM. Alack, alack!

MRS. DAIN. Come, come, we must see how it goes with her; I understand the disease.

LADY FID. Come!

PINCH. (*aside*) Well, there is no being too hard for women at their own weapon, lying, therefore I'll quit the field.   (*Exit.*)

MRS. SQUEAM. Here's an example of jealousy!

LADY FID. Indeed, as the world goes, I wonder there are no more jealous, since wives are so neglected.

MRS. DAIN. Pshaw! as the world goes, to what end should they be jealous?

LADY FID. Foh! 'tis a nasty world.

MRS. SQUEAM. That men of parts, great acquaintance, and quality, should take up with and spend themselves and fortunes in keeping little playhouse creatures, foh!

LADY FID. Nay, that women of understanding, great acquaintance, and good quality, should fall a-keeping too of little creatures, foh!

MRS. SQUEAM. Why, 'tis the men of quality's fault; they never visit women of honour and reputation as they used to do; and have not so much as common civility for ladies of our rank, but use us with the same indifferency and ill-breeding as if we were all married to 'em.

LADY FID. She says true; 'tis an arrant shame women of quality should be so slighted; methinks birth—birth should go for something; I have known men admired, courted, and followed for their titles only.

MRS. SQUEAM. Ay, one would think men of honour should not love, no more than marry, out of their own rank.

MRS. DAIN. Fy, fy, upon 'em! they are come to think cross breeding for themselves best, as well as for their dogs and horses.

LADY FID. They are dogs and horses for't.

MRS. SQUEAM. One would think, if not for love, for vanity a little.

MRS. DAIN. Nay, they do satisfy their vanity upon us sometimes; and are kind to us in their report, tell all the world they lie with us.

LADY FID. Damned rascals, that we should be only wronged by 'em! To report a man has had a person, when he has not had a person, is the greatest wrong in the whole world that can be done to a person.

MRS. SQUEAM. Well, 'tis an arrant shame noble persons should be so wronged and neglected.

LADY FID. But still 'tis an arranter shame for a noble person to neglect her own honour, and defame her own noble person with little inconsiderable fellows, foh!

MRS. DAIN. I suppose the crime against our honour is the same with a man of quality as with another.

LADY FID. How! no, sure, the man of quality is likest one's husband, and therefore the fault should be the less.

MRS. DAIN. But then the pleasure should be the less.

LADY FID. Fy, fy, fy, for shame, Sister! whither shall we ramble? Be continent in your discourse, or I shall hate you.

MRS. DAIN. Besides, an intrigue is so much the more notorious for the man's quality.

MRS. SQUEAM. 'Tis true, nobody takes notice of a private man, and therefore with him 'tis more secret; and the crime's the less when 'tis not known.

LADY FID. You say true; i'faith, I think you are in the right on't: 'tis not an injury to a husband till it be an injury to our honours; so that a woman of honour loses no honour with a private person; and to say truth——

MRS. DAIN. (*apart to* MRS. SQUEAMISH) So, the little fellow is grown a private person—with her——

LADY FID. But still my dear, dear honour——

Enter SIR JASPER, HORNER, *and* DORILANT

SIR JASP. Ay, my dear, dear of honour, thou hast still so much honour in thy mouth——

HORN. (*Aside*) That she has none elsewhere.

LADY FID. Oh, what d'ye mean to bring in these upon us?

MRS. DAIN. Foh! these are as bad as wits.

MRS. SQUEAM. Foh!

LADY FID. Let us leave the room.

SIR JASP. Stay, stay; faith, to tell you the naked truth——

LADY FID. Fy, Sir Jasper! do not use that word naked.

SIR JASP. Well, well, in short I have business at Whitehall, and cannot go to the play with you, therefore would have you go——

LADY FID. With those two to a play?

SIR JASP. No, not with t'other, but with Mr. Horner; there can be no more scandal to go with him than with Mr. Tattle, or Master Limberham.

LADY FID. With that nasty fellow! no—no.

SIR JASP. Nay, prithee, dear, hear me.

(*whispers to* LADY FIDGET)

HORN. Ladies——

(HORNER, DORILANT *drawing near* MRS. SQUEAMISH *and* MRS. DAINTY FIDGET)

MRS. DAIN. Stand off.

MRS. SQUEAM. Do not approach us.

MRS. DAIN. You herd with the wits, you are obscenity all over.

MRS. SQUEAM. And I would as soon look upon a picture of Adam and Eve without fig-leaves, as any of you, if I could help it; therefore keep off, and do not make us sick.

DOR. What a devil are these?

HORN. Why, these are pretenders to honour, as critics to wit, only by censuring others; and as every raw, peevish, out-of-humoured, affected, dull, tea-drinking, arithmetical fop, sets up for a wit by railing at men of sense, so these for honour, by railing at the court, and ladies of as great honour as quality.

SIR JASP. Come, Mr. Horner, I must desire you to go with these ladies to the play, Sir.

HORN. I, Sir?

SIR JASP. Ay, ay, come, Sir.

HORN. I must beg your pardon, Sir, and theirs; I will not be seen in women's company in public again for the world.

SIR JASP. Ha, ha, strange aversion!

MRS. SQUEAM. No, he's for women's company in private.

SIR JASP. He—poor man—he—ha! ha! ha!

MRS. DAIN. 'Tis a greater shame amongst lewd fellows to be seen in virtuous women's company, than for the women to be seen with them.

HORN. Indeed, Madam, the time was I only hated virtuous women, but now I hate the other too; I beg your pardon, ladies.

LADY FID. You are very obliging, Sir, because we would not be troubled with you.

SIR JASP. In sober sadness, he shall go.

DOR. Nay, if he wo' not, I am ready to wait upon the ladies, and I think I am the fitter man.

SIR JASP. You, Sir! no, I thank you for that. Master Horner is a privileged man amongst the virtuous ladies, 'twill be a great while before you are so; he! he! he! he's my wife's gallant; he! he! he! No, pray withdraw, Sir, for as I take it, the virtuous ladies have no business with you.

DOR. And I am sure he can have none with them. 'Tis strange a man can't come amongst virtuous women now, but upon the same terms as men are admitted into the Great Turk's seraglio. But heavens keep me from being an ombre player with 'em!—— But where is Pinchwife?   (*Exit.*)

SIR JASP. Come, come, man; what, avoid the sweet society of womankind? that sweet, soft, gentle, tame, noble creature, woman, made for man's companion——

HORN. So is that soft, gentle, tame, and more noble creature a spaniel, and has all their tricks; can fawn, lie down, suffer beating, and fawn the more; barks at your friends when they come to see you, makes your bed hard, gives you fleas, and the mange sometimes. And all the difference is, the spaniel's the more faithful animal, and fawns but upon one master.

SIR JASP. He! he! he!

MRS. SQUEAM. Oh the rude beast!

MRS. DAIN. Insolent brute!

LADY FID. Brute! stinking, mortified, rotten French wether, to dare——

SIR JASP. Hold, an't please your ladyship.——For shame, Master Horner! your mother was a woman—(*aside*) Now shall I never reconcile 'em.——(*aside to* LADY FIDGET) Hark you, Madam, take my advice in your anger. You know you often want one to make up your drolling pack of ombre players, and you may cheat him easily; for he's an ill gamester, and consequently loves play. Besides, you know you have but two old civil gentlemen (with stinking breaths too) to wait upon you abroad; take in the third into your service. The others are but crazy; and a lady should have a supernumerary gentleman-usher as a supernumerary coach-horse, lest sometimes you should be forced to stay at home.

LADY FID. But are you sure he loves play, and has money?

SIR JASP. He loves play as much as you, and has money as much as I.

LADY FID. Then I am contented to make him pay for his scurrility. Money makes up in a measure all other wants in men.—Those whom we cannot make hold for gallants, we make fine.

SIR JASP. (*aside*) So, so; now to mollify, to wheedle him.—— (*aside to* HORNER) Master Horner, will you never keep civil company? Methinks 'tis time now, since you are only fit for them. Come, come, man, you must e'en fall to visiting our wives, eating at our tables, drinking tea with our virtuous relations after dinner, dealing cards to 'em, reading plays and gazettes to 'em, picking fleas out of their shocks for 'em, collecting receipts, new songs, women, pages, and footmen for 'em.

HORN. I hope they'll afford me better employment, Sir.

SIR JASP. He! he! he! 'tis fit you know your work before you come into your place. And since you are unprovided of a lady to flatter, and a good house to eat at, pray frequent mine, and call my wife mistress, and she shall call you gallant, according to the custom.

HORN. Who, I?

SIR JASP. Faith, thou shalt for my sake; come, for my sake only.

HORN. For your sake——

SIR JASP. Come, come, here's a gamester for you; let him be a little familiar sometimes; nay, what if a little rude? Gamesters may be rude with ladies, you know.

LADY FID. Yes; losing gamesters have a privilege with women.

HORN. I always thought the contrary, that the winning gamester had most privilege with women; for when you have lost your
money to a man, you'll lose anything you have, all you have, they
say, and he may use you as he pleases.

SIR JASP. He! he! he! well, win or lose, you shall have your liberty with her.

LADY FID. As he behaves himself; and for your sake I'll give him
admittance and freedom.

HORN. All sorts of freedom, Madam?

SIR JASP. Ay, ay, ay, all sorts of freedom thou canst take. And
so go to her, begin thy new employment; wheedle her, jest with
her, and be better acquainted one with another.

HORN. (aside) I think I know her already; therefore may venture with her my secret for hers.

(HORNER and LADY FIDGET whisper.)

SIR JASP. Sister, cuz, I have provided an innocent playfellow for
you there.

MRS. DAIN. Who, he?

MRS. SQUEAM. There's a playfellow, indeed!

SIR JASP. Yes, sure. What, he is good enough to play at cards,
blindman's-buff, or the fool with, sometimes!

MRS. SQUEAM. Foh! we'll have no such playfellows.

MRS. DAIN. No, Sir; you shan't choose playfellows for us, we
thank you.

SIR JASP. Nay, pray hear me.   (whispering to them)

LADY FID. But, poor gentleman, could you be so generous, so
truly a man of honour, as for the sakes of us women of honour,
to cause yourself to be reported no man? No man! and to suffer
yourself the greatest shame that could fall upon a man, that none
might fall upon us women by your conversation? But, indeed, Sir,
as perfectly, perfectly the same man as before your going into
France, Sir? as perfectly, perfectly, Sir?

HORN. As perfectly, perfectly, Madam. Nay, I scorn you should
take my word; I desire to be tried only, Madam.

LADY FID. Well, that's spoken again like a man of honour: all
men of honour desire to come to the test. But, indeed, generally
you men report such things of yourselves, one does not know how
or whom to believe; and it is come to that pass we dare not take
your words no more than your tailor's, without some staid servant

of yours be bound with you. But I have so strong a faith in your honour, dear, dear, noble Sir, that I'd forfeit mine for yours, at any time, dear Sir.

HORN. No, Madam, you should not need to forfeit it for me; I have given you security already to save you harmless, my late reputation being so well known in the world, Madam.

LADY FID. But if upon any future falling-out, or upon a suspicion of my taking the trust out of your hands to employ some other, you yourself should betray your trust, dear Sir? I mean, if you'll give me leave to speak obscenely, you might tell, dear Sir.

HORN. If I did, nobody would believe me. The reputation of impotency is as hardly recovered again in the world as that of cowardice, dear Madam.

LADY FID. Nay, then, as one may say, you may do your worst, dear, dear Sir.

SIR JASP. Come, is your ladyship reconciled to him yet? have you agreed on matters? For I must be gone to Whitehall.

LADY FID. Why, indeed, Sir Jasper, Master Horner is a thousand, thousand times a better man than I thought him. Cousin Squeamish, sister Dainty, I can name him now. Truly, not long ago, you know, I thought his very name obscenity; and I would as soon have lain with him as have named him.

SIR JASP. Very likely, poor Madam.

MRS. DAIN. I believe it.

MRS. SQUEAM. No doubt on't.

SIR JASP. Well, well—that your ladyship is as virtuous as any she, I know, and him all the town knows—he! he! he! Therefore now you like him, get you gone to your business together; go, go to your business, I say, pleasure; whilst I go to my pleasure, business.

LADY FID. Come, then, dear gallant.

HORN. Come away, my dearest mistress.

SIR JASP. So, so; why, 'tis as I'd have it.   (*Exit.*)

HORN. And as I'd have it.

LADY FID.
Who for his business from his wife will run,
Takes the best care to have her business done.

                                        (*Exeunt omnes.*)

ACT III

SCENE I

ALITHEA *and* MRS. PINCHWIFE

ALITH. Sister, what ails you? You are grown melancholy.

MRS. PINCH. Would it not make any one melancholy to see you go every day fluttering about abroad, whilst I must stay at home like a poor lonely sullen bird in a cage?

ALITH. Ay, Sister, but you came young, and just from the nest to your cage, so that I thought you liked it, and could be as cheerful in't as others that took their flight themselves early, and are hopping abroad in the open air.

MRS. PINCH. Nay, I confess I was quiet enough till my husband told me what pure lives the London ladies live abroad, with their dancing, meetings, and junketings, and dressed every day in their best gowns; and I warrant you, play at nine-pins every day of the week, so they do.

Enter PINCHWIFE

PINCH. Come, what's here to do? You are putting the town-pleasures in her head, and setting her a-longing.

ALITH. Yes, after nine-pins. You suffer none to give her those longings you mean but yourself.

PINCH. I tell her of the vanities of the town like a confessor.

ALITH. A confessor! just such a confessor as he that, by forbidding a silly ostler to grease the horse's teeth, taught him to do't.

PINCH. Come, Mistress Flippant, good precepts are lost when bad examples are still before us: the liberty you take abroad makes her hanker after it, and out of humour at home. Poor wretch! she desired not to come to London; I would bring her.

ALITH. Very well.

PINCH. She has been this week in town, and never desired till this afternoon to go abroad.

ALITH. Was she not at a play yesterday?

PINCH. Yes, but she ne'er asked me; I was myself the cause of her going.

ALITH. Then if she ask you again, you are the cause of her asking, and not my example.

PINCH. Well, to-morrow night I shall be rid of you; and the
next day, before 'tis light, she and I'll be rid of the town, and my
dreadful apprehensions.——Come, be not melancholy; for thou
shalt go into the country after to-morrow, dearest.

ALITH. Great comfort!

MRS. PINCH. Pish! what d'ye tell me of the country for?

PINCH. How's this! what, pish at the country?

MRS. PINCH. Let me alone; I am not well.

PINCH. Oh, if that be all—what ails my dearest?

MRS. PINCH. Truly, I don't know: but I have not been well
since you told me there was a gallant at the play in love with me.

PINCH. Ha!——

ALITH. That's by my example too!

PINCH. Nay, if you are not well, but are so concerned because
a lewd fellow chanced to lie, and say he liked you, you'll make me
sick too.

MRS. PINCH. Of what sickness?

PINCH. Oh, of that which is worse than the plague, jealousy.

MRS. PINCH. Pish, you jeer! I'm sure there's no such disease in
our receipt-book at home.

PINCH. No, thou never met'st with it, poor innocent.—(*aside*)
Well, if thou cuckold me, 'twill be my own fault—for cuckolds
and bastards are generally makers of their own fortune.

MRS. PINCH. Well, but pray, bud, let's go to a play to-night.

PINCH. 'Tis just done, she comes from it. But why are you so
eager to see a play?

MRS. PINCH. Faith, dear, not that I care one pin for their talk
there; but I like to look upon the playermen, and would see, if
I could, the gallant you say loves me: that's all, dear bud.

PINCH. Is that all, dear bud?

ALITH. This proceeds from my example!

MRS. PINCH. But if the play be done, let's go abroad, however,
dear bud.

PINCH. Come, have a little patience and thou shalt go into the
country on Friday.

MRS. PINCH. Therefore I would see first some sights to tell my
neighbours of. Nay, I will go abroad, that's once.

ALITH. I'm the cause of this desire too!

PINCH. But now I think on't, who, who was the cause of Horner's coming to my lodgings to-day? That was you.

ALITH. No, you, because you would not let him see your handsome wife out of your lodging.

MRS. PINCH. Why, O Lord! did the gentleman come hither to see me indeed?

PINCH. No, no. You are not cause of that damned question too, Mistress Alithea?—(*aside*) Well, she's in the right of it. He is in love with my wife—and comes after her—'tis so—but I'll nip his love in the bud, lest he should follow us into the country, and break his chariot-wheel near our house, on purpose for an excuse to come to't. But I think I know the town.

MRS. PINCH. Come, pray, bud, let's go abroad before 'tis late; for I will go, that's flat and plain.

PINCH. (*aside*) So! the obstinacy already of the town-wife; and I must, whilst she's here, humour her like one.——Sister, how shall we do, that she may not be seen or known?

ALITH. Let her put on her mask.

PINCH. Pshaw! a mask makes people but the more inquisitive, and is as ridiculous a disguise as a stage-beard: her shape, stature, habit will be known. And if we should meet with Horner, he would be sure to take acquaintance with us, must wish her joy, kiss her, talk to her, leer upon her, and the devil and all. No, I'll not use her to a mask, 'tis dangerous, for masks have made more cuckolds than the best faces that ever were known.

ALITH. How will you do then?

MRS. PINCH. Nay, shall we go? The Exchange will be shut, and I have a mind to see that.

PINCH. So—I have it—I'll dress her up in the suit we are to carry down to her brother, little Sir James; nay, I understand the town-tricks. Come, let's go dress her. A mask! no—a woman masked, like a covered dish, gives a man curiosity and appetite; when, it may be, uncovered, 'twould turn his stomach: no, no.

ALITH. Indeed your comparison is something a greasy one: but I had a gentle gallant used to say, A beauty masked, like the sun in eclipse, gathers together more gazers than if it shined out.

(*Exeunt.*)

SCENE II

The Scene Changes to the New Exchange

Enter HORNER, HARCOURT, *and* DORILANT

DOR. Engaged to women, and not sup with us!

HORN. Ay, a pox on 'em all!

HAR. You were much a more reasonable man in the morning, and had as noble resolutions against 'em as a widower of a week's liberty.

DOR. Did I ever think to see you keep company with women in vain?

HORN. In vain: no—'tis since I can't love 'em, to be revenged on 'em.

HAR. Now your sting is gone, you looked in the box amongst all those women like a drone in the hive, all upon you; shoved and ill-used by 'em all, and thrust from one side to t'other.

DOR. Yet he must be buzzing amongst 'em still, like other old beetle-headed liquorish drones. Avoid 'em, and hate 'em, as they hate you.

HORN. Because I do hate 'em, and would hate 'em yet more, I'll frequent 'em. You may see by marriage, nothing makes a man hate a woman more than her constant conversation. In short, I converse with 'em, as you do with rich fools, to laugh at 'em and use 'em ill.

DOR. But I would no more sup with women unless I could lie with 'em than sup with a rich coxcomb unless I could cheat him.

HORN. Yes, I have known thee sup with a fool for his drinking; if he could set out your hand that way only, you were satisfied, and if he were a wine-swallowing mouth, 'twas enough.

HAR. Yes, a man drinks often with a fool, as he tosses with a marker, only to keep his hand in ure. But do the ladies drink?

HORN. Yes, Sir; and I shall have the pleasure at least of laying 'em flat with a bottle, and bring as much scandal that way upon 'em as formerly t'other.

HAR. Perhaps you may prove as weak a brother amongst 'em that way as t'other.

DOR. Foh! drinking with women is as unnatural as scolding with 'em. But 'tis a pleasure of decayed fornicators, and the basest way of quenching love.

HAR. Nay, 'tis drowning love, instead of quenching it. But leave us for civil women too!

DOR. Ay, when he can't be the better for 'em. We hardly pardon a man that leaves his friend for a wench, and that's a pretty lawful call.

HORN. Faith, I would not leave you for 'em, if they would not drink.

DOR. Who would disappoint his company at Lewis's for a gossiping?

HAR. Foh! Wine and women, good apart, together as nauseous as sack and sugar. But hark you, Sir, before you go, a little of your advice; an old maimed general, when unfit for action, is fittest for counsel. I have other designs upon women than eating and drinking with them; I am in love with Sparkish's mistress, whom he is to marry to-morrow: now how shall I get her?

Enter SPARKISH, *looking about*

HORN. Why, here comes one will help you to her.

HAR. He! he, I tell you, is my rival, and will hinder my love.

HORN. No; a foolish rival and a jealous husband assist their rival's designs, for they are sure to make their women hate them, which is the first step to their love for another man.

HAR. But I cannot come near his mistress but in his company.

HORN. Still the better for you; for fools are most easily cheated when they themselves are accessories, and he is to be bubbled of his mistress as of his money, the common mistress, by keeping him company.

SPARK. Who is that that is to be bubbled? Faith, let me snack; I han't met with a bubble since Christmas. 'Gad, I think bubbles are like their brother woodcocks, go out with the cold weather.

HAR. (*apart to* HORNER) A pox! he did not hear all, I hope.

SPARK. Come, you bubbling rogues you, where do we sup?——Oh, Harcourt, my mistress tells me you have been making fierce love to her all the play long: ha! ha! But I——

HAR. I make love to her!

SPARK. Nay, I forgive thee, for I think I know thee, and I know her; but I am sure I know myself.

HAR. Did she tell you so? I see all women are like these of the Exchange; who, to enhance the price of their commodities, report to their fond customers offers which were never made 'em.

HORN. Ay, women are as apt to tell before the intrigue, as men after it, and so show themselves the vainer sex. But hast thou a mistress, Sparkish? 'Tis as hard for me to believe it as that thou ever hadst a bubble, as you bragged just now.

SPARK. Oh, your servant, Sir: are you at your raillery, Sir? But we were some of us beforehand with you to-day at the play. The wits were something bold with you, Sir; did you not hear us laugh?

HORN. Yes; but I thought you had gone to plays to laugh at the poet's wit, not at your own.

SPARK. Your servant, Sir: no, I thank you. 'Gad, I go to a play as to a country treat; I carry my own wine to one, and my own wit to t'other, or else I'm sure I should not be merry at either. And the reason why we are so often louder than the players is because we think we speak more wit, and so become the poet's rivals in his audience: for to tell you the truth, we hate the silly rogues, nay, so much, that we find fault even with their bawdy upon the stage, whilst we talk nothing else in the pit as loud.

HORN. But why shouldst thou hate the silly poets? Thou hast too much wit to be one; and they, like whores, are only hated by each other: and thou dost scorn writing, I'm sure.

SPARK. Yes; I'd have you to know I scorn writing: but women, women, that make men do all foolish things, make 'em write songs too. Everybody does it. 'Tis even as common with lovers as playing with fans; and you can no more help rhyming to your Phyllis, than drinking to your Phyllis.

HAR. Nay, poetry in love is no more to be avoided than jealousy.

DOR. But the poets damned your songs, did they?

SPARK. Damn the poets! they turned 'em into burlesque, as they call it. That burlesque is a hocus-pocus trick they have got, which, by the virtue of *Hictius doctius, topsy turvy*, they make a wise and witty man in the world, a fool upon the stage you know not how: and 'tis therefore I hate 'em too, for I know not but it may be my own case; for they'll put a man into a play for looking asquint. Their predecessors were contented to make serving-men only their stage-fools: but these rogues must have gentlemen, with a pox to 'em, nay, knights; and, indeed, you shall hardly see a fool upon the stage but he's a knight. And to tell you the truth, they have kept me these six years from being a knight in earnest, for fear of being knighted in a play, and dubbed a fool.

DOR. Blame 'em not, they must follow their copy, the age.

HAR. But why shouldst thou be afraid of being in a play, who expose yourself every day in the playhouses, and as public places?

HORN. 'Tis but being on the stage, instead of standing on a bench in the pit.

DOR. Don't you give money to painters to draw you like? and are you afraid of your pictures at length in a playhouse, where all your mistresses may see you?

SPARK. A pox! painters don't draw the small-pox or pimples in one's face. Come, damn all your silly authors whatever, all books and booksellers, by the world, and all readers, courteous or uncourteous!

HAR. But who comes here, Sparkish?

Enter MR. PINCHWIFE *and his Wife in man's clothes,* ALITHEA, LUCY *her maid*

SPARK. Oh, hide me! There's my mistress too.

(SPARKISH *hides himself behind* HARCOURT.)

HAR. She sees you.

SPARK. But I will not see her. 'Tis time to go to Whitehall, and I must not fail the drawing-room.

HAR. Pray, first carry me, and reconcile me to her.

SPARK. Another time. Faith, the king will have supped.

HAR. Not with the worse stomach for thy absence. Thou art one of those fools that think their attendance at the king's meals as necessary as his physicians' when you are more troublesome to him than his doctors or his dogs.

SPARK. Pshaw! I know my interest, Sir. Prithee hide me.

HORN. Your servant, Pinchwife.——What, he knows us not!

PINCH. (*to his wife aside*) Come along.

MRS. PINCH. Pray, have you any ballads? give me sixpenny worth.

CLASP. We have no ballads.

MRS. PINCH. Then give me "Covent Garden Drollery," and a play or two—— Oh, here's "Tarugo's Wiles," and "The Slighted Maiden"; I'll have them.

PINCH. (*apart to her*) No; plays are not for your reading. Come along; will you discover yourself?

HORN. Who is that pretty youth with him, Sparkish?

SPARK. I believe his wife's brother, because he's something like her: but I never saw her but once.

HORN. Extremely handsome; I have seen a face like it too. Let us follow 'em.

(*Exeunt* PINCHWIFE, MRS. PINCHWIFE, ALITHEA, LUCY; HORNER, DORILANT *following them.*)

HAR. Come, Sparkish, your mistress saw you, and will be angry you go not to her. Besides, I would fain be reconciled to her, which none but you can do, dear friend.

SPARK. Well, that's a better reason, dear friend. I would not go near her now for hers or my own sake; but I can deny you nothing: for though I have known thee a great while, never go, if I do not love thee as well as a new acquaintance.

HAR. I am obliged to you indeed, dear friend. I would be well with her, only to be well with thee still; for these ties to wives usually dissolve all ties to friends. I would be contented she should enjoy you a-nights, but I would have you to myself a-days as I have had, dear friend.

SPARK. And thou shalt enjoy me a-days, dear, dear friend, never stir: and I'll be divorced from her, sooner than from thee. Come along.

HAR. (*aside*) So, we are hard put to't, when we make our rival our procurer; but neither she nor her brother would let me come near her now. When all's done, a rival is the best cloak to steal to a mistress under, without suspicion; and when we have once got to her as we desire, we throw him off like other cloaks.

(*Exit* SPARKISH, *and* HARCOURT *following him.*)

Re-enter PINCHWIFE, MRS. PINCHWIFE *in man's clothes*

PINCH (*to* ALITHEA) Sister, if you will not go, we must leave you.—(*aside*) The fool her gallant and she will muster up all the young saunterers of this place, and they will leave their dear seamstresses to follow us. What a swarm of cuckolds and cuckold-makers are here!—— Come, let's be gone, Mistress Margery.

MRS. PINCH. Don't you believe that; I han't half my bellyfull of sights yet.

PINCH. Then walk this way.

MRS. PINCH. Lord, what a power of brave signs are here! stay—
the Bull's-Head, the Ram's-Head, and the Stag's-Head, dear——

PINCH. Nay, if every husband's proper sign here were visible,
they would be all alike.

MRS. PINCH. What d'ye mean by that, bud?

PINCH. 'Tis no matter—no matter, bud.

MRS. PINCH. Pray tell me: nay, I will know.

PINCH. They would be all Bulls', Stags', and Rams'-heads.

(*Exeunt* MR. PINCHWIFE *and* MRS. PINCHWIFE.)

Re-enter SPARKISH, HARCOURT, ALITHEA, LUCY, *at t'other door*

SPARK. Come, dear Madam, for my sake you shall be reconciled
to him.

ALITH. For your sake I hate him.

HAR. That's something too cruel, Madam, to hate me for his
sake.

SPARK. Ay indeed, Madam, too, too cruel to me, to hate my
friend for my sake.

ALITH. I hate him because he is your enemy; and you ought to
hate him too, for making love to me, if you love me.

SPARK. That's a good one! I hate a man for loving you! If he
did love you, 'tis but what he can't help; and 'tis your fault, not
his, if he admires you. I hate a man for being of my opinion? I'll
n'er do't, by the world!

ALITH. Is it for your honour, or mine, to suffer a man to make
love to me, who am to marry you to-morrow?

SPARK. Is it for your honour, or mine, to have me jealous? That
he makes love to you, is a sign you are handsome; and that I am
not jealous, is a sign you are virtuous. That I think is for your
honour.

ALITH. But 'tis your honour too I am concerned for.

HAR. But why, dearest Madam, will you be more concerned
for his honour than he is himself? Let his honour alone, for my
sake and his. He! he has no honour——

SPARK. How's that?

HAR. But what my dear friend can guard himself.

SPARK. Oh ho—that's right again.

HAR. Your care of his honour argues his neglect of it, which is
no honour to my dear friend here. Therefore once more, let his
honour go which way it will, dear Madam.

SPARK. Ay, ay; were it for my honour to marry a woman whose
virtue I suspected, and could not trust her in a friend's hands?

ALITH. Are you not afraid to lose me?

HAR. He afraid to lose you, Madam! No, no—you may see how
the most estimable and most glorious creature in the world is
valued by him. Will you not see it?

SPARK. Right, honest Frank, I have that noble value for her
that I cannot be jealous of her.

ALITH. You mistake him. He means, you care not for me, nor
who has me.

SPARK. Lord, Madam, I see you are jealous! Will you wrest a
poor man's meaning from his words?

ALITH. You astonish me, Sir, with your want of jealousy.

SPARK. And you make me giddy, Madam, with your jealousy
and fears, and virtue and honour. 'Gad, I see virtue makes a
woman as troublesome as a little reading or learning.

ALITH. Monstrous!

LUCY. (*behind*) Well, to see what easy husbands these women
of quality can meet with! a poor chambermaid can never have
such ladylike luck. Besides, he's thrown away upon her. She'll
make no use of her fortune, her blessing, none to a gentleman,
for a pure cuckold, for it requires good breeding to be a cuckold.

ALITH. I tell you then plainly, he pursues me to marry me.

SPARK. Pshaw!

HAR. Come, Madam, you see you strive in vain to make him
jealous of me. My dear friend is the kindest creature in the world
to me.

SPARK. Poor fellow!

HAR. But his kindness only is not enough for me, without your
favour, your good opinion, dear Madam: 'tis that must perfect
my happiness. Good gentleman, he believes all I say: would you
would do so! Jealous of me! I would not wrong him nor you for
the world.

SPARK. Look you there. Hear him, hear him, and do not walk
away so.   (ALITHEA *walks carelessly to and fro.*)

HAR. I love you, Madam, so——

SPARK. How's that? Nay, now you begin to go too far indeed.

HAR. So much, I confess, I say, I love you, that I would not
have you miserable, and cast yourself away upon so unworthy
and inconsiderable a thing as what you see here.

                    (*clapping his hand on his breast, points at* SPARKISH)

SPARK. No, faith, I believe thou wouldst not: now his meaning
is plain; but I knew before thou wouldst not wrong me, nor her.

HAR. No, no, Heavens forbid the glory of her sex should fall
so low, as into the embraces of such a contemptible wretch, the
last of mankind—my dear friend here—I injure him!

(embracing SPARKISH)

ALITH. Very well.

SPARK. No, no, dear friend, I knew it.——Madam, you see he
will rather wrong himself than me, in giving himself such names.

ALITH. Do not you understand him yet?

SPARK. Yes: how modestly he speaks of himself, poor fellow!

ALITH. Methinks he speaks impudently of yourself, since—before yourself too; insomuch that I can no longer suffer his scurrilous abusiveness to you, no more than his love to me.

(offers to go)

SPARK. Nay, nay, Madam, pray stay—his love to you! Lord,
Madam, has he not spoke yet plain enough?

ALITH. Yes, indeed, I should think so.

SPARK. Well then, by the world, a man can't speak civilly to a
woman now, but presently she says he makes love to her. Nay,
Madam, you shall stay, with your pardon, since you have not yet
understood him, till he has made an *éclaircissement* of his love
to you, that is, what kind of love it is. Answer to thy catechism,
friend; do you love my mistress here?

HAR. Yes, I wish she would not doubt it.

SPARK. But how do you love her?

HAR. With all my soul.

ALITH. I thank him, methinks he speaks plain enough now.

SPARK. (*to* ALITHEA) You are out still.——But with what kind
of love, Harcourt?

HAR. With the best and the truest love in the world.

SPARK. Look you there then, that is with no matrimonial love,
I'm sure.

ALITH. How's that? do you say matrimonial love is not best?

SPARK. 'Gad, I went too far ere I was aware. But speak for thyself, Harcourt, you said you would not wrong me nor her.

HAR. No, no, Madam, e'en take him for Heaven's sake——

SPARK. Look you there, Madam.

HAR. Who should in all justice be yours, he that loves you most.

(claps his hand on his breast)

ALITH. Look you there, Mr. Sparkish, who's that?

SPARK. Who should it be?——Go on, Harcourt.

HAR. Who loves you more than women, titles, or fortune fools.
(*points at* SPARKISH)

SPARK. Look you there, he means me still, for he points at me.

ALITH. Ridiculous!

HAR. Who can only match your faith and constancy in love.

SPARK. Ay.

HAR. Who knows, if it be possible, how to value so much beauty and virtue.

SPARK. Ay.

HAR. Whose love can no more be equalled in the world, than that heavenly form of yours.

SPARK. No.

HAR. Who could no more suffer a rival than your absence, and yet could no more suspect your virtue than his own constancy in his love to you.

SPARK. No.

HAR. Who, in fine, loves you better than his eyes, that first made him love you.

SPARK. Ay—— Nay, Madam, faith, you shan't go till——

ALITH. Have a care, lest you make me stay too long.

SPARK. But till he has saluted you; that I may be assured you are friends, after his honest advice and declaration. Come, pray, Madam, be friends with him.

Enter MASTER PINCHWIFE, MRS. PINCHWIFE

ALITH. You must pardon me, Sir, that I am not yet so obedient to you.

PINCH. What, invite your wife to kiss men? Monstrous! Are you not ashamed? I will never forgive you.

SPARK. Are you not ashamed that I should have more confidence in the chastity of your family than you have? You must not teach me; I am a man of honour, Sir, though I am frank and free; I am frank, Sir——

PINCH. Very frank, Sir, to share your wife with your friends.

SPARK. He is an humble, menial friend, such as reconciles the differences of the marriage bed; you know man and wife do not always agree; I design him for that use, therefore would have him well with my wife.

PINCH. A menial friend!—you will get a great many menial friends, by showing your wife as you do.

SPARK. What then? It may be I have a pleasure in't, as I have to show fine clothes at a playhouse, the first day, and count money before poor rogues.

PINCH. He that shows his wife or money, will be in danger of having them borrowed sometimes.

SPARK. I love to be envied, and would not marry a wife that I alone could love; loving alone is as dull as eating alone. Is it not a frank age? and I am a frank person; and to tell you the truth, it may be I love to have rivals in a wife; they make her seem to a man still but as a kept mistress; and so good night, for I must to Whitehall.——Madam, I hope you are now reconciled to my friend; and so I wish you a good night, Madam, and sleep if you can: for to-morrow you know I must visit you early with a canonical gentleman. Good night, dear Harcourt.   (*Exit* SPARKISH.)

HAR. Madam, I hope you will not refuse my visit to-morrow, if it should be earlier with a canonical gentleman than Mr. Sparkish's.

PINCH. This gentlewoman is yet under my care, therefore you must yet forbear your freedom with her, Sir.

(*coming between* ALITHEA *and* HARCOURT)

HAR. Must, Sir?

PINCH. Yes, Sir, she is my sister.

HAR. 'Tis well she is, Sir—for I must be her servant, Sir.—— Madam——

PINCH. Come away, Sister, we had been gone, if it had not been for you, and so avoided these lewd rake-hells, who seem to haunt us.

Enter HORNER, DORILANT *to them*

HORN. How now, Pinchwife!

PINCH. Your servant.

HORN. What! I see a little time in the country makes a man turn wild and unsociable, and only fit to converse with his horses, dogs, and his herds.

PINCH. I have business, Sir, and must mind it; your business is pleasure; therefore you and I must go different ways.

HORN. Well, you may go on, but this pretty young gentle-man——   (*takes hold of* MRS. PINCHWIFE)

HAR. The lady——

DOR. And the maid——

HORN. Shall stay with us; for I suppose their business is the same with ours, pleasure.

PINCH. (aside) 'Sdeath, he knows her, she carries it so sillily! Yet if he does not, I should be more silly to discover it first.

ALITH. Pray, let us go, Sir.

PINCH. Come, come——

HORN. (to MRS. PINCHWIFE) Had you not rather stay with us?——Prithee, Pinchwife, who is this pretty young gentleman?

PINCH. One to whom I'm a guardian.—(aside) I wish I could keep her out of your hands.

HORN. Who is he? I never saw anything so pretty in all my life.

PINCH. Pshaw! do not look upon him so much, he's a poor bashful youth; you'll put him out of countenance.——Come away, brother. (offers to take her away)

HORN. Oh, your brother!

PINCH. Yes, my wife's brother.——Come, come, she'll stay supper for us.

HORN. I thought so, for he is very like her I saw you at the play with, whom I told you I was in love with.

MRS. PINCH. (aside) O jeminy! is this he that was in love with me? I am glad on't, I vow, for he's a curious fine gentleman, and I love him already, too.—(To PINCHWIFE.) Is this he, bud?

PINCH. (to his Wife) Come away, come away.

HORN. Why, what haste are you in? why won't you let me talk with him?

PINCH. Because you'll debauch him; he's yet young and innocent, and I would not have him debauched for anything in the world.—(aside) How she gazes on him! the devil!

HORN. Harcourt, Dorilant, look you here, this is the likeness of that dowdy he told us of, his wife; did you ever see a lovelier creature? The rogue has reason to be jealous of his wife, since she is like him, for she would make all that see her in love with her.

HAR. And, as I remember now, she is as like him here as can be.

DOR. She is indeed very pretty, if she be like him.

HORN. Very pretty? a very pretty commendation!—she is a glorious creature, beautiful beyond all things I ever beheld.

PINCH. So, so.

HAR. More beautiful than a poet's first mistress of imagination.

HORN. Or another man's last mistress of flesh and blood.

MRS. PINCH. Nay, now you jeer, Sir; pray don't jeer me.

PINCH. Come, come.—(*aside*) By Heavens, she'll discover herself!

HORN. I speak of your sister, Sir.

PINCH. Ay, but saying she was handsome, if like him, made him blush.—(*aside*) I am upon a rack!

HORN. Methinks he is so handsome he should not be a man.

PINCH. (*aside*) Oh, there 'tis out! he has discovered her! I am not able to suffer any longer.—(*To his Wife.*) Come, come away, I say.

HORN. Nay, by your leave, Sir, he shall not go yet.—(*aside to them*) Harcourt, Dorilant, let us torment this jealous rogue a little.

HAR. } How?
DOR. }

HORN. I'll show you.

PINCH. Come, pray let him go, I cannot stay fooling any longer; I tell you his sister stays supper for us.

HORN. Does she? Come then, we'll all go sup with her and thee.

PINCH. No, now I think on't, having stayed so long for us, I warrant she's gone to bed.—(*aside*) I wish she and I were well out of their hands.——Come, I must rise early to-morrow, come.

HORN. Well then, if she be gone to bed, I wish her and you a good night. But pray, young gentleman, present my humble service to her.

MRS. PINCH. Thank you heartily, Sir.

PINCH. (*aside*) 'Sdeath she will discover herself yet in spite of me.——He is something more civil to you, for your kindness to his sister, than I am, it seems.

HORN. Tell her, dear sweet little gentleman, for all your brother there, that you have revived the love I had for her at first sight in the playhouse.

MRS. PINCH. But did you love her indeed, and indeed?

PINCH. (*aside*) So, so.——Away, I say.

HORN. Nay, stay.—— Yes, indeed, and indeed, pray do you tell her so, and give her this kiss from me.   (*kisses her*)

PINCH. (*aside*) O Heavens! what do I suffer? Now 'tis too plain he knows her, and yet——

HORN. And this, and this———   (*kisses her again*)

MRS. PINCH. What do you kiss me for? I am no woman.

PINCH. (*aside*) So, there, 'tis out.——Come, I cannot, nor will stay any longer.

HORN. Nay, they shall send your lady a kiss too. Here, Harcourt, Dorilant, will you not?   (*They kiss her.*)

PINCH. (*aside*) How! do I suffer this? Was I not accusing another just now for this rascally patience, in permitting his wife to be kissed before his face? Ten thousand ulcers gnaw away their lips.——Come, come.

HORN. Good night, dear little gentleman; Madam, good night; farewell, Pinchwife.—(*apart to* HARCOURT *and* DORILANT) Did not I tell you I would raise his jealous gall?

       (*Exeunt* HORNER, HARCOURT, *and* DORILANT.)

PINCH. So, they are gone at last; stay, let me see first if the coach be at this door.   (*Exit.*)

HORNER, HARCOURT, *and* DORILANT *return*

HORN. What, not gone yet? Will you be sure to do as I desired you, sweet Sir?

MRS. PINCH. Sweet Sir, but what will you give me then?

HORN. Anything. Come away into the next walk.

       (*Exit, haling away* MRS. PINCHWIFE.)

ALITH. Hold! hold! what d'ye do?

LUCY. Stay, stay, hold——

HAR. Hold, Madam, hold, let him present him—he'll come presently; nay, I will never let you go till you answer my question.

       (ALITHEA, LUCY, *struggling with* HARCOURT *and* DORILANT)

LUCY. For God's sake, Sir, I must follow 'em.

DOR. No, I have something to present you with too, you shan't follow them.

PINCHWIFE *returns*

PINCH. Where?—how—what's become of?—gone!—whither?

LUCY. He's only gone with the gentleman, who will give him something, an't please your worship.

PINCH. Something!—give him something, with a pox!—where are they?

ALITH. In the next walk only, Brother.

PINCH. Only, only! where, where?

(Exit PINCHWIFE *and returns presently,
then goes out again.)*

HAR. What's the matter with him? Why so much concerned?
But, dearest Madam——

ALITH. Pray let me go, Sir; I have said and suffered enough
already.

HAR. Then you will not look upon, nor pity, my sufferings?

ALITH. To look upon 'em, when I cannot help 'em, were cruelty,
not pity; therefore, I will never see you more.

HAR. Let me then, Madam, have my privilege of a banished
lover, complaining or railing, and giving you but a farewell reason why, if you cannot condescend to marry me, you should not
take that wretch, my rival.

ALITH. He only, not you, since my honour is engaged so far to
him, can give me a reason why I should not marry him; but if he
be true, and what I think him to me, I must be so to him. Your
servant, Sir.

HAR. Have women only constancy when 'tis a vice, and, like
Fortune, only true to fools?

DOR. Thou shalt not stir, thou robust creature; you see I can
deal with you, therefore you should stay the rather, and be kind.

(to LUCY, *who struggles to get from him)*

Enter PINCHWIFE

PINCH. Gone, gone, not to be found! quite gone! ten thousand
plagues go with 'em! which way went they?

ALITH. But into t'other walk, Brother.

LUCY. Their business will be done presently sure, an't please
your worship; it can't be long in doing, I'm sure on't.

ALITH. Are they not there?

PINCH. No, you know where they are, you infamous wretch,
eternal shame of your family, which you do not dishonour enough
yourself you think, but you must help her to do it too, thou legion
of bawds!

ALITH. Good Brother——

PINCH. Damned, damned Sister!

ALITH. Look you here, she's coming.

Enter MRS. PINCHWIFE *in man's clothes, running, with her hat under her arm, full of oranges and dried fruit,* HORNER *following*

MRS. PINCH. O dear bud, look you here what I have got, see!

PINCH. (*aside, rubbing his forehead*) And what I have got here too, which you can't see.

MRS. PINCH. The fine gentleman has given me better things yet.

PINCH. Has he so?—(*aside*) Out of breath and coloured!—I must hold yet.

HORN. I have only given your little brother an orange, Sir.

PINCH. (*to* HORNER) Thank you, Sir.—(*aside*)You have only squeezed my orange, I suppose, and given it me again; yet I must have a city patience.—(*to his Wife*) Come, come away.

MRS. PINCH. Stay, till I have put up my fine things, bud.

Enter SIR JASPER FIDGET

SIR JASP. O, Master Horner, come, come, the ladies stay for you; your mistress, my wife, wonders you make not more haste to her.

HORN. I have stayed this half hour for you here, and 'tis your fault I am not now with your wife.

SIR JASP. But, pray, don't let her know so much; the truth on't is, I was advancing a certain project to his majesty about—I'll tell you.

HORN. No, let's go, and hear it at your house. Good night, sweet little gentleman; one kiss more, you'll remember me now, I hope.

(*kisses her*)

DOR. What, Sir Jasper, will you separate friends? He promised to sup with us, and if you take him to your house, you'll be in danger of our company too.

SIR JASP. Alas! gentlemen, my house is not fit for you; there are none but civil women there, which are not for your turn. He, you know, can bear with the society of civil women now, ha! ha! ha! besides, he's one of my family—he's—he! he! he!

DOR. What is he?

SIR JASP. Faith, my eunuch, since you'll have it; he! he! he!

(*Exeunt* SIR JASPER FIDGET *and* HORNER.)

DOR. I rather wish thou wert his or my cuckold. Harcourt, what a good cuckold is lost there for want of a man to make him one! Thee and I cannot have Horner's privilege, who can make use of it.

HAR. Ay, to poor Horner 'tis like coming to an estate at three-score, when a man can't be the better for't.

PINCH. Come.

MRS. PINCH. Presently, bud.

DOR. Come, let us go too.—(*to* ALITHEA) Madam, your servant.—(*to* LUCY) Good night, strapper.

HAR. Madam, though you will not let me have a good day or night, I wish you one; but dare not name the other half of my wish.

ALITH. Good night, Sir, for ever.

MRS. PINCH. I don't know where to put this here, dear bud, you shall eat it; nay, you shall have part of the fine gentleman's good things, or treat, as you call it, when we come home.

PINCH. Indeed, I deserve it, since I furnished the best part of it.
(*strikes away the orange*)
     The gallant treats presents, and gives the ball,
     But 'tis the absent cuckold pays for all.

ACT IV

SCENE I

In PINCHWIFE'S *House in the morning*

LUCY, ALITHEA *dressed in new clothes*

LUCY. Well, Madam,—now have I dressed you, and set you out with so many ornaments, and spent upon you ounces of essence and pulvillio; and all this for no other purpose but as people adorn and perfume a corpse for a stinking second-hand grave: such, or as bad, I think Master Sparkish's bed.

ALITH. Hold your peace.

LUCY. Nay, Madam, I will ask you the reason why you would banish poor Master Harcourt for ever from your sight; how could you be so hard-hearted?

ALITH. 'Twas because I was not hard-hearted.

LUCY. No, no; 'twas stark love and kindness, I warrant.

ALITH. It was so; I would see him no more because I love him.

LUCY. Hey day, a very pretty reason!

ALITH. You do not understand me.

LUCY. I wish you may yourself.

ALITH. I was engaged to marry, you see, another man, whom my justice will not suffer me to deceive or injure.

LUCY. Can there be a greater cheat or wrong done to a man than to give him your person without your heart? I should make a conscience of it.

ALITH. I'll retrieve it for him after I am married a while.

LUCY. The woman that marries to love better, will be as much mistaken as the wencher that marries to live better. No, Madam, marrying to increase love is like gaming to become rich; alas! you only lose what little stock you had before.

ALITH. I find by your rhetoric you have been bribed to betray me.

LUCY. Only by his merit, that has bribed your heart, you see, against your word and rigid honour. But what a devil is this honour! 'tis sure a disease in the head, like the megrim or falling-sickness, that always hurries people away to do themselves mischief. Men lose their lives by it; women, what's dearer to 'em, their love, the life of life.

ALITH. Come, pray talk you no more of honour, nor Master Harcourt; I wish the other would come to secure my fidelity to him and his right in me.

LUCY. You will marry him then?

ALITH. Certainly; I have given him already my word, and will my hand too, to make it good, when he comes.

LUCY. Well, I wish I may never stick pin more, if he be not an arrant natural to t'other fine gentleman.

ALITH. I own he wants the wit of Harcourt, which I will dispense withal for another want he has, which is want of jealousy, which men of wit seldom want.

LUCY. Lord, Madam, what should you do with a fool to your husband? You intend to be honest, don't you? then that husbandly virtue, credulity, is thrown away upon you.

ALITH. He only that could suspect my virtue should have cause to do it; 'tis Sparkish's confidence in my truth that obliges me to be so faithful to him.

LUCY. You are not sure his opinion may last.

ALITH. I am satisfied 'tis impossible for him to be jealous after the proofs I have had of him. Jealousy in a husband—Heaven defend me from it! it begets a thousand plagues to a poor woman, the loss of her honour, her quiet, and her——

LUCY. And her pleasure.

ALITH. What d'ye mean, impertinent?

LUCY. Liberty is a great pleasure, Madam.

ALITH. I say, loss of her honour, her quiet, nay, her life sometimes; and what's as bad almost, the loss of this town; that is, she is sent into the country, which is the last ill-usage of a husband to a wife, I think.

LUCY. (*aside*) Oh, does the wind lie there?—— Then of necessity, Madam, you think a man must carry his wife into the country, if he be wise. The country is as terrible, I find, to our young English ladies, as a monastery to those abroad; and, on my virginity, I think they would rather marry a London jailer than a high sheriff of a county, since neither can stir from his employment. Formerly women of wit married fools for a great estate, a fine seat, or the like; but now 'tis for a pretty seat only in Lincoln's Inn Fields, St. James's Fields, or the Pall Mall.

Enter to them SPARKISH, *and* HARCOURT, *dressed like a Parson*

SPARK. Madam, your humble servant, a happy day to you, and to us all.

HAR. Amen.

ALITH. Who have we here?

SPARK. My chaplain, faith—— O Madam, poor Harcourt remembers his humble service to you; and, in obedience to your last commands, refrains coming into your sight.

ALITH. Is not that he?

SPARK. No, fy, no; but to show that he ne'er intended to hinder our match, has sent his brother here to join our hands. When I get me a wife, I must get her a chaplain, according to the custom; this is his brother, and my chaplain.

ALITH. His brother!

LUCY. (*aside*) And your chaplain, to preach in your pulpit then——

ALITH. His brother!

SPARK. Nay, I knew you would not believe it.—— I told you, Sir, she would take you for your brother Frank.

ALITH. Believe it!

LUCY. (*aside*) His brother! ha! ha! he! he has a trick left still, it seems.

SPARK. Come, my dearest, pray let us go to church before the canonical hour is past.

ALITH. For shame, you are abused still.

SPARK. By the world, 'tis strange now you are so incredulous.

ALITH. 'Tis strange you are so credulous.

SPARK. Dearest of my life, hear me. I tell you this is Ned Harcourt of Cambridge, by the world; you see he has a sneaking college look. 'Tis true he's something like his brother Frank; and they differ from each other no more than in their age, for they were twins.

LUCY. Ha! ha! he!

ALITH. Your servant, Sir; I cannot be so deceived, though you are. But come, let's hear, how do you know what you affirm so confidently?

SPARK. Why, I'll tell you all. Frank Harcourt coming to me this morning to wish me joy, and present his service to you, I asked him if he could help me to a parson. Whereupon he told me he had a brother in town who was in orders; and he went straight away, and sent him, you see there, to me.

ALITH. Yes, Frank goes and puts on a black coat, then tells you he is Ned; that's all you have for't.

SPARK. Pshaw! pshaw! I tell you, by the same token, the midwife put her garter about Frank's neck, to know 'em asunder, they were so like.

ALITH. Frank tells you this too?

SPARK. Ay, and Ned there too: nay, they are both in a story.

ALITH. So, so; very foolish.

SPARK. Lord, if you won't believe one, you had best try him by your chambermaid there; for chambermaids must needs know chaplains from other men, they are so used to 'em.

LUCY. Let's see: nay, I'll be sworn he has the canonical smirk, and the filthy clammy palm of a chaplain.

ALITH. Well, most reverend Doctor, pray let us make an end of this fooling.

HAR. With all my soul, divine heavenly creature, when you please.

ALITH. He speaks like a chaplain indeed.

SPARK. Why, was there not soul, divine, heavenly, in what he said?

ALITH. Once more, most impertinent black coat, cease your persecution, and let us have a conclusion of this ridiculous love.

HAR. (aside) I had forgot; I must suit my style to my coat, or I wear it in vain.

ALITH. I have no more patience left; let us make once an end of this troublesome love, I say.

HAR. So be it, seraphic lady, when your honour shall think it meet and convenient so to do.

SPARK. 'Gad, I'm sure none but a chaplain could speak so, I think.

ALITH. Let me tell you, Sir, this dull trick will not serve your turn; though you delay our marriage, you shall not hinder it.

HAR. Far be it from me, munificent patroness, to delay your marriage; I desire nothing more than to marry you presently, which I might do, if you yourself would; for my noble, good-natured, and thrice generous patron here would not hinder it.

SPARK. No, poor man, not I, faith.

HAR. And now, Madam, let me tell you plainly nobody else shall marry you, by Heavens! I'll die first, for I'm sure I should die after it.

LUCY. How his love has made him forget his function, as I have seen it in real parsons!

ALITH. That was spoken like a chaplain too? Now you understand him, I hope.

SPARK. Poor man, he takes it heinously to be refused; I can't blame him, 'tis putting an indignity upon him, not to be suffered; but you'll pardon me, Madam, it shan't be; he shall marry us; come away, pray, Madam.

LUCY. Ha! ha! he! more ado! 'tis late.

ALITH. Invincible stupidity! I tell you, he would marry me as your rival, not as your chaplain.

SPARK. Come, come, Madam.   (pulling her away)

LUCY. I pray, Madam, do not refuse this reverend divine the honour and satisfaction of marrying you; for I dare say he has set his heart upon't, good doctor.

ALITH. What can you hope or design by this?

HAR. (aside) I could answer her, a reprieve for a day only,

often revokes a hasty doom. At worst, if she will not take mercy on me, and let me marry her, I have at least the lover's second pleasure, hindering my rival's enjoyment, though but for a time.

SPARK. Come, Madam, 'tis e'en twelve o'clock, and my mother charged me never to be married out of the canonical hours. Come, come; Lord, here's such a deal of modesty, I warrant, the first day.

LUCY. Yes, an't please your worship, married women show all their modesty the first day, because married men show all their love the first day.

(*Exeunt* SPARKISH, ALITHEA, HARCOURT, *and* LUCY.)

SCENE II

The Scene changes to a Bedchamber, where appear PINCHWIFE *and* MRS. PINCHWIFE

PINCH. Come, tell me, I say.

MRS. PINCH. Lord! han't I told it an hundred times over?

PINCH. (*aside*) I would try, if in the repetition of the ungrateful tale, I could find her altering it in the least circumstance; for if her story be false, she is so too.—— Come, how was't, baggage?

MRS. PINCH. Lord, what pleasure you take to hear it, sure!

PINCH. No, you take more in telling it, I find; but speak, how was't?

MRS. PINCH. He carried me up into the house next to the Exchange.

PINCH. So, and you two were only in the room!

MRS. PINCH. Yes, for he sent away a youth that was there, for some dried fruit, and China oranges.

PINCH. Did he so? Damn him for it—and for——

MRS. PINCH. But presently came up the gentlewoman of the house.

PINCH. Oh, 'twas well she did; but what did he do whilst the fruit came?

MRS. PINCH. He kissed me an hundred times, and told me he fancied he kissed my fine sister, meaning me, you know, whom he said he loved with all his soul, and bid me be sure to tell her so, and to desire her to be at her window, by eleven of the clock this morning, and he would walk under it at that time.

PINCH. (*aside*) And he was as good as his word, very punctual; a pox reward him for't.

MRS. PINCH. Well, and he said if you were not within, he would come up to her, meaning me, you know, bud, still.

PINCH. (*aside*) So—he knew her certainly; but for this confession, I am obliged to her simplicity.——But what, you stood very still when he kissed you?

MRS. PINCH. Yes, I warrant you; would you have had me discover myself?

PINCH. But you told me he did some beastliness to you, as you call it; what·was't?

MRS. PINCH. Why, he put——

PINCH. What?

MRS. PINCH. Why, he put the tip of his tongue between my lips, and so mousled me—and I said, I'd bite it.

PINCH. An eternal canker seize it, for a dog!

MRS. PINCH. Nay, you need not be so angry with him neither, for to say truth, he has the sweetest breath I ever knew.

PINCH. The devil! you were satisfied with it then, and would do it again?

MRS. PINCH. Not unless he should force me.

PINCH. Force you, changeling! I tell you, no woman can be forced.

MRS. PINCH. Yes, but she may sure, by such a one as he, for he's a proper, goodly, strong man; 'tis hard, let me tell you, to resist him.

PINCH. (*aside*) So, 'tis plain she loves him, yet she has not love enough to make her conceal it from me; but the sight of him will increase her aversion for me and love for him; and that love instruct her how to deceive me and satisfy him, all idiot as she is. Love! 'twas he gave women first their craft, their art of deluding. Out of Nature's hands they came plain, open, silly, and fit for slaves, as she and Heaven intended 'em; but damned Love— well—I must strangle that little monster whilst I can deal with him.—— Go fetch pen, ink, and paper out of the next room.

MRS. PINCH. Yes, bud.   (*Exit.*)

PINCH. Why should women have more invention in love than men? It can only be because they have more desires, more soliciting passions, more lust, and more of the devil.

MRS. PINCHWIFE *returns*

Come, minx, sit down and write.

MRS. PINCH. Ay, dear bud, but I can't do't very well.

PINCH. I wish you could not at all.

MRS. PINCH. But what should I write for?

PINCH. I'll have you write a letter to your lover.

MRS. PINCH. O Lord, to the fine gentleman a letter!

PINCH. Yes, to the fine gentleman.

MRS. PINCH. Lord, you do but jeer: sure you jest.

PINCH. I am not so merry: come, write as I bid you.

MRS. PINCH. What, do you think I am a fool?

PINCH. (*aside*) She's afraid I would not dictate any love to him, therefore she's unwilling.——But you had best begin.

MRS. PINCH. Indeed, and indeed, but I won't, so I won't.

PINCH. Why?

MRS. PINCH. Because he's in town; you may send for him if you will.

PINCH. Very well, you would have him brought to you; is it come to this? I say, take the pen and write, or you'll provoke me.

MRS. PINCH. Lord, what d'ye make a fool of me for? Don't I know that letters are never writ but from the country to London, and from London into the country? Now he's in town, and I am in town too; therefore I can't write to him, you know.

PINCH. (*aside*) So, I am glad it is no worse; she is innocent enough yet.—— Yes, you may, when your husband bids you, write letters to people that are in town.

MRS. PINCH. Oh, may I so? then I'm satisfied.

PINCH. Come, begin (*dictates*)—"Sir"——

MRS. PINCH. Shan't I say, "Dear Sir"? You know one says always something more than bare "Sir."

PINCH. Write as I bid you, or I will write whore with this penknife in your face.

MRS. PINCH. Nay, good bud (*She writes.*)—"Sir"——

PINCH. "Though I suffered last night your nauseous, loathed kisses and embraces"—— Write!

MRS. PINCH. Nay, why should I say so? You know I told you he had a sweet breath.

PINCH. Write!

MRS. PINCH. Let me but put out "loathed."

PINCH. Write, I say!

MRS. PINCH. Well then. *(writes)*

PINCH. Let's see, what have you writ?—*(takes the paper and reads)* "Though I suffered last night your kisses and embraces"—— Thou impudent creature! where is "nauseous" and "loathed"?

MRS. PINCH. I can't abide to write such filthy words.

PINCH. Once more write as I'd have you, and question it not, or I will spoil thy writing with this. I will stab out those eyes that cause my mischief. *(holds up the penknife)*

MRS. PINCH. O Lord! I will.

PINCH. So—so—let's see now.—*(reads)* "Though I suffered last night your nauseous, loathed kisses and embraces"—go on— "yet I would not have you presume that you shall ever repeat them"—so—— *(She writes.)*

MRS. PINCH. I have writ it.

PINCH. On, then—"I then concealed myself from your knowledge, to avoid your insolencies."—— *(She writes.)*

MRS. PINCH. So——

PINCH. "The same reason, now I am out of your hands"——
(She writes.)

MRS. PINCH. So——

PINCH. "Makes me own to you my unfortunate, though innocent frolic, of being in man's clothes"—— *(She writes.)*

MRS. PINCH. So——

PINCH. "That you may for evermore cease to pursue her, who hates and detests you"—— *(She writes on.)*

MRS. PINCH. So–h—— *(sighs)*

PINCH. What, do you sigh?—"detests you—as much as she loves her husband and her honour."

MRS. PINCH. I vow, husband, he'll ne'er believe I should write such a letter.

PINCH. What, he'd expect a kinder from you? Come, now your name only.

MRS. PINCH. What, shan't I say "Your most faithful humble servant till death"?

PINCH. No, tormenting fiend!—*(aside)* Her style, I find, would be very soft.—— Come, wrap it up now, whilst I go fetch wax and a candle; and write on the backside, "For Mr. Horner."

(Exit PINCHWIFE.)

MRS. PINCH. "For Mr. Horner."—— So, I am glad he has told me his name. Dear Mr. Horner! But why should I send thee such a letter that will vex thee, and make thee angry with me?—— Well, I will not send it.—— Ay, but then my husband will kill me—for I see plainly he won't let me love Mr. Horner—but what care I for my husband? I won't, so I won't, send poor Mr. Horner such a letter—— But then my husband—but oh, what if I writ at bottom my husband made me write it?—— Ay, but then my husband would see't—Can one have no shift? Ah, a London woman would have had a hundred presently. Stay—what if I should write a letter, and wrap it up like this, and write upon't too? Ay, but then my husband would see't—I don't know what to do.—But yet evads I'll try, so I will—for I will not send this letter to poor Mr. Horner, come what will on't.

"Dear, sweet Mr. Horner"—(*She writes and repeats what she hath writ.*)—so—"my husband would have me send you a base, rude, unmannerly letter; but I won't"—so—"and would have me forbid you loving me; but I won't"—so—"and would have me say to you, I hate you, poor Mr. Horner; but I won't tell a lie for him"—there—"for I'm sure if you and I were in the country at cards together"—so—"I could not help treading on your toe under the table"—so—"or rubbing knees with you, and staring in your face, till you saw me"—very well—"and then looking down, and blushing for an hour together"—so—"but I must make haste before my husband come: and now he has taught me to write letters, you shall have longer ones from me, who am, dear, dear, poor, dear Mr. Horner, your most humble friend, and servant to command till death,—Margery Pinchwife."

Stay, I must give him a hint at bottom—so—now wrap it up just like t'other—so—now write "For Mr. Horner"—But oh now, what shall I do with it? for here comes my husband.

Enter PINCHWIFE

PINCH. (*aside*) I have been detained by a sparkish coxcomb, who pretended a visit to me; but I fear 'twas to my wife—— What, have you done?

MRS. PINCH. Ay, ay, bud, just now.

PINCH. Let's see't: what d'ye tremble for? what, you would not have it go?

MRS. PINCH. Here—(*aside*) No, I must not give him that: so I had been served if I had given him this.

(*He opens and reads the first letter.*)

PINCH. Come, where's the wax and seal?

MRS. PINCH. (*aside*) Lord, what shall I do now? Nay, then I have it—— Pray let me see't. Lord, you think me so arrant a fool I cannot seal a letter; I will do't, so I will.

(*snatches the letter from him, changes it for the other, seals it, and delivers it to him*)

PINCH. Nay, I believe you will learn that, and other things too, which I would not have you.

MRS. PINCH. So, han't I done it curiously?—(*aside*) I think I have; there's my letter going to Mr. Horner, since he'll needs have me send letters to folks.

PINCH. 'Tis very well; but I warrant you would not have it go now?

MRS. PINCH. Yes, indeed, but I would, bud, now.

PINCH. Well, you are a good girl then. Come, let me lock you up in your chamber till I come back; and be sure you come not within three strides of the window when I am gone, for I have a spy in the street.—(*Exit* MRS. PINCHWIFE, PINCHWIFE *locks the door.*) At least, 'tis fit she think so. If we do not cheat women, they'll cheat us, and fraud may be justly used with secret enemies, of which a wife is the most dangerous; and he that has a handsome one to keep, and a frontier town, must provide against treachery, rather than open force. Now I have secured all within, I'll deal with the foe without, with false intelligence.

(*Holds up the letter. Exit* PINCHWIFE.)

SCENE III

The Scene changes to HORNER's *Lodging*

QUACK *and* HORNER

QUACK. Well, Sir, how fadges the new design? Have you not the luck of all your brother projectors, to deceive only yourself at last?

HORN. No, good domine Doctor, I deceive you, it seems, and

others too; for the grave matrons, and old, rigid husbands think me as unfit for love as they are; but their wives, sisters, and daughters know, some of 'em, better things already.

QUACK. Already!

HORN. Already, I say. Last night I was drunk with half-a-dozen of your civil persons, as you call 'em, and people of honour, and so was made free of their society and dressing-rooms for ever hereafter; and am already come to the privileges of sleeping upon their pallets, warming smocks, tying shoes and garters, and the like, Doctor, already, already, Doctor.

QUACK. You have made use of your time, Sir.

HORN. I tell thee, I am now no more interruption to 'em when they sing, or talk, bawdy, than a little squab French page who speaks no English.

QUACK. But do civil persons and women of honour drink, and sing bawdy songs?

HORN. Oh, amongst friends, amongst friends. For your bigots in honour are just like those in religion; they fear the eye of the world more than the eye of Heaven, and think there is no virtue but railing at vice, and no sin but giving scandal. They rail at a poor little kept player, and keep themselves some young modest pulpit comedian to be privy to their sins in their closets, not to tell 'em of them in their chapels.

QUACK. Nay, the truth on't is priests, amongst the women now, have quite got the better of us lay-confessors, physicians.

HORN. And they are rather their patients; but——

Enter MY LADY FIDGET, *looking about her*

Now we talk of women of honour, here comes one. Step behind the screen there, and but observe if I have not particular privileges with the women of reputation already, Doctor, already.

(QUACK *retires.*)

LADY FID. Well, Horner, am not I a woman of honour? You see, I'm as good as my word.

HORN. And you shall see, Madam, I'll not be behindhand with you in honour; and I'll be as good as my word too, if you please but to withdraw into the next room.

LADY FID. But first, my dear Sir, you must promise to have a care of my dear honour.

HORN. If you talk a word more of your honour, you'll make me incapable to wrong it. To talk of honour in the mysteries of love, is like talking of Heaven or the Deity in an operation of witch-craft just when you are employing the devil: it makes the charm impotent.

LADY FID. Nay, fy! let us not be smutty. But you talk of mys-teries and bewitching to me; I don't understand you.

HORN. I tell you, Madam, the word money in a mistress's mouth, at such a nick of time, is not a more disheartening sound to a younger brother, than that of honour to an eager lover like myself.

LADY FID. But you can't blame a lady of my reputation to be chary.

HORN. Chary! I have been chary of it already, by the report I have caused of myself.

LADY FID. Ay, but if you should ever let other women know that dear secret, it would come out. Nay, you must have a great care of your conduct; for my acquaintance are so censorious (oh, 'tis a wicked, censorious world, Mr. Horner!), I say, are so cen-sorious and detracting that perhaps they'll talk to the prejudice of my honour, though you should not let them know the dear secret.

HORN. Nay, Madam, rather than they shall prejudice your honour, I'll prejudice theirs; and, to serve you, I'll lie with 'em all, make the secret their own, and then they'll keep it. I am a Machiavel in love, Madam.

LADY FID. Oh, no, Sir, not that way.

HORN. Nay, the devil take me if censorious women are to be silenced any other way.

LADY FID. A secret is better kept, I hope, by a single person than a multitude; therefore pray do not trust anybody else with it, dear, dear Mr. Horner. *(embracing him)*

Enter SIR JASPER FIDGET

SIR JASP. How now!

LADY FID. *(aside)* Oh my husband!—prevented—and what's almost as bad, found with my arms about another man—that will appear too much—what shall I say?—— Sir Jasper, come hither: I am trying if Mr. Horner were ticklish, and he's as ticklish as can be. I love to torment the confounded toad; let you and I tickle him.

SIR JASP. No, your ladyship will tickle him better without me, I suppose. But is this your buying china? I thought you had been at the china-house.

HORN. (*aside*) China-house! that's my cue, I must take it.—— A pox! can't you keep your impertinent wives at home? Some men are troubled with the husbands, but I with the wives; but I'd have you to know, since I cannot be your journeyman by night, I will not be your drudge by day, to squire your wife about, and be your man of straw or scarecrow only to pies and jays, that would be nibbling at your forbidden fruit; I shall be shortly the hackney gentleman-usher of the town.

SIR JASP. (*aside*) He! he! he! poor fellow, he's in the right on't, faith. To squire women about for other folks is as ungrateful an employment, as to tell money for other folks.—— He! he! he! be'n't angry, Horner.

LADY FID. No, 'tis I have more reason to be angry, who am left by you to go abroad indecently alone; or, what is more indecent, to pin myself upon such ill-bred people of your acquaintance as this is.

SIR JASP. Nay, prithee, what has he done?

LADY FID. Nay, he has done nothing.

SIR JASP. But what d'ye take ill, if he has done nothing?

LADY FID. Ha! ha! ha! faith, I can't but laugh, however; why, d'ye think the unmannerly toad would come down to me to the coach? I was fain to come up to fetch him, or go without him, which I was resolved not to do; for he knows china very well, and has himself very good, but will not let me see it lest I should beg some; but I will find it out, and have what I came for yet.

HORN. (*apart to* LADY FIDGET) Lock the door, Madam.—(*Exit* LADY FIDGET, *and locks the door followed by* HORNER *to the door.*)—— So, she has got into my chamber and locked me out. Oh the impertinency of womankind! Well, Sir Jasper, plain-dealing is a jewel; if ever you suffer your wife to trouble me again here she shall carry you home a pair of horns, by my lord mayor she shall; though I cannot furnish you myself, you are sure, yet I'll find a way.

SIR JASP. Ha! ha! he!—(*aside*) At my first coming in, and finding her arms about him, tickling him it seems, I was half jealous, but now I see my folly.—— He! he! he! poor Horner.

HORN. Nay, though you laugh now, 'twill be my turn ere long.

Oh, women, more impertinent, more cunning, and more mischievous than their monkeys, and to me almost as ugly!—Now is she
throwing my things about and rifling all I have; but I'll get in to
her the back way, and so rifle her for it.

SIR JASP. Ha! ha! ha! poor angry Horner.

HORN. Stay here a little, I'll ferret her out to you presently, I
warrant.   (*Exit at t'other door.*)

> (SIR JASPER *calls through the door to his Wife;*
> *she answers from within.*)

SIR JASP. Wife! my Lady Fidget! wife! he is coming in to you
the back way.

LADY FID. Let him come, and welcome, which way he will.

SIR JASP. He'll catch you, and use you roughly, and be too
strong for you.

LADY FID. Don't you trouble yourself, let him if he can.

QUACK. (*behind*) This indeed I could not have believed from
him, nor any but my own eyes.

Enter MRS. SQUEAMISH

MRS. SQUEAM. Where's this woman-hater, this toad, this ugly,
greasy, dirty sloven?

SIR JASP. (*aside*) So, the women all will have him ugly: methinks he is a comely person, but his wants make his form contemptible to 'em; and 'tis e'en as my wife said yesterday, talking
of him, that a proper handsome eunuch was as ridiculous a thing
as a gigantic coward.

MRS. SQUEAM. Sir Jasper, your servant: where is the odious
beast?

SIR JASP. He's within in his chamber, with my wife; she's
playing the wag with him.

MRS. SQUEAM. Is she so? and he's a clownish beast, he'll give
her no quarter, he'll play the wag with her again, let me tell you:
come, let's go help her.—What, the door's locked?

SIR JASP. Ay, my wife locked it.

MRS. SQUEAM. Did she so? Let's break it open then.

SIR JASP. No, no; he'll do her no hurt.

MRS. SQUEAM. No.—(*aside*) But is there no other way to get
in to 'em? Whither goes this? I will disturb 'em.

> (*Exit* MRS. SQUEAMISH *at another door.*)

Enter OLD LADY SQUEAMISH

LADY SQUEAM. Where is this harlotry, this impudent baggage, this rambling tomrigg? O Sir Jasper, I'm glad to see you here; did you not see my vile grandchild come in hither just now?

SIR JASP. Yes.

LADY SQUEAM. Ay, but where is she then? where is she? Lord, Sir Jasper, I have e'en rattled myself to pieces in pursuit of her: but can you tell what she makes here? They say below, no woman lodges here.

SIR JASP. No.

LADY SQUEAM. No! what does she here then? Say, if it be not a woman's lodging, what makes she here? But are you sure no woman lodges here?

SIR JASP. No, nor no man neither; this is Mr. Horner's lodging.

LADY SQUEAM. Is it so, are you sure?

SIR JASP. Yes, yes.

LADY SQUEAM. So; then there's no hurt in't, I hope. But where is he?

SIR JASP. He's in the next room with my wife.

LADY SQUEAM. Nay, if you trust him with your wife, I may with my Biddy. They say he's a merry harmless man now, e'en as harmless a man as ever came out of Italy with a good voice, and as pretty, harmless company for a lady as a snake without his teeth.

SIR JASP. Ay, ay, poor man.

Enter MRS. SQUEAMISH

MRS. SQUEAM. I can't find 'em.——— Oh, are you here, Grandmother? I followed, you must know, my Lady Fidget hither; 'tis the prettiest lodging, and I have been staring on the prettiest pictures———

Enter LADY FIDGET *with a piece of china in her hand, and* HORNER *following*

LADY FID. And I have been toiling and moiling for the prettiest piece of china, my dear.

HORN. Nay, she has been too hard for me, do what I could.

MRS. SQUEAM. O Lord, I'll have some china too. Good Mr.

Horner, don't think to give other people china, and me none; come in with me too.

HORN. Upon my honour, I have none left now.

MRS. SQUEAM. Nay, nay, I have known you deny your china before now, but you shan't put me off so. Come.

HORN. This lady had the last there.

LADY FID. Yes, indeed, Madam, to my certain knowledge, he has no more left.

MRS. SQUEAM. Oh, but it may be he may have some you could not find.

LADY FID. What, d'ye think if he had had any left, I would not have had it too? for we women of quality never think we have china enough.

HORN. Do not take it ill, I cannot make china for you all, but I will have a roll-waggon for you too, another time.

MRS. SQUEAM. Thank you, dear toad.

LADY FID. (to HORNER aside) What do you mean by that promise?

HORN. (apart to LADY FIDGET) Alas, she has an innocent, literal understanding.

LADY SQUEAM. Poor Mr. Horner! he has enough to do to please you all, I see.

HORN. Ay, Madam, you see how they use me.

LADY SQUEAM. Poor gentleman, I pity you.

HORN. I thank you, Madam: I could never find pity but from such reverend ladies as you are; the young ones will never spare a man.

MRS. SQUEAM. Come, come, beast, and go dine with us; for we shall want a man at ombre after dinner.

HORN. That's all their use of me, Madam, you see.

MRS. SQUEAM. Come, sloven, I'll lead you, to be sure of you.
(pulls him by the cravat)

LADY SQUEAM. Alas, poor man, how she tugs him! Kiss, kiss her; that's the way to make such nice women quiet.

HORN. No, Madam, that remedy is worse than the torment; they know I dare suffer anything rather than do it.

LADY SQUEAM. Prithee kiss her, and I'll give you her picture in little, that you admired so last night; prithee do.

HORN. Well, nothing but that could bribe me: I love a woman

only in effigy and good painting, as much as I hate them. I'll do't, for I could adore the devil well painted.

                              (*kisses* MRS. SQUEAMISH)

MRS. SQUEAM. Foh, you filthy toad! nay, now I've done jesting.

LADY SQUEAM. Ha! ha! ha! I told you so.

MRS. SQUEAM. Foh! a kiss of his——

SIR JASP. Has no more hurt in't than one of my spaniel's.

MRS. SQUEAM. Nor no more good neither.

QUACK. (*behind*) I will now believe anything he tells me.

Enter PINCHWIFE

LADY FID. O Lord, here's a man! Sir Jasper, my mask, my mask! I would not be seen here for the world.

SIR JASP. What, not when I am with you?

LADY FID. No, no, my honour—let's be gone.

MRS. SQUEAM. O Grandmother, let us be gone; make haste, make haste, I know not how he may censure us.

LADY FID. Be found in the lodging of anything like a man!—Away.

    (*Exeunt* SIR JASPER FIDGET, LADY FIDGET, OLD LADY
                    SQUEAMISH, MRS. SQUEAMISH.)

QUACK. (*behind*) What's here? another cuckold? he looks like one, and none else sure have any business with him.

HORN. Well, what brings my dear friend hither?

PINCH. Your impertinency.

HORN. My impertinency!—why, you gentlemen that have got handsome wives think you have a privilege of saying anything to your friends, and are as brutish as if you were our creditors.

PINCH. No, Sir, I'll ne'er trust you any way.

HORN. But why not, dear Jack? Why diffide in me thou know'st so well?

PINCH. Because I do know you so well.

HORN. Han't I been always thy friend, honest Jack, always ready to serve thee, in love or battle, before thou wert married, and am so still?

PINCH. I believe so; you would be my second now, indeed.

HORN. Well then, dear Jack, why so unkind, so grum, so strange to me? Come, prithee, kiss me, dear rogue: gad, I was always, I say, and am still as much thy servant as——

PINCH. As I am yours, Sir. What, you would send a kiss to my wife, is that it?

HORN. So, there 'tis—a man can't show his friendship to a married man, but presently he talks of his wife to you. Prithee, let thy wife alone, and let thee and I be all one, as we were wont. What, thou art as shy of my kindness as a Lombard Street alderman of a courtier's civility at Locket's!

PINCH. But you are overkind to me, as kind as if I were your cuckold already; yet I must confess you ought to be kind and civil to me, since I am so kind, so civil to you, as to bring you this: look you there, Sir.   (delivers him a letter)

HORN. What is't?

PINCH. Only a love letter, Sir.

HORN. From whom?—how! this is from your wife—hum—and hum——   (reads)

PINCH. Even from my wife, Sir: am I not wondrous kind and civil to you now too?—(aside) But you'll not think her so.

HORN. (aside) Ha! is this a trick of his or hers?

PINCH. The gentleman's surprised I find.—What, you expected a kinder letter?

HORN. No faith, not I, how could I?

PINCH. Yes, yes, I'm sure you did. A man so well made as you are must needs be disappointed, if the women declare not their passion at first sight or opportunity.

HORN. (aside) But what should this mean? Stay, the postscript. —(reads aside) "Be sure you love me, whatsoever my husband says to the contrary, and let him not see this, lest he should come home and pinch me, or kill my squirrel."—It seems he knows not what the letter contains.

PINCH. Come, ne'er wonder at it so much.

HORN. Faith, I can't help it.

PINCH. Now, I think I have deserved your infinite friendship and kindness, and have showed myself sufficiently an obliging kind friend and husband; am I not so, to bring a letter from my wife to her gallant?

HORN. Ay, the devil take me, art thou, the most obliging, kind friend and husband in the world, ha! ha!

PINCH. Well, you may be merry, Sir; but in short I must tell you, Sir, my honour will suffer no jesting.

HORN. What dost thou mean?

PINCH. Does the letter want a comment? Then, know, Sir, though I have been so civil a husband as to bring you a letter from my wife, to let you kiss and court her to my face, I will not be a cuckold, Sir, I will not.

HORN. Thou art mad with jealousy. I never saw thy wife in my life but at the play yesterday, and I know not if it were she or no. I court her, kiss her!

PINCH. I will not be a cuckold, I say; there will be danger in making me a cuckold.

HORN. Why, wert thou not well cured of thy last clap?

PINCH. I wear a sword.

HORN. It should be taken from thee, lest thou shouldst do thyself a mischief with it; thou art mad, man.

PINCH. As mad as I am, and as merry as you are, I must have more reason from you ere we part. I say again, though you kissed and courted last night my wife in man's clothes, as she confesses in her letter——

HORN. (*aside*) Ha!

PINCH. Both she and I say you must not design it again, for you have mistaken your woman, as you have done your man.

HORN. (*aside*) Oh—I understand something now—— Was that thy wife! Why wouldst thou not tell me 'twas she? Faith, my freedom with her was your fault, not mine.

PINCH. (*aside*) Faith, so 'twas.

HORN. Fy! I'd never do't to a woman before her husband's face, sure.

PINCH. But I had rather you should do't to my wife before my face, than behind my back; and that you shall never do.

HORN. No—you will hinder me.

PINCH. If I would not hinder you, you see by her letter she would.

HORN. Well, I must e'en acquiesce then, and be contented with what she writes.

PINCH. I'll assure you 'twas voluntarily writ; I had no hand in't, you may believe me.

HORN. I do believe thee, faith.

PINCH. And believe her too, for she's an innocent creature, has no dissembling in her: and so fare you well, Sir.

HORN. Pray, however, present my humble service to her, and

tell her I will obey her letter to a tittle, and fulfil her desires, be what they will, or with what difficulty soever I do't; and you shall be no more jealous of me, I warrant her, and you.

PINCH. Well then, fare you well; and play with any man's honour but mine, kiss any man's wife but mine, and welcome.

(*Exit* MR. PINCHWIFE.)

HORN. Ha! ha! ha! Doctor.

QUACK. It seems he has not heard the report of you, or does not believe it.

HORN. Ha! ha!—now, Doctor, what think you?

QUACK. Pray let's see the letter—hum—(*reads the letter*)— "for—dear—love you——"

HORN. I wonder how she could contrive it! What say'st thou to't? 'Tis an original.

QUACK. So are your cuckolds, too, originals: for they are like no other common cuckolds, and I will henceforth believe it not impossible for you to cuckold the Grand Signior amidst his guards of eunuchs, that I say.

HORN. And I say for the letter, 'tis the first love letter that ever was without flames, darts, fates, destinies, lying and dissembling in't.

Enter SPARKISH *pulling in* MR. PINCHWIFE

SPARK. Come back, you are a pretty brother-in-law, neither go to church nor to dinner with your sister bride!

PINCH. My sister denies her marriage, and you see is gone away from you dissatisfied.

SPARK. Pshaw! upon a foolish scruple, that our parson was not in lawful orders, and did not say all the common prayer; but 'tis her modesty only I believe. But let women be never so modest the first day, they'll be sure to come to themselves by night, and I shall have enough of her then. In the meantime, Harry Horner, you must dine with me: I keep my wedding at my aunt's in the Piazza.

HORN. Thy wedding! what stale maid has lived to despair of a husband, or what young one of a gallant?

SPARK. Oh, your servant, Sir—this gentleman's sister then,— no stale maid.

HORN. I'm sorry for't.

PINCH. (*aside*) How comes he so concerned for her?

SPARK. You sorry for't? Why, do you know any ill by her?

HORN. No, I know none but by thee; 'tis for her sake, not yours, and another man's sake that might have hoped, I thought.

SPARK. Another man! another man! What is his name?

HORN. Nay, since 'tis past, he shall be nameless.—(*aside*) Poor Harcourt! I am sorry thou hast missed her.

PINCH. (*aside*) He seems to be much troubled at the match.

SPARK. Prithee, tell me—— Nay, you shan't go, Brother.

PINCH. I must of necessity, but I'll come to you to dinner.

(*Exit* PINCHWIFE.)

SPARK. But, Harry, what, have I a rival in my wife already? But with all my heart, for he may be of use to me hereafter; for though my hunger is now my sauce, and I can fall on heartily without, the time will come when a rival will be as good sauce for a married man to a wife, as an orange to veal.

HORN. O thou damned rogue! thou hast set my teeth on edge with thy orange.

SPARK. Then let's to dinner—there I was with you again. Come.

HORN. But who dines with thee?

SPARK. My friends and relations, my brother Pinchwife, you see, of your acquaintance.

HORN. And his wife?

SPARK. No, 'gad, he'll ne'er let her come amongst us good fellows; your stingy country coxcomb keeps his wife from his friends, as he does his little firkin of ale for his own drinking, and a gentleman can't get a smack on't; but his servants, when his back is turned, broach it at their pleasures, and dust it away, ha! ha! ha!—'Gad, I am witty, I think, considering I was married to-day, by the world; but come——

HORN. No, I will not dine with you, unless you can fetch her too.

SPARK. Pshaw! what pleasure canst thou have with women now, Harry?

HORN. My eyes are not gone; I love a good prospect yet, and will not dine with you unless she does too; go fetch her, therefore, but do not tell her husband 'tis for my sake.

SPARK. Well, I'll go try what I can do; in the meantime, come away to my aunt's lodging; 'tis in the way to Pinchwife's.

HORN. The poor woman has called for aid, and stretched forth

her hand, Doctor; I cannot but help her over the pale out of the
briars. (*Exeunt* SPARKISH, HORNER, QUACK.)

SCENE IV

The Scene changes to PINCHWIFE'S *House*

MRS. PINCHWIFE *alone, leaning on her elbow. A table, pen, ink,
and paper*

MRS. PINCH. Well, 'tis e'en so, I have got the London disease
they call love; I am sick of my husband, and for my gallant. I
have heard this distemper called a fever, but methinks 'tis liker
an ague; for when I think of my husband, I tremble, and am in
a cold sweat, and have inclinations to vomit; but when I think
of my gallant, dear Mr. Horner, my hot fit comes, and I am all
in a fever indeed; and, as in other fevers, my own chamber is
tedious to me, and I would fain be removed to his, and then
methinks I should be well. Ah, poor Mr. Horner! Well, I cannot,
will not stay here; therefore I'll make an end of my letter to him,
which shall be a finer letter than my last, because I have studied
it like anything. Oh sick, sick! (*takes the pen and writes*)

Enter PINCHWIFE, *who, seeing her writing, steals softly behind
her, and, looking over her shoulder, snatches the paper from
her.*

PINCH. What, writing more letters?
MRS. PINCH. O Lord, bud, why d'ye fright me so?
(*She offers to run out; he stops her, and reads.*)
PINCH. How's this? nay, you shall not stir, Madam:—"Dear,
dear, dear Mr. Horner"—very well—I have taught you to write
letters to good purpose—but let's see't. "First, I am to beg your
pardon for my boldness in writing to you, which I'd have you to
know I would not have done, had not you said first you loved me
so extremely, which if you do, you will never suffer me to lie in
the arms of another man whom I loathe, nauseate, and detest."
—Now you can write these filthy words. But what follows?—
"Therefore, I hope you will speedily find some way to free me
from this unfortunate match, which was never, I assure you, of

my choice, but I'm afraid 'tis already too far gone; however, if
you love me, as I do you, you will try what you can do; but you
must help me away before to-morrow, or else, alas! I shall be for
ever out of your reach, for I can defer no longer our—our——"
(*The letter concludes.*) what is to follow "our"?—speak, what?
Our journey into the country I suppose—Oh woman, damned
woman! and Love, damned Love, their old tempter! for this is
one of his miracles; in a moment he can make those blind that
could see, and those see that were blind, those dumb that could
speak, and those prattle who were dumb before; nay, what is
more than all, make these dough-baked, senseless, indocile ani-
mals, women, too hard for us, their politic lords and rulers, in a
moment. But make an end of your letter, and then I'll make an
end of you thus, and all my plagues together.   (*draws his sword*)

MRS. PINCH. O Lord, O Lord, you are such a passionate man,
bud!

Enter SPARKISH

SPARK. How now, what's here to do?

PINCH. This fool here now!

SPARK. What! drawn upon your wife? You should never do
that, but at night in the dark, when you can't hurt her. This is
my sister-in-law, is it not? ay, faith, e'en our country Margery
(*pulls aside her handkerchief*); one may know her. Come, she and
you must go dine with me; dinner's ready, come. But where's my
wife? Is she not come home yet? Where is she?

PINCH. Making you a cuckold; 'tis that they all do, as soon as
they can.

SPARK. What, the wedding-day? No, a wife that designs to
make a cully of her husband will be sure to let him win the first
stake of love, by the world. But come, they stay dinner for us:
come, I'll lead down our Margery.

MRS. PINCH. No—Sir, go, we'll follow you.

SPARK. I will not wag without you.

PINCH. (*aside*) This coxcomb is a sensible torment to me
amidst the greatest in the world.

SPARK. Come, come, Madam Margery.

PINCH. No; I'll lead her my way: what, would you treat your
friends with mine, for want of your own wife?—(*leads her to*

t'other door, and locks her in and returns) I am contented my
rage should take breath——

SPARK. (*aside*) I told Horner this.

PINCH. Come now.

SPARK. Lord, how shy you are of your wife! But let me tell
you, Brother, we men of wit have amongst us a saying that cuck-
olding, like the small-pox, comes with a fear; and you may keep
your wife as much as you will out of danger of infection, but if
her constitution incline her to't, she'll have it sooner or later, by
the world, say they.

PINCH (*aside*) What a thing is a cuckold, that every fool can
make him ridiculous!—— Well, Sir—but let me advise you,
now you are come to be concerned, because you suspect the
danger, not to neglect the means to prevent it, especially when
the greatest share of the malady will light upon your own head,
for

Hows'e'er the kind wife's belly comes to swell,
The husband breeds for her, and first is ill.

ACT V

SCENE I

MR. PINCHWIFE's *House*

Enter MR. PINCHWIFE *and* MRS. PINCHWIFE.
A table and candle

PINCH. Come, take the pen and make an end of the letter, just
as you intended; if you are false in a tittle, I shall soon perceive
it, and punish you with this as you deserve.—(*lays his hand
on his sword*) Write what was to follow—let's see—"You must
make haste, and help me away before to-morrow, or else I shall
be for ever out of your reach, for I can defer no longer our"—
What follows "our"?

MRS. PINCH. Must all out, then, bud?—Look you there, then.
                    (MRS. PINCHWIFE *takes the pen and writes.*)

PINCH. Let's see—"For I can defer no longer our—wedding
—Your slighted Alithea."—What's the meaning of this? my sister's name to't? Speak, unriddle.

MRS. PINCH. Yes, indeed, bud.

PINCH. But why her name to't? Speak—speak, I say.

MRS. PINCH. Ay, but you'll tell her then again. If you would not tell her again——

PINCH. I will not:—I am stunned, my head turns round.—Speak.

MRS. PINCH. Won't you tell her, indeed, and indeed?

PINCH. No; speak, I say.

MRS. PINCH. She'll be angry with me; but I had rather she should be angry with me than you, bud; and, to tell you the truth, 'twas she made me write the letter, and taught me what I should write.

PINCH. (*aside*) Ha! I thought the style was somewhat better than her own.—— But how could she come to you to teach you, since I had locked you up alone?

MRS. PINCH. Oh, through the keyhole, bud.

PINCH. But why should she make you write a letter for her to him, since she can write herself?

MRS. PINCH. Why, she said because—for I was unwilling to do it——

PINCH. Because what—because?

MRS. PINCH. Because, lest Mr. Horner should be cruel, and refuse her; or vain afterwards, and show the letter, she might disown it, the hand not being hers.

PINCH (*aside*) How's this? Ha!—then I think I shall come to myself again. This changeling could not invent this lie: but if she could, why should she? she might think I should soon discover it.—Stay—now I think on't too, Horner said he was sorry she had married Sparkish; and her disowning her marriage to me makes me think she has evaded it for Horner's sake: yet why should she take this course? But men in love are fools; women may well be so—— But hark you, Madam, your sister went out in the morning, and I have not seen her within since.

MRS. PINCH. Alack-a-day, she has been crying all day above, it seems, in a corner.

PINCH. Where is she? Let me speak with her.

MRS. PINCH. (*aside*) O Lord, then he'll discover all!—— Pray hold, bud; what, d'ye mean to discover me? she'll know I have told you then. Pray, bud, let me talk with her first.

PINCH. I must speak with her, to know whether Horner ever

made her any promise, and whether she be married to Sparkish
or no.

MRS. PINCH. Pray, dear bud, don't, till I have spoken with her,
and told her that I have told you all; for she'll kill me else.

PINCH. Go then, and bid her come out to me.

MRS. PINCH. Yes, yes, bud.

PINCH. Let me see——

MRS. PINCH. (*aside*) I'll go, but she is not within to come to
him: I have just got time to know of Lucy her maid, who first
set me on work, what lie I shall tell next; for I am e'en at my
wit's end.   (*Exit* MRS. PINCHWIFE.)

PINCH. Well, I resolve it, Horner shall have her: I'd rather
give him my sister than lend him my wife; and such an alliance
will prevent his pretensions to my wife, sure. I'll make him of kin
to her, and then he won't care for her.

MRS. PINCHWIFE returns

MRS. PINCH. O Lord, bud! I told you what anger you would
make me with my sister.

PINCH. Won't she come hither?

MRS. PINCH. No, no. Alack-a-day, she's ashamed to look you
in the face: and she says, if you go in to her, she'll run away
downstairs, and shamefully go herself to Mr. Horner, who has
promised her marriage, she says; and she will have no other, so
she won't.

PINCH. Did he so?—promise her marriage!—then she shall
have no other. Go tell her so; and if she will come and discourse
with me a little concerning the means, I will about it immediately. Go.—(*Exit* MRS. PINCHWIFE.) His estate is equal to
Sparkish's, and his extraction as much better than his as his
parts are; but my chief reason is I'd rather be akin to him by
the name of brother-in-law than that of cuckold.

Enter MRS. PINCHWIFE

Well, what says she now?

MRS. PINCH. Why, she says she would only have you lead her
to Horner's lodging; with whom she first will discourse the matter before she talks with you, which yet she cannot do; for alack,
poor creature, she says she can't so much as look you in the face,
therefore she'll come to you in a mask. And you must excuse her

if she make you no answer to any question of yours, till you have brought her to Mr. Horner; and if you will not chide her, nor question her, she'll come out to you immediately.

PINCH. Let her come: I will not speak a word to her, nor require a word from her.

MRS. PINCH. Oh, I forgot: besides, she says she cannot look you in the face, though through a mask; therefore would desire you to put out the candle.

PINCH. I agree to all. Let her make haste.—There, 'tis out.— (*Puts out the candle. Exit* MRS. PINCHWIFE.) My case is something better: I'd rather fight with Horner for not lying with my sister, than for lying with my wife; and of the two, I had rather find my sister too forward than my wife. I expected no other from her free education, as she calls it, and her passion for the town. Well, wife and sister are names which make us expect love and duty, pleasure and comfort; but we find 'em plagues and torments, and are equally, though differently, troublesome to their keeper; for we have as much ado to get people to lie with our sisters as to keep 'em from lying with our wives.

Enter MRS. PINCHWIFE *masked, and in hoods and scarfs, and a night-gown and petticoat of* ALITHEA'S, *in the dark.*

What, are you come, Sister? let us go then.—But first, let me lock up my wife. Mrs. Margery, where are you?

MRS. PINCH. Here, bud.

PINCH. Come hither, that I may lock you up: get you in.— (*locks the door*) Come, Sister, where are you now?

> (MRS. PINCHWIFE *gives him her hand; but when he lets her go, she steals softly on t'other side of him, and is led away by him for his sister,* ALITHEA.)

SCENE II

The Scene changes to HORNER'S *Lodging*

QUACK, HORNER

QUACK. What, all alone? not so much as one of your cuckolds here, nor one of their wives! They use to take their turns with you, as if they were to watch you.

HORN. Yes, it often happens that a cuckold is but his wife's spy, and is more upon family duty when he is with her gallant abroad, hindering his pleasure, than when he is at home with her playing the gallant. But the hardest duty a married woman imposes upon a lover is keeping her husband company always.

QUACK. And his fondness wearies you almost as soon as hers.

HORN. A pox! keeping a cuckold company, after you have had his wife, is as tiresome as the company of a country squire to a witty fellow of the town, when he has got all his money.

QUACK. And as at first a man makes a friend of the husband to get the wife, so at last you are fain to fall out with the wife to be rid of the husband.

HORN. Ay, most cuckold-makers are true courtiers; when once a poor man has cracked his credit for 'em, they can't abide to come near him.

QUACK. But at first, to draw him in, are so sweet, so kind, so dear! just as you are to Pinchwife. But what becomes of that intrigue with his wife?

HORN. A pox! he's as surly as an alderman that has been bit; and since he's so coy, his wife's kindness is in vain, for she's a silly innocent.

QUACK. Did she not send you a letter by him?

HORN. Yes; but that's a riddle I have not yet solved. Allow the poor creature to be willing, she is silly too, and he keeps her up so close——

QUACK. Yes, so close, that he makes her but the more willing, and adds but revenge to her love; which two, when met, seldom fail of satisfying each other one way or other.

HORN. What! here's the man we are talking of, I think.

Enter MR. PINCHWIFE, *leading in his Wife masked, muffled, and in her Sister's gown*

Pshaw!

QUACK. Bringing his wife to you is the next thing to bringing a love letter from her.

HORN. What means this?

PINCH. The last time, you know, Sir, I brought you a love letter; now, you see, a mistress; I think you'll say I am a civil man to you.

HORN. Ay, the devil take me, will I say thou art the civilest man I ever met with; and I have known some. I fancy I understand thee now better than I did the letter. But, hark thee, in thy ear——

PINCH. What?

HORN. Nothing but the usual question, man: is she sound, on thy word?

PINCH. What, you take her for a wench, and me for a pimp?

HORN. Pshaw! wench and pimp, paw words; I know thou art an honest fellow, and hast a great acquaintance among the ladies, and perhaps hast made love for me, rather than let me make love to thy wife.

PINCH. Come, Sir, in short, I am for no fooling.

HORN. Nor I neither: therefore prithee, let's see her face presently. Make her show, man: art thou sure I don't know her?

PINCH. I am sure you do know her.

HORN. A pox! why dost thou bring her to me then?

PINCH. Because she's a relation of mine——

HORN. Is she, faith, man? then thou art still more civil and obliging, dear rogue.

PINCH. Who desired me to bring her to you.

HORN. Then she is obliging, dear rogue.

PINCH. You'll make her welcome for my sake, I hope.

HORN. I hope she is handsome enough to make herself welcome. Prithee let her unmask.

PINCH. Do you speak to her; she would never be ruled by me.

HORN. Madam——(MRS. PINCHWIFE *whispers to* HORNER.) She says she must speak with me in private. Withdraw, prithee.

PINCH. (*aside*) She's unwilling, it seems, I should know all her undecent conduct in this business.—— Well then, I'll leave you together, and hope when I am gone, you'll agree; if not, you and I shan't agree, Sir.

HORN. What means the fool? if she and I agree 'tis no matter what you and I do.

(*whispers to* MRS. PINCHWIFE, *who makes*
signs with her hand for him to be gone)

PINCH. In the meantime I'll fetch a parson, and find out Sparkish and disabuse him. You would have me fetch a parson, would you not? Well then—now I think I am rid of her, and shall have

no more trouble with her—our sisters and daughters, like usurers'
money, are safest when put out; but our wives, like their writings, never safe but in our closets under lock and key.

(*Exit* MR. PINCHWIFE.)

Enter Boy

BOY. Sir Jasper Fidget, Sir, is coming up.   (*Exit.*)

HORN. Here's the trouble of a cuckold now we are talking of.
A pox on him! has he not enough to do to hinder his wife's sport,
but he must other women's too?—Step in here, Madam.

(*Exit* MRS. PINCHWIFE.)

Enter SIR JASPER

SIR JASP. My best and dearest friend.

HORN. (*aside to* QUACK) The old style, Doctor.——— Well, be
short, for I am busy. What would your impertinent wife have
now?

SIR JASP. Well guessed, i'faith; for I do come from her.

HORN. To invite me to supper! Tell her, I can't come: go.

SIR JASP. Nay, now you are out, faith; for my lady, and the
whole knot of the virtuous gang, as they call themselves, are resolved upon a frolic of coming to you tonight in masquerade.
and are all dressed already.

HORN. I shan't be at home.

SIR JASP. (*aside*) Lord, how churlish he is to women!——— Nay,
prithee don't disappoint 'em; they'll think 'tis my fault: prithee
don't. I'll send in the banquet and the fiddles. But make no noise
on't; for the poor virtuous rogues would not have it known, for
the world, that they go a-masquerading; and they would come
to no man's ball but yours.

HORN. Well, well—get you gone; and tell 'em, if they come,
'twill be at the peril of their honour and yours.

SIR JASP. He! he! he!—we'll trust you for that: farewell.

(*Exit* SIR JASPER.)

HORN.

Doctor, anon you too shall be my guest,
But now I'm going to a private feast.   (*Exeunt.*)

SCENE III

The Scene changes to the Piazza of Covent Garden

SPARKISH, PINCHWIFE

SPARK. (*with the letter in his hand*) But who would have thought a woman could have been false to me? By the world, I could not have thought it.

PINCH. You were for giving and taking liberty: she has taken it only, Sir, now you find in that letter. You are a frank person, and so is she, you see there.

SPARK. Nay, if this be her hand—for I never saw it.

PINCH. 'Tis no matter whether that be her hand or no; I am sure this hand, at her desire, led her to Mr. Horner, with whom I left her just now, to go fetch a parson to 'em at their desire too, to deprive you of her for ever; for it seems yours was but a mock marriage.

SPARK. Indeed, she would needs have it that 'twas Harcourt himself, in a parson's habit, that married us; but I'm sure he told me 'twas his brother Ned.

PINCH. Oh, there 'tis out; and you were deceived, not she: for you are such a frank person. But I must be gone.—You'll find her at Mr. Horner's. Go, and believe your eyes.

(*Exit* MR. PINCHWIFE.)

SPARK. Nay, I'll to her, and call her as many crocodiles, sirens, harpies, and other heathenish names as a poet would do a mistress who had refused to hear his suit, nay more, his verses on her.—But stay, is not that she following a torch at t'other end of the Piazza? and from Horner's certainly—'tis so.

Enter ALITHEA *following a torch, and* LUCY *behind*

You are well met, Madam, though you don't think so. What, you have made a short visit to Mr. Horner. But I suppose you'll return to him presently; by that time the parson can be with him.

ALITH. Mr. Horner and the parson, Sir!

SPARK. Come, Madam, no more dissembling, no more jilting; for I am no more a frank person.

ALITH. How's this?

LUCY. (*aside*) So, 'twill work, I see.

SPARK. Could you find out no easy country fool to abuse? none but me, a gentleman of wit and pleasure about the town? But it was your pride to be too hard for a man of parts, unworthy false woman! false as a friend that lends a man money to lose; false as dice, who undo those that trust all they have to 'em.

LUCY. (*aside*) He has been a great bubble, by his similes, as they say.

ALITH. You have been too merry, Sir, at your wedding-dinner, sure.

SPARK. What, d'ye mock me too?

ALITH. Or you have been deluded.

SPARK. By you.

ALITH. Let me understand you.

SPARK. Have you the confidence—I should call it something else, since you know your guilt—to stand my just reproaches? You did not write an impudent letter to Mr. Horner? who I find now has clubbed with you in deluding me with his aversion for women, that I might not, forsooth, suspect him for my rival.

LUCY. (*aside*) D'ye think the gentleman can be jealous now, Madam?

ALITH. I write a letter to Mr. Horner!

SPARK. Nay, Madam, do not deny it. Your brother showed it me just now; and told me likewise, he left you at Horner's lodging to fetch a parson to marry you to him: and I wish you joy, Madam, joy, joy; and to him, too, much joy; and to myself more joy, for not marrying you.

ALITH. (*aside*) So, I find my brother would break off the match; and I can consent to't, since I see this gentleman can be made jealous.——— O Lucy, by his rude usage and jealousy, he makes me almost afraid I am married to him. Art thou sure 'twas Harcourt himself, and no parson, that married us?

SPARK. No, Madam, I thank you. I suppose that was a contrivance too of Mr. Horner's and yours, to make Harcourt play the parson; but I would as little as you have him one now, no, not for the world. For shall I tell you another truth? I never had any passion for you till now, for now I hate you. 'Tis true, I might have married your portion, as other men of parts of the town do sometimes: and so, your servant. And to show my unconcerned-ness, I'll come to your wedding, and resign you with as much joy as I would a stale wench to a new cully; nay, with as much joy as I would after the first night, if I had been married to you. There's for you; and so your servant, servant.   (*Exit* SPARKISH.)

ALITH. How was I deceived in a man!

LUCY. You'll believe then a fool may be made jealous now? for that easiness in him that suffers him to be led by a wife, will likewise permit him to be persuaded against her by others.

ALITH. But marry Mr. Horner! my brother does not intend it, sure: if I thought he did, I would take thy advice, and Mr. Harcourt for my husband. And now I wish that if there be any overwise woman of the town, who, like me, would marry a fool for fortune, liberty, or title, first, that her husband may love play, and be a cully to all the town but her, and suffer none but Fortune to be mistress of his purse; then, if for liberty, that he may send her into the country, under the conduct of some huswifely mother-in-law; and if for title, may the world give 'em none but that of cuckold.

LUCY. And for her greater curse, Madam, may he not deserve it.

ALITH. Away, impertinent! Is not this my old Lady Lanterlu's?

LUCY. Yes, Madam.—(*aside*) And here I hope we shall find Mr. Harcourt.   (*Exeunt.*)

SCENE IV

The Scene changes again to HORNER's *Lodging.*

HORNER, LADY FIDGET, MRS. DAINTY FIDGET, MRS. SQUEAMISH

A table, banquet, and bottles

HORN. (*aside*) A pox! they are come too soon—before I have sent back my new mistress. All I have now to do is to lock her in, that they may not see her.

LADY FID. That we may be sure of our welcome, we have brought our entertainment with us, and are resolved to treat thee, dear toad.

MRS. DAIN. And that we may be merry to purpose, have left Sir Jasper and my old Lay Squeamish quarrelling at home at backgammon.

MRS. SQUEAM. Therefore let us make use of our time, lest they should chance to interrupt us.

LADY FID. Let us sit then.

HORN. First, that you may be private, let me lock this door and that, and I'll wait upon you presently.

LADY FID. No, Sir, shut 'em only, and your lips for ever; for we must trust you as much as our women.

HORN. You know all vanity's killed in me; I have no occasion for talking.

LADY FID. Now, ladies, supposing we had drank each of us our two bottles, let us speak the truth of our hearts.

MRS. DAIN. and MRS. SQUEAM. Agreed.

LADY FID. By this brimmer, for truth is nowhere else to be found—(*aside to* HORNER) not in thy heart, false man!

HORN. (*aside to* LADY FIDGET) You have found me a true man, I'm sure.

LADY FID. (*aside to* HORNER) Not every way.—— But let us sit and be merry.   (LADY FIDGET *sings*.)

1

Why should our damn'd tyrants oblige us to live
On the pittance of pleasure which they only give?
 We must not rejoice
 With wine and with noise:
In vain we must wake in a dull bed alone,
Whilst to our warm rival, the bottle, they're gone.
 Then lay aside charms,
 And take up these arms.*

2

'Tis wine only gives 'em their courage and wit;
Because we live sober, to men we submit.
 If for beauties you'd pass,
 Take a lick of the glass,
'Twill mend your complexions, and when they are gone,
 The best red we have is the red of the grape:
Then, sisters, lay't on,
 And damn a good shape.

* The glasses.

MRS. DAIN. Dear brimmer! Well, in token of our openness and plain-dealing, let us throw our masks over our heads.

HORN. So, 'twill come to the glasses anon.

MRS. SQUEAM. Lovely brimmer! let me enjoy him first.

LADY FID. No, I never part with a gallant till I've tried him. Dear brimmer! that makest our husbands short-sighted.

MRS. DAIN. And our bashful gallants bold.

MRS. SQUEAM. And, for want of a gallant, the butler lovely in our eyes.—— Drink, eunuch.

LADY FID. Drink, thou representative of a husband.—Damn a husband!

MRS. DAIN. And, as it were a husband, an old keeper.

MRS. SQUEAM. And an old grandmother.

HORN. And an English bawd, and a French chirurgeon.

LADY FID. Ay, we have all reason to curse 'em.

HORN. For my sake, ladies?

LADY FID. No, for our own; for the first spoils all young gallants' industry.

MRS. DAIN. And the other's art makes 'em bold only with common women.

MRS. SQUEAM. And rather run the hazard of the vile distemper amongst them, than of a denial amongst us.

MRS. DAIN. The filthy toads choose mistresses now as they do stuffs, for having been fancied and worn by others.

MRS. SQUEAM. For being common and cheap.

LADY FID. Whilst women of quality, like the richest stuffs, lie untumbled, and unasked for.

HORN. Ay, neat, and cheap, and new, often they think best.

MRS. DAIN. No, Sir, the beasts will be known by a mistress longer than by a suit.

MRS. SQUEAM. And 'tis not for cheapness neither.

LADY FID. No; for the vain fops will take up druggets and embroider 'em. But I wonder at the depraved appetites of witty men; they use to be out of the common road, and hate imitation. Pray tell me, beast, when you were a man, why you rather chose to club with a multitude in a common house for an entertainment than to be the only guest at a good table.

HORN. Why, faith, ceremony and expectation are unsufferable to those that are sharp bent. People always eat with the best stomach at an ordinary, where every man is snatching for the best bit.

LADY FID. Though he get a cut over the fingers.—But I have heard people eat most heartily of another man's meat, that is, what they do not pay for.

HORN. When they are sure of their welcome and freedom; for ceremony in love and eating is as ridiculous as in fighting: falling on briskly is all should be done on those occasions.

LADY FID. Well then, let me tell you, Sir, there is nowhere more freedom than in our houses; and we take freedom from a young person as a sign of good breeding; and a person may be as free as he pleases with us, as frolic, as gamesome, as wild as he will.

HORN. Han't I heard you all declaim against wild men?

LADY FID. Yes; but for all that, we think wildness in a man as desirable a quality as in a duck or rabbit: a tame man! foh!

HORN. I know not, but your reputations frightened me as much as your faces invited me.

LADY FID. Our reputation! Lord, why should you not think that we women make use of our reputation, as you men of yours, only to deceive the world with less suspicion? Our virtue is like the stateman's religion, the Quaker's word, the gamester's oath, and the great man's honour—but to cheat those that trust us.

MRS. SQUEAM. And that demureness, coyness, and modesty that you see in our faces in the boxes at plays, is as much a sign of a kind woman, as a vizard-mask in the pit.

MRS. DAIN. For, I assure you, women are least masked when they have the velvet vizard on.

LADY FID. You would have found us modest women in our denials only.

MRS. SQUEAM. Our bashfulness is only the reflection of the men's.

MRS. DAIN. We blush when they are shamefaced.

HORN. I beg your pardon, ladies, I was deceived in you devilishly. But why that mighty pretence to honour?

LADY FID. We have told you; but sometimes 'twas for the same reason you men pretend business often, to avoid ill company, to enjoy the better and more privately those you love.

HORN. But why would you ne'er give a friend a wink then?

LADY FID. Faith, your reputation frightened us as much as ours did you, you were so notoriously lewd.

HORN. And you so seemingly honest.

LADY FID. Was that all that deterred you?

HORN. And so expensive—you allow freedom, you say——

LADY FID. Ay, ay.

HORN. That I was afraid of losing my little money, as well as my little time, both which my other pleasures required.

LADY FID. Money! foh! you talk like a little fellow now: do such as we expect money?

HORN. I beg your pardon, Madam, I must confess, I have heard that great ladies, like great merchants, set but the higher prices upon what they have, because they are not in necessity of taking the first offer.

MRS. DAIN. Such as we make sale of our hearts?

MRS. SQUEAM. We bribed for our love? foh!

HORN. With your pardon, ladies, I know, like great men in offices, you seem to exact flattery and attendance only from your followers; but you have receivers about you, and such fees to pay a man is afraid to pass your grants. Besides, we must let you win at cards, or we lose your hearts; and if you make an assignation, 'tis at a goldsmith's, jeweller's, or china-house, where for your honour you deposit to him, he must pawn his to the punctual cit, and so paying for what you take up, pays for what he takes up.

MRS. DAIN. Would you not have us assured of our gallants' love?

MRS. SQUEAM. For love is better known by liberality than by jealousy.

LADY FID. For one may be dissembled, the other not.—(aside) But my jealousy can be no longer dissembled, and they are telling ripe.—— Come, here's to our gallants in waiting, whom we must name, and I'll begin. This is my false rogue.

(claps him on the back)

MRS. SQUEAM. How!

HORN. So, all will out now.

MRS. SQUEAM. (aside to HORNER) Did you not tell me 'twas for my sake only you reported yourself no man?

MRS. DAIN. (aside to HORNER) Oh, wretch! did you not swear to me, 'twas for my love and honour you passed for that thing you do?

HORN. So, so.

LADY FID. Come, speak, ladies: this is my false villain.

MRS. SQUEAM. And mine too.

MRS. DAIN. And mine.

HORN. Well then, you are all three my false rogues too, and there's an end on't.

LADY FID. Well then, there's no remedy; sister sharers, let us not fall out, but have a care of our honour. Though we get no presents, no jewels of him, we are savers of our honour, the jewel of most value and use, which shines yet to the world unsuspected, though it be counterfeit.

HORN. Nay, and is e'en as good as if it were true, provided the world think so; for honour, like beauty now, only depends on the opinion of others.

LADY FID. Well, Harry Common, I hope you can be true to three. Swear; but 'tis to no purpose to require your oath, for you are as often forsworn as you swear to new women.

HORN. Come, faith, Madam, let us e'en pardon one another; for all the difference I find betwixt we men and you women, we forswear ourselves at the beginning of an amour, you as long as it lasts.

Enter SIR JASPER FIDGET, *and* OLD LADY SQUEAMISH

SIR JASP. Oh, my Lady Fidget, was this your cunning, to come to Mr. Horner without me? But you have been nowhere else, I hope.

LADY FID. No, Sir Jasper.

LADY SQUEAM. And you came straight hither, Biddy?

MRS. SQUEAM. Yes, indeed, lady Grandmother.

SIR JASP. 'Tis well, 'tis well; I knew when once they were thoroughly acquainted with poor Horner, they'd ne'er be from him: you may let her masquerade it with my wife and Horner, and I warrant her reputation safe.

Enter Boy

BOY. O Sir, here's the gentleman come, whom you bid me not suffer to come up without giving you notice, with a lady too, and other gentlemen.

HORN. Do you all go in there, whilst I send 'em away; and,

boy, do you desire 'em to stay below till I come, which shall be immediately.

(*Exeunt* SIR JASPER, LADY SQUEAMISH, LADY FIDGET,
MRS. DAINTY, MRS. SQUEAMISH.)

BOY. Yes, sir. (*Exit.*)

(*Exit* HORNER *at t'other door, and
returns with* MRS. PINCHWIFE.)

HORN. You would not take my advice, to be gone home before your husband came back; he'll now discover all. Yet pray, my dearest, be persuaded to go home, and leave the rest to my management; I'll let you down the back way.

MRS. PINCH. I don't know the way home, so I don't.

HORN. My man shall wait upon you.

MRS. PINCH. No, don't you believe that I'll go at all; what, are you weary of me already?

HORN. No, my life, 'tis that I may love you long, 'tis to secure my love, and your reputation with your husband; he'll never receive you again else.

MRS. PINCH. What care I? d'ye think to frighten me with that? I don't intend to go to him again; you shall be my husband now.

HORN. I cannot be your husband, dearest, since you are married to him.

MRS. PINCH. Oh, would you make me believe that? Don't I see every day, at London here, women leave their first husbands, and go and live with other men as their wives? Pish, pshaw! you'd make me angry, but that I love you so mainly.

HORN. So, they are coming up—In again, in, I hear 'em.—(*Exit* MRS. PINCHWIFE.) Well, a silly mistress is like a weak place, soon got, soon lost, a man has scarce time for plunder; she betrays her husband first to her gallant, and then her gallant to her husband.

Enter PINCHWIFE, ALITHEA, HARCOURT,
SPARKISH, LUCY, *and a* PARSON

PINCH. Come, Madam, 'tis not the sudden change of your dress, the confidence of your asseverations, and your false witness there, shall persuade me I did not bring you hither just now; here's my witness, who cannot deny it, since you must be confronted.——
Mr. Horner, did not I bring this lady to you just now?

HORN. (*aside*) Now must I wrong one woman for another's

sake—but that's no new thing with me, for in these cases I am still on the criminal's side against the innocent.

ALITH. Pray speak, Sir.

HORN. (*aside*) It must be so. I must be impudent, and try my luck; impudence uses to be too hard for truth.

PINCH. What, you are studying an evasion or excuse for her! Speak, Sir.

HORN. No, faith, I am something backward only to speak in women's affairs or disputes.

PINCH. She bids you speak.

ALITH. Ah, pray, Sir, do, pray satisfy him.

HORN. Then truly, you did bring that lady to me just now.

PINCH. Oh ho!

ALITH. How, Sir?

HAR. How, Horner?

ALITH. What mean you, Sir? I always took you for a man of honour.

HORN. (*aside*) Ay, so much a man of honour, that I must save my mistress, I thank you, come what will on't.

SPARK. So, if I had had her, she'd have made me believe the moon had been made of a Christmas pie.

LUCY. (*aside*) Now could I speak, if I durst, and solve the riddle, who am the author of it.

ALITH. Oh unfortunate woman! A combination against my honour! which most concerns me now, because you share in my disgrace, Sir, and it is your censure, which I must now suffer, that troubles me, not theirs.

HAR. Madam, then have no trouble, you shall now see 'tis possible for me to love too, without being jealous; I will not only believe your innocence myself, but make all the world believe it. —(*apart to* HORNER) Horner, I must now be concerned for this lady's honour.

HORN. And I must be concerned for a lady's honour too.

HAR. This lady has her honour, and I will protect it.

HORN. My lady has not her honour, but has given it me to keep, and I will preserve it.

HAR. I understand you not.

HORN. I would not have you.

MRS. PINCH. (*peeping in behind*) What's the matter with 'em all?

PINCH. Come, come, Mr. Horner, no more disputing; here's the parson, I brought him not in vain.

HAR. No, Sir, I'll employ him, if this lady please.

PINCH. How! what d'ye mean?

SPARK. Ay, what does he mean?

HORN. Why, I have resigned your sister to him; he has my consent.

PINCH. But he has not mine, Sir; a woman's injured honour, no more than a man's, can be repaired or satisfied by any but him that first wronged it; and you shall marry her presently, or——
(lays his hand on his sword)

Enter to them MRS. PINCHWIFE

MRS. PINCH. *(aside)* O Lord, they'll kill poor Mr. Horner! besides, he shan't marry her whilst I stand by, and look on; I'll not lose my second husband so.

PINCH. What do I see?

ALITH. My sister in my clothes!

SPARK. Ha!

MRS. PINCH. *(to* MR. PINCHWIFE*)* Nay, pray now don't quarrel about finding work for the parson: he shall marry me to Mr. Horner; for now, I believe, you have enough of me.

HORNER. *(aside)* Damned, damned loving changeling!

MRS. PINCH. Pray, Sister, pardon me for telling so many lies of you.

HORN. I suppose the riddle is plain now.

LUCY. No, that must be my work.—— Good Sir, hear me.
(kneels to MR. PINCHWIFE, *who stands doggedly with his hat over his eyes)*

PINCH. I will never hear woman again, but make 'em all silent thus—— *(offers to draw upon his Wife)*

HORN. No, that must not be.

PINCH. You then shall go first, 'tis all one to me.
(offers to draw on HORNER, *stopped by* HARCOURT*)*

HAR. Hold!

Enter SIR JASPER FIDGET, LADY FIDGET, LADY SQUEAMISH, MRS. DAINTY FIDGET, MRS. SQUEAMISH

SIR JASP. What's the matter? what's the matter? pray, what's the matter, Sir? I beseech you communicate, Sir.

PINCH. Why, my wife has communicated, Sir, as your wife may
have done too, Sir, if she knows him, Sir.

SIR JASP. Pshaw, with him! ha! ha! he!

PINCH. D'ye mock me, Sir? A cuckold is a kind of a wild beast;
have a care, Sir.

SIR JASP. No, sure, you mock me, Sir. He cuckold you! it can't
be, ha! ha! he! why, I'll tell you, Sir——   (offers to whisper)

PINCH. I tell you again, he has whored my wife, and yours too,
if he knows her, and all the women he comes near; 'tis not his
dissembling, his hypocrisy, can wheedle me.

SIR JASP. How! does he dissemble? is he a hypocrite? Nay,
then—how—wife—sister, is he a hypocrite?

LADY SQUEAM. An hypocrite! a dissembler! Speak, young harlotry, speak, how?

SIR JASP. Nay, then—Oh my head too!—Oh thou libidinous
lady!

LADY SQUEAM. Oh thou harloting harlotry! hast thou done't
then?

SIR JASP. Speak, good Horner, art thou a dissembler, a rogue?
hast thou——

HORN. Soh!

LUCY. (apart to HORNER) I'll fetch you off, and her too, if she
will but hold her tongue.

HORN. (apart to LUCY) Can'st thou? I'll give thee——

LUCY (to MR. PINCHWIFE) Pray have but patience to hear me,
Sir, who am the unfortunate cause of all this confusion. Your
wife is innocent, I only culpable; for I put her upon telling you
all these lies concerning my mistress, in order to the breaking off
the match between Mr. Sparkish and her, to make way for Mr.
Harcourt.

SPARK. Did you so, eternal rotten tooth? Then, it seems, my
mistress was not false to me, I was only deceived by you. Brother,
that should have been, now man of conduct, who is a frank person now, to bring your wife to her lover, ha?

LUCY. I assure you, Sir, she came not to Mr. Horner out of love,
for she loves him no more——

MRS. PINCH. Hold, I told lies for you, but you shall tell none
for me, for I do love Mr. Horner with all my soul, and nobody
shall say me nay; pray, don't you go to make poor Mr. Horner
believe to the contrary; 'tis spitefully done of you, I'm sure.

HORN. (*aside to* MRS. PINCHWIFE) Peace, dear idiot.

MRS. PINCH. Nay, I will not peace.

PINCH. Not till I make you.

Enter DORILANT, QUACK

DOR. Horner, your servant; I am the doctor's guest, he must excuse our intrusion.

QUACK. But what's the matter, gentlemen? for Heaven's sake, what's the matter?

HORN. Oh, 'tis well you are come. 'Tis a censorious world we live in; you may have brought me a reprieve, or else I had died for a crime I never committed, and these innocent ladies had suffered with me; therefore, pray satisfy these worthy, honorable, jealous gentlemen—that——   (*whispers*)

QUACK. Oh, I understand you; is that all?—— Sir Jasper, by Heavens, and upon the word of a physician, Sir——
(*whispers to* SIR JASPER)

SIR JASP. Nay, I do believe you truly.—— Pardon me, my virtuous lady, and dear of honour.

LADY SQUEAM. What, then all's right again?

SIR JASP. Ay, ay, and now let us satisfy him too.
(*They whisper with* MR. PINCHWIFE.)

PINCH. An eunuch! Pray, no fooling with me.

QUACK. I'll bring half the chirurgeons in town to swear it.

PINCH. They!—they'll swear a man that bled to death through his wounds died of an apoplexy.

QUACK. Pray, hear me, Sir—why, all the town has heard the report of him.

PINCH. But does all the town believe it?

QUACK. Pray, inquire a little, and first of all these.

PINCH. I'm sure when I left the town, he was the lewdest fellow in't.

QUACK. I tell you, Sir, he has been in France since; pray, ask but these ladies and gentlemen, your friend Mr. Dorilant. Gentlemen and ladies, han't you all heard the late sad report of poor Mr. Horner?

ALL THE LADIES. Ay, ay, ay.

DOR. Why, thou jealous fool, dost thou doubt it? he's an arrant French capon.

MRS. PINCH. 'Tis false, Sir, you shall not disparage poor Mr. Horner, for to my certain knowledge——

LUCY. Oh, hold!

MRS. SQUEAM. (*aside to* LUCY) Stop her mouth!

LADY FID. (*to* PINCHWIFE) Upon my honour, Sir, 'tis as true——

MRS. DAIN. D'ye think we would have been seen in his company?

MRS. SQUEAM. Trust our unspotted reputations with him?

LADY FID. (*aside to* HORNER) This you get, and we too, by trusting your secret to a fool.

HORN. Peace, Madam.—(*aside to* QUACK) Well, Doctor, is not this a good design, that carries a man on unsuspected, and brings him off safe?

PINCH. (*aside*) Well, if this were true—but my wife——

(DORILANT *whispers with* MRS. PINCHWIFE.)

ALITH. Come, Brother, your wife is yet innocent, you see; but have a care of too strong an imagination, lest, like an over-concerned timorous gamester, by fancying an unlucky cast, it should come. Women and fortune are truest still to those that trust 'em.

LUCY. And any wild thing grows but the more fierce and hungry for being kept up, and more dangerous to the keeper.

ALITH. There's doctrine for all husbands, Mr. Harcourt.

HAR. I edify, Madam, so much, that I am impatient till I am one.

DOR. And I edify so much by example, I will never be one.

SPARK. And because I will not disparage my parts, I'll ne'er be one.

HORN. And I, alas! can't be one.

PINCH. But I must be one—against my will to a country wife, with a country murrain to me!

MRS. PINCH. (*aside*) And I must be a country wife still too, I find; for I can't, like a city one, be rid of my musty husband, and do what I list.

HORN. Now, Sir, I must pronounce your wife innocent, though I blush whilst I do it; and I am the only man by her now exposed to shame, which I will straight drown in wine, as you shall your suspicion; and the ladies' troubles we'll divert with a ballad.—— Doctor, where are your maskers?

LUCY. Indeed, she's innocent, Sir, I am her witness; and her end of coming out was but to see her sister's wedding; and what she has said to your face of her love to Mr. Horner was but the usual innocent revenge on a husband's jealousy—was it not, Madam, speak?

MRS. PINCH. (*aside to* LUCY *and* HORNER) Since you'll have me tell more lies—— Yes, indeed, bud.

PINCH.
For my own sake fain I would all believe;
Cuckolds, like lovers, should themselves deceive.
But—— (*sighs*) his honour is least safe (too late I find)
Who trusts it with a foolish wife or friend.

A *Dance of Cuckolds*

HORN.
Vain fops but court and dress, and keep a pother,
To pass for women's men with one another;
But he who aims by woman to be priz'd,
First by the men, you see, must be despis'd.

EPILOGUE

Spoken by MY LADY FIDGET

Now you the vigorous, who daily here ⎫
O'er vizard-mask in public domineer, ⎬
And what you'd do to her, if in place where; ⎭
Nay, have the confidence to cry, "Come out!"
Yet when she says, "Lead on!" you are not stout;
But to your well-dress'd brother straight turn round,
And cry, "Pox on her, Ned, she can't be sound!"
Then slink away, a fresh one to engage, ⎫
With so much seeming heat and loving rage, ⎬
You'd frighten listening actress on the stage; ⎭
Till she at last has seen you huffing come, ⎫
And talk of keeping in the tiring-room, ⎬
Yet cannot be provok'd to lead her home. ⎭
Next, you Falstaffs of fifty, who beset
Your buckram maidenheads, which your friends get;
And whilst to them you of achievements boast,

They share the booty, and laugh at your cost.
In fine, you essenc'd boys, both old and young, ⎫
Who would be thought so eager, brisk, and strong, ⎬
Yet do the ladies, not their husbands wrong; ⎭
Whose purses for your manhood make excuse,
And keep your Flanders mares for show, not use;
Encourag'd by our woman's man to-day,
A Horner's part may vainly think to play;
And may intrigues so bashfully disown,
That they may doubted be by few or none;
May kiss the cards at picquet, ombre, loo, ⎫
And so be thought to kiss the lady too; ⎬
But, gallants, have a care, faith, what you do. ⎭
The world, which to no man his due will give,
You by experience know you can deceive,
And men may still believe you vigorous,
But then we women—there's no cozening us.

The Man of Mode; or,

Sir Fopling Flutter

A COMEDY

By SIR GEORGE ETHEREGE

PROLOGUE

By Sir Car Scroope, Baronet

Like dancers on the ropes poor poets fare,
Most perish young, the rest in danger are;
This (one would think) should make our authors wary,
But, gamester-like, the giddy fools miscarry.
A lucky hand or two so tempts 'em on,
They cannot leave off play till they're undone.
With modest fears a Muse does first begin,
Like a young wench newly entic'd to sin;
But tickl'd once with praise, by her good will,
The wanton fool would never more lie still.
'Tis an old mistress you'll meet here to-night,
Whose charms you once have look'd on with delight.
But now of late such dirty drabs have known ye,
A Muse o'th' better sort's ashamed to own ye.
Nature well drawn, and wit, must now give place

To gaudy nonsense and to dull grimace;
Nor is it strange that you should like so much
That kind of wit, for most of yours is such.
But I'm afraid that while to France we go,
To bring you home fine dresses, dance, and show,
The stage, like you, will but more foppish grow.
Of foreign wares, why should we fetch the scum,
When we can be so richly serv'd at home?
For heav'n be thank'd, 'tis not so wise an age
But your own follies may supply the stage.
Tho' often plough'd, there's no great fear the soil
Should barren grow by the too frequent toil;
While at your doors are to be daily found
Such loads of dunghill to manure the ground.
'Tis by your follies that we players thrive,
As the physicians by diseases live;
And as each year some new distemper reigns,
Whose friendly poison helps to increase their gains,
So, among you, there starts up every day
Some new, unheard-of fool for us to play.
Then, for your own sakes be not too severe,
Nor what you all admire at home, damn here;
Since each is fond of his own ugly face,
Why should you, when we hold it, break the glass?

THE ACTORS' NAMES

GENTLEMEN:

MR. DORIMANT
MR. MEDLEY
OLD HARRY BELLAIR
YOUNG HARRY BELLAIR
SIR FOPLING FLUTTER

GENTLEWOMEN:

LADY TOWNLEY
EMILIA
MRS. LOVEIT
BELLINDA
LADY WOODVILL, *and*
HARRIET, *her daughter*

WAITING WOMEN·

PERT
and
BUSY

TOM, *a Shoemaker*
NAN, *an Orange-Woman*
Three Slovenly Bullies
Two Chairmen
MR. SMIRK, *a Parson*
HANDY, *a* Valet-de-chambre
Pages, Footmen, &c.

THE MAN OF MODE; OR,
SIR FOPLING FLUTTER

ACT I

SCENE: *A dressing-room; a table covered with a toilet,
clothes laid ready*

Enter DORIMANT *in his gown and slippers, with a note
in his hand, made up, repeating verses*

DOR.

Now for some ages had the pride of Spain
Made the sun shine on half the world in vain.

(then looking on the note)

"For Mrs. Loveit." What a dull, insipid thing is a billet-doux
written in cold blood, after the heat of the business is over! It is
a tax upon good nature which I have here been labouring to pay,
and have done it, but with as much regret as ever fanatic paid
the Royal Aid or church duties. 'Twill have the same fate, I
know, that all my notes to her have had of late: 'twill not be
thought kind enough. 'Faith, women are i'the right when they
jealously examine our letters, for in them we always first discover our decay of passion.—Hey! Who waits?

Enter HANDY

HAND. Sir——

DOR. Call a footman.

HAND. None of 'em are come yet.

DOR. Dogs! Will they ever lie snoring abed till noon?

HAND. 'Tis all one, Sir; if they're up, you indulge 'em so they're
ever poaching after whores all the morning.

DOR. Take notice henceforward who's wanting in his duty; the
next clap he gets, he shall rot for an example. What vermin are
those chattering without?

HAND. Foggy Nan, the orange-woman, and Swearing Tom, the
shoemaker.

DOR. Go, call in that overgrown jade with the flasket of guts
before her; fruit is refreshing in a morning. *(Exit* HANDY.*)*

It is not that I love you less
Than when before your feet I lay——

Enter Orange-Woman and HANDY

——How now, double tripe, what news do you bring?

OR. WOM. News! Here's the best fruit has come to town t'year; gad, I was up before four o'clock this morning and bought all the choice i'the market.

DOR. The nasty refuse of your shop.

OR. WOM. You need not make mouths at it; I assure you, 'tis all culled ware.

DOR. The citizens buy better on a holiday in their walk to Tottenham.

OR. WOM. Good or bad, 'tis all one; I never knew you commend anything. Lord! would the ladies had heard you talk of 'em as I have done! (*sets down the fruit*) Here, bid your man give me an angel.

DOR. Give the bawd her fruit again.

OR. WOM. Well, on my conscience, there never was the like of you! God's my life, I had almost forgot to tell you there is a young gentlewoman lately come to town with her mother, that is so taken with you.

DOR. Is she handsome?

OR. WOM. Nay, gad, there are few finer women, I tell you but so, and a hugeous fortune, they say. Here, eat this peach. It comes from the stone; 'tis better than any Newington y'have tasted.

DOR. (*taking the peach*) This fine woman, I'll lay my life, is some awkward, ill-fashioned country toad who, not having above four dozen of black hairs on her head, has adorned her baldness with a large, white fruz, that she may look sparkishly in the forefront of the King's box at an old play.

OR. WOM. Gad, you'd change your note quickly if you did but see her.

DOR. How came she to know me?

OR. WOM. She saw you yesterday at the Change; she told me you came and fooled with the woman at the next shop.

DOR. I remember there was a mask observed me, indeed. Fooled, did she say?

OR. WOM. Ay; I vow she told me twenty things you said, too, and acted with head and with her body so like you——

Enter MEDLEY

MED. Dorimant, my life, my joy, my darling sin! how dost thou?

OR. WOM. Lord, what a filthy trick these men have got of kissing one another! (*She spits.*)

MED. Why do you suffer this cartload of scandal to come near you and make your neighbors think you so improvident to need a bawd?

OR. WOM. Good, now! we shall have it you did but want him to help you! Come, pay me for my fruit.

MED. Make us thankful for it, huswife, bawds are as much out of fashion as gentlemen-ushers; none but old formal ladies use the one, and none but foppish old stagers employ the other. Go! You are an insignificant brandy bottle.

DOR. Nay, there you wrong her; three quarts of Canary is her business.

OR. WOM. What you please, gentlemen.

DOR. To him! give him as good as he brings.

OR. WOM. Hang him, there is not such another heathen in the town again, except it be the shoemaker without.

MED. I shall see you hold up your hand at the bar next sessions for murder, huswife; that shoemaker can take his oath you are in fee with the doctors to sell green fruit to the gentry that the crudities may breed diseases.

OR. WOM. Pray, give me my money.

DOR. Not a penny! When you bring the gentlewoman hither you spoke of, you shall be paid.

OR. WOM. The gentlewoman! the gentlewoman may be as honest as your sisters for aught as I know. Pray, pay me, Mr. Dorimant, and do not abuse me so; I have an honester way of living —you know it.

MED. Was there ever such a resty bawd?

DOR. Some jade's tricks she has, but she makes amends when she's in good humour.—— Come, tell me the lady's name and Handy shall pay you.

OR. WOM. I must not; she forbid me.

DOR. That's a sure sign she would have you.

MED. Where does she live?

OR. WOM. They lodge at my house.

MED. Nay, then she's in a hopeful way.

OR. WOM. Good Mr. Medley, say your pleasure of me, but take heed how you affront my house! God's my life!—"in a hopeful way"!

DOR. Prithee, peace! What kind of woman's the mother?

OR. WOM. A goodly grave gentlewoman. Lord, how she talks against the wild young men o' the town! As for your part, she thinks you an arrant devil; should she see you, on my conscience she would look if you had not a cloven foot.

DOR. Does she know me?

OR. WOM. Only by hearsay; a thousand horrid stories have been told her of you, and she believes 'em all.

MED. By the character this should be the famous Lady Wood-vill and her daughter Harriet.

OR. WOM. The devil's in him for guessing, I think.

DOR. Do you know 'em?

MED. Both very well; the mother's a great admirer of the forms and civility of the last age.

DOR. An antiquated beauty may be allowed to be out of hu-mour at the freedoms of the present. This is a good account of the mother; pray, what is the daughter?

MED. Why, first, she's an heiress—vastly rich.

DOR. And handsome?

MED. What alteration a twelvemonth may have bred in her I know not, but a year ago she was the beautifullest creature I ever saw: a fine, easy, clean shape; light brown hair in abun-dance; her features regular; her complexion clear and lively; large, wanton eyes; but above all, a mouth that has made me kiss it a thousand times in imagination; teeth white and even, and pretty, pouting lips, with a little moisture ever hanging on them, that look like the Provins rose fresh on the bush, ere the morning sun has quite drawn up the dew.

DOR. Rapture! mere rapture!

OR. WOM. Nay, gad, he tells you true; she's a delicate creature.

DOR. Has she wit?

MED. More than is usual in her sex, and as much malice. Then, she's as wild as you would wish her, and has a demureness in her looks that makes it so surprising.

DOR. Flesh and blood cannot hear this and not long to know her.

MED. I wonder what makes her mother bring her up to town; an old doting keeper cannot be more jealous of his mistress.

OR. WOM. She made me laugh yesterday; there was a judge came to visit 'em, and the old man, she told me, did so stare upon her, and when he saluted her smacked so heartily. Who would think it of 'em?

MED. God-a-mercy, judge!

DOR. Do 'em right; the gentlemen of the long robe have not been wanting by their good examples to countenance the crying sin o' the nation.

MED. Come, on with your trappings; 'tis later than you imagine.

DOR. Call in the shoemaker, Handy.

OR. WOM. Good Mr. Dorimant, pay me. Gad, I had rather give you my fruit than stay to be abused by that foul-mouthed rogue; what you gentlemen say, it matters not much, but such a dirty fellow does one more disgrace.

DOR. Give her ten shillings, and be sure you tell the young gentlewoman I must be acquainted with her.

OR. WOM. Now do you long to be tempting this pretty creature. Well, heavens mend you!

MED. Farewell, bog!   (*Exit Orange-Woman and* HANDY.) Dorimant, when did you see your *pisaller,* as you call her, Mrs. Loveit?

DOR. Not these two days.

MED. And how stand affairs between you?

DOR. There has been great patching of late, much ado; we make a shift to hang together.

MED. I wonder how her mighty spirit bears it.

DOR. Ill enough, on all conscience; I never knew so violent a creature.

MED. She's the most passionate in her love and the most extravagant in her jealousy of any woman I ever heard of. What note is that?

DOR. An excuse I am going to send her for the neglect I am guilty of.

MED. Prithee, read it.

DOR. No; but if you will take the pains, you may.

MED. (*reads*)

I never was a lover of business, but now I have a just reason to hate it, since it has kept me these two days from seeing you. I intend to wait upon you in the afternoon, and in the pleasure of your conversation forget all I have suffered during this tedious absence.

This business of yours, Dorimant, has been with a vizard at the playhouse; I have had an eye on you. If some malicious body should betray you, this kind note would hardly make your peace with her.

DOR. I desire no better.

MED. Why, would her knowledge of it oblige you?

DOR. Most infinitely; next to the coming to a good understanding with a new mistress, I love a quarrel with an old one. But the devil's in't, there has been such a calm in my affairs of late, I have not had the pleasure of making a woman so much as break her fan, to be sullen, or forswear herself, these three days.

MED. A very great misfortune. Let me see; I love mischief well enough to forward this business myself. I'll about it presently, and though I know the truth of what y'ave done will set her a-raving, I'll heighten it a little with invention, leave her in a fit o' the mother, and be here again before y'are ready.

DOR. Pray, stay; you may spare yourself the labour. The business is undertaken already by one who will manage it with as much address, and I think with a little more malice, than you can.

MED. Who i'the devil's name can this be!

DOR. Why, the vizard—that very vizard you saw me with.

MED. Does she love mischief so well as to betray herself to spite another?

DOR. Not so neither, Medley. I will make you comprehend the mystery: this mask, for a farther confirmation of what I have been these two days swearing to her, made me yesterday at the playhouse make her a promise before her face utterly to break off with Loveit, and, because she tenders my reputation and would not have me do a barbarous thing, has contrived a way to give me a handsome occasion.

MED. Very good.

DOR. She intends about an hour before me, this afternoon, to make Loveit a visit, and, having the privilege, by reason of a professed friendship between 'em, to talk of her concerns——

MED. Is she a friend?

DOR. Oh, an intimate friend!

MED. Better and better; pray, proceed.

DOR. She means insensibly to insinuate a discourse of me and artificially raise her jealousy to such a height that, transported with the first motions of her passion, she shall fly upon me with all the fury imaginable as soon as ever I enter; the quarrel being thus happily begun, I am to play my part, confess and justify all my roguery, swear her impertinence and ill-humour makes her intolerable, tax her with the next fop that comes into my head, and in a huff march away, slight her, and leave her to be taken by whosoever thinks it worth his time to lie down before her.

MED. This vizard is a spark and has a genius that makes her worthy of yourself, Dorimant.

Enter HANDY, *Shoemaker, and Footman*

DOR. You rogue there who sneak like a dog that has flung down a dish, if you do not mend your waiting, I'll uncase you and turn you loose to the wheel of fortune. Handy, seal this and let him run with it presently. (*Exit Footman.*)

MED. Since y'are resolved on a quarrel, why do you send her this kind note?

DOR. To keep her at home in order to the business.—(*to the Shoemaker*) How now, you drunken sot?

SHOEM. 'Zbud, you have no reason to talk; I have not had a bottle of sack of yours in my belly this fortnight.

MED. The orange-woman says your neighbours take notice what a heathen you are, and design to inform the bishop and have you burned for an atheist.

SHOEM. Damn her, dunghill, if her husband does not remove her, she stinks so, the parish intend to indict him for a nuisance.

MED. I advise you like a friend; reform your life. You have brought the envy of the world upon you by living above yourself. Whoring and swearing are vices too genteel for a shoemaker.

SHOEM. 'Zbud, I think you men of quality will grow as unreasonable as the women. You would ingross the sins of the nation; poor folks can no sooner be wicked but th'are railed at by their betters.

DOR. Sirrah, I'll have you stand i'the pillory for this libel!

SHOEM. Some of you deserve it, I'm sure; there are so many of 'em, that our journeymen nowadays, instead of harmless ballads, sing nothing but your damned lampoons.

DOR. Our lampoons, you rogue!

SHOEM. Nay, good Master, why should not you write your own commentaries as well as Cæsar?

MED. The rascal's read, I perceive.

SHOEM. You know the old proverb—ale and history.

DOR. Draw on my shoes, Sirrah.

SHOEM. Here's a shoe——!

DOR. Sits with more wrinkles than there are in an angry bully's forehead!

SHOEM. 'Zbud, as smooth as your mistress's skin does upon her! So; strike your foot in home. 'Zbud, if e'er a monsieur of 'em all make more fashionable ware, I'll be content to have my ears whipped off with my own paring knife.

MED. And served up in a ragout instead of coxcombs to a company of French shoemakers for a collation.

SHOEM. Hold, hold! Damn 'em, caterpillars! let 'em feed upon cabbage. Come Master, your health this morning next my heart now!

DOR. Go, get you home and govern your family better! Do not let your wife follow you to the ale-house, beat your whore, and lead you home in triumph.

SHOEM. 'Zbud, there's never a man i'the town lives more like a gentleman with his wife than I do. I never mind her motions, she never inquires into mine; we speak to one another civilly, hate one another heartily, and because 'tis vulgar to lie and soak together, we have each of us our several settle-bed.

DOR. Give him half a crown.

MED. Not without he will promise to be bloody drunk.

SHOEM. "Tope" 's the word i'the eye of the world, for my master's honor, Robin!

DOR. Do not debauch my servants, Sirrah.

SHOEM. I only tip him the wink; he knows an ale-house from a hovel. (*Exit Shoemaker.*)

DOR. My clothes, quickly.

MED. Where shall we dine today?

Enter YOUNG BELLAIR

DOR. Where you will; here comes a good third man.

Y. BELL. Your servant, gentlemen.

MED. Gentle Sir, how will you answer this visit to your honourable mistress? 'Tis not her interest you should keep company with men of sense who will be talking reason.

Y. BELL. I do not fear her pardon; do you but grant me yours for my neglect of late.

MED. Though y'ave made us miserable by the want of your good company, to show you I am free from all resentment, may the beautiful cause of our misfortune give you all the joys happy lovers have shared ever since the world began.

Y. BELL. You wish me in heaven, but you believe me on my journey to hell.

MED. You have a good strong faith, and that may contribute much towards your salvation. I confess I am but of an untoward constitution, apt to have doubts and scruples, and in love they are no less distracting than in religion. Were I so near marriage, I should cry out by fits as I ride in my coach, "Cuckold, cuckold!" with no less fury than the mad fanatic does "glory!" in Bethlem.

Y. BELL. Because religion makes some run mad must I live an atheist?

MED. Is it not great indiscretion for a man of credit, who may have money enough on his word, to go and deal with Jews, who for little sums make men enter into bonds and give judgments?

Y. BELL. Preach no more on this text. I am determined, and there is no hope of my conversion.

DOR. (*to* HANDY, *who is fiddling about him*) Leave your unnecessary fiddling; a wasp that's buzzing about a man's nose at dinner is not more troublesome than thou art.

HAND. You love to have your clothes hang just, Sir.

DOR. I love to be well dressed, Sir, and think it no scandal to my understanding.

HAND. Will you use the essence or orange flower water?

DOR. I will smell as I do to-day, no offence to the ladies' noses.

HAND. Your pleasure, Sir. (*Exit* HANDY.)

DOR. That a man's excellency should lie in neatly tying of a ribband or a cravat! How careful's nature in furnishing the world with necessary coxcombs!

Y. BELL. That's a mighty pretty suit of yours, Dorimant.

DOR. I am glad't has your approbation.

Y. BELL. No man in town has a better fancy in his clothes than you have.

DOR. You will make me have an opinion of my genius.

MED. There is a great critic, I hear, in these matters, lately arrived piping hot from Paris.

Y. BELL. Sir Fopling Flutter, you mean.

MED. The same.

Y. BELL. He thinks himself the pattern of modern gallantry.

DOR. He is indeed the pattern of modern foppery.

MED. He was yesterday at the play, with a pair of gloves up to his elbows, and a periwig more exactly curled than a lady's head newly dressed for a ball.

Y. BELL. What a pretty lisp he has!

DOR. Ho! that he affects in imitation of the people of quality of France.

MED. His head stands, for the most part, on one side, and his looks are more languishing than a lady's when she lolls at stretch in her coach or leans her head carelessly against the side of a box i'the playhouse.

DOR. He is a person indeed of great acquired follies.

MED. He is like many others, beholding to his education for making him so eminent a coxcomb; many a fool had been lost to the world had their indulgent parents wisely bestowed neither learning nor good breeding on 'em.

Y. BELL. He has been, as the sparkish word is, "brisk upon the ladies" already. He was yesterday at my Aunt Townley's and gave Mrs. Loveit a catalogue of his good qualities under the character of a complete gentleman, who, according to Sir Fopling, ought to dress well, dance well, fence well, have a genius for love letters, an agreeable voice for a chamber, be very amorous, something discreet, but not overconstant.

MED. Pretty ingredients to make an accomplished person!

DOR. I am glad he pitched upon Loveit.

Y. BELL. How so?

DOR. I wanted a fop to lay to her charge, and this is as pat as may be.

Y. BELL. I am confident she loves no man but you.

DOR. The good fortune were enough to make me vain, but that I am in my nature modest.

Y. BELL. Hark you, Dorimant.—— With your leave, Mr. Medley; 'tis only a secret concerning a fair lady.

MED. Your good breeding, Sir, gives you too much trouble; you might have whispered without all this ceremony.

Y. BELL. (*to* DORIMANT) How stand your affairs with Bellinda of late?

DOR. She's a little jilting baggage.

Y. BELL. Nay, I believe her false enough, but she's ne'er the worse for your purpose; she was with you yesterday in a disguise at the play.

DOR. There we fell out and resolved never to speak to one another more.

Y. BELL. The occasion?

DOR. Want of courage to meet me at the place appointed. These young women apprehend loving as much as the young men do fighting, at first; but, once entered, like them too, they all turn bullies straight.

Enter HANDY

HAND. (*to* YOUNG BELLAIR) Sir, your man without desires to speak with you.

Y. BELL. Gentlemen, I'll return immediately.

(*Exit* YOUNG BELLAIR.)

MED. A very pretty fellow this.

DOR. He's handsome, well-bred, and by much the most tolerable of all the young men that do not abound in wit.

MED. Ever well dressed, always complaisant, and seldom impertinent. You and he are grown very intimate, I see.

DOR. It is our mutual interest to be so: it makes the women think the better of his understanding, and judge more favourably of my reputation; it makes him pass upon some for a man of very good sense, and I upon others for a very civil person.

MED. What was that whisper?

DOR. A thing which he would fain have known, but I did not

think it fit to tell him; it might have frighted him from his honourable intentions of marrying.

MED. Emilia, give her her due, has the best reputation of any young woman about the town who has beauty enough to provoke detraction; her carriage is unaffected, her discourse modest, not at all censorious nor pretending, like the counterfeits of the age.

DOR. She's a discreet maid, and I believe nothing can corrupt her but a husband.

MED. A husband?

DOR. Yes, a husband: I have known many women make a difficulty of losing a maidenhead, who have afterwards made none of making a cuckold.

MED. This prudent consideration, I am apt to think, has made you confirm poor Bellair in the desperate resolution he has taken.

DOR. Indeed, the little hope I found there was of her, in the state she was in, has made me by my advice contribute something towards the changing of her condition.

Enter YOUNG BELLAIR

Dear Bellair, by heavens, I thought we had lost thee; men in love are never to be reckoned on when we would form a company.

Y. BELL. Dorimant, I am undone. My man has brought the most surprising news i'the world.

DOR. Some strange misfortune is befallen your love.

Y. BELL. My father came to town last night and lodges i'the very house where Emilia lies.

MED. Does he know it is with her you are in love?

Y. BELL. He knows I love, but knows not whom, without some officious sot has betrayed me.

DOR. Your Aunt Townley is your confidante and favours the business.

Y. BELL. I do not apprehend any ill office from her. I have received a letter in which I am commanded by my father to meet him at my aunt's this afternoon. He tells me farther he has made a match for me and bids me resolve to be obedient to his will or expect to be disinherited.

MED. Now's your time, Bellair; never had lover such an opportunity of giving a generous proof of his passion.

Y. BELL. As how, I pray?

MED. Why, hang an estate, marry Emilia out of hand, and provoke your father to do what he threatens; 'tis but despising a coach, humbling yourself to a pair of goloshes, being out of countenance when you meet your friends, pointed at and pitied wherever you go by all the amorous fops that know you, and your fame will be immortal.

Y. BELL. I could find in my heart to resolve not to marry at all.

DOR. Fie, fie! That would spoil a good jest and disappoint the well-natured town of an occasion of laughing at you.

Y. BELL. The storm I have so long expected hangs o'er my head and begins to pour down upon me; I am on the rack and can have no rest till I'm satisfied in what I fear. Where do you dine?

DOR. At Long's or Locket's.

MED. At Long's let it be.

Y. BELL. I'll run and see Emilia and inform myself how matters stand. If my misfortunes are not so great as to make me unfit for company, I'll be with you.   (*Exit* YOUNG BELLAIR.)

Enter a Footman with a letter

FOOT. (*to* DORIMANT) Here's a letter, Sir.

DOR. The superscription's right: "For Mr. Dorimant."

MED. Let's see; the very scrawl and spelling of a true-bred whore.

DOR. I know the hand; the style is admirable, I assure you.

MED. Prithee, read it.

DOR. (*reads*)

I told a you you dud not love me, if you dud, you would have seen me again ere now. I have no money and am very mallicolly; pray send me a guynie to see the operies.

Your servant to command,
Molly.

MED. Pray, let the whore have a favourable answer, that she may spark it in a box and do honour to her profession.

DOR. She shall, and perk up i'the face of quality. Is the coach at door?

HAND. You did not bid me send for it.

DOR. Eternal blockhead! (HANDY *offers to go out.*) Hey, sot——

HAND. Did you call me, Sir?

DOR. I hope you have no just exception to the name, Sir?

HAND. I have sense, Sir.

DOR. Not so much as a fly in winter.—— How did you come, Medley?

MED. In a chair.

FOOT. You may have a hackney coach if you please, Sir.

DOR. I may ride the elephant if I please, Sir. Call another chair and let my coach follow to Long's.

> Be calm, ye great parents, etc.

> (*Exeunt, singing.*)

ACT II

SCENE I

Enter my LADY TOWNLEY *and* EMILIA

L. TOWN. I was afraid, Emilia, all had been discovered.

EMIL. I tremble with the apprehension still.

L. TOWN. That my brother should take lodgings i'the very house where you lie!

EMIL. 'Twas lucky we had timely notice to warn the people to be secret. He seems to be a mighty good-humoured old man.

L. TOWN. He ever had a notable smirking way with him.

EMIL. He calls me rogue, tells me he can't abide me, and does so bepat me.

L. TOWN. On my word, you are much in his favour then.

EMIL. He has been very inquisitive, I am told, about my family, my reputation, and my fortune.

L. TOWN. I am confident he does not i'the least suspect you are the woman his son's in love with.

EMIL. What should make him, then, inform himself so particularly of me?

L. TOWN. He was always of a very loving temper himself; it may be he has a doting fit upon him—who knows?

EMIL. It cannot be.

Enter YOUNG BELLAIR

L. TOWN. Here comes my nephew.—— Where did you leave your father?

Y. BELL. *Writing a note within.* Emilia, this early visit loo
as if some kind jealousy would not let you rest at home.

EMIL. The knowledge I have of my rival gives me a little
cause to fear your constancy.

Y. BELL. My constancy! I vow——

EMIL. Do not vow. Our love is frail as is our life and full as
little in our power; and are you sure you shall outlive this day?

Y. BELL. I am not; but when we are in perfect health, 'twere
an idle thing to fright ourselves with the thoughts of sudden
death.

L. TOWN. Pray, what has passed between you and your father
i'the garden?

Y. BELL. He's firm in his resolution, tells me I must marry Mrs.
Harriet, or swears he'll marry himself and disinherit me. When
I saw I could not prevail with him to be more indulgent, I dissembled an obedience to his will, which has composed his passion and will give us time, and, I hope, opportunity, to deceive
him.

Enter OLD BELLAIR *with a note in his hand*

L. TOWN. Peace, here he comes!

O. BELL. Harry, take this and let your man carry it for me to
Mr. Fourbe's chamber, my lawyer i'the Temple.

(*Exit* YOUNG BELLAIR.)

(*to* EMILIA) Neighbour, a dod! I am glad to see thee here. Make
much of her, Sister; she's one of the best of your acquaintance.
I like her countenance and her behaviour well; she has a modesty that is not common i'this age, a dod, she has!

L. TOWN. I know her value, Brother, and esteem her accordingly.

O. BELL. Advise her to wear a little more mirth in her face;
a dod, she's too serious.

L. TOWN. The fault is very excusable in a young woman.

O. BELL. Nay, a dod, I like her ne'er the worse. A melancholy
beauty has her charms. I love a pretty sadness in a face, which
varies now and then, like changeable colours, into a smile.

L. TOWN. Methinks you speak very feelingly, Brother.

O. BELL. I am but five and fifty, Sister, you know, an age not
altogether unsensible.——(*to* EMILIA) Cheer up, sweetheart! I have
a secret to tell thee may chance to make thee merry. We three

ation together anon; i'the meantime, mum, I can't
, I can't abide you!

Enter YOUNG BELLAIR

Harry, ...l you must along with me to my Lady Woodvill's.
I am going to slip the boy at a mistress.

Y. BELL. At a wife, Sir, you would say.

O. BELL. You need not look so glum, Sir; a wife is no curse
when she brings the blessing of a good estate with her; but an
idle town flirt, with a painted face, a rotten reputation, and a
crazy fortune, a dod! is the devil and all, and such a one I hear
you are in league with.

Y. BELL. I cannot help detraction, Sir.

O. BELL. Out! A pise o' their breeches, there are keeping fools
enough for such flaunting baggages, and they are e'en too good
for 'em.—(*to* EMILIA) Remember 'night. Go, y'are a rogue, y'are
a rogue! Fare you well, fare you well!—— Come, come, come
along, Sir!   (*Exeunt* OLD *and* YOUNG BELLAIR.)

L. TOWN. On my word, the old man comes on apace; I'll lay
my life he's smitten.

EMIL. This is nothing but the pleasantness of his humour.

L. TOWN. I know him better than you. Let it work; it may
prove lucky.

Enter a Page

PAGE. Madam, Mr. Medley has sent to know whether a visit
will not be troublesome this afternoon.

L. TOWN. Send him word his visits never are so.   (*Exit Page.*)

EMIL. He's a very pleasant man.

L. TOWN. He's a very necessary man among us women; he's not
scandalous i'the least, perpetually contriving to bring good company together, and always ready to stop up a gap at ombre;
then, he knows all the little news o'the town.

EMIL. I love to hear him talk o'the intrigues; let 'em be never
so dull in themselves, he'll make 'em pleasant i'the relation.

L. TOWN. But he improves things so much one can take no
measure of the truth from him. Mr. Dorimant swears a flea or a
maggot is not made more monstrous by a magnifying glass than
a story is by his telling it.

Enter MEDLEY

EMIL. Hold, here he comes.

L. TOWN. Mr. Medley.

MED. Your servant, Madam.

L. TOWN. You have made yourself a stranger of late.

EMIL. I believe you took a surfeit of ombre last time you were here.

MED. Indeed, I had my bellyful of that termagant, Lady Dealer. There never was so unsatiable a carder; an old gleeker never loved to sit to't like her. I have played with her now at least a dozen times till she's worn out all her fine complexion and her tour would keep in curl no longer.

L. TOWN. Blame her not, poor woman; she loves nothing so well as a black ace.

MED. The pleasure I have seen her in when she has had hope in drawing for a matadore!

EMIL. 'Tis as pretty sport to her as persuading masks off is to you, to make discoveries.

L. TOWN. Pray, where's your friend Mr. Dorimant?

MED. Soliciting his affairs; he's a man of great employment, has more mistresses now depending than the most eminent lawyer in England has causes.

EMIL. Here has been Mrs. Loveit so uneasy and out of humour these two days.

L. TOWN. How strangely love and jealousy rage in that poor woman!

MED. She could not have picked out a devil upon earth so proper to torment her; he's made her break a dozen or two of fans already, tear half a score points in pieces, and destroy hoods and knots without number.

L. TOWN. We heard of a pleasant serenade he gave her t'other night.

MED. A Danish serenade with kettle-drums and trumpets.

EMIL. Oh, barbarous!

MED. What! You are of the number of the ladies whose ears are grown so delicate since our operas you can be charmed with nothing but *flûtes douces* and French hautboys?

EMIL. Leave your raillery, and tell us, is there any new wit come forth, songs or novels?

MED. A very pretty piece of gallantry, by an eminent author, called *The Diversions of Bruxelles,* very necessary to be read by all old ladies who are desirous to improve themselves at questions and commands, blindman's buff, and the like fashionable recreations.

EMIL. Oh, ridiculous!

MED. Then there is *The Art of Affectation,* written by a late beauty of quality, teaching you how to draw up your breasts, stretch up your neck, to thrust out your breech, to play with your head, to toss up your nose, to bite your lips, to turn up your eyes, to speak in a silly, soft tone of a voice, and use all the foolish French words that will infallibly make your person and conversation charming; with a short apology at the latter end in the behalf of young ladies who notoriously wash and paint though they have naturally good complexions.

EMIL. What a deal of stuff you tell us!

MED. Such as the town affords, Madam. The Russians, hearing the great respect we have for foreign dancing, have lately sent over some of their best balladines, who are now practising a famous ballet which will be suddenly danced at the Bear Garden.

L. TOWN. Pray, forbear your idle stories, and give us an account of the state of love as it now stands.

MED. Truly, there has been some revolutions in those affairs, great chopping and changing among the old, and some new lovers whom malice, indiscretion, and misfortune have luckily brought into play.

L. TOWN. What think you of walking into the next room and sitting down before you engage in this business?

MED. I wait upon you, and I hope (though women are commonly unreasonable) by the plenty of scandal I shall discover, to give you very good content, ladies.   (*Exeunt.*)

SCENE II

Enter MRS. LOVEIT *and* PERT. MRS. LOVEIT *putting up a letter, then pulling out her pocket-glass and looking in it*

LOV. Pert.

PERT. Madam?

LOV. I hate myself, I look so ill today.

PERT. Hate the wicked cause on't, that base man Mr. Dorimant, who makes you torment and vex yourself continually.

LOV. He is to blame, indeed.

PERT. To blame to be two days without sending, writing, or coming near you, contrary to his oath and covenant! 'Twas to much purpose to make him swear! I'll lay my life there's not an article but he has broken—talked to the vizards i'the pit, waited upon the ladies from the boxes to their coaches, gone behind the scenes, and fawned upon those little insignificant creatures, the players. 'Tis impossible for a man of his inconstant temper to forbear, I'm sure.

LOV. I know he is a devil, but he has something of the angel yet undefaced in him, which makes him so charming and agreeable that I must love him, be he never so wicked.

PERT. I little thought, Madam, to see your spirit tamed to this degree, who banished poor Mr. Lackwit but for taking up another lady's fan in your presence.

LOV. My knowing of such odious fools contributes to the making of me love Dorimant the better.

PERT. Your knowing of Mr. Dorimant, in my mind, should rather make you hate all mankind.

LOV. So it does, besides himself.

PERT. Pray, what excuse does he make in his letter?

LOV. He has had business.

PERT. Business in general terms would not have been a current excuse for another. A modish man is always very busy when he is in pursuit of a new mistress.

LOV. Some fop has bribed you to rail at him. He had business; I will believe it, and will forgive him.

PERT. You may forgive him anything, but I shall never forgive him his turning me into ridicule, as I hear he does.

LOV. I perceive you are of the number of those fools his wit has made his enemies.

PERT. I am of the number of those he's pleased to rally, Madam, and if we may believe Mr. Wagfan and Mr. Caperwell, he sometimes makes merry with yourself too, among his laughing companions.

LOV. Blockheads are as malicious to witty men as ugly women are to the handsome; 'tis their interest, and they make it their business to defame 'em.

PERT. I wish Mr. Dorimant would not make it his business to defame you.

LOV. Should he, I had rather be made infamous by him than owe my reputation to the dull discretion of those fops you talk of.

Enter BELLINDA

Bellinda!   (*running to her*)

BELL. My dear!

LOV. You have been unkind of late.

BELL. Do not say unkind—say unhappy.

LOV. I could chide you. Where have you been these two days?

BELL. Pity me rather, my dear, where I have been—so tired with two or three country gentlewomen, whose conversation has been more unsufferable than a country fiddle.

LOV. Are they relations?

BELL. No, Welsh acquaintance I made when I was last year at St. Winifred's. They have asked me a thousand questions of the modes and intrigues of the town, and I have told 'em almost as many things for news that hardly were so when their gowns were in fashion.

LOV. Provoking creatures! How could you endure 'em?

BELL. (*aside*) Now to carry on my plot. Nothing but love could make me capable of so much falsehood. 'Tis time to begin, lest Dorimant should come before her jealousy has stung her.—(*laughs, and then speaks on*) I was yesterday at a play with 'em, where I was fain to show 'em the living as the man at Westminster does the dead: "That is Mrs. Such-a-one, admired for her beauty; that is Mr. Such-a-one, cried up for a wit; that is sparkish Mr. Such-a-one, who keeps reverend Mrs. Such-a-one; and there sits fine Mrs. Such-a-one who was lately cast off by my Lord Such-a-one."

LOV. Did you see Dorimant there?

BELL. I did, and imagine you were there with him and have no mind to own it.

LOV. What should make you think so?

BELL. A lady masked in a pretty *déshabillé*, whom Dorimant entertained with more respect than the gallants do a common vizard.

LOV. (*aside*) Dorimant at the play entertaining a mask! Oh, heavens!

BELL. *(aside)* Good!

LOV. Did he stay all the while?

BELL. Till the play was done, and then led her out, which confirms me it was you.

LOV. Traitor!

PERT. Now you may believe he had business, and you may forgive him too.

LOV. Ingrateful, perjured man!

BELL. You seem so much concerned, my dear, I fear I have told you unawares what I had better have concealed for your quiet.

LOV. What manner of shape had she?

BELL. Tall and slender. Her motions were very genteel; certainly she must be some person of condition.

LOV. Shame and confusion be ever in her face when she shows it!

BELL. I should blame your discretion for loving that wild man, my dear, but they say he has a way so bewitching that few can defend their hearts who know him.

LOV. I will tear him from mine or die i'the attempt.

BELL. Be more moderate.

LOV. Would I had daggers, darts, or poisoned arrows in my breast, so I could but remove the thoughts of him from thence!

BELL. Fie, fie! your transports are too violent, my dear; this may be but an accidental gallantry, and 'tis likely ended at her coach.

PERT. Should it proceed farther, let your comfort be, the conduct Mr. Dorimant affects will quickly make you know your rival, ten to one let you see her ruined, her reputation exposed to the town—a happiness none will envy her but yourself, Madam.

LOV. Whoe'er she be, all the harm I wish her is, may she love him as well as I do and may he give her as much cause to hate him.

PERT. Never doubt the latter end of your curse, Madam.

LOV. May all the passions that are raised by neglected love—jealousy, indignation, spite, and thirst of revenge—eternally rage in her soul, as they do now in mine.

(walks up and down with a distracted air)

Enter a Page

PAGE. Madam, Mr. Dorimant——

LOV. I will not see him.

PAGE. I told him you were within, Madam.

LOV. Say you lied—say I'm busy—shut the door—say any-thing!

PAGE. He's here, Madam.

Enter DORIMANT

DOR. They taste of death who do at heaven arrive;
But we this paradise approach alive.

(*to* MISTRESS LOVEIT) What, dancing *The Galloping Nag* with-out a fiddle? (*offers to catch her by the hand; she flings away and walks on, he pursuing her*) I fear this restlessness of the body, Madam, proceeds from an unquietness of the mind. What unlucky accident puts you out of humour? A point ill washed, knots spoiled i'the making up, hair shaded awry, or some other little mistake in setting you in order?

PERT. A trifle, in my opinion, Sir, more inconsiderable than any you mention.

DOR. O Mrs. Pert! I never knew you sullen enough to be silent; come, let me know the business.

PERT. The business, Sir, is the business that has taken you up these two days. How have I seen you laugh at men of business, and now to become a man of business yourself!

DOR. We are not masters of our own affections; our inclina-tions daily alter: now we love pleasure, and anon we shall dote on business. Human frailty will have it so, and who can help it?

LOV. Faithless, inhuman, barbarous man——

DOR. (*aside*) Good! Now the alarm strikes.

LOV. Without sense of love, of honour, or of gratitude, tell me, for I will know, what devil masked she was you were with at the play yesterday?

DOR. Faith, I resolved as much as you, but the devil was obsti-nate and would not tell me.

LOV. False in this as in your vows to me!—you do know.

DOR. The truth is, I did all I could to know.

LOV. And dare you own it to my face? Hell and furies!

(*tears her fan in pieces*)

DOR. Spare your fan, Madam; you are growing hot and will want it to cool you.

LOV. Horror and distraction seize you! Sorrow and remorse gnaw your soul, and punish all your perjuries to me! (*weeps*)

DOR. (*turning to* BELLINDA)

> So thunder breaks the cloud in twain
> And makes a passage for the rain.

(*to* BELLINDA) Bellinda, you are the devil that have raised this storm; you were at the play yesterday and have been making discoveries to your dear.

BELL. Y'are the most mistaken man i'the world.

DOR. It must be so, and here I vow revenge—resolve to pursue and persecute you more impertinently than ever any loving fop did his mistress, hunt you i'the Park, trace you i'the Mail, dog you in every visit you make, haunt you at the plays and i'the drawing-room, hang my nose in your neck and talk to you whether you will or no, and ever look upon you with such dying eyes till your friends grow jealous of me, send you out of town, and the world suspect your reputation.—(*in a lower voice*) At my Lady Townley's when we go from hence.

> (*He looks kindly on* BELLINDA.)

BELL. I'll meet you there.

DOR. Enough.

LOV. (*pushing* DORIMANT *away*) Stand off! You sha' not stare upon her so.

DOR. Good; there's one made jealous already.

LOV. Is this the constancy you vowed?

DOR. Constancy at my years! 'Tis not a virtue in season; you might as well expect the fruit the autumn ripens i'the spring.

LOV. Monstrous principle!

DOR. Youth has a long journey to go, Madam; should I have set up my rest at the first inn I lodged at, I should never have arrived at the happiness I now enjoy.

LOV. Dissembler, damned dissembler!

DOR. I am so, I confess: good nature and good manners corrupt me. I am honest in my inclinations, and would not, wer't not to avoid offence, make a lady a little in years believe I think her young, willfully mistake art for nature, and seem as fond of a thing I am weary of as when I doted on't in earnest.

LOV. False man!

DOR. True woman!

LOV. Now you begin to show yourself.

DOR. Love gilds us over and makes us show fine things to one another for a time, but soon the gold wears off and then again the native brass appears.

LOV. Think on your oaths, your vows and protestations, perjured man!

DOR. I made 'em when I was in love.

LOV. And therefore ought they not to bind? Oh, impious!

DOR. What we swear at such a time may be a certain proof of a present passion, but, to say truth, in love there is no security to be given for the future.

LOV. Horrid and ingrateful, begone, and never see me more!

DOR. I am not one of those troublesome coxcombs who, because they were once well received, take the privilege to plague a woman with their love ever after. I shall obey you, Madam, though I do myself some violence.

(*He offers to go and* MRS. LOVEIT *pulls him back.*)

LOV. Come back! You sha' not go! Could you have the ill-nature to offer it?

DOR. When love grows diseased, the best thing we can do is to put it to a violent death. I cannot endure the torture of a lingering and consumptive passion.

LOV. Can you think mine sickly?

DOR. Oh, 'tis desperately ill. What worse symptoms are there than your being always uneasy when I visit you, your picking quarrels with me on slight occasions, and in my absence kindly listening to the impertinences of every fashionable fool that talks to you?

LOV. What fashionable fool can you lay to my charge?

DOR. Why, the very cock-fool of all those fools—Sir Fopling Flutter.

LOV. I never saw him in my life but once.

DOR. The worse woman you, at first sight to put on all your charms, to entertain him with that softness in your voice, and all that wanton kindness in your eyes you so notoriously affect when you design a conquest.

LOV. So damned a lie did never malice yet invent. Who told you this?

DOR. No matter. That ever I should love a woman that can

dote on a senseless caper, a tawdry French ribband, and a formal cravat!

LOV. You make me mad.

DOR. A guilty conscience may do much. Go on, be the game-mistress o' the town, and enter all our young fops as fast as they come from travel.

LOV. Base and scurrilous!

DOR. A fine mortifying reputation 'twill be for a woman of your pride, wit, and quality!

LOV. This jealousy's a mere pretence, a cursed trick of your own devising. I know you.

DOR. Believe it and all the ill of me you can: I would not have a woman have the least good thought of me that can think well of Fopling. Farewell! Fall to, and much good may do you with your coxcomb.

LOV. Stay, oh stay! and I will tell you all.

DOR. I have been told too much already.   (*Exit* DORIMANT.)

LOV. Call him again!

PERT. E'en let him go—a fair riddance.

LOV. Run, I say! call him again! I will have him called!

PERT. The devil should carry him away first were it my concern.   (*Exit* PERT.)

BELL. He's frighted me from the very thoughts of loving men. For heaven's sake, my dear, do not discover what I told you! I dread his tongue as much as you ought to have done his friendship.

Enter PERT

PERT. He's gone, Madam.

LOV. Lightning blast him!

PERT. When I told him you desired him to come back, he smiled, made a mouth at me, flung into his coach, and said——

LOV. What did he say?

PERT. "Drive away!" and then repeated verses.

LOV. Would I had made a contract to be a witch when first I entertained this greater devil, monster, barbarian! I could tear myself in pieces. Revenge—nothing but revenge can ease me. Plague, war, famine, fire—all that can bring universal ruin and misery on mankind—with joy I'd perish to have you in my power but this moment.   (*Exit* MRS. LOVEIT.)

PERT. Follow, Madam; leave her not in this outrageous passion! (PERT *gathers up the things.*)

BELL. (*aside*) He's given me the proof which I desired of his love,

> But 'tis a proof of his ill-nature too.
> I wish I had not seen him use her so.
> I sigh to think that Dorimant may be
> One day as faithless and unkind to me.

(*Exeunt.*)

ACT III

SCENE I

SCENE: LADY WOODVILL's *lodgings*

Enter HARRIET *and* BUSY, *her woman*

BUSY. Dear Madam, let me set that curl in order.

HAR. Let me alone; I will shake 'em all out of order.

BUSY. Will you never leave this wildness?

HAR. Torment me not.

BUSY. Look! There's a knot falling off.

HAR. Let it drop.

BUSY. But one pin, dear Madam.

HAR. How do I daily suffer under thy officious fingers!

BUSY. Ah, the difference that is between you and my Lady Dapper! how uneasy she is if the least thing be amiss about her!

HAR. She is indeed most exact; nothing is ever wanting to make her ugliness remarkable.

BUSY. Jeering people say so.

HAR. Her powdering, painting, and her patching never fail in public to draw the tongues and eyes of all the men upon her.

BUSY. She is, indeed, a little too pretending.

HAR. That women should set up for beauty as much in spite of nature as some men have done for wit!

BUSY. I hope without offence one may endeavour to make one's self agreeable.

HAR. Not when 'tis impossible. Women then ought to be no more fond of dressing than fools should be of talking; hoods and

modesty, masks and silence, things that shadow and conceal—
they should think of nothing else.

BUSY. Jesu! Madam, what will your mother think is become of
you? For heaven's sake go in again!

HAR. I won't.

BUSY. This is the extravagantest thing that ever you did in
your life, to leave her and a gentleman who is to be your husband.

HAR. My husband! Hast thou so little wit to think I spoke
what I meant when I overjoyed her in the country with a low
curtsey and "What you please, Madam; I shall ever be obedient"?

BUSY. Nay, I know not, you have so many fetches.

HAR. And this was one, to get her up to London! Nothing else,
I assure thee.

BUSY. Well, the man, in my mind, is a fine man.

HAR. The man indeed wears his clothes fashionably and has
a pretty, negligent way with him, very courtly and much affected; he bows, and talks, and smiles so agreeably, as he thinks.

BUSY. I never saw anything so genteel.

HAR. Varnished over with good breeding, many a blockhead
makes a tolerable show.

BUSY. I wonder you do not like him.

HAR. I think I might be brought to endure him, and that is all
a reasonable woman should expect in a husband; but there is
duty i'the case, and like the haughty Merab, I

> Find much aversion in my stubborn mind,

Which

> Is bred by being promis'd and design'd.

BUSY. I wish you do not design your own ruin. I partly guess
your inclinations, Madam—that Mr. Dorimant——

HAR. Leave your prating and sing some foolish song or other.

BUSY. I will—the song you love so well ever since you saw
Mr. Dorimant.

SONG

> When first Amintas charm'd my heart,
> My heedless sheep began to stray;
> The wolves soon stole the greatest part,
> And all will now be made a prey.

> Ah, let not love your thoughts possess,
> 'Tis fatal to a shepherdess;
> The dang'rous passion you must shun,
> Or else like me be quite undone.

HAR. Shall I be paid down by a covetous parent for a purchase? I need no land; no, I'll lay myself out all in love. It is decreed—

Enter YOUNG BELLAIR

Y. BELL. What generous resolution are you making, Madam?

HAR. Only to be disobedient, Sir.

Y. BELL. Let me join hands with you in that.

HAR. With all my heart; I never thought I should have given you mine so willingly. Here I, Harriet——

Y. BELL. And I, Harry——

HAR. Do solemnly protest——

Y. BELL. And vow——

HAR. That I with you——

Y. BELL. And I with you——

BOTH. Will never marry.

HAR. A match!

Y. BELL. And no match! How do you like this indifference now?

HAR. You expect I should take it ill, I see.

Y. BELL. 'Tis not unnatural for you women to be a little angry: you miss a conquest, though you would slight the poor man were he in your power.

HAR. There are some, it may be, have an eye like Bart'lomew—big enough for the whole fair; but I am not of the number, and you may keep your gingerbread. 'Twill be more acceptable to the lady whose dear image it wears, Sir.

Y. BELL. I must confess, Madam, you came a day after the fair.

HAR. You own then you are in love?

Y. BELL. I do.

HAR. The confidence is generous, and in return I could almost find in my heart to let you know my inclinations.

Y. BELL. Are you in love?

HAR. Yes, with this dear town, to that degree I can scarce endure the country in landscapes and in hangings.

Y. BELL. What a dreadful thing 'twould be to be hurried back to Hampshire!

HAR. Ah, name it not!

Y. BELL. As for us, I find we shall agree well enough. Would we could do something to deceive the grave people!

HAR. Could we delay their quick proceeding, 'twere well. A reprieve is a good step towards the getting of a pardon.

Y. BELL. If we give over the game, we are undone. What think you of playing it on booty?

HAR. What do you mean?

Y. BELL. Pretend to be in love with one another; 'twill make some dilatory excuses we may feign pass the better.

HAR. Let us do't, if it be but for the dear pleasure of dissembling.

Y. BELL. Can you play your part?

HAR. I know not what it is to love, but I have made pretty remarks by being now and then where lovers meet. Where did you leave their gravities?

Y. BELL. I'th' next room. Your mother was censuring our modern gallant.

Enter OLD BELLAIR *and* LADY WOODVILL

HAR. Peace! here they come. I will lean against this wall and look bashfully down upon my fan, while you, like an amorous spark, modishly entertain me.

L. WOOD. Never go about to excuse 'em; come, come, it was not so when I was a young woman.

O. BELL. A dod, they're something disrespectful——

L. WOOD. Quality was then considered, and not rallied by every fleering fellow.

O. BELL. Youth will have its jest, a dod, it will.

L. WOOD. 'Tis good breeding now to be civil to none but players and Exchange women; they are treated by 'em as much above their condition as others are below theirs.

O. BELL. Out! a pise on 'em! talk no more. The rogues ha' got an ill habit of preferring beauty no matter where they find it.

L. WOOD. See your son and my daughter; they have improved their acquaintance since they were within.

O. BELL. A dod, methinks they have! Let's keep back and observe.

Y. BELL. Now for a look and gestures that may persuade 'em I am saying all the passionate things imaginable.

HAR. Your head a little more on one side. Ease yourself on your left leg and play with your right hand.

Y. BELL. Thus, is it not?

HAR. Now set your right leg firm on the ground, adjust your belt, then look about you.

Y. BELL. A little exercising will make me perfect.

HAR. Smile, and turn to me again very sparkish.

Y. BELL. Will you take your turn and be instructed?

HAR. With all my heart!

Y. BELL. At one motion play your fan, roll your eyes, and then settle a kind look upon me.

HAR. So!

Y. BELL. Now spread your fan, look down upon it, and tell the sticks with a finger.

HAR. Very modish!

Y. BELL. Clap your hand up to your bosom, hold down your gown. Shrug a little, draw up your breasts, and let 'em fall again gently, with a sigh or two, etc.

HAR. By the good instructions you give, I suspect you for one of those malicious observers who watch people's eyes, and from innocent looks make scandalous conclusions.

Y. BELL. I know some, indeed, who out of mere love to mischief are as vigilant as jealousy itself, and will give you an account of every glance that passes at a play and i'th' Circle.

HAR. 'Twill not be amiss now to seem a little pleasant.

Y. BELL. Clap your fan, then, in both your hands, snatch it to your mouth, smile, and with a lively motion fling your body a little forwards. So! Now spread it, fall back on the sudden, cover your face with it and break out into a loud laughter—take up, look grave, and fall a-fanning of yourself.—Admirably well acted!

HAR. I think I am pretty apt at these matters.

O. BELL. A dod, I like this well!

L. WOOD. This promises something.

O. BELL. Come! there is love i'th' case, a dod there is, or will be. What say you, young lady?

HAR. All in good time, Sir; you expect we should fall to and love as game-cocks fight, as soon as we are set together. A dod, y'are unreasonable!

O. BELL. A dod, Sirrah, I like thy wit well.

Enter a Servant

SERV. The coach is at the door, Madam.

O. BELL. Go, get you and take the air together.

L. WOOD. Will not you go with us?

O. BELL. Out! a pise! A dod, I ha' business and cannot. We shall meet at night at my sister Townley's.

Y. BELL. (*aside*) He's going to Emilia. I overheard him talk of a collation.   (*Exeunt.*)

SCENE II

Enter LADY TOWNLEY, EMILIA, *and* MR. MEDLEY

L. TOWN. I pity the young lovers we last talked of, though to say truth their conduct has been so indiscreet they deserve to be unfortunate.

MED. Y'have had an exact account, from the great lady i'th' box down to the little orange wench.

EMIL. Y'are a living libel, a breathing lampoon. I wonder you are not torn in pieces.

MED. What think you of setting up an office of intelligence for these matters? The project may get money.

L. TOWN. You would have great dealings with country ladies.

MED. More than Muddiman has with their husbands.

Enter BELLINDA

L. TOWN. Bellinda, what has become of you? We have not seen you here of late with your friend Mrs. Loveit.

BELL. Dear creature, I left her but now so sadly afflicted!

L. TOWN. With her old distemper, jealousy!

MED. Dorimant has played her some new prank.

BELL. Well, that Dorimant is certainly the worst man breathing.

EMIL. I once thought so.

BELL. And do you not think so still?

EMIL. No, indeed!

BELL. Oh, Jesu!

EMIL. The town does him a great deal of injury, and I will never believe what it says of a man I do not know, again, for his sake.

BELL. You make me wonder.

L. TOWN. He's a very well-bred man.

BELL. But strangely ill-natured.

EMIL. Then he's a very witty man.

BELL. But a man of no principles.

MED. Your man of principles is a very fine thing, indeed.

BELL. To be preferred to men of parts by women who have regard to their reputation and quiet. Well, were I minded to play the fool, he should be the last man I'd think of.

MED. He has been the first in many ladies' favours, though you are so severe, Madam.

L. TOWN. What he may be for a lover, I know not; but he's a very pleasant acquaintance, I am sure.

BELL. Had you seen him use Mrs. Loveit as I have done, you would never endure him more.

EMIL. What, he has quarreled with her again!

BELL. Upon the slightest occasion; he's jealous of Sir Fopling.

L. TOWN. She never saw him in her life but yesterday, and that was here.

EMIL. On my conscience, he's the only man in town that's her aversion! How horribly out of humour she was all the while he talked to her!

BELL. And somebody has wickedly told him——

EMIL. Here he comes.

Enter DORIMANT

MED. Dorimant! you are luckily come to justify yourself: here's a lady——

BELL. Has a word or two to say to you from a disconsolate person.

DOR. You tender your reputation too much, I know, Madam, to whisper with me before this good company.

BELL. To serve Mrs. Loveit I'll make a bold venture.

DOR. Here's Medley, the very spirit of scandal.

BELL. No matter!

EMIL. 'Tis something you are unwilling to hear, Mr. Dorimant.

L. TOWN. Tell him, Bellinda, whether he will or no.

BELL. (*aloud*) Mrs. Loveit——

DOR. Softly! these are laughers; you do not know 'em.

BELL. (*to* DORIMANT *apart*) In a word, y'ave made me hate you, which I thought you never could have done.

DOR. In obeying your commands.

BELL. 'Twas a cruel part you played. How could you act it?

DOR. Nothing is cruel to a man who could kill himself to please you. Remember five o'clock to-morrow morning!

BELL. I tremble when you name it.

DOR. Be sure you come!

BELL. I sha'not.

DOR. Swear you will!

BELL. I dare not.

DOR. Swear, I say!

BELL. By my life—by all the happiness I hope for——

DOR. You will.

BELL. I will!

DOR. Kind!

BELL. I am glad I've sworn. I vow I think I should ha' failed you else!

DOR. Surprisingly kind! In what temper did you leave Loveit?

BELL. Her raving was prettily over, and she began to be in a brave way of defying you and all your works. Where have you been since you went from thence?

DOR. I looked in at the play.

BELL. I have promised, and must return to her again.

DOR. Persuade her to walk in the Mail this evening.

BELL. She hates the place and will not come.

DOR. Do all you can to prevail with her.

BELL. For what purpose?

DOR. Sir Fopling will be here anon; I'll prepare him to set upon her there before me.

BELL. You persecute her too much, but I'll do all you'll ha' me.

DOR. (*aloud*) Tell her plainly 'tis grown so dull a business I can drudge on no longer.

EMIL. There are afflictions in love, Mr. Dorimant.

DOR. You women make 'em, who are commonly as unreasonable in that as you are at play—without the advantage be on your side, a man can never quietly give over when he's weary.

MED. If you would play without being obliged to complaisance, Dorimant, you should play in public places.

DOR. Ordinaries were a very good thing for that, but gentlemen do not of late frequent 'em. The deep play is now in private houses.

(BELLINDA offering to steal away)

L. TOWN. Bellinda, are you leaving us so soon?

BELL. I am to go to the Park with Mrs. Loveit, Madam.

(Exit BELLINDA.)

L. TOWN. This confidence will go nigh to spoil this young creature.

MED. 'Twill do her good, Madam. Young men who are brought up under practising lawyers prove the abler counsel when they come to be called to the bar themselves.

DOR. The town has been very favourable to you this afternoon, my Lady Townley; you use to have an *embarras* of chairs and coaches at your door, an uproar of footmen in your hall, and a noise of fools above here.

L. TOWN. Indeed, my house is the general rendezvous, and next to the playhouse is the common refuge of all the young idle people.

EMIL. Company is a very good thing, Madam, but I wonder you do not love it a little more chosen.

L. TOWN. 'Tis good to have an universal taste; we should love wit, but for variety be able to divert ourselves with the extravagancies of those who want it.

MED. Fools will make you laugh.

EMIL. For once or twice, but the repetition of their folly after a visit or two grows tedious and unsufferable.

L. TOWN. You are a little too delicate, Emilia.

Enter a Page

PAGE. Sir Fopling Flutter, Madam, desires to know if you are to be seen.

L. TOWN. Here's the freshest fool in town, and one who has not cloyed you yet.—— Page!

PAGE. Madam!

L. TOWN. Desire him to walk up.   *(Exit Page.)*

DOR. Do not you fall on him, Medley, and snub him. Soothe him up in his extravagance; he will show the better.

MED. You know I have a natural indulgence for fools and need not this caution, Sir.

Enter SIR FOPLING FLUTTER *with his Page after him*

SIR FOP. Page, wait without. (*Exit Page.*) (*to* LADY TOWNLEY) Madam, I kiss your hands. I see yesterday was nothing of chance; the *belles assemblées* form themselves here every day. (*to* EMILIA) Lady, your servant.—— Dorimant, let me embrace thee! Without lying, I have not met with any of my acquaintance who retain so much of Paris as thou dost—the very air thou hadst when the marquise mistook thee i'th' Tuileries and cried, "Hey, Chevalier!" and then begged thy pardon.

DOR. I would fain wear in fashion as long as I can, Sir; 'tis a thing to be valued in men as well as baubles.

SIR FOP. Thou art a man of wit and understands the town. Prithee, let thee and I be intimate; there is no living without making some good man the confidant of our pleasures.

DOR. 'Tis true! but there is no man so improper for such a business as I am.

SIR FOP. Prithee, why hast thou so modest an opinion of thyself?

DOR. Why, first, I could never keep a secret in my life; and then, there is no charm so infallibly makes me fall in love with a woman as my knowing a friend loves her. I deal honestly with you.

SIR FOP. Thy humour's very gallant, or let me perish! I knew a French count so like thee!

L. TOWN. Wit, I perceive, has more power over you than beauty, Sir Fopling, else you would not have let this lady stand so long neglected.

SIR FOP. (*to* EMILIA) A thousand pardons, Madam; some civility's due of course upon the meeting a long absent friend. The *éclat* of so much beauty, I confess, ought to have charmed me sooner.

EMIL. The *brillant* of so much good language, Sir, has much more power than the little beauty I can boast.

SIR FOP. I never saw anything prettier than this high work on your *point d'Espagne.*

EMIL. 'Tis not so rich as *point de Venise.*

SIR FOP. Not altogether, but looks cooler and is more proper for the season.—— Dorimant, is not that Medley?

DOR. The same, Sir.

SIR FOP. Forgive me, Sir; in this *embarras* of civilities I could not come to have you in my arms sooner. You understand an equipage the best of any man in town, I hear.

MED. By my own you would not guess it.

SIR FOP. There are critics who do not write, Sir.

MED. Our peevish poets will scarce allow it.

SIR FOP. Damn 'em, they'll allow no man wit who does not play the fool like themselves and show it! Have you taken notice of the gallesh I brought over?

MED. Oh, yes! 't has quite another air than th' English makes.

SIR FOP. 'Tis as easily known from an English tumbril as an Inns of Court man is from one of us.

DOR. Truly; there is a *bel air* in galleshes as well as men.

MED. But there are few so delicate to observe it.

SIR FOP. The world is generally very *grossier* here, indeed.

L. TOWN. He's very fine.

EMIL. Extreme proper.

SIR FOP. A slight suit I made to appear in at my first arrival— not worthy your consideration, ladies.

DOR. The pantaloon is very well mounted.

SIR FOP. The tassels are new and pretty.

MED. I never saw a coat better cut.

SIR FOP. It makes me show long-waisted, and, I think, slender.

DOR. That's the shape our ladies dote on.

MED. Your breech, though, is a handful too high, in my eye, Sir Fopling.

SIR FOP. Peace, Medley! I have wished it lower a thousand times, but a pox on't! 'twill not be.

L. TOWN. His gloves are well fringed, large and graceful.

SIR FOP. I was always eminent for being *bien ganté*.

EMIL. He wears nothing but what are originals of the most famous hands in Paris.

SIR FOP. You are in the right, Madam.

L. TOWN. The suit!

SIR FOP. Barroy.

EMIL. The garniture!

SIR FOP. Le Gras.

MED. The shoes!

SIR FOP. Piccar.

DOR. The periwig!

SIR FOP. Chedreux.

L. TOWN. ⎱
EMIL.   ⎰ The gloves!

SIR FOP. Orangerie—you know the smell, ladies.—— Dorimant, I could find in my heart for an amusement to have a gallantry with some of our English ladies.

DOR. 'Tis a thing no less necessary to confirm the reputation of your wit than a duel will be to satisfy the town of your courage.

SIR FOP. Here was a woman yesterday——

DOR. Mistress Loveit.

SIR FOP. You have named her.

DOR. You cannot pitch on a better for your purpose.

SIR FOP. Prithee, what is she?

DOR. A person of quality, and one who has a rest of reputation enough to make the conquest considerable; besides, I hear she likes you too.

SIR FOP. Methoughts she seemed, though, very reserved and uneasy all the time I entertained her.

DOR. Grimace and affectation! You will see her i' th' Mail to-night.

SIR FOP. Prithee, let thee and I take the air together.

DOR. I am engaged to Medley, but I'll meet you at St. James's and give you some information upon the which you may regulate your proceedings.

SIR FOP. All the world will be in the Park to-night. Ladies, 'twere pity to keep so much beauty longer within doors and rob the Ring of all those charms that should adorn it.—— Hey, Page!

Enter Page

See that all my people be ready.   *(Page goes out again.)*
—Dorimant, *au revoir.*   *(Exit.)*

MED. A fine mettled coxcomb.

DOR. Brisk and insipid.

MED. Pert and dull.

EMIL. However you despise him, gentlemen, I'll lay my life he passes for a wit with many.

DOR. That may very well be; Nature has her cheats, stums a brain, and puts sophisticate dulness often on the tasteless multitude for true wit and good humour. Medley, come!

MED. I must go a little way; I will meet you i'the Mail.

DOR. I'll walk through the garden thither.—(*to the women*) We shall meet anon and bow.

L. TOWN. Not to-night. We are engaged about a business the knowledge of which may make you laugh hereafter.

MED. Your servant, ladies.

DOR. *Au revoir*, as Sir Fopling says.

(*Exeunt* MEDLEY *and* DORIMANT.)

L. TOWN. The old man will be here immediately.

EMIL. Let's expect him i'th' garden.

L. TOWN. Go! you are a rogue.

EMIL. I can't abide you.   (*Exeunt.*)

SCENE III

SCENE: *The Mail.*

Enter HARRIET *and* YOUNG BELLAIR, *she pulling him*

HAR. Come along.

Y. BELL. And leave your mother!

HAR. Busy will be sent with a hue and cry after us, but that's no matter.

Y. BELL. 'Twill look strangely in me.

HAR. She'll believe it a freak of mine and never blame your manners.

Y. BELL. What reverend acquaintance is that she has met?

HAR. A fellow-beauty of the last king's time, though by the ruins you would hardly guess it.   (*Exeunt.*)

Enter DORIMANT *and crosses the stage*
Enter YOUNG BELLAIR *and* HARRIET

Y. BELL. By this time your mother is in a fine taking.

HAR. If your friend Mr. Dorimant were but here now, that she might find me talking with him!

Y. BELL. She does not know him, but dreads him, I hear, of all mankind.

HAR. She concludes if he does but speak to a woman, she's

undone—is on her knees every day to pray heaven defend me from him.

Y. BELL. You do not apprehend him so much as she does?

HAR. I never saw anything in him that was frightful.

Y. BELL. On the contrary, have you not observed something extreme delightful in his wit and person?

HAR. He's agreeable and pleasant, I must own, but he does so much affect being so, he displeases me.

Y. BELL. Lord, Madam! all he does and says is so easy and so natural.

HAR. Some men's verses seem so to the unskillful, but labour i'the one and affectation in the other to the judicious plainly appear.

Y. BELL. I never heard him accused of affectation before.

Enter DORIMANT *and stares upon her*

HAR. It passes on the easy town, who are favourably pleased in him to call it humour.   (*Exeunt* YOUNG BELLAIR *and* HARRIET.)

DOR. 'Tis she! it must be she—that lovely hair, that easy shape, those wanton eyes, and all those melting charms about her mouth which Medley spoke of! I'll follow the lottery and put in for a prize with my friend Bellair.   (*Exeunt* DORIMANT *repeating:*

> In love the victors from the vanquish'd fly;
> They fly that wound, and they pursue that die.)

Enter YOUNG BELLAIR *and* HARRIET *and after them* DORIMANT *standing at a distance*

Y. BELL. Most people prefer High Park to this place.

HAR. It has the better reputation, I confess; but I abominate the dull diversions there—the formal bows, the affected smiles, the silly by-words and amorous tweers in passing. Here one meets with a little conversation now and then.

Y. BELL. These conversations have been fatal to some of your sex, Madam.

HAR. It may be so; because some who want temper have been undone by gaming, must others who have it wholly deny themselves the pleasure of play?

DOR. (*coming up gently and bowing to her*) Trust me, it were unreasonable, Madam.

HAR. (*She starts and looks grave.*) Lord, who's this?

Y. BELL. Dorimant!

DOR. Is this the woman your father would have you marry?

Y. BELL. It is.

DOR. Her name?

Y. BELL. Harriet.

DOR. I am not mistaken; she's handsome.

Y. BELL. Talk to her; her wit is better than her face. We were wishing for you but now.

DOR. (*to* HARRIET) Overcast with seriousness o'the sudden! A thousand smiles were shining in that face but now; I never saw so quick a change of weather.

HAR. (*aside*) I feel as great a change within, but he shall never know it.

DOR. You were talking of play, Madam. Pray, what may be your stint?

HAR. A little harmless discourse in public walks, or at most an appointment in a box, barefaced, at the playhouse: you are for masks and private meetings, where women engage for all they are worth, I hear.

DOR. I have been used to deep play, but I can make one at small game when I like my gamester well.

HAR. And be so unconcerned you'll ha' no pleasure in't.

DOR. Where there is a considerable sum to be won, the hope of drawing people in makes every trifle considerable.

HAR. The sordidness of men's natures, I know, makes 'em willing to flatter and comply with the rich, though they are sure never to be the better for 'em.

DOR. 'Tis in their power to do us good, and we despair not but at some time or other they may be willing.

HAR. To men who have fared in this town like you, 'twould be a great mortification to live on hope. Could you keep a Lent for a mistress?

DOR. In expectation of a happy Easter and, though time be very precious, think forty days well lost to gain your favour.

HAR. Mr. Bellair, let us walk; 'tis time to leave him. Men grow dull when they begin to be particular.

DOR. Y'are mistaken; flattery will not ensue, though I know y'are greedy of the praises of the whole Mail.

HAR. You do me wrong.

DOR. I do not. As I followed you, I observed how you were pleased when the fops cried, "She's handsome, very handsome! by God she is!" and whispered aloud your name; the thousand several forms you put your face into; then, to make yourself more agreeable, how wantonly you played with your head, flung back your locks, and looked smilingly over your shoulder at 'em!

HAR. I do not go begging the men's, as you do the ladies', good liking, with a sly softness in your looks and a gentle slowness in your bows as you pass by 'em—as thus, Sir. (*acts him*) Is not this like you?

Enter LADY WOODVILL *and* BUSY

Y. BELL. Your mother, Madam.

                              (*pulls* HARRIET; *she composes herself*)

L. WOOD. Ah, my dear child Harriet!

BUSY. Now is she so pleased with finding her again she cannot chide her.

L. WOOD. Come away!

DOR. 'Tis now but high Mail, Madam, the most entertaining time of all the evening.

HAR. I would fain see that Dorimant, Mother, you so cry out of for a monster; he's in the Mail, I hear.

L. WOOD. Come away then! The plague is here and you should dread the infection.

Y. BELL. You may be misinformed of the gentleman.

L. WOOD. Oh, no! I hope you do not know him. He is the prince of all the devils in the town—delights in nothing but in rapes and riots!

DOR. If you did but hear him speak, Madam!

L. WOOD. Oh, he has a tongue, they say, would tempt the angels to a second fall.

Enter SIR FOPLING *with his equipage,*
six Footmen and a Page

SIR FOP. Hey! Champagne, Norman, La Rose, La Fleur, La Tour, La Verdure!—— Dorimant——

L. WOOD. Here, here he is among this rout! He names him! Come away, Harriet; come away!

                              (*Exeunt* LADY WOODVILL, HARRIET,
                                   BUSY, *and* YOUNG BELLAIR.)

DOR. This fool's coming has spoiled all. She's gone, but she has left a pleasing image of herself behind that wanders in my soul—it must not settle there.

SIR FOP. What reverie is this? Speak, man!

DOR. Snatcht from myself, how far behind
Already I behold the shore!

Enter MEDLEY

MED. Dorimant, a discovery! I met with Bellair.

DOR. You can tell me no news, Sir; I know all.

MED. How do you like the daughter?

DOR. You never came so near truth in your life as you did in her description.

MED. What think you of the mother?

DOR. Whatever I think of her, she thinks very well of me, I find.

MED. Did she know you?

DOR. She did not; whether she does now or no, I know not. Here was a pleasant scene towards, when in came Sir Fopling, mustering up his equipage, and at the latter end named me and frighted her away.

MED. Loveit and Bellinda are not far off; I saw 'em alight at St. James's.

DOR. Sir Fopling! Hark you, a word or two. (*whispers*) Look you do not want assurance.

SIR FOP. I never do on these occasions.

DOR. Walk on; we must not be seen together. Make your advantage of what I have told you. The next turn you will meet the lady.

SIR FOP. Hey! Follow me all!

(*Exeunt* SIR FOPLING *and his equipage.*)

DOR. Medley, you shall see good sport anon between Loveit and this Fopling.

MED. I thought there was something toward, by that whisper.

DOR. You know a worthy principle of hers?

MED. Not to be so much as civil to a man who speaks to her in the presence of him she professes to love.

DOR. I have encouraged Fopling to talk to her to-night.

MED. Now you are here, she will go nigh to beat him.

DOR. In the humour she's in, her love will make her do some very extravagant thing doubtless.

MED. What was Bellinda's business with you at my Lady Townley's?

DOR. To get me to meet Loveit here in order to an *éclaircissement*. I made some difficulty of it and have prepared this rencounter to make good my jealousy.

MED. Here they come.

Enter MRS. LOVEIT, BELLINDA, *and* PERT

DOR. I'll meet her and provoke her with a deal of dumb civility in passing by, then turn short and be behind her when Sir Fopling sets upon her——

> See how unregarded now
> That piece of beauty passes.

(*Exeunt* DORIMANT *and* MEDLEY.)

BELL. How wonderful respectfully he bowed!

PERT. He's always over-mannerly when he has done a mischief.

BELL. Methoughts, indeed, at the same time he had a strange, despising countenance.

PERT. The unlucky look he thinks becomes him.

BELL. I was afraid you would have spoke to him, my dear.

LOV. I would have died first; he shall no more find me the loving fool he has done.

BELL. You love him still?

LOV. No!

PERT. I wish you did not.

LOV. I do not, and I will have you think so.—What made you hale me to this odious place, Bellinda?

BELL. I hate to be hulched up in a coach; walking is much better.

LOV. Would we could meet Sir Fopling now!

BELL. Lord, would you not avoid him?

LOV. I would make him all the advances that may be.

BELL. That would confirm Dorimant's suspicion, my dear.

LOV. He is not jealous; but I will make him so, and be revenged a way he little thinks on.

BELL. (*aside*) If she should make him jealous, that may make him fond of her again. I must dissuade her from it.—— Lord, my dear, this will certainly make him hate you.

LOV. 'Twill make him uneasy, though he does not care for me. I know the effects of jealousy on men of his proud temper.

BELL. 'Tis a fantastic remedy; its operations are dangerous and uncertain.

LOV. 'Tis the strongest cordial we can give to dying love: it often brings it back when there's no sign of life remaining. But I design not so much the reviving of his, as my revenge.

Enter SIR FOPLING *and his equipage*

SIR FOP. Hey! Bid the coachman send home four of his horses and bring the coach to Whitehall; I'll walk over the Park.—— Madam, the honour of kissing your fair hands is a happiness I missed this afternoon at my Lady Townley's.

LOV. You were very obliging, Sir Fopling, the last time I saw you there.

SIR FOP. The preference was due to your wit and beauty.—— Madam, your servant; there never was so sweet an evening.

BELL. 'T has drawn all the rabble of the town hither.

SIR FOP. 'Tis pity there's not an order made that none but the *beau monde* should walk here.

LOV. 'Twould add much to the beauty of the place. See what a sort of nasty fellows are coming!

Enter four ill-fashioned fellows, singing:

'Tis not for kisses alone, etc.

LOV. Fo! Their periwigs are scented with tobacco so strong——

SIR FOP. It overcomes our pulvillio. Methinks I smell the coffee-house they come from.

1 MAN. Dorimant's convenient, Madam Loveit.

2 MAN. I like the oily buttock with her.

3 MAN. What spruce prig is that?

1 MAN. A caravan lately come from Paris.

2 MAN. Peace! they smoke.

(*All of them coughing; exeunt singing:*
There's something else to be done, etc.)

Enter DORIMANT *and* MEDLEY

DOR. They're engaged.

MED. She entertains him as if she liked him!

DOR. Let us go forward—seem earnest in discourse and show ourselves; then you shall see how she'll use him.

BELL. Yonder's Dorimant, my dear.

LOV. (*aside*) I see him. He comes insulting, but I will disappoint him in his expectation. (*to* SIR FOPLING) I like this pretty, nice humour of yours, Sir Fopling.—— With what a loathing eye he looked upon those fellows!

SIR FOP. I sat near one of 'em at a play to-day and was almost poisoned with a pair of cordovan gloves he wears.

LOV. Oh, filthy cordovan! How I hate the smell!

(*laughs in a loud, affected way*)

SIR FOP. Did you observe, Madam, how their cravats hung loose an inch from their neck and what a frightful air it gave 'em?

LOV. Oh, I took particular notice of one that is always spruced up with a deal of dirty sky-coloured ribband.

BELL. That's one of the walking flageolets who haunt the Mail o'nights.

LOV. Oh, I remember him; h'has a hollow tooth enough to spoil the sweetness of an evening.

SIR FOP. I have seen the tallest walk the streets with a dainty pair of boxes neatly buckled on.

LOV. And a little foot-boy at his heels, pocket-high, with a flat cap, a dirty face——

SIR FOP. And a snotty nose.

LOV. Oh, odious!—There's many of my own sex with that Holborn equipage trig to Gray's Inn Walks and now and then travel hither on a Sunday.

MED. She takes no notice of you.

DOR. Damn her! I am jealous of a counterplot.

LOV. Your liveries are the finest, Sir Fopling—oh, that page! that page is the prettily'st dressed—they are all Frenchmen.

SIR FOP. There's one damned English blockhead among 'em; you may know him by his mien.

LOV. Oh, that's he—that's he! What do you call him?

SIR FOP. Hey—I know not what to call him——

LOV. What's your name?

FOOTM. John Trott, Madam.

SIR FOP. Oh, unsufferable! Trott, Trott, Trott! There's nothing
so barbarous as the names of our English servants.—— What
countryman are you, Sirrah?

FOOTM. Hampshire, Sir.

SIR FOP. Then Hampshire be your name. Hey, Hampshire!

LOV. Oh, that sound—that sound becomes the mouth of a
man of quality!

MED. Dorimant, you look a little bashful on the matter.

DOR. She dissembles better than I thought she could have
done.

MED. You have tempted her with too luscious a bait. She bites
at the coxcomb.

DOR. She cannot fall from loving me to that.

MED. You begin to be jealous in earnest.

DOR. Of one I do not love——

MED. You did love her.

DOR. The fit has long been over.

MED. But I have known men fàll into dangerous relapses
when they have found a woman inclining to another.

DOR. (*to himself*) He guesses the secret of my heart. I am
concerned, but dare not show it, lest Bellinda should mistrust
all I have done to gain her.

BELL. (*aside*) I have watched his look and find no alteration
there. Did he love her, some signs of jealousy would have appeared.

DOR. I hope this happy evening, Madam, has reconciled you
to the scandalous Mail. We shall have you now hankering here
again——

LOV. Sir Fopling, will you walk?

SIR FOP. I am all obedience, Madam.

LOV. Come along then, and let's agree to be malicious on all
the ill-fashioned things we meet.

SIR FOP. We'll make a critique on the whole Mail, Madam.

LOV. Bellinda, you shall engage——

BELL. To the reserve of our friends, my dear.

LOV. No! no exceptions!

SIR FOP. We'll sacrifice all to our diversion.

LOV. All—all.

SIR FOP. All.

BELL. All? Then let it be.

> (*Exeunt* SIR FOPLING, MRS. LOVEIT, BELLINDA,
> *and* PERT, *laughing.*)

MED. Would you had brought some more of your friends, Dorimant, to have been witnesses of Sir Fopling's disgrace and your triumph.

DOR. 'Twere unreasonable to desire you not to laugh at me; but pray do not expose me to the town this day or two.

MED. By that time you hope to have regained your credit.

DOR. I know she hates Fopling and only makes use of him in hope to work me on again; had it not been for some powerful considerations which will be removed to-morrow morning, I had made her pluck off this mask and show the passion that lies panting under.

Enter a Footman

MED. Here comes a man from Bellair with news of your last adventure.

DOR. I am glad he sent him; I long to know the consequence of our parting.

FOOTM. Sir, my master desires you to come to my Lady Townley's presently and bring Mr. Medley with you. My Lady Woodvill and her daughter are there.

MED. Then all's well, Dorimant.

FOOTM. They have sent for the fiddles and mean to dance. He bid me tell you, Sir, the old lady does not know you, and would have you own yourself to be Mr. Courtage. They are all prepared to receive you by that name.

DOR. That foppish admirer of quality, who flatters the very meat at honourable tables and never offers love to a woman below a lady-grandmother.

MED. You know the character you are to act, I see.

DOR. This is Harriet's contrivance—wild, witty, lovesome, beautiful, and young!—— Come along, Medley.

MED. This new woman would well supply the loss of Loveit.

DOR. That business must not end so; before to-morrow sun is set I will revenge and clear it.

And you and Loveit, to her cost, shall find,
I fathom all the depths of womankind.   (*Exeunt.*)

ACT IV

SCENE I

The Scene opens with the Fiddles playing a Country Dance.

Enter DORIMANT *and* LADY WOODVILL, YOUNG BELLAIR *and*
MRS. HARRIET, OLD BELLAIR *and* EMILIA, MR. MEDLEY
and LADY TOWNLEY, *as having just ended the Dance*

O. BELL. So, so, so!—a smart bout, a very smart bout, a dod!

L. TOWN. How do you like Emilia's dancing, Brother?

O. BELL. Not at all—not at all!

L. TOWN. You speak not what you think, I am sure.

O. BELL. No matter for that; go, bid her dance no more. It
don't become her—it don't become her. Tell her I say so. (*aside*)
A dod, I love her!

DOR. (*to* LADY WOODVILL) All people mingle nowadays,
Madam. And in public places women of quality have the least
respect showed 'em.

L. WOOD. I protest you say the truth, Mr. Courtage.

DOR. Forms and ceremonies, the only things that uphold quality and greatness, are now shamefully laid aside and neglected.

L. WOOD. Well, this is not the women's age, let 'em think what
they will. Lewdness is the business now; love was the business
in my time.

DOR. The women, indeed, are little beholding to the young
men of this age; they're generally only dull admirers of themselves, and make their court to nothing but their periwigs and
their cravats, and would be more concerned for the disordering
of 'em, though on a good occasion, than a young maid would
be for the tumbling of her head or handkercher.

L. WOOD. I protest you hit 'em.

DOR. They are very assiduous to show themselves at court,
well dressed, to the women of quality, but their business is with
the stale mistresses of the town, who are prepared to receive
their lazy addresses by industrious old lovers who have cast 'em
off and made 'em easy.

HAR. He fits my mother's humour so well, a little more and she'll dance a kissing dance with him anon.

MED. Dutifully observed, Madam.

DOR. They pretend to be great critics in beauty. By their talk you would think they liked no face, and yet can dote on an ill one if it belong to a laundress or a tailor's daughter. They cry, "A woman's past her prime at twenty, decayed at four-and-twenty, old and unsufferable at thirty."

L. WOOD. Unsufferable at thirty! That they are in the wrong, Mr. Courtage, at five-and-thirty, there are living proofs enough to convince 'em.

DOR. Ay, Madam. There's Mrs. Setlooks, Mrs. Droplip, and my Lady Lowd; show me among all our opening buds a face that promises so much beauty as the remains of theirs.

L. WOOD. The depraved appetite of this vicious age tastes nothing but green fruit, and loathes it when 'tis kindly ripened.

DOR. Else so many deserving women, Madam, would not be so untimely neglected.

L. WOOD. I protest, Mr. Courtage, a dozen such good men as you would be enough to atone for that wicked Dorimant and all the under debauchees of the town. (HARRIET, EMILIA, YOUNG BELLAIR, MEDLEY, LADY TOWNLEY *break out into a laughter.*)—— What's the matter there?

MED. A pleasant mistake, Madam, that a lady has made, occasions a little laughter.

O. BELL. Come, come, you keep 'em idle! They are impatient till the fiddles play again.

DOR. You are not weary, Madam?

L. WOOD. One dance more; I cannot refuse you, Mr. Courtage.

(*They dance. After the dance,* OLD BELLAIR, *singing and dancing up to* EMILIA.)

EMILIA. You are very active, Sir.

O. BELL. A dod, Sirrah! when I was a young fellow I could ha' capered up to my woman's gorget.

DOR. You are willing to rest yourself, Madam——

L. TOWN. We'll walk into my chamber and sit down.

MED. Leave us Mr. Courtage; he's a dancer, and the young ladies are not weary yet.

L. WOOD. We'll send him out again.

HAR. If you do not quickly, I know where to send for Mr. Dorimant.

L. WOOD. This girl's head, Mr. Courtage, is ever running on that wild fellow.

DOR. 'Tis well you have got her a good husband, Madam; that will settle it.

(*Exeunt* LADY TOWNLEY, LADY WOODVILL, *and* DORIMANT.)

O. BELL. (*to* EMILIA) A dod, sweetheart, be advised and do not throw thyself away on a young, idle fellow.

EMIL. I have no such intention, Sir.

O. BELL. Have a little patience! Thou shalt have the man I spake of. A dod, he loves thee and will make a good husband— but no words!

EMIL. But, Sir——

O. BELL. No answer—out a pise! peace! and think on't.

Enter DORIMANT

DOR. Your company is desired within, Sir.

O. BELL. I go, I go! Good Mr. Courtage, fare you well!—(*to* EMILIA) Go, I'll see you no more!

EMIL. What have I done, Sir?

O. BELL. You are ugly, you are ugly!—Is she not, Mr. Courtage?

EMIL. Better words or I shan't abide you.

O. BELL. Out a pise; a dod, what does she say? Hit her a pat for me there.   (*Exit* OLD BELLAIR.)

MED. You have charms for the whole family.

DOR. You'll spoil all with some unseasonable jest, Medley.

MED. You see I confine my tongue and am content to be a bare spectator, much contrary to my nature.

EMIL. Methinks, Mr. Dorimant, my Lady Woodvill is a little fond of you.

DOR. Would her daughter were!

MED. It may be you may find her so. Try her—you have an opportunity.

DOR. And I will not lose it.—— Bellair, here's a lady has something to say to you.

Y. BELL. I wait upon her.—— Mr. Medley, we have both business with you.

DOR. Get you all together then. (*to* HARRIET) That demure

curtsey is not amiss in jest, but do not think in earnest it becomes you.

HAR. Affectation is catching, I find; from your grave bow I got it.

DOR. Where had you all that scorn and coldness in your look?

HAR. From nature, Sir; pardon my want of art. I have not learnt those softnesses and languishings which now in faces are so much in fashion.

DOR. You need 'em not; you have a sweetness of your own, if you would but calm your frowns and let it settle.

HAR. My eyes are wild and wandering like my passions, and cannot yet be tied to rules of charming.

DOR. Women, indeed, have commonly a method of managing those messengers of love. Now they will look as if they would kill, and anon they will look as if they were dying. They point and rebate their glances, the better to invite us.

HAR. I like this variety well enough, but hate the set face that always looks as it would say, "Come love me!"—a woman who at plays makes the *doux yeux* to a whole audience and at home cannot forbear 'em to her monkey.

DOR. Put on a gentle smile and let me see how well it will become you.

HAR. I am sorry my face does not please you as it is, but I shall not be complaisant and change it.

DOR. Though you are obstinate, I know 'tis capable of improvement, and shall do you justice, Madam, if I chance to be at Court when the critics of the Circle pass their judgment; for thither you must come.

HAR. And expect to be taken in pieces, have all my features examined, every motion censured, and on the whole be condemned to be but pretty, or a beauty of the lowest rate. What think you?

DOR. The women—nay, the very lovers who belong to the drawing-room—will maliciously allow you more than that: they always grant what is apparent, that they may the better be believed when they name concealed faults they cannot easily be disproved in.

HAR. Beauty runs as great a risk exposed at Court as wit does on the stage, where the ugly and the foolish all are free to censure.

DOR. (*aside*) I love her and dare not let her know it; I fear sh'as an ascendant o'er me and may revenge the wrongs I have done her sex. (*to her*) Think of making a party, Madam; love will engage.

HAR. You make me start! I did not think to have heard of love from you.

DOR. I never knew what 'twas to have a settled ague yet, but now and then have had irregular fits.

HAR. Take heed! sickness after long health is commonly more violent and dangerous.

DOR. (*aside*) I have took the infection from her, and feel the disease now spreading in me. (*to her*) Is the name of love so frightful that you dare not stand it?

HAR. 'Twill do little execution out of your mouth on me, I am sure.

DOR. It has been fatal——

HAR. To some easy women, but we are not all born to one destiny. I was informed you use to laugh at love and not make it.

DOR. The time has been, but now I must speak——

HAR. If it be on that idle subject, I will put on my serious look, turn my head carelessly from you, drop my lip, let my eyelids fall and hang half o'er my eyes—thus—while you buzz a speech of an hour long in my ear, and I answer never a word. Why do you not begin?

DOR. That the company may take notice how passionately I make advances of love, and how disdainfully you receive 'em!

HAR. When your love's grown strong enough to make you bear being laughed at, I'll give you leave to trouble me with it. Till when pray forbear, Sir.

Enter SIR FOPLING *and others in masks*

DOR. What's here—masquerades?

HAR. I thought that foppery had been left off, and people might have been in private with a fiddle.

DOR. 'Tis endeavoured to be kept on foot still by some who find themselves the more acceptable the less they are known.

Y. BELL. This must be Sir Fopling.

MED. That extraordinary habit shows it.

Y. BELL. What are the rest?

MED. A company of French rascals whom he picked up in

Paris and has brought over to be his dancing equipage on these occasions. Make him own himself; a fool is very troublesome when he presumes he is incognito.

SIR FOP. (*to* HARRIET) Do you know me?

HAR. Ten to one but I guess at you?

SIR FOP. Are you women as fond of a vizard as we men are?

HAR. I am very fond of a vizard that covers a face I do not like, Sir.

Y, BELL. Here are no masks, you see, Sir, but those which came with you. This was intended a private meeting; but because you look like a gentleman, if you will discover yourself and we know you to be such, you shall be welcome.

SIR FOP. (*pulling off his mask*) Dear Bellair!

MED. Sir Fopling! How came you hither?

SIR FOP. Faith, as I was coming late from Whitehall, after the King's *couchée*, one of my people told me he had heard fiddles at my Lady Townley's, and——

DOR. You need not say any more, Sir.

SIR FOP. Dorimant, let me kiss thee.

DOR. Hark you, Sir Fopling——   (*whispers*)

SIR FOP. Enough, enough, Courtage.—— A pretty kind of young woman that, Medley. I observed her in the Mail—more *éveillée* than our English women commonly are. Prithee, what is she?

MED. The most noted coquette in town. Beware of her.

SIR FOP. Let her be what she will, I know how to take my measures. In Paris the mode is to flatter the *prude*, laugh at the *faux-prude*, make serious love to the *demi-prude*, and only rally with the *coquette*. Medley, what think you?

MED. That for all this smattering of the mathematics, you may be out in your judgment at tennis.

SIR FOP. What a *coq-à-l'âne* is this? I talk of women and thou answer'st tennis.

MED. Mistakes will be for want of apprehension.

SIR FOP. I am very glad of the acquaintance I have with this family.

MED. My lady truly is a good woman.

SIR FOP. Ah, Dorimant—Courtage, I would say—would thou hadst spent the last winter in Paris with me! When thou wert there, La Corneus and Sallyes were the only habitudes we had:

a comedian would have been a *bonne fortune*. No stranger ever
passed his time so well as I did some months before I came
over. I was well received in a dozen families where all the
women of quality used to visit; I have intrigues to tell thee more
pleasant than ever thou read'st in a novel.

HAR. Write 'em Sir, and oblige us women. Our language wants
such little stories.

SIR FOP. Writing, Madam, 's a mechanic part of wit. A gentleman should never go beyond a song or a *billet*.

HAR. Bussy was a gentleman.

SIR FOP. Who, d'Ambois?

MED. Was there ever such a brisk blockhead?

HAR. Not d'Ambois, Sir, but Rabutin—he who writ the loves
of France.

SIR FOP. That may be, Madam; many gentlemen do things
that are below 'em. Damn your authors, Courtage; women are
the prettiest things we can fool away our time with.

HAR. I hope ye have wearied yourself to-night at Court, Sir,
and will not think of fooling with anybody here.

SIR FOP. I cannot complain of my fortune there, Madam.——
Dorimant——

DOR. Again!

SIR FOP. Courtage—a pox on't!—I have something to tell
thee. When I had made my court within, I came out and flung
myself upon the mat under the state i'th' outward room, i'th'
midst of half a dozen beauties who were withdrawn to jeer
among themselves, as they called it.

DOR. Did you know 'em?

SIR FOP. Not one of 'em, by heavens!—not I. But they were
all your friends.

DOR. How are you sure of that?

SIR FOP. Why, we laughed at all the town—spared nobody but
yourself. They found me a man for their purpose.

DOR. I know you are malicious, to your power.

SIR FOP. And faith, I had occasion to show it, for I never saw
more gaping fools at a ball or on a birthday.

DOR. You learned who the women were?

SIR FOP. No matter; they frequent the drawing-room.

DOR. And entertain themselves pleasantly at the expense of all
the fops who come there.

SIR FOP. That's their business. Faith, I sifted 'em, and find they have a sort of wit among them.—— Ah, filthy!

(*pinches a tallow candle*)

DOR. Look, he has been pinching the tallow candle.

SIR FOP. How can you breathe in a room where there's grease frying?—— Dorimant, thou art intimate with my lady; advise her, for her own sake and the good company that comes hither, to burn wax lights.

HAR. What are these masquerades who stand so obsequiously at a distance?

SIR FOP. A set of balladines whom I picked out of the best in France and brought over with a *flûte-douce* or two—my servants. They shall entertain you.

HAR. I had rather see you dance yourself, Sir Fopling.

SIR FOP. And I had rather do it—all the company knows it—but, Madam——

MED. Come, come, no excuses, Sir Fopling!

SIR FOP. By heavens, Medley——

MED. Like a woman I find you must be struggled with before one brings you to what you desire.

HAR. (*aside*) Can he dance?

EMIL. And fence and sing too, if you'll believe him.

DOR. He has no more excellence in his heels than in his head. He went to Paris a plain, bashful English blockhead, and is returned a fine undertaking French fop.

MED. I cannot prevail.

SIR FOP. Do not think it want of complaisance, Madam.

HAR. You are too well bred to want that, Sir Fopling. I believe it want of power.

SIR FOP. By heavens, and so it is! I have sat up so damned late and drunk so cursed hard since I came to this lewd town, that I am fit for nothing but low dancing now—a *courante*, a *bourrée*, or a *menuet*. But St. André tells me, if I will but be regular, in one month I shall rise again. Pox on this debauchery!

(*endeavours at a caper*)

EMIL. I have heard your dancing much commended.

SIR FOP. It had the good fortune to please in Paris. I was judged to rise within an inch as high as the Basque in an entry I danced there.

HAR. I am mightily taken with this fool; let us sit.—— Here's a seat, Sir Fopling.

SIR FOP. At your feet, Madam; I can be nowhere so much at ease.—— By your leave, gown.

HAR.
EMIL. } Ah, you'll spoil it!

SIR FOP. No matter; my clothes are my creatures. I make 'em to make my court to you ladies.—— Hey! *Qu'on commence!* (*dance*)—— To an English dancer, English motions. I was forced to entertain this fellow, one of my set miscarrying.—— Oh, horrid! Leave your damned manner of dancing and put on the French air: have you not a pattern before you?—— Pretty well! imitation in time may bring him to something.

After the dance, enter OLD BELLAIR, LADY WOODVILL, *and* LADY TOWNLEY

O. BELL. Hey, a dod, what have we here—a mumming?

L. WOOD. Where's my daughter? Harriet!

DOR. Here, here, Madam! I know not but under these disguises there may be dangerous sparks; I gave the young lady warning.

L. WOOD. Lord! I am so obliged to you, Mr. Courtage.

HAR. Lord, how you admire this man!

L. WOOD. What have you to except against him?

HAR. He's a fop.

L. WOOD. He's not a Dorimant, a wild extravagant fellow of the times.

HAR. He's a man made up of forms and commonplaces sucked out of the remaining lees of the last age.

L. WOOD. He's so good a man that, were you not engaged——

L. TOWN. You'll have but little night to sleep in.

L. WOOD. Lord, 'tis perfect day.

DOR. (*aside*) The hour is almost come I appointed Bellinda, and I am not so foppishly in love here to forget. I am flesh and blood yet.

L. TOWN. I am very sensible, Madam.

L. WOOD. Lord, Madam!

HAR. Look! in what a struggle is my poor mother yonder!

Y. BELL. She has much ado to bring out the compliment.

DOR. She strains hard for it.

HAR. See, see! her head tottering, her eyes staring, and her under lip trembling——

DOR. Now—now she's in the very convulsions of her civility. (*aside*) 'Sdeath, I shall lose Bellinda! I must fright her hence; she'll be an hour in this fit of good manners else. (*to* LADY WOODVILL) Do you not know Sir Fopling, Madam?

L. WOOD. I have seen that face—oh, heaven! 'tis the same we met in the Mail. How came he here?

DOR. A fiddle, in this town, is a kind of fop-call; no sooner it strikes up but the house is besieged with an army of masquerades straight.

L. WOOD. Lord! I tremble, Mr. Courtage. For certain, Dorimant is in the company.

DOR. I cannot confidently say he is not. You had best be gone. I will wait upon you; your daughter is in the hands of Mr. Bellair.

L. WOOD. I'll see her before me.—— Harriet, come away.

Y. BELL. Lights! lights!

L. TOWN. Light, down there!

O. BELL. A dod, it needs not——

DOR. Call my Lady Woodvill's coach to the door quickly.

(*Exeunt* YOUNG BELLAIR, HARRIET, LADY TOWNLEY,
DORIMANT, *and* LADY WOODVILL.)

O. BELL. Stay, Mr. Medley: let the young fellows do that duty; we will drink a glass of wine together. 'Tis good after dancing. What mumming spark is that?

MED. He is not to be comprehended in few words.

SIR FOP. Hey, La Tour!

MED. Whither away, Sir Fopling?

SIR FOP. I have business with Courtage.

MED. He'll but put the ladies into their coach and come up again.

O. BELL. In the meantime I'll call for a bottle.

(*Exit* OLD BELLAIR.)

Enter YOUNG BELLAIR

MED. Where's Dorimant?

Y. BELL. Stolen home. He has had business waiting for him there all this night, I believe, by an impatience I observed in him.

MED. Very likely; 'tis but dissembling drunkenness, railing at his friends, and the kind soul will embrace the blessing and forget the tedious expectation.

SIR FOP. I must speak with him before I sleep.

Y. BELL. Emilia and I are resolved on that business.

MED. Peace! here's your father.

Enter OLD BELLAIR *and Butler with a bottle of wine*

O. BELL. The women are all gone to bed.—— Fill, boy!—— Mr. Medley, begin a health.

MED. (*whispers*) To Emilia!

O. BELL. Out a pise! she's a rogue, and I'll not pledge you.

MED. I know you will.

O. BELL. A dod, drink it, then!

SIR FOP. Let us have the new bacchic.

O. BELL. A dod, that is a hard word. What does it mean, Sir?

MED. A catch or drinking-song.

O. BELL. Let us have it then.

SIR FOP. Fill the glasses round and draw up in a body.—— Hey, music!   (*They sing.*)

The pleasures of love and the joys of good wine
To perfect our happiness wisely we join.
We to beauty all day
Give the sovereign sway
And her favourite nymphs devoutly obey.
At the plays we are constantly making our court,
And when they are ended we follow the sport
To the Mall and the Park,
Where we love till 'tis dark;
Then sparkling champagne
Puts an end to their reign;
It quickly recovers
Poor languishing lovers;
Makes us frolic and gay, and drowns all our sorrow.
But alas! we relapse again on the morrow.
    Let every man stand
    With his glass in his hand,
And briskly discharge at the word of command:
    Here's a health to all those
    Whom to-night we depose!
Wine and beauty by turns great souls should inspire;
Present all together! and now, boys, give fire!

o. BELL. A dod, a pretty business and very merry!

SIR FOP. Hark you, Medley, let you and I take the fiddles and go waken Dorimant.

MED. We shall do him a courtesy, if it be as I guess. For after the fatigue of this night he'll quickly have his belly full and be glad of an occasion to cry, "Take away, Handy!"

Y. BELL. I'll go with you, and there we'll consult about affairs, Medley.

o. BELL. (*looks on his watch*) A dod, 'tis six o'clock!

SIR FOP. Let's away, then.

o. BELL. Mr. Medley, my sister tells me you are an honest man—and a dod, I love you. Few words and hearty—that's the way with old Harry, old Harry.

SIR FOP. Light your flambeaux. Hey!

o. BELL. What does the man mean?

MED. 'Tis day, Sir Fopling.

SIR FOP. No matter; our serenade will look the greater.

(*Exeunt omnes.*)

SCENE II

SCENE: DORIMANT'S *lodging. A table, a candle, a toilet, etc.* HANDY, *tying up linen.*

Enter DORIMANT *in his gown, and* BELLINDA

DOR. Why will you be gone so soon?

BELL. Why did you stay out so late?

DOR. Call a chair, Handy.—— What makes you tremble so?

BELL. I have a thousand fears about me. Have I not been seen, think you?

DOR. By nobody but myself and trusty Handy.

BELL. Where are all your people?

DOR. I have dispersed 'em on sleeveless errands. What does that sigh mean?

BELL. Can you be so unkind to ask me? Well—(*sighs*)—were it to do again——

DOR. We should do it, should we not?

BELL. I think we should—the wickeder man you to make me love so well. Will you be discreet now?

DOR. I will.

BELL. You cannot.

DOR. Never doubt it.

BELL. I will not expect it.

DOR. You do me wrong.

BELL. You have no more power to keep the secret than I had not to trust you with it.

DOR. By all the joys I have had and those you keep in store——

BELL. You'll do for my sake what you never did before.

DOR. By that truth thou hast spoken, a wife shall sooner betray herself to her husband.

BELL. Yet I had rather you should be false in this than in another thing you promised me.

DOR. What's that?

BELL. That you would never see Loveit more but in public places—in the Park, at Court and plays.

DOR. 'Tis not likely a man should be fond of seeing a damned old play when there is a new one acted.

BELL. I dare not trust your promise.

DOR. You may——

BELL. This does not satisfy me. You shall swear you never will see her more.

DOR. I will, a thousand oaths. By all——

BELL. Hold! You shall not, now I think on't better.

DOR. I will swear!

BELL. I shall grow jealous of the oath and think I owe your truth to that, not to your love.

DOR. Then, by my love; no other oath I'll swear.

Enter HANDY

HAND. Here's a chair.

BELL. Let me go.

DOR. I cannot.

BELL. Too willingly, I fear.

DOR. Too unkindly feared. When will you promise me again?

BELL. Not this fortnight.

DOR. You will be better than your word.

BELL. I think I shall. Will it not make you love me less? (*starting*) Hark! what fiddles are these?   (*fiddles without*)

DOR. Look out, Handy.   (*Exit* HANDY *and returns.*)

HAND. Mr. Medley, Mr. Bellair, and Sir Fopling; they are coming up.

DOR. How got they in?

HAND. The door was open for the chair.

BELL. Lord, let me fly!

DOR. Here, here, down the back stairs! I'll see you into your chair.

BELL. No, no! Stay and receive 'em. And be sure you keep your word and never see Loveit more. Let it be a proof of your kindness.

DOR. It shall.—— Handy, direct her. (*kissing her hand*) Everlasting love go along with thee. (*Exeunt* BELLINDA *and* HANDY.)

Enter YOUNG BELLAIR, MEDLEY, *and* SIR FOPLING

Y. BELL. Not abed yet?

MED. You have had an irregular fit, Dorimant.

DOR. I have.

Y. BELL. And is it off already?

DOR. Nature has done her part, gentlemen; when she falls kindly to work, great cures are effected in little time, you know.

SIR FOP. We thought there was a wench in the case, by the chair that waited. Prithee, make us a *confidence*.

DOR. Excuse me.

SIR FOP. *Le sage* Dorimant! Was she pretty?

DOR. So pretty she may come to keep her coach and pay parish duties if the good humour of the age continue.

MED. And be of the number of the ladies kept by public-spirited men for the good of the whole town.

SIR FOP. (*dancing by himself*) Well said, Medley.

Y. BELL. See Sir Fopling dancing!

DOR. You are practising and have a mind to recover, I see.

SIR FOP. Prithee, Dorimant, why hast not thou a glass hung up here? A room is the dullest thing without one.

Y. BELL. Here is company to entertain you.

SIR FOP. But I mean in case of being alone. In a glass a man may entertain himself——

DOR. The shadow of himself, indeed.

SIR FOP. Correct the errors of his motions and his dress.

MED. I find, Sir Fopling, in your solitude you remember the saying of the wise man, and study yourself.

SIR FOP. 'Tis the best diversion in our retirements. Dorimant, thou art a pretty fellow and wear'st thy clothes well, but I never saw thee have a handsome cravat. Were they made up like mine, they'd give another air to thy face. Prithee, let me send my man to dress thee but one day; by heavens, an Englishman cannot tie a ribbon.

DOR. They are something clumsy fisted——

SIR FOP. I have brought over the prettiest fellow that ever spread a toilet. He served some time under Merille, the greatest *genie* in the world for a *valet-de-chambre*.

DOR. What! he who formerly belonged to the Duke of Candale?

SIR FOP. The same, and got him his immortal reputation.

DOR. Y'have a very fine brandenburgh on, Sir Fopling.

SIR FOP. It serves to wrap me up after the fatigue of a ball.

MED. I see you often in it, with your periwig tied up.

SIR FOP. We should not always be in a set dress; 'tis more *en cavalier* to appear now and then in a *deshabillé*.

MED. Pray, how goes your business with Loveit?

SIR FOP. You might have answered yourself in the Mail last night. Dorimant, did you not see the advances she made me? I have been endeavouring at a song.

DOR. Already!

SIR FOP. 'Tis my *coup d'essai* in English: I would fain have thy opinion of it.

DOR. Let's see it.

SIR FOP. Hey, page, give me my song.—— Bellair, here; thou hast a pretty voice—sing it.

Y. BELL. Sing it yourself, Sir Fopling.

SIR FOP. Excuse me.

Y. BELL. You learnt to sing in Paris.

SIR FOP. I did—of Lambert, the greatest master in the world. But I have his own fault, a weak voice, and care not to sing out of a *ruelle*.

DOR. (*aside*) A *ruelle* is a pretty cage for a singing fop, indeed.

Y. BELL. (*reads the song.*)

> How charming Phillis is, how fair!
>   Ah, that she were as willing
> To ease my wounded heart of care,
>   And make her eyes less killing.
> I sigh, I sigh, I languish now,

> And love will not let me rest;
> I drive about the Park and bow,
> Still as I meet my dearest.

SIR FOP. Sing it! sing it, man; it goes to a pretty new tune which I am confident was made by Baptiste.

MED. Sing it yourself, Sir Fopling; he does not know the tune.

SIR FOP. I'll venture.   (SIR FOPLING *sings*.)

DOR. Ay, marry! now 'tis something. I shall not flatter you, Sir Fopling; there is not much thought in't, but 'tis passionate and well turned.

MED. After the French way.

SIR FOP. That I aimed at. Does it not give you a lively image of the thing? Slap! down goes the glass, and thus we are at it.

DOR. It does, indeed, I perceive, Sir Fopling. You'll be the very head of the sparks who are lucky in compositions of this nature.

Enter SIR FOPLING's *Footman*

SIR FOP. La Tour, is the bath ready?

FOOTM. Yes, Sir.

SIR FOP. *Adieu donc, mes chers.*   (*Exit* SIR FOPLING.)

MED. When have you your revenge on Loveit, Dorimant?

DOR. I will but change my linen and about it.

MED. The powerful considerations which hindered have been removed then?

DOR. Most luckily this morning. You must along with me; my reputation lies at stake there.

MED. I am engaged to Bellair.

DOR. What's your business?

MED. Ma-tri-mony, an't like you.

DOR. It does not, Sir.

Y. BELL. It may in time, Dorimant: what think you of Mrs. Harriet?

DOR. What does she think of me?

Y. BELL. I am confident she loves you.

DOR. How does it appear?

Y. BELL. Why, she's never well but when she's talking of you— but then, she finds all the faults in you she can. She laughs at all who commend you—but then, she speaks ill of all who do not.

DOR. Women of her temper betray themselves by their over-cunning. I had once a growing love with a lady who would always quarrel with me when I came to see her, and yet was never quiet if I stayed a day from her.

Y. BELL. My father is in love with Emilia.

DOR. That is a good warrant for your proceedings. Go on and prosper; I must to Loveit. Medley, I am sorry you cannot be a witness.

MED. Make her meet Sir Fopling again in the same place and use him ill before me.

DOR. That may be brought about, I think. I'll be at your aunt's anon and give you joy, Mr. Bellair.

Y. BELL. You had not best think of Mrs. Harriet too much; without church security there's no taking up there.

DOR. I may fall into the snare too. But——

The wise will find a difference in our fate;
You wed a woman, I a good estate.   (*Exeunt.*)

SCENE III

Enter the chair with BELLINDA; *the men set it down
and open it.* BELLINDA *starting*

BELL. (*surprised*) Lord, where am I?—in the Mall! Whither have you brought me?

I CHAIRM. You gave us no directions, Madam.

BELL. (*aside*) The fright I was in made me forget it.

I CHAIRM. We use to carry a lady from the Squire's hither.

BELL. (*aside*) This is Loveit: I am undone if she sees me.—Quickly, carry me away!

I CHAIRM. Whither, an't like your honour?

BELL. Ask no questions——

Enter MRS. LOVEIT's *Footman*

FOOTM. Have you seen my lady, Madam?

BELL. I am just come to wait upon her.

FOOTM. She will be glad to see you, Madam. She sent me to you this morning to desire your company, and I was told you went out by five o'clock.

BELL. (*aside*) More and more unlucky!

FOOTM. Will you walk in, Madam?

BELL. I'll discharge my chair and follow. Tell your mistress I am here. (*Exit Footman.*) (*Gives the Chairmen money.*) Take this, and if ever you should be examined, be sure you say you took me up in the Strand over against the Exchange, as you will answer it to Mr. Dorimant.

CHAIRM. We will, an't like your honour. (*Exeunt Chairmen.*)

BELL. Now to come off, I must on——
In confidence and lies some hope is left;
'Twere hard to be found out in the first theft. (*Exit.*)

ACT V

SCENE I

Enter MRS. LOVEIT *and* PERT, *her woman*

PERT. Well! in my eyes Sir Fopling is no such despicable person.

LOV. You are an excellent judge!

PERT. He's as handsome a man as Mr. Dorimant, and as great a gallant.

LOV. Intolerable! Is't not enough I submit to his impertinences, but must I be plagued with yours too?

PERT. Indeed, Madam——

LOV. 'Tis false, mercenary malice——

Enter her Footman

FOOTM. Mrs. Bellinda, Madam.

LOV. What of her?

FOOTM. She's below.

LOV. How came she?

FOOTM. In a chair; Ambling Harry brought her.

LOV. He bring her! His chair stands near Dorimant's door and always brings me from thence.—— Run and ask him where he took her up. (*Exit Footman.*) Go! there is no truth in friendship neither. Women, as well as men, all are false——or all are so to me, at least.

PERT. You are jealous of her too?

LOV. You had best tell her I am. 'Twill become the liberty you take of late. This fellow's bringing of her, her going out by five o'clock—I know not what to think.

Enter BELLINDA

Bellinda, you are grown an early riser, I hear.

BELL. Do you not wonder, my dear, what made me abroad so soon?

LOV. You do not use to be so.

BELL. The country gentlewomen I told you of (Lord, they have the oddest diversions!) would never let me rest till I promised to go with them to the markets this morning to eat fruit and buy nosegays.

LOV. Are they so fond of a filthy nosegay?

BELL. They complain of the stinks of the town, and are never well but when they have their noses in one.

LOV. There are essences and sweet waters.

BELL. Oh, they cry out upon perfumes, they are unwholesome; one of 'em was falling into a fit with the smell of these *nerolii*.

LOV. Methinks in complaisance you should have had a nosegay too.

BELL. Do you think, my dear, I could be so loathsome to trick myself up with carnations and stock-gillyflowers? I begged their pardon and told them I never wore anything but orange flowers and tuberose. That which made me willing to go was a strange desire I had to eat some fresh nectarines.

LOV. And had you any?

BELL. The best I ever tasted.

LOV. Whence came you now?

BELL. From their lodgings, where I crowded out of a coach and took a chair to come and see you, my dear.

LOV. Whither did you send for that chair?

BELL. 'Twas going by empty.

LOV. Where do these country gentlewomen lodge, I pray?

BELL. In the Strand over against the Exchange.

PERT. That place is never without a nest of 'em. They are always, as one goes by, fleering in balconies or staring out of windows.

Enter Footman

LOV. (*to the Footman*) Come hither! (*whispers*)

BELL. (*aside*) This fellow by her order has been questioning the chairmen. I threatened 'em with the name of Dorimant; if they should have told truth, I am lost forever.

LOV. In the Strand, said you?

FOOTM. Yes, Madam; over against the Exchange.

(*Exit Footman.*)

LOV. (*aside*) She's innocent, and I am much to blame.

BELL. (*aside*) I am so frighted, my countenance will betray me.

LOV. Bellinda, what makes you look so pale?

BELL. Want of my usual rest and jolting up and down so long in an odious hackney.

Footman returns

FOOTM. Madam, Mr. Dorimant.

LOV. What makes him here?

BELL. (*aside*) Then I am betrayed, indeed. He's broke his word, and I love a man that does not care for me!

LOV. Lord, you faint, Bellinda!

BELL. I think I shall—such an oppression here on the sudden.

PERT. She has eaten too much fruit, I warrant you.

LOV. Not unlikely.

PERT. 'Tis that lies heavy on her stomach.

LOV. Have her into my chamber, give her some surfeit water, and let her lie down a little.

PERT. Come, Madam! I was a strange devourer of fruit when I was young—so ravenous——

(*Exeunt* BELLINDA, *and* PERT, *leading her off.*)

LOV. Oh, that my love would be but calm awhile, that I might receive this man with all the scorn and indignation he deserves!

Enter DORIMANT

DOR. Now for a touch of Sir Fopling to begin with. Hey, page, give positive order that none of my people stir. Let the *canaille* wait as they should do. Since noise and nonsense have such powerful charms,

I, that I may successful prove,
Transform myself to what you love.

LOV. If that would do, you need not change from what you are: you can be vain and loud enough.

DOR. But not with so good a grace as Sir Fopling. Hey, Hampshire! Oh, that sound, that sound becomes the mouth of a man of quality!

LOV. Is there a thing so hateful as a senseless mimic?

DOR. He's a great grievance indeed to all who, like yourself, Madam, love to play the fool in quiet.

LOV. A ridiculous animal, who has more of the ape than the ape has of the man in him!

DOR. I have as mean an opinion of a sheer mimic as yourself; yet were he all ape, I should prefer him to the gay, the giddy, brisk, insipid noisy fool you dote on.

LOV. Those noisy fools, however you despise 'em, have good qualities which weigh more (or ought at least) with us women than all the pernicious wit you have to boast of.

DOR. That I may hereafter have a just value for their merit, pray do me the favour to name 'em.

LOV. You'll despise 'em as the dull effects of ignorance and vanity; yet I care not if I mention some. First, they really admire us, while you at best but flatter us well.

DOR. Take heed! Fools can dissemble too.

LOV. They may, but not so artificially as you. There is no fear they should deceive us. Then, they are assiduous, Sir; they are ever offering us their service, and always waiting on our will.

DOR. You owe that to their excessive idleness. They know not how to entertain themselves at home, and find so little welcome abroad they are fain to fly to you who countenance 'em, as a refuge against the solitude they would be otherwise condemned to.

LOV. Their conversation, too, diverts us better.

DOR. Playing with your fan, smelling to your gloves, commending your hair, and taking notice how 'tis cut and shaded after the new way——

LOV. Were it sillier than you can make it, you must allow 'tis pleasanter to laugh at others than to be laughed at ourselves, though never so wittily. Then, though they want skill to flatter us, they flatter themselves so well they save us the labour. We need not take that care and pains to satisfy 'em of our love, which we so often lose on you.

DOR. They commonly, indeed, believe too well of themselves, and always better of you than you deserve.

LOV. You are in the right. They have an implicit faith in us which keeps 'em from prying narrowly into our secrets and saves us the vexatious trouble of clearing doubts which your subtle and causeless jealousies every moment raise.

DOR. There is an inbred falsehood in women which inclines 'em still to them whom they may most easily deceive.

LOV. The man who loves above his quality does not suffer more from the insolent impertinence of his mistress than the woman who loves above her understanding does from the arrogant presumptions of her friend.

DOR. You mistake the use of fools; they are designed for properties, and not for friends. You have an indifferent stock of reputation left yet. Lose it all like a frank gamester on the square; 'twill then be time enough to turn rook and cheat it up again on a good, substantial bubble.

LOV. The old and the ill-favoured are only fit for properties, indeed, but young and handsome fools have met with kinder fortunes.

DOR. They have, to the shame of your sex be it spoken! 'Twas this, the thought of this, made me by a timely jealousy endeavour to prevent the good fortune you are providing for Sir Fopling. But against a woman's frailty all our care is vain.

LOV. Had I not with a dear experience bought the knowledge of your falsehood, you might have fooled me yet. This is not the first jealousy you have feigned, to make a quarrel with me and get a week to throw away on some such unknown, inconsiderable slut as you have been lately lurking with at plays.

DOR. Women, when they would break off with a man, never want th' address to turn the fault on him.

LOV. You take a pride of late in using of me ill, that the town may know the power you have over me, which now (as unreasonably as yourself) expects that I (do me all the injuries you can) must love you still.

DOR. I am so far from expecting that you should, I begin to think you never did love me.

LOV. Would the memory of it were so wholly worn out in me, that I did doubt it too! What made you come to disturb my growing quiet?

DOR. To give you joy of your growing infamy.

LOV. Insupportable! Insulting devil!—this from you, the only

author of my shame! This from another had been but justice,
but from you 'tis a hellish and inhumane outrage. What have I
done?

DOR. A thing that puts you below my scorn, and makes my
anger as ridiculous as you have made my love.

LOV. I walked last night with Sir Fopling.

DOR. You did, Madam, and you talked and laughed aloud,
"Ha, ha, ha!"—Oh, that laugh! that laugh becomes the confidence of a woman of quality.

LOV. You who have more pleasure in the ruin of a
woman's reputation than in the endearments of her love, reproach me not with yourself—and I defy you to name the man
can lay a blemish on my fame.

DOR. To be seen publicly so transported with the vain follies
of that notorious fop, to me is an infamy below the sin of prostitution with another man.

LOV. Rail on! I am satisfied in the justice of what I did; you had
provoked me to't.

DOR. What I did was the effect of a passion whose extravagancies you have been willing to forgive.

LOV. And what I did was the effect of a passion you may
forgive if you think fit.

DOR. Are you so indifferent grown?

LOV. I am.

DOR. Nay, then 'tis time to part. I'll send you back your letters
you have so often asked for. I have two or three of 'em about me.

LOV. Give 'em me.

DOR. You snatch as if you thought I would not. There! and may
the perjuries in 'em be mine if e'er I see you more!

(offers to go; she catches him)

LOV. Stay!

DOR. I will not.

LOV. You shall.

DOR. What have you to say?

LOV. I cannot speak it yet.

DOR. Something more in commendation of the fool.——Death,.
I want patience; let me go!

LOV. I cannot. (aside) I can sooner part with the limbs that
hold him.—— I hate that nauseous fool; you know I do.

DOR. Was it the scandal you were fond of then?

LOV. Y'had raised my anger equal to my love—a thing you ne'er could do before, and in revenge I did—I know not what I did. Would you would not think on't any more!

DOR. Should I be willing to forget it, I shall be daily minded of it; 'twill be a commonplace for all the town to laugh at me, and Medley, when he is rhetorically drunk, will ever be declaiming on it in my ears.

LOV. 'Twill be believed a jealous spite. Come, forget it.

DOR. Let me consult my reputation; you are too careless of it. (*pauses*) You shall meet Sir Fopling in the Mail again to-night.

LOV. What mean you?

DOR. I have thought on it, and you must. 'Tis necessary to justify my love to the world. You can handle a coxcomb as he deserves when you are not out of humour, Madam.

LOV. Public satisfaction for the wrong I have done you! This is some new device to make me more ridiculous.

DOR. Hear me!

LOV. I will not.

DOR. You will be persuaded.

LOV. Never!

DOR. Are you so obstinate?

LOV. Are you so base?

DOR. You will not satisfy my love?

LOV. I would die to satisfy that; but I will not, to save you from a thousand racks, do a shameless thing to please your vanity.

DOR. Farewell, false woman!

LOV. Do! go!

DOR. You will call me back again.

LOV. Exquisite fiend, I knew you came but to torment me!

Enter BELLINDA *and* PERT

DOR. (*surprised*) Bellinda here!

BELL. (*aside*) He starts and looks pale! The sight of me has touched his guilty soul.

PERT. 'Twas but a qualm, as I said—a little indigestion; the surfeit water did it, Madam, mixed with a little mirabilis.

DOR. (*aside*) I am confounded, and cannot guess how she came hither!

LOV. 'Tis your fortune, Bellinda, ever to be here when I am abused by this prodigy of ill-nature.

BELL. I am amazed to find him here. How has he the face to come near you?

DOR. (*aside*) Here is fine work towards! I never was at such a loss before.

BELL. One who makes a public profession of breach of faith and ingratitude—I loathe the sight of him.

DOR. (*aside*) There is no remedy; I must submit to their tongues now, and some other time bring myself off as well as I can.

BELL. Other men are wicked, but then, they have some sense of shame. He is never well but when he triumphs—nay, glories to a woman's face in his villainies.

LOV. You are in the right, Bellinda, but methinks your kindness for me makes you concern yourself too much with him.

BELL. It does indeed, my dear. His barbarous carriage to you yesterday made me hope you ne'er would see him more, and the very next day to find him here again, provokes me strangely. But because I know you love him, I have done.

DOR. You have reproached me handsomely, and I deserve it for coming hither; but——

PERT. You must expect it, Sir. All women will hate you for my lady's sake.

DOR. (*aside to* BELLINDA) Nay, if she begins too, 'tis time to fly; I shall be scolded to death else.—— I am to blame in some circumstances, I confess; but as to the main, I am not so guilty as you imagine. I shall seek a more convenient time to clear myself.

LOV. Do it now. What impediments are here?

DOR. I want time, and you want temper.

LOV. These are weak pretences.

DOR. You were never more mistaken in your life; and so farewell.   (DORIMANT *flings off.*)

LOV. Call a footman, Pert, quickly; I will have him dogged.

PERT. I wish you would not, for my quiet and your own.

LOV. I'll find out the infamous cause of all our quarrels, pluck her mask off, and expose her barefaced to the world!

(*Exit* PERT.)

BELL. (*aside*) Let me but escape this time, I'll never venture more.

LOV. Bellinda, you shall go with me.

BELL. I have such a heaviness hangs on me with what I did this morning, I would fain go home and sleep, my dear.

LOV. Death and eternal darkness! I shall never sleep again. Raging fevers seize the world and make mankind as restless all as I am!   (*Exit* MRS. LOVEIT.)

BELL. I knew him false and helped to make him so. Was not her ruin enough to fright me from the danger? It should have been, but love can take no warning.   (*Exit* BELLINDA.)

SCENE II

SCENE: LADY TOWNLEY'S *house*

Enter MEDLEY, YOUNG BELLAIR, LADY TOWNLEY, EMILIA, *and Chaplain.*

MED. Bear up, Bellair, and do not let us see that repentance in thine we daily do in married faces.

L. TOWN. This wedding will strangely surprise my brother when he knows it.

MED. Your nephew ought to conceal it for a time, Madam; since marriage has lost its good name, prudent men seldom expose their own reputations till 'tis convenient to justify their wives.

O. BELL. (*without*) Where are you all there? Out, a dod! will nobody hear?

L. TOWN. My brother! Quickly, Mr. Smirk, into this closet! you must not be seen yet.   (SMIRK *goes into the closet.*)

Enter OLD BELLAIR *and* LADY TOWNLEY'S *Page*

O. BELL. Desire Mr. Fourbe to walk into the lower parlour; I will be with him presently. (*to* YOUNG BELLAIR) Where have you been, Sir, you could not wait on me to-day?

Y. BELL. About a business.

O. BELL. Are you so good at business? A dod, I have a business, too, you shall dispatch out of hand, Sir.—— Send for a parson, Sister; my Lady Woodvill and her daughter are coming.

L. TOWN. What need you huddle up things thus?

O. BELL. Out a pise! youth is apt to play the fool, and 'tis not good it should be in their power.

L. TOWN. You need not fear your son.

O. BELL. He's been idling this morning, and a dod, I do not like him. (*to* EMILIA) How dost thou do, sweetheart?

EMIL. You are very severe, Sir—married in such haste.

O. BELL. Go to, thou'rt a rogue, and I will talk with thee anon. Here's my Lady Woodvill come.

Enter LADY WOODVILL, HARRIET, *and* BUSY

Welcome, Madam; Mr. Fourbe's below with the writings.

L. WOOD. Let us down and make an end then.

O. BELL. Sister, show the way. (*to* YOUNG BELLAIR, *who is talking to* HARRIET) Harry, your business lies not there yet.—— Excuse him till we have done, lady, and then, a dod, he shall be for thee. Mr. Medley, we must trouble you to be a witness.

MED. I luckily came for that purpose, Sir.

(*Exeunt* OLD BELLAIR, MEDLEY, YOUNG BELLAIR,
LADY TOWNLEY, *and* LADY WOODVILL.)

BUSY. What will you do, Madam?

HAR. Be carried back and mewed up in the country again— run away here—anything rather than be married to a man I do not care for! Dear Emilia, do thou advise me.

EMIL. Mr. Bellair is engaged, you know.

HAR. I do, but know not what the fear of losing an estate may fright him to.

EMIL. In the desperate condition you are in, you should consult with some judicious man. What think you of Mr. Dorimant?

HAR. I do not think of him at all.

BUSY. (*aside*) She thinks of nothing else, I am sure.

EMIL. How fond your mother was of Mr. Courtage!

HAR. Because I contrived the mistake to make a little mirth, you believe I like the man.

EMIL. Mr. Bellair believes you love him.

HAR. Men are seldom in the right when they guess at a woman's mind. Would she whom he loves loved him no better!

BUSY. (*aside*) That's e'en well enough, on all conscience.

EMIL. Mr. Dorimant has a great deal of wit.

HAR. And takes a great deal of pains to show it.

EMIL. He's extremely well fashioned.

HAR. Affectedly grave, or ridiculously wild and apish.

BUSY. You defend him still against your mother!

HAR. I would not were he justly rallied, but I cannot hear anyone undeservedly railed at.

EMIL. Has your woman learnt the song you were so taken with?

HAR. I was fond of a new thing; 'tis dull at second hearing.

EMIL. Mr. Dorimant made it.

BUSY. She knows it, Madam, and has made me sing it at least a dozen times this morning.

HAR. Thy tongue is as impertinent as thy fingers.

EMIL. You have provoked her.

BUSY. 'Tis but singing the song and I shall appease her.

EMIL. Prithee, do.

HAR. She has a voice will grate your ears worse than a cat-call, and dresses so ill she's scarce fit to trick up a yeoman's daughter on a holiday.   (BUSY *sings*.)

SONG

BY SIR C. S.

As Amoret with Phillis sat,
    One evening on the plain,
And saw the charming Strephon wait
    To tell the nymph his pain;

The threat'ning danger to remove,
    She whisper'd in her ear,
"Ah, Phillis, if you would not love,
    This shepherd do not hear!

"None ever had so strange an art,
    His passion to convey
Into a list'ning virgin's heart,
    And steal her soul away.

"Fly, fly betimes, for fear you give
    Occasion for your fate."
"In vain," said she; "in vain I strive!
    Alas, 'tis now too late."

Enter DORIMANT

DOR. Music so softens and disarms the mind——

HAR. That not one arrow does resistance find.

DOR. Let us make use of the lucky minute, then.

HAR. (*aside, turning from* DORIMANT) My love springs with my blood into my face; I dare not look upon him yet.

DOR. What have we here? the picture of celebrated beauty giving audience in public to a declared lover?

HAR. Play the dying fop and make the piece complete, Sir.

DOR. What think you if the hint were well improved—the whole mystery of making love pleasantly designed and wrought in a suit of hangings?

HAR. 'Twere needless to execute fools in effigy who suffer daily in their own persons.

DOR. (*to* EMILIA, *aside*) Mrs. Bride, for such I know this happy day has made you——

EMIL. (*aside*) Defer the formal joy you are to give me, and mind your business with her. (*aloud*) Here are dreadful preparations, Mr. Dorimant—writings, sealing, and a parson sent for.

DOR. To marry this lady——

BUSY. Condemned she is, and what will become of her I know not, without you generously engage in a rescue.

DOR. In this sad condition, Madam, I can do no less than offer you my service.

HAR. The obligation is not great; you are the common sanctuary for all young women who run from their relations.

DOR. I have always my arms open to receive the distressed. But I will open my heart and receive you, where none yet did ever enter. You have filled it with a secret, might I but let you know it——

HAR. Do not speak it if you would have me believe it; your tongue is so famed for falsehood, 'twill do the truth an injury.
                                        (*turns away her head*)

DOR. Turn not away, then, but look on me and guess it.

HAR. Did you not tell me there was no credit to be given to faces? that women nowadays have their passions as much at will as they have their complexions, and put on joy and sadness, scorn and kindness, with the same ease they do their paint and patches? Are they the only counterfeits?

DOR. You wrong your own while you suspect my eyes. By all the hope I have in you, the inimitable colour in your cheeks is not more free from art than are the sighs I offer.

HAR. In men who have been long hardened in sin we have reason to mistrust the first signs of repentance.

DOR. The prospect of such a heaven will make me persevere and give you marks that are infallible.

HAR. What are those?

DOR. I will renounce all the joys I have in friendship and in wine, sacrifice to you all the interest I have in other women——

HAR. Hold! Though I wish you devout, I would not have you turn fanatic. Could you neglect these a while and make a journey into the country?

DOR. To be with you, I could live there and never send one thought to London.

HAR. Whate'er you say, I know all beyond High Park's a desert to you, and that no gallantry can draw you farther.

DOR. That has been the utmost limit of my love; but now my passion knows no bounds, and there's no measure to be taken of what I'll do for you from anything I ever did before.

HAR. When I hear you talk thus in Hampshire I shall begin to think there may be some truth enlarged upon.

DOR. Is this all? Will you not promise me——

HAR. I hate to promise; what we do then is expected from us and wants much of the welcome it finds when it surprises.

DOR. May I not hope?

HAR. That depends on you and not on me, and 'tis to no purpose to forbid it.   (*turns to* BUSY)

BUSY. Faith, Madam, now I perceive the gentleman loves you too, e'en let him know your mind, and torment yourselves no longer.

HAR. Dost think I have no sense of modesty?

BUSY. Think, if you lose this you may never have another opportunity.

HAR. May he hate me (a curse that frights me when I speak it), if ever I do a thing against the rules of decency and honour.

DOR. (*to* EMILIA) I am beholding to you for your good intentions, Madam.

EMIL. I thought the concealing of our marriage from her might have done you better service.

DOR. Try her again.

EMIL. What have you resolved, Madam? The time draws near.

HAR. To be obstinate and protest against this marriage.

Enter LADY TOWNLEY *in haste*

L. TOWN. (*to* EMILIA) Quickly, quickly! let Mr. Smirk out of the closet.   (SMIRK *come out of the closet.*)

HAR. A parson! Had you laid him in here?

DOR. I knew nothing of him.

HAR. Should it appear you did, your opinion of my easiness may cost you dear.

Enter OLD BELLAIR, YOUNG BELLAIR, MEDLEY,
and LADY WOODVILL

O. BELL. Out a pise! the canonical hour is almost past. Sister, is the man of God come?

L. TOWN. He waits your leisure.

O. BELL. By your favour, Sir.—— A dod, a pretty spruce fellow. What may we call him?

L. TOWN. Mr. Smirk—my Lady Biggot's chaplain.

O. BELL. A wise woman! a dod, she is. The man will serve for the flesh as well as the spirit. Please you, Sir, to commission a young couple to go to bed together a God's name?—— Harry!

Y. BELL. Here, Sir.

O. BELL. Out a pise! Without your mistress in your hand!

SMIRK. Is this the gentleman?

O. BELL. Yes, Sir.

SMIRK. Are you not mistaken, Sir?

O. BELL. A dod, I think not, Sir.

SMIRK. Sure, you are, Sir!

O. BELL. You look as if you would forbid the banns, Mr. Smirk. I hope you have no pretension to the lady.

SMIRK. Wish him joy, Sir; I have done him the good office to-day already.

O. BELL. Out a pise! What do I hear?

L. TOWN. Never storm, Brother; the truth is out.

O. BELL. How say you, Sir? Is this your wedding day?

Y. BELL. It is, Sir.

O. BELL. And a dod, it shall be mine too. (*to* EMILIA) Give me thy hand, sweetheart. What dost thou mean? Give me thy hand, I say.   (EMILIA *kneels and* YOUNG BELLAIR.)

L. TOWN. Come, come! give her your blessing; this is the woman your son loved and is married to.

O. BELL. Ha! cheated! cozened! and by your contrivance, Sister!

L. TOWN. What would you do with her? She's a rogue and you can't abide her.

MED. Shall I hit her a pat for you, Sir?

O. BELL. A dod, you are all rogues, and I never will forgive you.

L. TOWN. Whither? Whither away?

MED. Let him go and cool awhile.

L. WOOD. (*to* DORIMANT) Here's a business broke out now, Mr. Courtage; I am made a fine fool of.

DOR. You see the old gentleman knew nothing of it.

L. WOOD. I find he did not. I shall have some trick put upon me if I stay in this wicked town any longer.—— Harriet, dear child, where art thou? I'll into the country straight.

O. BELL. A dod, Madam, you shall hear me first.

Enter MRS. LOVEIT *and* BELLINDA

LOV. Hither my man dogged him.

BELL. Yonder he stands, my dear.

LOV. I see him (*aside*) and with him the face that has undone me. Oh, that I were but where I might throw out the anguish of my heart! Here it must rage within and break it.

L. TOWN. Mrs. Loveit! Are you afraid to come forward?

LOV. I was amazed to see so much company here in a morning. The occasion sure is extraordinary.

DOR. (*aside*) Loveit and Bellinda! The devil owes me a shame to-day and I think never will have done paying it.

LOV. Married! dear Emilia! How am I transported with the news!

HAR. (*to* DORIMANT) I little thought Emilia was the woman Mr. Bellair was in love with. I'll chide her for not trusting me with the secret.

DOR. How do you like Mrs. Loveit?

HAR. She's a famed mistress of yours, I hear.

DOR. She has been, on occasion.

O. BELL. (*to* LADY WOODVILL) A dod, Madam, I cannot help it.

L. WOOD. You need make no more apologies, Sir.

EMIL. (*to* MRS. LOVEIT) The old gentleman's excusing himself to my Lady Woodvill.

LOV. Ha, ha, ha! I never heard of anything so pleasant!

HAR. (*to* DORIMANT) She's extremely overjoyed at something.

DOR. At nothing. She is one of those hoyting ladies who gaily fling themselves about and force a laugh when their aching hearts are full of discontent and malice.

LOV. O heaven! I was never so near killing myself with laughing.—— Mr. Dorimant, are you a brideman?

L. WOOD. Mr. Dorimant!—Is this Mr. Dorimant, Madam?

LOV. If you doubt it, your daughter can resolve you, I suppose.

L. WOOD. I am cheated too—basely cheated!

O. BELL. Out a pise! what's here? More knavery yet?

L. WOOD. Harriet, on my blessing come away, I charge you!

HAR. Dear Mother, do but stay and hear me.

L. WOOD. I am betrayed and thou art undone, I fear.

HAR. Do not fear it; I have not, nor never will, do anything against my duty—believe me, dear Mother, do!

DOR. (*to* MRS. LOVEIT) I had trusted you with this secret but that I knew the violence of your nature would ruin my fortune, as now unluckily it has. I thank you, Madam.

LOV. She's an heiress, I know, and very rich.

DOR. To satisfy you, I must give up my interest wholly to my love. Had you been a reasonable woman, I might have secured 'em both and been happy.

LOV. You might have trusted me with anything of this kind— you know you might. Why did you go under a wrong name?

DOR. The story is too long to tell you now. Be satisfied, this is the business; this is the mask has kept me from you.

BELL. (*aside*) He's tender of my honour though he's cruel to my love.

LOV. Was it no idle mistress, then?

DOR. Believe me, a wife to repair the ruins of my estate, that needs it.

LOV. The knowledge of this makes my grief hang lighter on my soul, but I shall never more be happy.

DOR. Bellinda!

BELL. Do not think of clearing yourself with me; it is impossible. Do all men break their words thus?

DOR. Th'extravagant words they speak in love. 'Tis as unreasonable to expect we should perform all we promise then, as do all we threaten when we are angry. When I see you next——

BELL. Take no notice of me, and I shall not hate you.

DOR. How came you to Mrs. Loveit?

BELL. By a mistake the chairmen made for want of my giving them directions.

DOR. 'Twas a pleasant one. We must meet again.

BELL. Never.

DOR. Never!

BELL. When we do, may I be as infamous as you are false.

L. TOWN. Men of Mr. Dorimant's character always suffer in the general opinion of the world.

MED. You can make no judgment of a witty man from common fame, considering the prevailing faction, Madam.

O. BELL. A dod, he's in the right.

MED. Besides, 'tis a common error among women to believe too well of them they know, and too ill of them they don't.

O. BELL. A dod, he observes well.

L. TOWN. Believe me, Madam, you will find Mr. Dorimant as civil a gentleman as you thought Mr. Courtage.

HAR. If you would but know him better——

L. WOOD. You have a mind to know him better! Come away! You shall never see him more.

HAR. Dear Mother, stay!

L. WOOD. I wo'not be consenting to your ruin.

HAR. Were my fortune in your power——

L. WOOD. Your person is.

HAR. Could I be disobedient, I might take it out of yours and put it into his.

L. WOOD. 'Tis that you would be at; you would marry this Dorimant.

HAR. I cannot deny it; I would, and never will marry any other man.

L. WOOD. Is this the duty that you promised?

HAR. But I will never marry him against your will.

L. WOOD. (*aside*) She knows the way to melt my heart.—(*to* HARRIET) Upon yourself light your undoing!

MED. (*to* OLD BELLAIR) Come, Sir, you have not the heart any longer to refuse your blessing.

O. BELL. A dod, I ha' not.—— Rise, and God bless you both! Make much of her, Harry; she deserves thy kindness. (*to* EMILIA) A dod, Sirrah, I did not think it had been in thee.

Enter SIR FOPLING *and's Page*

SIR FOP. 'Tis a damned windy day.—— Hey, page, is my periwig right?

PAGE. A little out of order, Sir.

SIR FOP. Pox o' this apartment! It wants an antechamber to adjust oneself in. (*to* MRS. LOVEIT) Madam, I came from your house, and your servants directed me hither.

LOV. I will give order hereafter they shall direct you better.

SIR FOP. The great satisfaction I had in the Mail last night has given me much disquiet since.

LOV. 'Tis likely to give me more than I desire.

SIR FOP. (*aside*) What the devil makes her so reserved?—— Am I guilty of an indiscretion, Madam?

LOV. You will be of a great one if you continue your mistake, Sir.

SIR FOP. Something puts you out of humour.

LOV. The most foolish, inconsiderable thing that ever did.

SIR FOP. Is it in my power?

LOV. To hang or drown it. Do one of 'em and trouble me no more.

SIR FOP. So *fière? Serviteur*, Madam!—— Medley, where's Dorimant?

MED. Methinks the lady has not made you those advances to-day she did last night, Sir Fopling.

SIR FOP. Prithee, do not talk of her!

MED. She would be a *bonne fortune*.

SIR FOP. Not to me at present.

MED. How so?

SIR FOP. An intrigue now would be but a temptation to me to throw away that vigour on one which I mean shall shortly make my court to the whole sex in a ballet.

MED. Wisely considered, Sir Fopling.

SIR FOP. No one woman is worth the loss of a cut in a caper.

MED. Not when 'tis so universally designed.

L. WOOD. Mr. Dorimant, everyone has spoke so much in your behalf that I can no longer doubt but I was in the wrong.

LOV. There's nothing but falsehood and impertinence in this world; all men are villains or fools. Take example from my misfortunes. Bellinda, if thou wouldst be happy, give thyself wholly up to goodness.

HAR. (*to* MRS. LOVEIT) Mr. Dorimant has been your God Almighty long enough; 'tis time to think of another.

LOV. Jeered by her! I will lock myself up in my house and never see the world again.

HAR. A nunnery is the more fashionable place for such a retreat, and has been the fatal consequence of many a *belle passion*.

LOV. (*aside*) Hold, heart, till I get home! Should I answer, 'twould make her triumph greater.   (*is going out*)

DOR. Your hand, Sir Fopling——

SIR FOP. Shall I wait upon you, Madam?

LOV. Legion of fools, as many devils take thee!

                                        (*Exit* MRS. LOVEIT.)

MED. Dorimant, I pronounce thy reputation clear; and henceforward when I would know anything of woman, I will consult no other oracle.

SIR FOP. Stark mad, by all that's handsome!—— Dorimant, thou hast engaged me in a pretty business.

DOR. I have not leisure now to talk about it.

O. BELL. Out a pise! what does this man of mode do here again?

L. TOWN. He'll be an excellent entertainment within, Brother, and is luckily come to raise the mirth of the company.

L. WOOD. Madam, I take my leave of you.

L. TOWN. What do you mean, Madam?

L. WOOD. To go this afternoon part of my way to Hartly.

O. BELL. A dod, you shall stay and dine first! Come, we will all be good friends, and you shall give Mr. Dorimant leave to wait upon you and your daughter in the country.

L. WOOD. If his occasions bring him that way, I have now so good an opinion of him, he shall be welcome.

HAR. To a great rambling, lone house that looks as it were not inhabited, the family's so small. There you'll find my mother, an old lame aunt, and myself, Sir, perched up on chairs at a distance in a large parlour, sitting moping like three or four melancholy birds in a spacious volary. Does not this stagger your resolution?

DOR. Not at all, Madam. The first time I saw you you left me with the pangs of love upon me, and this day my soul has quite given up her liberty.

HAR. This is more dismal than the country! Emilia, pity me, who am going to that sad place. Methinks I hear the hateful noise of rooks already—kaw, kaw, kaw! There's music in the worst cry in London—My dill and cowcumbers to pickle!

O. BELL. Sister, knowing of this matter, I hope you have provided us some good cheer.

L. TOWN. I have, Brother, and the fiddles too.

O. BELL. Let 'em strike up, then; the young lady shall have a dance before she departs.   (*dance*)
(*after the dance*)—— So! now we'll in and make this an arrant wedding-day.   (*to the pit*)

> And if these honest gentlemen rejoice,
> A dod, the boy has made a happy choice.

                                      (*Exeunt omnes.*)

EPILOGUE

By Mr. Dryden

> Most modern wits such monstrous fools have shown,
> They seem'd not of heav'n's making, but their own.
> Those nauseous harlequins in farce may pass,
> But there goes more to a substantial ass.
> Something of man must be expos'd to view
> That, gallants, they may more resemble you.
> Sir Fopling is a fool so nicely writ,
> The ladies would mistake him for a wit;
> And when he sings, talks loud, and cocks, would cry,
> "I vow, methinks he's pretty company!

So brisk, so gay, so travell'd, so refin'd,
As he took pains to graff upon his kind."
True fops help nature's work and go to school,
To file and finish God A'mighty's fool.
Yet none Sir Fopling him, or him, can call;
He's knight o'th' shire, and represents ye all.
From each he meets, he culls whate'er he can;
Legion's his name, a people in a man.
His bulky folly gathers as it goes
And, rolling o'er you, like a snowball grows.
His various modes from various fathers follow;
One taught the toss, and one the new French wallow.
His sword-knot, this; his cravat, this design'd;
And this, the yard-long snake he twirls behind.
From one the sacred periwig he gain'd,
Which wind ne'er blew, nor touch of hat profan'd.
Another's diving bow he did adore,
Which with a shog casts all the hair before
Till he with full decorum brings it back,
And rises with a water spaniel shake.
As for his songs (the ladies' dear delight),
Those sure he took from most of you who write.
Yet every man is safe from what he feared,
For no one fool is hunted from the herd.

All for Love; or,

The World Well Lost

A TRAGEDY

By JOHN DRYDEN

Written in Imitation of Shakespeare's Style

*Facile est verbum aliquod ardens (ut ita dicam) notare:
idque restinctis animorum incendiis irridere.* *

PREFACE

The death of Antony and Cleopatra is a subject which has
been treated by the greatest wits of our nation, after Shakespeare; and by all so variously, that their example has given me
the confidence to try myself in this bow of Ulysses amongst the
crowd of suitors; and, withal, to take my own measures, in aim-

---

* It is an easy matter to seize out of context some expression all on
fire, so to speak, and make fun of it when the passions kindled by
the occasion have been quenched.—Cicero, *Orator*, 8,27.

ing at the mark. I doubt not but the same motive has prevailed with all of us in this attempt; I mean the excellency of the moral: for the chief persons represented were famous patterns of unlawful love, and their end accordingly was unfortunate. All reasonable men have long since concluded that the hero of the poem ought not to be a character of perfect virtue, for then he could not, without injustice, be made unhappy; nor yet altogether wicked, because he could not then be pitied. I have therefore steered the middle course; and have drawn the character of Antony as favourably as Plutarch, Appian, and Dion Cassius would give me leave; the like I have observed in Cleopatra. That which is wanting to work up the pity to a greater height was not afforded me by the story; for the crimes of love which they both committed were not occasioned by any necessity, or fatal ignorance, but were wholly voluntary; since our passions are, or ought to be, within our power. The fabric of the play is regular enough, as to the inferior parts of it; and the unities of time, place, and action, more exactly observed than, perhaps, the English theatre requires. Particularly, the action is so much one, that it is the only of the kind without episode, or underplot; every scene in the tragedy conducing to the main design, and every act concluding with a turn of it. The greatest error in the contrivance seems to be in the person of Octavia; for, though I might use the privilege of a poet to introduce her into Alexandria, yet I had not enough considered that the compassion she moved to herself and children was destructive to that which I reserved for Antony and Cleopatra; whose mutual love being founded upon vice, must lessen the favour of the audience to them, when virtue and innocence were oppressed by it. And, though I justified Antony in some measure, my making Octavia's departure to proceed wholly from herself, yet the force of the first machine still remained; and the dividing of pity, like the cutting of a river into many channels, abated the strength of the natural stream. But this is an objection which none of my critics have urged against me; and therefore I might have let it pass, if I could have resolved to have been partial to myself. The faults my enemies have found are rather cavils concerning little and not essential decencies, which a master of the ceremonies may decide betwixt us. The French poets, I confess, are strict observers of these punctilios. They would not, for example, have suffered Cleopatra and Octavia to have met; or, if they had met, there must only have passed betwixt them some cold civilities, but no eagerness of repartee, for fear of offending against the greatness of their characters, and the modesty of their sex. This objection I foresaw, and at the same time contemned; for I judged it both natural and probable that Octavia, proud of her new-gained conquest, would search out Cleopatra to triumph over her; and that Cleopatra, thus attacked, was not of a spirit to shun the encounter. And 'tis not unlikely that two exasperated rivals should use such satire as I have put into their mouths; for, after all, though the one were a Roman, and the other a queen, they were both women. 'Tis true, some actions, though natural, are not fit to be represented; and broad obscenities in words ought in good manners to be avoided: expressions therefore are a modest clothing of our thoughts, as breeches and petticoats are of our bodies. If I have kept myself within the bounds of modesty, all beyond it is but nicety and affectation; which is no more but modesty depraved into a vice: they betray themselves who are too quick of apprehension in such cases, and leave all reasonable men to imagine worse of them, than of the poet.

Honest Montaigne goes yet farther: *Nous ne sommes que cérémonie; la cérémonie nous emporte, et laissons la substance des choses. Nous nous tenons aux branches, et abandonnons le tronc et le corps. Nous avons appris aux dames de rougir, oyans seulement nommer ce qu'elles ne craignent aucunement à faire: Nous n'osons appeller à droit nos membres, et ne craignons pas de les employer à toute sorte de débauche. La cérémonie nous défend d'exprimer par paroles les choses licites et naturelles, et nous l'en croyons; la raison nous défend de n'en faire point d'illicites et mauvaises, et personne ne l'en croit.* My comfort is that by this opinion my enemies are but sucking critics, who would fain be nibbling ere their teeth are come.

Yet, in this nicety of manners does the excellency of French poetry consist; their heroes are the most civil people breathing; but their good breeding seldom extends to a word of sense. All their wit is in their ceremony; they want the genius which animates our stage; and therefore 'tis but necessary, when they cannot please, that they should take care not to offend. But as the civilest man in the company is commonly the dullest, so these authors, while they are afraid to make you laugh or cry, out of pure good manners make you sleep. They are so careful not to exasperate a critic that they never leave him any work; so busy with the broom, and make so clean a riddance, that there is little left either for censure or for praise: for no part of a poem is worth our discommending where the whole is insipid; as when we have once tasted of palled wine, we stay not to examine it glass by glass. But while they affect to shine in trifles, they are often careless in essentials. Thus, their Hippolytus is so scrupulous in point of decency, that he will rather expose himself to death than accuse his stepmother to his father; and my critics I am sure will commend him for it: but we of grosser apprehensions are apt to think that this excess of generosity is not practicable but with fools and madmen. This was good manners with a vengeance; and the audience is like to be much concerned at the misfortunes of this admirable hero: but take Hippolytus out of his poetic fit, and I suppose he would think it a wiser part to set the saddle on the right horse, and choose rather to live with the reputation of a plain-spoken, honest man, than to die with the infamy of an incestuous villain. In the meantime, we may take notice that where the poet ought to have preserved the character as it was delivered to us by antiquity, when he should have given us the picture of a rough young man, of the Amazonian strain, a jolly huntsman, and both by his profession and his early rising a mortal enemy to love, he has chosen to give him the turn of gallantry, sent him to travel from Athens to Paris, taught him to make love, and transformed the Hippolytus of Euripides into Monsieur Hippolyte. I should not have troubled myself thus far with French poets, but that I find our *Chedreux* critics wholly form their judgments by them. But for my part, I desire to be tried by the laws of my own country; for it seems unjust to me that the French should prescribe here, till they have conquered. Our little sonneteers, who follow them, have too narrow souls to judge of poetry. Poets themselves are the most proper, though I conclude not the only, critics. But till some genius as universal as Aristotle shall arise, one who can penetrate into all arts and sciences, without the practice of them, I shall think it reasonable that the judgment of an artificer in his own art should be preferable to the opinion of another man; at least where he is not bribed by interest, or prejudiced by malice. And this, I suppose, is manifest by plain induction: for, first, the crowd cannot be presumed to have more than a gross instinct of what pleases or displeases them. Every man will grant me this; but then, by a particular kindness to himself, he draws his own stake first, and will be distinguished from the multitude, of which other men may think him one. But, if I come closer to those who are allowed for witty men, either by the advantage of their quality, or by common fame, and affirm that neither are they qualified to decide sovereignly concerning poetry, I shall yet have a strong party of my opinion; for most of them severally will exclude the rest, either from the number of witty men, or at least of able judges. But here again they are all indulgent to themselves; and everyone who believes himself a wit, that is, every man, will pretend at the same time to a right of judging. But to press it yet farther, there are many witty men, but few poets; neither have all poets a taste of tragedy. And this is the rock on which they are daily splitting. Poetry, which is a picture of nature, must generally please; but 'tis not to be understood that all parts of it must please every man; therefore is not tragedy to be judged by a witty man whose taste is only confined to comedy. Nor is every man who loves tragedy a sufficient judge of it: he must understand the excellencies of it too, or he will only prove a blind admirer, not a critic. From hence it comes that so many satires on poets, and censures of their writings, fly abroad. Men of pleasant conversation (at least esteemed so), and endued with a trifling kind of fancy, perhaps helped out with some smattering of Latin, are ambitious to distinguish themselves from the herd of gentlemen by their poetry—

> *Rarus enim ferme sensus communis in illa*
> *Fortuna*[1]

And is not this a wretched affectation, not to be contented with what fortune has done for them, and sit down quietly with their estates, but they must call their wits in question, and needlessly expose their nakedness to public view? not considering that they are not to expect the same approbation from sober men, which they have found from their flatterers after the third bottle? If a little glittering in discourse has passed them on us for witty men, where was the necessity of undeceiving the world?

[1] For common sense is rare in that degree.

Would a man who has an ill title to an estate, but yet is in possession of it, would he bring it of his own accord to be tried at Westminster? We who write, if we want the talent, yet have the excuse that we do it for a poor subsistence; but what can be urged in their defence, who, not having the vocation of poverty to scribble, out of mere wantonness take pains to make themselves ridiculous? Horace was certainly in the right where he said that "no man is satisfied with his own condition." A poet is not pleased because he is not rich; and the rich are discontented because the poets will not admit them of their number. Thus the case is hard with writers: if they succeed not, they must starve; and if they do, some malicious satire is prepared to level them for daring to please without their leave. But while they are so eager to destroy the fame of others, their ambition is manifest in their concernment: some poem of their own is to be produced, and the slaves are to be laid flat with their faces on the ground, that the monarch may appear in the greater majesty.

Dionysius and Nero had the same longings, but with all their power they could never bring their business well about. 'Tis true, they proclaimed themselves poets by sound of trumpet; and poets they were, upon pain of death to any man who durst call them otherwise. The audience had a fine time on't, you may imagine; they sate in a bodily fear, and looked as demurely as they could: for 'twas a hanging matter to laugh unseasonably; and the tyrants were suspicious, as they had reason, that their subjects had 'em in the wind; so, every man, in his own defence, set as good a face upon the business as he could. 'Twas known beforehand that the monarchs were to be crowned laureates; but when the show was over, and an honest man was suffered to depart quietly, he took out his laughter which he had stifled, with a firm resolution never more to see an emperor's play, though he had been ten years a-making it. In the meantime the true poets were they who made the best markets, for they had wit enough to yield the prize with a good grace, and not contend with him who had thirty legions. They were sure to be rewarded if they confessed themselves bad writers, and that was somewhat better than to be martyrs for their reputation. Lucan's example was enough to teach them manners; and after he was put to death for overcoming Nero, the emperor carried it without dispute for the best poet in his dominions. No man was ambitious of that grinning honour; for if he heard the malicious trumpeter proclaiming his name before his betters, he knew there was but one way with him. Mæcenas took another course, and we know he was more than a great man, for he was witty too: but finding himself far gone in poetry, which Seneca assures us was not his talent, he thought it his best way to be well with Virgil and with Horace; that at least he might be a poet at the second hand; and we see how happily it has succeeded with him; for his own bad poetry is forgotten, and their panegyrics of him still remain. But they who should be our patrons are for no such expensive ways to fame; they have much of the poetry of Mæcenas, but little of his liberality. They are for persecuting Horace and Virgil, in the persons of their successors (for such is every man who has any part of their soul and fire, though in a less degree). Some of their little zanies yet go farther; for they are persecutors even of Horace himself, as far as they are able, by their ignorant and vile imitations of him; by making an unjust use of his authority, and turning his artillery against his friends. But how would he disdain to be copied by such hands! I dare answer for him, he would be more uneasy in their company than he was with Crispinus, their forefather, in the Holy Way; and would no more have allowed them a place amongst the critics than he would Demetrius the mimic, and Tigellius the buffoon;

> ———Demetri, teque, Tigelli,
> Discipulorum inter jubeo plorare cathedras.[2]

With what scorn would he look down on such miserable translators, who make doggerel of his Latin, mistake his meaning, misapply his censures, and often contradict their own? He is fixed as a landmark to set out the bounds of poetry,

> ——— Saxum antiquum ingens,
> Limes agro positus, litem ut discerneret arvis.[3]

[2] Demetrius and Tigellius, I bid you weep among your pupils' chairs.
[3] An antique stone he saw, the common bound
Of neighb'ring fields, and barrier of the ground.
[DRYDEN's translation]

But other arms than theirs, and other sinews, are required, to raise the weight of such an author; and when they would toss him against their enemies—

> *Genua labant, gelidus concrevit frigore sanguis,*
> *Tum lapis ipse viri vacuum per inane volutus,*
> *Nec spatium evasit totum, nec pertulit ictum.*[4]

For my part, I would wish no other revenge, either for myself, or the rest of the poets, from this rhyming judge of the twelve-penny gallery, this legitimate son of Sternhold, than that he would subscribe his name to his censure, or (not to tax him beyond his learning) set his mark: for, should he own himself publicly, and come from behind the lion's skin, they whom he condemns would be thankful to him, they whom he praises would choose to be condemned, and the magistrates whom he has elected would modestly withdraw from their employment to avoid the scandal of his nomination. The sharpness of his satire, next to himself, falls most heavily on his friends, and they ought never to forgive him for commending them perpetually the wrong way, and sometimes by contraries. If he have a friend whose hastiness in writing is his greatest fault, Horace would have taught him to have minced the matter, and to have called it readiness of thought, and a flowing fancy; for friendship will allow a man to christen an imperfection by the name of some neighbour virtue:

> *Vellem in amicitia sic erraremus; et isti*
> *Errori nomen virtus posuisset honestum.*[5]

But he would never have allowed him to have called a slow man hasty, or a hasty writer a slow drudge, as Juvenal explains it:

> ——— *Canibus pigris, scabieque vetusta*
> *Levibus, et siccæ lambentibus ora lucernæ,*

[4] His knocking knees are bent beneath the load,
And shiv'ring cold congeals his vital blood.
The stone drops from his arms, and, falling short
For want of vigour, mocks his vain effort.
        [DRYDEN's translation]

[5] Oh that we should err so in friendship, and that virtue had assigned an honourable name on that error.

Nomen erit Pardus, Tigris, Leo; si quid adhuc est
Quod fremit in terris violentius.[6]

Yet Lucretius laughs at a foolish lover, even for excusing the
imperfections of his mistress:

Nigra μελίχροος *est, immunda et fœtida* ἄκοσμος.
Balba loqui non quit, τραυλίζει; *muta pudens est,* etc.[7]

But to drive it *ad Æthiopem cygnum* is not to be endured. I
leave him to interpret this by the benefit of his French version
on the other side, and without farther considering him than I
have the rest of my illiterate censors, whom I have disdained to
answer, because they are not qualified for judges. It remains that
I acquaint the reader that I have endeavoured in this play to
follow the practice of the ancients, who, as Mr. Rymer has judi-
ciously observed, are and ought to be our masters. Horace likewise gives it for a rule in his art of poetry,

———— *Vos exemplaria Græca*
Nocturna versate manu, versate diurna.[8]

Yet, though their models are regular, they are too little for
English tragedy; which requires to be built in a larger compass.
I could give an instance in the *Œdipus Tyrannus,* which was the
masterpiece of Sophocles; but I reserve it for a more fit occasion,
which I hope to have hereafter. In my style, I have professed to
imitate the divine Shakespeare; which that I might perform more
freely, I have disencumbered myself from rhyme. Not that I condemn my former way, but that this is more proper to my present
purpose. I hope I need not to explain myself, that I have not

[6] Lazy dogs, hairless from chronic mange, and licking the rims
of an empty lamp—their name shall be Pard, Tiger, Lion, or whatever roars more violently on the earth.
[7] The sallow skin is for the swarthy put,
And love can make a slattern of a slut . . .
She stammers: O, what grace in lisping lies!
If she says nothing, to be sure she's wise.
                                    [DRYDEN's translation]
[8] Con your Greek models night and day.

copied my author servilely—words and phrases must of necessity receive a change in succeeding ages—but 'tis almost a miracle that much of his language remains so pure; and that he who began dramatic poetry amongst us, untaught by any, and as Ben Jonson tells us, without learning, should by the force of his own genius perform so much that in a manner he has left no praise for any who come after him. The occasion is fair, and the subject would be pleasant, to handle the difference of styles betwixt him and Fletcher, and wherein, and how far, they are both to be imitated. But since I must not be overconfident of my own performance after him, it will be prudence in me to be silent. Yet I hope I may affirm, and without vanity, that, by imitating him, I have excelled myself throughout the play; and particularly, that I prefer the scene betwixt Antony and Ventidius in the first act, to anything which I have written in this kind.

PROLOGUE

What flocks of critics hover here to-day, ⎱
As vultures wait on armies for their prey, ⎰
All gaping for the carcass of a play! ⎰
With croaking notes they bode some dire event,
And follow dying poets by the scent.
Ours gives himself for gone; y' have watch'd your time!
He fights this day unarm'd, without his rhyme,
And brings a tale which often has been told,
As sad as Dido's; and almost as old.
His hero, whom you wits his bully call,
Bates of his mettle, and scarce rants at all:
He's somewhat lewd; but a well-meaning mind;
Weeps much; fights little; but is wondrous kind.
In short, a pattern, and companion fit,
For all the keeping Tonies of the pit.
I could name more: a wife, and mistress too; ⎱
Both (to be plain) too good for most of you: ⎰
The wife well-natur'd, and the mistress true. ⎰
    Now, poets, if your fame has been his care,

Allow him all the candour you can spare.
A brave man scorns to quarrel once a day;
Like Hectors in at every petty fray.
Let those find fault whose wit's so very small,
They've need to show that they can think at all:
Errors like straws upon the surface flow;
He who would search for pearls must dive below.
Fops may have leave to level all they can,
As pigmies would be glad to lop a man.
Half-wits are fleas; so little and so light,
We scarce could know they live, but that they bite.
But, as the rich, when tir'd with daily feasts,
For change, become their next poor tenant's guests;
Drink hearty draughts of ale from plain brown bowls,
And snatch the homely rasher from the coals:
So you, retiring from much better cheer,
For once, may venture to do penance here.
And since that plenteous Autumn now is past,
Whose grapes and peaches have indulg'd your taste,
Take in good part, from our poor poet's board,
Such rivell'd fruits as winter can afford.

PERSONS REPRESENTED

MARK ANTONY
VENTIDIUS, *his general*
DOLABELLA, *his friend*
ALEXAS, *the Queen's eunuch*
SERAPION, *Priest of Isis*
MYRIS, *another priest*

Servants to Antony
CLEOPATRA, *Queen of Egypt*
OCTAVIA, *Antony's wife*
CHARMION,
IRAS, } *Cleopatra's maids*
Antony's two little daughters

SCENE: *Alexandria*

ALL FOR LOVE; OR,
THE WORLD WELL LOST

ACT I

SCENE: *The Temple of Isis*

Enter SERAPION, MYRIS, *Priests of Isis*

SERAP. Portents and prodigies are grown so frequent
That they have lost their name. Our fruitful Nile
Flow'd ere the wonted season, with a torrent
So unexpected, and so wondrous fierce,
That the wild deluge overtook the haste
Ev'n of the hinds that watch'd it: men and beasts
Were borne above the tops of trees, that grew
On th' utmost margin of the water-mark.
Then, with so swift an ebb the flood drove backward,
It slipt from underneath the scaly herd:
Here monstrous phocæ panted on the shore;
Forsaken dolphins there, with their broad tails,
Lay lashing the departing waves: hard by 'em,
Sea-horses flound'ring in the slimy mud,
Toss'd up their heads, and dash'd the ooze about 'em.

Enter ALEXAS *behind them*

MYR. Avert these omens, heav'n!
SERAP. Last night, between the hours of twelve and one,
In a lone aisle o' th' temple while I walk'd,
A whirlwind rose, that, with a violent blast,
Shook all the dome: the doors around me clapt;
The iron wicket, that defends the vault,
Where the long race of Ptolemies is laid,
Burst open, and disclos'd the mighty dead.
From out each monument, in order plac'd,
An armed ghost start up: the boy-king last
Rear'd his inglorious head. A peal of groans
Then follow'd, and a lamentable voice

Cried, "Egypt is no more!" My blood ran back,
My shaking knees against each other knock'd;
On the cold pavement down I fell entranc'd,
And so unfinish'd left the horrid scene.

ALEX. (*showing himself*) And dream'd you this? or did invent the story,
To frighten our Egyptian boys withal,
And train 'em up betimes in fear of priesthood?

SERAP. My Lord, I saw you not,
Nor meant my words should reach your ears; but what
I utter'd was most true.

ALEX.   A foolish dream,
Bred from the fumes of indigested feasts,
And holy luxury.

SERAP.   I know my duty:
This goes no farther.

ALEX.   'Tis not fit it should;
Nor would the times now bear it, were it true.
All southern, from yon hills, the Roman camp
Hangs o'er us black and threat'ning, like a storm
Just breaking on our heads.

SERAP. Our faint Egyptians pray for Antony;
But in their servile hearts they own Octavius.

MYR. Why then does Antony dream out his hours,
And tempts not fortune for a noble day
Which might redeem what Actium lost?

ALEX. He thinks 'tis past recovery.

SERAP.   Yet the foe
Seems not to press the siege.

ALEX.   Oh, there's the wonder.
Mæcenas and Agrippa, who can most
With Cæsar, are his foes. His wife Octavia,
Driv'n from his house, solicits her revenge;
And Dolabella, who was once his friend,
Upon some private grudge now seeks his ruin:
Yet still war seems on either side to sleep.

SERAP. 'Tis strange that Antony, for some days past,
Has not beheld the face of Cleopatra;
But here, in Isis' temple, lives retir'd,
And makes his heart a prey to black despair.

ALEX. 'Tis true; and we much fear he hopes by absence
To cure his mind of love.

SERAP.   If he be vanquish'd,
Or make his peace, Egypt is doom'd to be
A Roman province; and our plenteous harvests
Must then redeem the scarceness of their soil.
While Antony stood firm, our Alexandria
Rivall'd proud Rome (dominion's other seat),
And Fortune striding, like a vast Colossus,
Could fix an equal foot of empire here.

ALEX. Had I my wish, these tyrants of all nature
Who lord it o'er mankind, should perish—perish,
Each by the other's sword; but, since our will
Is lamely follow'd by our pow'r, we must
Depend on one, with him to rise or fall.

SERAP. How stands the queen affected?

ALEX.   Oh, she dotes,
She dotes, Serapion, on this vanquish'd man,
And winds herself about his mighty ruins,
Whom would she yet forsake, yet yield him up,
This hunted prey, to his pursuers' hands,
She might preserve us all; but 'tis in vain—
This changes my designs, this blasts my counsels,
And makes me use all means to keep him here,
Whom I could wish divided from her arms
Far as the earth's deep centre. Well, you know
The state of things; no more of your ill omens
And black prognostics; labour to confirm
The people's hearts.

Enter VENTIDIUS, *talking aside with a Gentleman of* ANTONY'S

SERAP.   These Romans will o'erhear us.
But who's that stranger? By his warlike port,
His fierce demeanor, and erected look,
He's of no vulgar note.

ALEX.   Oh, 'tis Ventidius,
Our emp'ror's great lieutenant in the East,
Who first show'd Rome that Parthia could be conquer'd.
When Antony return'd from Syria last,
He left this man to guard the Roman frontiers.

SERAP. You seem to know him well.

ALEX. Too well. I saw him in Cilicia first,
When Cleopatra there met Antony:
A mortal foe he was to us, and Egypt.
But, let me witness to the worth I hate,
A braver Roman never drew a sword;
Firm to his prince, but as a friend, not slave.
He ne'er was of his pleasures; but presides
O'er all his cooler hours, and morning counsels:
In short, the plainness, fierceness, rugged virtue
Of an old true-stamp'd Roman lives in him.
His coming bodes I know not what of ill
To our affairs. Withdraw, to mark him better;
And I'll acquaint you why I sought you here,
And what's our present work.

(*They withdraw to a corner of the stage; and* VENTIDIUS,
with the other, comes forwards to the front.)

VENT.   Not see him, say you?
I say, I must, and will.

GENT.   He has commanded,
On pain of death, none should approach his presence.

VENT. I bring him news will raise his drooping spirits,
Give him new life.

GENT.   He sees not Cleopatra.

VENT. Would he had never seen her!

GENT. He eats not, drinks not, sleeps not, has no use
Of anything, but thought; or, if he talks,
'Tis to himself, and then 'tis perfect raving:
Then he defies the world, and bids it pass;
Sometimes he gnaws his lip, and curses loud
The boy Octavius; then he draws his mouth
Into a scornful smile, and cries, "Take all,
The world's not worth my care."

VENT.   Just, just his nature.
Virtue's his path; but sometimes 'tis too narrow
For his vast soul; and then he starts out wide,
And bounds into a vice that bears him far
From his first course, and plunges him in ills:
But, when his danger makes him find his fault,
Quick to observe, and full of sharp remorse,

He censures eagerly his own misdeeds,
Judging himself with malice to himself,
And not forgiving what as man he did,
Because his other parts are more than man.
He must not thus be lost.

(ALEXAS *and the Priests come forward.*)

ALEX. You have your full instructions, now advance;
Proclaim your orders loudly.

SERAP. Romans, Egyptians, hear the queen's command.
Thus Cleopatra bids: "Let labour cease,
To pomp and triumphs give this happy day,
That gave the world a lord: 'tis Antony's."
Live, Antony; and Cleopatra live!
Be this the general voice sent up to heav'n,
And every public place repeat this echo.

VENT. (*aside*) Fine pageantry!

SERAP.   Set out before your doors
The images of all your sleeping fathers,
With laurels crown'd; with laurels wreathe your posts,
And strew with flow'rs the pavement; let the priests
Do present sacrifice; pour out the wine,
And call the Gods to join with you in gladness.

VENT. Curse on the tongue that bids this general joy!
Can they be friends of Antony, who revel
When Antony's in danger? Hide, for shame,
You Romans, your great grandsires' images,
For fear their souls should animate their marbles,
To blush at their degenerate progeny.

ALEX. A love which knows no bounds to Antony,
Would mark the day with honours, when all heaven
Laboured for him, when each propitious star
Stood wakeful in his orb, to watch that hour,
And shed his better influence. Her own birthday
Our queen neglected, like a vulgar fate
That passed obscurely by.

VENT.   Would it had slept,
Divided far from his, till some remote
And future age had call'd it out, to ruin
Some other prince, not him.

ALEX.   Your emperor,

Though grown unkind, would be more gentle than
T' upbraid my queen for loving him too well.
    VENT. Does the mute sacrifice upbraid the priest?
He knows him not his executioner.
Oh, she has deck'd his ruin with her love,
Led him in golden bands to gaudy slaughter,
And made perdition pleasing; she has left him
The blank of what he was;
I tell thee, eunuch, she has quite unmann'd him.
Can any Roman see, and know him now,
Thus alter'd from the lord of half mankind,
Unbent, unsinew'd, made a woman's toy,
Shrunk from the vast extent of all his honours,
And cramped within a corner of the world?
O Antony!
Thou bravest soldier, and thou best of friends!
Bounteous as nature; next to nature's God!
Couldst thou but make new worlds, so wouldst thou give em,
As bounty were thy being: rough in battle,
As the first Romans when they went to war;
Yet, after victory, more pitiful
Than all their praying virgins left at home!
    ALEX. Would you could add, to those more shining virtues,
His truth to her who loves him.
    VENT.   Would I could not!
But wherefore waste I precious hours with thee?
Thou art her darling mischief, her chief engine,
Antony's other fate. Go, tell thy queen,
Ventidius is arriv'd, to end her charms.
Let your Egyptian timbrels play alone;
Nor mix effeminate sounds with Roman trumpets.
You dare not fight for Antony; go pray,
And keep your cowards' holiday in temples.
                        (*Exeunt* ALEXAS, SERAPION.)

Enter a second Gentleman of MARK ANTONY

    2 GENT. The emperor approaches, and commands,
On pain of death, that none presume to stay.
    1 GENT. I dare not disobey him.   (*going out with the other*)
    VENT.   Well, I dare.

But I'll observe him first unseen, and find
Which way his humour drives: the rest I'll venture. (*withdraws*)

Enter ANTONY, *walking with a disturbed motion
before he speaks*

ANT. They tell me 'tis my birthday, and I'll keep it
With double pomp of sadness.
'Tis what the day deserves, which gave me breath.
Why was I rais'd the meteor of the world,
Hung in the skies, and blazing as I travell'd,
Till all my fires were spent; and then cast downward
To be trod out by Cæsar?
    VENT. (*aside*)   On my soul,
'Tis mournful, wondrous mournful!
    ANT.   Count thy gains.
Now, Antony, wouldst thou be born for this?
Glutton of fortune, thy devouring youth
Has starv'd thy wanting age.
    VENT. (*aside*)   How sorrow shakes him!
So, now the tempest tears him up by th' roots,
And on the ground extends the noble ruin.
    ANT. (*having thrown himself down*) Lie there, thou shadow
       of an emperor;
The place thou pressest on thy mother earth
Is all thy empire now: now it contains thee;
Some few days hence, and then 'twill be too large,
When thou'rt contracted in thy narrow urn,
Shrunk to a few cold ashes; then Octavia
(For Cleopatra will not live to see it)
Octavia then will have thee all her own,
And bear thee in her widow'd hand to Cæsar;
Cæsar will weep, the crocodile will weep,
To see his rival of the universe
Lie still and peaceful there. I'll think no more on't.
Give me some music; look that it be sad:
I'll soothe my melancholy till I swell
And burst myself with sighing.—(*soft music*)
'Tis somewhat to my humour. Stay, I fancy
I'm now turn'd wild, a commoner of nature,
Of all forsaken, and forsaking all;

Live in a shady forest's sylvan scene;
Stretch'd at my length beneath some blasted oak,
I lean my head upon the mossy bark,
And look just of a piece as I grew from it:
My uncomb'd locks, matted like mistletoe,
Hang o'er my hoary face; a murm'ring brook
Runs at my foot.
    VENT.   Methinks I fancy
Myself there too.
    ANT.   The herd come jumping by me,
And, fearless, quench their thirst, while I look on,
And take me for their fellow-citizen.
More of this image, more; it lulls my thoughts. (*soft music again*)
    VENT. I must disturb him; I can hold no longer.
                      (*stands before him*)
    ANT. (*starting up*) Art thou Ventidius?
    VENT.   Are you Antony?
I'm liker what I was, than you to him
I left you last.
    ANT.   I'm angry.
    VENT.   So am I.
    ANT. I would be private: leave me.
    VENT.   Sir, I love you,
And therefore will not leave you.
    ANT.   Will not leave me!
Where have you learnt that answer? Who am I?
    VENT. My emperor; the man I love next heaven:
If I said more, I think 'twere scarce a sin;
Y'are all that's good, and good-like.
    ANT.   All that's wretched.
You will not leave me then?
    VENT.   'Twas too presuming
To say I would not; but I dare not leave you:
And 'tis unkind in you to chide me hence
So soon, when I so far have come to see you.
    ANT. Now thou hast seen me, art thou satisfy'd?
For, if a friend, thou hast beheld enough;
And, if a foe, too much.
    VENT. (*weeping*) Look, Emperor, this is no common dew.
I have not wept this forty year; but now

My mother comes afresh into my eyes;
I cannot help her softness.

    ANT. By heav'n, he weeps, poor good old man, he weeps!
The big round drops course one another down
The furrows of his cheeks. Stop 'em, Ventidius,
Or I shall blush to death: they set my shame,
That caus'd 'em, full before me.

    VENT.   I'll do my best.

    ANT. Sure there's contagion in the tears of friends:
See, I have caught it too. Believe me, 'tis not
For my own griefs, but thine.—Nay, father.

    VENT.   Emperor.

    ANT. Emperor! Why, that's the style of victory;
The conqu'ring soldier, red with unfelt wounds,
Salutes his general so: but never more
Shall that sound reach my ears.

    VENT.   I warrant you.

    ANT. Actium, Actium! Oh!——

    VENT.   It sits too near you.

    ANT. Here, here it lies; a lump of lead by day,
And, in my short, distracted, nightly slumbers,
The hag that rides my dreams——

    VENT. Out with it; give it vent.

    ANT.   Urge not my shame.
I lost a battle.

    VENT.   So has Julius done.

    ANT. Thou favour'st me, and speak'st not half thou think'st;
For Julius fought it out, and lost it fairly:
But Antony——

    VENT.   Nay, stop not.

    ANT.   Antony,
(Well, thou wilt have it) like a coward, fled,
Fled while his soldiers fought; fled first, Ventidius.
Thou long'st to curse me, and I give thee leave.
I know thou cam'st prepar'd to rail.

    VENT.   I did.

    ANT. I'll help thee. I have been a man, Ventidius——

    VENT. Yes, and a brave one; but——

    ANT.   I know thy meaning.
But I have lost my reason, have disgrac'd

The name of soldier with inglorious ease.
In the full vintage of my flowing honours,
Sat still, and saw it press'd by other hands.
Fortune came smiling to my youth, and woo'd it,
And purple greatness met my ripen'd years.
When first I came to empire, I was borne
On tides of people, crowding to my triumphs,
The wish of nations; and the willing world
Receiv'd me as its pledge of future peace;
I was so great, so happy, so belov'd,
Fate could not ruin me; till I took pains,
And work'd against my fortune, chid her from me,
And turn'd her loose; yet still she came again.
My careless days, and my luxurious nights,
At length have weary'd her, and now she's gone,
Gone, gone, divorc'd for ever. Help me, soldier,
To curse this madman, this industrious fool,
Who labour'd to be wretched: pr'ythee, curse me.

 VENT. No.

 ANT. Why?

 VENT.   You are too sensible already
Of what y'have done, too conscious of your failings;
And, like a scorpion, whipp'd by others first
To fury, sting yourself in mad revenge.
I would bring balm, and pour it in your wounds,
Cure your distemper'd mind, and heal your fortunes.

 ANT. I know thou wouldst.

 VENT.   I will.

 ANT.   Ha, ha, ha, ha!

 VENT. You laugh.

 ANT.   I do, to see officious love
Give cordials to the dead.

 VENT.   You would be lost, then?

 ANT. I am.

 VENT. I say you are not. Try your fortune.

 ANT. I have, to th' utmost. Dost thou think me desperate
Without just cause? No, when I found all lost
Beyond repair, I hid me from the world,
And learn'd to scorn it here; which now I do

So heartily, I think it is not worth
The cost of keeping.

    VENT.   Cæsar thinks not so;
He'll thank you for the gift he could not take.
You would be kill'd like Tully, would you? Do,
Hold out your throat to Cæsar, and die tamely.

    ANT. No, I can kill myself; and so resolve.

    VENT. I can die with you too, when time shall serve;
But fortune calls upon us now to live,
To fight, to conquer.

    ANT.   Sure thou dream'st, Ventidius.

    VENT. No; 'tis you dream; you sleep away your hours
In desperate sloth, miscall'd philosophy.
Up, up, for honour's sake; twelve legions wait you,
And long to call you chief; by painful journeys
I led 'em, patient both of heat and hunger,
Down from the Parthian marches to the Nile.
'Twill do you good to see their sunburnt faces,
Their scarr'd cheeks, and chopp'd hands; there's virtue in 'em.
They'll sell those mangled limbs at dearer rates
Than yon trim bands can buy.

    ANT.   Where left you them?

    VENT. I said in Lower Syria.

    ANT.   Bring 'em hither;
There may be life in these.

    VENT.   They will not come.

    ANT. Why didst thou mock my hopes with promis'd aids,
To double my despair? They're mutinous.

    VENT. Most firm and loyal.

    ANT.   Yet they will not march
To succour me. O trifler!

    VENT.   They petition
You would make haste to head 'em.

    ANT.   I'm besieg'd.

    VENT. There's but one way shut up: how came I hither?

    ANT. I will not stir.

    VENT.   They would perhaps desire
A better reason.

    ANT.   I have never us'd

My soldiers to demand a reason of
My actions. Why did they refuse to march?
 VENT. They said they would not fight for Cleopatra.
 ANT. What was't they said?
 VENT. They said they would not fight for Cleopatra.
Why should they fight indeed, to make her conquer,
And make you more a slave? to gain you kingdoms,
Which, for a kiss, at your next midnight feast,
You'll sell to her? Then she new-names her jewels,
And calls this diamond such or such a tax;
Each pendant in her ear shall be a province.
 ANT. Ventidius, I allow your tongue free license
On all my other faults; but, on your life,
No word of Cleopatra: she deserves
More worlds than I can lose.
 VENT.   Behold, you pow'rs,
To whom you have intrusted humankind;
See Europe, Afric, Asia, put in balance,
And all weigh'd down by one light, worthless woman!
I think the Gods are Antonys, and give,
Like prodigals, this nether world away
To none but wasteful hands.
 ANT.   You grow presumptuous.
 VENT. I take the privilege of plain love to speak.
 ANT. Plain love! plain arrogance, plain insolence!
Thy men are cowards; thou, an envious traitor,
Who, under seeming honesty, hast vented
The burden of thy rank, o'erflowing gall.
Oh, that thou wert my equal, great in arms
As the first Cæsar was, that I might kill thee
Without a stain to honour!
 VENT.   You may kill me;
You have done more already—called me traitor.
 ANT. Art thou not one?
 VENT.   For showing you yourself,
Which none else durst have done? but had I been
That name, which I disdain to speak again,
I needed not have sought your abject fortunes,
Come to partake your fate, to die with you.

What hinder'd me t' have led my conqu'ring eagles
To fill Octavius's bands? I could have been
A traitor then, a glorious, happy traitor,
And not have been so call'd.

ANT.   Forgive me, soldier:
I've been too passionate.

VENT.   You thought me false;
Thought my old age betray'd you. Kill me, Sir;
Pray, kill me; yet you need not, your unkindness
Has left your sword no work.

ANT.   I did not think so;
I said it in my rage: pr'ythee, forgive me.
Why didst thou tempt my anger, by discovery
Of what I would not hear?

VENT.   No prince but you
Could merit that sincerity I us'd,
Nor durst another man have ventur'd it;
But you, ere love misled your wand'ring eyes,
Were sure the chief and best of human race,
Fram'd in the very pride and boast of nature,
So perfect, that the Gods, who form'd you, wonder'd
At their own skill, and cry'd, "A lucky hit
Has mended our design." Their envy hinder'd,
Else you had been immortal, and a pattern,
When heav'n would work for ostentation sake,
To copy out again.

ANT.   But Cleopatra——
Go on; for I can bear it now.

VENT.   No more.

ANT. Thou dar'st not trust my passion, but thou may'st;
Thou only lov'st, the rest have flatter'd me.

VENT. Heav'n's blessing on your heart for that kind word!
May I believe you love me? speak again.

ANT. Indeed I do. Speak this, and this, and this.

                                        (*hugging him*)

Thy praises were unjust; but I'll deserve 'em,
And yet mend all. Do with me what thou wilt;
Lead me to victory, thou know'st the way.

VENT. And, will you leave this——

ANT.   Pr'ythee, do not curse her,
And I will leave her; though, heav'n knows, I love
Beyond life, conquest, empire, all but honour;
But I will leave her.

VENT.   That's my royal master;
And, shall we fight?

ANT.   I warrant thee, old soldier,
Thou shalt behold me once again in iron,
And at the head of our old troops, that beat
The Parthians, cry aloud, "Come, follow me!"

VENT. Oh, now I hear my Emperor! in that word Octavius fell.
Gods, let me see that day,
And, if I have ten years behind, take all;
I'll thank you for th' exchange.

ANT.   O Cleopatra!

VENT. Again?

ANT.   I've done: in that last sigh, she went.
Cæsar shall know what 'tis to force a lover
From all he holds most dear.

VENT.   Methinks you breathe
Another soul: your looks are more divine;
You speak a hero, and you move a god.

ANT. Oh, thou hast fir'd me; my soul's up in arms,
And mans each part about me. Once again,
That noble eagerness of fight has seiz'd me;
That eagerness with which I darted upward
To Cassius's camp; in vain the steepy hill
Oppos'd my way; in vain a war of spears
Sung round my head, and planted all my shield;
I won the trenches, while my foremost men
Lagg'd on the plain below.

VENT.   Ye Gods, ye Gods,
For such another hour!

ANT.   Come on, my soldier!
Our hearts and arms are still the same: I long
Once more to meet our foes, that thou and I,
Like Time and Death, marching before our troops,
May taste fate to 'em; mow 'em out a passage,
    And, ent'ring where the foremost squadrons yield,
    Begin the noble harvest of the field.   (*Exeunt.*)

ACT II

CLEOPATRA, IRAS, *and* ALEXAS

CLEO. What shall I do, or whither shall I turn?
Ventidius has o'ercome, and he will go.

ALEX. He goes to fight for you.

CLEO. Then he would see me, ere he went to fight.
Flatter me not: if once he goes, he's lost,
And all my hopes destroy'd.

ALEX.   Does this weak passion
Become a mighty queen?

CLEO.   I am no queen:
Is this to be a queen, to be besieg'd
By yon insulting Roman, and to wait
Each hour the victor's chain? These ills are small:
For Antony is lost, and I can mourn
For nothing else but him. Now come, Octavius,
I have no more to lose; prepare thy bands;
I'm fit to be a captive: Antony
Has taught my mind the fortune of a slave.

IRAS. Call reason to assist you.

CLEO.   I have none,
And none would have: my love's a noble madness,
Which shows the cause deserv'd it. Moderate sorrow
Fits vulgar love, and for a vulgar man:
But I have lov'd with such transcendent passion,
I soar'd, at first, quite out of reason's view,
And now am lost above it. No, I'm proud
'Tis thus: would Antony could see me now!
Think you he would not sigh? Though he must leave me,
Sure he would sigh; for he is noble-natur'd,
And bears a tender heart: I know him well.
Ah, no, I know him not; I knew him once,
But now 'tis past.

IRAS.   Let it be past with you:
Forget him, Madam.

CLEO.   Never, never, Iras.
He once was mine; and once, though now 'tis gone,

Leaves a faint image of possession still.

ALEX. Think him unconstant, cruel, and ungrateful.

CLEO. I cannot: if I could, those thoughts were vain.
Faithless, ungrateful, cruel, though he be,
I still must love him.

Enter CHARMION

Now, what news, my Charmion?
Will he be kind? and will he not forsake me?
Am I to live, or die?—nay, do I live?
Or am I dead? for when he gave his answer,
Fate took the word, and then I liv'd or died.

CHAR. I found him, Madam——

CLEO.   A long speech preparing?
If thou bring'st comfort, haste, and give it me,
For never was more need.

IRAS.   I know he loves you.

CLEO. Had he been kind, her eyes had told me so
Before her tongue could speak it: now she studies,
To soften what he said; but give me death,
Just as he sent it, Charmion, undisguis'd,
And in the words he spoke.

CHAR.   I found him, then,
Incompass'd round, I think, with iron statues,
So mute, so motionless his soldiers stood,
While awfully he cast his eyes about,
And ev'ry leader's hopes or fears survey'd:
Methought he looked resolv'd, and yet not pleas'd.
When he beheld me struggling in the crowd,
He blush'd, and bade make way.

ALEX.   There's comfort yet.

CHAR. Ventidius fix'd his eyes upon my passage
Severely, as he meant to frown me back,
And sullenly gave place: I told my message,
Just as you gave it, broken and disorder'd;
I number'd in it all your sighs and tears,
And while I mov'd your pitiful request
That you but only begg'd a last farewell,
He fetch'd an inward groan, and ev'ry time
I nam'd you, sigh'd, as if his heart were breaking,

But shunn'd my eyes, and guiltily look'd down.
He seem'd not now that awful Antony
Who shook an arm'd assembly with his nod;
But, making show as he would rub his eyes,
Disguis'd and blotted out a falling tear.

CLEO. Did he then weep? and was I worth a tear?
If what thou hast to say be not as pleasing,
Tell me no more, but let me die contented.

CHAR. He bid me say he knew himself so well,
He could deny you nothing, if he saw you;
And therefore——

CLEO.   Thou wouldst say, he would not see me?

CHAR. And therefore begg'd you not to use a power,
Which he could ill resist; yet he should ever
Respect you as he ought.

CLEO.   Is that a word
For Antony to use to Cleopatra?
O that faint word, *respect!* how I disdain it!
Disdain myself, for loving after it!
He should have kept that word for cold Octavia.
Respect is for a wife. Am I that thing,
That dull, insipid lump, without desires,
And without pow'r to give 'em?

ALEX.   You misjudge;
You see through love, and that deludes your sight,
As what is straight seems crooked through the water;
But I, who bear my reason undisturb'd,
Can see this Antony, this dreaded man,
A fearful slave, who fain would run away,
And shuns his master's eyes: if you pursue him,
My life on't, he still drags a chain along,
That needs must clog his flight.

CLEO.   Could I believe thee!—

ALEX. By ev'ry circumstance I know he loves.
True, he's hard press'd, by int'rest and by honour;
Yet he but doubts, and parleys, and casts out
Many a long look for succour.

CLEO.   He sends word
He fears to see my face.

ALEX.   And would you more?

He shows his weakness who declines the combat,
And you must urge your fortune. Could he speak
More plainly? To my ears, the message sounds
"Come to my rescue, Cleopatra, come;
Come, free me from Ventidius, from my tyrant:
See me, and give me a pretence to leave him!"
I hear his trumpets. This way he must pass.
Please you, retire a while; I'll work him first,
That he may bend more easy.

    CLEO.   You shall rule me;
But all, I fear, in vain.   (*Exit with* CHARMION *and* IRAS.)

    ALEX.   I fear so too;
Though I conceal'd my thoughts, to make her bold;
But 'tis our utmost means, and fate befriend it!   (*withdraws*)

Enter Lictors with fasces, one bearing the eagle:
then enter ANTONY *with* VENTIDIUS, *followed by*
other Commanders

    ANT. Octavius is the minion of blind chance,
But holds from virtue nothing.

    VENT.   Has he courage?

    ANT. But just enough to season him from coward.
Oh, 'tis the coldest youth upon a charge,
The most deliberate fighter! if he ventures
(As in Illyria once they say he did
To storm a town), 'tis when he cannot choose,
When all the world have fix'd their eyes upon him,
And then he lives on that for seven years after;
But, at a close revenge he never fails.

    VENT. I heard you challeng'd him.

    ANT.   I did, Ventidius.
What think'st thou was his answer? 'Twas so tame!
He said he had more ways than one to die;
I had not.

    VENT.   Poor!

    ANT.   He has more ways than one;
But he would choose 'em all before that one.

    VENT. He first would choose an ague, or a fever.

    ANT. No; it must be an ague, not a fever;
He has not warmth enough to die by that.

VENT. Or old age and a bed.

ANT.   Aye, there's his choice,
He would live, like a lamp, to the last wink,
And crawl upon the utmost verge of life.
O Hercules! Why should a man like this,
Who dares not trust his fate for one great action,
Be all the care of heav'n? Why should he lord it
O'er fourscore thousand men, of whom each one
Is braver than himself?

VENT.   You conquer'd for him:
Philippi knows it; there you shar'd with him
That empire, which your sword made all your own.

ANT. Fool that I was, upon my eagle's wings
I bore this wren, till I was tir'd with soaring,
And now he mounts above me.
Good heav'ns, is this—is this the man who braves me?
Who bids my age make way, drives me before him,
To the world's ridge, and sweeps me off like rubbish?

VENT. Sir, we lose time; the troops are mounted all.

ANT. Then give the word to march:
I long to leave this prison of a town,
To join thy legions; and, in open field,
Once more to show my face. Lead, my deliverer.

Enter ALEXAS

ALEX. Great Emperor,
In mighty arms renown'd above mankind,
But, in soft pity to th' oppress'd, a god,
This message sends the mournful Cleopatra
To her departing lord.

VENT.   Smooth sycophant!

ALEX. A thousand wishes, and ten thousand prayers,
Millions of blessings wait you to the wars;
Millions of sighs and tears she sends you too,
And would have sent
As many dear embraces to your arms,
As many parting kisses to your lips;
But those, she fears, have weary'd you already.

VENT. (*aside*) False crocodile!

ALEX. And yet she begs not now, you would not leave her;

That were a wish too mighty for her hopes,
Too presuming
For her low fortune, and your ebbing love;
That were a wish for her more prosp'rous days,
Her blooming beauty, and your growing kindness.

ANT. (*aside*) Well, I must man it out!—What would the queen?

ALEX. First, to these noble warriors, who attend
Your daring courage in the chase of fame
(Too daring, and too dang'rous for her quiet),
She humbly recommends all she holds dear,
All her own cares and fears—the care of you.

VENT. Yes, witness Actium.

ANT.   Let him speak, Ventidius.

ALEX. You, when his matchless valour bears him forward,
With ardour too heroic, on his foes,
Fall down, as she would do, before his feet;
Lie in his way, and stop the paths of death.
Tell him, this God is not invulnerable;
That absent Cleopatra bleeds in him;
And, that you may remember her petition,
She begs you wear these trifles, as a pawn,
Which, at your wish'd return, she will redeem
                         (*gives jewels to the Commanders*)
With all the wealth of Egypt:
This to the great Ventidius she presents,
Whom she can never count her enemy
Because he loves her lord.

VENT.   Tell her, I'll none on't;
I'm not asham'd of honest poverty:
Not all the diamonds of the East can bribe
Ventidius from his faith. I hope to see
These, and the rest of all her sparkling store,
Where they shall more deservingly be plac'd.

ANT. And who must wear 'em then?

VENT.   The wrong'd Octavia.

ANT. You might have spar'd that word.

VENT.   And he that bribe.

ANT. But have I no remembrance?

ALEX.   Yes, a dear one:

Your slave the queen——

    ANT.   My mistress.

    ALEX.   Then your mistress;
Your mistress would, she says, have sent her soul,
But that you had long since; she humbly begs
This ruby bracelet, set with bleeding hearts
(The emblems of her own), may bind your arm.
                       (*presenting a bracelet*)

    VENT. Now, my best Lord, in honour's name, I ask you,
For manhood's sake, and for your own dear safety,
Touch not these poison'd gifts,
Infected by the sender; touch 'em not;
Myriads of bluest plagues lie underneath 'em,
And more than aconite has dipp'd the silk.

    ANT. Nay, now you grow too cynical, Ventidius:
A lady's favours may be worn with honour.
What, to refuse her bracelet! On my soul,
When I lie pensive in my tent alone,
'Twill pass the wakeful hours of winter nights,
To tell these pretty beads upon my arm,
To count for every one a soft embrace,
A melting kiss at such and such a time,
And now and then the fury of her love,
When—— And what harm's in this?

    ALEX.   None, none, my Lord,
But what's to her, that now 'tis past for ever.

    ANT. (*going to tie it*) We soldiers are so awkward—help me
    tie it.

    ALEX. In faith, my Lord, we courtiers too are awkward
In these affairs: so are all men indeed;
Ev'n I, who am not one. But shall I speak?

    ANT. Yes, freely.

    ALEX.   Then, my Lord, fair hands alone
Are fit to tie it; she, who sent it, can.

    VENT. Hell, death! this eunuch pander ruins you.
You will not see her?

               (ALEXAS *whispers an Attendant, who goes out.*)

    ANT.   But to take my leave.

    VENT. Then I have wash'd an Æthiope. Y'are undone;
Y'are in the toils; y'are taken; y'are destroy'd:

Her eyes do Cæsar's work.
    ANT.   You fear too soon.
I'm constant to myself; I know my strength;
And yet she shall not think me barbarous neither,
Born in the depths of Afric: I'm a Roman,
Bred to the rules of soft humanity.
A guest, and kindly us'd, should bid farewell.
    VENT. You do not know
How weak you are to her, how much an infant:
You are not proof against a smile, or glance;
A sigh will quite disarm you.
    ANT.   See, she comes!
Now you shall find your error. Gods, I thank you:
I form'd the danger greater than it was,
And now 'tis near, 'tis lessen'd.
    VENT.   Mark the end yet.

Enter CLEOPATRA, CHARMION, *and* IRAS

    ANT. Well, Madam, we are met.
    CLEO.   Is this a meeting?
Then, we must part?
    ANT.   We must.
    CLEO.   Who says we must?
    ANT. Our own hard fates.
    CLEO.   We make those fates ourselves.
    ANT. Yes, we have made 'em; we have lov'd each other
Into our mutual ruin.
    CLEO. The Gods have seen my joys with envious eyes;
I have no friends in heav'n; and all the world,
(As 'twere the bus'ness of mankind to part us)
Is arm'd against my love: ev'n you yourself
Join with the rest; you, you are arm'd against me.
    ANT. I will be justify'd in all I do
To late posterity, and therefore hear me.
If I mix a lie
With any truth, reproach me freely with it;
Else, favour me with silence.
    CLEO.   You command me,
And I am dumb.
    VENT. I like this well: he shows authority.

ANT. That I derive my ruin
From you alone——
    CLEO.   O heav'ns! I ruin you!
    ANT. You promis'd me your silence, and you break it
Ere I have scarce begun.
    CLEO.   Well, I obey you.
    ANT. When I beheld you first, it was in Egypt,
Ere Cæsar saw your eyes; you gave me love,
And were too young to know it; that I settled
Your father in his throne, was for your sake;
I left th' acknowledgment for time to ripen.
Cæsar stepp'd in, and with a greedy hand
Pluck'd the green fruit, ere the first blush of red,
Yet cleaving to the bough. He was my lord,
And was, beside, too great for me to rival;
But I deserv'd you first, though he enjoy'd you.
When, after, I beheld you in Cilicia,
An enemy to Rome, I pardon'd you.
    CLEO. I clear'd myself——
    ANT.   Again you break your promise.
I lov'd you still, and took your weak excuses,
Took you into my bosom, stain'd by Cæsar,
And not half mine. I went to Egypt with you,
And hid me from the bus'ness of the world,
Shut out enquiring nations from my sight,
To give whole years to you.
    VENT. (aside) Yes, to your shame be't spoken.
    ANT.   How I lov'd,
Witness, ye days and nights, and all your hours,
That danc'd away with down upon your feet,
As all your bus'ness were to count my passion!
One day pass'd by and nothing saw but love;
Another came, and still 'twas only love:
The suns were weary'd out with looking on,
And I untir'd with loving.
I saw you ev'ry day, and all the day;
And ev'ry day was still but as the first,
So eager was I still to see you more.
    VENT. 'Tis all too true.
    ANT.   Fulvia, my wife, grew jealous,

As she indeed had reason; rais'd a war
In Italy, to call me back.
    VENT.   But yet
You went not.
    ANT.   While within your arms I lay,
The world fell mould'ring from my hands each hour,
And left me scarce a grasp (I thank your love for't).
    VENT. Well push'd: that last was home.
    CLEO.   Yet may I speak?
    ANT. If I have urg'd a falsehood, yes; else, not.
Your silence says I have not. Fulvia died,
(Pardon, you Gods; with my unkindness died);
To set the world at peace, I took Octavia,
This Cæsar's sister; in her pride of youth
And flow'r of beauty did I wed that lady,
Whom blushing I must praise, because I left her.
You call'd; my love obey'd the fatal summons:
This rais'd the Roman arms; the cause was yours.
I would have fought by land, where I was stronger;
You hinder'd it: yet, when I fought at sea,
Forsook me fighting; and (Oh stain to honour!
Oh lasting shame!) I knew not that I fled,
But fled to follow you.
    VENT. What haste she made to hoist her purple sails!
And, to appear magnificent in flight,
Drew half our strength away.
    ANT.   All this you caus'd,
And would you multiply more ruins on me?
This honest man, my best, my only friend,
Has gather'd up the shipwrack of my fortunes;
Twelve legions I have left, my last recruits,
And you have watch'd the news, and bring your eyes
To seize them too. If you have aught to answer,
Now speak, you have free leave.
    ALEX. (*aside*)   She stands confounded:
Despair is in her eyes.
    VENT. Now lay a sigh i' th' way to stop his passage:
Prepare a tear, and bid it for his legions;
'Tis like they shall be sold.
    CLEO. How shall I plead my cause, when you, my judge,

Already have condemn'd me? Shall I bring
The love you bore me for my advocate?
That now is turn'd against me, that destroys me;
For love, once past, is, at the best, forgotten;
But oft'ner sours to hate: 'twill please my lord
To ruin me, and therefore I'll be guilty.
But, could I once have thought it would have pleas'd you,
That you would pry, with narrow searching eyes,
Into my faults, severe to my destruction,
And watching all advantages with care,
That serve to make me wretched? Speak, my Lord,
For I end here. Though I deserve this usage,
Was it like you to give it?

ANT.   Oh, you wrong me
To think I sought this parting, or desir'd
To accuse you more than what will clear myself,
And justify this breach.

CLEO.   Thus low I thank you.
And, since my innocence will not offend,
I shall not blush to own it.

VENT.   After this,
I think she'll blush at nothing.

CLEO.   You seem griev'd
(And therein you are kind) that Cæsar first
Enjoy'd my love, though you deserv'd it better;
I grieve for that, my Lord, much more than you;
For, had I first been yours, it would have sav'd
My second choice: I never had been his,
And ne'er had been but yours. But Cæsar first,
You say, possess'd my love. Not so, my Lord:
He first possess'd my person, you, my love:
Cæsar lov'd me; but I lov'd Antony.
If I endur'd him after, 'twas because
I judg'd it due to the first name of men;
And, half constrain'd, I gave, as to a tyrant,
What he would take by force.

VENT.   O siren! siren!
Yet grant that all the love she boasts were true,
Has she not ruin'd you? I still urge that,
The fatal consequence.

CLEO.   The consequence indeed,
For I dare challenge him, my greatest foe,
To say it was design'd: 'tis true, I lov'd you,
And kept you far from an uneasy wife—
Such Fulvia was.
Yes, but he'll say you left Octavia for me,
And, can you blame me to receive that love,
Which quitted such desert, for worthless me?
How often have I wish'd some other Cæsar,
Great as the first, and as the second young,
Would court my love, to be refus'd for you!

VENT. Words, words; but Actium, Sir, remember Actium.

CLEO. Ev'n there, I dare his malice. True, I counsell'd
To fight at sea; but I betray'd you not.
I fled, but not to the enemy. 'Twas fear;
Would I had been a man, not to have fear'd!
For none would then have envy'd me your friendship,
Who envy me your love.

ANT.   We're both unhappy:
If nothing else, yet our ill fortune parts us.
Speak; would you have me perish by my stay?

CLEO. If as a friend you ask my judgment, go;
If as a lover, stay. If you must perish—
'Tis a hard word—but stay.

VENT. See now th' effects of her so boasted love!
She strives to drag you down to ruin with her:
But, could she 'scape without you, oh, how soon
Would she let go her hold, and haste to shore,
And never look behind!

CLEO. Then judge my love by this.   (giving ANTONY a writing)
                              Could I have borne
A life or death, a happiness or woe,
From yours divided, this had giv'n me means.

ANT. By Hercules, the writing of Octavius!
I know it well: 'tis that proscribing hand,
Young as it was, that led the way to mine,
And left me but the second place in murder.——
See, see, Ventidius! here he offers Egypt,
And joins all Syria to it, as a present,
So, in requital, she forsake my fortunes,

And join her arms with his.

CLEO.   And yet you leave me!
You leave me, Antony; and yet I love you,
Indeed I do: I have refus'd a kingdom—
That's a trifle:
For I could part with life, with anything,
But only you. Oh, let me die but with you!
Is that a hard request?

ANT.   Next living with you,
'Tis all that heav'n can give.

ALEX. (*aside*)   He melts; we conquer.

CLEO. No, you shall go; your int'rest calls you hence;
Yes, your dear interest pulls too strong, for these
Weak arms to hold you here.—(*takes his hand*)
                                   Go; leave me, soldier
(For you're no more a lover); leave me dying:
Push me all pale and panting from your bosom,
And, when your march begins, let one run after,
Breathless almost for joy, and cry, "She's dead."
The soldiers shout; you then, perhaps, may sigh,
And muster all your Roman gravity:
Ventidius chides; and straight your brow clears up,
As I had never been.

ANT.   Gods, 'tis too much,
Too much for man to bear!

CLEO.   What is't for me then,
A weak, forsaken woman, and a lover?
Here let me breathe my last: envy me not
This minute in your arms: I'll die apace,
As fast as e'er I can, and end your trouble.

ANT. Die! rather let me perish: loosen'd nature
Leap from its hinges! Sink the props of heav'n,
And fall the skies to crush the nether world!
My eyes, my soul, my all!—   (*embraces her*)

VENT.   And what's this toy,
In balance with your fortune, honour, fame?

ANT. What is't, Ventidius?—it outweighs 'em all;
Why, we have more than conquer'd Cæsar now:
My queen's not only innocent, but loves me.
This, this is she who drags me down to ruin!

"But, could she 'scape without me, with what haste
Would she let slip her hold, and make to shore,
And never look behind!"
Down on thy knees, blasphemer as thou art,
And ask forgiveness of wrong'd innocence.

    VENT. I'll rather die, than take it. Will you go?

    ANT. Go! whither? Go from all that's excellent?
Faith, honour, virtue, all good things forbid
That I should go from her, who sets my love
Above the price of kingdoms. Give, you Gods,
Give to your boy, your Cæsar,
This rattle of a globe to play withal,
This gewgaw world, and put him cheaply off:
I'll not be pleas'd with less than Cleopatra.

    CLEO. She's wholly yours. My heart's so full of joy,
That I shall do some wild extravagance
Of love in public; and the foolish world,
Which knows not tenderness, will think me mad.

    VENT. O women! women! women! all the Gods
Have not such pow'r of doing good to man,
As you of doing harm.   (*Exit.*)

    ANT.   Our men are arm'd.
Unbar the gate that looks to Cæsar's camp;
I would revenge the treachery he meant me,
And long security makes conquest easy.
I'm eager to return before I go;
For all the pleasures I have known beat thick
On my remembrance. How I long for night!
    That both the sweets of mutual love may try,
    And once triumph o'er Cæsar ere we die.   (*Exeunt.*)

ACT III

At one door, enter CLEOPATRA, CHARMION, IRAS, *and* ALEXAS, *a
    train of Egyptians: at the other,* ANTONY *and Romans. The
    entrance on both sides is prepared by music, the trumpets
    first sounding on* ANTONY'S *part, then answered by timbrels,
    etc., on* CLEOPATRA'S. CHARMION *and* IRAS *hold a laurel*

wreath betwixt them. A dance of Egyptians. After the cere-mony, CLEOPATRA *crowns* ANTONY.

ANT. I thought how those white arms would fold me in,
And strain me close, and melt me into love;
So pleas'd with that sweet image, I sprung forwards,
And added all my strength to every blow.

CLEO. Come to me, come, my soldier, to my arms!
You've been too long away from my embraces;
But, when I have you fast, and all my own,
With broken murmurs, and with amorous sighs,
I'll say you were unkind, and punish you,
And mark you red with many an eager kiss.

ANT. My brighter Venus!

CLEO.   O my greater Mars!

ANT. Thou join'st us well, my love!
Suppose me come from the Phlegræan plains,
Where gasping giants lay, cleft by my sword,
And mountain-tops par'd off each other blow,
To bury those I slew. Receive me, Goddess!
Let Cæsar spread his subtile nets, like Vulcan;
In thy embraces I would be beheld
By heav'n and earth at once,
And make their envy what they meant their sport.
Let those who took us blush; I would love on
With awful state, regardless of their frowns,
As their superior God.
There's no satiety of love in thee;
Enjoy'd, thou still art new; perpetual spring
Is in thy arms; the ripen'd fruit but falls,
And blossoms rise to fill its empty place,
And I grow rich by giving.

Enter VENTIDIUS, *and stands apart*

ALEX. Oh, now the danger's past, your general comes!
He joins not in your joys, nor minds your triumphs;
But, with contracted brows, looks frowning on,
As envying your success.

ANT. Now, on my soul, he loves me, truly loves me;
He never flatter'd me in any vice,

But awes me with his virtue: ev'n this minute,
Methinks, he has a right of chiding me.——
Lead to the temple: I'll avoid his presence;
It checks too strong upon me.

> (*Exeunt the rest. As* ANTONY *is going,* VENTIDIUS
> *pulls him by the robe.*)

VENT.   Emperor!

ANT. (*looking back*) 'Tis the old argument; I pr'ythee, spare
me.

VENT. But this one hearing, Emperor.

ANT.   Let go
My robe; or, by my father Hercules——

VENT. By Hercules his father, that's yet greater,
I bring you somewhat you would wish to know.

ANT. Thou see'st we are observ'd; attend me here,
And I'll return.   (*Exit.*)

VENT. I'm waning in his favour, yet I love him;
I love this man, who runs to meet his ruin;
And sure the Gods, like me, are fond of him:
His virtues lie so mingled with his crimes
As would confound their choice to punish one,
And not reward the other.

Enter ANTONY

ANT.   We can conquer,
You see, without your aid.
We have dislodg'd their troops;
They look on us at distance, and, like curs
'Scaped from the lion's paws, they bay far off,
And lick their wounds, and faintly threaten war.
Five thousand Romans, with their faces upward,
Lie breathless on the plain.

VENT.   'Tis well: and he
Who lost 'em, could have spar'd ten thousand more.
Yet if, by this advantage, you could gain
An easier peace, while Cæsar doubts the chance
Of arms!——

ANT.   Oh, think not on't, Ventidius!
The boy pursues my ruin, he'll no peace;
His malice is considerate in advantage;

Oh, he's the coolest murderer! so staunch,
He kills and keeps his temper.

VENT.   Have you no friend
In all his army who has power to move him?
Mæcenas, or Agrippa, might do much.

ANT. They're both too deep in Cæsar's interests.
We'll work it out by dint of sword, or perish.

VENT. Fain I would find some other.

ANT.   Thank thy love.
Some four or five such victories as this
Will save thy farther pains.

VENT. Expect no more; Cæsar is on his guard:
I know, Sir, you have conquer'd against odds;
But still you draw supplies from one poor town,
And of Egyptians: he has all the world,
And, at his back, nations come pouring in
To fill the gaps you make. Pray, think again.

ANT. Why dost thou drive me from myself, to search
For foreign aids? to hunt my memory,
And range all o'er a waste and barren place
To find a friend? The wretched have no friends.——
Yet I had one, the bravest youth of Rome,
Whom Cæsar loves beyond the love of women;
He could resolve his mind, as fire does wax,
From that hard rugged image melt him down,
And mould him in what softer form he pleas'd.

VENT. Him would I see, that man of all the world;
Just such a one we want.

ANT.   He lov'd me too,
I was his soul; he liv'd not but in me;
We were so clos'd within each other's breasts
The rivets were not found that join'd us first.
That does not reach us yet: we were so mix'd,
As meeting streams, both to ourselves were lost;
We were one mass; we could not give or take,
But from the same; for he was I, I he!

VENT. (aside) He moves as I would wish him.

ANT.   After this,
I need not tell his name—'twas Dolabella.

VENT. He's now in Cæsar's camp.

ANT.   No matter where,
Since he's no longer mine. He took unkindly
That I forbade him Cleopatra's sight,
Because I fear'd he lov'd her: he confess'd
He had a warmth, which, for my sake, he stifled;
For 'twere impossible that two, so one,
Should not have lov'd the same. When he departed,
He took no leave; and that confirm'd my thoughts.

VENT. It argues that he lov'd you more than her,
Else he had stay'd; but he perceiv'd you jealous,
And would not grieve his friend: I know he loves you.

ANT. I should have seen him, then, ere now.

VENT.   Perhaps
He has thus long been lab'ring for your peace.

ANT. Would he were here!

VENT.   Would you believe he lov'd you?
I read your answer in your eyes; you would.
Not to conceal it longer, he has sent
A messenger from Cæsar's camp, with letters.

ANT. Let him appear.

VENT.   I'll bring him instantly.

(*Exit* VENTIDIUS, *and re-enters immediately with* DOLABELLA.)

ANT. 'Tis he himself! himself, by holy friendship!

                              (*runs to embrace him*)

Art thou return'd at last, my better half?
Come, give me all myself! Let me not live,
If the young bridegroom, longing for his night,
Was ever half so fond.

DOLA. I must be silent, for my soul is busy
About a nobler work: she's new come home,
Like a long-absent man, and wanders o'er
Each room, a stranger to her own, to look
If all be safe.

ANT.   Thou hast what's left of me;
For I am now so sunk from what I was
Thou find'st me at my lowest water-mark.
The rivers that ran in, and rais'd my fortunes,
Are all dried up, or take another course.
What I have left is from my native spring;
I've still a heart that swells, in scorn of fate,

And lifts me to my banks.

    DOLA. Still you are lord of all the world to me.

    ANT. Why, then I yet am so; for thou art all.
If I had any joy when thou wert absent,
I grudg'd it to myself; methought I robb'd
Thee of thy part. But, O my Dolabella!
Thou hast beheld me other than I am.
Hast thou not seen my morning chambers fill'd
With scepter'd slaves, who waited to salute me?
With eastern monarchs, who forgot the sun,
To worship my uprising? Menial kings
Ran coursing up and down my palace-yard,
Stood silent in my presence, watch'd my eyes,
And, at my least command, all started out,
Like racers to the goal.

    DOLA.   Slaves to your fortune.

    ANT. Fortune is Cæsar's now; and what am I?

    VENT. What you have made yourself; I will not flatter.

    ANT. Is this friendly done?

    DOLA. Yes, when his end is so, I must join with him;
Indeed I must, and yet you must not chide:
Why am I else your friend?

    ANT.   Take heed, young man,
How thou upbraid'st my love; the queen has eyes,
And thou too hast a soul. Canst thou remember,
When, swell'd with hatred, thou beheld'st her first,
As accessary to thy brother's death?

    DOLA. Spare my remembrance; 'twas a guilty day,
And still the blush hangs here.

    ANT.   To clear herself
For sending him no aid, she came from Egypt.
Her galley down the silver Cydnos row'd,
The tackling silk, the streamers wav'd with gold;
The gentle winds were lodg'd in purple sails;
Her nymphs, like Nereids, round her couch were plac'd,
Where she, another sea-born Venus, lay.

    DOLA. No more: I would not hear it.

    ANT.   Oh, you must!
She lay, and leant her cheek upon her hand,
And cast a look so languishingly sweet,

As if, secure of all beholders' hearts,
Neglecting, she could take 'em: boys, like Cupids,
Stood fanning with their painted wings the winds
That play'd about her face: but if she smil'd,
A darting glory seemed to blaze abroad,
That men's desiring eyes were never weary'd,
But hung upon the object. To soft flutes
The silver oars kept time; and while they play'd,
The hearing gave new pleasure to the sight,
And both to thought. 'Twas heav'n, or somewhat more;
For she so charm'd all hearts, that gazing crowds
Stood panting on the shore, and wanted breath
To give their welcome voice.
Then, Dolabella, where was then thy soul?
Was not thy fury quite disarm'd with wonder?
Didst thou not shrink behind me from those eyes,
And whisper in my ear, "Oh, tell her not
That I accus'd her of my brother's death"?
    DOLA. And should my weakness be a plea for yours?
Mine was an age when love might be excus'd,
When kindly warmth, and when my springing youth
Made it a debt to nature. Yours——
    VENT.   Speak boldly.
Yours, he would say, in your declining age,
When no more heat was left but what you forc'd,
When all the sap was needful for the trunk,
When it went down, then you constrain'd the course,
And robb'd from nature, to supply desire;
In you (I would not use so harsh a word)
But 'tis plain dotage.
    ANT.   Ha!
    DOLA.   'Twas urg'd too home.
But yet the loss was private that I made;
'Twas but myself I lost: I lost no legions;
I had no world to lose, no people's love.
    ANT. This from a friend?
    DOLA.   Yes, Antony, a true one;
A friend so tender that each word I speak
Stabs my own heart, before it reach your ear.

Oh, judge me not less kind because I chide!
To Cæsar I excuse you.

ANT.   O ye Gods!
Have I then liv'd to be excus'd to Cæsar?

DOLA. As to your equal.

ANT.   Well, he's but my equal;
While I wear this, he never shall be more.

DOLA. I bring conditions from him.

ANT.   Are they noble?
Methinks thou shouldst not bring 'em else; yet he
Is full of deep dissembling; knows no honour
Divided from his int'rest. Fate mistook him;
For nature meant him for an usurer:
He's fit indeed to buy, not conquer, kingdoms.

VENT. Then, granting this,
What pow'r was theirs who wrought so hard a temper
To honourable terms?

ANT. It was my Dolabella, or some God.

DOLA. Nor I, nor yet Mæcenas, nor Agrippa:
They were your enemies; and I, a friend,
Too weak alone; yet 'twas a Roman's deed.

ANT. 'Twas like a Roman done: show me that man,
Who has preserv'd my life, my love, my honour;
Let me but see his face.

VENT.   That task is mine,
And, heav'n, thou know'st how pleasing.   (*Exit* VENTIDIUS.)

DOLA.   You'll remember
To whom you stand oblig'd?

ANT.   When I forget it,
Be thou unkind, and that's my greatest curse.
My queen shall thank him too.

DOLA.   I fear she will not.

ANT. But she shall do't—the queen, my Dolabella!
Hast thou not still some grudgings of thy fever?

DOLA. I would not see her lost.

ANT.   When I forsake her,
Leave me, my better stars! for she has truth
Beyond her beauty. Cæsar tempted her,
At no less price than kingdoms, to betray me;

But she resisted all: and yet thou chid'st me
For loving her too well. Could I do so?

DOLA. Yes; there's my reason.

Re-enter VENTIDIUS, *with* OCTAVIA, *leading* ANTONY'S
two little daughters

ANT. (*starting back*) Where?—Octavia there!

VENT. What, is she poison to you? a disease?
Look on her, view her well, and those she brings:
Are they all strangers to your eyes? has nature
No secret call, no whisper they are yours?

DOLA. For shame, my Lord, if not for love, receive 'em
With kinder eyes. If you confess a man,
Meet 'em, embrace 'em, bid 'em welcome to you.
Your arms should open, ev'n without your knowledge,
To clasp 'em in; your feet should turn to wings,
To bear you to 'em; and your eyes dart out
And aim a kiss, ere you could reach the lips.

ANT. I stood amaz'd to think how they came hither.

VENT. I sent for 'em; I brought 'em in, unknown
To Cleopatra's guards.

DOLA.   Yet are you cold?

OCTAV. Thus long I have attended for my welcome,
Which, as a stranger, sure I might expect.
Who am I?

ANT.   Caesar's sister.

OCTAV.   That's unkind.
Had I been nothing more than Caesar's sister,
Know, I had still remain'd in Caesar's camp;
But your Octavia, your much injur'd wife,
Though banish'd from your bed, driv'n from your house,
In spite of Caesar's sister, still is yours.
'Tis true, I have a heart disdains your coldness,
And prompts me not to seek what you should offer;
But a wife's virtue still surmounts that pride:
I come to claim you as my own; to show
My duty first; to ask, nay beg, your kindness:
Your hand, my Lord; 'tis mine, and I will have it.

(*taking his hand*)

VENT. Do, take it; thou deserv'st it.

DOLA.   On my soul,
And so she does: she's neither too submissive,
Nor yet too haughty; but so just a mean
Shows, as it ought, a wife and Roman too.

 ANT. I fear, Octavia, you have begg'd my life.

 OCTAV. Begg'd it, my Lord?

 ANT.   Yes, begg'd it, my ambassadress,
Poorly and basely begg'd it of your brother.

 OCTAV. Poorly and basely I could never beg;
Nor could my brother grant.

 ANT. Shall I, who, to my kneeling slave, could say,
"Rise up, and be a king," shall I fall down
And cry, "Forgive me, Cæsar"? Shall I set
A man, my equal, in the place of Jove,
As he could give me being? No; that word,
"Forgive," would choke me up,
And die upon my tongue.

 DOLA.   You shall not need it.

 ANT. I will not need it. Come, you've all betray'd me—
My friend too!—to receive some vile conditions.
My wife has bought me, with her prayers and tears,
And now I must become her branded slave:
In every peevish mood, she will upbraid
The life she gave: if I but look awry,
She cries, "I'll tell my brother."

 OCTAV.   My hard fortune
Subjects me still to your unkind mistakes.
But the conditions I have brought are such
You need not blush to take: I love your honour,
Because 'tis mine; it never shall be said,
Octavia's husband was her brother's slave.
Sir, you are free—free, ev'n from her you loathe;
For, though my brother bargains for your love,
Makes me the price and cement of your peace,
I have a soul like yours; I cannot take
Your love as alms, nor beg what I deserve.
I'll tell my brother we are reconcil'd;
He shall draw back his troops, and you shall march
To rule the East: I may be dropp'd at Athens;
No matter where, I never will complain,

But only keep the barren name of wife,
And rid you of the trouble.

VENT. Was ever such a strife of sullen honour!
Both scorn to be oblig'd.

DOLA. Oh, she has touch'd him in the tender'st part;
See how he reddens with despite and shame,
To be outdone in generosity!

VENT. See how he winks! how he dries up a tear,
That fain would fall!

ANT. Octavia, I have heard you, and must praise
The greatness of your soul;
But cannot yield to what you have propos'd;
For I can ne'er be conquer'd but by love;
And you do all for duty. You would free me,
And would be dropp'd at Athens; was't not so?

OCTAV. It was, my Lord.

ANT.   Then I must be oblig'd
To one who loves me not, who, to herself,
May call me thankless and ungrateful man—
I'll not endure it; no.

VENT. (*aside*) I'm glad it pinches there.

OCTAV. Would you triumph o'er poor Octavia's virtue?
That pride was all I had to bear me up:
That you might think you ow'd me for your life,
And ow'd it to my duty, not my love.
I have been injur'd, and my haughty soul
Could brook but ill the man who slights my bed.

ANT. Therefore you love me not.

OCTAV.   Therefore, my Lord,
I should not love you.

ANT.   Therefore you would leave me?

OCTAV. And therefore I should leave you—if I could.

DOLA. Her soul's too great, after such injuries,
To say she loves; and yet she lets you see it.
Her modesty and silence plead her cause.

ANT. O Dolabella, which way shall I turn?
I find a secret yielding in my soul;
But Cleopatra, who would die with me,
Must she be left? Pity pleads for Octavia;
But does it not plead more for Cleopatra?

VENT. Justice and pity both plead for Octavia;
For Cleopatra, neither.
One would be ruin'd with you, but she first
Had ruin'd you: the other, you have ruin'd,
And yet she would preserve you.
In everything their merits are unequal.

ANT. Oh my distracted soul!

OCTAV.   Sweet heav'n compose it!
Come, come, my Lord, if I can pardon you,
Methinks you should accept it. Look on these;
Are they not yours? Or stand they thus neglected,
As they are mine? Go to him, children, go;
Kneel to him, take him by the hand, speak to him;
For you may speak, and he may own you too,
Without a blush; and so he cannot all
His children: go, I say, and pull him to me,
And pull him to yourselves, from that bad woman.
You, Agrippina, hang upon his arms;
And you, Antonia, clasp about his waist:
If he will shake you off, if he will dash you
Against the pavement, you must bear it, children;
For you are mine, and I was born to suffer.

                        (*Here the Children go to him, etc.*)

VENT. Was ever sight so moving?—Emperor!

DOLA. Friend!

OCTAV.   Husband!

BOTH CHILD.   Father!

ANT.   I am vanquish'd; take me,
Octavia; take me, children; share me all.   (*embracing them*)
I've been a thriftless debtor to your loves,
And run out much, in riot, from your stock;
But all shall be amended.

OCTAV.   Oh blest hour!

DOLA. O happy change!

VENT.   My joy stops at my tongue;
But it has found two channels here for one,
And bubbles out above.

ANT. (*to* OCTAVIA) This is thy triumph; lead me where thou
    wilt,

Ev'n to thy brother's camp.
    OCTAV.   All there are yours.

Enter ALEXAS *hastily*

    ALEX. The queen, my mistress, Sir, and yours——
    ANT.   'Tis past.——
Octavia, you shall stay this night; to-morrow,
Cæsar and we are one.
                    (*Exit leading* OCTAVIA; DOLABELLA *and*
                             the Children follow.)
    VENT. There's news for you; run, my officious eunuch,
Be sure to be the first; haste forward;
Haste, my dear eunuch, haste!   (*Exit.*)
    ALEX. This downright fighting fool, this thick-skull'd hero,
This blunt, unthinking instrument of death,
With plain dull virtue has outgone my wit.
Pleasure forsook my earliest infancy;
The luxury of others robb'd my cradle,
And ravish'd thence the promise of a man.
Cast out from nature, disinherited
Of what her meanest children claim by kind,
Yet greatness kept me from contempt: that's gone.
Had Cleopatra follow'd my advice,
Then he had been betray'd who now forsakes.
She dies for love, but she has known its joys:
Gods, is this just, that I, who know no joys,
Must die, because she loves?

Enter CLEOPATRA, CHARMION, IRAS, *and train*

O Madam, I have seen what blasts my eyes!
Octavia's here!
    CLEO.   Peace with that raven's note.
I know it too; and now am in
The pangs of death.
    ALEX.   You are no more a queen;
Egypt is lost.
    CLEO.   What tell'st thou me of Egypt?
My life, my soul is lost! Octavia has him!
O fatal name to Cleopatra's love!
My kisses, my embraces now are hers;

While I—— But thou hast seen my rival; speak,
Does she deserve this blessing? Is she fair?
Bright as a goddess? And is all perfection
Confin'd to her? It is. Poor I was made
Of that coarse matter, which, when she was finish'd,
The Gods threw by, for rubbish.

   ALEX. She's indeed a very miracle.

   CLEO. Death to my hopes, a miracle!

   ALEX. (*bowing*)   A miracle;
I mean of goodness; for in beauty, Madam,
You make all wonders cease.

   CLEO.   I was too rash:
Take this in part of recompense. But, oh!   (*giving a ring*)
I fear thou flatter'st me.

   CHAR. She comes! she's here!

   IRAS.   Fly, Madam, Cæsar's sister!

   CLEO. Were she the sister of the thund'rer Jove,
And bore her brother's lightning in her eyes,
Thus would I face my rival.

        (*Meets* OCTAVIA *with* VENTIDIUS. OCTAVIA *bears up to*
        her. Their trains come up on either side.)

   OCTAV. I need not ask if you are Cleopatra;
Your haughty carriage——

   CLEO.   Shows I am a queen:
Nor need I ask you who you are.

   OCTAV.   A Roman:
A name that makes and can unmake a queen.

   CLEO. Your lord, the man who serves me, is a Roman.

   OCTAV. He was a Roman, till he lost that name,
To be a slave in Egypt; but I come
To free him thence.

   CLEO.   Peace, peace, my lover's Juno.
When he grew weary of that household clog,
He chose my easier bonds.

   OCTAV.   I wonder not
Your bonds are easy; you have long been practis'd
In that lascivious art: he's not the first
For whom you spread your snares: let Cæsar witness.

   CLEO. I lov'd not Cæsar; 'twas but gratitude
I paid his love. The worst your malice can,

Is but to say the greatest of mankind
Has been my slave. The next, but far above him
In my esteem, is he whom law calls yours,
But whom his love made mine.

OCTAV. (*coming up close to her*) I would view nearer
That face which has so long usurp'd my right,
To find th' inevitable charms that catch
Mankind so sure, that ruin'd my dear lord.

CLEO. Oh, you do well to search; for had you known
But half these charms, you had not lost his heart.

OCTAV. Far be their knowledge from a Roman lady,
Far from a modest wife! Shame of our sex,
Dost thou not blush to own those black endearments
That make sin pleasing?

CLEO.   You may blush, who want 'em.
If bounteous nature, if indulgent heav'n
Have giv'n me charms to please the bravest man,
Should I not thank 'em? Should I be asham'd,
And not be proud? I am, that he has lov'd me;
And, when I love not him, heav'n change this face
For one like that.

OCTAV.   Thou lov'st him not so well.

CLEO. I love him better, and deserve him more.

OCTAV. You do not, cannot: you have been his ruin.
Who made him cheap at Rome, but Cleopatra?
Who made him scorn'd abroad, but Cleopatra?
At Actium, who betray'd him? Cleopatra.
Who made his children orphans, and poor me
A wretched widow? only Cleopatra.

CLEO. Yet she who loves him best is Cleopatra.
If you have suffer'd, I have suffer'd more.
You bear the specious title of a wife
To gild your cause, and draw the pitying world
To favour it: the world contemns poor me,
For I have lost my honour, lost my fame,
And stain'd the glory of my royal house,
And all to bear the branded name of mistress.
There wants but life, and that too I would lose
For him I love.

OCTAV.   Be't so, then; take thy wish.   (*Exit cum suis.*)

CLEO. And 'tis my wish,
Now he is lost for whom alone I liv'd.
My sight grows dim, and every object dances
And swims before me, in the maze of death.
My spirits, while they were oppos'd, kept up;
They could not sink beneath a rival's scorn:
But now she's gone, they faint.

ALEX.   Mine have had leisure
To recollect their strength, and furnish counsel,
To ruin her, who else must ruin you.

CLEO.   Vain promiser!
Lead me, my Charmion; nay, your hand too, Iras:
My grief has weight enough to sink you both.
Conduct me to some solitary chamber,
And draw the curtains round;
Then leave me to myself, to take alone
My fill of grief.

There I till death will his unkindness weep;
As harmless infants moan themselves asleep.   (*Exeunt.*)

ACT IV

ANTONY, DOLABELLA

DOLA. Why would you shift it from yourself on me?
Can you not tell her you must part?

ANT.   I cannot.
I could pull out an eye, and bid it go,
And t'other should not weep. O Dolabella,
How many deaths are in this word "depart"!
I dare not trust my tongue to tell her so:
One look of hers would thaw me into tears,
And I should melt till I were lost again.

DOLA. Then let Ventidius;
He's rough by nature.

ANT.   Oh, he'll speak too harshly;
He'll kill her with the news: thou, only thou.

DOLA. Nature has cast me in so soft a mould,
That but to hear a story feign'd for pleasure
Of some sad lover's death, moistens my eyes,

And robs me of my manhood. I should speak
So faintly, with such fear to grieve her heart,
She'd not believe it earnest.

ANT.   Therefore, therefore
Thou only, thou art fit; think thyself me,
And when thou speak'st (but let it first be long),
Take off the edge from every sharper sound,
And let our parting be as gently made
As other loves begin: wilt thou do this?

DOLA. What you have said so sinks into my soul,
That, if I must speak, I shall speak just so.

ANT. I leave you then to your sad task. Farewell!
I sent her word to meet you.

                              (*goes to the door, and comes back*)
                              I forgot;
Let her be told I'll make her peace with mine:
Her crown and dignity shall be preserv'd,
If I have pow'r with Cæsar. Oh, be sure
To think on that.

DOLA.   Fear not, I will remember.

          (ANTONY *goes again to the door, and comes back.*)

ANT. And tell her, too, how much I was constrain'd;
I did not this, but with extremest force:
Desire her not to hate my memory,
For I still cherish hers; insist on that.

DOLA. Trust me, I'll not forget it.

ANT.   Then that's all.
                              (*goes out, and returns again*)
Wilt thou forgive my fondness this once more?
Tell her, though we shall never meet again,
If I should hear she took another love,
The news would break my heart.—Now I must go;
For every time I have return'd, I feel
My soul more tender; and my next command
Would be to bid her stay, and ruin both.   (*Exit.*)

DOLA. Men are but children of a larger growth;
Our appetites as apt to change as theirs,
And full as craving too, and full as vain;
And yet the soul, shut up in her dark room,
Viewing so clear abroad, at home sees nothing;

But, like a mole in earth, busy and blind,
Works all her folly up, and casts it outward
To the world's open view: thus I discover'd,
And blam'd the love of ruin'd Antony;
Yet wish that I were he, to be so ruin'd.

Enter VENTIDIUS *above*

VENT. Alone? and talking to himself? concern'd too?
Perhaps my guess is right; he lov'd her once
And may pursue it still.
DOLA.   Oh friendship! friendship!
Ill canst thou answer this, and reason, worse:
Unfaithful in th' attempt, hopeless to win,
And if I win, undone: mere madness all.
And yet th' occasion's fair. What injury
To him, to wear the robe which he throws by?
VENT. None, none at all. This happens as I wish,
To ruin her yet more with Antony.

Enter CLEOPATRA, *talking with* ALEXAS; CHARMION, IRAS,
on the other side

DOLA. She comes! What charms have sorrow on that face!
Sorrow seems pleas'd to dwell with so much sweetness;
Yet, now and then, a melancholy smile
Breaks loose, like lightning in a winter's night,
And shows a moment's day.
VENT. If she should love him too! her eunuch there!
That porcpisce bodes ill weather. Draw, draw nearer,
Sweet devil, that I may hear.
ALEX.   Believe me; try
          (DOLABELLA *goes over to* CHARMION *and* IRAS;
               seems to talk with them.)
To make him jealous; jealousy is like
A polish'd glass held to the lips when life's in doubt:
If there be breath, 'twill catch the damp, and show it.
CLEO. I grant you, jealousy's a proof of love,
But 'tis a weak and unavailing med'cine;
It puts out the disease, and makes it show,
But has no pow'r to cure.
ALEX. 'Tis your last remedy, and strongest too:

And then this Dolabella—who so fit
To practise on? He's handsome, valiant, young,
And looks as he were laid for nature's bait
To catch weak women's eyes.
He stands already more than half suspected
Of loving you: the least kind word or glance
You give this youth will kindle him with love:
Then, like a burning vessel set adrift,
You'll send him down amain before the wind,
To fire the heart of jealous Antony.

    CLEO. Can I do this? Ah, no; my love's so true
That I can neither hide it where it is
Nor show it where it is not. Nature meant me
A wife, a silly, harmless, household dove,
Fond without art, and kind without deceit;
But Fortune, that has made a mistress of me,
Has thrust me out to the wide world, unfurnish'd
Of falsehood to be happy.

    ALEX.   Force yourself.
Th' event will be your lover will return
Doubly desirous to possess the good
Which once he fear'd to lose.

    CLEO.   I must attempt it;
But oh, with what regret!   (*Exit* ALEXAS.)
        (*She comes up to* DOLABELLA.)
    VENT. So, now the scene draws near; they're in my reach.
    CLEO. (*to* DOLABELLA) Discoursing with my women! might
  not I
Share in your entertainment?

    CHAR.   You have been
The subject of it, Madam.

    CLEO.   How! and how?
    IRAS. Such praises of your beauty!

    CLEO.   Mere poetry.
Your Roman wits, your Gallus and Tibullus,
Have taught you this from Cytheris and Delia.

    DOLA. Those Roman wits have never been in Egypt;
Cytheris and Delia else had been unsung:
I, who have seen—had I been born a poet,
Should choose a nobler name.

CLEO.   You flatter me.
But, 'tis your nation's vice: all of your country
Are flatterers, and all false. Your friend's like you.
I'm sure he sent you not to speak these words.

   DOLA. No, Madam; yet he sent me——

   CLEO.   Well, he sent you——

   DOLA. Of a less pleasing errand.

   CLEO.   How less pleasing?
Less to yourself, or me?

   DOLA.   Madam, to both;
For you must mourn, and I must grieve to cause it.

   CLEO. You, Charmion, and your fellow, stand at distance.—
(*aside*) Hold up, my spirits.—— Well, now your mournful
    matter;
For I'm prepar'd, perhaps can guess it too.

   DOLA. I wish you would; for 'tis a thankless office
To tell ill news: and I, of all your sex,
Most fear displeasing you.

   CLEO.   Of all your sex,
I soonest could forgive you, if you should.

   VENT. Most delicate advances! Woman! Woman!
Dear, damn'd, inconstant sex!

   CLEO.   In the first place,
I am to be forsaken; is't not so?

   DOLA. I wish I could not answer to that question.

   CLEO. Then pass it o'er, because it troubles you:
I should have been more griev'd another time.
Next, I'm to lose my kingdom.——Farewell, Egypt!
Yet, is there any more?

   DOLA.   Madam, I fear
Your too deep sense of grief has turn'd your reason.

   CLEO. No, no, I'm not run mad; I can bear fortune:
And love may be expell'd by other love,
As poisons are by poisons.

   DOLA. You o'erjoy me, Madam,
To find your griefs so moderately borne.
You've heard the worst; all are not false like him.

   CLEO. No; heav'n forbid they should.

   DOLA.   Some men are constant.

   CLEO. And constancy deserves reward, that's certain.

DOLA. Deserves it not; but give it leave to hope.

VENT. I'll swear thou hast my leave. I have enough.
But how to manage this! Well, I'll consider.   (*Exit.*)

DOLA.   I came prepar'd
To tell you heavy news; news, which I thought
Would fright the blood from your pale cheeks to hear:
But you have met it with a cheerfulness
That makes my task more easy; and my tongue,
Which on another's message was employ'd,
Would gladly speak its own.

CLEO.   Hold, Dolabella.
First tell me, were you chosen by my lord?
Or sought you this employment?

DOLA. He pick'd me out; and, as his bosom friend,
He charg'd me with his words.

CLEO.   The message then
I know was tender, and each accent smooth,
To mollify that rugged word "depart."

DOLA. Oh, you mistake: he chose the harshest words;
With fiery eyes, and with contracted brows,
He coin'd his face in the severest stamp,
And fury shook his fabric, like an earthquake;
He heaved for vent, and burst like bellowing Ætna,
In sounds scarce human, "Hence, away for ever:
Let her begone, the blot of my renown,
And bane of all my hopes!

> (*All the time of this speech,* CLEOPATRA *seems more
> and more concerned, till she sinks quite down.*)

Let her be driv'n as far as men can think
From man's commerce! She'll poison to the centre."

CLEO. Oh, I can bear no more!

DOLA. Help, help!—O wretch! O cursed, cursed wretch!
What have I done!

CHAR.   Help, chafe her temples, Iras.

IRAS. Bend, bend her forward quickly.

CHAR.   Heav'n be prais'd,
She comes again.

CLEO.   Oh, let him not approach me.
Why have you brought me back to this loath'd being,

Th' abode of falsehood, violated vows,
And injur'd love? For pity, let me go;
For, if there be a place of long repose,
I'm sure I want it. My disdainful lord
Can never break that quiet, nor awake
The sleeping soul with holloing in my tomb
Such words as fright her hence. Unkind, unkind!

DOLA. (*kneeling*) Believe me, 'tis against myself I speak,
That sure deserves belief; I injur'd him:
My friend ne'er spoke those words. Oh, had you seen
How often he came back, and every time
With something more obliging and more kind,
To add to what he said; what dear farewells;
How almost vanquish'd by his love he parted,
And lean'd to what unwillingly he left!
I, traitor as I was, for love of you
(But what can you not do, who made me false!)
I forg'd that lie; for whose forgiveness kneels
This self-accus'd, self-punish'd criminal.

CLEO. With how much ease believe we what we wish!
Rise, Dolabella; if you have been guilty,
I have contributed, and too much love
Has made me guilty too.
Th' advance of kindness which I made was feign'd,
To call back fleeting love by jealousy;
But 'twould not last. Oh, rather let me lose,
Than so ignobly trifle with his heart.

DOLA. I find your breast fenc'd round from human reach,
Transparent as a rock of solid crystal,
Seen through, but never pierc'd. My friend, my friend!
What endless treasure hast thou thrown away,
And scatter'd, like an infant, in the ocean,
Vain sums of wealth, which none can gather thence!

CLEO. Could you not beg
An hour's admittance to his private ear?
Like one who wanders through long barren wilds,
And yet foreknows no hospitable inn
Is near to succour hunger, eats his fill
Before his painful march,

So would I feed a while my famish'd eyes
Before we part; for I have far to go,
If death be far, and never must return.

VENTIDIUS with OCTAVIA, behind

VENT. From hence you may discover—oh, sweet, sweet!
Would you indeed? the pretty hand in earnest?
  DOLA. I will, for this reward.—(takes her hand) Draw it not
back,
'Tis all I e'er will beg.
  VENT. They turn upon us.
  OCTAV.   What quick eyes has guilt!
  VENT. Seem not to have observ'd 'em, and go on.

They enter

  DOLA. Saw you the emperor, Ventidius?
  VENT.   No.
I sought him; but I heard that he was private,
None with him but Hipparchus, his freedman.
  DOLA. Know you his bus'ness?
  VENT.   Giving him instructions,
And letters to his brother Cæsar.
  DOLA.   Well,
He must be found.   (Exeunt DOLABELLA and CLEOPATRA.)
  OCTAV.   Most glorious impudence!
  VENT. She look'd, methought,
As she would say, "Take your old man, Octavia;
Thank you, I'm better here." Well, but what use
Make we of this discovery?
  OCTAV.   Let it die.
  VENT. I pity Dolabella; but she's dangerous:
Her eyes have pow'r beyond Thessalian charms
To draw the moon from heav'n; for eloquence,
The sea-green Sirens taught her voice their flatt'ry,
And, while she speaks, night steals upon the day,
Unmark'd of those that hear. Then she's so charming,
Age buds at sight of her, and swells to youth:
The holy priests gaze on her when she smiles,
And with heav'd hands, forgetting gravity,
They bless her wanton eyes: even I, who hate her,

With a malignant joy behold such beauty,
And, while I curse, desire it. Antony
Must needs have some remains of passion still,
Which may ferment into a worse relapse,
If now not fully cur'd. I know, this minute,
With Cæsar he's endeavouring her peace.

    OCTAV. You have prevail'd:—but for a farther purpose
                                        (*walks off*)
I'll prove how he will relish this discovery.
What, make a strumpet's peace! it swells my heart:
It must not, sha' not be.
    VENT.   His guards appear.
Let me begin, and you shall second me.

Enter ANTONY

    ANT. Octavia, I was looking you, my love:
What, are your letters ready? I have giv'n
My last instructions.
    OCTAV.   Mine, my Lord, are written.
    ANT. Ventidius!   (*drawing him aside*)
    VENT.   My Lord?
    ANT.   A word in private.
When saw you Dolabella?
    VENT.   Now, my Lord,
He parted hence; and Cleopatra with him.
    ANT. Speak softly.—'Twas by my command he went,
To bear my last farewell.
    VENT. (*aloud*)   It look'd indeed
Like your farewell.
    ANT.   More softly.—My farewell?
What secret meaning have you in those words
Of "my farewell"? He did it by my order.
    VENT. (*aloud*) Then he obey'd your order. I suppose
You bid him do it with all gentleness,
All kindness, and all——love.
    ANT.   How she mourn'd,
The poor forsaken creature!
    VENT. She took it as she ought; she bore your parting
As she did Cæsar's, as she would another's,
Were a new love to come.

ANT. (*aloud*)   Thou dost belie her;
Most basely, and maliciously belie her.

VENT. I thought not to displease you; I have done.

OCTAV. (*coming up*) You seem disturb'd, my Lord.

ANT.   A very trifle.
Retire, my love.

VENT.   It was indeed a trifle.
He sent——

ANT. (*angrily*) No more. Look how thou disobey'st me;
Thy life shall answer it.

OCTAV.   Then 'tis no trifle.

VENT. (*to* OCTAVIA) 'Tis less, a very nothing; you too saw it
As well as I, and therefore 'tis no secret.

ANT. She saw it!

VENT.   Yes: she saw young Dolabella——

ANT. Young Dolabella!

VENT.   Young, I think him young,
And handsome too; and so do others think him.
But what of that? He went by your command,
Indeed 'tis probable, with some kind message;
For she receiv'd it graciously; she smil'd;
And then he grew familiar with her hand,
Squeez'd it, and worry'd it with ravenous kisses;
She blush'd, and sigh'd, and smil'd, and blush'd again;
At last she took occasion to talk softly,
And brought her cheek up close, and lean'd on his;
At which, he whisper'd kisses back on hers;
And then she cried aloud that constancy
Should be rewarded.

OCTAV.   This I saw and heard.

ANT. What woman was it, whom you heard and saw
So playful with my friend? Not Cleopatra?

VENT. Ev'n she, my Lord.

ANT.   My Cleopatra?

VENT. Your Cleopatra;
Dolabella's Cleopatra;
Every man's Cleopatra.

ANT. Thou li'st.

VENT.   I do not lie, my Lord.
Is this so strange? Should mistresses be left,

And not provide against a time of change?
You know she's not much used to lonely nights.
   ANT. I'll think no more on't.
I know 'tis false, and see the plot betwixt you.
You needed not have gone this way, Octavia.
What harms it you that Cleopatra's just?
She's mine no more. I see, and I forgive:
Urge it no farther, love.
   OCTAV.   Are you concern'd,
That she's found false?
   ANT.   I should be, were it so;
For, though 'tis past, I would not that the world
Should tax my former choice, that I lov'd one
Of so light note; but I forgive you both.
   VENT. What has my age deserv'd, that you should think
I would abuse your ears with perjury?
If heav'n be true, she's false.
   ANT.   Though heav'n and earth
Should witness it, I'll not believe her tainted.
   VENT. I'll bring you, then, a witness
From hell, to prove her so. (*seeing* ALEXAS *just entering, and
       starting back*)—Nay, go not back;
For stay you must and shall.
   ALEX.   What means my Lord?
   VENT. To make you do what most you hate—speak truth.
You are of Cleopatra's private counsel,
Of her bed-counsel, her lascivious hours,
Are conscious of each nightly change she makes,
And watch her, as Chaldeans do the moon;
Can tell what signs she passes through, what day.
   ALEX. My noble Lord!
   VENT.   My most illustrious pander,
No fine set speech, no cadence, no turn'd periods,
But a plain homespun truth, is what I ask:
I did, myself, o'erhear your queen make love
To Dolabella. Speak; for I will know,
By your confession, what more pass'd betwixt 'em;
How near the bus'ness draws to your employment;
And when the happy hour.
   ANT. Speak truth, Alexas; whether it offend

Or please Ventidius, care not: justify
Thy injur'd queen from malice: dare his worst.

OCTAV. (*aside*) See how he gives him courage! how he fears
To find her false! and shuts his eyes to truth,
Willing to be misled!

ALEX. As far as love may plead for woman's frailty,
Urg'd by desert and greatness of the lover,
So far, divine Octavia, may my queen
Stand ev'n excus'd to you for loving him
Who is your lord: so far, from brave Ventidius,
May her past actions hope a fair report.

ANT. 'Tis well, and truly spoken: mark, Ventidius.

ALEX. To you, most noble Emperor, her strong passion
Stands not excus'd, but wholly justify'd.
Her beauty's charms alone, without her crown,
From Ind and Meroe drew the distant vows
Of sighing kings; and at her feet were laid
The sceptres of the earth, expos'd on heaps,
To choose where she would reign:
She thought a Roman only could deserve her,
And, of all Romans, only Antony.
And, to be less than wife to you, disdain'd
Their lawful passion.

ANT.   'Tis but truth.

ALEX. And yet, though love, and your unmatch'd desert,
Have drawn her from the due regard of honour,
At last heav'n open'd her unwilling eyes
To see the wrongs she offer'd fair Octavia,
Whose holy bed she lawlessly usurp'd.
The sad effects of this improsperous war
Confirm'd those pious thoughts.

VENT. (*aside*)   Oh, wheel you there?
Observe him now; the man begins to mend,
And talk substantial reason.—— Fear not, eunuch;
The emperor has giv'n thee leave to speak.

ALEX. Else had I never dar'd t'offend his ears
With what the last necessity has urg'd
On my forsaken mistress; yet I must not
Presume to say her heart is wholly alter'd.

ANT. No, dare not for thy life, I charge thee dare not

Pronounce that fatal word!

OCTAV. (*aside*) Must I bear this? Good heav'n, afford me
patience.

VENT. On, sweet eunuch; my dear half-man, proceed.

ALEX. Yet Dolabella
Has lov'd her long; he, next my god-like Lord,
Deserves her best; and should she meet his passion,
Rejected, as she is, by him she lov'd——

ANT. Hence, from my sight! for I can bear no more:
Let Furies drag thee quick to hell; let all
The longer damn'd have rest; each torturing hand
Do thou employ, till Cleopatra comes;
Then join thou too, and help to torture her!

(*Exit* ALEXAS, *thrust out by* ANTONY.)

OCTAV. 'Tis not well,
Indeed, my Lord, 'tis much unkind to me,
To show this passion, this extreme concernment,
For an abandon'd, faithless prostitute.

ANT. Octavia, leave me: I am much disorder'd.
Leave me, I say.

OCTAV.   My Lord!

ANT.   I bid you leave me.

VENT. Obey him, Madam: best withdraw a while,
And see how this will work.

OCTAV. Wherein have I offended you, my Lord,
That I am bid to leave you? Am I false,
Or infamous? Am I a Cleopatra?
Were I she,
Base as she is, you would not bid me leave you,
But hang upon my neck, take slight excuses,
And fawn upon my falsehood.

ANT.   'Tis too much,
Too much, Octavia; I am press'd with sorrows
Too heavy to be borne; and you add more:
I would retire, and recollect what's left
Of man within, to aid me.

OCTAV.   You would mourn,
In private, for your love, who has betray'd you;
You did but half return to me: your kindness
Linger'd behind with her. I hear, my Lord,

You make conditions for her,
And would include her treaty. Wondrous proofs
Of love to me!
    ANT.   Are you my friend, Ventidius?
Or are you turn'd a Dolabella too,
And let this Fury loose?
    VENT.   Oh, be advis'd,
Sweet Madam, and retire.
    OCTAV. Yes, I will go; but never to return.
You shall no more be haunted with this Fury.
My Lord, my Lord, love will not always last,
When urg'd with long unkindness and disdain;
Take her again whom you prefer to me;
She stays but to be call'd. Poor cozen'd man!
Let a feign'd parting give her back your heart,
Which a feign'd love first got; for injur'd me,
Though my just sense of wrongs forbid my stay,
My duty shall be yours.
To the dear pledges of our former love
My tenderness and care shall be transferr'd,
And they shall cheer, by turns, my widow'd nights:
So, take my last farewell; for I despair
To have you whole, and scorn to take you half.   (*Exit.*)
    VENT. I combat heav'n, which blasts my best designs:
My last attempt must be to win her back;
But oh! I fear, in vain.   (*Exit.*)
    ANT. Why was I fram'd with this plain, honest heart
Which knows not to disguise its griefs and weakness,
But bears its workings outward to the world?
I should have kept the mighty anguish in,
And forc'd a smile at Cleopatra's falsehood:
Octavia had believ'd it, and had stay'd.
But I am made a shallow-forded stream,
Seen to the bottom, all my clearness scorn'd,
And all my faults expos'd!—— See where he comes,

Enter DOLABELLA

Who has profan'd the sacred name of friend,
And worn it into vileness!
With how secure a brow, and specious form,

He gilds the secret villain! Sure that face
Was meant for honesty; but heav'n mismatch'd it,
And furnish'd treason out with nature's pomp,
To make its work more easy.

DOLA.   O my friend!

ANT. Well, Dolabella, you perform'd my message?

DOLA. I did, unwillingly.

ANT.   Unwillingly?
Was it so hard for you to bear our parting?
You should have wish'd it.

DOLA.   Why?

ANT.   Because you love me.
And she receiv'd my message with as true,
With as unfeign'd a sorrow as you brought it?

DOLA. She loves you, ev'n to madness.

ANT.   Oh, I know it.
You, Dolabella, do not better know
How much she loves me. And should I
Forsake this beauty, this all-perfect creature?

DOLA. I could not, were she mine.

ANT.   And yet you first
Persuaded me: how come you alter'd since?

DOLA. I said at first I was not fit to go;
I could not hear her sighs, and see her tears,
But pity must prevail: and so, perhaps,
It may again with you; for I have promis'd
That she should take her last farewell: and, see,
She comes to claim my word.

Enter CLEOPATRA

ANT.   False Dolabella!

DOLA. What's false, my Lord?

ANT.   Why, Dolabella's false,
And Cleopatra's false; both false and faithless.
Draw near, you well-join'd wickedness, you serpents,
Whom I have in my kindly bosom warm'd
Till I am stung to death.

DOLA.   My Lord, have I
Deserv'd to be thus used?

CLEO.   Can heav'n prepare

A newer torment? Can it find a curse
Beyond our separation?
    ANT.   Yes, if fate
Be just, much greater: heav'n should be ingenious
In punishing such crimes. The rolling stone,
And gnawing vulture, were slight pains, invented
When Jove was young, and no examples known
Of mighty ills; but you have ripen'd sin
To such a monstrous growth 'twill pose the Gods
To find an equal torture. Two, two such!—
Oh, there's no farther name, two such!—to me,
To me, who lock'd my soul within your breasts,
Had no desires, no joys, no life, but you;
When half the globe was mine, I gave it you
In dowry with my heart; I had no use,
No fruit of all, but you: a friend and mistress
Was what the world could give. O Cleopatra!
O Dolabella! how could you betray
This tender heart, which with an infant fondness
Lay lull'd betwixt your bosoms, and there slept,
Secure of injur'd faith?
    DOLA.   If she has wrong'd you,
Heav'n, hell, and you revenge it.
    ANT.   If she wrong'd me!
Thou wouldst evade thy part of guilt; but swear
Thou lov'st not her.
    DOLA.   Not so as I love you.
    ANT. Not so! Swear, swear, I say; thou dost not love her.
    DOLA. No more than friendship will allow.
    ANT.   No more?
Friendship allows thee nothing: thou art perjur'd—
And yet thou didst not swear thou lov'dst her not;
But not so much, no more. O trifling hypocrite,
Who dar'st not own to her, thou dost not love,
Nor own to me, thou dost! Ventidius heard it;
Octavia saw it.
    CLEO.   They are enemies.
    ANT. Alexas is not so: he, he confess'd it:
He, who, next hell, best knew it, he avow'd it.
(*to* DOLABELLA) Why do I seek a proof beyond yourself?

You, whom I sent to bear my last farewell,
Return'd to plead her stay.
DOLA.   What shall I answer?
If to have lov'd be guilt, then I have sinn'd;
But if to have repented of that love
Can wash away my crime, I have repented.
Yet, if I have offended past forgiveness,
Let not her suffer: she is innocent.
   CLEO. Ah, what will not a woman do, who loves!
What means will she refuse, to keep that heart
Where all her joys are plac'd? 'Twas I encourag'd,
'Twas I blew up the fire that scorch'd his soul,
To make you jealous, and by that regain you.
But all in vain; I could not counterfeit.
In spite of all the dams my love broke o'er,
And drown'd my heart again. Fate took th' occasion;
And thus one minute's feigning has destroy'd
My whole life's truth.
   ANT.   Thin cobweb arts of falsehood,
Seen, and broke through at first.
   DOLA.   Forgive your mistress.
   CLEO. Forgive your friend.
   ANT.   You have convinc'd yourselves,
You plead each other's cause. What witness have you
That you but meant to raise my jealousy?
   CLEO. Ourselves, and heav'n.
   ANT. Guilt witnesses for guilt. Hence, love and friendship!
You have no longer place in human breasts;
These two have driv'n you out. Avoid my sight!
I would not kill the man whom I have lov'd,
And cannot hurt the woman; but avoid me—
I do not know how long I can be tame,
For, if I stay one minute more to think
How I am wrong'd, my justice and revenge
Will cry so loud within me, that my pity
Will not be heard for either.
   DOLA.   Heav'n has but
Our sorrow for our sins; and then delights
To pardon erring man: sweet mercy seems
Its darling attribute, which limits justice,

As if there were degrees in infinite,
And infinite would rather want perfection
Than punish to extent.

ANT.   I can forgive
A foe, but not a mistress and a friend.
Treason is there in its most horrid shape,
Where trust is greatest: and the soul resign'd
Is stabb'd by its own guards. I'll hear no more;
Hence from my sight for ever!

CLEO.   How? for ever!
I cannot go one moment from your sight,
And must I go for ever?
My joys, my only joys, are centred here.
What place have I to go to? My own kingdom?
That I have lost for you. Or to the Romans?
They hate me for your sake. Or must I wander
The wide world o'er, a helpless, banish'd woman,
Banish'd for love of you, banish'd from you?
Aye, there's the banishment! Oh, hear me! hear me,
With strictest justice, for I beg no favour;
And if I have offended you, then kill me,
But do not banish me.

ANT.   I must not hear you.
I have a fool within me takes your part;
But honour stops my ears.

CLEO.   For pity hear me!
Would you cast off a slave who follow'd you?
Who crouch'd beneath your spurn?——He has no pity!
See, if he gives one tear to my departure,
One look, one kind farewell: O iron heart!
Let all the Gods look down, and judge betwixt us,
If he did ever love!

ANT.   No more.——Alexas!

DOLA. A perjur'd villain!

ANT. (to CLEOPATRA)   Your Alexas, yours!

CLEO. Oh, 'twas his plot, his ruinous design,
T' engage you in my love by jealousy.
Hear him; confront him with me; let him speak.

ANT. I have; I have.

CLEO.   And if he clear me not——

ANT. Your creature! one who hangs upon your smiles!
Watches your eye, to say or to unsay
Whate'er you please! I am not to be mov'd.

CLEO. Then must we part? Farewell, my cruel Lord!
Th' appearance is against me; and I go,
Unjustify'd, for ever from your sight.
How I have lov'd, you know; how yet I love,
My only comfort is, I know myself:
I love you more, ev'n now you are unkind,
Than when you lov'd me most: so well, so truly,
I'll never strive against it; but die pleas'd,
To think you once were mine.

ANT. Good heav'n, they weep at parting!
Must I weep too? That calls 'em innocent.
I must not weep; and yet I must, to think
That I must not forgive.——
Live, but live wretched; 'tis but just you should,
Who made me so. Live from each other's sight:
Let me not hear you meet: set all the earth,
And all the seas, betwixt your sunder'd loves:
View nothing common but the sun and skies.
Now, all take several ways;
   And each your own sad fate, with mine, deplore;
   That you were false, and I could trust no more.

(*Exeunt severally.*)

ACT V

CLEOPATRA, CHARMION, IRAS

CHAR. Be juster, heav'n: such virtue punish'd thus,
Will make us think that chance rules all above,
And shuffles, with a random hand, the lots
Which man is forc'd to draw.

CLEO. I could tear out these eyes, that gain'd his heart,
And had not pow'r to keep it. Oh the curse
Of doting on, ev'n when I find it dotage!
Bear witness, Gods, you heard him bid me go;
You, whom he mock'd with imprecating vows
Of promis'd faith!——I'll die; I will not bear it.

(*She pulls out her dagger, and they hold her.*)

You may hold me——
But I can keep my breath; I can die inward,
And choke this love.

Enter ALEXAS

IRAS.   Help, O Alexas, help!
The queen grows desperate; her soul struggles in her
With all the agonies of love and rage,
And strives to force its passage.

CLEO.   Let me go.
Art thou there, traitor!—Oh!
Oh, for a little breath, to vent my rage!
Give, give me way, and let me loose upon him.

ALEX. Yes, I deserve it, for my ill-tim'd truth.
Was it for me to prop
The ruins of a falling majesty?
To place myself beneath the mighty flaw,
Thus to be crush'd, and pounded into atoms,
By its o'erwhelming weight? 'Tis too presuming
For subjects to preserve that wilful pow'r
Which courts its own destruction.

CLEO.   I would reason
More calmly with you. Did not you o'errule,
And force my plain, direct, and open love
Into these crooked paths of jealousy?
Now, what's th' event? Octavia is remov'd;
But Cleopatra's banish'd. Thou, thou, villain,
Hast push'd my boat to open sea, to prove,
At my sad cost, if thou canst steer it back.
It cannot be; I'm lost too far; I'm ruin'd!
Hence, thou impostor, traitor, monster, devil!
I can no more: thou, and my griefs, have sunk
Me down so low, that I want voice to curse thee.

ALEX. Suppose some shipwrack'd seaman near the shore,
Dropping and faint with climbing up the cliff,
If, from above, some charitable hand
Pull him to safety, hazarding himself
To draw the other's weight, would he look back,
And curse him for his pains? The case is yours;
But one step more, and you have gain'd the height.

CLEO. Sunk, never more to rise.

ALEX. Octavia's gone, and Dolabella banish'd.
Believe me, Madam, Antony is yours.
His heart was never lost, but started off
To jealousy, love's last retreat and covert;
Where it lies hid in shades, watchful in silence,
And list'ning for the sound that calls it back.
Some other, any man ('tis so advanc'd),
May perfect this unfinish'd work, which I
(Unhappy only to myself) have left
So easy to his hand.

CLEO.   Look well thou do't; else——

ALEX. Else, what your silence threatens.—Antony
Is mounted up the Pharos, from whose turret
He stands surveying our Egyptian galleys,
Engag'd with Cæsar's fleet. Now death or conquest!
If the first happen, fate acquits my promise;
If we o'ercome, the conqueror is yours.   (*a distant shout within*)

CHAR. Have comfort, Madam: did you mark that shout?

                                        (*second shout nearer*)

IRAS. Hark! they redouble it.

ALEX.   'Tis from the port.
The loudness shows it near: good news, kind heavens!

CLEO. Osiris make it so!

Enter SERAPION

SERAP.   Where, where's the queen?

ALEX. How frightfully the holy coward stares!
As if not yet recover'd of th' assault,
When all his Gods, and, what's more dear to him,
His offerings, were at stake.

SERAP.   Oh horror, horror!
Egypt has been; our latest hour is come:
The queen of nations, from her ancient seat,
Is sunk for ever in the dark abyss:
Time has unroll'd her glories to the last,
And now clos'd up the volume.

CLEO.   Be more plain:
Say whence thou com'st (though fate is in thy face,
Which from thy haggard eyes looks wildly out,

And threatens ere thou speak'st).

    SERAP.   I come from Pharos;
From viewing (spare me, and imagine it)
Our land's last hope, your navy——

    CLEO.   Vanquish'd?

    SERAP.   No.
They fought not.

    CLEO.   Then they fled?

    SERAP.   Nor that. I saw,
With Antony, your well-appointed fleet
Row out; and thrice he wav'd his hand on high,
And thrice with cheerful cries they shouted back:
'Twas then false Fortune, like a fawning strumpet,
About to leave the bankrupt prodigal,
With a dissembled smile would kiss at parting,
And flatter to the last; the well-tim'd oars
Now dipp'd from every bank, now smoothly run
To meet the foe; and soon indeed they met,
But not as foes. In few, we saw their caps
On either side thrown up; th' Egyptian galleys
(Receiv'd like friends) pass'd through, and fell behind
The Roman rear; and now they all come forward,
And ride within the port.

    CLEO.   Enough, Serapion:
I've heard my doom.—This needed not, you Gods:
When I lost Antony your work was done;
'Tis but superfluous malice.—Where's my lord?
How bears he this last blow?

    SERAP. His fury cannot be express'd by words:
Thrice he attempted headlong to have fall'n
Full on his foes, and aim'd at Cæsar's galley:
Withheld, he raves on you; cries he's betrayed.
Should he now find you——

    ALEX.   Shun him; seek your safety,
Till you can clear your innocence.

    CLEO.   I'll stay.

    ALEX. You must not; haste you to your monument,
While I make speed to Cæsar.

    CLEO.   Cæsar! No,
I have no business with him.

ALEX.   I can work him
To spare your life, and let this madman perish.

CLEO. Base fawning wretch! wouldst thou betray him too?
Hence from my sight! I will not hear a traitor;
'Twas thy design brought all this ruin on us.
Serapion, thou art honest; counsel me:
But haste, each moment's precious.

SERAP. Retire; you must not yet see Antony.
He who began this mischief,
'Tis just he tempt the danger: let him clear you;
And, since he offer'd you his servile tongue
To gain a poor precarious life from Cæsar,
Let him expose that fawning eloquence,
And speak to Antony.

ALEX.   O heavens! I dare not;
I meet my certain death.

CLEO.   Slave, thou deserv'st it.—
Not that I fear my lord, will I avoid him;
I know him noble: when he banish'd me,
And thought me false, he scorn'd to take my life;
But I'll be justify'd, and then die with him.

ALEX. Oh pity me, and let me follow you!

CLEO. To death, if thou stir hence. Speak, if thou canst,
Now for thy life, which basely thou wouldst save;
While mine I prize at—this! Come, good Serapion.

             (*Exeunt* CLEOPATRA, SERAPION, CHARMION, IRAS.)

ALEX. Oh that I less could fear to lose this being,
Which, like a snowball in my coward hand,
The more 'tis grasp'd, the faster melts away.
Poor reason! what a wretched aid art thou!
For still, in spite of thee,
These two long lovers, soul and body, dread
Their final separation. Let me think:
What can I say, to save myself from death?
No matter what becomes of Cleopatra.

ANT. (*within*) Which way? where?

VENT. (*within*)   This leads to th' monu-
    ment.

ALEX. Ah me! I hear him; yet I'm unprepar'd:
My gift of lying's gone;

And this court-devil, which I so oft have raised,
Forsakes me at my need. I dare not stay;
Yet cannot far go hence.   (*Exit.*)

Enter ANTONY *and* VENTIDIUS

ANT. O happy Cæsar! thou hast men to lead:
Think not 'tis thou hast conquer'd Antony,
But Rome has conquer'd Egypt. I'm betray'd.
    VENT. Curse on this treach'rous train!
Their soil and heav'n infect 'em all with baseness:
And their young souls come tainted to the world
With the first breath they draw.
    ANT. Th' original villain sure no God created;
He was a bastard of the sun, by Nile,
Ap'd into man; with all his mother's mud
Crusted about his soul.
    VENT.   The nation is
One universal traitor, and their queen
The very spirit and extract of 'em all.
    ANT. Is there yet left
A possibility of aid from valour?
Is there one God unsworn to my destruction?
The least unmortgag'd hope? for, if there be,
Methinks I cannot fall beneath the fate
Of such a boy as Cæsar.
The world's one half is yet in Antony;
And from each limb of it that's hew'd away,
The soul comes back to me.
    VENT.   There yet remain
Three legions in the town: the last assault
Lopp'd off the rest. If death be your design
(As I must wish it now), these are sufficient
To make a heap about us of dead foes,
An honest pile for burial.
    ANT.   They're enough.
We'll not divide our stars; but side by side
Fight emulous, and with malicious eyes
Survey each other's acts: so every death
Thou giv'st, I'll take on me, as a just debt,
And pay thee back a soul.

VENT. Now you shall see I love you. Not a word
Of chiding more. By my few hours of life,
I am so pleas'd with this brave Roman fate,
That I would not be Cæsar, to outlive you.
When we put off this flesh, and mount together,
I shall be shown to all th' ethereal crowd,
"Lo, this is he who died with Antony!"

ANT. Who knows but we may pierce through all their troops,
And reach my veterans yet? 'Tis worth the tempting,
T' o'erleap this gulf of fate,
And leave our wond'ring destinies behind.

Enter ALEXAS, *trembling*

VENT. See, see, that villain!
See Cleopatra stamp'd upon that face,
With all her cunning, all her arts of falsehood!
How she looks out through those dissembling eyes!
How he has set his count'nance for deceit
And promises a lie, before he speaks!
Let me dispatch him first.   (*drawing*)

ALEX.   O, spare me, spare me!

ANT. Hold; he's not worth your killing.——On thy life
(Which thou may'st keep, because I scorn to take it),
No syllable to justify thy queen;
Save thy base tongue its office.

ALEX.   Sir, she's gone,
Where she shall never be molested more
By love, or you.

ANT.   Fled to her Dolabella!
Die, traitor! I revoke my promise! die!   (*going to kill him*)

ALEX. O hold! she is not fled.

ANT.   She is: my eyes
Are open to her falsehood; my whole life
Has been a golden dream of love and friendship.
But, now I wake, I'm like a merchant rous'd
From soft repose, to see his vessel sinking,
And all his wealth cast o'er. Ingrateful woman!
Who follow'd me, but as the swallow summer,
Hatching her young ones in my kindly beams,
Singing her flatt'ries to my morning wake;

But, now my winter comes, she spreads her wings,
And seeks the spring of Cæsar.
  ALEX.   Think not so:
Her fortunes have, in all things, mix'd with yours.
Had she betray'd her naval force to Rome,
How easily might she have gone to Cæsar,
Secure by such a bribe!
  VENT.   She sent it first,
To be more welcome after.
  ANT.   'Tis too plain;
Else would she have appear'd, to clear herself.
  ALEX. Too fatally she has; she could not bear
To be accus'd by you, but shut herself
Within her monument, look'd down and sigh'd,
While, from her unchang'd face, the silent tears
Dropp'd, as they had not leave, but stole their parting.
Some undistinguish'd words she inly murmur'd;
At last, she rais'd her eyes; and, with such looks
As dying Lucrece cast——
  ANT.   My heart forbodes——
  VENT. All for the best; go on.
  ALEX.   She snatch'd her poniard,
And, ere we could prevent the fatal blow,
Plung'd it within her breast: then turn'd to me:
"Go, bear my lord," said she, "my last farewell;
And ask him if he yet suspect my faith."
More she was saying, but death rush'd betwixt.
She half pronounc'd your name with her last breath,
And bury'd half within her.
  VENT.   Heav'n be prais'd!
  ANT. Then art thou innocent, my poor dear love,
And art thou dead?
O those two words! their sound should be divided:
Hadst thou been false, and died; or hadst thou liv'd
And hadst been true.—But innocence and death!
This shows not well above. Then what am I,
The murderer of this truth, this innocence!
Thoughts cannot form themselves in words so horrid
As can express my guilt!
  VENT. Is't come to this? The Gods have been too gracious:

And thus you thank 'em for't!

ANT. (*to* ALEXAS)   Why stay'st thou here?
Is it for thee to spy upon my soul,
And see its inward mourning? Get thee hence!
Thou art not worthy to behold what now
Becomes a Roman emperor to perform.

ALEX. (*aside*) He loves her still:
His grief betrays it. Good! The joy to find
She's yet alive, completes the reconcilement.
I've sav'd myself, and her. But, oh! the Romans!
Fate comes too fast upon my wit,
Hunts me too hard, and meets me at each double.   (*Exit.*)

VENT. Would she had died a little sooner, though,
Before Octavia went; you might have treated:
Now 'twill look tame, and would not be receiv'd.
Come, rouse yourself, and let's die warm together.

ANT. I will not fight: there's no more work for war.
The bus'ness of my angry hours is done.

VENT. Cæsar is at your gates.

ANT.   Why, let him enter;
He's welcome now.

VENT. What lethargy has crept into your soul?

ANT. 'Tis but a scorn of life, and just desire
To free myself from bondage.

VENT.   Do it bravely.

ANT. I will; but not by fighting O Ventidius!
What should I fight for now? My queen is dead.
I was but great for her; my pow'r, my empire,
Were but my merchandise to buy her love,
And conquer'd kings, my factors. Now she's dead,
Let Cæsar take the world,—
An empty circle, since the jewel's gone
Which made it worth my strife: my being's nauseous;
For all the bribes of life are gone away.

VENT. Would you be taken?

ANT.   Yes, I would be taken;
But, as a Roman ought—dead, my Ventidius:
For I'll convey my soul from Cæsar's reach,
And lay down life myself. 'Tis time the world
Should have a lord, and know whom to obey.

We two have kept its homage in suspense,
And bent the globe, on whose each side we trod,
Till it was dinted inwards. Let him walk
Alone upon't; I'm weary of my part.
My torch is out; and the world stands before me
Like a black desert at th' approach of night:
I'll lay me down, and stray no farther on.

    VENT. I could be griev'd,
But that I'll not outlive you: choose your death;
For I have seen him in such various shapes,
I care not which I take: I'm only troubled
The life I bear is worn to such a rag
'Tis scarce worth giving. I could wish, indeed,
We threw it from us with a better grace,
That, like two lions taken in the toils,
We might at least thrust out our paws, and wound
The hunters that inclose us.

    ANT.   I have thought on't.
Ventidius, you must live.

    VENT.   I must not, Sir.

    ANT. Wilt thou not live, to speak some good of me?
To stand by my fair fame, and guard th' approaches
From the ill tongues of men?

    VENT.   Who shall guard mine,
For living after you?

    ANT.   Say, I command it.

    VENT. If we die well, our deaths will speak themselves
And need no living witness.

    ANT.   Thou hast lov'd me,
And fain I would reward thee. I must die;
Kill me, and take the merit of my death
To make thee friends with Cæsar.

    VENT.   Thank your kindness.
You said I lov'd you; and, in recompense,
You bid me turn a traitor. Did I think
You would have us'd me thus?—that I should die
With a hard thought of you?

    ANT.   Forgive me, Roman.
Since I have heard of Cleopatra's death,
My reason bears no rule upon my tongue,

But lets my thoughts break all at random out.
I've thought better; do not deny me twice.

    VENT. By heav'n, I will not.
Let it not be t' outlive you.

    ANT.   Kill me first,
And then die thou; for 'tis but just thou serve
Thy friend, before thyself.

    VENT.   Give me your hand.
We soon shall meet again. Now, farewell, Emperor!—

                                          (embrace)
Methinks that word's too cold to be my last:
Since death sweeps all distinctions, farewell, friend!
That's all.——
I will not make a bus'ness of a trifle;
And yet I cannot look on you, and kill you;
Pray turn your face.

    ANT.   I do: strike home, be sure.

    VENT. Home as my sword will reach.   *(kills himself)*

    ANT.   Oh, thou mistak'st!
That wound was none of thine: give it me back:
Thou robb'st me of my death!

    VENT.   I do indeed;
But think 'tis the first time I e'er deceiv'd you,
If that may plead my pardon. And you, Gods,
Forgive me, if you will; for I die perjur'd,
Rather than kill my friend.   *(dies)*

    ANT. Farewell! Ever my leader, ev'n in death!
My queen and thou have got the start of me,
And I'm the lag of honour.—Gone so soon?
Is Death no more? He us'd him carelessly,
With a familiar kindness; ere he knock'd,
Ran to the door, and took him in his arms,
As who should say, "Y'are welcome at all hours,
A friend need give no warning." Books had spoil'd him;
For all the learn'd are cowards by profession.
'Tis not worth
My farther thought; for death, for aught I know,
Is but to think no more. Here's to be satisfied.

                              (falls on his sword)
I've missed my heart. O unperforming hand!

Thou never couldst have err'd in a worse time.
My fortune jades me to the last; and Death,
Like a great man, takes state, and makes me wait
For my admittance.—— *(trampling within)*
        Some, perhaps from Cæsar:
If he should find me living, and suspect
That I played booty with my life! I'll mend
My work, ere they can reach me. *(rises upon his knees)*

     Enter CLEOPATRA, CHARMION, IRAS

CLEO. Where is my lord! where is he?
CHAR.   There he lies.
And dead Ventidius by him.
CLEO. My fears were prophets; I am come too late.
O that accurst Alexas! *(runs to him)*
ANT.   Art thou living?
Or am I dead before I knew, and thou
The first kind ghost that meets me?
CLEO.   Help me seat him.
Send quickly, send for help! *(They place him in a chair.)*
ANT.   I am answer'd.
We live both. Sit thee down, my Cleopatra:
I'll make the most I can of life, to stay
A moment more with thee.
CLEO. How is it with you?
ANT.   'Tis as with a man
Removing in a hurry; all pack'd up,
But one dear jewel that his haste forgot;
And he, for that, returns upon the spur:
So I come back, for thee.
CLEO. Too long, you heav'ns, you have been cruel to me;
Now show your mended faith, and give me back
His fleeting life!
ANT.   It will not be, my love.
I keep my soul by force.
Say but thou art not false.
CLEO.   'Tis now too late
To say I'm true: I'll prove it, and die with you.
Unknown to me, Alexas feign'd my death:
Which, when I knew, I hasted to prevent

This fatal consequence. My fleet betray'd
Both you and me.

ANT.   And Dolabella——

CLEO.   Scarce
Esteem'd before he lov'd; but hated now.

ANT. Enough: my life's not long enough for more.
Thou say'st thou wilt come after: I believe thee;
For I can now believe whate'er thou say'st
That we may part more kindly.

CLEO.   I will come:
Doubt not, my life, I'll come, and quickly too:
Cæsar shall triumph o'er no part of thee.

ANT. But grieve not, while thou stay'st,
My last disastrous times:
Think we have had a clear and glorious day,
And heav'n did kindly to delay the storm,
Just till our close of ev'ning. Ten years' love,
And not a moment lost, but all improv'd
To th' utmost joys—what ages have we liv'd!
And now to die each other's; and, so dying,
While hand in hand we walk in groves below,
Whole troops of lovers' ghosts shall flock about us,
And all the train be ours.

CLEO. Your words are like the notes of dying swans,
Too sweet to last. Were there so many hours
For your unkindness, and not one for love?

ANT. No, not a minute.—This one kiss—more worth
Than all I leave to Cæsar.   (*dies*)

CLEO. Oh, tell me so again,
And take ten thousand kisses for that word.
My Lord, my Lord! speak, if you yet have being;
Sigh to me, if you cannot speak; or cast
One look! Do anything that shows you live.

IRAS. He's gone too far to hear you;
And this you see, a lump of senseless clay,
The leavings of a soul.

CHAR.   Remember, Madam,
He charg'd you not to grieve.

CLEO.   And I'll obey him.
I have not lov'd a Roman not to know

What should become his wife; his wife, my Charmion,
For 'tis to that high title I aspire,
And now I'll not die less! Let dull Octavia
Survive, to mourn him dead: my nobler fate
Shall knit our spousals with a tie too strong
For Roman laws to break.

IRAS.   Will you then die?
CLEO. Why shouldst thou make that question?
IRAS. Cæsar is merciful.
CLEO.   Let him be so
To those that want his mercy: my poor lord
Made no such cov'nant with him, to spare me
When he was dead. Yield me to Cæsar's pride?
What! to be led in triumph through the streets,
A spectacle to base plebeian eyes;
While some dejected friend of Antony's,
Close in a corner, shakes his head, and mutters
A secret curse on her who ruin'd him?
I'll none of that.

CHAR.   Whatever you resolve,
I'll follow, ev'n to death. .
IRAS.   I only fear'd
For you, but more should fear to live without you.
CLEO. Why, now 'tis as it should be. Quick, my friends,
Dispatch; ere this, the town's in Cæsar's hands:
My lord looks down concern'd and fears my stay.
Lest I should be surpris'd;
Keep him not waiting for his love too long.
You, Charmion, bring my crown and richest jewels;
With 'em, the wreath of victory I made
(Vain augury!) for him who now lies dead.
You, Iras, bring the cure of all our ills.

IRAS. The aspics, Madam?
CLEO.   Must I bid you twice?
                         (*Exeunt* CHARMION *and* IRAS.)
'Tis sweet to die when they would force life on me,
To rush into the dark abode of Death,
And seize him first; if he be like my love,
He is not frightful, sure.
We're now alone, in secrecy and silence;

And is not this like lovers? I may kiss
These pale, cold lips; Octavia does not see me;
And, oh! 'tis better far to have him thus,
Than see him in her arms.—Oh, welcome, welcome!

Enter CHARMION *and* IRAS

CHAR. What must be done?
CLEO.   Short ceremony, friends;
But yet it must be decent. First, this laurel
Shall crown my hero's head: he fell not basely,
Nor left his shield behind him. Only thou
Couldst triumph o'er thyself, and thou alone
Wert worthy so to triumph.
CHAR.   To what end
These ensigns of your pomp and royalty?
CLEO. Dull that thou art! why, 'tis to meet my love;
As when I saw him first, on Cydnos' bank,
All sparkling, like a Goddess: so adorn'd,
I'll find him once again: my second spousals
Shall match my first in glory. Haste, haste, both,
And dress the bride of Antony.
CHAR.   'Tis done.
CLEO. Now seat me by my lord. I claim this place;
For I must conquer Cæsar too, like him,
And win my share o' th' world.—Hail, you dear relics
Of my immortal love!
Oh, let no impious hand remove you hence;
But rest for ever here! Let Egypt give
His death that peace, which it deny'd his life.—
Reach me the casket.
IRAS.   Underneath the fruit
The aspic lies.
CLEO. (*putting aside the leaves*) Welcome, thou kind deceiver!
Thou best of thieves, who, with an easy key,
Dost open life, and, unperceiv'd by us,
Ev'n steal us from ourselves; discharging so
Death's dreadful office better than himself,
Touching our limbs so gently into slumber,
That Death stands by, deceiv'd by his own image,
And thinks himself but Sleep.

SERAP. (*within*)   The queen, where is she?
The town is yielded, Cæsar's at the gates.
CLEO. He comes too late t' invade the rites of death.
Haste, bare my arm, and rouse the serpent's fury.

(holds out her arm, and draws it back)

Coward flesh,
Wouldst thou conspire with Cæsar to betray me,
As thou wert none of mine? I'll force thee to't,
And not be sent by him,
But bring, myself, my soul to Antony.

(turns aside, and then shows her arm bloody)

Take hence; the work is done.
SERAP. (*within*)   Break ope the door,
And guard the traitor well.
CHAR.   The next is ours.
IRAS. Now, Charmion, to be worthy
Of our great queen and mistress.   (*They apply the aspics.*)
CLEO. Already, death, I feel thee in my veins;
I go with such a will to find my lord
That we shall quickly meet.
A heavy numbness creeps through every limb,
And now 'tis at my head: my eyelids fall,
And my dear love is vanish'd in a mist.
Where shall I find him, where? Oh turn me to him.
And lay me on his breast!—Cæsar, thy worst;
Now part us, if thou canst.   (*dies*)

(IRAS sinks down at her feet, and dies;
CHARMION stands behind her chair,
as dressing her head.)

Enter SERAPION, *two Priests,* ALEXAS *bound, Egyptians*

2 PRIESTS.   Behold, Serapion,
What havoc death has made!
SERAP.   'Twas what I feared.——
Charmion, is this well done?
CHAR. Yes, 'tis well done, and like a queen, the last
Of her great race: I follow her.   (*sinks down; dies*)
ALEX.   'Tis true,
She has done well: much better thus to die,
Than live to make a holiday in Rome.

SERAP. See,
See how the lovers sit in state together,
As they were giving laws to half mankind!
Th' impression of a smile, left in her face,
Shows she dy'd pleas'd with him for whom she liv'd,
And went to charm him in another world.
Cæsar's just ent'ring: grief has now no leisure.
Secure that villain, as our pledge of safety,
To grace th' imperial triumph.——Sleep, blest pair,
Secure from human chance, long ages out,
While all the storms of fate fly o'er your tomb,
    And fame to late posterity shall tell,
    No lovers liv'd so great, or died so well.

EPILOGUE

Poets, like disputants, when reasons fail,
Have one sure refuge left—and that's to rail.
Fop, coxcomb, fool, are thunder'd through the pit;
And this is all their equipage of wit.
We wonder how the devil this diff'rence grows,
Betwixt our fools in verse, and yours in prose:
For, 'faith, the quarrel rightly understood,
'Tis civil war with their own flesh and blood.
The threadbare author hates the gaudy coat,
And swears at the gilt coach, but swears afoot:
For 'tis observ'd of every scribbling man,
He grows a fop as fast as e'er he can;
Prunes up, and asks his oracle, the glass,
If pink or purple best become his face.
For our poor wretch, he neither rails nor prays;⎫
Nor likes your wit just as you like his plays; ⎬
He has not yet so much of Mr. Bayes.   ⎭
He does his best; and if he cannot please,
Would quietly sue out his *writ of ease*.
Yet, if he might his own grand jury call,
By the fair sex he begs to stand or fall.
Let Cæsar's pow'r the men's ambition move,
But grace you him who lost the world for love!

Yet if some antiquated lady say,
The last age is not copy'd in his play,
Heav'n help the man who for that face must drudge,
Which only has the wrinkles of a judge.
Let not the young and beauteous join with those;
For should you raise such numerous hosts of foes,
Young wits and sparks he to his aid must call;
'Tis more than one man's work to please you all.

Venice Preserved; or,

A Plot Discovered

A TRAGEDY

By THOMAS OTWAY

PROLOGUE

In these distracted times, when each man dreads
The bloody stratagems of busy heads;
When we have fear'd three years we know not what,⎫
Till witnesses begin to die o' th' rot, ⎬
What made our poet meddle with a plot? ⎭
Was't that he fancy'd, for the very sake
And name of plot, his trifling play might take?
For there's not in't one inch-board evidence, ⎫
But 'tis, he says, to reason plain and sense, ⎬
And that he thinks a plausible defence. ⎭
Were truth by sense and reason to be tried,
Sure all our swearers might be laid aside:
No, of such tools our author has no need,
To make his plot, or make his play succeed;
He of black bills has no prodigious tales,
Or Spanish pilgrims cast ashore in Wales;
Here's not one murder'd magistrate at least,

Kept rank like ven'son for a city feast,
Grown four days stiff the better to prepare
And fit his pliant limbs to ride in chair.
Yet here's an army rais'd, though underground,
But no man seen, nor one commission found;
Here is a traitor too, that's very old,
Turbulent, subtle, mischievous, and bold,
Bloody, revengeful, and, to crown his part,
Loves fumbling with a wench with all his heart;
Till after having many changes pass'd,
In spite of age (thanks, heaven) is hang'd at last.
Next is a senator that keeps a whore,
In Venice none a higher office bore;
To lewdness every night the lecher ran, ⎫
Show me, all London, such another man; ⎬
Match him at Mother Creswold's if you can. ⎭
O Poland, Poland! had it been thy lot,
T'have heard in time of this Venetian plot,
Thou surely chosen hadst one king from thence,
And honour'd them as thou hast England since.

PERSONS REPRESENTED

DUKE OF VENICE	*Conspirators*	
PRIULI, *father to Belvidera, a Senator*	RENAULT	DURAND
	BEDAMAR	MEZZANA
ANTONIO, *a fine speaker in the Senate*	SPINOSA	BRAINVEIL
	THEODORE	TERNON
JAFFEIR	ELIOT	RETROSI
PIERRE	REVILLIDO	BRABE

BELVIDERA
AQUILINA

Two Women, attendants or   *The Council of Ten*
   Belvidera   *Officer*
Two Women, servants to   *Guards*
   Aquilina   *Friar*
                          Executioner and Rabble

SCENE: *Venice.*

VENICE PRESERVED; OR,
A PLOT DISCOVERED

ACT I

Enter PRIULI *and* JAFFEIR

PRIU. No more! I'll hear no more; begone and leave.

JAFF. Not hear me! by my sufferings, but you shall!
My Lord, my Lord! I'm not that abject wretch
You think me. Patience! where's the distance throws
Me back so far, but I may boldly speak
In right, though proud oppression will not hear me!

PRIU. Have you not wrong'd me?

JAFF.   Could my nature e'er
Have brook'd injustice or the doing wrongs,
I need not now thus low have bent myself
To gain a hearing from a cruel father!
Wrong'd you?

PRIU.   Yes! wrong'd me, in the nicest point,
The honour of my house; you have done me wrong.
You may remember (for I now will speak,
And urge its baseness) when you first came home
From travel, with such hopes as made you look'd on
By all men's eyes, a youth of expectation;
Pleas'd with your growing virtue, I receiv'd you,
Courted, and sought to raise you to your merits:
My house, my table, nay, my fortune, too,
My very self, was yours; you might have us'd me
To your best service. Like an open friend,
I treated, trusted you, and thought you mine;
When in requital of my best endeavours,
You treacherously practis'd to undo me,
Seduc'd the weakness of my age's darling,
My only child, and stole her from my bosom.
O Belvidera!

JAFF.   'Tis to me you owe her;
Childless you had been else, and in the grave,
Your name extinct, nor no more Priuli heard of.

You may remember, scarce five years are past
Since in your brigandine you sail'd to see
The Adriatic wedded by our Duke,
And I was with you: your unskilful pilot
Dash'd us upon a rock; when to your boat
You made for safety, entered first yourself;
The affrighted Belvidera following next,
As she stood trembling on the vessel side,
Was by a wave wash'd off into the deep;
When instantly I plung'd into the sea,
And buffeting the billows to her rescue,
Redeem'd her life with half the loss of mine.
Like a rich conquest in one hand I bore her,
And with the other dash'd the saucy waves
That throng'd and press'd to rob me of my prize:
I brought her, gave her to your despairing arms.
Indeed you thank'd me; but a nobler gratitude
Rose in her soul: for from that hour she lov'd me,
Till for her life she paid me with herself.

PRIU. You stole her from me; like a thief you stole her,
At dead of night; that cursed hour you chose
To rifle me of all my heart held dear.
May all your joys in her prove false like mine;
A sterile fortune and a barren bed
Attend you both: continual discord make
Your days and nights bitter and grievous: still
May the hard hand of a vexatious need
Oppress and grind you; till at last you find
The curse of disobedience all your portion.

JAFF. Half of your curse you have bestow'd in vain;
Heav'n has already crown'd our faithful loves
With a young boy, sweet as his mother's beauty.
May he live to prove more gentle than his grandsire,
And happier than his father!

PRIU.   Rather live
To bait thee for his bread, and din your ears
With hungry cries, whilst his unhappy mother
Sits down and weeps in bitterness of want.

JAFF. You talk as if it would please you.

PRIU.   'Twould, by heav'n!

Once she was dear indeed; the drops that fell
From my sad heart when she forgot her duty,
The fountain of my life was not so precious:
But she is gone, and if I am a man,
I will forget her.

JAFF. Would I were in my grave.

PRIU.   And she, too, with thee;
For, living here, you're but my curs'd remembrancers
I once was happy.

JAFF. You use me thus because you know my soul
Is fond of Belvidera. You perceive
My life feeds on her, therefore thus you treat me.
Oh! could my soul ever have known satiety,
Were I that thief, the doer of such wrongs
As you upbraid me with, what hinders me
But I might send her back to you with contumely,
And court my fortune where she would be kinder!

PRIU. You dare not do't.

JAFF.   Indeed, my Lord, I dare not.
My heart, that awes me, is too much my master.
Three years are past since first our vows were plighted,
During which time, the world must bear me witness,
I have treated Belvidera like your daughter,
The daughter of a senator of Venice;
Distinction, place, attendance, and observance,
Due to her birth, she always has commanded;
Out of my little fortune I have done this,
Because (though hopeless e'er to win your nature)
The world might see I lov'd her for herself,
Not as the heiress of the great Priuli.——

PRIU. No more!

JAFF.   Yes! all, and then adieu forever!
There's not a wretch that lives on common charity
But's happier than me: for I have known
The luscious sweets of plenty; every night
Have slept with soft content about my head,
And never wak'd but to a joyful morning,
Yet now must fall like a full ear of corn,
Whose blossom 'scaped, yet's wither'd in the ripening.

PRIU. Home, and be humble; study to retrench;

Discharge the lazy vermin of thy hall,
Those pageants of thy folly;
Reduce the glittering trappings of thy wife
To humble weeds, fit for thy little state;
Then to some suburb cottage both retire;
Drudge, to feed loathsome life; get brats, and starve—
Home, home, I say!   (*Exit* PRIULI.)

   JAFF.   Yes, if my heart would let me—
This proud, this swelling heart. Home I would go
But that my doors are hateful to my eyes,
Fill'd and damm'd up with gaping creditors,
Watchful as fowlers when their game will spring;
I have now not fifty ducats in the world,
Yet still I am in love, and pleas'd with ruin.
O Belvidera! oh, she's my wife—
And we will bear our wayward fate together,
But ne'er know comfort more.

Enter PIERRE

   PIERRE.   My friend, good morrow!
How fares the honest partner of my heart?
What! melancholy? not a word to spare me?
   JAFF. I'm thinking, Pierre, how that damn'd starving quality
Call'd honesty, got footing in the world.
   PIERRE. Why, pow'rful villainy first set it up,
For its own ease and safety: honest men
Are the soft easy cushions on which knaves
Repose and fatten. Were all mankind villains,
They'd starve each other; lawyers would want practice,
Cut-throats rewards; each man would kill his brother
Himself; none would be paid or hang'd for murder.
Honesty was a cheat invented first
To bind the hands of bold deserving rogues,
That fools and cowards might sit safe in power,
And lord it uncontroll'd above their betters.
   JAFF. Then honesty is but a notion.
   PIERRE.   Nothing else;
Like wit, much talk'd of, not to be defin'd:
He that pretends to most, too, has least share in't;

'Tis a ragged virtue. Honesty!—no more on't.

JAFF. Sure, thou art honest?

PIERRE.   So indeed men think me.
But they're mistaken, Jaffeir; I am a rogue
As well as they—
A fine, gay, bold-fac'd villain, as thou seest me.
'Tis true, I pay my debts when they're contracted;
I steal from no man; would not cut a throat
To gain admission to a great man's purse,
Or a whore's bed; I'd not betray my friend,
To get his place or fortune; I scorn to flatter
A blown-up fool above me, or crush the wretch beneath me;
Yet, Jaffeir, for all this, I am a villain!

JAFF. A villain——

PIERRE.   Yes, a most notorious villain
To see the suff'rings of my fellow creatures,
And own myself a man; to see our senators
Cheat the deluded people with a show
Of liberty, which yet they ne'er must taste of;
They say by them our hands are free from fetters,
Yet whom they please they lay in basest bonds;
Bring whom they please to infamy and sorrow;
Drive us like wracks down the rough tide of power,
Whilst no hold's left to save us from destruction.
All that bear this are villains; and I one,
Not to rouse up at the great call of nature
And check the growth of these domestic spoilers
That make us slaves and tell us 'tis our charter.

JAFF. O Aquilina! Friend, to lose such beauty,
The dearest purchase of thy noble labours!
She was thy right by conquest, as by love.

PIERRE. O Jaffeir! I'd so fix'd my heart upon her
That wheresoe'er I fram'd a scheme of life
For time to come, she was my only joy
With which I wish'd to sweeten future cares;
I fancy'd pleasures, none but one that loves
And dotes as I did, can imagine like 'em:
When in the extremity of all these hopes,
In the most charming hour of expectation,

Then when our eager wishes soar the highest
Ready to stoop and grasp the lovely game,
A haggard owl, a worthless kite of prey,
With his foul wings sail'd in and spoil'd my quarry.

JAFF. I know the wretch, and scorn him as thou hat'st him.

PIERRE. Curse on the common good that's so protected,
Where every slave that heaps up wealth enough
To do much wrong, becomes a lord of right!
I, who believ'd no ill could e'er come near me,
Found in the embraces of my Aquilina
A wretched, old, but itching senator;
A wealthy fool, that had bought out my title,
A rogue that uses beauty like a lambskin,
Barely to keep him warm. That filthy cuckoo, too,
Was in my absence crept into my nest,
And spoiling all my brood of noble pleasure.

JAFF. Didst thou not chase him thence?

PIERRE.   I did, and drove
The rank old bearded Hirco stinking home.
The matter was complain'd of in the Senate;
I, summon'd to appear, and censur'd basely,
For violating something they call *privilege*—
This was the recompense of my service.
Would I'd been rather beaten by a coward!
A soldier's mistress, Jaffeir, 's his religion;
When that's profan'd, all other ties are broken;
That even dissolves all former bonds of service,
And from that hour I think myself as free
To be the foe as e'er the friend of Venice—
Nay, dear Revenge, whene'er thou call'st I'm ready.

JAFF. I think no safety can be here for virtue,
And grieve, my friend, as much as thou to live
In such a wretched state as this of Venice,
Where all agree to spoil the public good,
And villains fatten with the brave man's labours.

PIERRE. We have neither safety, unity, nor peace,
For the foundation's lost of common good;
Justice is lame as well as blind amongst us;
The laws (corrupted to their ends that make 'em)
Serve but for instruments of some new tyranny,

That every day starts up to enslave us deeper.
Now could this glorious cause but find out friends
To do it right! O Jaffeir! then mightst thou
Not wear these seals of woe upon thy face;
The proud Priuli should be taught humanity,
And learn to value such a son as thou art.
I dare not speak! But my heart bleeds this moment.
 JAFF. Curst be the cause, though I thy friend be part on't!
Let me partake the troubles of thy bosom,
For I am us'd to misery, and perhaps
May find a way to sweeten't to thy spirit.
 PIERRE. Too soon it will reach thy knowledge——
 JAFF.   Then from thee
Let it proceed. There's virtue in thy friendship
Would make the saddest tale of sorrow pleasing,
Strengthen my constancy, and welcome ruin.
 PIERRE. Then thou art ruin'd!
 JAFF.   That I long since knew;
I and ill fortune have been long acquainted.
 PIERRE. I pass'd this very moment by thy doors,
And found them guarded by a troop of villains;
The sons of public rapine were destroying;
They told me, by the sentence of the law,
They had commission to seize all thy fortune,
Nay, more, Priuli's cruel hand hath sign'd it.
Here stood a ruffian with a horrid face
Lording it o'er a pile of massy plate
Tumbled into a heap for public sale.
There was another making villainous jests
At thy undoing; he had ta'en possession
Of all thy ancient, most domestic ornaments,
Rich hangings intermix'd and wrought with gold;
The very bed which on thy wedding night
Receiv'd thee to the arms of Belvidera,
The scene of all thy joys, was violated
By the coarse hands of filthy dungeon villains,
And thrown amongst the common lumber.
 JAFF. Now thanks, heav'n——
 PIERRE. Thank heav'n! for what?
 JAFF.   That I'm not worth a ducat.

PIERRE. Curse thy dull stars and the worse fate of Venice!
Where brothers, friends, and fathers, all are false;
Where there's no trust, no truth; where innocence
Stoops under vile oppression, and vice lords it.
Hadst thou but seen, as I did, how at last
Thy beauteous Belvidera, like a wretch
That's doom'd to banishment, came weeping forth,
Shining through tears, like April suns in showers
That labour to o'ercome the cloud that loads 'em;
Whilst two young virgins, on whose arms she lean'd,
Kindly look'd up, and at her grief grew sad,
As if they catch'd the sorrows that fell from her:
Even the lewd rabble that were gather'd round
To see the sight, stood mute when they beheld her,
Govern'd their roaring throats, and grumbled pity.
I could have hugg'd the greasy rogues; they pleas'd me.

JAFF. I thank thee for this story from my soul,
Since now I know the worst that can befall me.
Ah, Pierre! I have a heart that could have borne
The roughest wrong my fortune could have done me;
But when I think what Belvidera feels,
The bitterness her tender spirit tastes of,
I own myself a coward. Bear my weakness,
If throwing thus my arms about thy neck,
I play the boy and blubber in thy bosom.
Oh! I shall drown thee with my sorrows!

PIERRE.   Burn!
First burn, and level Venice to thy ruin!
What! starve like beggar's brats in frosty weather
Under a hedge, and whine ourselves to death!
Thou, or thy cause, shall never want assistance
Whilst I have blood or fortune fit to serve thee;
Command my heart: thou art every way its master.

JAFF. No! There's a secret pride in bravely dying.

PIERRE. Rats die in holes and corners, dogs run mad;
Man knows a braver remedy for sorrow:
Revenge! the attribute of gods; they stamp'd it
With their great image on our natures. Die!
Consider well the cause that calls upon thee,

And if thou art base enough, die then; remember
Thy Belvidera suffers. Belvidera!
Die—damn first! What! be decently interr'd
In a churchyard, and mingle thy brave dust
With stinking rogues that rot in dirty winding sheets—
Surfeit-slain fools, the common dung o'th' soil?

JAFF. Oh!

PIERRE. Well said! out with't; swear a little——
                                                           Swear!

By sea and air! by earth, by heaven and hell,
I will revenge my Belvidera's tears!
Hark thee, my friend: Priuli—is—a senator!

PIERRE. A dog!

JAFF.   Agreed.

PIERRE.   Shoot him.

JAFF.   With all my heart.
No more. Where shall we meet at night?

PIERRE.   I'll tell thee:
On the Rialto every night at twelve
I take my evening's walk of meditation;
There we two will meet, and talk of precious
Mischief——

JAFF.   Farewell.

PIERRE.   At twelve.

JAFF.   At any hour; my plagues
Will keep me waking.   (*Exit* PIERRE.)
                Tell me why, good heav'n,
Thou mad'st me what I am, with all the spirit,
Aspiring thoughts, and elegant desires
That fill the happiest man? Ah! rather why
Didst thou not form me sordid as my fate,
Base-minded, dull, and fit to carry burdens?
Why have I sense to know the curse that's on me?
Is this just dealing, Nature?—— Belvidera!

Enter BELVIDERA *with Attendants*

Poor Belvidera!

BELV.   Lead me, lead me, my virgins,
To that kind voice! My Lord, my love, my refuge!

yes when they behold thy face:
art will leave its doleful beating
ee, and bound with sprightful joys.
when our loves were in their spring,
And cheer my fainting soul!

JAFF.   As when our loves
Were in their spring? has then my fortune chang'd?
Art thou not Belvidera, still the same,
Kind, good, and tender, as my arms first found thee?
If thou art alter'd, where shall I have harbour?
Where ease my loaded heart? oh! where complain?

BELV. Does this appear like change, or love decaying,
When thus I throw myself into thy bosom
With all the resolution of a strong truth?
Beats not my heart as 'twould alarm thine
To a new charge of bliss? I joy more in thee
Than did thy mother when she hugg'd thee first,
And bless'd the gods for all her travail past.

JAFF. Can there in woman be such glorious faith?
Sure, all ill stories of thy sex are false.
O woman! lovely woman! Nature made thee
To temper man; we had been brutes without you.
Angels are painted fair, to look like you;
There's in you all that we believe of heav'n—
Amazing brightness, purity, and truth,
Eternal joy, and everlasting love.

BELV. If love be treasure, we'll be wondrous rich:
I have so much, my heart will surely break with't.
Vows cannot express it: when I would declare
How great's my joy, I'm dumb with the big thought:
I swell and sigh, and labour with my longing.
Oh, lead me to some desert wide and wild,
Barren as our misfortunes, where my soul
May have its vent; where I may tell aloud
To the high heavens and every list'ning planet
With what a boundless stock my bosom's fraught;
Where I may throw my eager arms about thee,
Give loose to love with kisses, kindling joy,
And let off all the fire that's in my heart.

JAFF. O Belvidera! doubly I'm a beggar—
Undone by fortune, and in debt to thee.
Want! worldly want! that hungry, meagre fiend
Is at my heels and chases me in view.
Canst thou bear cold and hunger? Can these limbs,
Fram'd for the tender offices of love,
Endure the bitter gripes of smarting poverty?
When banish'd by our miseries abroad,
(As suddenly we shall be) to seek out
(In some far climate where our names are strangers)
For charitable succour; wilt thou then,
When in a bed of straw we shrink together,
And the bleak winds shall whistle round our heads,
Wilt thou then talk thus to me? Wilt thou then
Hush my cares thus, and shelter me with love?

BELV. Oh, I will love thee, even in madness love thee.
Though my distracted senses should forsake me,
I'd find some intervals when my poor heart
Should 'suage itself, and be let loose to thine.
Though the bare earth be all our resting-place,
Its roots our food, some clift our habitation,
I'll make this arm a pillow for thy head;
As thou sighing li'st, and swell'd with sorrow,
Creep to thy bosom, pour the balm of love
Into thy soul, and kiss thee to thy rest;
Then praise our God, and watch thee till the morning.

JAFF. Hear this, you heav'ns, and wonder how you made her!
Reign, reign, ye monarchs that divide the world!
Busy rebellion ne'er will let you know
Tranquillity and happiness like mine.
Like gaudy ships, th'obsequious billows fall
And rise again, to lift you in your pride;
They wait but for a storm and then devour you:
I, in my private bark, already wreck'd,
Like a poor merchant driven on unknown land,
That had by chance pack'd up his choicest treasure
In one dear casket, and sav'd only that,

      Since I must wander further on the shore,
      Thus hug my little, but my precious store;
      Resolv'd to scorn, and trust my fate no more.   *(Exeunt.)*

ACT II

SCENE I

Enter PIERRE *and* AQUILINA

AQUIL. By all thy wrongs, thou art dearer to my arms
Than all the wealth of Venice; prithee, stay,
And let us love to-night.

PIERRE.   No: there's fool,
There's fool about thee. When a woman sells
Her flesh to fools, her beauty's lost to me;
They leave a taint, a sully where th'ave pass'd;
There's such a baneful quality about 'em,
Even spoils complexions with their own nauseousness;
They infect all they touch; I cannot think
Of tasting anything a fool has pall'd.

AQUIL. I loathe and scorn that fool thou mean'st as much
Or more than thou canst; but the beast has gold
That makes him necessary; power too,
To qualify my character, and poise me
Equal with peevish virtue, that beholds
My liberty with envy. In their hearts,
Are loose as I am; but an ugly power
Sits in their faces, and frights pleasures from 'em.

PIERRE. Much good may't do you, Madam, with your senator.

AQUIL. My senator! why, canst thou think that wretch
E'er filled thy Aquilina's arms with pleasure?
Think'st thou, because I sometimes give him leave
To foil himself at what he is unfit for,
Because I force myself to endure and suffer him,
Think'st thou I love him? No, by all the joys
Thou ever gav'st me, his presence is my penance;
The worst thing an old man can be's a lover,
A mere *memento mori* to poor woman.
I never lay by his decrepit side
But all that night I ponder'd on my grave.

PIERRE. Would he were well sent thither!

AQUIL.   That's my wish, too:

For then, my Pierre, I might have cause with pleasure
To play the hypocrite. Oh! how I could weep
Over the dying dotard, and kiss him too,
In hopes to smother him quite; then, when the time
Was come to pay my sorrows at his funeral—
For he has already made me heir to treasures
Would make me out-act a real widow's whining—
How could I frame my face to fit my mourning!
With wringing hands attend him to his grave;
Fall swooning on his hearse; take mad possession
Even of the dismal vault where he lay bury'd;
There like the Ephesian matron dwell, till thou,
My lovely soldier, comest to my deliverance;
Then throwing up my veil, with open arms
And laughing eyes, run to new-dawning joy.

    PIERRE. No more! I have friends to meet me here to-night,
And must be private. As you prize my friendship,
Keep up your coxcomb. Let him not pry nor listen
Nor fisk about the house as I have seen him,
Like a tame mumping squirrel with a bell on.
Curs will be abroad to bite him, if you do.

    AQUIL. What friends to meet? may I not be of your council?

    PIERRE. How! a woman ask questions out of bed?
Go to your senator, ask him what passes
Amongst his brethren; he'll hide nothing from you.
But pump not me for politics. No more!
Give order that whoever in my name
Comes here, receive admittance; so, good night.

    AQUIL. Must we ne'er meet again? embrace no more?
Is love so soon and utterly forgotten?

    PIERRE. As you henceforward treat your fool, I'll think on't.

    AQUIL. (*aside*) Curst be all fools, and doubly curst myself,
The worst of fools.—I die if he forsakes me;
And now to keep him, heav'n or hell instruct me.   (*Exeunt.*)

SCENE II

SCENE: *The Rialto*

Enter JAFFEIR

JAFF. I am here; and thus, the shades of night around me,
I look as if all hell were in my heart,
And I in hell. Nay, surely, 'tis so with me;
For every step I tread methinks some fiend
Knocks at my breast and bids it not be quiet.
I've heard how desperate wretches like myself
Have wander'd out at this dead time of night
To meet the foe of mankind in his walk:
Sure, I'm so curst that, though of heav'n forsaken,
No minister of darkness cares to tempt me.
Hell! Hell! why sleepest thou?

Enter PIERRE

PIERRE. Sure, I have stay'd too long;
The clock has struck, and I may lose my proselyte.
—— Speak, who goes there?
JAFF.   A dog that comes to howl
At yonder moon. What's he that asks the question?
PIERRE. A friend to dogs, for they are honest creatures,
And ne'er betray their masters; never fawn
On any that they love not. Well met, friend.
—Jaffeir!
JAFF. The same. O Pierre! thou art come in season:
I was just going to pray.
PIERRE.   Ah, that's mechanic:
Priests make a trade on't, and yet starve by't, too:
No praying; it spoils business, and time's precious.
Where's Belvidera?
JAFF.   For a day or two
I've lodg'd her privately, till I see farther
What fortune will do with me. Prithee, friend,
If thou wouldst have me fit to hear good counsel,
Speak not of Belvidera——

PIERRE.   Speak not of her?

JAFF. Oh, no!

PIERRE.   Nor name her? Maybe I wish her well.

JAFF. Who well?

PIERRE.   Thy wife, thy lovely Belvidera;
I hope a man may wish his friend's wife well,
And no harm done!

JAFF.   Y'are merry, Pierre!

PIERRE.   I am so.
Thou shalt smile too, and Belvidera smile;
We'll all rejoice.   (*gives him a purse*)
               Here's something to buy pins;
Marriage is chargeable.

JAFF.   I but half wished
To see the devil, and he's here already.
—— Well!
What must this buy—rebellion, murder, treason?
Tell me which way I must be damn'd for this.

PIERRE. When last we parted, we had no qualms like these,
But entertain'd each other's thoughts like men
Whose souls were well acquainted. Is the world
Reform'd since our last meeting? What new miracles
Have happen'd? Has Priuli's heart relented?
Can he be honest?

JAFF.   Kind heav'n! let heavy curses
Gall his old age! cramps, aches, rack his bones,
And bitterest disquiet wring his heart!
Oh, let him live till life become his burden;
Let him groan under't long, linger an age
In the worst agonies and pangs of death,
And find its ease but late!

PIERRE.   Nay, couldst thou not
As well, my friend, have stretch'd the curse to all
The Senate round, as to one single villain?

JAFF. But curses stick not. Could I kill with cursing
By heav'n, I know not thirty heads in Venice
Should not be blasted; senators should rot
Like dogs on dunghills, but their wives and daughters
Die of their own diseases. Oh for a curse
To kill with!

PIERRE.   Daggers, daggers, are much better.

JAFF. Ha!

PIERRE.   Daggers.

JAFF.   But where are they?

PIERRE.   Oh, a thousand
May be dispos'd in honest hands in Venice.

JAFF. Thou talk'st in clouds.

PIERRE.   But yet a heart half wrong'd
As thine has been, would find the meaning, Jaffeir.

JAFF. A thousand daggers, all in honest hands,
And have not I a friend will stick one here?

PIERRE. Yes, if I thought thou were not to be cherish'd
To a nobler purpose, I'd be that friend.
But thou hast better friends, friends whom thy wrongs
Have made thy friends, friends worthy to be call'd so.
I'll trust thee with a secret: there are spirits
This hour at work. But as thou art a man
Whom I have pick'd and chosen from the world,
Swear that thou wilt be true to what I utter;
And when I have told thee that which only gods
And men like gods are privy to, then swear
No chance or change shall wrest it from thy bosom.

JAFF. When thou wouldst bind me, is there need of oaths?
(Green-sickness girls lose maidenheads with such counters!)
For thou art so near my heart that thou mayst see
Its bottom, sound its strength and firmness to thee.
Is coward, fool, or villain in my face?
If I seem none of these, I dare believe
Thou wouldst not use me in a little cause,
For I am fit for honour's toughest task,
Nor ever yet found fooling was my province;
And for a villainous, inglorious enterprise,
I know thy heart so well, I dare lay mine
Before thee, set it to what point thou wilt.

PIERRE. Nay, it's a cause thou wilt be fond of, Jaffeir,
For it is founded on the noblest basis—
Our liberties, our natural inheritance.
There's no religion, no hypocrisy in't;
We'll do the business, and ne'er fast and pray for't;
Openly act a deed the world shall gaze

With wonder at, and envy when 'tis done.
   JAFF. For liberty!
   PIERRE.   For liberty, my friend!
Thou shalt be freed from base Priuli's tyranny,
And thy sequestred fortunes heal'd again.
I shall be freed from opprobrious wrongs
That press me now and bend my spirit downward:
All Venice free, and every growing merit
Succeed to its just right: fools shall be pull'd
From wisdom's seat—those baleful, unclean birds,
Those lazy owls, who (perch'd near fortune's top)
Sit only watchful with their heavy wings
To cuff down new fledg'd virtues, that would rise
To nobler heights and make the grove harmonious.
   JAFF. What can I do?
   PIERRE.   Canst thou not kill a senator?
   JAFF. Were there one wise or honest, I could kill him
For herding with that nest of fools and knaves.
By all my wrongs, thou talk'st as if revenge
Were to be had, and the brave story warms me.
   PIERRE. Swear then!
   JAFF.   I do, by all those glittering stars
And yond great ruling planet of the night!
By all good pow'rs above, and ill below,
By love and friendship, dearer than my life,
No pow'r or death shall make me false to thee!
   PIERRE. Here we embrace, and I'll unlock my heart.
A council's held hard by, where the destruction
Of this great empire's hatching: there I'll lead thee!
But be a man, for thou art to mix with men
Fit to disturb the peace of all the world,
And rule it when it's wildest.
   JAFF.   I give thee thanks
For this kind warning. Yes, I will be a man,
And charge thee, Pierre, whene'er thou see'st my fears
Betray me less, to rip this heart of mine
Out of my breast, and show it for a coward's.
Come, let's begone, for from this hour I chase
All little thoughts, all tender human follies
Out of my bosom. Vengeance shall have room—

Revenge!

PIERRE. And liberty!

JAFF.   Revenge! Revenge——   (*Exeunt.*)

SCENE III

The scene changes to AQUILINA'S *house, the Greek courtesan*

Enter RENAULT

REN. Why was my choice ambition the worst ground
A wretch can build on? It's indeed at distance
A good prospect, tempting to the view;
The height delights us, and the mountain top
Looks beautiful, because it's nigh to heav'n.
But we ne'er think how sandy's the foundation,
What storm will batter, and what tempest shake us!
——Who's there?

Enter SPINOSA

SPIN. Renault, good morrow! for by this time
I think the scale of night has turn'd the balance
And weighs up morning. Has the clock struck twelve?
REN. Yes, clocks will go as they are set. But man,
Irregular man's ne'er constant, never certain.
I've spent at least three precious hours of darkness
In waiting dull attendance; 'tis the curse
Of diligent virtue to be mix'd, like mine,
With giddy tempers, souls but half resolv'd.
SPIN. Hell seize that soul amongst us it can frighten.
REN. What's then the cause that I am here alone?
Why are we not together?

Enter ELIOT

O Sir, welcome!
You are an Englishman: when treason's hatching
One might have thought you'd not have been behindhand.
In what whore's lap have you been lolling?
Give but an Englishman his whore and ease,
Beef and a sea-coal fire, he's yours forever.

ELIOT. Frenchman, you are saucy.
REN.   How!

Enter BEDAMAR *the ambassador,* THEODORE, BRAINVEIL,
DURAND, BRABE, REVILLIDO, MEZZANA, TERNON,
RETROSI, *Conspirators*

BEDA.   At difference?—fie!
Is this a time for quarrels? Thieves and rogues
Fall out and brawl. Should men of your high calling,
Men separated by the choice of Providence
From this gross heap of mankind, and set here
In this great assembly as in one great jewel,
T'adorn the bravest purpose it e'er smil'd on—
Should you like boys wrangle for trifles?
REN.   Boys!
BEDA. Renault, thy hand!
REN.   I thought I'd given my heart
Long since to every man that mingles here,
But grieve to find it trusted with such tempers,
That can't forgive my froward age its weakness.
BEDA. Eliot, thou once hadst virtue; I have seen
Thy stubborn temper bend with godlike goodness,
Not half thus courted. 'Tis thy nation's glory,
To hug the foe that offers brave alliance.
Once more embrace, my friends—we'll all embrace.
United thus, we are the mighty engine
Must twist this rooted empire from its basis!
Totters it not already?
ELIOT.   Would it were tumbling.
BEDA. Nay, it shall down: this night we seal its ruin.

Enter PIERRE

O Pierre! thou art welcome!
Come to my breast, for by its hopes thou look'st
Lovelily dreadful, and the fate of Venice
Seems on thy sword already. O my Mars!
The poets that first feign'd a god of war
Sure prophesy'd of thee.
PIERRE.   Friends! was not Brutus,
(I mean that Brutus who in open senate

Stabb'd the first Cæsar that usurp'd the world)
A gallant man?

REN.   Yes, and Catiline too,
Though story wrong his fame: for he conspir'd
To prop the reeling glory of his country:
His cause was good.

BEDA.   And ours as much above it
As, Renault, thou art superior to Cethegus,
Or Pierre to Cassius.

PIERRE.   Then to what we aim at.
When do we start? or must we talk forever?

BEDA. No, Pierre, the deed's near birth: Fate seems to have set
The business up and given it to our care.
I hope there's not a heart nor hand amongst us
But is firm and ready.

ALL. All! We'll die with Bedamar.

BEDA.   O men,
Matchless as will your glory be hereafter!
The game is for a matchless prize, if won;
If lost, disgraceful ruin.

REN.   What can lose it?
The public stock's a beggar; one Venetian
Trusts not another. Look into their stores
Of general safety: empty magazines,
A tatter'd fleet, a murmuring unpaid army,
Bankrupt nobility, a harass'd commonalty,
A factious, giddy, and divided senate,
Is all the strength of Venice. Let's destroy it;
Let's fill their magazines with arms to awe them,
Man out their fleet, and make their trade maintain it;
Let loose the murmuring army on their masters,
To pay themselves with plunder; lop their nobles
To the base roots, whence most of 'em first sprung;
Enslave the rout, whom smarting will make humble;
Turn out their droning senate, and possess
That seat of empire which our souls were fram'd for.

PIERRE. Ten thousand men are armed at your nod,
Commanded all by leaders fit to guide
A battle for the freedom of the world;
This wretched state has starv'd them in its service,

And by your bounty quicken'd, they're resolv'd
To serve your glory, and revenge their own.
They've all their different quarters in this city,
Watch for th' alarm, and grumble 'tis so tardy.
    BEDA. I doubt not, friend, but thy unweary'd diligence
Has still kept waking, and it shall have ease;
After this night it is resolv'd we meet
No more till Venice own us for her lords.
    PIERRE. How lovely the Adriatic whore,
Dress'd in her flames, will shine!—devouring flames,
Such as shall burn her to the watery bottom
And hiss in her foundation!
    BEDA.   Now if any
Amongst us that owns this glorious cause
Have friends or interest he'd wish to save,
Let it be told. The general doom is seal'd,
But I'd forgo the hopes of a world's empire,
Rather than wound the bowels of my friend.
    PIERRE. I must confess you there have touch'd my weakness.
I have a friend; hear it, such a friend!
My heart was ne'er shut to him. Nay, I'll tell you.
He knows the very business of this hour,
But he rejoices in the cause and loves it:
We've chang'd a vow to live and die together,
And he's at hand to ratify it here.
    REN.   How! all betray'd?
    PIERRE. No—I've dealt nobly with you.
I've brought my all into the public stock;
I had but one friend, and him I'll share amongst you!
Receive and cherish him; or if, when seen
And search'd, you find him worthless, as my tongue
Has lodg'd this secret in his faithful breast,
To ease your fears I wear a dagger here
Shall rip it out again, and give you rest.
——Come forth, thou only good I e'er could boast of!

Enter JAFFEIR *with a dagger*

    BEDA. His presence bears the show of manly virtue.
    JAFF. I know you'll wonder all, that thus uncall'd
I dare approach this place of fatal councils;

But I am amongst you, and by heav'n it glads me
To see so many virtues thus united
To restore justice and dethrone oppression.
Command this sword, if you would have it quiet,
Into this breast; but if you think it worthy
To cut the throats of reverend rogues in robes,
Send me into the curst, assembled Senate:
It shrinks not, though I meet a father there.
Would you behold this city flaming? Here's
A hand shall bear a lighted torch at noon
To the arsenal, and set its gates on fire.

    REN. You talk this well, Sir.

    JAFF.   Nay—by heav'n, I'll do this!
Come, come, I read distrust in all your faces;
You fear me a villain, and indeed it's odd
To hear a stranger talk thus at first meeting,
Of matters that have been so well debated;
But I come ripe with wrongs as you with councils.
I hate this Senate, am a foe to Venice,
A friend to none but men resolv'd like me
To push on mischief. Oh, did you but know me,
I need not talk thus!

    BEDA.   Pierre! I must embrace him;
My heart beats to this man as if it knew him.

    REN. I never lov'd these huggers.

    JAFF.   Still I see
The cause delights me not. Your friends survey me
As I were dang'rous—but I come arm'd
Against all doubts, and to your trust will give
A pledge worth more than all the world can pay for.
——My Belvidera! Ho! my Belvidera!

    BEDA. What wonder next?

    JAFF.   Let me entreat you
As I have henceforth hopes to call ye friends,
That all but the ambassador, this
Grave guide of councils, with my friend that owns me,
Withdraw awhile to spare a woman's blushes.

        (*Exeunt all but* BEDAMAR, RENAULT, JAFFEIR, PIERRE.)

    BEDA. Pierre, whither will this ceremony lead us?

    JAFF. My Belvidera! Belvidera!

Enter BELVIDERA

BELV.   Who?
Who calls so loud at this late, peaceful hour?
That voice was wont to come in gentler whispers,
And fill my ears with the soft breath of love.
Thou hourly image of my thoughts, where art thou?
    JAFF. Indeed, 'tis late.
    BELV.   Oh! I have slept, and dreamt,
And dreamt again. Where hast thou been, thou loiterer?
Though my eyes clos'd, my arms have still been open'd,
Stretch'd every way betwixt my broken slumbers,
To search if thou wert come to crown my rest;
There's no repose without thee. Oh, the day
Too soon will break, and wake us to our sorrow;
Come, come to bed, and bid thy cares good night.
    JAFF. O Belvidera! we must change the scene
In which the past delights of life were tasted.
The poor sleep little; we must learn to watch
Our labours late, and early every morning,
Midst winter frosts, thin clad and fed with sparing,
Rise to our toils, and drudge away the day.
    BELV. Alas! where am I? whither is't you lead me?
Methinks I read distraction in your face,
Something less gentle than the fate you tell me!
You shake and tremble too! your blood runs cold!
Heavens, guard my love, and bless his heart with patience.
    JAFF. That I have patience, let our fate bear witness,
Who has ordain'd it so that thou and I
(Thou the divinest good man e'er possess'd,
And I the wretched'st of the race of man)
This very hour, without one tear, must part.
    BELV. Part! must we part? Oh! am I then forsaken?
Will my love cast me off? have my misfortunes
Offended him so highly that he'll leave me?
Why drag you from me? whither are you going?
My dear! my life! my love!
    JAFF.   Oh, friends!
    BELV. Speak to me.
    JAFF.   Take her from my heart,

She'll gain such hold else I shall ne'er get loose.
I charge thee take her, but with tender'st care,
Relieve her troubles, and assuage her sorrows.

    REN. Rise, Madam! and command amongst your servants.

    JAFF. To you, Sirs, and your honours, I bequeath her,
And with her this. When I prove unworthy—   (*gives a dagger*)
You know the rest—then strike it to her heart;
And tell her, he who three whole happy years
Lay in her arms, and each kind night repeated
The passionate vows of still increasing love,
Sent that reward for all her truth and sufferings.

    BELV. Nay, take my life, since he has sold it cheaply;
Or send me to some distant clime your slave;
But let it be far off, lest my complainings
Should reach his guilty ears, and shake his peace.

    JAFF. No, Belvidera, I've contrived thy honour;
Trust to my faith, and be but Fortune kind
To me, as I'll preserve that faith unbroken,
When next we meet, I'll lift thee to a height
Shall gather all the gazing world about thee
To wonder what strange virtue plac'd thee there.
But if we ne'er meet more——

    BELV.   Oh, thou unkind one,
Never meet more! Have I deserv'd this from you?
Look on me, tell me, tell me, speak, thou dear deceiver,
Why am I separated from thy love?
If I am false, accuse me; but if true,
Don't, prithee, don't in poverty forsake me,
But pity the sad heart that's torn with parting.
Yet hear me! yet recall me——

                (*Exeunt* RENAULT, BEDAMAR, *and* BELVIDERA.)

    JAFF.   O my eyes,
Look not that way, but turn yourselves awhile
Into my heart, and be wean'd altogether!
——My friend, where art thou?

    PIERRE.   Here, my honour's brother.

    JAFF. Is Belvidera gone?

    PIERRE.   Renault has led her
Back to her own apartment: but, by heav'n!
Thou must not see her more till our work's over.

JAFF. No.

PIERRE.   Not for your life.

JAFF.   O Pierre, wert thou but she,
How I could pull thee down into my heart,
Gaze on thee till my eye-strings crack'd with love,
Till all my sinews with its fire extended,
Fix'd me upon the rack of ardent longing;
   Then swelling, sighing, raging to be blest,
   Come like a panting turtle to thy breast;
   On thy soft bosom, hovering, bill and play,
   Confess the cause why last I fled away;
   Own 'twas a fault, but swear to give it o'er,
   And never follow false ambition more.   (*Exeunt ambo.*)

ACT III

SCENE I

Enter AQUILINA *and her Maid*

AQUIL. Tell him I am gone to bed; tell him I am not at
home; tell him I've better company with me, or anything; tell
him in short I will not see him, the eternal troublesome, vexatious
fool! He's worse company than an ignorant physician—I'll not
be disturbed at these unseasonable hours!

MAID. But, Madam, he's here already, just entered the doors.

AQUIL. Turn him out again, you unnecessary, useless, giddy-
brained ass! If he will not begone, set the house afire and burn us
both. I had rather meet a toad in my dish than that old hideous
animal in my chamber to-night.

Enter ANTONIO

ANT. Nacky, Nacky, Nacky—how dost do, Nacky? Hurry
durry. I am come, little Nacky; past eleven a-clock, a late hour;
time in all conscience to go to bed, Nacky—Nacky, did I say?
Aye, Nacky; Aquilina, lina, lina, quilina, quilina, quilina, Aquilina, Naquilina, Naquilina, Acky, Acky, Nacky, Nacky, queen
Nacky—come, let's to bed—you fubbs, you pugg, you—you little
puss—purree tuzzey—I am a senator.

AQUIL. You are a fool, I am sure.

ANT. Maybe so, too, sweetheart. Never the worse senator for all that. Come Nacky, Nacky, let's have a game at rump, Nacky.

AQUIL. You would do well, Signior, to be troublesome here no longer, but leave me to myself, be sober, and go home, Sir.

ANT. Home, Madonna!

AQUIL. Aye, home, Sir. Who am I?

ANT. Madonna, as I take it you are my—you are—thou art my little Nicky Nacky—that's all!

AQUIL. I find you are resolved to be troublesome; and so to make short of the matter in few words, I hate you, detest you, loathe you, I am weary of you, sick of you—hang you, you are an old, silly, impertinent, impotent, solicitous coxcomb, crazy in your head and lazy in your body, love to be meddling with everything, and if you had not money, you are good for nothing.

ANT. Good for nothing! Hurry durry, I'll try that presently. Sixty-one years old, and good for nothing; that's brave! (to the Maid)——Come, come, come, Mistress Fiddle-faddle, turn you out for a season. Go, turn out, I say, it is our will and pleasure to be private some moments—out, out when you are bid to! (puts her out and locks the door)——"Good for nothing," you say.

AQUIL. Why, what are you good for?

ANT. In the first place, Madam, I am old, and consequently very wise, very wise, Madonna, d'e mark that? In the second place, take notice, if you please, that I am a senator, and when I think fit can make speeches, Madonna. Hurry durry, I can make a speech in the Senate-house now and then—would make your hair stand on end, Madonna.

AQUIL. What care I for your speeches in the Senate-house? If you would be silent here, I should thank you.

ANT. Why, I can make speeches to thee, too, my lovely Madonna; for example: "My cruel fair one (takes out a purse of gold, and at every pause shakes it), since it is my fate that you should with your servant angry prove; though late at night—I hope 'tis not too late with this to gain reception for my love."—— There's for thee, my little Nicky Nacky—take it, here take it— I say take it, or I'll throw it at your head. How now, rebel!

AQUIL. Truly, my illustrious senator, I must confess your honour is at present most profoundly eloquent, indeed.

ANT. Very well: come now, let's sit down and think upon't a little. Come sit, I say—sit down by me a little, my Nicky Nacky, hah—(*sits down*). Hurry durry—"good for nothing!"

AQUIL. No, Sir; if you please, I can know my distance, and stand.

ANT. Stand! How? Nacky up, and I down! Nay, then, let me exclaim with the poet,

> Show me a case more pitiful who can,
> A standing woman, and a falling man.

Hurry durry—not sit down!—See this, ye gods.—You won't sit down?

AQUIL. No, Sir.

ANT. Then look you now, suppose me a bull, a Basan-bull, the bull of bulls, or any bull. Thus up I get and with my brows thus bent—I broo, I say I broo, I broo, I broo. You won't sit down, will you?—I broo——

(*bellows like a bull, and drives her about*)

AQUIL. Well, Sir, I must endure this. (*She sits down.*) Now your honour has been a bull, pray what beast will your worship please to be next?

ANT. Now I'll be a senator again, and thy lover, little Nicky Nacky! (*He sits by her.*) Ah, toad, toad, toad, toad! spit in my face a little, Nacky—spit in my face, prithee, spit in my face, never so little. Spit but a little bit—spit, spit, spit, spit when you are bid, I say; do, prithee, spit—now, now, now, spit. What, you won't spit, will you? Then I'll be a dog.

AQUIL. A dog, my Lord?

ANT. Aye, a dog—and I'll give thee this t'other purse to let me be a dog—and to use me like a dog a little. Hurry durry—I will—here 'tis. (*gives the purse*)

AQUIL. Well, with all my heart. But let me beseech your dog-ship to play your tricks over as fast as you can, that you may come to stinking the sooner and be turned out of doors as you deserve.

ANT. Aye, aye—no matter for that—that shan't move me. (*He gets under the table.*) Now, bough waugh waugh, bough waugh—— (*barks like a dog*)

AQUIL. Hold, hold, hold, Sir, I beseech you: what is't you do?

If curs bite, they must be kicked, Sir.—Do you see, kicked thus?

ANT. Aye, with all my heart. Do kick, kick on; now I am under the table, kick again—kick harder—harder yet, bough waugh waugh, waugh, bough—'odd, I'll have a snap at thy shins—bough waugh bough, waugh, bough!—'Odd, she kicks bravely.——

AQUIL. Nay, then, I'll go another way to work with you; and I think here's an instrument fit for the purpose. (*fetches a whip and bell*)——What, bite your mistress, Sirrah! out, out of doors, you dog, to kennel and be hanged—bite your mistress by the legs, you rogue! (*She whips him.*)

ANT. Nay, prithee, Nacky, now thou art too loving! Hurry durry, 'odd! I'll be a dog no longer.

AQUIL. Nay, none of your fawning and grinning, but begone, or here's the discipline! What, bite your mistress by the legs, you mongrel? Out of doors—hout hout, to kennel, Sirrah! go!

ANT. This is very barbarous usage, Nacky, very barbarous. Look you, I will not go—I will not stir from the door; that I resolve—hurry durry—what, shut me out? (*She whips him out.*)

AQUIL. Aye, and if you come here any more to-night, I'll have my footmen lug you, you cur. What, bite your poor mistress Nacky, Sirrah?

Enter Maid

MAID. Heav'ns, Madam! what's the matter?
(*He howls at the door like a dog.*)

AQUIL. Call my footmen hither presently.

Enter two Footmen

MAID. They are here already, Madam; the house is all alarmed with a strange noise that nobody knows what to make of.

AQUIL. Go, all of you, and turn that troublesome beast in the next room out of my house. If I ever see him within these walls again, without my leave for his admittance, you sneaking rogues —I'll have you poisoned all—poisoned like rats! Every corner of the house shall stink of one of you; go! and learn hereafter to know my pleasure. So now for my Pierre:

Thus when godlike lover was displeas'd,
We sacrifice our fool and he's appeas'd. (*Exeunt.*)

Enter BELVIDERA

BELV. I'm sacrific'd! I am sold! betray'd to shame!
Inevitable ruin has inclos'd me!
No sooner was I to my bed repair'd,
To weigh, and (weeping) ponder my condition,
But the old hoary wretch to whose false care
My peace and honour was entrusted, came
(Like Tarquin) ghastly with infernal lust.
O thou Roman Lucrece! thou couldst find friends to vindicate thy
    wrong!
I never had but one, and he's prov'd false;
He that should guard my virtue has betray'd it,
Left me! undone me! Oh, that I could hate him!
Where shall I go? oh, whither, whither wander?

Enter JAFFEIR

JAFF. Can Belvidera want a resting place
When these poor arms are open to receive her?
Oh, 'tis in vain to struggle with desires
Strong as my love to thee; for every moment
I am from thy sight, the heart within my bosom
Moans like a tender infant in its cradle,
Whose nurse had left it. Come, and with the songs
Of gentle love persuade it to its peace.

BELV. I fear the stubborn wanderer will not own me;
'Tis grown a rebel to be rul'd no longer,
Scorns the indulgent bosom that first lull'd it,
And like a disobedient child disdains
The soft authority of Belvidera.

JAFF. There was a time——

BELV.   Yes, yes, there was a time
When Belvidera's tears, her cries, and sorrows
Were not despis'd; when if she chanc'd to sigh,
Or look but sad—there was indeed a time
When Jaffeir would have ta'en her in his arms,
Eas'd her declining head upon his breast,

_r till he found the cause.

385

weep seas,

_d the earth, sigh till she burst

_nder—still he bears it all,

_ wind, and as the rocks unshaken.

_ave I been deaf? am I that rock unmov'd,

Agai_ whose root tears beat and sighs are sent
In vain? have I beheld thy sorrows calmly?
Witness against me, heav'ns; have I done this?
Then bear me in a whirlwind back again,
And let that angry dear one ne'er forgive me!
Oh, thou too rashly censur'st of my love!
Couldst thou but think how I have spent this night,
Dark and alone, no pillow to my head,
Rest in my eyes, nor quiet in my heart,
Thou wouldst not, Belvidera, sure thou wouldst not
Talk to me thus, but like a pitying angel
Spreading thy wings, come settle on my breast
And hatch warm comfort there ere sorrows freeze it.

    BELV. Why, then, poor mourner, in what baleful corner
Hast thou been talking with that witch, the Night?
On what cold stone hast thou been stretch'd along,
Gathering the grumbling winds about thy head,
To mix with theirs the accents of thy woes?
Oh, now I find the cause my love forsakes me!
I am no longer fit to bear a share
In his concernments: my weak, female virtue
Must not be trusted; 'tis too frail and tender.

    JAFF. O Portia! Portia! what a soul was thine!

    BELV. That Portia was a woman, and when Brutus,
Big with the fate of Rome (heav'n guard thy safety!),
Conceal'd from her the labours of his mind,
She let him see her blood was great as his,
Flow'd from a spring as noble, and a heart
Fit to partake his troubles, as his love.
Fetch, fetch that dagger back, the dreadful dower
Thou gav'st last night in parting with me; strike it
Here to my heart, and as the blood flows from it,
Judge if it run not pure as Cato's daughter's.

    JAFF. Thou art too good, and I indeed unworthy,

Unworthy so much virtue. Teach me how
I may deserve such matchless love as thine,
And see with what attention I'll obey thee.

    BELV. Do not despise me: that's the all I ask.

    JAFF. Despise thee! hear me——

    BELV.   Oh, thy charming tongue
Is but too well acquainted with my weakness;
Knows, let it name but love, my melting heart
Dissolves within my breast, till with clos'd eyes
I reel into thy arms, and all's forgotten.

    JAFF. What shall I do?

    BELV.   Tell me! be just, and tell me
Why dwells that busy cloud upon thy face?
Why am I made a stranger? why that sigh,
And I not know the cause? Why, when the world
Is wrapp'd in rest, why chooses then my love
To wander up and down in horrid darkness,
Loathing his bed and these desiring arms?
Why are these eyes bloodshot with tedious watching?
Why starts he now? and looks as if he wish'd
His fate were finish'd? Tell me, ease my fears;
Lest, when we next time meet, I want the power
To search into the sickness of thy mind,
But talk as wildly then as thou look'st now.

    JAFF. O Belvidera!

    BELV. Why was I last night deliver'd to a villain?

    JAFF. Hah, a villain!

    BELV. Yes! to a villain! Why at such an hour
Meets that assembly all made up of wretches
That look as hell had drawn 'em into league?
Why, I in this hand, and in that a dagger,
Was I deliver'd with such dreadful ceremonies?
"To you, Sirs, and to your honour I bequeath her,
And with her this: whene'er I prove unworthy—
You know the rest—then strike it to her heart"?
Oh! why's that *rest* conceal'd from me? Must I
Be made the hostage of a hellish trust?
For such I know I am; that's all my value!
But by the love and loyalty I owe thee,
I'll free thee from the bondage of these slaves;

Straight to the Senate, tell 'em all I know,
All that I think, all that my fears inform me.

JAFF. Is this the Roman virtue? this the blood
That boasts it purity with Cato's daughter?
Would she have e'er betray'd her Brutus?

BELV.   No,
For Brutus trusted her; wert thou so kind,
What would not Belvidera suffer for thee!

JAFF. I shall undo myself and tell thee all.

BELV. Look not upon me as I am, a woman,
But as a bone, thy wife, thy friend, who long
Has had admission to thy heart, and there
Studied the virtues of thy gallant nature;
Thy constancy, thy courage, and thy truth
Have been my daily lesson: I have learnt them,
Am bold as thou, can suffer or despise
The worst of fates for thee, and with thee share them.

JAFF. O you divinest powers! look down and hear
My prayers! instruct me to reward this virtue!
Yet think a little ere thou tempt me further:
Think I have a tale to tell will shake thy nature,
Melt all this boasted constancy thou talk'st of
Into vile tears and despicable sorrows:
Then if thou shouldst betray me——!

BELV.   Shall I swear?

JAFF. No: do not swear. I would not violate
Thy tender nature with so rude a bond;
But as thou hop'st to see me live my days
And love thee long, lock this within thy breast.
I've bound myself by all the strictest sacraments,
Divine and human——

BELV.   Speak!——

JAFF.   To kill thy father——

BELV. My father!

JAFF.   Nay, the throats of the whole Senate
Shall bleed, my Belvidera. He amongst us
That spares his father, brother, or his friend,
Is damn'd. How rich and beauteous will the face
Of ruin look, when these wide streets run blood;
I and the glorious partners of my fortune

Shouting, and striding o'er the prostrate dead,
Still to new waste; whilst thou, far off in safety
Smiling, shall see the wonders of our daring;
And when night comes, with praise and love receive me.

    BELV. Oh!

    JAFF.   Have a care, and shrink not, even in thought,
For if thou dost——

    BELV.   I know it—thou wilt kill me.
Do, strike thy sword into this bosom. Lay me
Dead on the earth, and then thou wilt be safe.
Murder my father! though his cruel nature
Has persecuted me to my undoing,
Driven me to basest wants, can I behold him
With smiles of vengeance, butcher'd in his age?
The sacred fountain of my life destroy'd?
And canst thou shed the blood that gave me being?
Nay, be a traitor too, and sell thy country?
Can thy great heart descend so vilely low,
Mix with hir'd slaves, bravoes, and common stabbers,
Nose-slitters, alley-lurking villains? join
With such a crew, and take a ruffian's wages,
To cut the throats of wretches as they sleep?

    JAFF. Thou wrong'st me, Belvidera! I've engag'd
With men of souls, fit to reform the ills
Of all mankind. There's not a heart amongst them
But's as stout as death, yet honest as the nature
Of man first made, ere fraud and vice were fashions.

    BELV. What's he to whose curst hands last night thou gav'st
      me?
Was that well done? Oh! I could tell a story
Would rouse thy lion heart out of its den,
And make it rage with terrifying fury.

    JAFF. Speak on, I charge thee!

    BELV.   O my love! if e'er
Thy Belvidera's peace deserv'd thy care,
Remove me from this place! Last night, last night!

    JAFF. Distract me not, but give me all the truth.

    BELV. No sooner wert thou gone, and I alone,
Left in the pow'r of that old son of mischief;
No sooner was I lain on my sad bed,

But that vile wretch approach'd me; loose, unbutton'd,
Ready for violation. Then my heart
Throbb'd with its fears. Oh, how I wept and sigh'd
And shrunk and trembled; wish'd in vain for him
That should protect me. Thou, alas, wert gone!

    JAFF. Patience, sweet heav'n! till I make vengeance sure.

    BELV. He drew the hideous dagger forth thou gav'st him,
And with upbraiding smiles he said, "Behold it;
This is the pledge of a false husband's love."
And in my arms then press'd, and would have clasp'd me;
But with my cries I scar'd his coward heart,
Till he withdrew and mutter'd vows to hell.
These are thy friends! with these thy life, thy honour,
Thy love—all's stak'd, and all will go to ruin.

    JAFF. No more. I charge thee keep this secret close;
Clear up thy sorrows, look as if thy wrongs
Were all forgot, and treat him like a friend,
As no complaint were made. No more; retire,
Retire, my life, and doubt not of my honour;
I'll heal its failings and deserve thy love.

    BELV. Oh, should I part with thee, I fear thou wilt
In anger leave me, and return no more.

    JAFF. Return no more! I would not live without thee
Another night, to purchase the creation.

    BELV. When shall we meet again?

    JAFF.   Anon at twelve!
I'll steal myself to thy expecting arms,
Come like a travell'd dove and bring thee peace.

    BELV. Indeed!

    JAFF.   By all our loves!

    BELV.   'Tis hard to part:
But sure, no falsehood e'er look'd so fairly.
Farewell.—Remember twelve!   (*Exit* BELVIDERA.)

    JAFF.   Let heav'n forget me
When I remember not thy truth, thy love.
How curst is my condition, toss'd and jostled
From every corner; Fortune's common fool,
The jest of rogues, an instrumental ass
For villains to lay loads of shame upon,
And drive about just for their ease and scorn!

Enter PIERRE

PIERRE. Jaffeir!

JAFF.   Who calls?

PIERRE.   A friend, that could have wish'd
T'have found thee otherwise employ'd. What, hunt
A wife on the dull foil! sure, a staunch husband
Of all hounds is the dullest! Wilt thou never,
Never be wean'd from caudles and confections?
What feminine tale hast thou been listening to,
Of unair'd shirts, catarrhs, and tooth-ache got
By thin-sol'd shoes? Damnation! that a fellow
Chosen to be sharer in the destruction
Of a whole people, should sneak thus in corners
To ease his fulsome lusts and fool his mind.

JAFF. May not a man, then, trifle out an hour
With a kind woman and not wrong his calling?

PIERRE. Not in a cause like ours.

JAFF.   Then, friend, our cause
Is in a damn'd condition; for I'll tell thee,
That canker-worm called lechery has touch'd it;
'Tis tainted vilely. Wouldst thou think it? Renault
(That mortify'd, old, wither'd, winter rogue)
Loves simple fornication like a priest.
I found him out for watering at my wife:
He visited her last night like a kind guardian.
Faith, she has some temptations, that's the truth on't.

PIERRE. He durst not wrong his trust!

JAFF.   'Twas something late,
   though,
To take the freedom of a lady's chamber.

PIERRE. Was she in bed?

JAFF.   Yes, faith, in virgin sheets
White as her bosom, Pierre, dish'd neatly up,
Might tempt a weaker appetite to taste.
Oh, how the old fox stunk, I warrant thee,
When the rank fit was on him!

PIERRE.   Patience guide me!
He us'd no violence?

JAFF.   No, no! out on't, violence!

Play'd with her neck, brush'd her with his gray beard,
Struggled and towz'd, tickled her till she squeak'd a little,
Maybe, or so—but not a jot of violence——

    PIERRE. Damn him!

    JAFF.   Aye, so say I; but hush, no more on't!
All hitherto is well, and I believe
Myself no monster yet, though no man knows
What fate he's born to. Sure, 'tis near the hour
We all should meet for our concluding orders.
Will the ambassador be here in person?

    PIERRE. No: he has sent commission to that villain, Renault,
To give the executing charge.
I'll have thee be a man if possible,
And keep thy temper; for a brave revenge
Ne'er comes too late.

    JAFF.   Fear not; I am cool as patience.
Had he completed my dishonour, rather
Than hazard the success our hopes are ripe for,
I'd bear it all with mortifying virtue.

    PIERRE. He's yonder, coming this way through the hall;
His thoughts seem full.

    JAFF.   Prithee retire, and leave me
With him alone. I'll put him to some trial,
See how his rotten part will bear the touching.

    PIERRE. Be careful then.   (*Exit* PIERRE.)

    JAFF.   Nay, never doubt, but trust me.
What, be a devil? take a damning oath
For shedding native blood? can there be a sin
In merciful repentance? Oh, this villain!

Enter RENAULT

    REN. (*aside*) Perverse and peevish! What a slave is man!
To let his itching flesh thus get the better of him!
Dispatch the tool, her husband—that were well.
——Who's there?

    JAFF.   A man.

    REN.   My friend, my near ally!
The hostage of your faith, my beauteous charge,
Is very well.

    JAFF.   Sir, are you sure of that?

Stands she in perfect health? beats her pulse even?
Neither too hot nor cold?

REN.   What means that question?

JAFF. Oh, women have fantastic constitutions,
Inconstant as their wishes, always wavering,
And ne'er fix'd. Was it not boldly done
Even at first sight to trust the thing I lov'd
(A tempting treasure too!) with youth so fierce
And vigorous as thine? But thou art honest.

REN. Who dares accuse me?

JAFF.   Curst be him that doubts
Thy virtue! I have try'd it, and declare,
Were I to choose a guardian of my honour,
I'd put it in thy keeping; for I know thee.

REN. Know me!

JAFF.   Aye, know thee. There's no falsehood in thee.
Thou look'st just as thou art. Let us embrace.
Now wouldst thou cut my throat or I cut thine?

REN. You dare not do't.

JAFF.   You lie, Sir.

REN.   How!

JAFF.   No more.
'Tis a base world, and must reform, that's all.

Enter SPINOSA, THEODORE, ELIOT, REVILLIDO, DURAND,
     BRAINVEIL, *and the rest of the Conspirators*

REN. Spinosa! Theodore!

SPIN.   The same.

REN.   You are welcome!

SPIN. You are trembling, Sir.

REN.   'Tis a cold night, indeed; I am
     aged,
Full of decay and natural infirmities.
We shall be warm, my friend, I hope to-morrow.

PIERRE *re-enters*

PIERRE. 'Twas not well done; thou shouldst have strok'd him
And not have gall'd him.

JAFF.   Damn him, let him chew on't.
Heav'n! where am I? beset with cursed fiends,

That wait to damn me. What a devil's man
When he forgets his nature—— Hush, my heart.
   REN. My friends, 'tis late; are we assembled all?
Where's Theodore?
   THEODORE.   At hand.
   REN.   Spinosa.
   SPIN.   Here.
   REN. Brainveil.
   BRAINVEIL.   I am ready.
   REN.   Durand and Brabe.
   DURAND.   Command us;
We are both prepar'd!
   REN.   Mezzana, Revillido,
Ternon, Retrosi; oh, you are men, I find,
Fit to behold your fate and meet her summons.
To-morrow's rising sun must see you all
Deck'd in your honours! Are the soldiers ready?
   OMNES. All, all.
   REN. You, Durand, with your thousand must possess
St. Mark's. You, Captain, know your charge already;
'Tis to secure the Ducal Palace. You,
Brabe, with a hundred more must gain the Secque:
With the like number, Brainveil, to the Procuralle.
Be all this done with the least tumult possible,
Till in each place you post sufficient guards:
Then sheathe your swords in every breast you meet.
   JAFF. (aside) Oh, reverend cruelty! damn'd, bloody villain!
   REN. During this execution, Durand, you
Must in the midst keep your battalia fast.
And, Theodore, be sure to plant the cannon
That may command the streets; whilst Revillido,
Mezzana, Ternon and Retrosi, guard you.
This done, we'll give the general alarm,
Apply petards, and force the Ars'nal gates;
Then fire the city round in several places,
Or with our cannon (if it dare resist)
Batter't to ruin. But above all I charge you,
Shed blood enough; spare neither sex nor age,
Name nor condition; if there live a senator
After to-morrow, though the dullest rogue

That e'er said nothing, we have lost our ends;
If possible, let's kill the very name
Of senator, and bury it in blood.
  JAFF. (*aside*) Merciless, horrid slave!—Aye, blood enough!
Shed blood enough, old Renault: how thou charm'st me!
  REN. But one thing more, and then farewell till fate
Join us again or separate us ever.
First, let's embrace; heav'n knows who next shall thus
Wing ye together. But let's all remember
We wear no common cause upon our swords:
Let each man think that on his single virtue
Depends the good and fame of all the rest—
Eternal honour or perpetual infamy.
Let's remember through what dreadful hazards
Propitious Fortune hitherto has led us,
How often on the brink of some discovery
Have we stood tottering, and yet still kept our ground
So well, the busiest searchers ne'er could follow
Those subtle tracks which puzzled all suspicion.
——You droop, Sir!
  JAFF.   No: with a most profound attention
I've heard it all, and wonder at thy virtue.
  REN. Though there be yet few hours 'twixt them and ruin,
Are not the Senate lull'd in full security,
Quiet and satisfy'd, as fools are always?
Never did so profound repose forerun
Calamity so great! Nay, our good fortune
Has blinded the most piercing of mankind,
Strengthen'd the fearfull'st, charm'd the most suspectful,
Confounded the most subtle: for we live,
We live, my friends, and quickly shall our life
Prove fatal to these tyrants. Let's consider
That we destroy oppression, avarice,
A people nurs'd up equally with vices
And loathsome lusts, which Nature most abhors,
And such as without shame she cannot suffer.
  JAFF. (*aside*) O Belvidera, take me to thy arms,
And show me where's my peace, for I've lost it. (*Exit* JAFFEIR.)
  REN. Without the least remorse, then, let's resolve
With fire and sword t'exterminate these tyrants;

And when we shall behold those curst tribunals,
Stain'd by the tears and sufferings of the innocent,
Burning with flames rather from heav'n than ours,
The raging, furious, and unpitying soldier
Pulling his reeking dagger from the bosoms
Of gasping wretches; death in every quarter,
With all that sad disorder can produce,
To make a spectacle of horror—then,
Then let's call to mind, my dearest friends,
That there is nothing pure upon the earth;
That the most valu'd things have most alloys;
And that in change of all those vile enormities
Under whose weight this wretched country labours,
The means are only in our hands to crown them.

    PIERRE. And may those powers above that are propitious
To gallant minds record this cause and bless it.

    REN. Thus happy, thus secure of all we wish for,
Should there, my friends, be found amongst us one
False to this glorious enterprise, what fate,
What vengeance, were enough for such a villain?

    ELIOT. Death here without repentance, hell hereafter.

    REN. Let that be my lot, if as here I stand
Listed by fate amongst her darling sons,
Though I had one only brother, dear by all
The strictest ties of nature; though one hour
Had given us birth, one fortune fed our wants,
One only love, and that but of each other,
Still fill'd our minds: could I have such a friend
Join'd in this cause, and had but ground to fear
Meant foul play, may this right hand drop from me,
If I'd not hazard all my future peace,
And stab him to the heart before you. Who
Would do less? wouldst not thou, Pierre, the same?

    PIERRE. You have singled me, Sir, out for this hard question,
As if 'twere started only for my sake!
Am I the thing you fear? Here, here's my bosom;
Search it with all your swords! Am I a traitor?

    REN. No: but I fear your late commended friend
Is little less. Come, Sirs, 'tis now no time
To trifle with our safety. Where's this Jaffeir?

SPIN. He left the room just now in strange disorder.

REN. Nay, there is danger in him: I observ'd him
During the time I took for explanation;
He was transported from most deep attention
To a confusion which he could not smother.
His looks grew full of sadness and surprise,
All which betray'd a wavering spirit in him,
That labour'd with reluctancy and sorrow.
What's requisite for safety must be done
With speedy execution: he remains
Yet in our power. I for my own part wear
A dagger.

PIERRE. Well.

REN.   And I could wish it——

PIERRE.   Where?

REN. Bury'd in his heart.

PIERRE.   Away! w'are yet all friends!
No more of this; 'twill breed ill blood amongst us!

SPIN. Let us all draw our swords, and search the house,
Pull him from the dark hole where he sits brooding
O'er his cold fears, and each man kill his share of him.

PIERRE. Who talks of killing? Who's he'll shed the blood
That's dear to me?—Is't you? or you? or you, Sir?
What, not one speak? how you stand gaping all
On your grave oracle, your wooden god there;
Yet not a word? (*to* RENAULT) Then, Sir, I'll tell you a secret:
Suspicion's but at best a coward's virtue!

REN. A coward——   (*handles his sword*)

PIERRE.   Put, put up thy sword, old man,
Thy hand shakes at it; come, let's heal this breach,
I am too hot; we yet may live friends.

SPIN. Till we are safe, our friendship cannot be so.

PIERRE. Again! Who's that?

SPIN.   'Twas I.

THEO.   And I.

REVILL.   And I.

ELIOT.   And all.

REN. Who are on my side?

SPIN.   Every honest sword.
Let's die like men and not be sold like slaves.

PIERRE. One such word more, by heav'n, I'll to the Senate
And hang ye all, like dogs in clusters!
Why peep your coward swords half out their shells?
Why do you not all brandish them like mine?
You fear to die, and yet dare talk of killing.
REN. Go to the Senate and betray us! Hasten,
Secure thy wretched life; we fear to die
Less than thou dar'st be honest.
PIERRE.   That's rank falsehood!
Fear'st not thou death? fie, there's a knavish itch
In that salt blood, an utter foe to smarting.
Had Jaffeir's wife prov'd kind, he had still been true.
Foh—how that stinks!
Thou die! thou kill my friend!—or thou—or thou
—Or thou, with that lean, wither'd, wretched face!
Away! disperse all to your several charges,
And meet to-morrow where your honour calls you;
I'll bring that man whose blood you so much thirst for,
And you shall see him venture for you fairly—
Hence, hence, I say!   (*Exit* RENAULT *angrily.*)
SPIN.   I fear we have been to blame,
And done too much.
THEO. 'Twas too far urg'd against the man you lov'd.
REVILL. Here, take our swords and crush 'em with your feet.
SPIN. Forgive us, gallant friend.
PIERRE.   Nay, now y'have found
The way to melt and cast me as you will,
I'll fetch this friend and give him to your mercy:
Nay, he shall die if you will take him from me;
For your repose I'll quit my heart's jewel,
But would not have him torn away by villains
And spiteful villainy.
SPIN.   No, may you both
Forever live and fill the world with fame!
PIERRE. Now you are too kind. Whence rose all this discord?
Oh, what a dangerous precipice have we 'scap'd!
How near a fall was all we had long been building!
What an eternal blot had stain'd our glories,
If one, the bravest and the best of men,
Had fallen a sacrifice to rash suspicion,

Butcher'd by those whose cause he came to cherish!
Oh, could you know him all as I have known him,
How good he is, how just, how true, how brave,
You would not leave this place till you had seen him;
Humbled yourselves before him, kiss'd his feet,
And gained remission for the worst of follies.
Come but to-morrow, all your doubts shall end,
And to your loves me better recommend,
That I've preserv'd your fame, and sav'd my friend.

(Exeunt omnes.)

ACT IV

SCENE I

Enter JAFFEIR *and* BELVIDERA

JAFF. Where dost thou lead me? Every step I move,
Methinks I tread upon some mangled limb
Of a rack'd friend. O my dear charming ruin!
Where are we wand'ring?
BELV.   To eternal honour;
To do a deed shall chronicle thy name
Among the glorious legends of those few
That have sav'd sinking nations. Thy renown
Shall be the future song of all the virgins
Who by thy piety have been preserv'd
From horrid violation. Every street
Shall be adorn'd with statues to thy honour,
And at thy feet this great inscription written,
Remember him that propp'd the fall of Venice.
JAFF. Rather, remember him who, after all
The sacred bonds of oaths and holier friendship,
In fond compassion to a woman's tears,
Forgot his manhood, virtue, truth and honour,
To sacrifice the bosom that reliev'd him.
Why wilt thou damn me?
BELV.   O inconstant man!
How will you promise? how will you deceive?
Do, return back, replace me in my bondage,

ends how dangerously thou lov'st me,
agger do its bloody office.
d dagger, Jaffeir, how 'twill look
gh my heart, drench'd in my blood to th'hilts!
e poor dying eyes shall with their tears
No mo. orment thee, then thou wilt be free.
Or if thou think'st it nobler, let me live
Till I am a victim to the hateful lust
Of that infernal devil, that old fiend
That's damn'd himself and would undo mankind:
Last night, my love!

JAFF.   Name, name it not again.
It shows a beastly image to my fancy
Will wake me into madness. Oh, the villain!
That durst approach such purity as thine
On terms so vile! Destruction, swift destruction
Fall on my coward head, and make my name
The common scorn of fools if I forgive him!
If I forgive him, if I not revenge
With utmost rage, and most unstaying fury,
Thy sufferings, thou dear darling of my life, love!

BELV. Delay no longer then, but to the Senate;
And tell the dismal'st story e'er was utter'd:
Tell 'em what bloodshed, rapines, desolations,
Have been prepar'd, how near's the fatal hour!
Save thy poor country, save the reverend blood
Of all its nobles, which to-morrow's dawn
Must else see shed. Save the poor, tender lives
Of all those little infants which the swords
Of murderers are whetting for this moment.
Think thou already hear'st their dying screams,
Think that thou seest their sad, distracted mothers
Kneeling before thy feet, and begging pity,
With torn, dishevell'd hair and streaming eyes,
Their naked, mangled breasts besmear'd with blood,
And even the milk with which their fondled babes
Softly they hush'd, dropping in anguish from 'em.
Think thou seest this, and then consult thy heart.

JAFF. Oh!

BELV.   Think too, if thou lose this present minute,

What miseries the next day bring upon thee.
Imagine all the horrors of that night,
Murder and rapine, waste and desolation,
Confusedly ranging. Think what then may prove
My lot! The ravisher may then come safe,
And 'midst the terror of the public ruin
Do a damn'd deed—perhaps to lay a train
May catch thy life; then where will be revenge,
The dear revenge that's due to such a wrong?
  JAFF. By all heaven's powers, prophetic truth dwells in thee;
For every word thou speak'st strikes through my heart
Like a new light, and shows it how't has wander'd.
Just what th'hast made me, take me, Belvidera,
And lead me to the place where I'm to say
This bitter lesson, where I must betray
My truth, my virtue, constancy, and friends.
Must I betray my friends? Ah, take me quickly,
Secure me well before that thought's renew'd;
If I relapse once more, all's lost forever.
  BELV. Hast thou a friend more dear than Belvidera?
  JAFF. No, th'art my soul itself; wealth, friendship, honour,
All present joys, and earnest of all future,
Are summ'd in thee: methinks, when in thy arms
Thus leaning on thy breast, one minute's more
Than a long thousand years of vulgar hours.
Why was such happiness not given me pure?
Why dash'd with cruel wrongs, and bitter wantings?
Come, lead me forward now like a tame lamb
To sacrifice; thus in his fatal garlands,
Deck'd fine, and pleas'd, the wanton skips and plays,
  Trots by th'enticing, flatt'ring priestess' side,
  And much transported with his little pride,
  Forgets his dear companions of the plain
  Till by her, bound, he's on the altar lain;
  Yet then too hardly bleats, such pleasure's in the pain.

Enter Officer and Six Guards

OFFIC. Stand! Who goes there?
BELV.   Friends.
JAFF. Friends, Belvidera! Hide me from my friends.

By heaven, I'd rather see the face of hell
Than meet the man I love.

   OFFIC.   But what friends are you?

   BELV. Friends to the Senate and the state of Venice.

   OFFIC. My orders are to seize on all I find
At this late hour, and bring 'em to the Council,
Who now are sitting.

   JAFF.   Sir, you shall be obey'd.
Hold, brutes, stand off! none of your paws upon me!
Now the lot's cast, and, Fate, do what thou wilt.

                            (Exeunt guarded.)

SCENE II

SCENE: *The Senate-house,*

where appear sitting the DUKE OF VENICE, PRIULI,
ANTONIO, *and eight other Senators*

   DUKE. Anthony, Priuli, senators of Venice,
Speak; why are we assembled here this night?
What have you to inform us of, concerns
The state of Venice, honour, or its safety?

   PRIU. Could words express the story I have to tell you,
Fathers, these tears were useless—these sad tears
That fall from my old eyes; but there is cause
We all should weep, tear off these purple robes,
And wrap ourselves in sack-cloth, sitting down
On the sad earth, and cry aloud to heaven.
Heaven knows if yet there be an hour to come
Ere Venice be no more!

   ALL SENATORS.   How!

   PRIU.   Nay, we stand
Upon the very brink of gaping ruin.
Within this city's formed a dark conspiracy
To massacre us all, our wives and children,
Kindred and friends, our palaces and temples
To lay in ashes—nay, the hour, too, fix'd;
The swords, for aught I know, drawn even this moment,
And the wild waste begun. From unknown hands

I had this warning: but if we are men,
Let's not be tamely butcher'd, but do something
That may inform the world in after ages,
Our virtue was not ruin'd, though we were.
> (*a noise without:* "Room, room, make room for some
> prisoners!")

2D SEN. Let's raise the city!

Enter Officer and Guard

PRIU.   Speak there—what disturbance?
OFFIC. Two prisoners have the guard seiz'd in the streets,
Who say they come to inform this reverend Senate
About the present danger.

Enter JAFFEIR *and* BELVIDERA, *guarded*

ALL.   Give 'em entrance—
Well, who are you?
JAFF.   A villain.
ANT.   Short and pithy.
The man speaks well.
JAFF.   Would every man that hears me
Would deal so honestly, and own his title.
DUKE. 'Tis rumour'd that a plot has been contriv'd
Against this state; that you have a share in't, too.
If you are a villain, to redeem your honour,
Unfold the truth and be restor'd with mercy.
JAFF. Think not that I to save my life come hither—
I know its value better—but in pity
To all those wretches whose unhappy dooms
Are fix'd and seal'd. You see me here before you,
The sworn and covenanted foe of Venice.
But use me as my dealings may deserve,
And I may prove a friend.
DUKE.   The slave capitulates.
Give him the tortures.
JAFF.   That you dare not do;
Your fears won't let you, nor the longing itch
To hear a story which you dread the truth of—
Truth which the fear of smart shall ne'er get from me.
Cowards are scar'd with threat'nings. Boys are whipp'd

Into confessions: but a steady mind
Acts of itself, ne'er asks the body counsel.
"Give him the tortures!" Name but such a thing
Again, by heaven, I'll shut these lips forever.
Not all your racks, your engines, or your wheels
Shall force a groan away—that you may guess at.

ANT. A bloody-minded fellow, I'll warrant;
A damn'd bloody-minded fellow.

DUKE. Name your conditions.

JAFF.   For myself, full pardon,
Besides the lives of two and twenty friends   (*delivers a list*)
Whose names are here enroll'd. Nay, let their crimes
Be ne'er so monstrous, I must have the oaths
And sacred promise of this reverend Council,
That in a full assembly of the Senate
The thing I ask be ratify'd. Swear this,
And I'll unfold the secrets of your danger.

ALL. We'll swear.

DUKE.   Propose the oath.

JAFF.   By all the hopes
Ye have of peace and happiness hereafter,
Swear!

ALL. We all swear.

JAFF.   To grant me what I've ask'd,
Ye swear.

ALL.   We swear.

JAFF.   And as ye keep the oath,
May you and your posterity be blest
Or curst forever.

ALL.   Else be curst forever!

JAFF. (*delivers another paper*) Then here's the list, and with't
    the full disclose
Of all that threatens you.
Now, Fate, thou hast caught me.

ANT. Why, what a dreadful catalogue of cut-throats is here!
I'll warrant you not one of these fellows but has a face like a
    lion.
I dare not so much as read their names over.

DUKE. Give orders that all diligent search be made
To seize these men; their characters are public.

The paper intimates their rendezvous
To be at the house of a fam'd Grecian courtesan
Called Aquilina; see that place secur'd.

ANT. (*aside*) What! My Nicky Nacky, Hurry Durry,
Nicky Nacky in the plot? I'll make a speech.
—— Most noble senators,
What headlong apprehension drives you on,
Right noble, wise, and truly solid senators,
To violate the laws and right of nations?
The lady is a lady of renown.
'Tis true, she holds a house of fair reception,
And though I say't myself, as many more
Can say as well as I.

2D SEN.   My Lord, long speeches
Are frivolous here when dangers are so near us.
We all well know your interest in that lady;
The world talks loud on't.

ANT.   Verily, I have done.
I say no more.

DUKE.   But, since he has declar'd
Himself concern'd, pray, Captain, take great caution
To treat the fair one as becomes her character,
And let her bed-chamber be search'd with decency.
You, Jaffeir, must with patience bear till morning
To be our prisoner.

JAFF.   Would the chains of death
Had bound me fast ere I had known this minute!
I've done a deed will make my story hereafter
Quoted in competition with all ill ones:
The history of my wickedness shall run
Down through the low traditions of the vulgar,
And boys be taught to tell the tale of Jaffeir.

DUKE. Captain, withdraw your prisoner.

JAFF.   Sir, if possible,
Lead me where my own thoughts themselves may lose me;
Where I may doze out what I've left of life,
Forget myself and this day's guilt and falsehood.
Cruel remembrance, how shall I appease thee!   (*Exit guarded.*)
           (*noise without:* "More traitors; room, room, make room
                there!")

DUKE. How's this? Guards——
Where are our guards? Shut up the gates; the treason's
Already at our doors!

Enter Officer

OFFIC.   My Lords, more traitors—
Seiz'd in the very act of consultation;
Furnish'd with arms and instruments of mischief.
Bring in the prisoners.

Enter PIERRE, RENAULT, THEODORE, ELIOT, REVILLIDO,
and other Conspirators, in fetters, guarded

PIERRE.   You, my Lords and fathers
(As you are pleas'd to call yourselves) of Venice,
If you sit here to guide the course of justice,
Why these disgraceful chains upon the limbs
That have so often labour'd in your service?
Are these the wreaths of triumphs ye bestow
On those that bring you conquests home and honours?
     DUKE. Go on; you shall be heard, Sir.
     ANT. And be hang'd too, I hope.
     PIERRE. Are these the trophies I've deserv'd for fighting
Your battles with confederated powers,
When winds and seas conspir'd to overthrow you,
And brought the fleets of Spain to your own harbours?
When you, great Duke, shrunk trembling in your palace,
And saw your wife, th'Adriatic, plough'd
Like a lewd whore by bolder prows than yours,
Stepp'd not I forth, and taught your loose Venetians
The task of honour and the way to greatness,
Rais'd you from your capitulating fears,
To stipulate the terms of su'd-for peace—
And this my recompense! If I am a traitor,
Produce my charge; or show the wretch that's base enough
And brave enough to tell me I am a traitor.
     DUKE. Know you one Jaffeir?

                              (*All the Conspirators murmur.*)
     PIERRE.   Yes, and know his virtue.
His justice, truth, his general worth and sufferings
From a hard father taught me first to love him.

Enter JAFFEIR, *guarded*

DUKE. See him brought forth.

PIERRE.   My friend, too, bound? nay, then
Our fate has conquer'd us, and we must fall.
Why droops the man whose welfare's so much mine
They're but one thing? These reverend tyrants, Jaffeir,
Call us all traitors; art thou one, my brother?

JAFF. To thee I am the falsest, veriest slave
That e'er betray'd a generous, trusting friend,
And gave up honour to be sure of ruin.
All our fair hopes which morning was to have crown'd,
Has this curst tongue o'erthrown.

PIERRE.   So, then all's over:
Venice has lost her freedom; I, my life.
No more. Farewell!

DUKE.   Say, will you make confession
Of your vile deeds and trust the Senate's mercy?

PIERRE. Curst be your Senate; curst your Constitution.
The curse of growing factions and division
Still vex your councils, shake your public safety,
And make the robes of government you wear
Hateful to you as these base chains to me!

DUKE. Pardon, or death?

PIERRE.   Death—honourable death!

REN. Death's the best thing we ask or you can give.

ALL CONSPIR. No shameful bonds, but honourable death!

DUKE. Break up the council. Captain, guard your prisoners.
Jaffeir, y'are free, but these must wait for judgment.
                    (*Exeunt all the Senators.*)

PIERRE. Come, where's my dungeon? Lead me to my straw.
It will not be the first time I've lodg'd hard
To do your Senate service.

JAFF.   Hold one moment!

PIERRE. Who's he disputes the judgment of the Senate?
Presumptuous rebel—on—   (*strikes* JAFFEIR)

JAFF.   By heaven, you stir not.
I must be heard, I must have leave to speak:
Thou hast disgrac'd me, Pierre, by a vile blow.
Had not a dagger done thee nobler justice?

But use me as thou wilt, thou canst not wrong me,
For I am fallen beneath the basest injuries;
Yet look upon me with an eye of mercy,
With pity and with charity behold me;
Shut not thy heart against a friend's repentance,
But as there dwells a godlike nature in thee,
Listen with mildness to my supplications.

    PIERRE. What whining monk art thou? what holy cheat
That wouldst encroach upon my credulous ears,
And cant'st thus vilely? Hence! I know thee not.
Dissemble and be nasty: leave me, hypocrite.

    JAFF. Not know me, Pierre?
    PIERRE.   No, know thee not. What art thou?

    JAFF. Jaffeir, thy friend, thy once lov'd, valu'd friend,
Though now deservedly scorn'd, and us'd most hardly.

    PIERRE. Thou Jaffeir; thou my once lov'd, valu'd friend!
By heavens, thou li'st! The man so call'd, my friend,
Was generous, honest, faithful, just and valiant,
Noble in mind, and in his person lovely,
Dear to my eyes and tender to my heart:
But thou, a wretched, base, false, worthless coward,
Poor even in soul, and loathsome in thy aspect,
All eyes must shun thee, and all hearts detest thee.
Prithee avoid, nor longer cling thus round me
Like something baneful, that my nature's chill'd at.

    JAFF. I have not wrong'd thee—by these tears I have not!
But still am honest, true, and hope, too, valiant;
My mind still full of thee; therefore, still noble.
Let not thy eyes then shun me, nor thy heart
Detest me utterly. Oh, look upon me!
Look back and see my sad, sincere submission!
How my heart swells, as even 'twould burst my bosom,
Fond of its gaol, and labouring to be at thee!
What shall I do, what say, to make thee hear me?

    PIERRE. Hast thou not wrong'd me? dar'st thou call thyself
Jaffeir, that once lov'd, valu'd friend of mine,
And swear thou hast not wrong'd me? Whence these chains?
Whence the vile death, which I may meet this moment?
Whence this dishonour but from thee, thou false one?

    JAFF. All's true; yet grant one thing, and I've done asking.

PIERRE. What's that?

JAFF.   To take thy life on such conditions
The Council have propos'd. Thou and thy friends
May yet live long, and to be better treated.

PIERRE. Life! ask my life! confess! record myself
A villain for the privilege to breathe
And carry up and down this cursed city
A discontented and repining spirit,
Burdensome to itself, a few years longer,
To lose, it may be, at last in a lewd quarrel
For some new friend, treacherous and false as thou art!
No, this vile world and I have long been jangling,
And cannot part on better terms than now,
When only men like thee are fit to live in't.

JAFF. By all that's just——

PIERRE.   Swear by some other powers,
For thou hast broke that sacred oath too lately.

JAFF. Then by that hell I merit, I'll not leave thee
Till to thyself, at least, thou'rt reconcil'd,
However thy resentments deal with me.

PIERRE. Not leave me!

JAFF.   No, thou shalt not force me from thee.
Use me reproachfully, and like a slave;
Tread on me, buffet me, heap wrongs on wrongs
On my poor head; I'll bear it all with patience
Shall weary out thy most unfriendly cruelty,
Lie at thy feet and kiss 'em though they spurn me,
Till, wounded by my sufferings, thou relent,
And raise me to thy arms with dear forgiveness.

PIERRE. Art thou not——

JAFF.   What?

PIERRE.   A traitor?

JAFF.   Yes.

PIERRE.   A villain?

JAFF. Granted.

PIERRE.   A coward—a most scandalous coward,
Spiritless, void of honour, one who has sold
Thy everlasting fame for shameless life?

JAFF. All, all, and more—much more: my faults are number-
     less.

PIERRE. And wouldst thou have me live on terms like thine?
Base as thou art false——

JAFF.   No, 'tis to me that's granted;
The safety of thy life was all I aim'd at,
In recompense for faith and trust so broken.

PIERRE. I scorn it more because preserv'd by thee.
And as, when first my foolish heart took pity
On thy misfortunes, sought thee in thy miseries,
Reliev'd thy wants, and rais'd thee from thy state
Of wretchedness in which thy fate had plung'd thee,
To rank thee in my list of noble friends,
All I receiv'd in surety for thy truth,
Were unregarded oaths; and this, this dagger,
Given with a worthless pledge, thou since hast stol'n:
So I restore it back to thee again,
Swearing by all those powers which thou hast violated,
Never from this curst hour to hold communion,
Friendship, or interest with thee, though our years
Were to exceed those limited the world.
Take it—farewell—for now I owe thee nothing.

JAFF. Say thou wilt live, then.

PIERRE.   For my life, dispose it
Just as thou wilt, because 'tis what I'm tir'd with.

JAFF. O Pierre!

PIERRE.   No more.

JAFF.   My eyes won't lose the sight of thee,
But languish after thine, and ache with gazing.

PIERRE. Leave me.—Nay, then, thus, thus, I throw thee from
me,
And curses, great as is thy falsehood, catch thee!   (*Exit.*)

JAFF. Amen. He's gone, my father, friend, preserver,
And here's the portion he has left me.   (*holds the dagger up*)
This dagger, well remember'd—with this dagger
I gave a solemn vow of dire importance,
Parted with this and Belvidera together;
Have a care, Mem'ry, drive that thought no farther;
No, I'll esteem it as a friend's last legacy,
Treasure it up in this wretched bosom,
Where it may grow acquainted with my heart,
That when they meet, they start not from each other.

So: now for thinking. A blow; call'd traitor, villain,
Coward, dishonourable coward—fogh!
Oh, for a long, sound sleep, and so forget it!
Down, busy devil——

Enter BELVIDERA

BELV.   Whither shall I fly?
Where hide me and my miseries together?
Where's now the Roman constancy I boasted?
Sunk into trembling fears and desperation!
Not daring now to look up to that dear face
Which us'd to smile even on my faults, but down
Bending these miserable eyes to earth,
Must move in penance, and implore much mercy.

JAFF. Mercy!—Kind heaven has surely endless stores
Hoarded for thee of blessings yet untasted;
Let wretches loaded hard with guilt as I am,
Bow with the weight, and groan beneath the burden,
Creep with a remnant of that strength th'have left
Before the footstool of that heaven th'have injur'd.
O Belvidera! I'm the wretched'st creature
E'er crawl'd on earth! Now if thou hast virtue, help me;
Take me into thy arms, and speak the words of peace
To my divided soul that wars within me,
And raises every sense to my confusion.
By heav'n, I am tottering to the very brink
Of peace; and thou art all the hold I've left.

BELV. Alas! I know thy sorrows are most mighty.
I know th'hast cause to mourn—to mourn, my Jaffeir,
With endless cries, and never-ceasing wailings;
Th'hast lost——

JAFF.   Oh, I have lost what can't be counted!
My friend, too, Belvidera, that dear friend,
Who, next to thee, was all my health rejoic'd in,
Has us'd me like a slave—shamefully us'd me.
'Twould break thy pitying heart to hear the story.
What shall I do? resentment, indignation,
Love, pity, fear, and mem'ry, how I've wrong'd him,
Distract my quiet with the very thought on't,
And tear my heart to pieces in my bosom.

BELV. What has he done?

JAFF.   Thou'dst hate me should I tell thee.

BELV. Why?

JAFF. Oh, he has us'd me! Yet, by heaven, I bear it!
He has us'd me, Belvidera—but first swear
That when I've told thee, thou'lt not loathe me utterly,
Though vilest blots and stains appear upon me;
But still at least with charitable goodness,
Be near me in the pangs of my affliction,
Not scorn me, Belvidera, as he has done.

BELV. Have I then e'er been false that now I am doubted?
Speak, what's the cause I'm grown into distrust?
Why thought unfit to hear my love's complainings?

JAFF. Oh!

BELV.   Tell me.

JAFF.   Bear my failings, for they are many,
O my dear angel! In that friend I've lost
All my soul's peace; for every thought of him
Strikes my sense hard, and deads in it my brains.
Wouldst thou believe it?

BELV.   Speak.

JAFF.   Before we parted,
Ere yet his guards had led him to his prison,
Full of severest sorrows for his suff'rings,
With eyes o'erflowing and a bleeding heart
Humbling myself almost beneath my nature,
As at his feet I kneel'd and su'd for mercy,
Forgetting all our friendship, all the dearness
In which w'have liv'd so many years together,'
With a reproachful hand he dash'd a blow—
He struck me, Belvidera, by heaven, he struck me,
Buffeted, called me traitor, villain, coward!
Am I a coward? am I a villain? Tell me:
Th'art the best judge, and mad'st me, if I am so.
Damnation—coward!

BELV.   Oh! forgive him, Jaffeir.
And if his sufferings wound thy heart already,
What will they do to-morrow?

JAFF.   Hah!

BELV.   To-morrow,

When thou shalt see him stretch'd in all the agonies
Of a tormenting and a shameful death,
His bleeding bowels, and his broken limbs,
Insulted o'er by a vile, butchering villain;
What will thy heart do then? Oh, sure 'twill stream
Like my eyes now.

JAFF. What means thy dreadful story?
Death, and to-morrow? broken limbs and bowels?
Insulted o'er by a vile, butchering villain?
By all my fears, I shall start out to madness
With barely guessing if the truth's hid longer.

BELV. The faithless senators, 'tis they 've decreed it:
They say, according to our friend's request,
They shall have death, and not ignoble bondage:
Declare their promis'd mercy all as forfeited,
False to their oaths, and deaf to intercession;
Warrants are pass'd for public death to-morrow.

JAFF. Death! doom'd to die! condemn'd unheard! unpleaded!

BELV. Nay, cruel'st racks and torments are preparing,
To force confessions from their dying pangs.
Oh, do not look so terribly upon me!
How your lips shake, and all your face disorder'd!
What means my love?

JAFF. Leave me! I charge thee, leave me—strong temptations
Wake in my heart.

BELV. For what?

JAFF. No more, but leave me

BELV. Why?

JAFF. Oh! by heaven, I love thee with that fondness
I would not have thee stay a moment longer
Near these curst hands. Are they not cold upon thee?
  (*pulls the dagger half out of his bosom and puts it back again*)

BELV. No, everlasting comfort's in thy arms;
To lean thus on thy breast is softer ease
Than downy pillows deck'd with leaves of roses.

JAFF. Alas, thou think'st not of the thorns 'tis fill'd with:
Fly ere they gall thee: there's a lurking serpent
Ready to leap and sting thee to thy heart;
Art thou not terrify'd?

BELV No.

JAFF.   Call to mind
What thou hast done, and whither thou hast brought me.
  BELV. Hah!
  JAFF.   Where's my friend? my friend, thou smiling mis-
    chief?
Nay, shrink not, now 'tis too late, thou shouldst have fled
When thy guilt first had cause, for dire revenge
Is up and raging for my friend. He groans,
Hark, how he groans! His screams are in my ears
Already; see, th'have fix'd him on the wheel,
And now they tear him.—Murder! perjur'd Senate!
Murder—Oh!—hark thee, trait'ress, thou hast done this;
Thanks to thy tears and false persuading love.
How her eyes speak! O thou bewitching creature!
                              (fumbling for his dagger)
Madness cannot hurt thee. Come, thou little trembler,
Creep, even into my heart, and there lie safe:
'Tis thy own citadel.—Hah—yet stand off!
Heaven must have justice, and my broken vows
Will sink me else beneath its reaching mercy.
I'll wink and then 'tis done——
  BELV.   What means the lord
Of me, my life and love? What's in thy bosom
Thou grasp'st at so? Nay, why am I thus treated?
                    (draws the dagger; offers to stab her)
What wilt thou do? Ah, do not kill me, Jaffeir!
Pity these panting breasts, and trembling limbs,
That us'd to clasp thee when thy looks were milder—
That yet hang heavy on my unpurg'd soul;
And plunge it not into eternal darkness.
  JAFF. No, Belvidera, when we parted last,
I gave this dagger with thee as in trust
To be thy portion if I e'er prov'd false.
On such condition was my truth believ'd;
But now 'tis forfeited and must be paid for.
                              (offers to stab her again)
  BELV. (kneeling) Oh, mercy!
  JAFF.   Nay, no struggling.
  BELV. (leaps upon his neck and kisses him) Now then kill me!
While thus I cling about thy cruel neck,

Kiss thy revengeful lips and die in joys
Greater than any I can guess hereafter.

JAFF. I am, I am a coward; witness't, heaven,
Witness it, earth, and every being, witness!
'Tis but one blow; yet—by immortal love,
I cannot longer bear a thought to harm thee!
                    (*He throws away the dagger and embraces her.*)
The seal of Providence is sure upon thee,
And thou wert born for yet unheard-of wonders:
Oh, thou wert either born to save or damn me!
By all the power that's given thee o'er my soul,
By thy resistless tears and conquering smiles,
By the victorious love that still waits on thee,
Fly to thy cruel father: save my friend,
Or all our future quiet's lost forever:
Fall at his feet; cling round his reverend knees;
Speak to him with thy eyes, and with thy tears
Melt his hard heart, and wake dead nature in him.
Crush him in th' arms, and torture him with thy softness:
    Nor, till thy prayers are granted, set him free,
    But conquer him, as thou hast vanquish'd me. (*Exeunt ambo.*)

ACT V

SCENE I

Enter PRIULI, *solus*

PRIU. Why, cruel heaven, have my unhappy days
Been lengthen'd to this sad one? Oh! dishonour
And deathless infamy is fall'n upon me.
Was it my fault? Am I a traitor? No.
But then, my only child, my daughter, wedded;
There my best blood runs foul, and a disease
Incurable has seiz'd upon my memory,
To make it rot and stink to after ages.
Curst be the fatal minute when I got her;
Or would that I'd been anything but man,
And rais'd an issue which would ne'er have wrong'd me.
The miserablest creatures (man excepted)

Are not the less esteem'd, though their posterity
Degenerate from the virtues of their fathers;
The vilest beasts are happy in their offsprings,
While only man gets traitors, whores, and villains.
Curst be the names, and some swift blow from fate
Lay his head deep, where mine may be forgotten!

Enter BELVIDERA *in a long mourning veil*

BELV. He's there—my father, my inhuman father,
That, for three years, has left an only child
Expos'd to all the outrages of fate,
And cruel ruin.—Oh!——
 PRIU.   What child of sorrow
Art thou, that com'st thus wrapp'd in weeds of sadness,
And mov'st as if thy steps were towards a grave?
 BELV. A wretch who from the very top of happiness
Am fallen into the lowest depths of misery,
And want your pitying hand to raise me up again.
 PRIU. Indeed, thou talk'st as thou hadst tasted sorrows;
Would I could help thee!
 BELV.   'Tis greatly in your power.
The world, too, speaks you charitable, and I,
Who ne'er asked alms before, in that dear hope
Am come a-begging to you, Sir.
 PRIU.   For what?
 BELV. Oh, well regard me! Is this voice a strange one?
Consider, too, when beggars once pretend
A case like mine, no little will content 'em.
 PRIU. What wouldst thou beg for?
 BELV.   Pity and forgiveness.
           (*throws up her veil*)
By the kind tender names of child and father,
Hear my complaints, and take me to your love.
 PRIU. My daughter?
 BELV.   Yes, your daughter, by a mother
Virtuous and noble, faithful to your honour,
Obedient to your will, kind to your wishes,
Dear to your arms. By all the joys she gave you,
When in her blooming years she was your treasure,

Look kindly on me; in my face behold
The lineaments of hers y'have kissed so often,
Pleading the cause of your poor cast-off child.

PRIU. Thou art my daughter.

BELV.   Yes—and y'have oft told me
With smiles of love and chaste, paternal kisses,
I'd much resemblance of my mother.

PRIU.   Oh!
Hadst thou inherited her matchless virtues,
I'd been too blest.

BELV.   Nay, do not call to memory
My disobedience, but let pity enter
Into your heart, and quite deface the impression;
For could you think how mine's perplex'd, what sadness,
Fears, and despairs distract the peace within me,
Oh, you would take me in your dear, dear arms,
Hover with strong compassion o'er your young one,
To shelter me with a protecting wing
From the black gather'd storm that's just, just breaking!

PRIU. Don't talk thus.

BELV.   Yes, I must; and you must hear too.
I have a husband——

PRIU.   Damn him!

BELV.   Oh, do not curse him!
He would not speak so hard a word towards you
On any terms, howe'er he deal with me.

PRIU. Hah! what means my child?

BELV. Oh, there's but this short moment
'Twixt me and fate. Yet send me not with curses
Down to my grave; afford me one kind blessing
Before we part: just take me in your arms
And recommend me with a prayer to heaven,
That I may die in peace; and when I'm dead——

PRIU. How my soul's catch'd!

BELV.   Lay me, I beg you, lay me
By the dear ashes of my tender mother.
She would have pity'd me, had fate yet spar'd her.

PRIU. By heaven, my aching heart forebodes much mischief.
Tell me thy story, for I'm still thy father.

contented.

Speak.

No matter.

Tell me.

heaven, my heart runs o'er with fondness.

BEL.

PRIU. Utter't.

BELV. Oh, my husband, my dear husband
Carries a dagger in his once kind bosom
To pierce the heart of your poor Belvidera.

PRIU. Kill thee!

BELV. Yes, kill me. When he pass'd his faith
And covenant against your state and Senate,
He gave me up as hostage for his truth,
With me a dagger and a dire commission,
Whene'er he fail'd, to plunge it through this bosom.
I learnt the danger, chose the hour of love
T'attempt his heart, and bring it back to honour.
Great love prevail'd and bless'd me with success.
He came, confess'd, betray'd his dearest friends
For promis'd mercy; now they're doom'd to suffer.
Gall'd with remembrance of what then was sworn,
If they are lost, he vows t'appease the gods
With this poor life, and make my blood th'atonement.

PRIU. Heavens!

BELV. Think you saw what pass'd at our last parting;
Think you beheld him like a raging lion,
Pacing the earth and tearing up his steps,
Fate in his eyes, and roaring with the pain
Of burning fury; think you saw his one hand
Fix'd on my throat, while the extended other
Grasp'd a keen, threat'ning dagger. Oh, 'twas thus
We last embrac'd; when, trembling with revenge,
He dragg'd me to the ground, and at my bosom
Presented horrid death, cried out, "My friends,
Where are my friends?" swore, wept, rag'd, threaten'd, lov'd,
For he yet lov'd, and that dear love preserv'd me
To this last trial of a father's pity.
I fear not death, but cannot bear a thought

That that dear hand should do th' unfriendly office;
If I was ever then your care, now hear me;
Fly to the Senate, save the promis'd lives
Of his dear friends, ere mine be made the sacrifice.

PRIU. Oh, my heart's comfort!

BELV. Will you not, my father?
Weep not, but answer me.

PRIU. By heaven, I will!
Not one of 'em but what shall be immortal.
Canst thou forgive me all my follies past,
I'll henceforth be indeed a father; never,
Never more thus expose, but cherish thee,
Dear as the vital warmth that feeds my life,
Dear as these eyes that weep in fondness o'er thee.
Peace to thy heart! Farewell.

BELV. Go, and remember,
'Tis Belvidera's life her father pleads for. (*Exeunt severally.*)

Enter ANTONIO

ANT. Hum, hum, hah. Signior Priuli, my lord Priuli, my lord, my lord, my lord. How we lords love to call one another by our titles. My lord, my lord, my lord.—Pox on him, I am a lord as well as he. And so let him fiddle.—I'll warrant him he's gone to the Senate-house, and I'll be there too, soon enough for somebody. Odd!—here's a tickling speech about the plot. I'll prove there's a plot with a vengeance—would I had it without book. Let me see—"Most reverend senators, That there is a plot, surely by this time, no man that hath eyes or understanding in his head will presume to doubt; 'tis as plain as the light in the cowcumber"—no—hold there—cowcumber does not come in yet—" 'tis as plain as the light in the sun, or as the man in the moon, even at noonday. It is, indeed, a pumpkin-plot, which, just as it was mellow, we have gathered; and now we have gathered it, pre-pared and dressed it, shall we throw it like a pickled cowcumber out at the window? No! That it is not only a bloody, horrid, excrable, damnable, and audacious plot, but it is, as I may so say, a saucy plot; and we all know, most reverend fathers, that what is sauce for a goose is sauce for a gander: therefore, I say, as those blood-thirsty ganders of the conspiracy would have

destroyed us geese of the Senate, let us make haste to destroy
them. So I humbly move for hanging"—Hah, hurry durry, I
think this will do, though I was something out, at first, about the
sun and the cowcumber.

Enter AQUILINA

AQUIL. Good morrow, Senator.

ANT. Nacky, my dear Nacky, morrow, Nacky; odd, I am very
brisk, very merry, very pert, very jovial—ha-a-a-a-a—kiss me,
Nacky; how dost thou do, my little Tory, rory strumpet? Kiss
me, I say, hussy, kiss me.

AQUIL. "Kiss me, Nacky!" Hang you, Sir! coxcomb, hang you,
Sir!

ANT. Hayty tayty, is it so indeed, with all my heart, faith—
(sings) Hey then, up go we, faith—hey then, up go we, dum
dum derum dump.

AQUIL. Signior.

ANT. Madonna.

AQUIL. Do you intend to die in your bed—?

ANT. About threescore years hence; much may be done, my
   dear.

AQUIL. You'll be hanged, Signior.

ANT. Hanged, sweetheart? Prithee, be quiet. Hanged, quoth-a,
that's a merry conceit, with all my heart. Why, thou jok'st, Nacky;
thou art given to joking, I'll swear. Well, I protest, Nacky—nay,
I must protest, and will protest that I love joking dearly, man.
And I love thee for joking, and I'll kiss thee for joking, and touse
thee for joking—and odd, I have a devilish mind to take thee
aside about that business for joking, too—odd, I have! and
(sings) Hey then, up go we, dum dum derum dump.

AQUIL. (draws a dagger) See you this, Sir?

ANT. O Laud, a dagger! O Laud! it is naturally my aversion;
I cannot endure the sight on't; hide it, for heaven's sake! I cannot
look that way till it be gone—hide it, hide it, oh, oh, hide it!

AQUIL. Yes, in your heart, I'll hide it.

ANT. My heart! What, hide a dagger in my heart's blood!

AQUIL. Yes, in thy heart, thy throat, thou pamper'd devil!
Thou hast help'd to spoil my peace, and I'll have vengeance
On thy curst life for all the bloody Senate,
The perjur'd, faithless Senate. Where's my lord,

My happiness, my love, my god, my hero?
Doom'd by thy accursed tongue, amongst the rest,
T'a shameful wrack? By all the rage that's in me,
I'll be whole years in murdering thee!

ANT. Why, Nacky, wherefore so passionate? What have I done? What's the matter, my dear Nacky? Am not I thy love, thy happiness, thy lord, thy hero, thy senator, and everything in the world, Nacky?

AQUIL. Thou! Thinkst thou, thou art fit to meet my joys,
To bear the eager clasps of my embraces?
Give me my Pierre, or——

ANT. Why, he's to be hanged, little Nacky, trussed up for treason, and so forth, child.

AQUIL. Thou li'st! stop down thy throat that hellish sentence,
Or 'tis thy last. Swear that my love shall live,
Or thou art dead.

ANT.   Ah-h-h-h.

AQUIL.   Swear to recall his doom,
Swear at my feet, and tremble at my fury.

ANT. I do—— Now, if she would but kick a little bit, one kick now, ah-h-h-h.

AQUIL. Swear, or——

ANT. I do, by these dear fragrant foots and little toes, sweet as —e-e-e-e, my Nacky, Nacky, Nacky.

AQUIL. How!

ANT. Nothing but untie thy shoestring, a little, faith and troth; that's all, that's all, as I hope to live, Nacky, that's all.

AQUIL. Nay, then——

ANT. Hold, hold! thy love, thy lord, thy hero
Shall be preserv'd and safe.

AQUIL.   Or may this poniard
Rust in thy heart!

ANT.   With all my soul.

AQUIL.   Farewell——

(*Exit* AQUILINA.)

ANT. Adieu. Why, what a bloody-minded, inveterate, ter-magant strumpet have I been plagued with! Oh-h-h, yet more! nay, then, I die, I die—I am dead already.

(*stretches himself out*)

SCENE II

Enter JAFFEIR

JAFF. Final destruction seize on all the world!
Bend down, ye heavens, and shutting round this earth,
Crush the vile globe into its first confusion;
Scorch it with elemental flames to one curst cinder,
And all us little creepers in't, call'd men,
Burn, burn to nothing: but let Venice burn
Hotter than all the rest: here kindle hell
Ne'er to extinguish, and let souls hereafter
Groan here, in all those pains which mine feels now.

Enter BELVIDERA

BELV. (*meeting him*) My life——
JAFF. (*turning from her*)   My plague——
BELV.   Nay, then
I see my ruin,
If I must die!
          JAFF.   No, Death's this day too busy;
Thy father's ill-tim'd mercy came too late.
I thank thee for thy labours, though, and him, too,
But all my poor, betray'd, unhappy friends
Have summons to prepare for fate's black hour;
And yet I live.
          BELV.   Then be the next my doom.
I see thou hast pass'd my sentence in thy heart,
And I'll no longer weep or plead against it,
But with the humblest, most obedient patience
Meet thy dear hands, and kiss 'em when they wound me;
Indeed I am willing, but I beg thee do it
With some remorse; and where thou giv'st the blow,
View me with eyes of a relenting love,
And show me pity, for 'twill sweeten justice.
          JAFF. Show pity to thee?
          BELV.   Yes, and when thy hands,
Charg'd with my fate, come trembling to the deed,
As thou hast done a thousand, thousand dear times
To this poor breast, when kinder rage has brought thee,

When our sting'd hearts have leap'd to meet each other,
And melting kisses seal'd our lips together,
When joys have left me gasping in thy arms,
So let my death come now, and I'll not shrink from't.
    JAFF. Nay, Belvidera, do not fear my cruelty,
Nor let the thoughts of death perplex thy fancy,
But answer me to what I shall demand,
With a firm temper and unshaken spirit.
    BELV. I will when I've done weeping——
    JAFF.   Fie, no more on't!
How long is't since the miserable day
We wedded first——
    BELV.   Oh-h-h.
    JAFF.   Nay, keep in thy tears,
Lest they unman me, too.
    BELV.   Heaven knows I cannot;
The words you utter sound so very sadly
These streams will follow——
    JAFF.   Come, I'll kiss 'em dry, then.
    BELV. But was't a miserable day?
    JAFF.   A curst one.
    BELV. I thought it otherwise, and you've oft sworn
In the transporting hours of warmest love,
When sure you spoke the truth, you've sworn you bless'd it.
    JAFF. 'Twas a rash oath.
    BELV.   Then why am I not curst too?
    JAFF. No, Belvidera; by th'eternal truth,
I dote with too much fondness.
    BELV.   Still so kind?
Still then do you love me?
    JAFF.   Nature, in her workings,
Inclines not with more ardour to creation
Than I do now towards thee; man ne'er was blest
Since the first pair first met, as I have been.
    BELV. Then sure you will not curse me.
    JAFF.   No, I'll bless thee·
I came on purpose, Belvidera, to bless thee.
'Tis now, I think, three years w'have liv'd together.
    BELV. And may no fatal minute ever part us
Till, reverend grown for age and love, we go

Down to one grave as our last bed, together;
There sleep in peace till an eternal morning.

JAFF. (*sighing*) When will that be?

BELV.   I hope long ages hence.

JAFF. Have I not hitherto (I beg thee tell me
Thy very fears) us'd thee with tender'st love?
Did e'er my soul rise up in wrath against thee?
Did I e'er frown when Belvidera smil'd,
Or, by the least unfriendly word, betray
A bating passion? Have I ever wrong'd thee?

BELV. No.

JAFF.   Has my heart, or have my eyes e'er wandred
To any other woman?

BELV.   Never, never—
I were the worst of false ones, should I accuse thee.
I own I've been too happy, blest above
My sex's charter.

JAFF. Did I not say I came to bless thee?

BELV. Yes.

JAFF.   Then hear me, bounteous heaven!
Pour down your blessings on this beauteous head,
Where everlasting sweets are always springing.
With a continual giving hand, let peace,
Honour, and safety always hover round her;
Feed her with plenty; let her eyes ne'er see
A sight of sorrow, nor her heart know mourning;
Crown all her days with joy, her nights with rest,
Harmless as her own thoughts, and prop her virtue
To bear the loss of one that too much lov'd,
And comfort her with patience in our parting.

BELV. How—parting, parting!

JAFF.   Yes, forever parting.
I have sworn, Belvidera, by yon heaven,
That best can tell how much I lose to leave thee,
We part this hour forever.

BELV.   Oh, call back
Your cruel blessings; stay with me and curse me!

JAFF. No, 'tis resolv'd.

BELV.   Then hear me, too, just heaven!

Pour down your curses on this wretched head
With never-ceasing vengeance; let despair,
Danger, or infamy, nay all, surround me;
Starve me with wantings; let my eyes ne'er see
A sight of comfort, nor my heart know peace,
But dash my days with sorrow, nights with horrors
Wild as my own thoughts now, and let loose fury
To make me mad enough for what I lose,
If I must lose him. If I must!—I will not.
Oh, turn and hear me!
    JAFF.   Now hold, heart, or never!
    BELV. By all the tender days we have liv'd together,
By all our charming nights, and joys that crown'd 'em,
Pity my sad condition—speak, but speak!
    JAFF. Oh-h-h!
    BELV.   By these arms that now cling round thy neck,
By this dear kiss and by ten thousand more,
By these poor streaming eyes——
    JAFF.   Murder! unhold me.
By th'immortal destiny that doom'd me   (*draws his dagger*)
To this curst minute, I'll not live one longer.
Resolve to let me go or see me fall——
    BELV. Hold, Sir; be patient.   (*Passing-bell tolls.*)
    JAFF.   Hark, the dismal bell
Tolls out for death! I must attend its call, too;
For my poor friend, my dying Pierre, expects me:
He sent a message to require I'd see him
Before he died, and take his last forgiveness.
Farewell forever.   (*going out, looks back at her*)
    BELV.   Leave thy dagger with me;
Bequeath me something.—Not one kiss at parting?
O my poor heart, when wilt thou break?
    JAFF.   Yet stay!
We have a child, as yet a tender infant.
Be a kind mother to him when I am gone;
Breed him in virtue and the paths of honour,
But let him never know his father's story.
I charge thee guard him from the wrongs my fate
May do his future fortune or his name.

Now—nearer yet——   (*approaching each other*)
                    Oh, that my arms were riveted
Thus round thee ever! But my friends, my oath!   (*kisses her*)
This and no more.
    BELV.   Another, sure another,
For that poor little one you've ta'en care of;
I'll give't him truly.
    JAFF.   So, now farewell.
    BELV.   Forever?
    JAFF. Heaven knows, forever; all good angels guard thee.
                                    (*Exit.*)

    BELV. All ill ones sure had charge of me this moment.
Curst be my days, and doubly curst my nights,
Which I must now mourn out in widow'd tears;
Blasted be every herb and fruit and tree;
Curst be the rain that falls upon the earth,
And may the general curse reach man and beast.
Oh, give me daggers, fire, or water!
How I could bleed, how burn, how drown, the waves
Huzzing and booming round my sinking head,
Till I descended to the peaceful bottom!
Oh, there's all quiet; here, all rage and fury:
The air's too thin, and pierces my weak brain:
I long for thick, substantial sleep. Hell, hell,
Burst from the centre, rage and roar aloud
If thou art half so hot, so mad as I am.

Enter PRIULI *and Servants*

Who's there?
    PRIU.   Run, seize and bring her safely home.
                                    (*They seize her.*)
Guard her as you would life. Alas, poor creature!
    BELV. What? To my husband then conduct me quickly.
Are all things ready? Shall we die most gloriously?
Say not a word of this to my old father.
Murmuring streams, soft shades, and springing flowers,
Lutes, laurels, seas of milk, and ships of amber.   (*Exeunt.*)

SCENE III

Scene opening, discovers a scaffold and a wheel prepared for the executing of PIERRE; *then enter Officers,* PIERRE, *and Guards, a Friar, Executioner, and a great Rabble*

OFFIC. Room, room there! Stand all by; make room for the prisoner.

PIERRE. My friend not come yet?

FATH.   Why are you so obstinate?

PIERRE. Why you so troublesome, that a poor wretch cannot die in peace,

But you, like ravens, will be croaking round him?

FATH. Yet, heaven——

PIERRE.   I tell thee, heaven and I are friends.

I ne'er broke peace with't yet by cruel murders,

Rapine, or perjury, or vile deceiving;

But liv'd in moral justice towards all men,

Nor am a foe to the most strong believers,

Howe'er my own short-sighted faith confine me.

FATH. But an all-seeing Judge——

PIERRE.   You say my conscience

Must be mine accuser: I have search'd that conscience,

And find no records there of crimes that scare me.

FATH. 'Tis strange you should want faith.

PIERRE.   You want to lead

My reason blindfold, like a hamper'd lion,

Check'd of its nobler vigour; then, when baited

Down to obedient tameness, make it couch,

And show strange tricks which you call signs of faith.

So silly souls are gull'd and you get money.

Away, no more!—Captain, I'd have hereafter

This fellow write no lies of my conversion,

Because he has crept upon my troubled hours.

Enter JAFFEIR

JAFF. Hold. Eyes, be dry; heart, strengthen me to bear

This hideous sight, and humble me to take

The last forgiveness of a dying friend,

Betray'd by my vile falsehood to his ruin!

—O Pierre!

PIERRE. Yet nearer.

JAFF.   Crawling on my knees,
And prostrate on the earth, let me approach thee.
How shall I look up to thy injur'd face,
That always us'd to smile with friendship on me?
It darts an air of so much manly virtue,
That I, methinks, look little in thy sight,
And stripes are fitter for me than embraces.

PIERRE. Dear to my arms, though thou hast undone my fame,
I cannot forget to love thee: prithee, Jaffeir,
Forgive that filthy blow my passion dealt thee;
I am now preparing for the land of peace,
And fain would have the charitable wishes
Of all good men, like thee, to bless my journey.

JAFF. Good! I am the vilest creature, worse than e'er
Suffer'd the shameful fate thou art going to taste of.
Why was I sent for to be us'd thus kindly?
Call, call me villain, as I am, describe
The foul complexion of my hateful deeds;
Lead me to the rack, and stretch me in thy stead;
I've crimes enough to give it its full load,
And do it credit. Thou wilt but spoil the use on't,
And honest men hereafter bear its figure
About 'em as a charm from treacherous friendship.

OFFIC. The time grows short; your friends are dead already.

JAFF. Dead!

PIERRE. Yes, dead, Jaffeir; they've all died like men too,
Worthy their character.

JAFF.   And what must I do?

PIERRE. O Jaffeir!

JAFF.   Speak aloud thy burthen'd soul,
And tell thy troubles to thy tortur'd friend.

PIERRE. Friend! Couldst thou yet be a friend, a generous
    friend,
I might hope comfort from thy noble sorrows.
Heav'n knows I want a friend.

JAFF.   And I a kind one,
That would not thus scorn my repenting virtue,

Or think, when he is to die, my thoughts are idle.

PIERRE. No! live, I charge thee, Jaffeir.

JAFF.   Yes, I will live,
But it shall be to see thy fall reveng'd
At such a rate as Venice long shall groan for.

PIERRE. Wilt thou?

JAFF.   I will, by heav'n!

PIERRE.   Then still thou'rt noble,
And I forgive thee. Oh—yet—shall I trust thee?

JAFF. No: I've been false already.

PIERRE.   Dost thou love me?

JAFF. Rip up my heart, and satisfy thy doubtings.

PIERRE. Curse on this weakness!   (*He weeps.*)

JAFF.   Tears! Amazement! Tears!
I never saw thee melted thus before;
And know there's something lab'ring in thy bosom
That must have vent: though I'm a villain, tell me.

PIERRE. (*pointing to the wheel*) Seest thou that engine?

JAFF. Why?

PIERRE. Is't fit a soldier who has liv'd with honour,
Fought nations' quarrels, and been crown'd with conquest,
Be expos'd a common carcass on a wheel?

JAFF. Hah!

PIERRE.   Speak! is't fitting?

JAFF.   Fitting?

PIERRE.   Yes, is't fitting?

JAFF. What's to be done?

PIERRE.   I'd have thee undertake
Something that's noble, to preserve my memory
From the disgrace that's ready to attaint it.

OFFIC. The day grows late, Sir.

PIERRE.   I'll make haste.—— O Jaffeir,
Though thou'st betray'd me, do me some way justice.

JAFF. No more of that. Thy wishes shall be satisfy'd.
I have a wife, and she shall bleed; my child, too,
Yield up his little throat, and all t'appease thee——
                        (*Going away,* PIERRE *holds him.*)

PIERRE. No—this—no more!   (*He whispers* JAFFEIR.)

JAFF.   Hah! is't then so?

PIERRE. Most certainly.

JAFF. I'll do't.

PIERRE. Remember!

OFFIC. Sir.

PIERRE. Come, now I'm ready.

(He and JAFFEIR *ascend the scaffold.)*

Captain, you should be a gentleman of honour;
Keep off the rabble, that I may have room
To entertain my fate, and die with decency.
Come!

(Takes off his gown. Executioner prepares to bind him.)

FATH. Son!

PIERRE. Hence, tempter!

OFFIC. Stand off, priest!

PIERRE. I thank you, Sir.

(to JAFFEIR*)* You'll think on't?

JAFF. 'Twon't grow stale before to-morrow.

PIERRE. Now, Jaffeir! now I am going. Now———

(Executioner having bound him)

JAFF. Have at thee,
Thou honest heart, then—here——— *(stabs him)*
And this is well, too. *(then stabs himself)*

FATH. Damnable deed!

PIERRE. Now thou hast indeed been faithful.
This was done nobly.—We have deceiv'd the Senate.

JAFF. Bravely.

PIERRE. Ha, ha, ha—Oh, oh——— *(dies)*

JAFF. Now, ye curst rulers,
Thus of the blood y'have shed I make libation,
And sprinkle't mingling. May it rest upon you,
And all your race. Be henceforth peace a stranger
Within your walls; let plagues and famine waste
Your generations.——— Oh, poor Belvidera!
Sir, I have a wife; bear this in safety to her—
A token that with my dying breath I blest her,
And the dear little infant left behind me.
I am sick—I'm quiet——— *(*JAFFEIR *dies.)*

OFFIC. Bear this news to the Senate,
And guard their bodies till there's farther order.
Heav'n grant I die so well——— *(Scene shuts upon them.)*

SCENE IV

Soft music. Enter BELVIDERA *distracted, led by two
of her Women,* PRIULI, *and Servants*

PRIU. Strengthen her heart with patience, pitying heav'n.
BELV. Come, come, come, come, come! Nay, come to bed,
Prithee, my love. The winds! hark, how they whistle!
And the rain beats: oh, how the weather shrinks me!
You are angry now; who cares? pish, no indeed.
Choose then. I say you shall not go, you shall not!
Whip your ill nature; get you gone then! (JAFFEIR's *Ghost rises.*)
                                        Oh,
Are you return'd? See, Father, here he's come again!
Am I to blame to love him? Oh, thou dear one! (*Ghost sinks.*)
Why do you fly me? Are you angry still, then?
Jaffeir! where art thou?—— Father, why do you do thus?
Stand off, don't hide him from me! He's here somewhere.
Stand off, I say!—— What, gone? Remember't, tyrant!
I may revenge myself for this trick one day.
I'll do't—I'll do't. Renault's a nasty fellow.
Hang him, hang him, hang him!

Enter Officer and others

PRIU. News—what news?   (*Officer whispers* PRIULI.)
OFFIC.   Most sad, Sir.
Jaffeir, upon the scaffold, to prevent
A shameful death, stabb'd Pierre, and next himself:
Both fell together.
PRIU.   Daughter——
(*The Ghosts of* JAFFEIR *and* PIERRE *rise together, both bloody.*)
BELV.   Hah, look there!
My husband bloody, and his friend, too! Murder!
Who has done this? Speak to me, thou sad vision;
On these poor trembling knees I beg it.   (*Ghosts sink.*)
                        Vanished—
Here they went down. Oh, I'll dig, dig the den up.
You shan't delude me thus. Hoa, Jaffeir, Jaffeir!
Peep up and give me but a look.—— I have him!
I've got him, Father; oh, now how I'll smuggle him!

My love! my dear! my blessing! help me, help me!
They have hold on me, and drag me to the bottom!
Nay—now they pull so hard—farewell——   (*She dies.*)
   MAID.   She's dead,
Breathless and dead.
   PRIU.   Then guard me from the sight on't:
Lead me into some place that's fit for mourning;
Where the free air, light, and the cheerful sun
May never enter. Hang it round with black;
Set up one taper that may last a day—
As long as I've to live; and there all leave me,
  Sparing no tears when you this tale relate,
  But bid all cruel fathers dread my fate.
                (*Curtain falls. Exeunt omnes.*)

EPILOGUE

The text is done, and now for application,
And when that's ended, pass your approbation.
Though the conspiracy's prevented here,
Methinks I see another hatching there;
And there's a certain faction fain would sway,
If they had strength enough, and damn this play.
But this the author bade me boldly say:
If any take his plainness in ill part,
He's glad on't from the bottom of his heart;
Poets in honour of the truth should write,
With the same spirit brave men for it fight;
And though against him causeless hatreds rise,
And daily where he goes of late he spies
The scowls of sullen and revengeful eyes,
'Tis what he knows with much contempt to bear,
And serves a cause too good to let him fear:
He fears no poison from an incens'd drab,
No ruffian's five-foot-sword, nor rascal's stab,
Nor any other snares of mischief laid,
Not a Rose-alley cudgel-ambuscade,
From any private cause where malice reigns,
Or general pique all blockheads have to brains:

Nothing shall daunt his pen when truth does call,
No, not the picture-mangler* at Guildhall.
The rebel-tribe, of which that vermin's one,
Have now set forward and their course begun;
And while that prince's figure they deface,
   As they before had massacred his name,
Durst their base fears but look him in the face,
   They'd use his person as they've used his fame;
A face, in which such lineaments they read
Of that great martyr's whose rich blood they shed,
That their rebellious hate they still retain,
And in his son would murder him again.
With indignation then, let each brave heart,
Rouse and unite to take his injur'd part;
Till royal love and goodness call him home,
And songs of triumph meet him as he come;
Till heaven his honour and our peace restore,
And villains never wrong his virtue more.

* 'The rascal that cut the Duke of York's picture.'

The Relapse; or,

Virtue in Danger

By SIR JOHN VANBRUGH

BEING THE SEQUEL OF

THE FOOL IN FASHION

THE PREFACE

To go about to excuse half the defects this abortive brat is come
into the world with, would be to provoke the town with a long
useless preface, when 'tis, I doubt, sufficiently soured already by
a tedious play.

I do therefore (with all the humility of a repenting sinner)
confess it wants everything—but length; and in that, I hope, the
severest critic will be pleased to acknowledge I have not been
wanting. But my modesty will sure atone for everything, when
the world shall know it is so great I am even to this day insensible
of those two shining graces in the play (which some part of the
town is pleased to compliment me with) blasphemy and bawdy.

For my part, I cannot find 'em out: if there was any obscene
expressions upon the stage, here they are in the print; for I have
dealt fairly, I have not sunk a syllable that could (though by
racking of mysteries) be ranged under that head; and yet I

415

believe with a steady faith, there is not one woman of a real reputation in town but when she has read it impartially over in her closet will find it so innocent she'll think it no affront to her prayer-book to lay it upon the same shelf. So to them (with all manner of deference) I entirely refer my cause; and I'm confident they'll justify me against those pretenders to good manners, who, at the same time, have so little respect for the ladies they would extract a bawdy jest from an ejaculation, to put 'em out of countenance. But I expect to have these well-bred persons always my enemies, since I'm sure I shall never write anything lewd enough to make 'em my friends.

As for the saints (your thorough-paced ones, I mean, with screwed faces and wry mouths) I despair of them; for they are friends to nobody. They love nothing but their altars and themselves. They have too much zeal to have any charity; they make debauches in piety, as sinners do in wine, and are as quarrelsome in their religion as other people are in their drink: so I hope nobody will mind what they say. But if any man (with flat plod shoes, a little band, greasy hair, and a dirty face, who is wiser than I, at the expense of being forty years older) happens to be offended at a story of a cock and a bull, and a priest and a bull-dog, I beg his pardon with all my heart; which, I hope, I shall obtain by eating my words, and making this public recantation. I do therefore, for his satisfaction, acknowledge I lied when I said they never quit their hold; for in that little time I have lived in the world, I thank God I have seen 'em forced to 't more than once; but next time I'll speak with more caution and truth, and only say they have very good teeth.

If I have offended any honest gentleman of the town whose friendship or good word is worth the having, I am very sorry for it; I hope they'll correct me as gently as they can, when they consider I have had no other design, in running a very great risk, than to divert (if possible) some part of their spleen, in spite of their wives and their taxes.

One word more about the bawdy, and I have done. I own, the first night this thing was acted some indecencies had like to have happened; but 'twas not my fault.

The fine gentleman of the play, drinking his mistress's health in Nantes brandy, from six in the morning to the time he waddled on upon the stage in the evening, had toasted himself up to such a pitch of vigour, I confess I once gave Amanda for gone, and I am since (with all due respect to Mrs. Rogers) very sorry she scaped; for I am confident a certain lady (let no one take it to herself that's handsome) who highly blames the play for the barrenness of the conclusion, would then have allowed it a very natural close.

PROLOGUE

SPOKEN BY MISS HOYDEN

Ladies, this play in too much haste was writ
To be o'ercharg'd with either plot or wit;
'Twas got, conceiv'd, and born in six weeks' space,
And wit, you know, 's as slow in growth—as grace.
Sure it can ne'er be ripen'd to your taste;
I doubt 'twill prove our author bred too fast:
For mark 'em well, who with the Muses marry,
They rarely do conceive, but they miscarry.
'Tis the hard fate of those wh'are big with rhyme,
Still to be brought to bed before their time.
Of our late poets, Nature few has made;
The greatest part—are only so by trade.
Still want of something brings the scribbling fit; ⎫
For want of money some of 'em have writ,   ⎬
And others do't, you see—for want of wit.   ⎭
Honour, they fancy, summons 'em to write,   ⎫
So out they lug in resty Nature's spite,   ⎬
As some of you spruce beaux do—when you fight. ⎭
Yet let the ebb of wit be ne'er so low,   ⎫
Some glimpse of it a man may hope to show,   ⎬
Upon a theme so ample—as a beau.   ⎭
So, howsoe'er true courage may decay,   ⎫
Perhaps there's not one smock-face here to-day,   ⎬
But's bold as Cæsar—to attack a play.   ⎭
Nay, what's yet more, with an undaunted face,   ⎫
To do the thing with more heroic grace,   ⎬
'Tis six to four y'attack the strongest place.   ⎭
You are such Hotspurs in this kind of venture,
Where there's no breach, just there you needs must enter.

But be advis'd.
E'en give the hero and the critic o'er,
For Nature sent you on another score;
She formed her beau for nothing but her whore.

PERSONS REPRESENTED

MEN

SIR NOVELTY FASHION, *newly created Lord Foppington*
YOUNG FASHION, *his brother*
LOVELESS, *husband to Amanda*
WORTHY, *a gentleman of the town*
SIR TUNBELLY CLUMSEY, *a country gentleman*
SIR JOHN FRIENDLY, *his neighbour*
COUPLER, *a matchmaker*
BULL, *chaplain to Sir Tunbelly*
SERRINGE, *a surgeon*
LORY, *servant to Young Fashion*
Shoemaker, Tailor, Periwig-maker, &c.

WOMEN

AMANDA, *wife to Loveless*
BERINTHIA, *her cousin, a young widow*
MISS HOYDEN, *a great fortune, daughter to Sir Tunbelly*
Nurse, *her gouvernante*
MRS. CALLICOE, *a seamstress*
ABIGAIL, *maid to Berinthia*
Maid to Amanda

THE RELAPSE; OR,
VIRTUE IN DANGER

ACT I

SCENE I

Enter LOVELESS, *reading*

LOV. How true is that philosophy which says
Our heaven is seated in our minds!
Through all the roving pleasures of my youth
(Where nights and days seem'd all consum'd in joy,
Where the false face of luxury display'd such charms
As might have shaken the most holy hermit,
And made him totter at his altar),
I never knew one moment's peace like this.
Here—in this little soft retreat,
My thoughts unbent from all the cares of life,
Content with fortune,
Eas'd from the grating duties of dependence,
From envy free, ambition under foot,
The raging flame of wild destructive lust
Reduc'd to a warm pleasing fire of lawful love,
My life glides on, and all is well within.

Enter AMANDA

LOV. (*meeting her kindly*) How does the happy cause of my
    content, my dear Amanda?
You find me musing on my happy state,
And full of grateful thoughts to heaven, and you.
AMAN. Those grateful offerings heaven can't receive
With more delight than I do:
Would I could share with it as well
The dispensations of its bliss,
That I might search its choicest favours out,
And shower 'em on your head for ever.
LOV. The largest boons that heaven thinks fit to grant

419

To things it has decreed shall crawl on earth,
Are in the gift of women form'd like you.
Perhaps, when time shall be no more,
When the aspiring soul shall take its flight,
And drop this pond'rous lump of clay behind it,
It may have appetites we know not of,
And pleasures as refin'd as its desires—
But till that day of knowledge shall instruct me,
The utmost blessing that my thought can reach,

                              (*taking her in his arms*)

Is folded in my arms, and rooted in my heart.

AMAN. There let it grow for ever.

LOV. Well said, Amanda—let it be for ever—
Would heaven grant that——

AMAN.   'Twere all the heaven I'd ask.
But we are clad in black mortality,
And the dark curtain of eternal night
At last must drop between us.

LOV. It must: that mournful separation we must see. A bitter
pill it is to all; but doubles its ungrateful taste, when lovers are
to swallow it.

AMAN. Perhaps that pain may only be my lot;
You possibly may be exempted from it.
Men find out softer ways to quench their fires.

LOV. Can you then doubt my constancy, Amanda?
You'll find 'tis built upon a steady basis—
The rock of reason now supports my love,
On which it stands so fix'd
The rudest hurricane of wild desire
Would, like the breath of a soft slumb'ring babe,
Pass by, and never shake it.

AMAN. Yet still 'tis safer to avoid the storm;
The strongest vessels, if they put to sea,
May possibly be lost.
Would I could keep you here in this calm port for ever!
Forgive the weakness of a woman,
I am uneasy at your going to stay so long in town;
I know its false insinuating pleasures;
I know the force of its delusions;

I know the strength of its attacks;
I know the weak defence of nature;
I know you are a man—and I—a wife.
 LOV. You know then all that needs to give you rest,
For wife's the strongest claim that you can urge.
When you would plead your title to my heart,
On this you may depend; therefore be calm,
Banish your fears, for they are traitors to your peace;
Beware of 'em: they are insinuating busy things
That gossip to and fro,
And do a world of mischief where they come:
But you shall soon be mistress of 'em all;
I'll aid you with such arms for their destruction
They never shall erect their heads again.
You know the business is indispensable,
That obliges me to go for London,
And you have no reason that I know of
To believe I'm glad of the occasion:
For my honest conscience is my witness,
I have found a due succession of such charms
In my retirement here with you,
I have never thrown one roving thought that way;
But since, against my will, I'm dragg'd once more
To that uneasy theatre of noise,
I am resolv'd to make such use on't,
As shall convince you 'tis an old cast mistress,
Who has been so lavish of her favours
She's now grown bankrupt of her charms,
And has not one allurement left to move me.
 AMAN. Her bow, I do believe, is grown so weak,
Her arrows (at this distance) cannot hurt you,
But in approaching 'em you give 'em strength:
The dart that has not far to fly will put
The best of armour to a dangerous trial.
 LOV. That trial past, and y'are at ease for ever;
When you have seen the helmet prov'd,
You'll apprehend no more for him that wears it:
Therefore to put a lasting period to your fears,
I am resolv'd, this once, to launch into temptation.

I'll give you an essay of all my virtues;
My former boon companions of the bottle
Shall fairly try what charms are left in wine:
I'll take my place amongst 'em, they shall hem me in,
Sing praises to their god, and drink his glory;
Turn wild enthusiasts for his sake,
And beasts to do him honour:
Whilst I, a stubborn atheist,
Sullenly look on,
Without one reverend glass to his divinity.
That for my temperance: then for my constancy——
      AMAN. Ay, there take heed.
      LOV.   Indeed the danger's small.
      AMAN. And yet my fears are great.
      LOV.   Why are you so timorous?
      AMAN. Because you are so bold.
      LOV. My courage should disperse your apprehensions.
      AMAN. My apprehensions should alarm your courage.
      LOV. Fy, fy, Amanda, it is not kind thus to distrust me.
      AMAN. And yet my fears are founded on my love.
      LOV. Your love then is not founded as it ought;
For if you can believe 'tis possible
I should again relapse to my past follies,
I must appear to you a thing
Of such an undigested composition,
That but to think of me with inclination
Would be a weakness in your taste
Your virtue scarce could answer.
      AMAN. 'Twould be a weakness in my tongue,
My prudence could not answer,
If I should press you farther with my fears;
I'll therefore trouble you no longer with 'em.
      LOV. Nor shall they trouble you much longer;
A little time shall show you they were groundless.
This winter shall be the fiery trial of my virtue,
Which, when it once has past,
You'll be convinc'd 'twas of no false alloy;
There all your cares will end.
      AMAN.   Pray heaven they may!
                              (*Exeunt hand in hand.*)

SCENE II

SCENE: *Whitehall*

Enter YOUNG FASHION, LORY, *and Waterman*

Y. FAS. Come, pay the waterman, and take the portmantle.

LO. Faith, Sir, I think the waterman had as good take the portmantle and pay himself.

Y. FAS. Why, sure there's something left in't!

LO. But a solitary old waistcoat, upon honour, Sir.

Y. FAS. Why, what's become of the blue coat, Sirrah?

LO. Sir, 'twas eaten at Gravesend; the reckoning came to thirty shillings, and your privy purse was worth but two half-crowns.

Y. FAS. 'Tis very well.

WAT. Pray, Master, will you please to dispatch me?

Y. FAS. Ay, here a—canst thou change me a guinea?

LO. (*aside*) Good!

WAT. Change a guinea, Master! Ha, ha, your honour's pleased to compliment.

Y. FAS. I'gad I don't know how I shall pay thee then, for I have nothing but gold about me.

LO. (*aside*) Hum, hum.

Y. FAS. What dost thou expect, friend?

WAT. Why, Master, so far against wind and tide is richly worth half a piece.

Y. FAS. Why, faith, I think thou art a good conscionable fellow. I'gad, I begin to have so good an opinion of thy honesty, I care not if I leave my portmantle with thee, till I send thee thy money.

WAT. Ha! God bless your honour; I should be as willing to trust you, Master, but that you are, as a man may say, a stranger to me, and these are nimble times. There are a great many sharpers stirring. (*taking up the portmantle*) Well, Master, when your worship sends the money, your portmantle shall be forthcoming; my name's Tugg; my wife keeps a brandy-shop in Drab Alley at Wapping.

Y. FAS. Very well; I'll send for't to-morrow. (*Exit Waterman.*)

LO. So! Now, Sir, I hope you'll own yourself a happy man; you have outlived all your cares.

Y. FAS. How so, Sir?

LO. Why you have nothing left to take care of.

Y. FAS. Yes, Sirrah, I have myself and you to take care of still.

LO. Sir, if you could but prevail with somebody else to do that for you, I fancy we might both fare the better for't.

Y. FAS. Why, if thou canst tell me where to apply myself, I have at present so little money, and so much humility about me, I don't know but I may follow a fool's advice.

LO. Why then, Sir, your fool advises you to lay aside all animosity and apply to Sir Novelty, your elder brother.

Y. FAS. Damn my elder brother!

LO. With all my heart; but get him to redeem your annuity, however.

Y. FAS. My annuity! 'Sdeath, he's such a dog, he would not give his powder-puff to redeem my soul.

LO. Look you, Sir, you must wheedle him, or you must starve.

Y. FAS. Look you, Sir, I will neither wheedle him nor starve.

LO. Why? What will you do then?

Y. FAS. I'll go into the army.

LO. You can't take the oaths; you are a Jacobite.

Y. FAS. Thou may'st as well say I can't take orders because I'm an atheist.

LO. Sir, I ask your pardon; I find I did not know the strength of your conscience so well as I did the weakness of your purse.

Y. FAS. Methinks, Sir, a person of your experience should have known that the strength of the conscience proceeds from the weakness of the purse.

LO. Sir, I am very glad to find you have a conscience able to take care of us, let it proceed from what it will; but I desire you'll please to consider that the army alone will be but a scanty maintenance for a person of your generosity (at least as rents now are paid); I shall see you stand in damnable need of some auxiliary guineas for your *menus plaisirs;* I will therefore turn fool once more for your service, and advise you to go directly to your brother.

Y. FAS. Art thou then so impregnable a blockhead to believe he'll help me with a farthing?

LO. Not if you treat him *de haut en bas,* as you use to do.

Y. FAS. Why, how would'st have me treat him?

LO. Like a trout—tickle him.

Y. FAS. I can't flatter.

LO. Can you starve?

Y. FAS. Yes.

LO. I can't; good-by t'ye, Sir—— *(going)*

Y. FAS. Stay, thou wilt distract me. What would'st thou have me say to him?

LO. Say nothing to him: apply yourself to his favourites; speak to his periwig, his cravat, his feather, his snuff-box, and when you are well with them—desire him to lend you a thousand pounds. I'll engage you prosper.

Y. FAS. 'Sdeath and Furies! why was that coxcomb thrust into the world before me? O Fortune—Fortune—thou art a bitch, by Gad! *(Exeunt.)*

SCENE III

SCENE: *A dressing-room*

Enter LORD FOPPINGTON *in his night-gown*

L. FOP. Page!

Enter Page

PAGE. Sir.

L. FOP. "Sir!" Pray, Sir, do me the favour to teach your tongue the title the king has thought fit to honour me with.

PAGE. I ask your Lordship's pardon, my Lord.

L. FOP. Oh, you can pronounce the word, then; I thought it would have choked you. D'ye hear?

PAGE. My Lord.

L. FOP. Call La Vérole; I would dress—— *(Exit Page.)* *(solus)* Well, 'tis an unspeakable pleasure to be a man of quality —strike me dumb!—"My Lord!"—"Your Lordship!"—"My Lord Foppington!"—*Ah! c'est quelque chose de beau, que le diable m'emporte.* Why, the ladies were ready to puke at me whilst I had nothing but Sir Navelty to recommend me to 'em. Sure, whilst I was but a knight, I was a very nauseous fellow. Well, 'tis ten thousand pawnd well given—stap my vitals——

Enter LA VÉROLE

L. V. Me Lord, de shoemaker, de tailor, de hosier, de seamstress, de barber, be all ready, if your Lordship please to be dress.

L. FOP. 'Tis well; admit 'em.

L. V. *Hey, messieurs, entrez.*

Enter Tailor, etc.

L. FOP. So, gentlemen, I hope you have all taken pains to
show yourselves masters in your professions.

TAI. I think I may presume to say, Sir——

L. V. "My Lord"—you clawn, you!

TAI. Why, is he made a lord?——My Lord, I ask your Lordship's pardon, my Lord; I hope, my Lord, your Lordship will
please to own I have brought your Lordship as accomplished a
suit of clothes as ever peer of England trod the stage in, my Lord:
will your Lordship please to try 'em now?

L. FOP. Ay, but let my people dispose the glasses so that I may
see myself before and behind; for I love to see myself all
raund——

Whilst he puts on his clothes, enter YOUNG FASHION *and* LORY

Y. FAS. Hey-dey, what the devil have we here? Sure my
gentleman's grown a favourite at Court, he has got so many
people at his levee.

LO. Sir, these people come in order to make him a favourite
at Court; they are to establish him with the ladies.

Y. FAS. Good God! to what an ebb of taste are women fallen,
that it should be in the power of a laced coat to recommend a
gallant to 'em.

LO. Sir, tailors and periwig-makers are now become the bawds
of the nation: 'tis they debauch all the women.

Y. FAS. Thou sayest true; for there's that fop now has not by
nature wherewithal to move a cook-maid, and by that time these
fellows have done with him, i'gad, he shall melt down a countess.

But now for my reception: I'll engage it shall be as cold a one
as a courtier's to his friend, who comes to put him in mind of his
promise.

L. FOP. (*to his tailor*) Death and eternal tartures! Sir, I say
the packet's too high by a foot.

TAI. My Lord, if it had been an inch lower it would not have held your Lordship's pocket-handkerchief.

L. FOP. Rat my pocket-handkerchief! Have not I a page to carry it? You may make him a packet up to his chin a purpose for it; but I will not have mine come so near my face.

TAI. 'Tis not for me to dispute your Lordship's fancy.

Y. FAS. (*to* LORY) His Lordship! Lory, did you observe that?

LO. Yes, Sir; I always thought 'twould end there. Now, I hope, you'll have a little more respect for him.

Y. FAS. Respect! Damn him for a coxcomb; now has he ruined his estate to buy a title, that he may be a fool of the first rate. But let's accost him. (*to* LORD FOPPINGTON) Brother, I'm your humble servant.

L. FOP. O Lard, Tam; I did not expect you in England: Brother, I am glad to see you.—(*turning to his tailor*) Look you, Sir, I shall never be reconciled to this nauseous packet; therefore pray get me another suit with all manner of expedition, for this is my eternal aversion. Mrs. Callicoe, are not you of my mind?
(*Exit Tailor.*)

SEAM. Oh, directly, my Lord; it can never be too low.

L. FOP. You are positively in the right on't, for the packet becomes no part of the body but the knee.

SEAM. I hope your Lordship is pleased with your steenkirk.

L. FOP. In love with it, stap my vitals. Bring your bill, you shall be paid to-marrow.

SEAM. I humbly thank your honour.   (*Exit Seamstress.*)

L. FOP. Hark thee, shoemaker, these shoes a'n't ugly, but they don't fit me.

SHOE. My Lord, my thinks they fit you very well.

L. FOP. They hurt me just below the instep.

SHOE. (*feeling his foot*) My Lord, they don't hurt you there.

L. FOP. I tell thee, they pinch me execrably.

SHOE. My Lord, if they pinch you, I'll be bound to be hanged, that's all.

L. FOP. Why, wilt thou undertake to persuade me I cannot feel?

SHOE. Your Lordship may please to feel what you think fit, but that shoe does not hurt you; I think I understand my trade.

L. FOP. Now by all that's great and powerful, thou art an incomprehensible coxcomb; but thou makest good shoes, and so I'll bear with thee.

SHOE. My Lord, I have worked for half the people of quality in town these twenty years; and 'twere very hard I should not know when a shoe hurts and when it don't.

L. FOP. Well, prithee begone about thy business.

(*Exit Shoemaker.*)

(*to the hosier*) Mr. Mend-legs, a word with you; the calves of these stockings are thickened a little too much. They make my legs look like a chairman's.

MEND. My Lord, my thinks they look mighty well.

L. FOP. Ay, but you are not so good a judge of these things as I am; I have studied 'em all my life; therefore pray let the next be the thickness of a crawnpiece less.——(*aside*) If the town takes notice my legs are fallen away, 'twill be attributed to the violence of some new intrigue.   (*Exit Hosier.*)

(*to the Periwig-maker*) Come, Mr. Foretop, let me see what you have done, and then the fatigue of the marning will be over.

FORETOP. My Lord, I have done what I defy any prince in Europe t' out-do; I have made you a periwig so long, and so full of hair, it will serve you for hat and cloak in all weathers.

L. FOP. Then thou hast made me thy friend to eternity: come, comb it out.

Y. FAS. Well, Lory, what dost think on't? A very friendly reception from a brother after three years' absence!

LO. Why, Sir, it's your own fault: we seldom care for those that don't love what we love; if you would creep into his heart, you must enter into his pleasures. Here have you stood ever since you came in, and have not commended any one thing that belongs to him.

Y. FAS. Nor never shall, whilst they belong to a coxcomb.

LO. Then, Sir, you must be content to pick a hungry bone.

Y. FAS. No, Sir, I'll crack it, and get to the marrow before I have done.

L. FOP. Gad's curse! Mr. Foretop, you don't intend to put this upon me for a full periwig?

FORE. Not a full one, my Lord? I don't know what your Lordship may please to call a full one, but I have crammed twenty ounces of hair into it.

L. FOP. What it may be by weight, Sir, I shall not dispute; but by tale, there are not nine hairs of a side.

FORE. O Lord! O Lord! O Lord! Why, as Gad shall judge me, your honour's side-face is reduced to the tip of your nose.

L. FOP. My side-face may be in eclipse for aught I know; but I'm sure my full-face is like the full moon

FORE. (*rubbing his eyes*) Heaven bless my eyesight! Sure I look through the wrong end of the perspective, for by my faith, an't please your honour, the broadest place I see in your face does not seem to me to be two inches diameter.

L. FOP. If it did, it would be just two inches too broad; far a periwig to a man should be like a mask to a woman: nothing should be seen but his eyes.

FORE. My Lord, I have done; if you please to have more hair in your wig, I'll put it in.

L. FOP. Passitively, yes.

FORE. Shall I take it back now, my Lord?

L. FOP. No: I'll wear it to-day, though it show such a manstrous pair of cheeks: stap my vitals, I shall be taken for a trumpeter.

(*Exit* FORETOP.)

Y. FAS. Now your people of business are gone, Brother, I hope I may obtain a quarter of an hour's audience of you.

L. FOP. Faith, Tam, I must beg you'll excuse me at this time, for I must away to the House of Lards immediately; my Lady Teaser's case is to come on to-day, and I would not be absent for the salvation of mankind.—— Hey, page! is the coach at the door?

PAGE. Yes, my Lord.

L. FOP. You'll excuse me, Brother. (*going*)

Y. FAS. Shall you be back at dinner?

L. FOP. As Gad shall jidge me, I can't tell; for 'tis passible I may dine with some of aur House at Lacket's.

Y. FAS. Shall I meet you there? for I must needs talk with you.

L. FOP. That, I'm afraid, mayn't be so praper; far the lards I commonly eat with are people of a nice conversation; and you know, Tam, your education has been a little at large: but if you'll stay here, you'll find a family dinner.—— Hey, fellow! What is there for dinner? There's beef: I suppose my brother will eat beef.—— Dear Tam, I'm glad to see thee in England, stap my vitals. (*Exit with his equipage.*)

Y. FAS. Hell and Furies, is this to be borne?

LO. Faith, Sir, I could almost have given him a knock o' th' pate myself.

Y. FAS. 'Tis enough; I will now show thee the excess of my passion by being very calm. Come, Lory, lay your loggerhead to mine, and in cool blood let us contrive his destruction.

LO. Here comes a head, Sir, would contrive it better than us both, if he would but join in the confederacy.

Enter COUPLER

Y. FAS. By this light, old Coupler alive still! Why, how now, matchmaker, art thou here still to plague the world with matrimony? You old bawd, how have you the impudence to be hobbling out of your grave twenty years after you are rotten!

COUP. When you begin to rot, Sirrah, you'll go off like a pippin; one winter will send you to the devil. What mischief brings you home again? Ha! you young lascivious rogue, you! let me put my hand in your bosom, Sirrah.

Y. FAS. Stand off, old Sodom.

COUP. Nay, prithee, now, don't be so coy.

Y. FAS. Keep your hands to yourself, you old dog you, or I'll wring your nose off.

COUP. Hast thou then been a year in Italy, and brought home a fool at last? By my conscience, the young fellows of this age profit no more by their going abroad than they do by their going to church. Sirrah, Sirrah, if you are not hanged before you come to my years, you'll know a cock from a hen. But come, I'm still a friend to thy person, though I have a contempt of thy understanding; and therefore I would willingly know thy condition, that I may see whether thou stand'st in need of my assistance; for widows swarm, my boy, the town's infected with 'em.

Y. FAS. I stand in need of anybody's assistance that will help me to cut my elder brother's throat, without the risk of being hanged for him.

COUP. I'gad, Sirrah, I could help thee to do him almost as good a turn, without the danger of being burnt in the hand for't.

Y. FAS. Sayest thou so, old Satan? Show me but that, and my soul is thine.

COUP. Pox o' thy soul! give me thy warm body, Sirrah; I shall have a substantial title to't when I tell thee my project.

Y. FAS. Out with it then, dear Dad, and take possession as soon as thou wilt.

COUP. Sayest thou so, my Hephestion? Why, then, thus lies the scene—but hold! who's that? if we are heard we are undone.

Y. FAS. What, have you forgot Lory?

COUP. Who? trusty Lory, is it thee?

LO. At your service, Sir.

COUP. Give me thy hand, old boy; i'gad, I did not know thee again; but I remember thy honesty, though I did not thy face; I think thou hadst like to have been hanged once or twice for thy master.

LO. Sir, I was very near once having that honour.

COUP. Well, live and hope; don't be discouraged; eat with him, and drink with him, and do what he bids thee, and it may be thy reward at last as well as another's. (*to* YOUNG FASHION) Well, Sir, you must know I have done you the kindness to make up a match for your brother.

Y. FAS. Sir, I am very much beholding to you, truly.

COUP. You may be, Sirrah, before the wedding-day yet; the lady is a great heiress; fifteen hundred pound a year, and a great bag of money; the match is concluded, the writings are drawn, and the pipkin's to be cracked in a fortnight. Now you must know, stripling (with respect to your mother), your brother's the son of a whore.

Y. FAS. Good!

COUP. He has given me a bond of a thousand pounds for helping him to this fortune, and has promised me as much more in ready money upon the day of marriage, which, I understand by a friend, he ne'er designs to pay me. If therefore you will be a generous young dog, and secure me five thousand pounds, I'll be a covetous old rogue, and help you to the lady.

Y. FAS. I'gad, if thou canst bring this about, I'll have thy statue cast in brass. But don't you dote, you old pander, you, when you talk at this rate?

COUP. That your youthful parts shall judge of. This plump partridge that I tell you of lives in the country, fifty miles off, with her honoured parents, in a lonely old house which nobody comes near; she never goes abroad, nor sees company at home; to prevent all misfortunes, she has her breeding within doors: the parson of the parish teaches her to play upon the bass-viol,

the clerk to sing, her nurse to dress, and her father to dance. In
short, nobody can give you admittance there but I; nor can I do
it any other way than by making you pass for your brother.

Y. FAS. And how the devil wilt thou do that?

COUP. Without the devil's aid, I warrant thee. Thy brother's
face not one of the family ever saw; the whole business has been
managed my me, and all the letters go through my hands: the
last that was writ to Sir Tunbelly Clumsey (for that's the old
gentleman's name) was to tell him his Lordship would be down
in a fortnight to consummate. Now you shall go away immediately, pretend you writ that letter only to have the romantic
pleasure of surprising your mistress, fall desperately in love as
soon as you see her; make that your plea for marrying her immediately, and when the fatigue of the wedding-night's over you
shall send me a swinging purse of gold, you dog, you.

Y. FAS. I'gad, old Dad, I'll put my hand in thy bosom now.

COUP. Ah, you young hot lusty thief, let me muzzle you—
(*kissing*)—Sirrah, let me muzzle you.

Y. FAS. (*aside*) Psha, the old lecher——

COUP. Well, I'll warrant thou hast not a farthing of money in
thy pocket now, no; one may see it in thy face——

Y. FAS. Not a souse, by Jupiter.

COUP. Must I advance then. Well, Sirrah, be at my lodgings in
half an hour, and I'll see what may be done; we'll sign and seal,
and eat a pullet, and when I have given thee some farther instructions, thou shalt hoist sail and be gone. (*kissing*) T'other
buss, and so adieu.

Y. FAS. Um, psha.

COUP. Ah, you young warm dog, you; what a delicious night
will the bride have on't!   (*Exit* COUPLER.)

Y. FAS. So, Lory: Providence, thou seest at last, takes care of
men of merit: we are in a fair way to be great people.

LO. Ay, Sir, if the devil don't step between the cup and the
lip, as he uses to do.

Y. FAS. Why, faith, he has played me many a damned trick to
spoil my fortune, and, i'gad, I'm almost afraid he's at work about
it again now; but if I should tell thee how, thou'dst wonder at
me.

LO. Indeed, Sir, I should not.

Y. FAS. How dost know?

LO. Because, Sir, I have wondered at you so often, I can wonder at you no more.

Y. FAS. No? what wouldst thou say if a qualm of conscience should spoil my design?

LO. I would eat my words, and wonder more than ever.

Y. FAS. Why, faith, Lory, though I am a young rake-hell, and have played many a roguish trick, this is so full-grown a cheat, I find I must take pains to come up to't; I have scruples.

LO. They are strong symptoms of death; if you find they increase, pray, Sir, make your will.

Y. FAS. No, my conscience shan't starve me, neither. But thus far I will harken to it, before I execute this project. I'll try my brother to the bottom; I'll speak to him with the temper of a philosopher; my reasons (though they press him home) shall yet be clothed with so much modesty, not one of all the truths they urge shall be so naked to offend his sight: if he has yet so much humanity about him as to assist me (though with a moderate aid) I'll drop my project at his feet, and show him I can—do for him much more than what I ask he'd do for me. This one conclusive trial of him I resolve to make.

Succeed or no, still victory's my lot;
If I subdue his heart, 'tis well; if not,
I shall subdue my conscience to my plot.   (*Exeunt.*)

ACT II

Enter LOVELESS *and* AMANDA

LOV. How do you like these lodgings, my dear? For my part, I am so well pleased with 'em, I shall hardly remove whilst we stay in town, if you are satisfied.

AMAN. I am satisfied with everything that pleases you; else I had not come to town at all.

LOV. Oh, a little of the noise and bustle of the world sweetens the pleasures of retreat: we shall find the charms of our retirement doubled when we return to it.

AMAN. That pleasing prospect will be my chiefest entertainment, whilst (much against my will) I am obliged to stand surrounded with these empty pleasures which 'tis so much the fashion to be fond of.

LOV. I own most of 'em are indeed but empty; nay, so empty, that one would wonder by what magic power they act, when they induce us to be vicious for their sakes. Yet some there are we may speak kindlier of: there are delights (of which a private life is destitute) which may divert an honest man, and be a harmless entertainment to a virtuous woman. The conversation of the town is one; and truly (with some small allowances) the plays, I think, may be esteemed another.

AMAN. The plays, I must confess, have some small charms, and would have more would they restrain that loose, obscene encouragement to vice which shocks, if not the virtue of some women, at least the modesty of all.

LOV. But till that reformation can be made I would not leave the wholesome corn for some intruding tares that grow amongst it. Doubtless the moral of a well-wrought scene is of prevailing force. Last night there happened one that moved me strangely.

AMAN. Pray, what was that?

LOV. Why, 'twas about—but 'tis not worth repeating.

AMAN. Yes, pray let me know it.

LOV. No, I think 'tis as well let alone.

AMAN. Nay, now you make me have a mind to know.

LOV. 'Twas a foolish thing: you'd perhaps grow jealous should I tell it you, though without cause, heaven knows.

AMAN. I shall begin to think I have cause, if you persist in making it a secret.

LOV. I'll then convince you you have none, by making it no longer so. Know then, I happened in the play to find my very character, only with the addition of a relapse, which struck me so I put a sudden stop to a most harmless entertainment which till then diverted me between the acts. 'Twas to admire the workmanship of Nature in the face of a young lady that sate some distance from me, she was so exquisitely handsome.

AMAN. "So exquisitely handsome!"

LOV. Why do you repeat my words, my dear?

AMAN. Because you seemed to speak 'em with such pleasure I thought I might oblige you with their echo.

LOV. Then you are alarmed, Amanda?

AMAN. It is my duty to be so, when you are in danger.

LOV. You are too quick in apprehending for me; all will be

well when you have heard me out. I do confess I gazed upon her, nay, eagerly I gazed upon her.

AMAN. Eagerly? That's with desire.

LOV. No, I desired her not: I viewed her with a world of admiration, but not one glance of love.

AMAN. Take heed of trusting to such nice distinctions.

LOV. I did take heed; for, observing in the play that he who seemed to represent me there was, by an accident like this unwarily surprised into a net in which he lay a poor entangled slave, and brought a train of mischiefs on his head, I snatched my eyes away; they pleaded hard for leave to look again, but I grew absolute, and they obeyed.

AMAN. Were they the only things that were inquisitive? Had I been in your place, my tongue, I fancy, had been curious, too: I should have asked her name, and where she lived (yet still without design). Who was she, pray?

LOV. Indeed I cannot tell.

AMAN. You will not tell.

LOV. By all that's sacred, then, I did not ask.

AMAN. Nor do you know what company was with her?

LOV. I do not.

AMAN. Then I am calm again.

LOV. Why were you disturbed?

AMAN. Had I then no cause?

LOV. None, certainly.

AMAN. I thought I had.

LOV. But you thought wrong, Amanda; for turn the case, and let it be your story. Should you come home, and tell me you had seen a handsome man, should I grow jealous because you had eyes?

AMAN. But should I tell you he were exquisitely so; that I had gazed on him with admiration; that I had looked with eager eyes upon him; should you not think 'twere possible I might go one step farther, and enquire his name?

LOV. (*aside*) She has reason on her side: I have talked too much; but I must turn it off another way. (*to* AMANDA) Will you then make no difference, Amanda, between the language of our sex and yours? There is a modesty restrains your tongues which makes you speak by halves when you commend; but rov-

ing flattery gives a loose to ours, which makes us still speak
double what we think: you should not therefore in so strict a
sense take what I said to her advantage.

AMAN. Those flights of flattery, Sir, are to our faces only: when
women once are out of hearing, you are as modest in your com-
mendations as we are. But I shan't put you to the trouble of
farther excuses; if you please, this business shall rest here. Only
give me leave to wish, both for your peace and mine, that you
may never meet this miracle of beauty more.

LOV. I am content.

Enter Servant

SERV. Madam, there's a young lady at the door in a chair, desires to know whether your ladyship sees company. I think her
name is Berinthia.

AMAN. Oh dear! 'tis a relation I have not seen these five
years.—— Pray her to walk in.   (*Exit Servant.*)
(*to* LOVELESS) Here's another beauty for you. She was young
when I saw her last; but I hear she's grown extremely handsome.

LOV. Don't you be jealous now, for I shall gaze upon her too.

Enter BERINTHIA

LOV. (*aside*) Ha! By heavens, the very woman!

BER. (*saluting* AMANDA) Dear Amanda, I did not expect to
meet with you in town.

AMAN. Sweet Cousin, I'm overjoyed to see you. (*to* LOVELESS)
Mr. Loveless, here's a relation and a friend of mine I desire
you'll be better acquainted with.

LOV. (*saluting* BERINTHIA) If my wife never desires a harder
thing, Madam, her request will be easily granted.

BER. (*to* AMANDA) I think, Madam, I ought to wish you joy.

AMAN. Joy! Upon what?

BER. Upon your marriage: you were a widow when I saw you
last.

LOV. You ought rather, Madam, to wish me joy upon that,
since I am the only gainer.

BER. If she has got so good a husband as the world reports,
she has gained enough to expect the compliments of her friends
upon it.

LOV. If the world is so favourable to me, to allow I deserve that title, I hope 'tis so just to my wife to own I derive it from her.

BER. Sir, it is so just to you both, to own you are, and deserve to be, the happiest pair that live in it.

LOV. I'm afraid we shall lose that character, Madam, whenever you happen to change your condition.

Enter Servant

SERV. Sir, my Lord Foppington presents his humble service to you, and desires to know how you do. He but just now heard you were in town. He's at the next door; and if it be not inconvenient, he'll come and wait upon you.

LOV. Lord Foppington! I know him not.

BER. Not his dignity, perhaps, but you do his person. 'Tis Sir Novelty; he has bought a barony in order to marry a great fortune: his patent has not been passed eight-and-forty hours, and he has already sent how-do-ye's to all the town, to make 'em acquainted with his title.

LOV. Give my service to his Lordship, and let him know I am proud of the honour he intends me.   (*Exit Servant.*)
Sure this addition of quality must have so improved this coxcomb, he can't but be very good company for a quarter of an hour.

AMAN. Now it moves my pity more than my mirth, to see a man whom nature has made no fool be so very industrious to pass for an ass.

LOV. No, there you are wrong, Amanda; you should never bestow your pity upon those who take pains for your contempt. Pity those whom nature abuses, but never those who abuse nature.

BER. Besides, the town would be robbed of one of its chief diversions, if it should become a crime to laugh at a fool.

AMAN. I could never yet perceive the town inclined to part with any of its diversions for the sake of their being crimes; but I have seen it very fond of some I think had little else to recommend 'em.

BER. I doubt, Amanda, you are grown its enemy, you speak with so much warmth against it.

AMAN. I must confess I am not much its friend.

BER. Then give me leave to make you mine, by not engaging in its quarrel.

AMAN. You have many stronger claims than that, Berinthia, whenever you think fit to plead your title.

LOV. You have done well to engage a second, my dear; for here comes one will be apt to call you to an account for your country principles.

Enter LORD FOPPINGTON

L. FOP. (*to* LOVELESS) Sir, I am your most humble servant.

LOV. I wish you joy, my Lord.

L. FOP. O Lard, Sir!—— Madam, your Ladyship's welcome to tawn.

AMAN. I wish your Lordship joy.

L. FOP. O heavens, Madam!

LOV. My Lord, this young lady is a relation of my wife's.

L. FOP. (*saluting her*) The beautifullest race of people upon earth, rat me. Dear Loveless, I am overjoyed to see you have braught your family to tawn again: I am, stap my vitals—(*aside*) far I design to lie with your wife. (*to* AMANDA) Far Gad's sake, Madam, haw has your Ladyship been able to subsist thus long under the fatigue of a country life?

AMAN. My life has been very far from that, my Lord; it has been a very quiet one.

L. FOP. Why, that's the fatigue I speak of, Madam, for 'tis impossible to be quiet without thinking: now thinking is to me the greatest fatigue in the world.

AMAN. Does not your Lordship love reading, then?

L. FOP. Oh, passionately, Madam—but I never think of what I read.

BER. Why, can your Lordship read without thinking?

L. FOP. O Lard—can your Ladyship pray without devotion— Madam?

AMAN. Well, I must own I think books the best entertainment in the world.

L. FOP. I am so much of your Ladyship's mind, Madam, that I have a private gallery, where I walk sometimes, is furnished with nothing but books and looking-glasses. Madam, I have gilded 'em, and ranged 'em so prettily, before Gad, it is the most entertaining thing in the world to walk and look upon 'em.

AMAN. Nay, I love a neat library too; but 'tis, I think, the inside of the book should recommend it most to us.

L. FOP. That, I must confess, I am nat altogether so fand of. Far to mind the inside of a book is to entertain one's self with the forced product of another man's brain. Naw I think a man of quality and breeding may be much better diverted with the natural sprauts of his own. But to say the truth, Madam, let a man love reading never so well, when once he comes to know this tawn he finds so many better ways of passing the four-and-twenty hours that 'twere ten thousand pities he should consume his time in that. Far example, Madam, my life; my life, Madam, is a perpetual stream of pleasure, that glides through such a variety of entertainments I believe the wisest of our ancestors never had the least conception of any of 'em. I rise, Madam, about ten a'clack. I don't rise sooner, because 'tis the worst thing in the world for the complexion; nat that I pretend to be a beau, but a man must endeavour to look wholesome, lest he make so nauseous a figure in the side-box, the ladies should be compelled to turn their eyes upon the play. So at ten a'clack, I say, I rise. Naw, if I find 'tis a good day, I resalve to take a turn in the park, and see the fine women; so huddle on my clothes, and get dressed by one. If it be nasty weather, I take a turn in the chocolate-hause, where, as you walk, Madam, you have the prettiest prospect in the world; you have looking-glasses all round you.——But I'm afraid I tire the company?

BER. Not at all. Pray go on.

L. FOP. Why then, ladies, from thence I go to dinner at Lacket's, where you are so nicely and delicately served that, stap my vitals, they shall compose you a dish no bigger than a saucer, shall come to fifty shillings. Between eating my dinner, and washing my mauth, ladies, I spend my time till I go to the play, where, till nine a'clack, I entertain myself with looking upon the company; and usually dispose of one hour more in leading 'em aut. So there's twelve of the four-and-twenty pretty well over. The other twelve, Madam, are disposed of in two articles: in the first four I toast myself drunk, and in t'other eight I sleep myself sober again. Thus, ladies, you see my life is an eternal raund O of delights.

LOV. 'Tis a heavenly one, indeed.

AMAN. But I thought, my Lord, you beaux spent a great deal

of your time in intrigues: you have given us no account of them yet.

L. FOP. (*aside*) Soh! she would enquire into my amours—that's jealousy—she begins to be in love with me. (*to* AMANDA) Why, Madam—as to time for my intrigues, I usually make detachments of it from my other pleasures, according to the exigency. Far your Ladyship may please to take notice that those who intrigue with women of quality have rarely occasion far above half an hour at a time: people of that rank being under those decorums they can seldom give you a langer view than will just serve to shoot 'em flying. So that the course of my other pleasures is not very much interrupted by my amours.

LOV. But your Lordship now is become a pillar of the state; you must attend the weighty affairs of the nation.

L. FOP. Sir—as to weighty affairs—I leave them to weighty heads. I never intend mine shall be a burthen to my body.

LOV. Oh, but you'll find the House will expect your attendance.

L. FOP. Sir, you'll find the House will compound for my appearance.

LOV. But your friends will take it ill if you don't attend their particular causes.

L. FOP. Not, Sir, if I come time enough to give 'em my particular vote.

BER. But pray, my Lord, how do you dispose of yourself on Sundays? for that, methinks, is a day should hang wretchedly upon your hands.

L. FOP. Why, faith, Madam—Sunday—is a vile day, I must confess. I intend to move for leave to bring in a bill that the players may work upon it, as well as the hackney coaches. Though this I must say for the Government, it leaves us the churches to entertain us—but then again, they begin so abominably early, a man must rise by candle-light to get dressed by the psalm.

BER. Pray, which church does your Lordship most oblige with your presence?

L. FOP. Oh, St. James's, Madam—there's much the best company.

AMAN. Is there good preaching too?

L. FOP. Why, faith, Madam—I can't tell. A man must have very little to do there, that can give an account of the sermon.

BER. You can give us an account of the ladies, at least?

L. FOP. Or I deserve to be excommunicated. There is my Lady
Tattle, my Lady Prate, my Lady Titter, my Lady Leer, my Lady
Giggle, and my Lady Grin. These sit in the front of the boxes,
and all church-time are the prettiest company in the world, stap
my vitals. (*to* AMANDA) Mayn't we hope for the honour to see
your Ladyship added to our society, Madam?

AMAN. Alas, my Lord, I am the worst company in the world at
church: I'm apt to mind the prayers, or the sermon, or——

L. FOP. One is indeed strangely apt at church to mind what
one should not do. But I hope, Madam, at one time or other,
I shall have the honour to lead your Ladyship to your coach there.
(*aside*) Methinks she seems strangely pleased with everything
I say to her. 'Tis a vast pleasure to receive encouragement from
a woman before her husband's face—I have a good mind to
pursue my conquest, and speak the thing plainly to her at once.
I'gad, I'll do 't, and that in so cavalier a manner she shall be
surprised at it.—— Ladies, I'll take my leave; I'm afraid I begin
to grow troublesome with the length of my visit.

AMAN. Your Lordship's too entertaining to grow troublesome
anywhere.

L. FOP. (*aside*) That now was as much as if she had said "Pray
lie with me." I'll let her see I'm quick of apprehension. (*to*
AMANDA) O Lard, Madam, I had like to have forgot a secret I
must needs tell your ladyship. (*to* LOVELESS) Ned, you must not
be so jealous now as to listen.

LOV. Not I, my Lord; I am too fashionable a husband to pry
into the secrets of my wife.

L. FOP. (*to* AMANDA, *squeezing her hand*) I am in love with
you to desperation, strike me speechless.

AMAN. (*giving him a box o' th' ear*) Then thus I return your
passion—an impudent fool!

L. FOP. Gad's curse, Madam, I'm a peer of the realm.

LOV. Hey; what the devil! do you affront my wife, Sir? Nay,
then——

(*They draw and fight. The women run shrieking for help.*)

AMAN. Ah! What has my folly done? Help! Murder, help! Part
'em, for heaven's sake!

L. FOP. (*falling back, and leaning upon his sword*) Ah—quite
through the body—stap my vitals.

Enter Servants

LOV. (*running to him*) I hope I han't killed the fool, however.
—— Bare him up!—— Where's your wound?

L. FOP. Just through the guts.

LOV. Call a surgeon there: unbutton him quickly.

L. FOP. Ay, pray make haste.   (*Exit Servant.*)

LOV. This mischief you may thank yourself for.

L. FOP. I may so—love's the devil indeed, Ned.

Enter SERRINGE *and Servant*

SERV. Here's Mr. Serringe, Sir, was just going by the door.

L. FOP. He's the welcom'st man alive.

SER. Stand by, stand by, stand by. Pray, gentlemen, stand by.
Lord have mercy upon us! did you never see a man run through
the body before? Pray stand by.

L. FOP. Ah, Mr. Serringe—I'm a dead man.

SER. A dead man, and I by—I should laugh to see that, i'gad.

LOV. Prithee don't stand prating, but look upon his wound.

SER. Why, what if I won't look upon his wound this hour, Sir?

LOV. Why, then he'll bleed to death, Sir.

SER. Why, then I'll fetch him to life again, Sir.

LOV. 'Slife, he's run through the guts, I tell thee.

SER. Would he were run through the heart: I should get the
more credit by his cure. Now I hope you're satisfied?—— Come,
now let me come at him; now let me come at him. (*viewing his
wound*) Oons, what a gash is here!—— Why, Sir, a man may
drive a coach and six horses into your body.

L. FOP. Ho!——

SER. Why, what the devil! have you run the gentleman through
with a scythe?—— (*aside*) A little prick between the skin and
the ribs, that's all.

LOV. Let me see his wound.

SER. Then you shall dress it, Sir; for if anybody looks upon it,
I won't.

LOV. Why, thou art the veriest coxcomb I ever saw.

SER. Sir, I am not master of my trade for nothing.

L. FOP. Surgeon!

SER. Well, Sir?

L. FOP. Is there any hopes?

SER. Hopes? I can't tell. What are you willing to give for your cure?

L. FOP. Five hundred paunds with pleasure.

SER. Why, then perhaps there may be hopes. But we must avoid farther delay. Here, help the gentleman into a chair, and carry him to my house presently: that's the properest place—(*aside*) to bubble him out of his money.—— Come, a chair, a chair quickly—there, in with him.

(They put him into a chair.)

L. FOP. Dear Loveless—adieu. If I die—I forgive thee; and if I live—I hope thou'lt do as much by me. I'm very sorry you and I should quarrel; but I hope here's an end on't, for if you are satisfied—I am.

LOV. I shall hardly think it worth my prosecuting any farther, so you may be at rest, Sir.

L. FOP. Thou art a generous fellow, strike me dumb. (*aside*) But thou hast an impertinent wife, stap my vitals.

SER. So, carry him off, carry him off; we shall have him prate himself into a fever by and by; carry him off.

(Exit SERRINGE *with* LORD FOPPINGTON.)

AMAN. Now on my knees, my dear, let me ask your pardon for my indiscretion: my own I never shall obtain.

LOV. Oh! there's no harm done: you served him well.

AMAN. He did indeed deserve it. But I tremble to think how dear my indiscreet resentment might have cost you.

LOV. Oh, no matter; never trouble yourself about that.

BER. For heaven's sake, what was't he did to you?

AMAN. Oh, nothing; he only squeezed me kindly by the hand and frankly offered me a coxcomb's heart. I know I was to blame to resent it as I did, since nothing but a quarrel could ensue. But the fool so surprised me with his insolence I was not mistress of my fingers.

BER. Now I dare swear he thinks you had 'em at great command, they obeyed you so readily.

Enter WORTHY

WOR. Save you, save you, good people; I'm glad to find you all alive; I met a wounded peer carrying off. For heaven's sake, what was the matter?

LOV. Oh, a trifle: he would have lain with my wife before my face, so she obliged him with a box o' the ear, and I run him through the body: that was all.

WOR. Bagatelle on all sides. But, pray, Madam, how long has this noble lord been an humble servant of yours?

AMAN. This is the first I have heard on't. So I suppose 'tis his quality, more, than his love, has brought him into this adventure. He thinks his title an authentic passport to every woman's heart, below the degree of a peeress.

WOR. He's coxcomb enough to think anything. But I would not have you brought into trouble for him: I hope there's no danger of his life?

LOV. None at all: he's fallen into the hands of a roguish surgeon I perceive designs to frighten a little money out of him. But I saw his wound—'tis nothing; he may got to the play to-night if he pleases.

WOR. I am glad you have corrected him without farther mischief. And now, Sir, if these ladies have no farther service for you, you'll oblige me if you can go to the place I spoke to you of t'other day.

LOV. With all my heart. (*aside*) Though I could wish, methinks, to stay and gaze a little longer on that creature. Good gods! how beautiful she is!—but what have I to do with beauty? I have already had my portion, and must not covet more. (*to* WORTHY) Come, Sir, when you please.

WOR. Ladies, your servant.

AMAN. Mr. Loveless, pray one word with you before you go.

LOV. (*to* WORTHY) I'll overtake you, Sir. (*Exit* WORTHY.)——What would my dear?

AMAN. Only a woman's foolish question; how do you like my cousin here?

LOV. Jealous already, Amanda?

AMAN. Not at all; I ask you for another reason.

LOV. (*aside*) Whate'er her reason be, I must not tell her true. (*to* AMANDA) Why, I confess she's handsome. But you must not think I slight your kinswoman if I own to you, of all the women who may claim that character she is the last would triumph in my heart.

AMAN. I'm satisfied.

LOV. Now tell me why you asked.

AMAN. At night I will. Adieu.

LOV. (*kissing her*) I'm yours. (*Exit* LOVELESS.)

AMAN. (*aside*) I'm glad to find he does not like her; for I have a great mind to persuade her to come and live with me. (*to* BERINTHIA) Now, dear Berinthia, let me enquire a little into your affairs: for I do assure you I am enough your friend to interest myself in everything that concerns you.

BER. You formerly have given me such proofs on't I should be very much to blame to doubt it. I am sorry I have no secrets to trust you with, that I might convince you how entire a confidence I durst repose in you.

AMAN. Why, is it possible that one so young and beautiful as you should live and have no secrets?

BER. What secrets do you mean?

AMAN. Lovers.

BER. Oh, twenty; but not one secret one amongst 'em. Lovers in this age have too much honour to do anything underhand; they do all aboveboard.

AMAN. That, now, methinks, would make me hate a man.

BER. But the women of the town are of another mind: for by this means a lady may, with the expense of a few coquet glances, lead twenty fools about in a string for two or three years together. Whereas, if she should allow 'em greater favours, and oblige 'em to secrecy, she would not keep one of 'em a fortnight.

AMAN. There's something indeed in that to satisfy the vanity of a woman, but I can't comprehend how the men find their account in it.

BER. Their entertainment, I must confess, is a riddle to me. For there's very few of 'em ever get farther than a bow and an ogle. I have half a score for my share, who follow me all over the town; and at the play, the park, and the church do (with their eyes) say the violent'st things to me—but I never hear any more of 'em.

AMAN. What can be the reason of that?

BER. One reason is they don't know how to go farther. They have had so little practice they don't understand the trade. But besides their ignorance, you must know there is not one of my half-score lovers but what follows half a score mistresses. Now their affections, being divided amongst so many, are not strong enough for any one to make 'em pursue her to the purpose. Like a young puppy in a warren, they have a flirt at all, and catch none.

AMAN. Yet they seem to have a torrent of love to dispose of.

BER. They have so: but 'tis like the rivers of a modern philosopher (whose works, though a woman, I have read): it sets out with a violent stream, splits in a thousand branches, and is all lost in the sands.

AMAN. But do you think this river of love runs all its course without doing any mischief? Do you think it overflows nothing?

BER. Oh yes; 'tis true, it never breaks into anybody's ground that has the least fence about it; but it overflows all the commons that lie in its way. And this is the utmost achievement of those dreadful champions in the field of love—the beaux.

AMAN. But prithee, Berinthia, instruct me a little farther, for I'm so great a novice, I am almost ashamed on't. My husband's leaving me whilst I was young and fond threw me into that depth of discontent that ever since I have led so private and recluse a life my ignorance is scarce conceivable. I therefore fain would be instructed; not, heaven knows, that what you call intrigues have any charms for me: my love and principles are too well fixed. The practic part of all unlawful love is——

BER. Oh, 'tis abominable: but for the speculative—that we must all confess is entertaining. The conversation of all the virtuous women in the town turns upon that and new clothes.

AMAN. Pray be so just then to me to believe 'tis with a world of innocency I would enquire whether you think those women we call women of reputation do really 'scape all other men, as they do those shadows of 'em, the beaux.

BER. Oh no, Amanda; there are a sort of men make dreadful work amongst 'em: men that may be called the beaux' antipathy, for they agree in nothing but walking upon two legs.

These have brains: the beau has none.

These are in love with their mistress: the beau with himself.

They take care of her reputation: he's industrious to destroy it.

They are decent: he's a fop.

They are sound: he's rotten.

They are men: he's an ass.

AMAN. If this be their character, I fancy we had here e'en now a pattern of 'em both.

BER. His Lordship and Mr. Worthy?

AMAN. The same.

BER. As for the lord, he's eminently so: and for the ▨
assure you there's not a man in town who has a be▨
with the women that are worth having an interest wi▨
all private: he's like a back-stair minister at Court, wh▨ ▨ust
the reputed favourites are sauntering in the bed-chamber, is
ruling the roast in the closet.

AMAN. He answers then the opinion I had ever of him.
Heavens! what a difference there is between a man like him and
that vain, nauseous fop, Sir Novelty! (*taking her hand*) I must
acquaint you with a secret, Cousin. 'Tis not that fool alone has
talked to me of love: Worthy has been tampering too. 'Tis true,
he has done't in vain: not all his charms or art have power to
shake me. My love, my duty, and my virtue are such faithful
guards, I need not fear my heart should e'er betray me. But
what I wonder at is this: I find I did not start at his proposal,
as when it came from one whom I contemned. I therefore mention his attempt that I may learn from you whence it proceeds
that vice, which cannot change its nature, should so far change
at least its shape as that the self-same crime proposed from one
shall seem a monster gaping at your ruin, when from another it
shall look so kind as though it were your friend, and never meant
to harm you.

Whence, think you, can this difference proceed? For 'tis not
love, heaven knows.

BER. Oh, no. I would not for the world believe it were. But
possibly, should there a dreadful sentence pass upon you to
undergo the rage of both their passions, the pain you'd apprehend from one might seem so trivial to the other, the danger
would not quite so much alarm you.

AMAN. Fy, fy, Berinthia! You would indeed alarm me, could
you incline me to a thought that all the merit of mankind combined could shake that tender love I bear my husband. No, he
sits triumphant in my heart, and nothing can dethrone him.

BER. But should he abdicate again, do you think you should
preserve the vacant throne ten tedious winters more, in hopes of
his return?

AMAN. Indeed I think I should. Though I confess, after those
obligations he has to me, should he abandon me once more, my

...art would grow extremely urgent with me to root him thence, and cast him out forever.

BER. Were I that thing they call a slighted wife, somebody should run the risk of being that thing they call—a husband.

AMAN. Oh fy, Berinthia! No revenge should ever be taken against a husband: but to wrong his bed is a vengeance, which of all vengeance——

BER. Is the sweetest—ha, ha, ha! Don't I talk madly?

AMAN. Madly indeed.

BER. Yet I'm very innocent.

AMAN. That I dare swear you are. I know how to make allowances for your humour: you were always very entertaining company; but I find since marriage and widowhood have shown you the world a little, you are very much improved.

BER. (aside) Alack-a-day, there has gone more than that to improve me, if she knew all.

AMAN. For heaven's sake, Berinthia, tell me what way I shall take to persuade you to come and live with me.

BER. Why, one way in the world there is—and but one.

AMAN. Pray which is that?

BER. It is to assure me—I shall be very welcome.

AMAN. If that be all, you shall e'en lie here to-night.

BER. To-night?

AMAN. Yes, to-night.

BER. Why, the people where I lodge will think me mad.

AMAN. Let 'em think what they please.

BER. Say you so, Amanda? Why then they shall think what they please: for I'm a young widow, and I care not what anybody thinks. Ah, Amanda, it's a delicious thing to be a young widow.

AMAN. You'll hardly make me think so.

BER. Phu, because you are in love with your husband: but that is not every woman's case.

AMAN. I hope 'twas yours, at least.

BER. Mine, say ye? Now have I a great mind to tell you a lie, but I should do it so awkwardly you'd find me out.

AMAN. Then e'en speak the truth.

BER. Shall I? Then after all, I did love him, Amanda—as a nun does penance.

AMAN. Why did not you refuse to marry him, then?

BER. Because my mother would have whipped me.

AMAN. How did you live together?

BER. Like man and wife—asunder;
He loved the country, I the town:
He hawks and hounds, I coaches and equipage:
He eating and drinking, I carding and playing:
He the sound of a horn, I the squeak of a fiddle.
We were dull company at table, worse abed.
Whenever we met, we gave one another the spleen.
And never agreed but once, which was about lying alone.

AMAN. But tell me one thing truly and sincerely.

BER. What's that?

AMAN. Notwithstanding all these jars, did not his death at last —extremely trouble you?

BER. Oh, yes: not that my present pangs were so very violent, but the after-pains were intolerable. I was forced to wear a beastly widow's band a twelve-month for't.

AMAN. Women, I find, have different inclinations.

BER. Women, I find, keep different company. When your husband ran away from you, if you had fallen into some of my acquaintance, 'twould have saved you many a tear. But you go and live with a grandmother, a bishop, and an old nurse, which was enough to make any woman break her heart for her husband. Pray, Amanda, if ever you are a widow again, keep yourself so as I do.

AMAN. Why, do you then resolve you'll never marry?

BER. Oh, no; I resolve I will.

AMAN. How so?

BER. That I never may.

AMAN. You banter me.

BER. Indeed I don't. But I consider I'm a woman, and form my resolutions accordingly.

AMAN. Well, my opinion is, form what resolution you will, matrimony will be the end on't.

BER. Faith it won't.

AMAN. How do you know?

BER. I'm sure on't.

AMAN. Why, do you think 'tis impossible for you to fall in love?

BER. No.

AMAN. Nay, but to grow so passionately fond that nothing but the man you love can give you rest?

BER. Well, what then?

AMAN. Why, then you'll marry him.

BER. How do you know that?

AMAN. Why, what can you do else?

BER. Nothing—but sit and cry.

AMAN. Psha!

BER. Ah, poor Amanda, you have led a country life: but if you'll consult the widows of this town, they'll tell you you should never take a lease of a house you can hire for a quarter's warning.

(*Exeunt.*)

ACT III

SCENE I

Enter LORD FOPPINGTON *and Servant*

L. FOP. Hey, fellow, let the coach come to the door.

SERV. Will your Lordship venture so soon to expose yourself to the weather?

L. FOP. Sir, I will venture as soon as I can to expose myself to the ladies: though give me my cloak, however, for in that side-box, what between the air that comes in at the door on one side, and the intolerable warmth of the masks on t'other, a man gets so many heats and colds, 'twould destroy the canstitution of a harse.

SERV. (*putting on his cloak*) I wish your Lordship would please to keep house a little longer; I'm afraid your honour does not well consider your wound.

L. FOP. My wound?—I would not be in eclipse another day, though I had as many wounds in my guts as I have had in my heart.

Enter YOUNG FASHION

Y. FAS. Brother, your servant: how do you find yourself to-day?

L. FOP. So well that I have ardered my coach to the door: so there's no great danger of death this baut, Tam.

Y. FAS. I'm very glad of it.

L. FOP. (*aside*) That I believe's a lie.—— Prithee, Tam, tell me one thing: did nat your heart cut a caper up to your mauth, when you heard I was run through the bady?

Y. FAS. Why do you think it should?

L. FOP. Because I remember mine did so, when I heard my father was shat through the head.

Y. FAS. It then did very ill.

L. FOP. Prithee, why so?

Y. FAS. Because he used you very well.

L. FOP. Well?—naw strike me dumb, he starved me. He has let me want a thausand women for want of a thausand paund.

Y. FAS. Then he hindered you from making a great many ill bargains, for I think no woman is worth money that will take money.

L. FOP. If I were a younger brother, I should think so too.

Y. FAS. Why, is it possible you can value a woman that's to be bought?

L. FOP. Prithee, why not as well as a pad-nag?

Y. FAS. Because a woman has a heart to dispose of; a horse has none.

L. FOP. Look you, Tam, of all things that belang to a woman, I have an aversion to her heart; far when once a woman has given you her heart—you can never get rid of the rest of her bady.

Y. FAS. This is strange doctrine. But pray, in your amours how is it with your own heart?

L. FOP. Why, my heart in my amours—is like my heart aut of my amours: *à la glace.*

My bady, Tam, is a watch, and my heart is the pendulum to it; whilst the finger runs raund to every hour in the circle, that still beats the same time.

Y. FAS. Then you are seldom much in love?

L. FOP. Never, stap my vitals.

Y. FAS. Why then did you make all this bustle about Amanda?

L. FOP. Because she was a woman of an insolent virtue, and I thought myself picked in honour to debauch her.

Y. FAS. Very well. (*aside*) Here's a rare fellow for you, to have the spending of five thousand pounds a year. But now for my business with him. (*To* LORD FOPPINGTON.)—Brother, though I know to talk to you of business (especially of money) is a theme not quite so entertaining to you as that of the ladies, my necessities are such I hope you'll have patience to hear me.

L. FOP. The greatness of your necessities, Tam, is the worst argument in the world far your being patiently heard. I do believe you are going to make me a very good speech, but, strike me dumb, it has the worst beginning of any speech I have heard this twelvemonth.

Y. FAS. I'm very sorry you think so.

L. FOP. I do believe thau art. But come, let's know thy affair quickly; far 'tis a new play, and I shall be so rumpled and squeezed with pressing through the crawd to get to my servant the women will think I have lain all night in my clothes.

Y. FAS. Why then (that I may not be the author of so great a misfortune) my case in a word is this: the necessary expenses of my travels have so much exceeded the wretched income of my annuity that I have been forced to mortgage it for five hundred pounds, which is spent; so that unless you are so kind to assist me in redeeming it, I know no remedy but to go take a purse.

L. FOP. Why, faith, Tam—to give you my sense of the thing, I do think taking a purse the best remedy in the world; for if you succeed, you are relieved that way; if you are taken—you are relieved t'other.

Y. FAS. I'm glad to see you are in so pleasant a humour; I hope I shall find the effects on't.

L. FOP. Why, do you then really think it a reasonable thing I should give you five hundred paunds?

Y. FAS. I do not ask it as a due, Brother; I am willing to receive it as a favour.

L. FOP. Thau art willing to receive it any haw, strike me speechless. But these are damned times to give money in: taxes are so great, repairs so exorbitant, tenants such rogues, and periwigs so dear, that the devil take me, I am reduced to that extremity in my cash I have been forced to retrench in that one article of sweet pawder, till I have braught it dawn to five guineas a manth. Naw judge, Tam, whether I can spare you five hundred paunds?

Y. FAS. If you can't, I must starve, that's all. (*aside*) Damn him!

L. FOP. All I can say is, you should have been a better husband.

Y. FAS. 'Oons, if you can't live upon five thousand a year, how do you think I should do't upon two hundred?

L. FOP. Don't be in a passion, Tam, far passion is the most unbecoming thing in the world—to the face. Look you, I don't love to say anything to you to make you melancholy; but upon this occasion I must take leave to put you in mind that a running horse does require more attendance than a coach-horse. Nature has made some difference 'twixt you and I.

Y. FAS. Yes, she has made you older. (*aside*) Pox take her!

L. FOP. That is nat all, Tam.

Y. FAS. Why, what is there else?

L. FOP. (*looking first upon himself, then upon his brother*) Ask the ladies.

Y. FAS. Why, thou essence bottle, thou musk-cat, dost thou then think thou hast any advantage over me but what fortune has given thee?

L. FOP. I do—stap my vitals.

Y. FAS. Now, by all that's great and powerful, thou art the prince of coxcombs.

L. FOP. Sir—I am praud of being at the head of so prevailing a party.

Y. FAS. Will nothing then provoke thee?—— Draw, coward!

L. FOP. Look you, Tam, you know I have always taken you for a mighty dull fellow, and here is one of the foolishest plats broke out that I have seen a long time. Your paverty makes your life so burthensome to you you would provoke me to a quarrel, in hopes either to slip through my lungs into my estate, or to get yourself run through the guts, to put an end to your pain. But I will disappoint you in both your designs; far with the temper of a philasapher, and the discretion of a statesman—I will go to the play with my sword in my scabbard.

(*Exit* LORD FOPPINGTON.)

Y. FAS. So! Farewell, snuff-box. And now, conscience, I defy thee. Lory!

Enter LORY

LO. Sir.

Y. FAS. Here's rare news, Lory; his Lordship has given me a pill has purged off all my scruples.

LO. Then my heart's at ease again: for I have been in a lamentable fright, Sir, ever since your conscience had the impudence to intrude into your company.

Y. FAS. Be at peace, it will come there no more: my brother has given it a wring by the nose, and I have kicked it down stairs. So run away to the inn; get the horses ready quickly, and bring 'em to old Coupler's, without a moment's delay.

LO. Then, Sir, you are going straight about the fortune?

Y. FAS. I am: away! fly, Lory!

LO. The happiest day I ever saw. I'm upon the wing already.
(*Exeunt several ways.*)

SCENE II

SCENE: *A garden*

Enter LOVELESS *and Servant*

LOV. Is my wife within?

SERV. No, Sir, she has been gone out this half hour.

LOV. 'Tis well; leave me.

(*solus*) Sure, fate has yet some business to be done,
Before Amanda's heart and mine must rest;
Else why, amongst those legions of her sex,
Which throng the world,
Should she pick out for her companion
The only one on earth
Whom nature has endow'd for her undoing?
"Undoing" was't I said?—Who shall undo her?
Is not her empire fix'd? Am I not hers?
Did she not rescue me, a grov'ling slave?
When, chain'd and bound by that black tyrant, Vice,
I labour'd in his vilest drudgery,
Did she not ransom me, and set me free?
Nay, more:
When by my follies sunk
To a poor tatter'd, despicable beggar,
Did she not lift me up to envy'd fortune?
Give me herself, and all that she possessed?
Without a thought of more return,
Than what a poor repenting heart might make her.

Han't she done this? And if she has,
Am I not strongly bound to love her for it?
To love her!—Why, do I not love her then?
By earth and heaven, I do!
Nay, I have demonstration that I do:
For I would sacrifice my life to serve her.
Yet hold:—if laying down my life
Be demonstration of my love,
What is't I feel in favour of Berinthia?
For should she be in danger, methinks, I could incline
To risk it for her service too; and yet I do not love her.
How then subsists my proof?—
—Oh, I have found it out.
What I would do for one is demonstration of my love;
And if I'd do as much for t'other,
If there is demonstration of my friendship—
Ay—It must be so.
I find I'm very much her friend.
—Yet let me ask myself one puzzling question more:
Whence springs this mighty friendship all at once?
For our acquaintance is of later date.
Now friendship's said to be a plant of tedious growth,
Its root compos'd of tender fibres,
Nice in their taste, cautious in spreading,
Check'd with the least corruption in the soil;
Long ere it take, and longer still ere it appear to do so.
Whilst mine is in a moment shot so high,
And fix'd so fast, it seems beyond the power
Of storms to shake it. I doubt it thrives too fast.   (*musing*)

Enter BERINTHIA

Ha! she here! Nay, then,
Take heed, my heart, for there are dangers towards.

BER. What makes you look so thoughtful, Sir? I hope you are
not ill?

LOV. I was debating, Madam, whether I was so or not; and
that was it which made me look so thoughtful.

BER. Is it then so hard a matter to decide? I thought all people
had been acquainted with their own bodies, though few people
know their own minds.

LOV. What if the distemper I suspect be in the mind?

BER. Why, then I'll undertake to prescribe you a cure.

LOV. Alas, you undertake you know not what.

BER. So far at least then allow me to be a physician.

LOV. Nay, I'll allow you so yet farther: for I have reason to believe should I put myself into your hands you would increase my distemper.

BER. Perhaps I might have reasons from the college not to be too quick in your cure; but 'tis possible I might find ways to give you often ease, Sir.

LOV. Were I but sure of that, I'd quickly lay my case before you.

BER. Whether you are sure of it or no, what risk do you run in trying?

LOV. Oh, a very great one.

BER. How?

LOV. You might betray my distemper to my wife.

BER. And so lose all my practice.

LOV. Will you then keep my secret?

BER. I will, if it don't burst me.

LOV. Swear.

BER. I do.

LOV. By what?

BER. By woman.

LOV. That's swearing by my deity. Do it by your own, or I shan't believe you.

BER. By man, then.

LOV. I'm satisfied. Now hear my symptoms,
And give me your advice. The first were these:
When 'twas my chance to see you at the play,
A random glance you threw, at first alarm'd me;
I could not turn my eyes from whence the danger came:
I gaz'd upon you, till you shot again,
And then my fears came on me.
My heart began to pant, my limbs to tremble,
My blood grew thin, my pulse beat quick,
My eyes grew hot and dim, and all the frame of nature
Shook with apprehension.
'Tis true, some small recruits of resolution
My manhood brought to my assistance,

And by their help I made a stand a while,
But found at last your arrows flew so thick,
They could not fail to pierce me;
So left the field,
And fled for shelter to Amanda's arms.
What think you of these symptoms, pray?

BER. Feverish, every one of 'em.
But what relief, pray, did your wife afford you?

LOV. Why, instantly she let me blood,
Which for the present much assuag'd my flame.
But when I saw you, out it burst again,
And rag'd with greater fury than before.
Nay, since you now appear, 'tis so encreas'd
That in a moment, if you do not help me,
I shall, whilst you look on, consume to ashes.

                                    (*taking hold of her hand*)

BER. (*breaking from him*) O Lard, let me go:
'Tis the plague, and we shall all be infected.

LOV. (*catching her in his arms, and kissing her*)
Then we'll die together, my charming angel.

BER. O Ged—the devil's in you.
Lord, let me go, here's somebody coming.

Enter Servant

SERV. Sir, my lady's come home, and desires to speak with you:
she's in her chamber.

LOV. Tell her I'm coming.   (*Exit Servant.*)
(*to* BERINTHIA) But before I go, one glass of nectar more to drink
her health.

BER. Stand off, or I shall hate you, by heavens.

LOV. (*kissing her*) In matters of love, a woman's oath is no
more to be minded than a man's.

BER. Um——

Enter WORTHY

WOR. (*aside*) Ha! What's here? my old mistress, and so close,
i'faith? I would not spoil her sport for the universe. (*He retires.*)

BER. O Ged—— Now do I pray to heaven, (*exit* LOVELESS
running) with all my heart and soul, that the devil in hell may
take me, if ever—I was better pleased in my life—this man has

bewitch'd me, that's certain. (*sighing*) Well, I am condemn'd, but, thanks to heaven, I feel myself each moment more and more prepar'd for my execution—nay, to that degree, I don't perceive I have the least fear of dying. No, I find, let the—executioner be but a man, and there's nothing will suffer with more resolution than a woman. Well, I never had but one intrigue yet: but I confess I long to have another. Pray heaven it end as the first did, though, that we may both grow weary at a time; for 'tis a melancholy thing for lovers to outlive one another.

Enter WORTHY

WOR. (*aside*) This discovery's a lucky one; I hope to make a happy use on't. That gentlewoman there is no fool, so I shall be able to make her understand her interest.—(*to* BERINTHIA) Your servant, Madam; I need not ask you how you do, you have got so good a colour.

BER. No better than I used to have, I suppose?

WOR. A little more blood in your cheeks.

BER. The weather's hot.

WOR. If it were not, a woman may have a colour.

BER. What do you mean my that?

WOR. Nothing.

BER. Why do you smile then?

WOR. Because the weather's hot.

BER. You'll never leave roguing, I see that.

WOR. (*putting his finger to his nose*) You'll never leave——I see that.

BER. Well, I can't imagine what you drive at. Pray tell me what you mean?

WOR. Do you tell me; it's the same thing.

BER. I can't.

WOR. Guess!

BER. I shall guess wrong.

WOR. Indeed you won't.

BER. Psha! either tell, or let it alone.

WOR. Nay, rather than let it alone, I will tell. But first I must put you in mind that, after what has past 'twixt you and I, very few things ought to be secrets between us.

BER. Why, what secrets do we hide? I know of none.

WOR. Yes, there are two; one I have hid from you, and t'other

ACT III, SCENE II

459

you would hide from me. You are fond of Loveless, which I have discovered; and I am fond of his wife——

BER. Which I have discovered.

WOR. Very well, now I confess your discovery to be true: what do you say to mine?

BER. Why, I confess—I would swear 'twere false, if I thought you were fool enough to believe me.

WOR. Now am I almost in love with you again. Nay, I don't know but I might be quite so, had I made one short campaign with Amanda. Therefore, if you find 'twould tickle your vanity to bring me down once more to your lure, e'en help me quickly to dispatch her business, that I may have nothing else to do but to apply myself to yours.

BER. Do you then think, Sir, I am old enough to be a bawd?

WOR. No, but I think you are wise enough to——

BER. To do what?

WOR. To hoodwink Amanda with a gallant, that she mayn't see who is her husband's mistress.

BER. (aside) He has reason: the hint's a good one.

WOR. Well, Madam, what think you on't?

BER. I think you are so much a deeper politician in these affairs than I am, that I ought to have a very great regard to your advice.

WOR. Then give me leave to put you in mind that the most easy, safe, and pleasant situation for your own amour is the house in which you now are, provided you keep Amanda from any sort of suspicion: that the way to do that is to engage her in an intrigue of her own, making yourself her confidante: and the way to bring her to intrigue, is to make her jealous of her husband in a wrong place; which the more you foment, the less you'll be suspected.

This is my scheme, in short; which if you follow as you should do (my dear Berinthia) we may all four pass the winter very pleasantly.

BER. Well, I could be glad to have nobody's sins to answer for but my own. But where there is a necessity——

WOR. Right as you say; where there is a necessity, a Christian is bound to help his neighbour. So, good Berinthia, lose no time, but let us begin the dance as fast as we can.

BER. Not till the fiddles are in tune, pray, Sir. Your lady's strings will be very apt to fly, I can tell you that, if they are wound up too hastily. But if you'll have patience to screw 'em to their pitch by degrees, I don't doubt but she may endure to be played upon.

wor. Ay, and will make admirable music, too, or I'm mistaken. But have you had no private closet discourse with her yet about males and females, and so forth, which may give you hopes in her constitution? for I know her morals are the devil against us.

ber. I have had so much discourse with her that I believe were she once cured of her fondness to her husband, the fortress of her virtue would not be so impregnable as she fancies.

wor. What? she runs, I'll warrant you, into that common mistake of fond wives, who conclude themselves virtuous because they can refuse a man they don't like when they have got one they do.

ber. True, and therefore I think 'tis a presumptuous thing in a woman to assume the name of virtuous till she has heartily hated her husband and been soundly in love with somebody else, whom if she has withstood—then—much good may it do her!

wor. Well, so much for her virtue. Now, one word of her inclinations, and everyone to their post. What opinion do you find she has of me?

ber. What you could wish; she thinks you handsome and discreet.

wor. Good! that's thinking half-seas over. One tide more brings us into port.

ber. Perhaps it may, though still remember there's a difficult bar to pass.

wor. I know there is, but I don't question I shall get well over it, by the help of such a pilot.

ber. You may depend upon your pilot, she'll do the best she can; so weigh anchor, and be gone as soon as you please.

wor. I'm under sail already. Adieu.   (*Exit* worthy.)

ber. *Bon voyage.* (*sola*) So, here's fine work. What a business have I undertaken! I'm a very pretty gentlewoman, truly; but there was no avoiding it: he'd have ruined me if I had refused him. Besides, faith, I begin to fancy there may be as much pleasure in carrying on another body's intrigue as one's own. This at least is certain, it exercises almost all the entertaining faculties of a woman: for there's employment for hypocrisy, invention, deceit, flattery, mischief, and lying.

Enter AMANDA, *her Woman following her*

WOM. If you please, Madam, only to say, whether you'll have me buy 'em or not.

AMAN. Yes, no, go fiddle! I care not what you do. Prithee leave me.

WOM. I have done. (*Exit Woman.*)

BER. What in the name of Jove's the matter with you?

AMAN. The matter, Berinthia! I'm almost mad, I'm plagued to death.

BER. Who is it that plagues you?

AMAN. Who do you think should plague a wife but her husband?

BER. O ho, is it come to that? We shall have you wish yourself a widow by and by.

AMAN. Would I were anything but what I am! A base ungrateful man, after what I have done for him, to use me thus!

BER. What! he has been ogling now, I'll warrant you?

AMAN. Yes, he has been ogling.

BER. And so you are jealous? Is that all?

AMAN. That all! Is jealousy then nothing?

BER. It should be nothing, if I were in your case.

AMAN. Why, what would you do?

BER. I'd cure myself.

AMAN. How?

BER. Let blood in the fond vein: care as little for my husband as he did for me.

AMAN. That would not stop his course.

BER. Nor nothing else, when the wind's in the warm corner. Look you, Amanda, you may build castles in the air, and fume, and fret, and grow thin and lean and pale and ugly, if you please. But I tell you, no man worth having is true to his wife, or can be true to his wife, or ever was, or ever will be so.

AMAN. Do you then really think he's false to me? for I did but suspect him.

BER. Think so? I know he's so.

AMAN. Is it possible? Pray tell me what you know.

BER. Don't press me then to name names, for that I have sworn I won't do.

AMAN. Well, I won't; but let me know all you can without perjury.

BER. I'll let you know enough to prevent any wise woman's dying of the pip; and I hope you'll pluck up your spirits, and show, upon occasion, you can be as good a wife as the best of 'em.

AMAN. Well, what a woman can do I'll endeavour.

BER. Oh, a woman can do a great deal, if once she sets her mind to it. Therefore pray don't stand trifling any longer, and teasing yourself with this and that, and your love and your virtue, and I know not what. But resolve to hold up your head, get a-tiptoe, and look over 'em all; for to my certain knowledge your husband is a-pickering elsewhere.

AMAN. You are sure on't?

BER. Positively; he fell in love at the play.

AMAN. Right, the very same; do you know the ugly thing?

BER. Yes, I know her well enough; but she's no such an ugly thing, neither.

AMAN. Is she very handsome?

BER. Truly, I think so.

AMAN. Hey ho!

BER. What do you sigh for now?

AMAN. Oh, my heart!

BER. (aside) Only the pangs of nature! she's in labour of her love; heaven send her a quick delivery; I'm sure she has a good midwife.

AMAN. I'm very ill, I must go to my chamber. Dear Berinthia, don't leave me a moment.

BER. No, don't fear. (aside) I'll see you safe brought to bed, I'll warrant you.   (Exeunt, AMANDA leaning upon BERINTHIA.)

SCENE III

SCENE: *A country house*

Enter YOUNG FASHION *and* LORY

Y. FAS. So, here's our inheritance, Lory, if we can but get into possession. But methinks the seat of our family looks like Noah's ark, as if the chief part on't were designed for the fowls of the air and the beasts of the field.

LO. Pray, Sir, don't let your head run upon the orders of building here; get but the heiress, let the devil take the house.

Y. FAS. Get but the house, let the devil take the heiress, I say; at least if she be as old Coupler describes her. But come, we have no time to squander. Knock at the door. (LORY *knocks two or three times.*) What the devil, have they got no ears in this house? Knock harder.

LO. I'gad, Sir, this will prove some enchanted castle; we shall have the giant come out by and by with his club, and beat our brains out.   (*knocks again*)

Y. FAS. Hush! they come.

(*From within*) Who is there?

LO. Open the door and see: is that your country breeding?

(*Within*) Ay, but two words to a bargain: Tummas, is the blunderbuss primed?

Y. FAS. Oons, give 'em good words, Lory; we shall be shot here a fortune-catching.

LO. I'gad, Sir, I think y'are in the right on't.—— Ho, Mr. What d'ye-call-um.

          (*Servant appears at the window with a blunderbuss.*)

SERV. Weall naw what's yare business?

Y. FAS. Nothing, Sir, but to wait upon Sir Tunbelly, with your leave.

SERV. To weat upon Sir Tunbelly? Why, you'll find that's just as Sir Tunbelly pleases.

Y. FAS. But will you do me the favour, Sir, to know whether Sir Tunbelly pleases or not?

SERV. Why, look you, do you see, with good words much may be done.—— Ralph, go thy weas, and ask Sir Tunbelly if he pleases to be waited upon. And, dost hear? call to nurse, that she may lock up Miss Hoyden before the geats open.

Y. FAS. D'ye hear that, Lory?

LO. Ay, sir, I'm afraid we shall find a difficult job on't. Pray heaven that old rogue Coupler han't sent us to fetch milk out of the gunroom!

Y. FAS. I'll warrant thee all will go well: see, the door opens.

Enter SIR TUNBELLY, *with his Servants armed with
guns, clubs, pitchforks, scythes, etc.*

LO. (*running behind his master*) O Lord, O Lord, O Lord, we
are both dead men!

Y. FAS. Take heed, fool; thy fear will ruin us.

LO. My fear, Sir—'sdeath, Sir, I fear nothing. (*aside*) Would I
were well up to the chin in a horse-pond!

SIR TUN. Who is it here has any business with me?

Y. FAS. Sir, 'tis I, if your name be Sir Tunbelly Clumsey.

SIR TUN. Sir, my name is Sir Tunbelly Clumsey, whether you
have any business with me or not. So you see I am not ashamed of
my name—nor my face, neither.

Y. FAS. Sir, you have no cause that I know of.

SIR. TUN. Sir, if you have no cause neither, I desire to know
who you are; for till I know your name, I shall not ask you to
come into my house; and when I know your name—'tis six to
four I don't ask you neither.

Y. FAS. (*giving him a letter*) Sir, I hope you'll find this letter
an authentic passport.

SIR TUN. Cod's my life, I ask your Lordship's pardon ten
thousand times. (*to his Servants*) Here, run in a-doors quickly:
get a Scotch coal fire in the great parlour; set all the Turkey-
work chairs in their places; get the great brass candlesticks out,
and be sure stick the sockets full of laurel; run! (*turning to*
YOUNG FASHION) My Lord, I ask your Lordship's pardon. (*to
other Servants*) And do you hear, run away to nurse, bid her let
Miss Hoyden loose again, and if it was not shifting-day, let her
put on a clean tucker—quick! (*Exeunt Servants confusedly.*) (*to*
YOUNG FASHION) I hope your honour will excuse the disorder of
my family; we are not used to receive men of your Lordship's
great quality every day; pray, where are your coaches and servants, my Lord?

Y. FAS. Sir, that I might give you and your fair daughter a proof
how impatient I am to be nearer akin to you, I left my equipage
to follow me, and came away post with only one servant.

SIR TUN. Your Lordship does me too much honour; it was ex-
posing your person to too much fatigue and danger, I protest it
was; but my daughter shall endeavour to make you what amends

she can; and though I say it, that should not say it—Hoyden has charms.

Y. FAS. Sir, I am not a stranger to them, though I am to her; common fame has done her justice.

SIR. TUN. My Lord, I am common fame's very grateful humble servant. My Lord—my girl's young: Hoyden is young, my Lord; but this I must say for her, what she wants in art, she has by nature; what she wants in experience, she has in breeding; and what's wanting in her age is made good in her constitution. So pray, my Lord, walk in; pray, my Lord, walk in.

Y. FAS. Sir, I wait upon you.   (*Exeunt.*)

SCENE IV

MISS HOYDEN, *sola*

Sure, never nobody was used as I am. I know well enough what other girls do, for all they think to make a fool of me: it's well I have a husband a-coming, or i'cod, I'd marry the baker, I would so. Nobody can knock at the gate, but presently I must be locked up; and here's the young greyhound bitch can run loose about the house all day long, she can; 'tis very well.

NURSE (*without opening the door*) Miss Hoyden! Miss, Miss, Miss; Miss Hoyden!

Enter Nurse

MISS. Well, what do you make such a noise for, ha? What do you din a body's ears for? Can't one be at quiet for you!

NURSE. What do I din your ears for? Here's one come will din your ears for you.

MISS. What care I who's come? I care not a fig who comes, nor who goes, as long as I must be locked up like the ale-cellar.

NURSE. That, Miss, is for fear you should be drank before you are ripe.

MISS. Oh, don't you trouble your head about that: I'm as ripe as you, though not so mellow.

NURSE. Very well; now have I a good mind to lock you up again, and not let you see my Lord to-night.

MISS. My Lord? Why, is my husband come?

NURSE. Yes, marry is he, and a goodly person too.

MISS. (*hugging Nurse*) O my dear nurse, forgive me this once, and I'll never misuse you again; no, if I do, you shall give me three thumps on the back, and a great pinch by the cheek.

NURSE. Ah, the poor thing, see how it melts; it's as full of good-nature as an egg's full of meat.

MISS. But, my dear nurse, don't lie now; is he come, by your troth?

NURSE. Yes, by my truly, is he.

MISS. O Lord! I'll go put on my laced smock, though I'm whipped till the blood run down my heels for't.   (*Exit running.*)

NURSE. Eh—the Lord succour thee, how thou art delighted!
(*Exit after her.*)

SCENE V

Enter SIR TUNBELLY *and* YOUNG FASHION.
A Servant with wine

SIR TUN. My Lord, I am proud of the honour to see your Lordship within my doors, and I humbly crave leave to bid you welcome in a cup of sack wine.

Y. FAS. Sir, to your daughter's health.   (*drinks*)

SIR TUN. Ah, poor girl, she'll be scared out of her wits on her wedding night; for, honestly speaking, she does not know a man from a woman, but by his beard and his britches.

Y. FAS. Sir, I don't doubt but she has a virtuous education, which, with the rest of her merit, makes me long to see her mine. I wish you would dispense with the canonical hour, and let it be this very night.

SIR TUN. Oh, not so soon, neither; that's shooting my girl before you bid her stand. No, give her fair warning: we'll sign and seal to-night if you please, and this day seven-night—let the jade look to her quarters.

Y. FAS. This day sennight?—Why, what! do you take me for a ghost, Sir? 'Slife, Sir, I'm made of flesh and blood, and bones and sinews, and can no more live a week without your daughter —(*aside*) than I can live a month with her.

SIR TUN. Oh, I'll warrant you, my hero; young men are hot, I know, but they don't boil over at that rate, neither; besides, my wench's wedding gown is not come home yet.

Y. FAS. Oh, no matter, Sir; I'll take her in her shift. (*aside*) A pox of this old fellow; he'll delay the business till my damned star finds me out, and discovers me. (*to* SIR TUNBELLY) Pray, Sir, let it be done without ceremony; 'twill save money.

SIR TUN. Money?—save money when Hoyden's to be married? Udswoons, I'll give my wench a wedding dinner, though I go to grass with the King of Assyria for't; and such a dinner it shall be, as is not to be cooked in the poaching of an egg. Therefore, my noble Lord, have a little patience; we'll go and look over our deeds and settlements immediately; and as for your bride, though you may be sharp set before she's quite ready, I'll engage for my girl she stays your stomach at last. *(Exeunt.)*

ACT IV

SCENE I

Enter MISS HOYDEN *and Nurse*

NURSE. Well, Miss, how do you like your husband that is to be?

MISS. O Lord, nurse, I'm so overjoyed, I can scarce contain myself.

NURSE. Oh, but you must have a care of being too fond, for men nowadays hate a woman that loves 'em.

MISS. Love him? Why, do you think I love him, nurse? I'cod, I would not care if he were hanged, so I were but once married to him. No—that which pleases me is to think what work I'll make when I get to London; for when I am a wife and a lady both, nurse, i'cod, I'll flaunt it with the best of 'em.

NURSE. Look, look, if his honour be not coming again to you; now if I were sure you would behave yourself handsomely, and not disgrace me that have brought you up, I'd leave you alone together.

MISS. That's my best nurse: do as you would be done by; trust us together this once, and if I don't show my breeding from the head to the foot of me, may I be twice married, and die a maid!

NURSE. Well, this once I'll venture you; but if you disparage me——

MISS. Never fear; I'll show him my parts, I'll warrant him.

(Exit Nurse.)

(Sola.) These old women are so wise when they get a poor girl

in their clutches, but ere it be long I shall know what's what, as
well as the best of 'em.

Enter YOUNG FASHION

Y. FAS. Your servant, Madam: I'm glad to find you alone, for
I have something of importance to speak to you about.

MISS. Sir (my Lord, I meant) you may speak to me about what
you please; I shall give you a civil answer.

Y. FAS. You give me so obliging a one, it encourages me to tell
you in few words what I think both for your interest and mine.
Your father, I suppose you know, has resolved to make me happy
in being your husband, and I hope I may depend upon your
consent to perform what he desires.

MISS. Sir, I never disobey my father in anything but eating of
green gooseberries.

Y. FAS. So good a daughter must needs make an admirable
wife; I am therefore impatient till you are mine, and hope you
will so far consider the violence of my love that you won't have
the cruelty to defer my happiness so long as your father designs it.

MISS. Pray, my Lord, how long is that?

Y. FAS. Madam, a thousand year—a whole week.

MISS. A week!—why, I shall be an old woman by that time.

Y. FAS. And I an old man, which you'll find a greater misfortune than t'other.

MISS. Why, I thought 'twas to be to-morrow morning, as soon
as I was up; I'm sure nurse told me so.

Y. FAS. And it shall be to-morrow morning still, if you'll consent.

MISS. If I'll consent? Why, I thought I was to obey you as my
husband.

Y. FAS. That's when we are married; till then I am to obey you.

MISS. Why then, if we are to take it by turns, it's the same
thing: I'll obey you now, and when we are married, you shall
obey me.

Y. FAS. With all my heart; but I doubt we must get nurse on
our side, or we shall hardly prevail with the chaplain.

MISS. No more we shan't, indeed, for he loves her better than
he loves his pulpit, and would always be a-preaching to her, by
his good will.

Y. FAS. Why then, my dear little bedfellow, if you'll call her hither, we'll try to persuade her presently.

MISS. O Lord, I can tell you a way how to persuade her to anything.

Y. FAS. How's that?

MISS. Why, tell her she's a wholesome, comely woman—and give her half a crown.

Y. FAS. Nay, if that will do, she shall have half a score of 'em.

MISS. O Gemini! for half that she'd marry you herself: I'll run and call her. (Exit MISS HOYDEN.)

Y. FAS. (solus) So, matters go swimmingly; this is a rare girl, i'faith; I shall have a fine time on't with her at London. I'm much mistaken if she don't prove a March hare all the year round. What a scamp'ring chase will she make on't, when she finds the whole kennel of beaux at her tail! hey to the park, and the play, and the church, and the devil; she'll show 'em sport, I'll warrant 'em. But no matter: she brings an estate will afford me a separate maintenance.

Enter MISS HOYDEN and Nurse

Y. FAS. How do you do, good Mistress Nurse; I desired your young lady would give me leave to see you, that I might thank you for your extraordinary care and conduct in her education; pray accept of this small acknowledgment for it at present, and depend upon my farther kindness when I shall be that happy thing, her husband.

NURSE (aside) Gold, by makings!—— Your honour's goodness is too great: alas! all I can boast of is, I gave her pure good milk, and so your honour would have said, an you had seen how the poor thing sucked it—Eh, God's blessing on the sweet face on't! how it used to hang at this poor tett, and suck and squeeze, and kick and sprawl it would, till the belly on't was so full it would drop off like a leech.

MISS. (to Nurse, taking her angrily aside) Pray one word with you; prithee, nurse, don't stand ripping up old stories, to make one ashamed before one's love: do you think such a fine proper gentleman as he cares for a fiddlecome tale of a draggle-tailed girl? if you have a mind to make him have a good opinion of a woman, don't tell him what one did then: tell him what one can do now. (To YOUNG FASHION.) I hope your honour will excuse my mismanners to whisper before you; it was only to give some orders about the family.

Y. FAS. Oh, everything, Madam, is to give way to business; besides, good housewifery is a very commendable quality in a young lady.

MISS. Pray, Sir, are the young ladies good housewives at London town? do they darn their own linen?

Y. FAS. Oh, no; they study how to spend money, not to save it.

MISS. I'cod, I don't know but that may be better sport than t'other; ha, nurse?

Y. FAS. Well, you shall have your choice when you come there.

MISS. Shall I?—then by my troth I'll get there as fast as I can. (*to Nurse*) His honour desires you'll be so kind as to let us be married to-morrow.

NURSE. To-morrow, my dear Madam?

Y. FAS. Yes, to-morrow, sweet nurse, privately; young folks, you know, are impatient, and Sir Tunbelly would make us stay a week for a wedding-dinner. Now all things being signed and sealed and agreed, I fancy there could be no great harm in practising a scene or two of matrimony in private, if it were only to give us the better assurance when we come to play it in public.

NURSE. Nay, I must confess stol'n pleasures are sweet; but if you should be married now, what will you do when Sir Tunbelly calls for you to be wed?

MISS. Why, then we'll be married again.

NURSE. What, twice, my child?

MISS. I'cod, I don't care how often I'm married, not I.

Y. FAS. Pray, nurse, don't you be against your young lady's good; for by this means she'll have the pleasure of two wedding-days.

MISS. (*to Nurse softly*) And of two wedding-nights, too, nurse.

NURSE. Well, I'm such a tender-hearted fool, I find I can refuse nothing; so you shall e'en follow your own inventions.

MISS. Shall I? (*aside*) O Lord, I could leap over the moon.

Y. FAS. Dear nurse, this goodness of yours shan't go unrewarded; but now you must employ your power with Mr. Bull, the chaplain, that he may do us his friendly office too, and then we shall all be happy; do you think you can prevail with him?

NURSE. Prevail with him?—or he shall never prevail with me, I can tell him that.

MISS. My Lord, she has had him upon the hip this seven year.

Y. FAS. I'm glad to hear it; however, to strengthen your interest with him, you may let him know I have several fat livings in my gift, and that the first that falls shall be in your disposal.

NURSE. Nay, then I'll make him marry more folks than one, I'll promise him.

MISS. Faith, do, nurse, make him marry you too; I'm sure he'll do't for a fat living; for he loves eating more than he loves his Bible; and I have often heard him say a fat living was the best meat in the world.

NURSE. Ay, and I'll make him commend the sauce too, or I'll bring his gown to a cassock, I will so.

Y. FAS. Well, nurse, whilst you go and settle matters with him, then your lady and I will go take a walk in the garden.

NURSE. I'll do your honour's business in the catching up of a garter. (*Exit Nurse.*)

Y. FAS. (*giving her his hand*) Come, Madam, dare you venture yourself alone with me?

MISS. Oh dear, yes, Sir; I don't think you'll do anything to me I need be afraid on. (*Exeunt.*)

SCENE II

Enter AMANDA *and* BERINTHIA

A Song

I

"I SMILE at love, and all its arts,"
   The charming Cynthia cried;
"Take heed, for Love has piercing darts,"
   A wounded swain replied.
"Once free and blest as you are now,
   I trifled with his charms;
I pointed at his little bow,
   And sported with his arms:
Till urg'd too far, 'Revenge!' he cries,
   A fatal shaft he drew;
It took its passage through your eyes,
   And to my heart it flew.

II

"To tear it thence I tried in vain;
        To strive, I quickly found,
Was only to encrease the pain,
        And to enlarge the wound.
Ah! much too well I fear you know
        What pain I'm to endure,
Since what your eyes alone could do,
        Your heart alone can cure.
And that (grant heaven I may mistake)
        I doubt is doom'd to bear
A burthen for another's sake,
        Who ill rewards its care."

AMAN. Well, now, Berinthia, I'm at leisure to hear what 'twas you had to say to me.

BER. What I had to say was only to echo the sighs and groans of a dying lover.

AMAN. Phu, will you never learn to talk in earnest of anything?

BER. Why, this shall be in earnest, if you please; for my part, I only tell you matter of fact—you may take it which way you like best, but if you'll follow the women of the town, you'll take it both ways; for when a man offers himself to one of them, first she takes him in jest, and then she takes him in earnest.

AMAN. I'm sure there's so much jest and earnest in what you say to me, I scarce know how to take it; but I think you have bewitched me, for I don't find it possible to be angry with you, say what you will.

BER. I'm very glad to hear it, for I have no mind to quarrel with you, for more reasons than I'll brag of; but quarrel or not, smile or frown, I must tell you what I have suffered upon your account.

AMAN. Upon my account?

BER. Yes, upon yours; I have been forced to sit still and hear you commended for two hours together, without one compliment to myself; now don't you think a woman had a blessed time of that?

AMAN. Alas! I should have been unconcerned at it; I never knew where the pleasure lay of being praised by the men: but pray who was this that commended me so?

BER. One you have a mortal aversion to—Mr. Worthy; he used you like a text, he took you all to pieces, but spoke so learnedly upon every point, one might see the spirit of the church was in him: if you are a woman, you'd have been in an ecstasy to have heard how feelingly he handled your hair, your eyes, your nose, your mouth, your teeth, your tongue, your chin, your neck, and so forth. Thus he preached for an hour, but when he came to use an application, he observed that all these, without a gallant, were nothing. Now consider of what has been said, and heaven give you grace to put it in practice!

AMAN. Alas! Berinthia, did I incline to a gallant (which you know I do not), do you think a man so nice as he could have the least concern for such a plain unpolished thing as I am? It is impossible!

BER. Now have you a great mind to put me upon commending you.

AMAN. Indeed that was not my design.

BER. Nay, if it were, it's all one, for I won't do't; I'll leave that to your looking-glass. But to show you I have some good-nature left, I'll commend him, and maybe that may do as well.

AMAN. You have a great mind to persuade me I am in love with him.

BER. I have a great mind to persuade you you don't know what you are in love with.

AMAN. I am sure I am not in love with him, nor never shall be; so let that pass: but you were saying something you would commend him for.

BER. Oh, you'd be glad to hear a good character of him, however.

AMAN. Psha!

BER. "Psha!"—Well, 'tis a foolish undertaking for women, in these kind of matters, to pretend to deceive one another—have not I been bred a woman as well as you?

AMAN. What then?

BER. Why, then I understand my trade so well, that whenever I am told of a man I like, I cry, "Psha!" But that I may spare you the pains of putting me a second time in mind to commend him, I'll proceed, and give you this account of him: that though 'tis possible he may have had women with as good faces as your Ladyship's (no discredit to it neither), yet you must know your cautious behaviour, with that reserve in your humour, has given him his death's wound; he mortally hates a coquette; he says 'tis impossible to love where we cannot esteem; and that no woman can be esteemed by a man who has sense if she makes herself cheap in the eye of a fool. That pride to a woman is as necessary as humility to a divine; and that far-fetched and dear bought is meat for gentlemen as well as for ladies—in short, that every woman who has beauty may set a price upon herself, and that by underselling the market they ruin the trade. This is his doctrine: how do you like it?

AMAN. So well that, since I never intend to have a gallant for myself, if I were to recommend one to a friend, he should be the man.

Enter WORTHY

Bless me, he's here! pray heaven he did not hear me!

BER. If he did, it won't hurt your reputation; your thoughts are as safe in his heart as in your own.

WOR. I venture in at an unseasonable time of night, ladies; I hope if I'm troublesome you'll use the same freedom in turning me out again.

AMAN. I believe it can't be late, for Mr. Loveless is not come home yet, and he usually keeps good hours.

WOR. Madam, I'm afraid he'll transgress a little to-night; for he told me about half an hour ago he was going to sup with some company he doubted would keep him out till three or four o'clock in the morning, and desired I would let my servant acquaint you with it, that you might not expect him: but my fellow's a blunder-head, so, lest he should make some mistake, I thought it my duty to deliver the message myself.

AMAN. I'm very sorry he should give you that trouble, Sir: but——

BER. But since he has, will you give me leave, Madam, to keep him to play at ombre with us?

AMAN. Cousin, you know you command my house.

WOR. (to BERINTHIA) And, Madam, you know you command me, though I'm a very wretched gamester.

BER. Oh, you play well enough to lose your money, and that's all the ladies require; so without any more ceremony let us go into the next room and call for the cards.

AMAN. With all my heart.   (*Exit* WORTHY *leading* AMANDA.)
BER. (*sola*) Well, how this business will end, heaven knows;
but she seems to me to be in as fair a way—as a boy is to be a
rogue, when he's put clerk to an attorney.   (*Exit* BERINTHIA.)

SCENE III

SCENE: BERINTHIA'S *chamber*

Enter LOVELESS *cautiously in the dark*

LOV. So, thus far all's well. I'm got into her bed-chamber, and
I think nobody has perceived me steal into the house; my wife
don't expect me home till four o'clock; so if Berinthia comes to
bed by eleven, I shall have a chase of five hours. Let me see,
where shall I hide myself? under her bed? No; we shall have her
maid searching there for something or other; her closet's a better
place, and I have a master key will open it: I'll e'en in there,
and attack her just when she comes to her prayers: that's the
most likely to prove her critical minute, for then the devil will
be there to assist me.

> (*He opens the closet, goes in, and shuts the door after
> him.*)

Enter BERINTHIA *with a candle in her hand*

BER. Well, sure I am the best-natured woman in the world.
I that love cards so well (there is but one thing upon earth I
love better) have pretended letters to write, to give my friends—
a *tête-à-tête*; however, I'm innocent, for picquet is the game I
set 'em to: at her own peril be it, if she ventures to play with
him at any other. But now what shall I do with myself? I don't
know how in the world to pass my time; would Loveless were
here to *badiner* a little. Well, he's a charming fellow; I don't
wonder his wife's so fond of him. What if I should sit down and
think of him till I fall asleep, and dream of the Lord knows what?
Oh, but then if I should dream we were married, I should be
frightened out of my wits. (*seeing a book*) What's this book? I
think I had best go read. Oh, *splénétique!* it's a sermon. Well,
I'll go into my closet, and read *The Plotting Sisters*. (*She opens*

the closet, sees LOVELESS, *and shrieks out.*) O Lord, a ghost, a ghost, a ghost, a ghost!

Enter LOVELESS, *running to her*

LOV. Peace, my dear; it's no ghost; take it in your arms, you'll find 'tis worth a hundred of 'em.

BER. Run in again; here's somebody coming.

(*Exit* LOVELESS.)

Enter her Maid

MAID. Lord, Madam, what's the matter?

BER. O heavens! I'm almost frighted out of my wits: I thought verily I had seen a ghost, and 'twas nothing but the white curtain, with a black hood pinned up against it; you may be gone again, I am the fearfullest fool.   (*Exit Maid.*)

Re-enter LOVELESS

LOV. Is the coast clear?

BER. The coast clear! I suppose you are clear, you'd never play such a trick as this else.

LOV. I am very well pleased with my trick thus far, and shall be so till I have played it out, if it ben't your fault: where's my wife?

BER. At cards.

LOV. With whom?

BER. With Worthy.

LOV. Then we are safe enough.

BER. Are you so? Some husbands would be of another mind, if he were at cards with their wives.

LOV. And they'd be in the right on't too. But I dare trust mine. Besides I know he's in love in another place, and he's not one of those who court half a dozen at a time.

BER. Nay, the truth on't is you'd pity him if you saw how uneasy he is at being engaged with us; but 'twas my malice: I fancied he was to meet his mistress somewhere else, so did it to have the pleasure of seeing him fret.

LOV. What says Amanda to my staying abroad so late?

BER. Why, she's as much out of humour as he; I believe they wish one another at the devil.

LOV. Then I'm afraid they'll quarrel at play, and soon throw up the cards; (*offering to pull her into the closet*) therefore, my dear charming angel, let us make a good use of our time.

BER. Heavens, what do you mean?

LOV. Pray, what do you think I mean?

BER. I don't know.

LOV. I'll show you.

BER. You may as well tell me.

LOV. No, that would make you blush worse than t'other.

BER. Why, do you intend to make me blush?

LOV. Faith, I can't tell that; but if I do, it shall be in the dark.

(*pulling her*)

BER. O, heavens! I would not be in the dark with you for all the world.

LOV. I'll try that.   (*puts out the candle*)

BER. O Lord! are you mad? What shall I do for light?

LOV. You'll do as well without it.

BER. Why, one can't find a chair to sit down!

LOV. Come into the closet, Madam: there's moonshine upon the couch.

BER. Nay, never pull, for I will not go.

LOV. Then you must be carried.   (*carrying her*)

BER. (*very softly*) Help, help, I'm ravished, ruined, undone! O Lord, I shall never be able to bear it.   (*Exeunt.*)

SCENE IV

SCENE: SIR TUNBELLY'S *house*

Enter MISS HOYDEN, *Nurse*, YOUNG FASHION, *and* BULL

Y. FAS. This quick dispatch of yours, Mr. Bull, I take so kindly, it shall give you a claim to my favour as long as I live, I do assure you.

MISS. And to mine too, I promise you.

BULL. I must humbly thank your honours, and I hope, since it has been my lot to join you in the holy bands of wedlock, you will so well cultivate the soil which I have craved a blessing on that your children may swarm about you like bees about a honeycomb.

MISS. I'cod, with all my heart: the more the merrier, I say; ha, nurse?

Enter LORY, *taking his master hastily aside*

LO. One word with you, for heaven's sake.

Y. FAS. What the devil's the matter?

LO. Sir, your fortune's ruined, and I don't think your life's worth a quarter of an hour's purchase: yonder's your brother arrived with two coaches and six horses, twenty footmen and pages, a coat worth fourscore pound, and a periwig down to his knees: so judge what will become of your lady's heart.

Y. FAS. Death and Furies! 'tis impossible.

LO. Fiends and spectres, Sir! 'tis true.

Y. FAS. Is he in the house yet?

LO. No, they are capitulating with him at the gate; the porter tells him he's come to run away with Miss Hoyden, and has cocked the blunderbuss at him; your brother swears, Gad damme, they are a parcel of clawns, and he has a good mind to break off the match; but they have given the word for Sir Tunbelly, so I doubt all will come out presently. Pray, Sir, resolve what you'll do this moment, for i'gad they'll maul you.

Y. FAS. Stay a little.—— (*to* MISS HOYDEN) My dear, here's a troublesome business my man tells me of; but don't be frightened, we shall be too hard for the rogue. Here's an impudent fellow at the gate (not knowing I was come hither *incognito*) has taken my name upon him, in hopes to run away with you.

MISS. Oh, the brazen-faced varlet! it's well we are married, or maybe we might never a been so.

Y. FAS. (*aside*) I'gad, like enough!—— Prithee, dear Doctor, run to Sir Tunbelly and stop him from going to the gate before I speak with him.

BULL. I fly, my good Lord——   (*Exit* BULL.)

NURSE. An't please your honour, my lady and I had best lock ourselves up till the danger be over.

Y. FAS. Ay, by all means.

MISS. Not so fast: I won't be locked up any more. I'm married.

Y. FAS. Yes, pray, my dear, do, till we have seized this rascal.

MISS. Nay, if you pray me, I'll do any thing.

(*Exeunt* MISS HOYDEN *and Nurse.*)

Y. FAS. Oh! here's Sir Tunbelly coming. (*To* LORY.) Hark you,

Sirrah, things are better than you imagine: the wedding's over.

LO. The devil it is, Sir.

Y. FAS. Not a word, all's safe: but Sir Tunbelly don't know it, nor must not yet; so I am resolved to brazen the business out, and have the pleasure of turning the impostor upon his Lordship, which I believe may easily be done.

Enter SIR TUNBELLY, *Chaplain and Servants armed*

Y. FAS. Did you ever hear, Sir, of so impudent an undertaking?

SIR TUN. Never, by the mass; but we'll tickle him, I'll warrant him.

Y. FAS. They tell me, Sir, he has a great many people with him disguised like servants.

SIR. TUN. Ay, ay, rogues enough; but I'll soon raise the posse upon 'em.

Y. FAS. Sir, if you'll take my advice, we'll go a shorter way to work; I find, whoever this spark is, he knows nothing of my being privately here; so if you pretend to receive him civilly, he'll enter without suspicion; and as soon as he is within the gate we'll whip up the drawbridge upon his back, let fly the blunderbuss to disperse his crew, and so commit him to gaol.

SIR TUN. I'gad, your Lordship is an ingenious person, and a very great general; but shall we kill any of 'em, or not?

Y. FAS. No, no, fire over their heads only to fright 'em; I'll warrant the regiment scours when the colonel's a prisoner.

SIR TUN. Then come along, my boys, and let your courage be great—for your danger is but small. (*Exeunt.*)

SCENE V

SCENE: *The gate*

Enter LORD FOPPINGTON *and Followers*

LORD FOP. A pax of these bumpkinly people!—will they open the gate, or do they desire I should grow at their moat-side like a willow? (*to the Porter*) Hey, fellow—prithee do me the favour, in as few words as thou canst find to express thyself, to tell me whether thy master will admit me or not, that I may turn about my coach and be gone.

POR. Here's my master himself now at hand; he's of age, he'll give you his answer.

Enter SIR TUNBELLY *and Servants*

SIR TUN. My most noble Lord, I crave your pardon for making your honour wait so long; but my orders to my servants have been to admit nobody without my knowledge, for fear of some attempt upon my daughter, the times being full of plots and roguery.

LORD FOP. Much caution, I must confess, is a sign of great wisdom: but, stap my vitals, I have got a cold enough to destroy a porter—he, hem——

SIR TUN. I am very sorry for't, indeed, my Lord; but if your Lordship please to walk in, we'll help you to some brown sugar-candy. My Lord, I'll show you the way.

LORD FOP. Sir, I follow you with pleasure.   (*Exeunt.*)

(*As* LORD FOPPINGTON's *Servants go to follow him in, they clap the door against* LA VÉROLE.)

SERVANTS (*within*) Nay, hold you me there, Sir.

LA VÉR. *Jernie die, qu'est ce que veut dire ça?*

SIR TUN. (*within*)——Fire, porter.

PORT. (*fires*) Have among ye, my masters!

LA VÉR. *Ah, je suis mort*——   (*The Servants all run off.*)

PORT. Not one soldier left, by the mass.

SCENE VI

Scene changes to the hall

Enter SIR TUNBELLY, *the Chaplain and Servants, with* LORD FOPPINGTON *disarmed*

SIR TUN. Come, bring him along, bring him along.

LORD FOP. What the pax do you mean, gentlemen? is it fair time, that you are all drunk before dinner?

SIR TUN. Drunk, Sirrah? Here's an impudent rogue for you! Drunk or sober, bully, I'm a justice of the peace, and know how to deal with strollers.

LORD FOP. Strollers!

SIR TUN. Ay, strollers; come, give an account of yourself;

what's your name? where do you live? Do you pay scot and lot? Are you a Williamite, or a Jacobite? Come.

LORD FOP. And why dost thou ask me so many impertinent questions?

SIR TUN. Because I'll make you answer 'em before I have done with you, you rascal you.

LORD FOP. Before Gad, all the answer I can make thee to 'em, is, that thou art a very extraordinary old fellow; stap my vitals——

SIR TUN. Nay, if you are for joking with deputy-lieutenants, we'st know how to deal with you.—Here, draw a warrant for him immediately.

LORD FOP. A warrant—what the devil is't thou wouldst be at, old gentleman?

SIR TUN. I would be at you, Sirrah (if my hands were not tied as a magistrate), and with these two double fists beat your teeth down your throat, you dog you.

LORD FOP. And why would'st thou spoil my face at that rate?

SIR TUN. For your design to rob me of my daughter, villain.

LORD FOP. Rab thee of thy daughter!—(aside) Now do I begin to believe I am abed and asleep, and that all this is but a dream. If it be, 'twill be an agreeable surprise enough to waken by and by and instead of the impertinent company of a nasty country justice, find myself, perhaps, in the arms of a woman of quality. (to SIR TUNBELLY) Prithee, old father, wilt thou give me leave to ask thee one question?

SIR TUN. I can't tell whether I will or not, till I know what it is.

LORD FOP. Why, then, it is whether thou didst not write to my Lord Foppington to come down and marry thy daughter.

SIR TUN. Yes, marry did I, and my Lord Foppington is come down, and shall marry my daughter before she's a day older.

LORD FOP. Now give me thy hand, dear Dad: I thought we should understand one another at last.

SIR TUN. This fellow's mad—here, bind him hand and foot.
(They bind him down.)

LORD FOP. Nay, prithee, knight, leave fooling: thy jest begins to grow dull.

SIR TUN. Bind him, I say, he's mad—bread and water, a dark room, and a whip, may bring him to his senses again.

LORD FOP. (*aside*) I'gad, if I don't waken quickly, bv all I can see, this is like to prove one of the most impertinent dreams that ever I dreamt in my life.

Enter MISS HOYDEN *and Nurse*

MISS. (*going up to him*) Is this he that would have run away with me? Fough, how he stinks of sweets! Pray, Father, let him be dragged through the horse-pond.

LORD FOP. (*aside*) This must be my wife, by her natural inclination to her husband.

MISS. Pray, Father, what do you intend to do with him? hang him?

SIR TUN. That at least, child.

NURSE. Ay, and it's e'en too good for him too.

LORD FOP. (*aside*) *Madame la gouvernante,* I presume: hitherto this appears to me to be one of the most extraordinary families that ever man of quality matched into.

SIR TUN. What's become of my Lord, daughter?

MISS. He's just coming, Sir.

LORD FOP. (*aside*) "My Lord!"—what does he mean by that, now?

Enter YOUNG FASHION *and* LORY

(*seeing him*) Stap my vitals—Tam! Now the dream's out.

Y. FAS. Is this the fellow, Sir, that designed to trick me of your daughter?

SIR TUN. This is he, my Lord: how do you like him? Is not he a pretty fellow to get a fortune?

Y. FAS. I find by his dress, he thought your daughter might be taken with a beau.

MISS. O Gemini! Is this a beau? let me see him again—ha! I find a beau is no such ugly thing, neither.

Y. FAS. I'gad, she'll be in love with him presently; I'll e'en have him sent away to gaol. (*to* LORD FOPPINGTON) Sir, though your undertaking shows you are a person of no extraordinary modesty, I suppose you han't confidence enough to expect much favour from me?

LORD FOP. Strike me dumb, Tam, thou art a very impudent fellow.

NURSE. Look if the varlet has not the frontery to call his Lordship plain Thomas.

BULL. The business is, he would feign himself mad, to avoid going to gaol.

LORD FOP. (*aside*) That must be the chaplain, by his unfolding of mysteries.

SIR TUN. Come, is the warrant writ?

CLERK. Yes, Sir.

SIR TUN. Give me the pen, I'll sign it—so!—now, Constable, away with him.

LORD FOP. Hold one moment—pray, gentlemen! My Lord Foppington, shall I beg one word with your Lordship?

NURSE. O ho, it's "my Lord" with him now; see how afflictions will humble folks.

MISS. Pray, my Lord, don't let him whisper too close, lest he bite your ear off.

LORD FOP. I am not altogether so hungry as your Ladyship is pleased to imagine. (*to* YOUNG FASHION) Look you, Tam, I am sensible I have not been so kind to you as I ought, but I hope you'll forget what's past, and accept of the five thousand pounds I offer; thou may'st live in extreme splendour with it, stap my vitals.

Y. FAS. It's a much easier matter to prevent a disease than to cure it; a quarter of that sum would have secured your mistress; twice as much won't redeem her.   (*leaving him*)

SIR TUN. Well, what says he?

Y. FAS. Only the rascal offered me a bribe to let him go.

SIR TUN. Ay, he shall go, with a pox to him.—— Lead on, Constable.

LORD FOP. One word more, and I have done.

SIR TUN. Before Gad, thou art an impudent fellow to trouble the court at this rate, after thou art condemned; but speak once for all.

LORD FOP. Why then once for all, I have at last luckily called to mind that there is a gentleman of this country, who I believe cannot live far from this place, if he were here would satisfy you I am Navelty, Baron of Foppington, with five thousand pounds a year, and that fellow there a rascal not worth a groat.

SIR TUN. Very well; now who is this honest gentleman you are so well acquainted with? (*to* YOUNG FASHION) Come, Sir, we shall hamper him.

LORD FOP. 'Tis Sir John Friendly.

SIR TUN. So: he lives within half a mile, and came down into the country but last night; this bold-faced fellow thought he had been at London still, and so quoted him; now we shall display him in his colours: I'll send for Sir John immediately.——— Here, fellow, away presently, and desire my neighbour he'll do me the favour to step over, upon an extraordinary occasion; (*exit Servant*)—and in the meanwhile you had best secure this sharper in the gate-house.

CONST. An't please your Worship, he may chance to give us the slip thence: if I were worthy to advise, I think the dog-kennel's a surer place.

SIR TUN. With all my heart, anywhere.

LORD FOP. Nay, for heaven's sake, Sir, do me the favour to put me in a clean room, that I mayn't daub my clothes.

SIR TUN. Oh, when you have married my daughter, her estate will afford you new ones.——— Away with him.

LORD FOP. A dirty country justice is a barbarous magistrate, stap my vitals!   (*Exit Constable with* LORD FOPPINGTON.)

Y. FAS. (*aside*) I'gad, I must prevent this knight's coming, or the house will grow soon too hot to hold me. (*To* SIR TUNBELLY.) Sir, I fancy 'tis not worth while to trouble Sir John upon this impertinent fellow's desire: I'll send and call the messenger back———

SIR TUN. Nay, with all my heart; for to be sure he thought he was far enough off, or the rogue would never have named him.

Enter Servant

SERV. Sir, I met Sir John just lighting at the gate; he's come to wait upon you.

SIR TUN. Nay, then it happens as one could wish.

Y. FAS. (*aside*) The devil it does!——— Lory, you see how things are: here will be a discovery presently, and we shall have our brains beat out, for my brother will be sure to swear he don't know me: therefore run into the stable, take the two first horses you can light on: I'll slip out at the back door, and we'll away immediately.

LO. What, and leave your lady, Sir?

Y. FAS. There's no danger in that, as long as I have taken possession; I shall know how to treat with 'em well enough, if once I am out of their reach: away, I'll steal after thee.

> (*Exit* LORY: *his master follows him out at one door, as* SIR JOHN *enters at t'other.*)

Enter SIR JOHN

SIR TUN. Sir John, you are the welcom'st man alive; I had just sent a messenger to desire you'd step over, upon a very extraordinary occasion—we are all in arms here.

SIR JOHN. How so?

SIR TUN. Why, you must know—a finical sort of a tawdry fellow here (I don't know who the devil he is, not I) hearing, I suppose, that the match was concluded between my Lord Foppington and my girl Hoyden, comes impudently to the gate, with a whole pack of rogues in liveries, and would have passed upon me for his Lordship: but what does I? I comes up to him boldly at the head of his guards, takes him by the throat, strikes up his heels, binds him hand and foot, dispatches a warrant, and commits him prisoner to the dog-kennel.

SIR JOHN. So, but how do you know but this was my Lord? for I was told he set out from London the day before me, with a very fine retinue, and intended to come directly hither.

SIR TUN. Why now to show you how many lies people raise in that damned town, he came two nights ago post, with only one servant, and is now in the house with me. But you don't know the cream of the jest yet; this same rogue (that lies yonder neck and heels among the hounds) thinking you were out of the country, quotes you for his acquaintance, and said if you were here you'd justify him to be Lord Foppington, and I know not what.

SIR JOHN. Pray will you let me see him?

SIR TUN. Ay, that you shall presently.—— Here, fetch the prisoner.   (*Exit Servant.*)

SIR JOHN. I wish there ben't some mistake in this business; where's my Lord? I know him very well.

SIR TUN. He was here just now—— see for him, Doctor, tell him Sir John is here to wait upon him.   (*Exit Chaplain.*)

SIR JOHN. I hope, Sir Tunbelly, the young lady is not married yet.

SIR TUN. No, things won't be ready this week; but why do you say you hope she is not married?

SIR JOHN. Some foolish fancies only; perhaps I'm mistaken.

Re-enter Chaplain

BULL. Sir, his Lordship is just rid out to take the air.

SIR TUN. To take the air! is that his London breeding, to go take the air when gentlemen come to visit him?

SIR JOHN. 'Tis possible he might want it: he might not be well, some sudden qualm perhaps.

Enter Constable, etc., with LORD FOPPINGTON

LORD FOP. Stap my vitals, I'll have satisfaction.

SIR JOHN (running to him) My dear Lord Foppington!

LORD FOP. Dear Friendly, thou art come in the critical minute, strike me dumb.

SIR JOHN. Why, I little thought I should have found you in fetters.

LORD FOP. Why truly, the world must do me the justice to confess I do use to appear a little more *dégagé:* but this old gentleman, not liking the freedom of my air, has been pleased to skewer down my arms like a rabbit.

SIR TUN. Is it then possible that this should be the true Lord Foppington at last?

LORD FOP. Why, what do you see in his face to make you doubt of it? Sir, without presuming to have any extraordinary opinion of my figure, give me leave to tell you, if you had seen as many lords as I have done, you would not think it impossible a person of a worse *taille* than mine might be a modern man of quality.

SIR TUN. Unbind him, slaves.—— My Lord, I'm struck dumb: I can only beg pardon by signs; but if a sacrifice will appease you, you shall have it.—— Here, pursue this Tartar, bring him back—away, I say!—a dog, oons!—I'll cut off his ears and his tail, I'll draw out all his teeth, pull his skin over his head—and —and what shall I do more?

SIR JOHN. He does indeed deserve to be made an example of.

LORD FOP. He does deserve to be *châtré,* stap my vitals.

SIR TUN. May I then hope I have your honour's pardon?

LORD FOP. Sir, we courtiers do nothing without a bribe; that fair young lady might do miracles.

SIR TUN. Hoyden, come hither, Hoyden.

LORD FOP. Hoyden is her name, Sir?

SIR TUN. Yes, my Lord.

LORD FOP. The prettiest name for a song I ever heard.

SIR TUN. My Lord—here's my girl, she's yours; she has a wholesome body and a virtuous mind; she's a woman complete, both in flesh and in spirit; she has a bag of milled crowns, as scarce as they are, and fifteen hundred a year stitched fast to her tail: so go thy ways, Hoyden.

LORD FOP. Sir, I do receive her like a gentleman.

SIR TUN. Then I'm a happy man, I bless heaven, and if your Lordship will give me leave, I will, like a good Christian at Christmas, be very drunk by way of thanksgiving. Come, my noble peer, I believe dinner's ready; if your honour pleases to follow me, I'll lead you on to the attack of a venison pasty.

(*Exit* SIR TUNBELLY.)

LORD FOP. Sir, I wait upon you.—— Will your Ladyship do me the favour of your little finger, Madam?

MISS. My Lord, I'll follow you presently: I have a little business with my nurse.

LORD FOP. Your Ladyship's most humble servant.—— Come, Sir John, the ladies have *des affaires*.

(*Exeunt* LORD FOPPINGTON *and* SIR JOHN.)

MISS. So, nurse, we are finely brought to bed! What shall we do now?

NURSE. Ah, dear miss, we are all undone! Mr. Bull, you were used to help a woman to a remedy.   (*crying*)

BULL. Alack-a-day, but it's past my skill now; I can do nothing.

NURSE. Who would have thought that ever your invention should have been drained so dry?

MISS. Well, I have often thought old folks fools, and now I'm sure they are so; I have found a way myself to secure us all.

NURSE. Dear lady, what's that?

MISS. Why, if you two will be sure to hold your tongues, and not say a word of what's past, I'll e'en marry this lord too.

NURSE. What! two husbands, my dear?

MISS. Why you have had three, good nurse; you may hold your tongue.

NURSE. Ay, but not all together, sweet child.

MISS. Psha, if you had, you'd ne'er a thought much on't.

NURSE. Oh, but 'tis a sin—sweeting.

BULL. Nay, that's my business to speak to, nurse: I do confess, to take two husbands for the satisfaction of the flesh is to commit the sin of exorbitancy, but to do it for the peace of the spirit is no more than to be drunk by way of physic: besides, to prevent a parent's wrath is to avoid the sin of disobedience; for when the parent's angry the child is froward. So that upon the whole matter, I do think, though Miss should marry again, she may be saved.

MISS. I'cod, and I will marry again then, and so there's an end of the story.   (*Exeunt.*)

ACT V

SCENE I

SCENE: *London*

Enter COUPLER, YOUNG FASHION, *and* LORY

COUP. Well, and so Sir John coming in——?

Y. FAS. And so Sir John coming in, I thought it might be manners in me to go out, which I did, and getting on horseback as fast as I could, rid away as if the devil had been at the rear of me; what has happened since, heav'n knows.

COUP. I'gad, Sirrah, I know as well as heaven.

Y. FAS. What do you know?

COUP. That you are a cuckold.

Y. FAS. The devil I am! by who?

COUP. By your brother.

Y. FAS. My brother! which way?

COUP. The old way—he has lain with your wife.

Y. FAS. Hell and Furies, what dost thou mean?

COUP. I mean plainly; I speak no parable.

Y. FAS. Plainly! Thou dost not speak common sense; I cannot understand one word thou say'st.

COUP. You will do soon, youngster. In short, you left your wife a widow, and she married again.

Y. FAS. It's a lie.

COUP.——I'cod, if I were a young fellow, I'd break your head, Sirrah.

Y. FAS. Dear Dad, don't be angry, for I'm as mad as Tom of Bedlam.

COUP. Then I had fitted you with a wife, you should have kept her.

Y. FAS. But is it possible the young strumpet could play me such a trick?

COUP. A young strumpet, Sir—can play twenty tricks.

Y. FAS. But prithee instruct me a little farther; whence comes thy intelligence!

COUP. From your brother, in this letter: there you may read it.

Y. FAS. (*reads*) "DEAR COUPLER, (*pulling off his hat*) I have only time to tell thee in three lines, or thereabouts, that here has been the devil: that rascal Tam, having stole the letter thou hadst formerly writ for me to bring to Sir Tunbelly, formed a damnable design upon my mistress, and was in a fair way of success when I arrived. But after having suffered some indignities (in which I have all daubed my embroidered coat) I put him to flight. I sent out a party of horse after him, in hopes to have made him my prisoner, which if I had done, I would have qualified him for the seraglio, stap my vitals.

"The danger I have thus narrowly 'scaped has made me fortify myself against further attempts by entering immediately into an association with the young lady, by which we engage to stand by one another as long as we both shall live.

"In short, the papers are sealed and the contract is signed, so the business of the lawyer is *achevé;* but I defer the divine part of the thing till I arrive at London, not being willing to consummate in any other bed but my own.

"POSTSCRIPT. 'Tis passible I may be in tawn as soon as this letter, for I find the lady is so violently in love with me, I have determined to make her happy with all the dispatch that is practicable, without disardering my coach harses."

So, here's rare work, i'faith!

LO. I'gad, Miss Hoyden has laid about her bravely.

COUP. I think my country girl has played her part as well as if she had been born and bred in St. James's parish.

Y. FAS. ——That rogue the chaplain!

LO. And then that jade the nurse, Sir.

Y. FAS. And then that drunken sot, Lory, Sir, that could not keep himself sober to be a witness to the marriage.

LO. Sir—with respect—I know very few drunken sots that do keep themselves sober.

Y. FAS. Hold your prating, Sirrah, or I'll break your head. Dear Coupler, what's to be done?

COUP. Nothing's to be done till the bride and bridegroom come to town.

Y. FAS. Bride and bridegroom? Death and Furies, I can't bear that thou shouldst call 'em so.

COUP. Why, what shall I call 'em, dog and cat?

Y. FAS. Not for the world; that sounds more like man and wife than t'other.

COUP. Well, if you'll hear of 'em in no language, we'll leave 'em for the nurse and the chaplain.

Y. FAS. The devil and the witch.

COUP. When they come to town——

LO. We shall have stormy weather.

COUP. Will you hold your tongues, gentlemen, or not?

LO. Mum.

COUP. I say, when they come we must find what stuff they are made of—whether the churchman be chiefly composed of the flesh or the spirit; I presume the former, for as chaplains now go, 'tis probable he eats three pound of beef to the reading of one chapter; this gives him carnal desires: he wants money, preferment, wine, a whore; therefore we must invite him to supper, give him fat capons, sack and sugar, a purse of gold, and a plump sister. Let this be done, and I'll warrant thee, my boy, he speaks truth like an oracle.

Y. FAS. Thou art a profound statesman, I allow it; but how shall we gain the nurse?

COUP. Oh, never fear the nurse, if once you have got the priest, for the devil always rides the hag.

Well, there's nothing more to be said of the matter at this time, that I know of; so let us go and enquire if there's any news of our people yet; perhaps they may be come.

But let me tell you one thing by the way, Sirrah: I doubt you have been an idle fellow; if thou hadst behaved thyself as thou shouldst have done, the girl would never have left thee.

(*Exeunt.*)

SCENE: BERINTHIA's *apartment*

Enter her Maid, passing the stage, followed by WORTHY

WOR. Hem, Mrs. Abigail, is your mistress to be spoken with?

AB. By you, Sir, I believe she may.

WOR. Why 'tis by me I would have her spoken with.

AB. I'll acquaint her, Sir.   (*Exit* ABIGAIL.)

WOR. (*solus*) One lift more I must persuade her to give me, and then I'm mounted. Well, a young bawd and a handsome one for my money: 'tis they do the execution; I'll never go to an old one, but when I have occasion for a witch.

Lewdness looks heavenly to a woman when an angel appears in its cause, but when a hag is advocate, she thinks it comes from the devil.

An old woman has something so terrible in her looks, that whilst she is persuading your mistress to forget she has a soul, she stares hell and damnation full in her face.

Enter BERINTHIA

BER. Well, Sir, what news bring you?

WOR. No news, Madam: there's a woman going to cuckold her husband.

BER. Amanda?

WOR. I hope so.

BER. Speed her well.

WOR. Ay, but there must be more than a Godspeed, or your charity won't be worth a farthing.

BER. Why, han't I done enough already?

WOR. Not quite.

BER. What's the matter?

WOR. The lady has a scruple still, which you must remove.

BER. What's that?

WOR. Her virtue—she says.

BER. And do you believe her?

WOR. No, but I believe it's what she takes for her virtue; it's some relics of lawful love: she is not yet fully satisfied her husband has got another mistress, which unless I can convince her of, I have opened the trenches in vain, for the breach must be wider before I dare storm the town.

BER. And so I'm to be your engineer?

WOR. I'm sure you know best how to manage the battery.

BER. What think you of springing a mine? I have a thought just now come into my head, how to blow her up at once.

WOR. That would be a thought, indeed!

BER. ——Faith, I'll do't, and thus the execution of it shall be. We are all invited to my Lord Foppington's to-night to supper; he's come to town with his bride, and makes a ball, with an entertainment of music. Now you must know, my undoer here, Loveless, says he must needs meet me about some private business (I don't know what 'tis) before we go to the company. To which end he has told his wife one lie, and I have told her another. But to make her amends, I'll go immediately and tell her a solemn truth.

WOR. What's that?

BER. Why, I'll tell her that to my certain knowledge her husband has a rendezvous with his mistress this afternoon; and that if she'll give me her word she'll be satisfied with the discovery without making any violent inquiry after the woman, I'll direct her to a place where she shall see 'em meet. Now, friend, this I fancy may help you to a critical minute. For home she must go again to dress. You, with your good breeding, come to wait upon us to the ball, find her all alone, her spirit enflamed against her husband for his treason, and her flesh in a heat from some contemplations upon the treachery; her blood on a fire, her conscience in ice; a lover to draw, and the devil to drive—— Ah, poor Amanda!

WOR. (kneeling) Thou angel of light, let me fall down and adore thee!

BER. Thou minister of darkness, get up again, for I hate to see the devil at his devotions.

WOR. Well, my incomparable Berinthia—how shall I requite you?

BER. Oh, ne'er trouble yourself about that: Virtue is its own reward: there's a pleasure in doing good, which sufficiently pays itself. Adieu.

WOR. Farewell, thou best of women.   (*Exeunt several ways.*)

Enter AMANDA, *meeting* BERINTHIA

AMAN. Who was that went from you?

BER. A friend of yours.

AMAN. What does he want?

BER. Something you might spare him, and be ne'er the poorer.

AMAN. I can spare him nothing but my friendship; my love already's all disposed of: though, I confess, to one ungrateful to my bounty.

BER. Why, there's the mystery: you have been so bountiful you have cloyed him. Fond wives do by their husbands as barren wives do by their lap-dogs: cram 'em with sweetmeats till they spoil their stomachs.

AMAN. Alas! Had you but seen how passionately fond he has been since our last reconciliation, you would have thought it were impossible he ever should have breathed an hour without me.

BER. Ay, but there you thought wrong again, Amanda; you should consider that in matters of love men's eyes are always bigger than their bellies. They have violent appetites, 'tis true, but they have soon dined.

AMAN. Well; there's nothing upon earth astonishes me more than men's inconstancy.

BER. Now there's nothing upon earth astonishes me less, when I consider what they and we are composed of. For nature has made them children, and us babies. Now, Amanda, how we used our babies, you may remember. We were mad to have 'em as soon as we saw 'em; kissed 'em to pieces as soon as we got 'em; then pulled off their clothes, saw 'em naked, and so threw 'em away.

AMAN. But do you think all men are of this temper?

BER. All but one.

AMAN. Who is that?

BER. Worthy.

AMAN. Why, he's weary of his wife too, you see.

BER. Ay, that's no proof.

AMAN. What can be a greater?

BER. Being weary of his mistress.

AMAN. Don't you think 'twere possible he might give you that too?

BER. Perhaps he might, if he were my gallant; not if he were yours.

AMAN. Why do you think he should be more constant to me than he would to you? I'm sure I'm not so handsome.

BER. Kissing goes by favour; he likes you best.

AMAN. Suppose he does: that's no demonstration he would be constant to me.

BER. No, that I'll grant you: but there are other reasons to expect it; for you must know after all, Amanda, the inconstancy we commonly see in men of brains does not so much proceed from the uncertainty of their temper as from the misfortunes of their love. A man sees perhaps a hundred women he likes well enough for an intrigue and away, but possibly, through the whole course of his life, does not find above one who is exactly what he could wish her: now her, 'tis a thousand to one, he never gets. Either she is not to be had at all (though that seldom happens, you'll say) or he wants those opportunities that are necessary to gain her. Either she likes somebody else much better than him or uses him like a dog because he likes nobody so well as her. Still something or other fate claps in the way between them and the woman they are capable of being fond of: and this makes them wander about from mistress to mistress, like a pilgrim from town to town, who every night must have a fresh lodging, and 's in haste to be gone in the morning.

AMAN. 'Tis possible there may be something in what you say; but what do you infer from it, as to the man we were talking of?

BER. Why, I infer that you being the woman in the world the most to his humour, 'tis not likely he would quit you for one that is less.

AMAN. That is not to be depended upon, for you see Mr. Loveless does so.

BER. What does Mr. Loveless do?

AMAN. Why, he runs after something for variety, I'm sure he does not like so well as he does me.

BER. That's more than you know, Madam.

AMAN. No, I'm sure on't: I'm not very vain, Berinthia, and yet

I'd lay my life, if I could look into his heart, he thinks I deserve to be preferred to a thousand of her.

BER. Don't be too positive in that, neither: a million to one, but she has the same opinion of you. What would you give to see her?

AMAN. Hang her, dirty trull! though I really believe she's so ugly she'd cure me of my jealousy.

BER. All the men of sense about town say she's handsome.

AMAN. They are as often out in those things as any people.

BER. Then I'll give you farther proof—all the women about town say she's a fool: now I hope you're convinced?

AMAN. Whate'er she be, I'm satisfied he does not like her well enough to bestow anything more than a little outward gallantry upon her.

BER. Outward gallantry?——(aside) I can't bear this. (To AMANDA.) Don't you think she's a woman to be fobbed off so. Come, I'm too much your friend to suffer you should be thus grossly imposed upon by a man who does not deserve the least part about you, unless he knew how to set a greater value upon it. Therefore, in one word, to my certain knowledge he is to meet her, now, within a quarter of an hour, somewhere about that Babylon of wickedness, Whitehall. And if you'll give me your word that you'll be content with seeing her masked in his hand, without pulling her headclothes off, I'll step immediately to the person from whom I have my intelligence, and send you word whereabouts you may stand to see 'em meet. My friend and I'll watch 'em from another place, and dodge 'em to their private lodging: but don't you offer to follow 'em, lest you do it awkwardly, and spoil all. I'll come home to you again, as soon as I have earthed 'em, and give you an account in what corner of the house the scene of their lewdness lies.

AMAN. If you can do this, Berinthia, he's a villain.

BER. I can't help that: men will be so.

AMAN. Well! I'll follow your directions, for I shall never rest till I know the worst of this matter.

BER. Pray, go immediately, and get yourself ready, then. Put on some of your woman's clothes, a great scarf and a mask, and you shall presently receive orders. (calls within) Here, who's there? get me a chair quickly.

Enter Servant.

SERV. There are chairs at the door, Madam.

BER. 'Tis well; I'm coming.   (*Exit Servant.*)

AMAN. But pray, Berinthia, before you go, tell me how I may know this filthy thing, if she should be so forward (as I suppose she will) to come to the rendezvous first; for methinks I would fain view her a little.

BER. Why, she's about my height, and very well shaped.

AMAN. I thought she had been a little crooked?

BER. Oh no, she's as straight as I am. But we lose time: come away.   (*Exeunt.*)

SCENE III

Enter YOUNG FASHION, *meeting* LORY

Y. FAS. Well, will the doctor come?

LO. Sir, I sent a porter to him as you ordered me. He found him with a pipe of tobacco and a great tankard of ale, which he said he would dispatch while I could tell three, and be here.

Y. FAS. He does not suspect 'twas I that sent for him?

LO. Not a jot, Sir; he divines as little for himself as he does for other folks.

Y. FAS. Will he bring nurse with him?

LO. Yes.

Y. FAS. That's well; where's Coupler?

LO. He's half way up the stairs taking breath; he must play his bellows a little before he can get to the top.

Enter COUPLER

Y. FAS. Oh, here he is. Well, old phthisic? The doctor's coming.

COUP. Would the pox had the doctor—I'm quite out of wind. (*to* LORY) Set me a chair, Sirrah. Ah! (*sits down. To* YOUNG FASHION) Why the plague canst not thou lodge upon the ground floor?

Y. FAS. Because I love to lie as near heaven as I can.

COUP. Prithee let heaven alone; ne'er affect tending that way: thy centre's downwards.

Y. FAS. That's impossible. I have too much ill luck in this world to be damned in the next.

COUP. Thou art out in thy logic. Thy major is true, but thy minor is false; for thou art the luckiest fellow in the universe.

Y. FAS. Make out that.

COUP. I'll do't: last night the devil ran away with the parson of Fatgoose living.

Y. FAS. If he had run away with the parish too, what's that to me?

COUP. I'll tell thee what it's to thee. This living is worth five hundred pound a year, and the presentation of it is thine, if thou canst prove thyself a lawful husband to Miss Hoyden.

Y. FAS. Say'st thou so, my protector? then i'cad I shall have a brace of evidences here presently.

COUP. The nurse and the doctor?

Y. FAS. The same: the devil himself won't have interest enough to make 'em withstand it.

COUP. That we shall see presently: here they come.

Enter Nurse and Chaplain; they start back, seeing
YOUNG FASHION

NURSE. Ah goodness, Roger, we are betrayed.

Y. FAS. (*laying hold on 'em*) Nay, nay, ne'er flinch for the matter, for I have you safe. Come, to your trials immediately: I have no time to give you copies of your indictment. There sits your judge.

BOTH. (*kneeling*) Pray, Sir, have compassion on us.

NURSE. I hope, Sir, my years will move your pity; I am an aged woman.

COUP. That is a moving argument, indeed.

BULL. I hope, Sir, my character will be considered; I am heaven's ambassador.

COUP. (*to* BULL) Are not you a rogue of sanctity?

BULL. Sir, with respect to my function, I do wear a gown.

COUP. Did not you marry this vigorous young fellow to a plump young buxom wench?

NURSE. (*to* BULL) Don't confess, Roger, unless you are hard put to it, indeed.

COUP. Come, out with't!—— Now is he chewing the cud of his roguery, and grinding a lie between his teeth.

BULL. Sir—I cannot positively say—I say, Sir—positively I cannot say——

COUP. Come, no equivocations, no Roman turns upon us. Consider thou standest upon Protestant ground, which will slip from under thee like a Tyburn cart; for in this country we have always ten hangmen for one Jesuit.

BULL. (*to* YOUNG FASHION) Pray, Sir, then will you but permit me to speak one word in private with nurse?

Y. FAS. Thou art always for doing something in private with nurse.

COUP. But pray let his betters be served before him for once. I would do something in private with her myself. Lory, take care of this reverend gownman in the next room a little. Retire, priest. (*Exit* LORY *with* BULL.)—— Now, virgin, I must put the matter home to you a little: do you think it might not be possible to make you speak truth?

NURSE. Alas! Sir, I don't know what you mean by truth.

COUP. Nay, 'tis possible thou may'st be a stranger to it.

Y. FAS. Come, nurse, you and I were better friends when we saw one another last and I still believe you are a very good woman in the bottom. I did deceive you and your young lady, 'tis true, but I always designed to make a very good husband to her, and to be a very good friend to you. And 'tis possible, in the end she might have found herself happier and you richer than ever my brother will make you.

NURSE. Brother! Why, is your Worship then his Lordship's brother?

Y. FAS. I am; which you should have known, if I durst have stayed to have told you; but I was forced to take horse a little in haste, you know.

NURSE. You were, indeed, Sir: poor young man, how he was bound to scour for't. Now won't your Worship be angry if I confess the truth to you: when I found you were a cheat (with respect be it spoken) I verily believed Miss had got some pitiful skip-jack varlet or other to her husband, or I had ne'er let her think of marrying again.

COUP. But where was your conscience all this while, woman? Did not that stare in your face with huge saucer-eyes, and a great horn upon the forehead? Did not you think you should be damned for such a sin? Ha?

Y. FAS. Well said, divinity: pass that home upon her.

NURSE. Why, in good truly, Sir, I had some fearful thoughts

on't, and could never be brought to consent, till Mr. Bull said it
was a *peckadilla,* and he'd secure my soul for a tithe-pig.

Y. FAS. There was a rogue for you!

COUP. And he shall thrive accordingly: he shall have a good
living. Come, honest nurse, I see you have butter in your compound: you can melt. Some compassion you can have of this
handsome young fellow.

NURSE. I have, indeed, Sir.

Y. FAS. Why, then, I'll tell you what you shall do for me. You
know what a warm living here is fallen, and that it must be in
the disposal of him who has the disposal of Miss. Now if you
and the doctor will agree to prove my marriage, I'll present him
to it, upon condition he makes you his bride.

NURSE. Naw the blessing of the Lord follow your good Worship both by night and by day! Let him be fetched in by the ears;
I'll soon bring his nose to the grindstone.

COUP. (*aside*) Well said, old white-leather.—— Hey; bring in
the prisoner there.

Enter LORY *with* BULL

COUP. Come, advance, holy man! Here's your duck, does not
think fit to retire with you into the chancel at this time; but she
has a proposal to make to you in the face of the congregation.
Come, nurse, speak for yourself; you are of age.

NURSE. Roger, are not you a wicked man, Roger, to set your
strength against a weak woman, and persuade her it was no sin
to conceal Miss's nuptials? My conscience flies in my face for it,
thou priest of Baal; and I find by woful experience, thy absolution is not worth an old cassock. Therefore I am resolved to confess the truth to the whole world, though I die a beggar for it.
But his worship overflows with his mercy and his bounty: he is
not only pleased to forgive us our sins, but designs thou shalt
squat thee down in Fatgoose living; and, which is more than all,
has prevailed with me to become the wife of thy bosom.

Y. FAS. All this I intend for you, Doctor. What you are to do
for me, I need not tell you.

BULL. Your Worship's goodness is unspeakable. Yet there is
one thing seems a point of conscience, and conscience is a tender
babe. If I should bind myself, for the sake of this living, to marry

nurse, and maintain her afterwards, I doubt it might be looked on as a kind of simony.

COUP. (*rising up*) If it were sacrilege, the living's worth it: therefore no more words, good Doctor, but with the parish—here (*giving Nurse to him*)—take the parsonage-house. 'Tis true, 'tis a little out of repair; some dilapidations there are to be made good; the windows are broke, the wainscot is warped, the ceilings are peeled, and the walls are cracked; but a little glazing, painting, whitewash, and plaster will make it last thy time.

BULL. Well, Sir, if it must be so, I shan't contend: what Providence orders, I submit to.

NURSE. And so do I, with all humility.

COUP. Why, that now was spoke like good people: come, my turtle-doves, let us go help this poor pigeon to his wandering mate again; and after institution and induction you shall all go a-cooing together. (*Exeunt.*)

SCENE IV

Enter AMANDA, *in a scarf, etc., as just returned, her Woman following her*

AMAN. Prithee, what care I who has been here?

WOM. Madam, 'twas my Lady Bridle and my Lady Tiptoe.

AMAN. My Lady Fiddle and my Lady Faddle. What dost stand troubling me with the visits of a parcel of impertinent women? when they are well seamed with the small-pox they won't be so fond of showing their faces. There are more coquettes about this town——

WOM. Madam, I suppose they only came to return your Ladyship's visit, according to the custom of the world.

AMAN. Would the world were on fire, and you in the middle on't! Begone: leave me. (*Exit Woman.*)

AMAN. (*sola*) At last I am convinc'd. My eyes are testimonies of his falsehood.
The base, ungrateful, perjur'd villain——
Good gods—what slippery stuff are men compos'd of?
Sure the account of their creation's false,
And 'twas the woman's rib that they were form'd of.
But why am I thus angry?
This poor relapse should only move my scorn.

'Tis true, the roving flights of his unfinish'd youth
Had strong excuse from the plea of Nature:
Reason had thrown the reins loose on his neck,
And slipt him to unlimited desire.
If therefore he went wrong, he had a claim
To my forgiveness, and I did him right.
But since the years of manhood rein him in,
And reason, well digested into thought,
Has pointed out the course he ought to run;
If now he strays?
'Twould be as weak and mean in me to pardon,
As it has been in him t'offend. But hold:
'Tis an ill cause indeed, where nothing's to be said for't.
My beauty possibly is in the wane:
Perhaps sixteen has greater charms for him:
Yes, there's the secret. But let him know,
My quiver's not entirely empty'd yet,
I still have darts, and I can shoot 'em too;
They're not so blunt, but they can enter still;
The want's not in my power, but in my will.
Virtue's his friend; or, through another's heart,
I yet could find the way to make his smart.

(*Going off, she meets* WORTHY.)

Ha! He here?
Protect me, heaven, for this looks ominous.
    WOR. You seem disorder'd, Madam;
I hope there's no misfortune happen'd to you?
        AMAN. None that will long disorder me, I hope.
    WOR. Whate'er it be disturbs you,
I would to heaven 'twere in my power
To bear the pain till I were able to remove the cause.
        AMAN. I hope ere long it will remove itself.
At least, I have given it warning to be gone.
    WOR. Would I durst ask, where 'tis the thorn torments you?
Forgive me if I grow inquisitive;
'Tis only with desire to give you ease.
        AMAN. Alas! 'tis in a tender part.
It can't be drawn without a world of pain:
Yet out it must;
For it begins to fester in my heart.

wor. If 'tis the sting of unrequited love, remove it instantly:
I have a balm will quickly heal the wound.

aman. You'll find the undertaking difficult:
The surgeon who already has attempted it
Has much tormented me.

wor.   I'll aid him with a gentler hand
—If you will give me leave.

aman.   How soft soe'er the hand may be,
There still is terror in the operation.

wor. Some few preparatives would make it easy,
Could I persuade you to apply 'em.
Make home reflections, Madam, on your slighted love.
Weigh well the strength and beauty of your charms:
Rouse up that spirit women ought to bear,
And slight your god, if he neglects his angel.
With arms of ice receive his cold embraces,
And keep your fire for those who come in flames.
Behold a burning lover at your feet,
His fever raging in his veins.
See how he trembles, how he pants!
See how he glows, how he consumes!
Extend the arms of mercy to his aid;
His zeal may give him title to your pity,
Although his merit cannot claim your love.

aman. Of all my feeble sex,
Sure I must be the weakest,
Should I again presume to think on love.
(sighing) Alas! my heart has been too roughly treated.

wor. 'Twill find the greater bliss in softer usage.

aman. But where's that usage to be found?

wor.   'Tis here,
Within this faithful breast; which, if you doubt,
I'll rip it up before your eyes,
Lay all its secrets open to your view,
And then you'll see 'twas sound.

aman. With just such honest words as these
The worst of men deceiv'd me.

wor.   He therefore merits
All revenge can do; his fault is such,
The extent and stretch of vengeance cannot reach it.

Oh, make me but your instrument of justice;
You'll find me execute it with such zeal
As shall convince you I abhor the crime.

AMAN. The rigour of an executioner
Has more the face of cruelty than justice,
And he who puts the cord about the wretch's neck
Is seldom known to exceed him in his morals.

WOR. What proof then can I give you of my truth?

AMAN. There is on earth but one.

WOR.   And is that in my power?

AMAN.   It is.
And one that would so thoroughly convince me,
I should be apt to rate your heart so high,
I possibly might purchas't with a part of mine.

WOR. Then, heav'n, thou art my friend, and I am blest;
For if 'tis in my power, my will, I'm sure,
Will reach it. No matter what the terms may be,
When such a recompense is offer'd.
Oh, tell me quickly what this proof must be.
What is it will convince you of my love?

AMAN. I shall believe you love me as you ought
If from this moment you forbear to ask
Whatever is unfit for me to grant.
——You pause upon it, Sir—I doubt, on such hard terms
A woman's heart is scarcely worth the having.

WOR. A heart like yours on any terms is worth it;
'Twas not on that I paus'd. But I was thinking (*drawing nearer to
        her*)
Whether some things there may not be
Which women cannot grant without a blush,
And yet which men may take without offense.
(*taking her hand*) Your hand, I fancy, may be of the number:
Oh, pardon me, if I commit a rape
Upon it (*kissing it eagerly*) and thus devour it with my kisses!

AMAN. O heavens! let me go!

WOR. Never, whilst I have strength to hold you here.
(*forcing her to sit down on a couch*) My life, my soul, my god-
        dess—Oh, forgive me!

AMAN. Oh, whither am I going? Help, heaven, or I am lost.

WOR. Stand neuter, gods, this once I do invoke you.

AMAN. Then save me, virtue, and the glory's thine.

WOR. Nay, never strive!

AMAN.   I will, and conquer, too.
My forces rally bravely to my aid, (*breaking from him*)
And thus I gain the day.

WOR. Then mine as bravely double their attack, (*seizing her
    again*)
And thus I wrest it from you. Nay, struggle not,
For all's in vain: or death or victory,
I am determined.

AMAN.   And so am I. (*rushing from him*)
Now keep your distance, or we part forever.

WOR. (*offering again*) For heaven's sake——

AMAN. (*going*)   Nay, then farewell.

WOR. (*kneeling and holding by her clothes*) Oh, stay, and see
    the magic force of love:
Behold this raging lion at your feet,
Struck dead with fear, and tame as charms can make him.
What must I do to be forgiven by you?

AMAN. Repent, and never more offend.

WOR. Repentance for past crimes is just and easy;
But sin no more's a task too hard for mortals.

AMAN. Yet those who hope for heaven
Must use their best endeavours to perform it.

WOR. Endeavours we may use; but flesh and blood
Are got in t'other scale,
And they are pond'rous things.

AMAN. Whate'er they are,
There is a weight in resolution
Sufficient for their balance. The soul, I do confess,
Is usually so careless of its charge,
So soft, and so indulgent to desire,
It leaves the reins in the wild hand of Nature,
Who, like a Phaeton, drives the fiery chariot,
And sets the world on flame.
Yet still the sovereignty is in the mind,
Whene'er it pleases to exert its force.
Perhaps you may not think it worth your while
To take such mighty pains for my esteem;
But that I leave to you.

You see the price I set upon my heart; ⎤
Perhaps 'tis dear: but spite of all your art, ⎬ (*Exit* AMANDA.)
You'll find on cheaper terms we ne'er shall part. ⎦

   WOR. (*solus*) Sure there's divinity about her;
And sh'as dispens'd some portion on't to me.
For what but now was the wild flame of love,
Or (to dissect that specious term)
The vile, the gross desires of flesh and blood,
Is in a moment turned to adoration.
The coarser appetite of nature's gone,
And 'tis, methinks, the food of angels I require:
How long this influence may last, heaven knows.
But in this moment of my purity
I could on her own terms accept her heart.
Yes, lovely woman, I can accept it,
For now 'tis doubly worth my care.
Your charms are much encreas'd, since thus adorn'd.
When truth's extorted from us, then we own
The robe of virtue is a graceful habit.
Could women but our secret counsels scan,
Could they but reach the deep reserves of man,
They'd wear it on, that that of love might last;
For when they throw off one, we soon the other cast.
Their sympathy is such——
The fate of one the other scarce can fly;
They live together, and together die.   (*Exit.*)

Enter MISS HOYDEN *and Nurse*

   MISS. But is it sure and certain, say you, he's my Lord's own brother?

   NURSE. As sure as he's your lawful husband.

   MISS. I'cod, if I had known that in time, I don't know but I might have kept him; for between you and I, nurse, he'd have made a husband worth two of this I have. But which do you think you should fancy most, nurse?

   NURSE. Why, truly, in my poor fancy, Madam, your first husband is the prettier gentleman.

   MISS. I don't like my Lord's shapes, nurse.

NURSE. Why, in good truly, as a body may say, he is but a slam.

MISS. What do you think now he puts me in mind of? Don't you remember a long, loose, shambling sort of a horse my father called Washy?

NURSE. As like as two twin brothers.

MISS. I'cod, I have thought so a hundred times: 'faith, I'm tired of him.

NURSE. Indeed, Madam, I think you had e'en as good stand to your first bargain.

MISS. Oh, but, nurse, we han't considered the main thing yet. If I leave my Lord, I must leave "my Lady" too: and when I rattle about the streets in my coach, they'll only say, There goes Mistress—Mistress—Mistress what? What's this man's name I have married, nurse?

NURSE. Squire Fashion.

MISS. Squire Fashion, is it?—— Well, Squire, that's better than nothing: do you think one could not get him made a knight, nurse?

NURSE. I don't know but one might, Madam, when the king's in a good humour.

MISS. I'cod, that would do rarely. For then he'd be as good a man as my father, you know.

NURSE. By'r Lady, and that's as good as the best of 'em.

MISS. So 'tis, faith; for then I shall be "my Lady" and "your Ladyship" at every word, and that's all I have to care for. Ha, nurse! but hark you me, one thing more, and then I have done. I'm afraid, if I change my husband again, I shan't have so much money to throw about, nurse.

NURSE. Oh, enough's as good as a feast: besides, Madam, one don't know but as much may fall to your share with the younger brother as with the elder. For though these lords have a power of wealth, indeed, yet as I have heard say, they give it all to their sluts and their trulls, who joggle it about in their coaches, with a murrain to 'em, whilst poor madam sits sighing and wishing, and knotting and crying, and has not a spare half-crown to buy her a *Practice of Piety*.

MISS. Oh, but for that, don't deceive yourself, nurse. For this I must say for my Lord, and a——(*snapping her fingers*) for him: he's as free as an open house at Christmas. For this very morning he told me I should have two hundred a year to buy pins.

Now, nurse, if he gives me two hundred a year to buy pins, what do you think he'll give me to buy fine petticoats?

NURSE. Ah, my dearest, he deceives thee faully, and he's no better than a rogue for his pains. These Londoners have got a gibberidge with 'em, would confound a gipsy. That which they call pin-money is to buy their wives everything in the varsal world, dawn to their very shoe-ties: nay, I have heard folks say that some ladies, if they will have gallants, as they call 'um, are forced to find them out of their pin-money too.

MISS. Has he served me so, say ye?—then I'll be his wife no longer, so that's fixed. Look, here he comes, with all the fine folk at 's heels. I'cod, nurse, these London ladies will laugh till they crack again, to see me slip my collar, and run away from my husband. But, d'ye hear? pray take care of one thing: when the business comes to break out, be sure you get between me and my father, for you know his tricks; he'll knock me down.

NURSE. I'll mind him, ne'er fear, Madam.

Enter LORD FOPPINGTON, LOVELESS, WORTHY,
AMANDA, *and* BERINTHIA

LORD FOP. Ladies and gentlemen, you are all welcome. (*to* LOVELESS) Loveless—that's my wife; prithee do me the favour to salute her: and dost hear, (*aside to him*) if thau hast a mind to try thy fartune, to be revenged of me, I won't take it ill, stap my vitals.

LOV. You need not fear, Sir: I'm too fond of my own wife to have the least inclination to yours.   (*All salute* MISS HOYDEN.)

LORD FOP. (*aside*) I'd give a thausand paund he would make love to her, that he may see she has sense enough to prefer me to him, though his own wife has not: (*viewing him*)—he's a very beastly fellow, in my opinion.

MISS. (*aside*) What a power of fine men there are in this London! He that kissed me first is a goodly gentleman, I promise you: sure those wives have a rare time on't, that live here always!

Enter SIR TUNBELLY, *with Musicians, Dancers, etc.*

SIR TUN. Come; come in, good people, come in; come, tune your fiddles, tune your fiddles. (*to the Hautboys*) Bag-pipes, make ready there. Come, strike up! (*sings*)

> For this is Hoyden's wedding-day;
> And therefore we keep holy-day,
> And come to be merry.

Ha! there's my wench, i'faith: touch and take, I'll warrant her; she'll breed like a tame rabbit.

MISS. (aside) I'cod, I think my father's gotten drunk before supper.

SIR TUN. (to LOVELESS and WORTHY) Gentlemen, you are welcome. (saluting AMANDA and BERINTHIA) Ladies, by your leave.—— Ha—they bill like turtles. Udsookers, they set my old blood afire; I shall cuckold somebody before morning.

LORD FOP. (to SIR TUNBELLY) Sir, you being master of the entertainment, will you desire the company to sit?

SIR TUN. Oons, Sir—I'm the happiest man on this side the Ganges.

LORD FOP. (aside) This is a mighty unaccountable old fellow. (to SIR TUNBELLY) I said, Sir, it would be convenient to ask the company to sit.

SIR TUN. Sit?—with all my heart.—— Come, take your places, ladies; take your places, gentlemen: come, sit down, sit down; a pox of ceremony, take your places.

> (They sit, and the masque begins.)

DIALOGUE BETWEEN CUPID AND HYMEN

CUPID.   1

Thou bane to my empire, thou spring of contest,
Thou source of all discord, thou period to rest;
Instruct me what wretches in bondage can see,
That the aim of their life is still pointed to thee.

HYMEN.   2

Instruct me, thou little impertinent god,
From whence all thy subjects have taken the mode
To grow fond of a change, to whatever it be,
And I'll tell thee why those would be bound, who are free.

Chorus

For change, w'are for change, to whatever it be,
We are neither contented with freedom nor thee.

Constancy's an empty sound.
Heaven and earth and all go round;
All the works of nature move,
And the joys of life and love
      Are in variety.

CUPID.   3

Were love the reward of a painstaking life,
Had a husband the art to be fond of his wife,
Were virtue so plenty, a wife could afford,
These very hard times, to be true to her lord;
Some specious account might be given of those
Who are tied by the tail, to be led by the nose.

4

But since 'tis the fate of a man and his wife
To consume all their days in contention and strife:
Since whatever the bounty of heaven may create her,
He's morally sure he shall heartily hate her;
I think 'twere much wiser to ramble at large,
And the volleys of love on the herd to discharge.

HYMEN.   5

Some colour of reason thy counsel might bear,
Could a man have no more than his wife to his share:
Or were I a monarch so cruelly just,
To oblige a poor wife to be true to her trust;
But I have not pretended, for many years past,
By marrying of people, to make 'em grow chaste.

6

I therefore advise thee to let me go on,
Thou'lt find I'm the strength and support of thy throne;
For hadst thou but eyes, thou would'st quickly perceive it,
   How smoothly thy dart
   Slips into the heart
   Of a woman that's wed;
   Whilst the shivering maid
Stands trembling, and wishing, but dare not receive it.

Chorus

For change, *etc.*

The masque ended, enter YOUNG FASHION,
COUPLER, *and* BULL

SIR TUN. So, very fine, very fine, i'faith; this is something like a wedding; now if supper were but ready, I'd say a short grace; and if I had such a bedfellow as Hoyden to-night—I'd say as short prayers. (*seeing* YOUNG FASHION) How now—what have we got here? a ghost? Nay, it must be so, for his flesh and his blood could never have dared to appear before me. (*to him*) Ah, rogue——!

LORD FOP. Stap my vitals, Tam again.

SIR TUN. My Lord, will you cut his throat? or shall I?

LORD FOP. Leave him to me, Sir, if you please.—— Prithee, Tam, be so ingenuous, now, as to tell me what thy business is here?

Y. FAS. 'Tis with your bride.

LORD FOP. Thau art the impudent'st fellow that nature has yet spawned into the warld, strike me speechless.

Y. FAS. Why, you know my modesty would have starved me; I sent it a-begging to you, and you would not give it a groat.

LORD FOP. And dost thau expect by an excess of assurance to extart a maintenance fram me?

Y. FAS. (*taking* MISS HOYDEN *by the hand*) I do intend to extort your mistress from you, and that I hope will prove one.

LORD FOP. I ever thaught Newgate or Bedlam would be his fartune, and naw his fate's decided. Prithee, Loveless, dost know of ever a mad-doctor hard by?

Y. FAS. There's one at your elbow will cure you presently. (*to* BULL) Prithee, Doctor, take him in hand quickly.

LORD FOP. Shall I beg the favour of you, Sir, to pull your fingers out of my wife's hand?

Y. FAS. His wife! Look you there; now I hope you are all satisfied he's mad?

LORD FOP. Naw is it nat possible far me to penetrate what species of fally it is thau art driving at.

SIR TUN. Here, here, here, let me beat out his brains, and that will decide all.

LORD FOP. No, pray, Sir, hold: we'll destray him presently according to law.

Y. FAS. (*to* BULL) Nay, then advance, Doctor; come, you are a man of conscience; answer boldly to the questions I shall ask: Did not you marry me to this young lady, before ever that gentleman there saw her face?

BULL. Since the truth must out, I did.

Y. FAS. Nurse, sweet nurse, were not you a witness to it?

NURSE. Since my conscience bids me speak—I was.

Y. FAS. (*to* MISS HOYDEN) Madam, am not I your lawful husband?

MISS. Truly I can't tell, but you married me first.

Y. FAS. Now I hope you are all satisfied?

SIR TUN. (*offering to strike him, is held by* LOVELESS *and* WORTHY) Oons and thunder, you lie.

LORD FOP. Pray, Sir, be calm: the battle is in disarder, but requires more canduct than courage to rally our forces.—— Pray, Dactar, one word with you. (*to* BULL *aside*) Look you, Sir, though I will not presume to calculate your notions of damnation fram the description you give us of hell, yet since there is at least a passibility you may have a pitchfark thrust in your backside, methinks it should not be worth your while to risk your saul in the next warld far the sake of a beggarly yaunger brather who is nat able to make your bady happy in this.

BULL. Alas! my Lord, I have no worldly ends; I speak the truth, heaven knows.

LORD FOP. Nay, prithee, never engage heaven in the matter, far, by all I can see, 'tis like to prove a business for the devil.

Y. FAS. Come, pray, Sir, all above-board: no corrupting of evidences, if you please; this young lady is my lawful wife, and I'll justify it in all the courts of England; so your Lordship (who always had a passion for variety) may go seek a new mistress, if you think fit.

LORD FOP. I am struck dumb with his impudence, and cannot passitively tell whether ever I shall speak again or nat.

SIR TUN. Then let me come and examine the business a little: I'll jerk the truth out of 'em presently; here, give me my dog-whip.

Y. FAS. Look you, old gentleman, 'tis in vain to make a noise; if you grow mutinous, I have some friends within call have swords by their sides above four foot long; therefore be calm, hear the evidence patiently, and when the jury have given their verdict, pass sentence according to law: here's honest Coupler shall be foreman, and ask as many questions as he pleases.

COUP. All I have to ask is whether nurse persists in her evidence? The parson, I dare swear, will never flinch from his.

NURSE. (*to* SIR TUNBELLY, *kneeling*) I hope in heaven your Worship will pardon me; I have served you long and faithfully, but in this thing I was overreached; your Worship, however, was deceived as well as I, and if the wedding-dinner had been ready, you had put Madam to bed to him with your own hands.

SIR TUN. But how durst you do this, without acquainting of me?

NURSE. Alas! if your Worship had seen how the poor thing begged, and prayed, and clung, and twined about me, like ivy to an old wall, you would say I, who had suckled it, and swaddled it, and nursed it both wet and dry, must have had a heart of adamant to refuse it.

SIR TUN. Very well!

Y. FAS. Foreman, I expect your verdict.

COUP. Ladies and gentlemen, what's your opinions?

ALL. A clear case, a clear case.

COUP. Then, my young folks, I wish you joy.

SIR TUN. (*to* YOUNG FASHION) Come hither, stripling; if it be true, then, that thou hast married my daughter, prithee tell me who thou art?

Y. FAS. Sir, the best of my condition is, I am your son-in-law; and the worst of it is, I am brother to that noble peer there.

SIR TUN. Art thou brother to that noble peer? Why then, that noble peer, and thee, and thy wife, and the nurse, and the priest —may all go and be damned together. (*Exit* SIR TUNBELLY.)

LORD FOP. (*aside*) Now, for my part, I think the wisest thing a man can do with an aching heart, is to put on a serene countenance, for a philosophical air is the most becoming thing in the world to the face of a person of quality; I will therefore bear my disgrace like a great man, and let the people see I am above an affront. (*to* YOUNG FASHION) Dear Tam, since things are thus fallen aut, prithee give me leave to wish thee jay: I do it *de bon cœur*, strike me dumb: you have married a woman beautiful in her person, charming in her airs, prudent in her canduct, canstant in her inclinations, and of a nice marality, split my windpipe.

Y. FAS. Your Lordship may keep up your spirits with your grimace, if you please; I shall support mine with this lady and two thousand pound a year.

(*Taking* MISS HOYDEN.) Come, Madam:
  We once again, you see, are man and wife,
  And now, perhaps, the bargain's struck for life;
  If I mistake, and we should part again,
  At least you see you may have choice of men:
  Nay, should the war at length such havoc make
  That lovers should grow scarce, yet for your sake,
  Kind heaven always will preserve a beau:
  (*pointing to* LORD FOPPINGTON)
  You'll find his Lordship ready to come to.

LORD FOP. Her ladyship shall stap my vitals if I do.

EPILOGUE

Spoken by Lord Foppington

  Gentlemen and ladies,
  These people have regal'd you here to-day
  (In my opinion) with a saucy play,
  In which the author does presume to show
  That coxcomb, *ab origine*—was beau.
  Truly I think the thing of so much weight,
  That if some smart chastisement ben't his fate,
  Gad's curse, it may in time destroy the state.
  I hold no one its friend, I must confess,
  Who would discauntenance your men of dress.
  Far, give me leave t'abserve, good clothes are things
  Have ever been of great support to kings:
  All treasons come fram slovens; it is nat
  Within the reach of gentle beaux to plat.
  They have no gall, no spleen, no teeth, no stings,
  Of all Gad's creatures, the most harmless things.
  Through all recard, no prince was ever slain
  By one who had a feather in his brain.

They're men of too refin'd an education,
To squabble with a court—for a vile dirty nation.
I'm very passitive, you never saw
A through republican a finish'd beau.
Nor truly shall you very often see
A Jacobite much better dress'd than he;
In shart, through all the courts that I have been in,
Your men of mischief—still are in faul linen.
Did ever one yet dance the Tyburn jig
With a free air, ar a well pawdered wig?
Did ever highway-man yet bid you stand
With a sweet bawdy snuff-bax in his hand;
Ar do you ever find they ask your purse
As men of breeding do?—Ladies, Gad's curse,
This author is a dag, and 'tis not fit
You should allow him ev'n one grain of wit.
To which, that his pretence may ne'er be nam'd,
My humble motion is—he may be damn'd.

The Way of the World

A COMEDY

By WILLIAM CONGREVE

Audire est operæ pretium, procedere recte
Qui mœchis non vultis HORACE, *Satires*[1]
Metuat doti deprensa Ibid.[2]

DEDICATION

TO THE RIGHT HONOURABLE RALPH, EARL OF MONTAGUE, &C.

My Lord,

Whether the world will arraign me of vanity, or not, that I have presumed to dedicate this comedy to your Lordship, I am yet in doubt; though it may be it is some degree of vanity even to doubt of it. One who has at any time had the honour of your Lordship's conversation cannot be supposed to think very meanly

---

[1] O ye who wish adulterers ill, it is worth your while to give your ear and hear how badly in every way they fare.

Horace, *Satires*, 1,2,37-38

[2] The woman, caught in the act, fears for her dowry.

Horace, *Satires*, 1,2,131

of that which he would prefer to your perusal; yet it were to incur the imputation of too much sufficiency to pretend to such a merit as might abide the test of your Lordship's censure.

Whatever value may be wanting to this play while yet it is mine will be sufficiently made up to it when it is once become your Lordship's; and it is my security that I cannot have over-rated it more by my dedication, than your Lordship will dignify it by your patronage.

That it succeeded on the stage was almost beyond my expectation, for but little of it was prepared for that general taste which seems now to be predominant in the palates of our audience.

Those characters which are meant to be ridiculous in most of our comedies are of fools so gross that, in my humble opinion, they should rather disturb than divert the well-natured and reflecting part of an audience; they are rather objects of charity than contempt; and instead of moving our mirth, they ought very often to excite our compassion.

This reflection moved me to design some characters which should appear ridiculous, not so much through a natural folly (which is incorrigible, and therefore not proper for the stage) as through an affected wit; a wit, which at the same time that it is affected, is also false. As there is some difficulty in the formation of a character of this nature, so there is some hazard which attends the progress of its success upon the stage: for many come to a play so overcharged with criticism, that they very often let fly their censure when through their rashness they have mistaken their aim. This I had occasion lately to observe: for this play had been acted two or three days before some of these hasty judges could find the leisure to distinguish betwixt the character of a Witwoud and a Truewit.

I must beg your Lordship's pardon for this digression from the true course of this epistle; but that it may not seem altogether impertinent, I beg that I may plead the occasion of it, in part of that excuse of which I stand in need, for recommending this comedy to your protection. It is only by the countenance of your Lordship, and the *few* so qualified, that such who write with care and pains can hope to be distinguished: for the prostituted name of *poet* promiscuously levels all that bear it.

Terence, the most correct writer in the world, had a Scipio

and a Lælius, if not to assist him, at least to support him in his reputation: and notwithstanding his extraordinary merit, it may be their countenance was not more than necessary.

The purity of his style, the delicacy of his turns, and the justness of his characters, were all of them beauties which the greater part of his audience were incapable of tasting; some of the coarsest strokes of Plautus, so severely censured by Horace, were more likely to affect the multitude; such, who come with expectation to laugh out the last act of a play, and are better entertained with two or three unseasonable jests, than with the artful solution of the *fable*.

As Terence excelled in his performances, so had he great advantages to encourage his undertakings; for he built most on the foundations of Menander: his plots were generally modelled, and his characters ready drawn to his hand. He copied Menander; and Menander had no less light in the formation of his characters, from the observations of Theophrastus, of whom he was a disciple; and Theophrastus, it is known, was not only the disciple, but the immediate successor of Aristotle, the first and greatest judge of poetry. These were great models to design by; and the further advantage which Terence possessed, towards giving his plays the due ornaments of purity of style, and justness of manners, was not less considerable from the freedom of conversation, which was permitted him with Lælius and Scipio, two of the greatest and most polite men of his age. And indeed, the privilege of such a conversation is the only certain means of attaining to the perfection of dialogue.

If it has happened in any part of this comedy that I have gained a turn of style or expression more correct, or at least more corrigible, than in those which I have formerly written, I must, with equal pride and gratitude, ascribe it to the honour of your Lordship's admitting me into your conversation, and that of a society where everybody else was so well worthy of you, in your retirement last summer from the town; for it was immediately after that this comedy was written. If I have failed in my performance, it is only to be regretted, where there were so many, not inferior either to a Scipio or a Lælius, that there should be one wanting equal to the capacity of a Terence.

If I am not mistaken, poetry is almost the only art which has not yet laid claim to your Lordship's patronage. Architecture, and painting, to the great honour of our country, have flourished under your influence and protection. In the meantime, poetry, the eldest sister of all arts, and parent of most, seems to have resigned her birthright, by having neglected to pay her duty to your Lordship, and by permitting others of a later extraction to prepossess that place in your esteem, to which none can pretend a better title. Poetry, in its nature, is sacred to the good and great; the relation between them is reciprocal, and they are ever propitious to it. It is the privilege of poetry to address to them, and it is their prerogative alone to give it protection.

This received maxim is a general apology for all writers who consecrate their labours to great men: but I could wish at this time that this address were exempted from the common pretence of all dedications; and that as I can distinguish your Lordship even among the most deserving, so this offering might become remarkable by some particular instance of respect, which should assure your Lordship that I am, with all due sense of your extreme worthiness and humanity, my Lord, your Lordship's most obedient and most obliged humble servant,

WILL. CONGREVE.

PROLOGUE

Spoken by MR. FAINALL

Of those few fools, who with ill stars are curs'd,
Sure scribbling fools, call'd poets, fare the worst,
For they're a sort of fools which Fortune makes,
And, after she has made 'em fools, forsakes.
With Nature's oafs 'tis quite a diff'rent case,
For Fortune favours all her idiot race;
In her own nest the cuckoo-eggs we find,
O'er which she broods to hatch the changeling kind.
No portion for her own she has to spare,
So much she dotes on her adopted care.
    Poets are bubbles, by the town drawn in,
Suffer'd at first some trifling stakes to win;
But what unequal hazards do they run!
Each time they write they venture all they've won; ⎫
The squire that's butter'd still is sure to be undone. ⎭

This author, heretofore, has found your favour,
But pleads no merit from his past behaviour.
To build on that might prove a vain presumption,
Should grants to poets made admit resumption;
And in Parnassus he must lose his seat
If that be found a forfeited estate.

He owns, with toil he wrote the following scenes,
But if they're naught ne'er spare him for his pains.
Damn him the more: have no commiseration
For dulness on mature deliberation.
He swears he'll not resent one hissed-off scene, ⎱
Nor, like those peevish wits, his play maintain, ⎰
Who, to assert their sense, your taste arraign. ⎰
Some plot we think he has, and some new thought,
Some humour, too, no farce—but that's a fault.
Satire, he thinks, you ought not to expect:
For so reform'd a town who dares correct?
To please this time has been his sole pretence;
He'll not instruct, lest it should give offence.
Should he by chance a knave or fool expose,
That hurts none here; sure here are none of those.
In short, our play shall (with your leave to show it)
Give you one instance of a passive poet,
Who to your judgments yields all resignation:
So save or damn, after your own discretion.

PERSONS REPRESENTED

MEN:

FAINALL, *in love with Mrs. Marwood*
MIRABELL, *in love with Mrs. Millamant*
WITWOUD, ⎱
PETULANT, ⎰ *followers of Mrs. Millamant*
SIR WILFULL WITWOUD, *half-brother to Witwoud, and nephew to Lady Wishfort*
WAITWELL, *servant to Mirabell*

WOMEN:

LADY WISHFORT, *enemy to Mirabell, for having falsely pretended love to her*

MRS. MILLAMANT, *a fine lady, niece to Lady Wishfort, and loves Mirabell*

MRS. MARWOOD, *friend to Mr. Fainall, and likes Mirabell*

MRS. FAINALL, *daughter to Lady Wishfort, and wife to Fainall, formerly friend to Mirabell*

FOIBLE, *woman to Lady Wishfort*

MINCING, *woman to* MRS. MILLAMANT

Dancers, Footmen, and Attendants

SCENE: *London*

The time equal to that of the presentation

THE WAY OF THE WORLD

ACT I

SCENE: *A chocolate-house*

MIRABELL *and* FAINALL, *rising from cards.*
BETTY *waiting*

MIRA. You are a fortunate man, Mr. Fainall.

FAIN. Have we done?

MIRA. What you please. I'll play on to entertain you.

FAIN. No, I'll give you your revenge another time, when you are not so indifferent; you are thinking of something else now, and play too negligently; the coldness of a losing gamester lessens the pleasure of the winner: I'd no more play with a man that slighted his ill fortune, than I'd make love to a woman who undervalued the loss of her reputation.

MIRA. You have a taste extremely delicate, and are for refining on your pleasures.

FAIN. Prithee, why so reserved? Something has put you out of humour.

MIRA. Not at all: I happen to be grave to-day, and you are gay; that's all.

FAIN. Confess, Millamant and you quarrelled last night, after I left you; my fair cousin has some humours that would tempt the patience of a Stoic. What! some coxcomb came in, and was well received by her, while you were by?

MIRA. Witwoud and Petulant; and what was worse, her aunt, your wife's mother, my evil genius; or to sum up all in her own name, my old Lady Wishfort came in.

FAIN. Oh, there it is then! She has a lasting passion for you, and with reason. What! then my wife was there?

MIRA. Yes, and Mrs. Marwood and three or four more, whom I never saw before; seeing me, they all put on their grave faces, whispered one another, then complained aloud of the vapours, and after fell into a profound silence.

FAIN. They had a mind to be rid of you.

MIRA. For which reason I resolved not to stir. At last the good old lady broke through her painful taciturnity with an invective against lóng visits. I would not have understood her, but Milla- mant joining in the argument, I rose and with a constrained smile told her I thought nothing was so easy as to know when a visit began to be troublesome; she reddened and I withdrew, without expecting her reply.

FAIN. You were to blame to resent what she spoke only in com- pliance with her aunt.

MIRA. She is more mistress of herself than to be under the necessity of such a resignation.

FAIN. What? though half her fortune depends upon her marry- ing with my lady's approbation?

MIRA. I was then in such a humour, that I should have been better pleased if she had been less discreet.

FAIN. Now I remember, I wonder not they were weary of you; last night was one of their cabal-nights; they have 'em three times a week, and meet by turns, at one another's apartments, where they come together like the coroner's inquest to sit upon the murdered reputations of the week. You and I are excluded; and it was once proposed that all the male sex should be ex- cepted; but somebody moved that to avoid scandal there might be one man of the cōmmunity; upon which motion Witwould and Petulant were enrolled members.

MIRA. And who may have been the foundress of this sect? My Lady Wishfort, I warrant, who publishes her detestation of man- kind; and full of the vigour of fifty-five, declares for a friend and ratafia; and let posterity shift for itself, she'll breed no more.

FAIN. The discovery of your sham addresses to her, to conceal your love to her niece, has provoked this separation: had you dissembled better, things might have continued in the state of nature.

MIRA. I did as much as man could, with any reasonable con- science; I proceeded to the very last act of flattery with her, and was guilty of a song in her commendation. Nay, I got a friend to put her into a lampoon, and compliment her with the imputation of an affair with a young fellow, which I carried so far that I told her the malicious town took notice that she was grown fat of a sudden; and when she lay in of a dropsy, persuaded her she was reported to be in labour. The devil's in't, if an old woman is to be flattered further, unless a man should endeavour downright personally to debauch her; and that my virtue forbade me. But for the discovery of that amour, I am indebted to your friend, or your wife's friend, Mrs. Marwood.

FAIN. What should provoke her to be your enemy, without she has made you advances which you have slighted? Women do not easily forgive omissions of that nature.

MIRA. She was always civil to me, till of late. I confess I am not one of those coxcombs who are apt to interpret a woman's good manners to her prejudice, and think that she who does not refuse 'em everything, can refuse 'em nothing.

FAIN. You are a gallant man, Mirabell; and though you may have cruelty enough not to satisfy a lady's longing, you have too much generosity not to be tender of her honour. Yet you speak with an indifference which seems to be affected; and confesses you are conscious of a negligence.

MIRA. You pursue the argument with a distrust that seems to be unaffected, and confesses you are conscious of a concern for which the lady is more indebted to you than your wife.

FAIN. Fie, fie, friend, if you grow censorious I must leave you. I'll look upon the gamesters in the next room.

MIRA. Who are they?

FAIN. Petulant and Witwoud. (*to* BETTY) Bring me some chocolate.   (*Exit.*)

MIRA. Betty, what says your clock?

BET. Turned of the last canonical hour, Sir.   (*Exit.*)

MIRA. How pertinently the jade answers me! Ha! almost one o'clock! (*looking on his watch*) Oh, y'are come——

Enter a Servant

Well, is the grand affair over? You have been something tedious.

SERV. Sir, there's such coupling at Pancras that they stand behind one another, as 'twere in a country dance. Ours was the last couple to lead up; and no hopes appearing of dispatch, besides, the parson growing hoarse, we were afraid his lungs would have failed before it came to our turn; so we drove round to Duke's Place; and there they were riveted in a trice.

MIRA. So, so, you are sure they are married?

SERV. Married and bedded, Sir: I am witness.

MIRA. Have you the certificate?

SERV. Here it is, Sir.

MIRA. Has the tailor brought Waitwell's clothes home, and the new liveries?

SERV. Yes, Sir.

MIRA. That's well. Do you go home again, d'ee hear, and adjourn the consummation till farther order; bid Waitwell shake his ears, and Dame Partlet rustle up her feathers, and meet me at one o'clock by Rosamond's Pond, that I may see her before she returns to her lady; and as you tender your ears be secret.

(*Exit Servant.*)

Re-enter FAINALL

FAIN. Joy of your success, Mirabell; you look pleased.

MIRA. Ay; I have been engaged in a matter of some sort of mirth, which is not yet ripe for discovery. I am glad this is not a cabal-night. I wonder, Fainall, that you who are married, and of consequence should be discreet, will suffer your wife to be of such a party.

FAIN. Faith, I am not jealous. Besides, most who are engaged are women and relations; and for the men, they are of a kind too contemptible to give scandal.

MIRA. I am of another opinion. The greater the coxcomb, always the more the scandal: for a woman who is not a fool can have but one reason for associating with a man that is.

FAIN. Are you jealous as often as you see Witwoud entertained by Millamant?

MIRA. Of her understanding I am, if not of her person.

FAIN. You do her wrong; for to give her her due, she has wit.

MIRA. She has beauty enough to make any man think so, and complaisance enough not to contradict him who shall tell her so.

FAIN. For a passionate lover, methinks you are a man somewhat too discerning in the failings of your mistress.

MIRA. And for a discerning man, somewhat too passionate a lover; for I like her with all her faults; nay, like her for her faults. Her follies are so natural, or so artful, that they become her; and those affectations which in another woman would be odious serve but to make her more agreeable. I'll tell thee, Fainall, she once used me with that insolence that in revenge I took her to pieces; sifted her and separated her failings; I studied 'em, and got 'em by rote. The catalogue was so large, that I was not without hopes, one day or other, to hate her heartily: to which end I so used myself to think of 'em, that at length, contrary to my design and expectation, they gave me every hour less and less disturbance; till in a few days it became habitual to me to remember 'em without being displeased. They are now grown as familiar to me as my own frailties; and in all probability in a little time longer I shall like 'em as well.

FAIN. Marry her, marry her; be half as well acquainted with her charms as you are with her defects, and my life on't, you are your own man again.

MIRA. Say you so?

FAIN. Ay, ay; I have experience: I have a wife, and so forth.

Enter Messenger

MESS. Is one Squire Witwoud here?

BET. Yes; what's your business?

MESS. I have a letter for him, from his brother, Sir Wilfull, which I am charged to deliver into his own hands.

BET. He's in the next room, friend—that way.

(Exit Messenger.)

MIRA. What, is the chief of that noble family in town, Sir Wilfull Witwoud?

FAIN. He is expected to-day. Do you know him?

MIRA. I have seen him; he promises to be an extraordinary person; I think you have the honour to be related to him.

FAIN. Yes; he is half-brother to this Witwoud by a former wife, who was sister to my Lady Wishfort, my wife's mother. If you marry Millamant, you must call cousins too.

MIRA. I had rather be his relation than his acquaintance.

FAIN. He comes to town in order to equip himself for travel.

MIRA. For travel! Why the man that I mean is above forty.

FAIN. No matter for that; 'tis for the honour of England that all Europe should know we have blockheads of all ages.

MIRA. I wonder there is not an act of Parliament to save the credit of the nation, and prohibit the exportation of fools.

FAIN. By no means, 'tis better as 'tis; 'tis better to trade with a little loss than to be quite eaten up with being overstocked.

MIRA. Pray, are the follies of this knight-errant, and those of the squire his brother, anything related?

FAIN. Not at all; Witwoud grows by the knight like a medlar grafted on a crab. One will melt in your mouth, and t'other set your teeth on edge; one is all pulp, and the other all core.

MIRA. So one will be rotten before he be ripe, and the other will be rotten without ever being ripe at all.

FAIN. Sir Wilfull is an odd mixture of bashfulness and obstinacy. But when he's drunk, he's as loving as the monster in *The Tempest,* and much after the same manner. To give the t'other his due, he has something of good nature, and does not always want wit.

MIRA. Not always, but as often as his memory fails him, and his commonplace of comparisons. He is a fool with a good memory, and some few scraps of other folks' wit. He is one whose conversation can never be approved, yet it is now and then to be endured. He has indeed one good quality, he is not exceptious; for he so passionately affects the reputation of understanding raillery, that he will construe an affront into a jest, and call downright rudeness and ill language, satire and fire.

FAIN. If you have a mind to finish his picture, you have an opportunity to do it at full length. Behold the original.

Enter WITWOUD

WIT. Afford me your compassion, my dears; pity me, Fainall, Mirabell, pity me.

MIRA. I do from my soul.

FAIN. Why, what's the matter?

WIT. No letters for me, Betty?

BET. Did not the messenger bring you one but now, Sir?

WIT. Ay, but no other?

BET. No, Sir.

WIT. That's hard, that's very hard;—a messenger, a mule, a beast of burden: he has brought me a letter from the fool my brother, as heavy as a panegyric in a funeral sermon or a copy of commendatory verses from one poet to another. And what's worse, 'tis as sure a forerunner of the author as an epistle dedicatory.

MIRA. A fool, and your brother, Witwoud!

WIT. Ay, ay, my half-brother. My half-brother he is, no nearer upon honour.

MIRA. Then 'tis possible he may be but half a fool.

WIT. Good, good, Mirabell, *le drôle!* Good, good!—hang him, don't let's talk of him.—— Fainall, how does your lady? Gad, I say anything in the world to get this fellow out of my head. I beg pardon that I should ask a man of pleasure, and the town, a question at once so foreign and domestic. But I talk like an old maid at a marriage, I don't know what I say: but she's the best woman in the world.

FAIN. 'Tis well you don't know what you say, or else your commendation would go near to make me either vain or jealous.

WIT. No man in town lives well with a wife but Fainall. Your judgment, Mirabell.

MIRA. You had better step and ask his wife, if you would be credibly informed.

WIT. Mirabell.

MIRA. Ay.

WIT. My dear, I ask ten thousand pardons.—Gad, I have forgot what I was going to say to you.

MIRA. I thank you heartily, heartily.

WIT. No, but prithee excuse me—my memory is such a memory.

MIRA. Have a care of such apologies, Witwoud; for I never knew a fool but he affected to complain either of the spleen or his memory.

FAIN. What have you done with Petulant?

WIT. He's reckoning his money—my money it was; I have no luck to-day.

FAIN. You may allow him to win of you at play, for you are sure to be too hard for him at repartee: since you monopolize the wit that is between you, the fortune must be his of course.

MIRA. I don't find that Petulant confesses the superiority of wit to be your talent, Witwoud.

WIT. Come, come, you are malicious now, and would breed debates. Petulant's my friend, and a very honest fellow, and a very pretty fellow, and has a smattering—faith and troth, a pretty deal of an odd sort of a small wit. Nay, I'll do him justice. I'm his friend, I won't wrong him, neither. And if he had but any judgment in the world, he would not be altogether contemptible. Come, come, don't detract from the merits of my friend.

FAIN. You don't take your friend to be over-nicely bred.

wit. No, no, hang him, the rogue has no manners at all, that I must own—no more breeding than a bum-baily, that I grant you. 'Tis pity, faith; the fellow has fire and life.

mira. What, courage?

wit. Hum, faith I don't know as to that—I can't say as to that. Yes, faith, in a controversy he'll contradict anybody.

mira. Though 'twere a man whom he feared, or a woman whom he loved.

wit. Well, well, he does not always think before he speaks. We have all our failings; you're too hard upon him, you are, faith. Let me excuse him—I can defend most of his faults, except one or two; one he has, that's the truth on't, if he were my brother, I could not acquit him. That, indeed, I could wish were otherwise.

mira. Ay, marry, what's that, Witwoud?

wit. Oh, pardon me! Expose the infirmities of my friend? No, my dear, excuse me there.

fain. What! I warrant, he's unsincere, or 'tis some such trifle.

wit. No, no, what if he be? 'Tis no matter for that, his wit will excuse that: a wit should no more be sincere than a woman constant; one argues a decay of parts, as t'other of beauty.

mira. Maybe you think him too positive?

wit. No, no, his being positive is an incentive to argument, and keeps up conversation.

fain. Too illiterate.

wit. That! that's his happiness. His want of learning gives him the more opportunities to show his natural parts.

mira. He wants words.

wit. Ay; but I like him for that now; for his want of words gives me the pleasure very often to explain his meaning.

fain. He's impudent.

wit. No, that's not it.

mira. Vain.

wit. No.

mira. What, he speaks unseasonable truths sometimes, because he has not wit enough to invent an evasion?

wit. Truths! Ha, ha, ha! No, no, since you will have it—I mean, he never speaks truth at all—that's all. He will lie like a chambermaid, or a woman of quality's porter. Now that is a fault.

Enter Coachman

COACH. Is Master Petulant here, Mistress?

BET. Yes.

COACH. Three gentlewomen in the coach would speak with him.

FAIN. O brave Petulant, three!

BET. I'll tell him.

COACH. You must bring two dishes of chocolate and a glass of cinnamon-water.   (*Exeunt* BETTY *and Coachman.*)

WIT. That should be for two fasting strumpets and a bawd troubled with wind. Now you may know what the three are.

MIRA. You are very free with your friend's acquaintance.

WIT. Ay, ay, friendship without freedom is as dull as love without enjoyment, or wine without toasting; but to tell you a secret, these are trulls that he allows coach-hire, and something more by the week, to call on him once a day at public places.

MIRA. How!

WIT. You shall see he won't go to 'em because there's no more company here to take notice of him. Why, this is nothing to what he used to do; before he found out this way, I have known him call for himself——

FAIN. Call for himself? What dost thou mean?

WIT. Mean?—why, he would slip you out of this chocolate-house, just when you had been talking to him. As soon as your back was turned—whip he was gone; then trip to his lodging, clap on a hood and scarf, and mask, slap into a hackney-coach, and drive hither to the door again in a trice; where he would send in for himself—that I mean—call for himself, wait for himself, nay and what's more, not finding himself, sometimes leave a letter for himself.

MIRA. I confess this is something extraordinary—I believe he waits for himself now, he is so long a-coming. Oh, I ask his pardon!

Enter PETULANT *and* BETTY

BET. Sir, the coach stays.   (*Exit.*)

PET. Well, well; I come.—— 'Sbud, a man had as good be a professed midwife as a professed whoremaster, at this rate; to be knocked up and raised at all hours, and in all places! Pox on 'em,

I won't come. D'ee hear, tell 'em I won't come. Let 'em snivel and cry their hearts out.

FAIN. You are very cruel, Petulant.

PET. All's one, let it pass—I have a humour to be cruel.

MIRA. I hope they are not persons of condition that you use at this rate.

PET. Condition! condition's a dried fig, if I am not in humour. By this hand, if they were your—a—a—your what-d'ee-call-'ems themselves, they must wait or rub off, if I want appetite.

MIRA. What-d'ee-call-'ems! What are they, Witwoud?

WIT. Empresses, my dear—by your what-d'ee-call-'ems he means sultana queens.

PET. Ay, Roxolanas.

MIRA. Cry you mercy.

FAIN. Witwoud says they are——

PET. What does he say th'are?

WIT. I—fine ladies, I say.

PET. Pass on, Witwoud.—— Hark'ee, by this light, his relations—two co-heiresses his cousins, and an old aunt, that loves caterwauling better than a conventicle.

WIT. Ha, ha, ha! I had a mind to see how the rogue would come off. Ha, ha, ha! Gad I can't be angry with him, if he said they were my mother and my sisters.

MIRA. No!

WIT. No; the rogue's wit and readiness of invention charm me: dear Petulant.

Re-enter BETTY

BET. They are gone, Sir, in great anger.

PET. Enough, let 'em trundle. Anger helps complexion, saves paint.

FAIN. This continence is all dissembled; this is in order to have something to brag of the next time he makes court to Millamant, and swear he has abandoned the whole sex for her sake.

MIRA. Have you not left off your impudent pretensions there yet? I shall cut your throat, sometime or other, Petulant, about that business.

PET. Ay, ay, let that pass—there are other throats to be cut——

MIRA. Meaning mine, Sir?

PET. Not I—I mean nobody—I know nothing. But there are uncles and nephews in the world—and they may be rivals. What then? All's one for that——

MIRA. How! Hark 'ee, Petulant, come hither. Explain, or I shall call your interpreter.

PET. Explain! I know nothing. Why, you have an uncle, have you not, lately come to town, and lodges by my Lady Wishfort's?

MIRA. True.

PET. Why, that's enough. You and he are not friends; and if he should marry and have a child, you may be disinherited, ha?

MIRA. Where hast thou stumbled upon all this truth?

PET. All's one for that; why, then, say I know something.

MIRA. Come, thou art an honest fellow, Petulant, and shalt make love to my mistress, thou shalt, faith. What hast thou heard of my uncle?

PET. I? nothing I. If throats are to be cut, let swords clash; snug's the word, I shrug and am silent.

MIRA. O raillery, raillery. Come, I know thou art in the women's secrets. What, you're a cabalist; I know you stayed at Millamant's last night, after I went. Was there any mention made of my uncle, or me? Tell me; if thou hadst but good nature equal to thy wit, Petulant, Tony Witwoud, who is now thy competitor in fame, would show as dim by thee as a dead whiting's eye by a pearl of Orient; he would no more be seen by thee, than Mercury is by the sun. Come, I'm sure thou wo't tell me.

PET. If I do, will you grant me common sense then, for the future?

MIRA. Faith, I'll do what I can for thee; and I'll pray that heaven may grant it thee in the meantime.

PET. Well, hark'ee.

FAIN. Petulant and you both will find Mirabell as warm a rival as a lover.

WIT. Pshaw, pshaw, that she laughs at Petulant is plain. And for my part—but that it is almost a fashion to admire her, I should—hark'ee—to tell you a secret, but let it go no further—between friends, I shall never break my heart for her.

FAIN. How!

WIT. She's handsome; but she's a sort of an uncertain woman.

FAIN. I thought you had died for her.

WIT. Umh—no——

FAIN. She has wit.

WIT. 'Tis what she will hardly allow anybody else. Now, demme, I should hate that, if she were as handsome as Cleopatra. Mirabell is not so sure of her as he thinks for.

FAIN. Why do you think so?

WIT. We stayed pretty late there last night, and heard something of an uncle to Mirabell, who is lately come to town, and is between him and the best part of his estate. Mirabell and he are at some distance, as my Lady Wishfort has been told; and you know she hates Mirabell worse than a Quaker hates a parrot, or than a fishmonger hates a hard frost. Whether this uncle has seen Mrs. Millamant or not I cannot say, but there were items of such a treaty being in embryo; and if it should come to life, poor Mirabell would be in some sort unfortunately fobbed i'faith.

FAIN. 'Tis impossible Millamant should hearken to it.

WIT. Faith, my dear, I can't tell; she's a woman and a kind of a humorist.

MIRA. And this is the sum of what you could collect last night?

PET. The quintessence. Maybe Witwoud knows more; he stayed longer. Besides, they never mind him; they say anything before him.

MIRA. I thought you had been the greatest favourite.

PET. Ay, *tête-à-tête;* but not in public, because I make remarks.

MIRA. Do you?

PET. Ay, ay; pox, I'm malicious, man. Now, he's soft, you know; they are not in awe of him. The fellow's well bred, he's what you call a—what-d'ee-call-'em. A fine gentleman, but he's silly withal.

MIRA. I thank you, I know as much as my curiosity requires.—— Fainall, are you for the Mall?

FAIN. Ay, I'll take a turn before dinner.

WIT. Ay, we'll all walk in the Park; the ladies talked of being there.

MIRA. I thought you were obliged to watch for your brother Sir Wilfull's arrival.

WIT. No, no, he comes to his aunt's, my Lady Wishfort; pox on him, I shall be troubled with him too; what shall I do with the fool?

PET. Beg him for his estate, that I may beg you afterwards, and so have but one trouble with you both.

WIT. O rare Petulant! thou art as quick as a fire in a frosty morning; thou shalt to the Mall with us, and we'll be very severe.

PET. Enough! I'm in a humour to be severe.

MIRA. Are you? Pray then walk by yourselves—let not us be accessary to your putting the ladies out of countenance with your senseless ribaldry, which you roar out aloud as often as they pass by you; and when you have made a handsome woman blush, then you think you have been severe.

PET. What, what? Then let 'em either show their innocence by not understanding what they hear, or else show their discretion by not hearing what they would not be thought to understand.

MIRA. But hast not thou then sense enough to know that thou ought'st to be most ashamed thyself, when thou hast put another out of countenance?

PET. Not I, by this hand—I always take blushing either for a sign of guilt, or ill breeding.

MIRA. I confess you ought to think so. You are in the right, that you may plead the error of your judgment in defence of your practice.

Where modesty's ill manners, 'tis but fit

That impudence and malice pass for wit.   (*Exeunt.*)

ACT II

SCENE: *St. James's Park*

Enter MRS. FAINALL *and* MRS. MARWOOD

MRS. FAIN. Ay, ay, dear Marwood, if we will be happy, we must find the means in ourselves, and among ourselves. Men are ever in extremes; either doting or averse. While they are lovers, if they have fire and sense, their jealousies are insupportable: and when they cease to love (we ought to think at least) they loathe; they look upon us with horror and distaste; they meet us like the ghosts of what we were, and as such, fly from us.

MRS. MAR. True, 'tis an unhappy circumstance of life that love should ever die before us; and that the man so often should out-live the lover. But say what you will, 'tis better to be left than never to have been loved. To pass our youth in dull indifference, to refuse the sweets of life because they once must leave us, is as preposterous as to wish to have been born old, because we one day must be old. For my part, my youth may wear and waste, but it shall never rust in my possession.

MRS. FAIN. Then it seems you dissemble an aversion to mankind, only in compliance with my mother's humour.

MRS. MAR. Certainly. To be free; I have no taste of those insipid dry discourses, with which our sex of force must entertain themselves, apart from men. We may affect endearments to each other, profess eternal friendships, and seem to dote like lovers; but 'tis not in our natures long to persevere. Love will resume his empire in our breasts, and every heart, or soon or late, receive and readmit him as its lawful tyrant.

MRS. FAIN. Bless me, how have I been deceived! Why, you profess a libertine.

MRS. MAR. You see my friendship by my freedom. Come, be as sincere, acknowledge that your sentiments agree with mine.

MRS. FAIN. Never.

MRS. MAR. You hate mankind.

MRS. FAIN. Heartily, inveterately.

MRS. MAR. Your husband.

MRS. FAIN. Most transcendently; ay, though I say it, meritoriously.

MRS. MAR. Give me your hand upon it.

MRS. FAIN. There.

MRS. MAR. I join with you; what I have said has been to try you.

MRS. FAIN. Is it possible? Dost thou hate those vipers, men?

MRS. MAR. I have done hating 'em, and am now come to despise 'em; the next thing I have to do, is eternally to forget 'em.

MRS. FAIN. There spoke the spirit of an Amazon, a Penthesilea.

MRS. MAR. And yet I am thinking sometimes to carry my aversion further.

MRS. FAIN. How?

MRS. MAR. Faith, by marrying; if I could but find one that loved me very well, and would be thoroughly sensible of ill usage, I think I should do myself the violence of undergoing the ceremony.

MRS. FAIN. You would not make him a cuckold?

MRS. MAR. No; but I'd make him believe I did, and that's as bad.

MRS. FAIN. Why, had not you as good do it?

MRS. MAR. Oh, if he should ever discover it, he would then know the worst, and be out of his pain; but I would have him ever to continue upon the rack of fear and jealousy.

MRS. FAIN. Ingenious mischief! Would thou wert married to Mirabell.

MRS. MAR. Would I were.

MRS. FAIN. You change colour.

MRS. MAR. Because I hate him.

MRS. FAIN. So do I; but I can hear him named. But what reason have you to hate him in particular?

MRS. MAR. I never loved him; he is, and always was, insufferably proud.

MRS. FAIN. By the reason you give for your aversion, one would think it dissembled; for you have laid a fault to his charge of which his enemies must acquit him.

MRS. MAR. Oh, then it seems you are one of his favourable enemies. Methinks you look a little pale, and now you flush again.

MRS. FAIN. Do I? I think I am a little sick o' the sudden.

MRS. MAR. What ails you?

MRS. FAIN. My husband. Don't you see him? He turned short upon me unawares, and has almost overcome me.

Enter FAINALL *and* MIRABELL

MRS. MAR. Ha, ha, ha! he comes opportunely for you.

MRS. FAIN. For you, for he has brought Mirabell with him.

FAIN. My dear.

MRS. FAIN. My soul.

FAIN. You don't look well to-day, child.

MRS. FAIN. D'ee think so?

MIRA. He is the only man that does, Madam.

MRS. FAIN. The only man that would tell me so at least; and the only man from whom I could hear it without mortification.

FAIN. O my dear, I am satisfied of your tenderness; I know you cannot resent anything from me; especially what is an effect of my concern.

MRS. FAIN. Mr. Mirabell, my mother interrupted you in a pleasant relation last night: I would fain hear it out.

MIRA. The persons concerned in that affair have yet a tolerable reputation. I am afraid Mr. Fainall will be censorious.

MRS. FAIN. He has a humour more prevailing than his curiosity, and will willingly dispense with the hearing of one scandalous story, to avoid giving an occasion to make another by being seen to walk with his wife. This way, Mr. Mirabell, and I dare promise you will oblige us both.

(*Exeunt* MRS. FAINALL *and* MIRABELL.)

FAIN. Excellent creature! Well, sure if I should live to be rid of my wife, I should be a miserable man.

MRS. MAR. Ay!

FAIN. For having only that one hope, the accomplishment of it, of consequence, must put an end to all my hopes; and what a wretch is he who must survive his hopes! Nothing remains when that day comes, but to sit down and weep like Alexander when he wanted other worlds to conquer.

MRS. MAR. Will you not follow 'em?

FAIN. Faith, I think not.

MRS. MAR. Pray let us; I have a reason.

FAIN. You are not jealous?

MRS. MAR. Of whom?

FAIN. Of Mirabell.

MRS. MAR. If I am, is it inconsistent with my love to you that I am tender of your honour?

FAIN. You would intimate, then, as if there were a fellow-feeling between my wife and him.

MRS. MAR. I think she does not hate him to that degree she would be thought.

FAIN. But he, I fear, is too insensible.

MRS. MAR. It may be you are deceived.

FAIN. It may be so. I do now begin to apprehend it.

MRS. MAR. What?

FAIN. That I have been deceived, Madam, and you are false.

MRS. MAR. That I am false! What mean you?

FAIN. To let you know I see through all your little arts. Come, you both love him; and both have equally dissembled your aversion. Your mutual jealousies of one another have made you clash till you have both struck fire. I have seen the warm confession reddening on your cheeks, and sparkling from your eyes.

MRS. MAR. You do me wrong.

FAIN. I do not. 'Twas for my ease to oversee and wilfully neglect the gross advances made him by my wife, that by permitting her to be engaged, I might continue unsuspected in my pleasures, and take you oftener to my arms in full security. But could you think, because the nodding husband would not wake, that e'er the watchful lover slept?

MRS. MAR. And wherewithal can you reproach me?

FAIN. With infidelity, with loving of another, with love of Mirabell.

MRS. MAR. 'Tis false. I challenge you to show an instance that can confirm your groundless accusation. I hate him.

FAIN. And wherefore do you hate him? He is insensible, and your resentment follows his neglect. An instance? The injuries you have done him are a proof: your interposing in his love. What cause had you to make discoveries of his pretended passion? To undeceive the credulous aunt, and be the officious obstacle of his match with Millamant?

MRS. MAR. My obligations to my lady urged me: I had professed a friendship to her; and could not see her easy nature so abused by that dissembler.

FAIN. What, was it conscience then? Professed a friendship! Oh, the pious friendships of the female sex!

MRS. MAR. More tender, more sincere, and more enduring, than all the vain and empty vows of men, whether professing love to us, or mutual faith to one another.

FAIN. Ha, ha, ha! you are my wife's friend too.

MRS. MAR. Shame and ingratitude! Do you reproach me? You, you upbraid me! Have I been false to her, through strict fidelity to you, and sacrificed my friendship to keep my love inviolate? And have you the baseness to charge me with the guilt, unmindful of the merit! To you it should be meritorious that I have been vicious: and do you reflect that guilt upon me, which should lie buried in your bosom?

FAIN. You misinterpret my reproof. I meant but to remind you of the slight account you once could make of strictest ties, when set in competition with your love to me.

MRS. MAR. 'Tis false, you urged it with deliberate malice—
'twas spoke in scorn, and I never will forgive it.

FAIN. Your guilt, not your resentment, begets your rage. If yet
you loved, you could forgive a jealousy: but you are stung to
find you are discovered.

MRS. MAR. It shall be all discovered. You too shall be discovered; be sure you shall. I can but be exposed. If I do it myself
I shall prevent your baseness.

FAIN. Why, what will you do?

MRS. MAR. Disclose it to your wife; own what has passed
between us.

FAIN. Frenzy!

MRS. MAR. By all my wrongs I'll do't!—I'll publish to the world
the injuries you have done me, both in my fame and fortune.
With both I trusted you, you bankrupt in honour, as indigent of
wealth!

FAIN. Your fame I have preserved. Your fortune has been
bestowed as the prodigality of your love would have it, in
pleasures which we both have shared. Yet, had not you been
false, I had ere this repaid it. 'Tis true. Had you permitted
Mirabell with Millamant to have stolen their marriage, my lady
had been incensed beyond all means of reconcilement: Millamant had forfeited the moiety of her fortune, which then would
have descended to my wife; and wherefore did I marry, but to
make lawful prize of a rich widow's wealth, and squander it on
love and you?

MRS. MAR. Deceit and frivolous pretence!

FAIN. Death, am I not married? What's pretence? Am I not
imprisoned, fettered? Have I not a wife? Nay, a wife that was
a widow, a young widow, a handsome widow; and would be
again a widow, but that I have a heart of proof, and something
of a constitution to bustle through the ways of wedlock and
this world. Will you yet be reconciled to truth and me?

MRS. MAR. Impossible. Truth and you are inconsistent—I hate
you, and shall forever.

FAIN. For loving you?

MRS. MAR. I loathe the name of love after such usage; and
next to the guilt with which you would asperse me, I scorn you
most. Farewell.

FAIN. Nay, we must not part thus.

MRS. MAR. Let me go.

FAIN. Come, I'm sorry.

MRS. MAR. I care not—let me go—break my hands, do—I'd leave 'em to get loose.

FAIN. I would not hurt you for the world. Have I no other hold to keep you here?

MRS. MAR. Well, I have deserved it all.

FAIN. You know I love you.

MRS. MAR. Poor dissembling!—Oh, that—well, it is not yet——

FAIN. What? What is it not? What is it not yet? It is not yet too late——

MRS. MAR. No, it is not yet too late—I have that comfort.

FAIN. It is, to love another.

MRS. MAR. But not to loathe, detest, abhor mankind, myself, and the whole treacherous world.

FAIN. Nay, this is extravagance. Come, I ask your pardon —no tears—I was to blame, I could not love you and be easy in my doubts. Pray forbear—I believe you; I'm convinced I've done you wrong; and any way, every way will make amends; I'll hate my wife yet more, damn her, I'll part with her, rob her of all she's worth, and will retire somewhere, anywhere, to another world. I'll marry thee—be pacified.—— 'Sdeath, they come; hide your face, your tears. You have a mask, wear it a moment. This way, this way, be persuaded.   (*Exeunt.*)

Enter MIRABELL *and* MRS. FAINALL

MRS. FAIN. They are here yet.

MIRA. They are turning into the other walk.

MRS. FAIN. While I only hated my husband, I could bear to see him; but since I have despised him, he's too offensive.

MIRA. Oh, you should hate with prudence.

MRS. FAIN. Yes, for I have loved with indiscretion.

MIRA. You should have just so much disgust for your husband as may be sufficient to make you relish your lover.

MRS. FAIN. You have been the cause that I have loved without bounds, and would you set limits to that aversion of which you have been the occasion? Why did you make me marry this man?

MIRA. Why do we daily commit disagreeable and dangerous actions? To save that idol, reputation. If the familiarities of our loves had produced that consequence of which you were apprehensive, where could you have fixed a father's name with credit, but on a husband? I knew Fainall to be a man lavish of his morals, an interested and professing friend, a false and a designing lover; yet one whose wit and outward fair behaviour have gained a reputation with the town, enough to make that woman stand excused who has suffered herself to be won by his addresses. A better man ought not to have been sacrificed to the occasion; a worse had not answered to the purpose. When you are weary of him, you know your remedy.

MRS. FAIN. I ought to stand in some degree of credit with you, Mirabell.

MIRA. In justice to you, I have made you privy to my whole design, and put it in your power to ruin or advance my fortune.

MRS. FAIN. Whom have you instructed to represent your pretended uncle?

MIRA. Waitwell, my servant.

MRS. FAIN. He is an humble servant to Foible, my mother's woman, and may win her to your interest.

MIRA. Care is taken for that. She is won and worn by this time. They were married this morning.

MRS. FAIN. Who?

MIRA. Waitwell and Foible. I would not tempt my servant to betray me by trusting him too far. If your mother, in hopes to ruin me, should consent to marry my pretended uncle, he might, like Mosca in *The Fox*, stand upon terms; so I made him sure beforehand.

MRS. FAIN. So, if my poor mother is caught in a contract, you will discover the imposture betimes, and release her by producing a certificate of her gallant's former marriage.

MIRA. Yes, upon condition she consent to my marriage with her niece, and surrender the moiety of her fortune in her possession.

MRS. FAIN. She talked last night of endeavouring at a match between Millamant and your uncle.

MIRA. That was by Foible's direction, and my instruction, that she might seem to carry it more privately.

MRS. FAIN. Well, I have an opinion of your success, for I believe my lady will do anything to get a husband; and when she has this, which you have provided for her, I suppose she will submit to anything to get rid of him.

MIRA. Yes, I think the good lady would marry anything that resembled a man, though 'twere no more than what a butler could pinch out of a napkin.

MRS. FAIN. Female frailty! We must all come to it, if we live to be old, and feel the craving of a false appetite when the true is decayed.

MIRA. An old woman's appetite is depraved like that of a girl. 'Tis the green-sickness of a second childhood; and like the faint offer of a latter spring, serves but to usher in the fall, and withers in an affected bloom.

MRS. FAIN. Here's your mistress.

Enter MRS. MILLAMANT, WITWOUD, *and* MINCING

MIRA. Here she comes, i'faith, full sail, with her fan spread and her streamers out, and a shoal of fools for tenders. Ha, no, I cry her mercy!

MRS. FAIN. I see but one poor empty sculler; and he tows her woman after him.

MIRA. You seem to be unattended, Madam. You used to have the *beau monde* throng after you, and a flock of gay fine perukes hovering round you.

WIT. Like moths about a candle.—I had like to have lost my comparison for want of breath.

MILLA. Oh, I have denied myself airs to-day. I have walked as fast through the crowd——

WIT. As a favourite in disgrace; and with as few followers.

MILLA. Dear Mr. Witwoud, truce with your similitudes: for I am as sick of 'em——

WIT. As a physician of a good air.—I cannot help it, Madam, though 'tis against myself.

MILLA. Yet again! Mincing, stand between me and his wit.

WIT. Do, Mrs. Mincing, like a screen before a great fire. I confess I do blaze to-day, I am too bright.

MRS. FAIN. But, dear Millamant, why were you so long?

MILLA. Long! Lord, have I not made violent haste? I have asked every living thing I met for you; I have enquired after you as after a new fashion.

WIT. Madam, truce with your similitudes. No, you met her husband, and did not ask him for her.

MIRA. By your leave, Witwoud, that were like enquiring after an old fashion, to ask a husband for his wife.

WIT. Hum, a hit, a hit, a palpable hit, I confess it.

MRS. FAIN. You were dressed before I came abroad.

MILLA. Ay, that's true—oh, but then I had—Mincing, what had I? Why was I so long?

MINC. O Mem, your la'ship stayed to peruse a pecquet of letters.

MILLA. Oh, ay, letters—I had letters—I am persecuted with letters—I hate letters. Nobody knows how to write letters; and yet one has 'em, one does not know why. They serve one to pin up one's hair.

WIT. Is that the way? Pray, Madam, do you pin up your hair with all your letters? I find I must keep copies.

MILLA. Only with those in verse, Mr. Witwoud. I never pin up my hair with prose. I fancy one's hair would not curl if it were pinned up with prose. I think I tried once, Mincing.

MINC. O Mem, I shall never forget it.

MILLA. Ay, poor Mincing tift and tift all the morning.

MINC. Till I had the cremp in my fingers, I'll vow, Mem. And all to no purpose. But when your la'ship pins it up with poetry, it sits so pleasant the next day as anything, and is so pure and so crips.

WIT. Indeed, so "crips"?

MINC. You're such a critic, Mr. Witwoud.

MILLA. Mirabell, did not you take exceptions last night? Oh, ay, and went away. Now I think on't I'm angry.—No, now I think on't I'm pleased—for I believe I gave you some pain.

MIRA. Does that please you?

MILLA. Infinitely; I love to give pain.

MIRA. You would affect a cruelty which is not in your nature; your true vanity is in the power of pleasing.

MILLA. Oh, I ask your pardon for that. One's cruelty is one's power, and when one parts with one's cruelty, one parts with one's power; and when one has parted with that, I fancy one's old and ugly.

MIRA. Ay, ay, suffer your cruelty to ruin the object of your power, to destroy your lover—and then how vain, how lost a thing you'll be! Nay, 'tis true: you are no longer handsome when you've lost your lover; your beauty dies upon the instant: for beauty is the lover's gift; 'tis he bestows your charms—your glass is all a cheat. The ugly and the old, whom the looking-glass mortifies, yet after commendation can be flattered by it, and discover beauties in it: for that reflects our praises, rather than your face.

MILLA. Oh, the vanity of these men! Fainall, d'ee hear him? If they did not commend us, we were not handsome! Now you must know they could not commend one if one was not handsome. Beauty the lover's gift—Lord, what is a lover, that it can give? Why, one makes lovers as fast as one pleases, and they live as long as one pleases, and they die as soon as one pleases: and then if one pleases, one makes more.

WIT. Very pretty. Why you make no more of making of lovers, Madam, than of making so many card-matches.

MILLA. One no more owes one's beauty to a lover, than one's wit to an echo: they can but reflect what we look and say; vain empty things if we are silent or unseen, and want a being.

MIRA. Yet, to those two vain empty things you owe two the greatest pleasures of your life.

MILLA. How so?

MIRA. To your lover you owe the pleasure of hearing yourselves praised; and to an echo the pleasure of hearing yourselves talk.

WIT. But I know a lady that loves talking so incessantly she won't give an echo fair play; she has that everlasting rotation of tongue that an echo must wait till she dies, before it can catch her last words.

MILLA. Oh, fiction! Fainall, let us leave these men.

MIRA. (*aside to* MRS. FAINALL) Draw off Witwoud.

MRS. FAIN. Immediately.—— I have a word or two for Mr. Witwoud.

MIRA. I would beg a little private audience too.

(*Exeunt* WITWOUD *and* MRS. FAINALL.)

You had the tyranny to deny me last night; though you knew I came to impart a secret to you that concerned my love.

MILLA. You saw I was engaged.

MIRA. Unkind. You had the leisure to entertain a herd of fools; things who visit you from their excessive idleness, bestowing on your easiness that time which is the incumbrance of their lives.

How can you find delight in such society? It is impossible they should admire you, they are not capable: or if they were, it should be to you as a mortification, for sure to please a fool is some degree of folly.

MILLA. I please myself—besides, sometimes to converse with fools is for my health.

MIRA. Your health! Is there a worse disease than the conversation of fools?

MILLA. Yes, the vapours; fools are physic for it, next to asafœtida.

MIRA. You are not in a course of fools?

MILLA. Mirabell, if you persist in this offensive freedom, you'll displease me. I think I must resolve, after all, not to have you. We shan't agree.

MIRA. Not in our physic, it may be.

MILLA. And yet our distemper in all likelihood will be the same; for we shall be sick of one another. I shan't endure to be reprimanded, nor instructed; 'tis so dull to act always by advice, and so tedious to be told of one's faults—I can't bear it. Well, I won't have you, Mirabell—I'm resolved—I think—you may go —ha, ha, ha! What would you give, that you could help loving me?

MIRA. I would give something that you did not know I could not help it.

MILLA. Come, don't look grave then. Well, what do you say to me?

MIRA. I say that a man may as soon make a friend by his wit, or a fortune by his honesty, as win a woman with plain dealing and sincerity.

MILLA. Sententious Mirabell! Prithee, don't look with that violent and inflexible wise face, like Solomon at the dividing of the child in an old tapestry hanging.

MIRA. You are merry, Madam, but I would persuade you for one moment to be serious.

MILLA. What, with that face? No, if you keep your countenance, 'tis impossible I should hold mine. Well, after all, there is something very moving in a lovesick face. Ha, ha, ha!—well, I won't laugh, don't be peevish—heigho! Now I'll be melancholy, as melancholy as a watch-light. Well, Mirabell, if ever you will win me, woo me now.—Nay, if you are so tedious, fare you well; I see they are walking away.

MIRA. Can you not find in the variety of your disposition one moment——

MILLA. To hear you tell me that Foible's married, and your plot like to speed? No.

MIRA. But how you came to know it——

MILLA. Unless by the help of the devil, you can't imagine; unless she should tell me herself. Which of the two it may have been, I will leave you to consider; and when you have done thinking of that, think of me. (*Exit.*)

MIRA. I have something more—— Gone!—Think of you! To think of a whirlwind, though 'twere in a whirlwind, were a case of more steady contemplation; a very tranquillity of mind and mansion. A fellow that lives in a windmill has not a more whimsical dwelling than the heart of a man that is lodged in a woman. There is no point of the compass to which they cannot turn, and by which they are not turned, and by one as well as another; for motion, not method, is their occupation. To know this, and yet continue to be in love, is to be made wise from the dictates of reason,. and yet persevere to play the fool by the force of instinct. Oh, here come my pair of turtles!—— What, billing so sweetly! Is not Valentine's Day over with you yet?

Enter WAITWELL *and* FOIBLE

Sirrah Waitwell, why sure you think you were married for your own recreation, and not for my conveniency.

WAIT. Your pardon, Sir. With submission, we have indeed been solacing in lawful delights; but still with an eye to business, Sir. I have instructed her as well as I could. If she can take your directions as readily as my instructions, Sir, your affairs are in a prosperous way.

MIRA. Give you joy, Mrs. Foible.

FOIB. O 'las, Sir, I'm so ashamed—I'm afraid my lady has been in a thousand inquietudes for me. But I protest, Sir, I made as much haste as I could.

WAIT. That she did indeed, Sir. It was my fault that she did not make more.

MIRA. That I believe.

FOIB. But I told my lady as you instructed me, Sir. That I had a prospect of seeing Sir Rowland, your uncle; and that I would put her ladyship's picture in my pocket to show him; which I'll be sure to say has made him so enamoured of her beauty that he burns with impatience to lie at her ladyship's feet and worship the original.

MIRA. Excellent Foible! Matrimony has made you eloquent in love.

WAIT. I think she has profited, Sir. I think so.

FOIB. You have seen Madam Millamant, Sir?

MIRA. Yes.

FOIB. I told her, Sir, because I did not know that you might find an opportunity; she had so much company last night.

MIRA. Your diligence will merit more. In the meantime——
                                              (*gives money*)

FOIB. O dear Sir, your humble servant.

WAIT. Spouse!

MIRA. Stand off, Sir, not a penny.—— Go on and prosper, Foible. The lease shall be made good and the farm stocked, if we succeed.

FOIB. I don't question your generosity, Sir: and you need not doubt of success. If you have no more commands, Sir, I'll be gone; I'm sure my lady is at her toilet, and can't dress 'till I come.—— Oh dear, I'm sure that (*looking out*) was Mrs. Marwood that went by in a mask; if she has seen me with you I'm sure she'll tell my lady. I'll make haste home and prevent her. Your servant, Sir. B'w'y, Waitwell.   (*Exit* FOIBLE.)

WAIT. Sir Rowland, if you please. The jade's so pert upon her preferment she forgets herself.

MIRA. Come, Sir, will you endeavour to forget yourself—and transform into Sir Rowland.

WAIT. Why, Sir, it will be impossible I should remember myself—married, knighted, and attended all in one day! 'Tis enough to make any man forget himself. The difficulty will be how to recover my acquaintance and familiarity with my former self, and fall from my transformation to a reformation into Waitwell. Nay, I shan't be quite the same Waitwell neither—for now I remember me, I am married, and can't be my own man again.

　　Ay, there's the grief; that's the sad change of life;
　　To lose my title, and yet keep my wife.   (*Exeunt.*)

ACT III

SCENE: *A room in* LADY WISHFORT'S *house*

LADY WISHFORT *at her toilet,* PEG *waiting*

LADY WISH. Merciful, no news of Foible yet?

PEG. No, Madam.

LADY WISH. I have no more patience. If I have not fretted myself till I am pale again, there's no veracity in me. Fetch me the red—the red, do you hear, sweetheart? An arrant ash color, as I'm a person. Look you how this wench stirs! Why dost thou not fetch me a little red? Didst thou not hear me, mopus?

PEG. The red ratafia does your Ladyship mean, or the cherry-brandy?

LADY WISH. Ratafia, fool! No, fool. Not the ratafia, fool—grant me patience! I mean the Spanish paper, idiot—complexion, darling. Paint, paint, paint, dost thou understand that, changeling, dangling thy hands like bobbins before thee? Why dost thou not stir, puppet? thou wooden thing upon wires!

PEG. Lord, Madam, your Ladyship is so impatient. I cannot come at the paint, Madam; Mrs. Foible has locked it up, and carried the key with her.

LADY WISH. A pox take you both! Fetch me the cherry-brandy then. (*Exit* PEG.) I'm as pale and as faint, I look like Mrs. Qualmsick the curate's wife, that's always breeding.—— Wench, come, come, wench, what art thou doing, sipping? tasting? Save thee, dost thou not know the bottle?

Enter PEG *with a bottle and china cup*

PEG. Madam, I was looking for a cup.

LADY WISH. A cup, save thee, and what a cup hast thou brought! Dost thou take me for a fairy, to drink out of an acorn? Why didst thou not bring thy thimble? Hast thou ne'er a brass thimble clinking in thy pocket with a bit of nutmeg? I warrant thee. Come, fill, fill.—So—again. (*One knocks.*) See who that is. Set down the bottle first. Here, here, under the table. What, wouldst thou go with the bottle in thy hand like a tapster? (*Exit* PEG.) As I'm a person, this wench has lived in an inn upon the road, before she came to me, like Maritornes the Asturian in *Don Quixote*. (*Re-enter* PEG.) No Foible yet?

PEG. No, Madam, Mrs. Marwood.

LADY WISH. Oh, Marwood! let her come in. Come in, good Marwood.

Enter MRS. MARWOOD

MRS. MAR. I'm surprised to find your Ladyship in dishabille at this time of day.

LADY WISH. Foible's a lost thing; has been abroad since morning, and never heard of since.

MRS. MAR. I saw her but now, as I came masked through the Park, in conference with Mirabell.

LADY WISH. With Mirabell! You call my blood into my face, with mentioning that traitor. She durst not have the confidence. I sent her to negotiate an affair, in which if I'm detected I'm undone. If that wheedling villain has wrought upon Foible to detect me, I'm ruined. Oh, my dear friend, I'm a wretch of wretches if I'm detected.

MRS. MAR. O Madam, you cannot suspect Mrs. Foible's integrity.

LADY WISH. Oh, he carries poison in his tongue that would corrupt integrity itself. If she has given him an opportunity, she has as good as put her integrity into his hands. Ah, dear Marwood, what's integrity to an opportunity?—— Hark! I hear her. —— Go, you thing, and send her in! (*Exit* PEG.) Dear friend, retire into my closet, that I may examine her with more freedom. —You'll pardon me, dear friend, I can make bold with you.— There are books over the chimney—Quarles and Prynne, and *The Short View of the Stage*, with Bunyan's works, to entertain you.   (*Exit* MARWOOD.)

Enter FOIBLE

O Foible, where hast thou been? What hast thou been doing?

FOIB. Madam, I have seen the party.

LADY WISH. But what hast thou done?

FOIB. Nay, 'tis your Ladyship has done, and are to do; I have only promised. But a man so enamoured—so transported! Well, here it is, all that is left; all that is not kissed away. Well, if worshipping of pictures be a sin—poor Sir Rowland, I say.

LADY WISH. The miniature has been counted like—— But hast thou not betrayed me, Foible? Hast thou not detected me to that faithless Mirabell? What hadst thou to do with him in the Park? Answer me, has he got nothing out of thee?

FOIB. So, the devil has been beforehand with me: what shall I say?—— Alas, Madam, could I help it, if I met that confident thing? Was I in fault? If you had heard how he used me, and all upon your Ladyship's account, I'm sure you would not suspect my fidelity. Nay, if that had been the worst, I could have borne: but he had a fling at your Ladyship too; and then I could not hold, but, i'faith, I gave him his own.

LADY WISH. Me? What did the filthy fellow say?

FOIB. O Madam, 'tis a shame to say what he said—with his taunts and his fleers, tossing up his nose. "Humh!" says he, "what, you are a-hatching some plot," says he, "you are so early abroad, or catering," says he, "ferreting for some disbanded officer, I warrant—half pay is but thin subsistence," says he. "Well, what pension does your lady propose? Let me see," says he; "what, she must come down pretty deep now: she's superannuated," says he, "and——"

LADY WISH. Ods my life, I'll have him—I'll have him murdered. I'll have him poisoned. Where does he eat? I'll marry a drawer to have him poisoned in his wine. I'll send for Robin from Locket's immediately.

FOIB. Poison him? Poisoning's too good for him. Starve him, Madam, starve him; marry Sir Rowland and get him disinherited. Oh, you would bless yourself, to hear what he said.

LADY WISH. A villain! "superannuated!"

FOIB. "Humh!" says he, "I hear you are laying designs against me, too," says he, "and Mrs. Millamant is to marry my uncle";—(he does not suspect a word of your ladyship);—"but," says he, "I'll fit you for that, I warrant you," says he, "I'll hamper you for that," says he, "you and your old frippery, too," says he, "I'll handle you——"

LADY WISH. Audacious villain! handle me! Would he durst!—"Frippery? old frippery!" Was there ever such a foul-mouthed fellow? I'll be married to-morrow, I'll be contracted to-night.

FOIB. The sooner the better, Madam.

LADY WISH. Will Sir Rowland be here, say'st thou? When, Foible?

FOIB. Incontinently, Madam. No new sheriff's wife expects the return of her husband after knighthood with that impatience in which Sir Rowland burns for the dear hour of kissing your Ladyship's hands after dinner.

LADY WISH. "Frippery? superannuated frippery!" I'll frippery the villain; I'll reduce him to frippery and rags. A tatterdemalion! —I hope to see him hung with tatters, like a Long Lane pent-house, or a gibbet-thief. A slander-mouthed railer: I warrant the spendthrift prodigal's in debt as much as the million lottery, or the whole court upon a birthday. I'll spoil his credit with his tailor. Yes, he shall have my niece with her fortune, he shall.

FOIB. He! I hope to see him lodge in Ludgate first, and angle into Blackfriars for brass farthings with an old mitten.

LADY WISH. Ay, dear Foible; thank thee for that, dear Foible. He has put me out of all patience. I shall never recompose my features to receive Sir Rowland with any economy of face. This wretch has fretted me that I am absolutely decayed. Look, Foible.

FOIB. Your Ladyship has frowned a little too rashly, indeed, Madam. There are some cracks discernible in the white varnish.

LADY WISH. Let me see the glass.—Cracks, say'st thou? Why, I am arrantly flayed. I look like an old peeled wall. Thou must repair me, Foible, before Sir Rowland comes, or I shall never keep up to my picture.

FOIB. I warrant you, Madam; a little art once made your picture like you; and now a little of the same art must make you like your picture. Your picture must sit for you, Madam.

LADY WISH. But art thou sure Sir Rowland will not fail to come? Or will a not fail when he does come? Will he be importunate, Foible, and push? For if he should not be importunate—I shall never break decorums—I shall die with confusion, if I am forced to advance—oh no, I can never advance—I shall swoon if he should expect advances. No, I hope Sir Rowland is better bred than to put a lady to the necessity of breaking her forms. I won't be too coy neither. I won't give him despair—but a little disdain is not amiss; a little scorn is alluring.

FOIB. A little scorn becomes your Ladyship.

LADY WISH. Yes, but tenderness becomes me best—a sort of a dyingness. You see that picture has a sort of a—ha, Foible?— a swimminess in the eyes. Yes, I'll look so. My niece affects it; but she wants features. Is Sir Rowland handsome? Let my toilet be removed—I'll dress above. I'll receive Sir Rowland here. Is he handsome? Don't answer me. I won't know: I'll be surprised. I'll be taken by surprise.

FOIB. By storm, Madam. Sir Rowland's a brisk man.

LADY WISH. Is he! Oh, then he'll importune, if he's a brisk man. I shall save decorums if Sir Rowland importunes. I have a mortal terror at the apprehension of offending against decorums. Nothing but importunity can surmount decorums. Oh, I'm glad he's a brisk man! Let my things be removed, good Foible.

(*Exit.*)

Enter MRS. FAINALL

MRS. FAIN. O Foible, I have been in a fright lest I should come too late. That devil, Marwood, saw you in the Park with Mirabell, and I'm afraid will discover it to my lady.

FOIB. Discover what, Madam?

MRS. FAIN. Nay, nay, put not on that strange face. I am privy to the whole design, and know that Waitwell, to whom thou wert this morning married, is to personate Mirabell's uncle, and as such, winning my lady, to involve her in those difficulties from which Mirabell only must release her, by his making his conditions to have my cousin and her fortune left to her own disposal.

FOIB. O dear Madam, I beg your pardon. It was not my confidence in your Ladyship that was deficient; but I thought the former good correspondence between your Ladyship and Mr. Mirabell might have hindered his communicating this secret.

MRS. FAIN. Dear Foible, forget that.

FOIB. O dear Madam, Mr. Mirabell is such a sweet winning gentleman—but your Ladyship is the pattern of generosity. Sweet Lady, to be so good! Mr. Mirabell cannot choose but be grateful. I find your Ladyship has his heart still. Now, Madam, I can safely tell your Ladyship our success; Mrs. Marwood had told my lady, but I warrant I managed myself. I turned it all for the better. I told my lady that Mr. Mirabell railed at her. I laid horrid things to his charge, I'll vow; and my lady is so incensed that she'll be contracted to Sir Rowland to-night, she says; I warrant I worked her up that he may have her for asking for, as they say of a Welsh maidenhead.

MRS. FAIN. O rare Foible!

FOIB. Madam, I beg your Ladyship to acquaint Mr. Mirabell of his success. I would be seen as little as possible to speak to him; besides, I believe Madam Marwood watches me. She has a month's mind, but I know Mr. Mirabell can't abide her. (*Enter Footman.*) John, remove my lady's toilet. Madam, your servant. My lady is so impatient, I fear she'll come for me, if I stay.

MRS. FAIN. I'll go with you up the back stairs, lest I should meet her. (*Exeunt.*)

Enter MRS. MARWOOD

MRS. MAR. Indeed, Mrs. Engine, is it thus with you? Are you become a go-between of this importance? Yes, I shall watch you. Why, this wench is the *passe-partout*, a very master-key to everybody's strong box. My friend Fainall, have you carried it so swimmingly? I thought there was something in it; but it seems it's over with you. Your loathing is not from a want of appetite then, but from a surfeit. Else you could never be so cool to fall from a principal to be an assistant, to procure for him! A pattern of generosity, that I confess. Well, Mr. Fainall, you have met with your match.—— O man, man! Woman, woman! The devil's an ass: if I were a painter, I would draw him like an idiot, a driveler, with a bib and bells. Man should have his head and horns, and woman the rest of him. Poor simple fiend! "Madam Marwood has a month's mind, but he can't abide her."—'Twere better for him you had not been his confessor in that affair, without you could have kept his counsel closer. I shall not prove another pattern of generosity and stalk for him, till he takes his stand to aim at a fortune; he has not obliged me to that with those excesses of himself; and now I'll have none of him. Here comes the good lady, panting ripe; with a heart full of hope, and a head full of care, like any chemist upon the day of projection.

Enter LADY WISHFORT

LADY WISH. O dear Marwood, what shall I say for this rude forgetfulness? But my dear friend is all goodness.

MRS. MAR. No apologies, dear Madam. I have been very well entertained.

LADY WISH. As I'm a person, I am in a very chaos to think I should so forget myself—but I have such an olio of affairs, really I know not what to do.—— (*calls*) Foible!—— I expect my

nephew Sir Wilfull every moment too.—— Why, Foible!——
He means to travel for improvement.

MRS. MAR. Methinks Sir Wilfull should rather think of marrying than travelling at his years. I hear he is turned of forty.

LADY WISH. Oh, he's in less danger of being spoiled by his
travels. I am against my nephew's marrying too young. It will be
time enough when he comes back, and has acquired discretion to
choose for himself.

MRS. MAR. Methinks Mrs. Millamant and he would make a
very fit match. He may travel afterwards. 'Tis a thing very usual
with young gentlemen.

LADY WISH. I promise you I have thought on't—and since 'tis
your judgment, I'll think on't again. I assure you I will; I value
your judgment extremely. On my word, I'll propose it.

Enter FOIBLE

Come, come, Foible—I had forgot my nephew will be here before dinner. I must make haste.

FOIB. Mr. Witwoud and Mr. Petulant are come to dine with
your Ladyship.

LADY WISH. Oh dear, I can't appear till I'm dressed. Dear
Marwood, shall I be free with you again, and beg you to enter-
tain 'em? I'll make all imaginable haste. Dear friend, excuse me.
(*Exeunt* LADY WISHFORT *and* FOIBLE.)

Enter MRS. MILLAMANT *and* MINCING

MILLA. Sure never anything was so unbred as that odious man.
—— Marwood, your servant.

MRS. MAR. You have a colour; what's the matter?

MILLA. That horrid fellow, Petulant, has provoked me into a
flame. I have broke my fan.—— Mincing, lend me yours. Is not
all the powder out of my hair?

MRS. MAR. No. What has he done?

MILLA. Nay, he has done nothing; he has only talked. Nay, he
has said nothing neither; but he has contradicted everything that
has been said. For my part, I thought Witwoud and he would
have quarrelled.

MINC. I vow, Mem, I thought once they would have fit.

MILLA. Well, 'tis a lamentable thing, I'll swear, that one has not the liberty of choosing one's acquaintance as one does one's clothes.

MRS. MAR. If we had the liberty, we should be as weary of one set of acquaintance, though never so good, as we are of one suit, though never so fine. A fool and a doily stuff would now and then find days of grace, and be worn for variety.

MILLA. I could consent to wear 'em, if they would wear alike; but fools never wear out—they are such *drap-de-Berry* things!— without one could give 'em to one's chambermaid after a day or two.

MRS. MAR. 'Twere better so indeed. Or what think you of the playhouse? A fine gay glossy fool should be given there, like a new masking habit, after the masquerade is over, and we have done with the disguise. For a fool's visit is always a disguise; and never admitted by a woman of wit but to blind her affair with a lover of sense. If you would but appear barefaced now, and own Mirabell, you might as easily put off Petulant and Witwoud as your hood and scarf. And indeed 'tis time, for the town has found it: the secret is grown too big for the pretence. 'Tis like Mrs. Primly's great belly; she may lace it down before, but it burnishes on her hips. Indeed, Millamant, you can no more conceal it than my Lady Strammel can her face, that goodly face, which in defiance of her Rhenish-wine tea, will not be comprehended in a mask.

MILLA. I'll take my death, Marwood, you are more censorious than a decayed beauty, or a discarded toast.—— Mincing, tell the men they may come up. My aunt is not dressing.—— Their folly is less provoking than your malice. The town has found it! (*Exit* MINCING.) What has it found? That Mirabell loves me is no more a secret, than it is a secret that you discovered it to my aunt, or than the reason why you discovered it is a secret.

MRS. MAR. You are nettled.

MILLA. You're mistaken. Ridiculous!

MRS. MAR. Indeed, my dear, you'll tear another fan, if you don't mitigate those violent airs.

MILLA. O silly! Ha, ha, ha! I could laugh immoderately. Poor Mirabell! His constancy to me has quite destroyed his complaisance for all the world beside. I swear, I never enjoined it him, to be so coy. If I had the vanity to think he would obey me, I would command him to show more gallantry. 'Tis hardly well bred to be so particular on one hand, and so insensible on the other. But I despair to prevail, and so let him follow his own way. Ha, ha, ha! Pardon me, dear creature, I must laugh, ha, ha, ha!—though I grant you 'tis a little barbarous, ha, ha, ha!

MRS. MAR. What pity 'tis, so much fine raillery, and delivered with so significant gesture, should be so unhappily directed to miscarry.

MILLA. Heh? Dear creature, I ask your pardon—I swear I did not mind you.

MRS. MAR. Mr. Mirabell and you both may think it a thing impossible, when I shall tell him by telling you——

MILLA. O dear, what? for it is the same thing, if I hear it—ha, ha, ha!

MRS. MAR. That I detest him, hate him, Madam.

MILLA. O Madam, why so do I—and yet the creature loves me, ha, ha, ha! How can one forbear laughing to think of it? I am a sibyl if I am not amazed to think what he can see in me. I'll take my death, I think you are handsomer—and within a year or two as young. If you could but stay for me, I should over-take you—but that cannot be. Well, that thought makes me melancholy. Now I'll be sad.

MRS. MAR. Your merry note may be changed sooner than you think.

MILLA. D'ee say so? Then I'm resolved I'll have a song to keep up my spirits.

Enter MINCING

MINC. The gentlemen stay but to comb, Madam, and will wait on you.

MILLA. Desire Mrs.—— that is in the next room to sing the song I would have learnt yesterday. You shall hear it, Madam—not that there's any great matter in it—but 'tis agreeable to my humour.

SONG

Set by Mr. John Eccles, and sung by Mrs. Hodgson

I

> Love's but the frailty of the mind,
> When 'tis not with ambition join'd;

A sickly flame, which if not fed expires;
And feeding, wastes in self-consuming fires.

II

'Tis not to wound a wanton boy
Or am'rous youth, that gives the joy;
But 'tis the glory to have pierc'd a swain,
For whom inferior beauties sigh'd in vain.

III

Then I alone the conquest prize,
When I insult a rival's eyes:
If there's delight in love, 'tis when I see
That heart which others bleed for, bleed for me.

Enter PETULANT *and* WITWOUD

MILLA. Is your animosity composed, gentlemen?

WIT. Raillery, raillery, Madam; we have no animosity—we hit off a little wit now and then, but no animosity. The falling out of wits is like the falling out of lovers. We agree in the main, like treble and bass. Ha, Petulant?

PET. Ay, in the main. But when I have a humour to contradict——

WIT. Ay, when he has a humour to contradict, then I contradict too. What, I know my cue. Then we contradict one another like two battledores, for contradictions beget one another like Jews.

PET. If he says black's black—if I have a humour to say 'tis blue—let that pass—all's one for that. If I have a humour to prove it, it must be granted.

WIT. Not positively must—but it may—it may.

PET. Yes, it positively must, upon proof positive.

WIT. Ay, upon proof positive it must; but upon proof presumptive it only may. That's a logical distinction now, Madam.

MRS. MAR. I perceive your debates are of importance and very learnedly handled.

PET. Importance is one thing, and learning's another; but a debate's a debate, that I assert.

WIT. Petulant's an enemy to learning; he relies altogether on his parts.

PET. No, I'm no enemy to learning; it hurts not me.

MRS. MAR. That's a sign indeed it's no enemy to you.

PET. No, no, it's no enemy to anybody but them that have it.

MILLA. Well, an illiterate man's my aversion. I wonder at the impudence of any illiterate man, to offer to make love.

WIT. That I confess I wonder at too.

MILLA. Ah! to marry an ignorant that can hardly read or write!

PET. Why should a man be ever the further from being married though he can't read, any more than he is from being hanged? The ordinary's paid for setting the psalm, and the parish-priest for reading the ceremony. And for the rest which is to follow in both cases, a man may do it without book—so all's one for that.

MILLA. D'ee hear the creature? Lord, here's company, I'll be gone.   (*Exeunt* MILLAMANT *and* MINCING.)

WIT. In the name of Bartlemew and his fair, what have we here?

MRS. MAR. 'Tis your brother, I fancy. Don't you know him?

WIT. Not I—yes, I think it is he—I've almost forgot him; I have not seen him since the Revolution.

Enter SIR WILFULL WITWOUD *in a country riding habit, and Servant to* LADY WISHFORT

SERV. Sir, my lady's dressing. Here's company, if you please to walk in, in the meantime.

SIR WIL. Dressing! What, it's but morning here I warrant with you in London; we should count it towards afternoon in our parts, down in Shropshire. Why then belike my aunt han't dined yet—ha, friend?

SERV. Your aunt, Sir?

SIR WIL. My aunt, Sir, yes, my aunt, Sir, and your lady, Sir; your lady is my aunt, Sir. Why, what, dost thou not know me, friend? Why, then send somebody here that does. How long hast thou lived with thy lady, fellow, ha?

SERV. A week, Sir; longer than anybody in the house, except my lady's woman.

SIR WIL. Why then belike thou dost not know thy lady, if thou seest her, ha, friend?

SERV. Why truly, Sir, I cannot safely swear to her face in a morning, before she is dressed. 'Tis like I may give a shrewd guess at her by this time.

SIR WIL. Well, prithee try what thou canst do; if thou canst not guess, enquire her out, dost hear, fellow? And tell her, her nephew, Sir Wilful Witwoud, is in the house.

SERV. I shall, Sir.

SIR WIL. Hold ye, hear me, friend; a word with you in your ear; prithee who are these gallants?

SERV. Really, Sir, I can't tell; there come so many here, 'tis hard to know 'em all.   (*Exit Servant.*)

SIR WIL. Oons, this fellow knows less than a starling; I don't think a' knows his own name.

MRS. MAR. Mr. Witwoud, your brother is not behindhand in forgetfulness—I fancy he has forgot you too.

WIT. I hope so—the devil take him that remembers first, I say.

SIR WIL. Save you, gentlemen and lady.

MRS. MAR. For shame, Mr. Witwoud; why won't you speak to him?—— And you, Sir.

WIT. Petulant, speak.

PET. And you, Sir.

SIR WIL. No offence, I hope.   (*salutes* MARWOOD)

MRS. MAR. No, sure, Sir.

WIT. This is a vile dog, I see that already. No offence! Ha, ha, ha! To him; to him, Petulant, smoke him.

PET. It seems as if you had come a journey, Sir; hem, hem.
                                    (*surveying him round*)

SIR WIL. Very likely, Sir, that it may seem so.

PET. No offence, I hope, Sir.

WIT. Smoke the boots, the boots, Petulant, the boots; ha, ha, ha!

SIR WIL. Maybe not, Sir; thereafter as 'tis meant, Sir.

PET. Sir, I presume upon the information of your boots.

SIR WIL. Why, 'tis like you may, Sir: if you are not satisfied with the information of my boots, Sir, if you will step to the stable, you may enquire further of my horse, Sir.

PET. Your horse, Sir! Your horse is an ass, Sir!

SIR WIL. Do you speak by way of offence, Sir?

MRS. MAR. The gentleman's merry, that's all, Sir.—— 'Slife, we shall have a quarrel betwixt an horse and an ass, before they find one another out.——— You must not take anything amiss from your friends, Sir. You are among your friends here, though it may be you don't know it. If I am not mistaken, you are Sir Wilfull Witwoud.

SIR WIL. Right, Lady; I am Sir Wilfull Witwoud, so I write myself; no offence to anybody, I hope; and nephew to the Lady Wishfort of this mansion.

MRS. MAR. Don't you know this gentleman, Sir?

SIR WIL. Hum! What, sure 'tis not.—Yea, by'r Lady, but 'tis.—'Sheart, I know not whether 'tis or no.—Yea, but 'tis, by the Wrekin. Brother Anthony! What, Tony, i'faith! What, dost thou not know me? By'r Lady, nor I thee, thou art so becravatted and beperiwigged.—'Sheart, why dost not speak? Art thou o'erjoyed?

WIT. Odso, Brother, is it you? Your servant, Brother.

SIR WIL. Your servant! Why yours, Sir. Your servant again.—'Sheart, and your friend and servant to that—and a—(puff) and a flap-dragon for your service, Sir, and a hare's foot, and a hare's scut for your service, Sir, an you be so cold and so courtly!

WIT. No offence, I hope, Brother.

SIR WIL. 'Sheart, Sir, but there is, and much offence. A pox, is this your Inns o' Court breeding, not to know your friends and your relations, your elders, and your betters?

WIT. Why, brother Wilfull of Salop, you may be as short as a Shrewsbury cake, if you please. But I tell you 'tis not modish to know relations in town. You think you're in the country, where great lubberly brothers slabber and kiss one another when they meet, like a call of serjeants. 'Tis not the fashion here; 'tis not indeed, dear Brother.

SIR WIL. The fashion's a fool; and you're a fop, dear Brother. 'Sheart, I've suspected this. By'r Lady, I conjectured you were a fop, since you began to change the style of your letters, and writ in a scrap of paper gilt round the edges, no broader than a *subpœna*. I might expect this when you left off "Honoured Brother," and "hoping you are in good health," and so forth—to begin with a "Rat me, knight, I'm so sick of a last night's debauch"—Od's heart, and then tell a familiar tale of a cock and a bull, and a whore and a bottle, and so conclude. You could write news before you were out of your time, when you lived with honest Pumple Nose, the attorney of Furnival's Inn. You could intreat to be remembered then to your friends round the Wrekin. We could have gazettes then, and Dawks's Letter, and the weekly bill, till of late days.

PET. 'Slife, Witwoud, were you ever an attorney's clerk? Of the family of the Furnivals. Ha, ha, ha!

WIT. Ay, ay, but that was for a while. Not long, not long. Pshaw! I was not in my own power then. An orphan, and this fellow was my guardian; ay, ay, I was glad to consent to that man to come to London. He had the disposal of me then. If I had not agreed to that, I might have been bound prentice to a felt-maker in Shrewsbury; this fellow would have bound me to a maker of felts.

SIR WIL. 'Sheart, and better than to be bound to a maker of fops; where, I suppose, you have served your time and now you may set up for yourself.

MRS. MAR. You intend to travel, Sir, as I'm informed.

SIR WIL. Belike I may, Madam. I may chance to sail upon the salt seas, if my mind hold.

PET. And the wind serve.

SIR WIL. Serve or not serve, I shan't ask license of you, Sir; nor the weather-cock your companion. I direct my discourse to the lady, Sir. 'Tis like my aunt may have told you, Madam—yes, I have settled my concerns, I may say now, and am minded to see foreign parts. If an how that the peace holds, whereby, that is, taxes abate.

MRS. MAR. I thought you had designed for France at all adventures.

SIR WIL. I can't tell that; 'tis like I may, and 'tis like I may not. I am somewhat dainty in making a resolution, because when I make it I keep it. I don't stand shill I, shall I, then; if I say't, I'll do't: but I have thoughts to tarry a small matter in town, to learn somewhat of your lingo first, before I cross the seas. I'd gladly have a spice of your French, as they say, whereby to hold discourse in foreign countries.

MRS. MAR. Here is an academy in town for that use.

SIR WIL. There is? 'Tis like there may.

MRS. MAR. No doubt you will return very much improved.

WIT. Yes, refined, like a Dutch skipper from a whale-fishing.

Enter LADY WISHFORT *and* FAINALL

LADY WISH. Nephew, you are welcome.

SIR WIL. Aunt, your servant.

FAIN. Sir Wilfull, your most faithful servant.

SIR WIL. Cousin Fainall, give me your hand.

LADY WISH. Cousin Witwould, your servant; Mr. Petulant, your servant.—— Nephew, you are welcome again. Will you drink anything after your journey, Nephew, before you eat? Dinner's almost ready.

SIR WIL. I'm very well, I thank you, Aunt—however, I thank you for your courteous offer. 'Sheart, I was afraid you would have been in the fashion too, and have remembered to have forgot your relations. Here's your Cousin Tony, belike, I mayn't call him Brother for fear of offence.

LADY WISH. Oh, he's a rallier, Nephew—my cousin's a wit; and your great wits always rally their best friends to choose. When you have been abroad, Nephew, you'll understand raillery better.

(FAINALL *and* MRS. MARWOOD *talk apart.*)

SIR WIL. Why then let him hold his tongue in the meantime; and rail when that day comes.

Enter MINCING

MINC. Mem, I come to acquaint your La'ship that dinner is impatient.

SIR WIL. Impatient? Why then belike it won't stay till I pull off my boots. Sweetheart, can you help me to a pair of slippers? My man's with his horses, I warrant.

LADY WISH. Fie, fie, Nephew, you would not pull off your boots here. Go down into the hall—dinner shall stay for you.—— My nephew's a little unbred, you'll pardon him, Madam.—— Gentlemen, will you walk? Marwood——

MRS. MAR. I'll follow you, Madam, before Sir Wilfull is ready.

(*Manent* MRS. MARWOOD *and* FAINALL.)

FAIN. Why then Foible's a bawd, an arrant, rank, matchmaking bawd. And I, it seems, am a husband, a rank husband; and my wife a very arrant, rank wife—all in the way of the world. 'Sdeath, to be an anticipated cuckold, a cuckold in embryo! Sure I was born with budding antlers like a young satyr, or a citizen's child. 'Sdeath, to be out-witted, to be out-jilted—

out-matrimonied! If I had kept my speed like a stag, 'twere somewhat, but to crawl after with my horns like a snail, and be out-
stripped by my wife—'tis scurvy wedlock.

MRS. MAR. Then shake it off: you have often wished for an
opportunity to part, and now you have it. But first prevent their
plot—the half of Millamant's fortune is too considerable to be
parted with to a foe, to Mirabell.

FAIN. Damn him, that had been mine, had you not made that
fond discovery—that had been forfeited, had they been married.
My wife had added lustre to my horns, by that increase of fortune; I could have worn 'em tipt with gold, though my forehead
had been furnished like a deputy-lieutenant's hall.

MRS. MAR. They may prove a cap of maintenance to you still,
if you can away with your wife. And she's no worse than when
you had her—I dare swear she had given up her game before
she was married.

FAIN. Hum! That may be. She might throw up her cards; but
I'll be hanged if she did not put Pam in her pocket.

MRS. MAR. You married her to keep you; and if you can contrive to have her keep you better than you expected, why should
you not keep her longer than you intended?

FAIN. The means, the means!

MRS. MAR. Discover to my lady your wife's conduct; threaten
to part with her. My lady loves her, and will come to any composition to save her reputation. Take the opportunity of breaking it, just upon the discovery of this imposture. My lady will be
enraged beyond bounds, and sacrifice niece, and fortune, and all
at that conjuncture. And let me alone to keep her warm; if she
should flag in her part, I will not fail to prompt her.

FAIN. Faith, this has an appearance.

MRS. MAR. I'm sorry I hinted to my lady to endeavour a match
between Millamant and Sir Wilfull; that may be an obstacle.

FAIN. Oh, for that matter leave me to manage him; I'll disable
him for that; he will drink like a Dane: after dinner, I'll set his
hand in.

MRS. MAR. Well, how do you stand affected towards your lady?

FAIN. Why, faith, I'm thinking of it.—Let me see—I am married already, so that's over; my wife has played the jade with
me—well, that's over too; I never loved her, or if I had, why
that would have been over too by this time.—Jealous of her I

cannot be, for I am certain—so there's an end of jealousy. Weary
of her, I am, and shall be—no, there's no end of that; no, no, that
were too much to hope. Thus far concerning my repose. Now
for my reputation. As to my own, I married not for it; so that's
out of the question. And as to my part in my wife's—why, she
had parted with hers before; so bringing none to me, she can
take none from me; 'tis against all rule of play that I should lose
to one who has not wherewithal to stake.

MRS. MAR. Besides, you forget, marriage is honourable.

FAIN. Hum! Faith, and that's well thought on; marriage is
honourable, as you say; and if so, wherefore should cuckoldom
be a discredit, being derived from so honourable a root?

MRS. MAR. Nay, I know not; if the root be honourable, why
not the branches?

FAIN. So, so, why this point's clear. Well, how do we proceed?

MRS. MAR. I will contrive a letter which shall be delivered to
my lady at the time when that rascal who is to act Sir Rowland
is with her. It shall come as from an unknown hand—for the less
I appear to know of the truth, the better I can play the incen-
diary. Besides, I would not have Foible provoked if I could help
it, because you know she knows some passages. Nay, I expect
all will come out—but let the mine be sprung first, and then I
care not if I'm discovered.

FAIN. If the worst come to the worst, I'll turn my wife to grass.
I have already a deed of settlement of the best part of her estate,
which I wheedled out of her, and that you shall partake at least.

MRS. MAR. I hope you are convinced that I hate Mirabell; now
you'll be no more jealous.

FAIN. Jealous, no!—by this kiss—let husbands be jealous, but
let the lover still believe; or if he doubt, let it be only to endear
his pleasure, and prepare the joy that follows, when he proves
his mistress true; but let husbands' doubts convert to endless jealousy; or if they have belief, let it corrupt to superstition, and
blind credulity. I am single, and will herd no more with 'em.
True, I wear the badge, but I'll disown the order. And since I
take my leave of 'em, I care not if I leave 'em a common motto
to their common crest:

All husbands must, or pain, or shame, endure;
The wise too jealous are, fools too secure.   (*Exeunt.*)

ACT IV

Scene continues

Enter LADY WISHFORT and FOIBLE

LADY WISH. Is Sir Rowland coming, say'st thou, Foible? and are things in order?

FOIB. Yes, Madam. I have put waxlights in the sconces, and placed the footmen in a row in the hall, in their best liveries, with the coachman and postilion to fill up the equipage.

LADY WISH. Have you pulvilled the coachman and postilion, that they may not stink of the stable when Sir Rowland comes by?

FOIB. Yes, Madam.

LADY WISH. And are the dancers and the music ready, that he may be entertained in all points with correspondence to his passion?

FOIB. All is ready, Madam.

LADY WISH. And—well—and how do I look, Foible?

FOIB. Most killing well, Madam.

LADY WISH. Well, and how shall I receive him? In what figure shall I give his heart the first impression? There is a great deal in the first impression. Shall I sit?—No, I won't sit—I'll walk—ay, I'll walk from the door upon his entrance; and then turn full upon him.—No, that will be too sudden. I'll lie—ay, I'll lie down—I'll receive him in my little dressing-room; there's a couch—yes, yes, I'll give the first impression on a couch.—I won't lie neither, but loll and lean upon one elbow, with one foot a little dangling off, jogging in a thoughtful way—yes—and then as soon as he appears, start, ay, start and be surprised, and rise to meet him in a pretty disorder—yes—oh, nothing is more alluring than a levee from a couch in some confusion. It shows the foot to advantage, and furnishes with blushes, and recomposing airs beyond comparison. Hark! There's a coach.

FOIB. 'Tis he, Madam.

LADY WISH. Oh dear, has my nephew made his addresses to Millamant? I ordered him.

FOIB. Sir Wilfull is set in to drinking, Madam, in the parlour.

LADY WISH. Ods my life, I'll send him to her. Call her down, Foible; bring her hither. I'll send him as I go. When they are together, then come to me, Foible, that I may not be too long alone with Sir Rowland.   (*Exit.*)

Enter MRS. MILLAMANT *and* MRS. FAINALL

FOIB. Madam, I stayed here, to tell your Ladyship that Mr. Mirabell has waited this half-hour for an opportunity to talk with you. Though my lady's orders were to leave you and Sir Wilfull together. Shall I tell Mr. Mirabell that you are at leisure?

MILLA. No—what would the dear man have? I am thoughtful, and would amuse myself—bid him come another time.

(*repeating and walking about*)

There never yet was woman made,
  Nor shall, but to be curst.

That's hard!

MRS. FAIN. You are very fond of Sir John Suckling to-day, Millamant, and the poets.

MILLA. Heh? Ay, and filthy verses—so I am.

FOIB. Sir Wilfull is coming, Madam. Shall I send Mr. Mirabell away?

MILLA. Ay, if you please, Foible, send him away—or send him hither—just as you will, dear Foible.—I think I'll see him.— Shall I? Ay, let the wretch come.   (*repeating*)

Thyrsis, a youth of the inspired train.

Dear Fainall, entertain Sir Wilfull—thou hast philosophy to undergo a fool; thou art married, and hast patience.—I would confer with my own thoughts.

MRS. FAIN. I am obliged to you, that you would make me your proxy in this affair; but I have business of my own.

Enter SIR WILFULL

O Sir Wilfull, you are come at the critical instant. There's your mistress up to the ears in love and contemplation; pursue your point, now or never.

SIR WIL. Yes; my aunt would have it so. I would gladly have been encouraged with a bottle or two, because I'm somewhat wary at first, before I am acquainted.—(*this while* MILLAMANT *walks about repeating to herself*) But I hope, after a time, I shall break my mind—that is, upon further acquaintance. So for the present, Cousin, I'll take my leave—if so be you'll be so kind to make my excuse, I'll return to my company——

MRS. FAIN. Oh, fie, Sir Wilfull! What, you must not be daunted.

SIR WIL. Daunted! no, that's not it, it is not so much for that—for if so be that I set on't, I'll do't. But only for the present, 'tis sufficient till further acquaintance, that's all—your servant.

MRS. FAIN. Nay, I'll swear you shall never lose so favourable an opportunity, if I can help it. I'll leave you together, and lock the door.   (*Exit.*)

SIR WIL. Nay, nay, Cousin—I have forgot my gloves. What d'ee do? 'Sheart, a' has locked the door indeed, I think. Nay, Cousin Fainall, open the door.—Pshaw, what a vixen trick is this?—Nay, now a' has seen me too.—— Cousin, I made bold to pass through as it were—I think this door's inchanted——

MILLA. (*repeating*)

> I prithee spare me, gentle boy,
> Press me no more for that slight toy—

SIR WIL. Anan? Cousin, your servant.

MILLA. (*repeating*)

> That foolish trifle of a heart——

Sir Wilfull!

SIR WIL. Yes—your servant. No offence, I hope, Cousin.

MILLA. (*repeating*)

> I swear it will not do its part,
> Though thou dost thine, employ'st thy power and art.

Natural, easy Suckling!

SIR WIL. Anan? Suckling? No such suckling neither, Cousin, nor stripling: I thank heaven, I'm no minor.

MILLA. Ah, rustic, ruder than Gothic!

SIR. WIL. Well, well, I shall understand your lingo one of these days, Cousin; in the meanwhile I must answer in plain English.

MILLA. Have you any business with me, Sir Wilfull?

SIR WIL. Not at present, Cousin.—Yes, I made bold to see, to come and know if that how you were disposed to fetch a walk this evening, if so be that I might not be troublesome, I would have sought a walk with you.

MILLA. A walk? What then?

SIR WIL. Nay, nothing—only for the walk's sake, that's all——

MILLA. I nauseate walking; 'tis a country diversion; I loathe the country and everything that relates to it.

SIR WIL. Indeed! Hah! Look ye, look ye, you do? Nay, 'tis like you may. Here are choice of pastimes here in town, as plays and the like; that must be confessed indeed.

MILLA. *Ah, l'étourdie!* I hate the town too.

SIR WIL. Dear heart, that's much. Hah! that you should hate 'em both! Hah! 'tis like you may; there are some can't relish the town, and others can't away with the country—'tis like you may be one of those, Cousin.

MILLA. Ha, ha, ha! Yes, 'tis like I may. You have nothing further to say to me?

SIR WIL. Not at present, Cousin. 'Tis like when I have an opportunity to be more private, I may break my mind in some measure—I conjecture you partly guess. However, that's as time shall try—but spare to speak and spare to speed, as they say.

MILLA. If it is of no great importance, Sir Wilfull, you will oblige me to leave me: I have just now a little business——

SIR WIL. Enough, enough, Cousin: yes, yes, all a case. When you're disposed, when you're disposed. Now's as well as another time; and another time as well as now. All's one for that—yes, yes, if your concerns call you, there's no haste; it will keep cold as they say. Cousin, your servant.—I think this door's locked.

MILLA. You may go this way, Sir.

SIR WIL. Your servant! then with your leave I'll return to my company.   (*Exit.*)

MILLA. Ay, ay; ha, ha, ha!

Like Phœbus sung the no less am'rous boy.

Enter MIRABELL

MIRA.

Like Daphne she, as lovely and as coy.

Do you lock yourself up from me, to make my search more curious? Or is this pretty artifice contrived, to signify that here the chase must end and my pursuit be crowned, for you can fly no further?

MILLA. Vanity! No—I'll fly and be followed to the last moment. Though I am upon the very verge of matrimony, I expect you should solicit me as much as if I were wavering at the grate of a monastery, with one foot over the threshold. I'll be solicited to the very last, nay, and afterwards.

MIRA. What, after the last?

MILLA. Oh, I should think I was poor and had nothing to bestow if I were reduced to an inglorious ease, and freed from the agreeable fatigues of solicitation.

MIRA. But do not you know that when favours are conferred upon instant and tedious solicitation, that they diminish in their value, and that both the giver loses the grace, and the receiver lessens his pleasure?

MILLA. It may be in things of common application; but never sure in love. Oh, I hate a lover that can dare to think he draws a moment's air independent on the bounty of his mistress. There is not so impudent a thing in nature as the saucy look of an assured man, confident of success. The pedantic arrogance of a very husband has not so pragmatical an air. Ah! I'll never marry unless I am first made sure of my will and pleasure.

MIRA. Would you have 'em both before marriage? Or will you be contented with the first now, and stay for the other till after grace?

MILLA. Ah, don't be impertinent.—My dear liberty, shall I leave thee? My faithful solitude, my darling contemplation, must I bid you then adieu? Ay-h, adieu—my morning thoughts, agreeable wakings, indolent slumbers, all ye *douceurs*, ye *sommeils du matin*, adieu?—I can't do't, 'tis more than impossible. Positively, Mirabell, I'll lie abed in a morning as long as I please.

MIRA. Then I'll get up in a morning as early as I please.

MILLA. Ah! Idle creature, get up when you will. And d'ee hear, I won't be called names after I'm married; positively I won't be called names.

MIRA. Names!

MILLA. Ay, as wife, spouse, my dear, joy, jewel, love, sweetheart, and the rest of that nauseous cant in which men and their wives are so fulsomely familiar—I shall never bear that. Good Mirabell, don't let us be familiar or fond, nor kiss before folks, like my Lady Fadler and Sir Francis: nor go to Hyde Park together the first Sunday in a new chariot to provoke eyes and whispers, and then never to be seen there together again, as if

we were proud of one another the first week, and ashamed of
one another for ever after. Let us never visit together, nor go to
a play together, but let us be very strange and well bred: let us
be as strange as if we had been married a great while; and as
well bred as if we were not married at all.

MIRA. Have you any more conditions to offer? Hitherto your
demands are pretty reasonable.

MILLA. Trifles—as liberty to pay and receive visits to and from
whom I please; to write and receive letters, without interrogatories or wry faces on your part. To wear what I please; and
choose conversation with regard only to my own taste; to have
no obligation upon me to converse with wits that I don't like,
because they are your acquaintance; or to be intimate with fools,
because they may be your relations. Come to dinner when I
please, dine in my dressing-room when I'm out of humour, without giving a reason. To have my closet inviolate; to be sole em-
press of my tea-table, which you must never presume to approach
without first asking leave. And lastly, wherever I am, you shall
always knock at the door before you come in. These articles subscribed, if I continue to endure you a little longer, I may by
degrees dwindle into a wife.

MIRA. Your bill of fare is something advanced in this latter
account. Well, have I liberty to offer conditions—that when you
are dwindled into a wife, I may not be beyond measure enlarged
into a husband?

MILLA. You have free leave; propose your utmost, speak and
spare not.

MIRA. I thank you. *Imprimis* then, I covenant that your acquaintance be general; that you admit no sworn confidante, or
intimate of your own sex; no she-friend to screen her affairs under your countenance, and tempt you to make trial of a mutual
secrecy. No decoy-duck to wheedle you a "fop-scrambling" to the
play in a mask—then bring you home in a pretended fright,
when you think you shall be found out—and rail at me for missing the play, and disappointing the frolic which you had, to
pick me up and prove my constancy.

MILLA. Detestable *imprimis!* I go to the play in a mask!

MIRA. *Item,* I article that you continue to like your own face
as long as I shall; and while it passes current with me, that you

endeavour not to new-coin it. To which end, together with all vizards for the day, I prohibit all masks for the night, made of oiled-skins and I know not what—hog's bones, hare's gall, pig-water, and the marrow of a roasted cat. In short, I forbid all commerce with the gentlewoman in What-d'ye-call-it Court. *Item,* I shut my doors against all bawds with baskets, and pennyworths of muslin, china, fans, atlases, etc.—*Item,* when you shall be breeding——

MILLA. Ah! name it not.

MIRA. Which may be presumed, with a blessing on our endeavours——

MILLA. Odious endeavours!

MIRA. I denounce against all strait lacing, squeezing for a shape, till you mould my boy's head like a sugar-loaf, and instead of a man-child, make me the father to a crooked billet. Lastly, to the dominion of the tea-table I submit, but with *proviso* that you exceed not in your province, but restrain yourself to native and simple tea-table drinks, as tea, chocolate, and coffee, as likewise to genuine and authorized tea-table talk—such as mending of fashions, spoiling reputations, railing at absent friends, and so forth—but that on no account you encroach upon the men's prerogative, and presume to drink healths, or toast fellows; for prevention of which I banish all foreign forces, all auxiliaries to the tea-table, as orange-brandy, all aniseed, cinnamon, citron, and Barbadoes waters, together with ratafia and the most noble spirit of clary, but for cowslip-wine, poppy water, and all dormitives, those I allow. These *provisos* admitted, in other things I may prove a tractable and complying husband.

MILLA. Oh, horrid *provisos!* filthy strong waters! I toast fellows, odious men! I hate your odious *provisos.*

MIRA. Then we're agreed. Shall I kiss your hand upon the contract? And here comes one to be a witness to the sealing of the deed.

Enter MRS. FAINALL

MILLA. Fainall, what shall I do? Shall I have him? I think I must have him.

MRS. FAIN. Ay, ay, take him, take him, what should you do?

MILLA. Well then—I'll take my death, I'm in a horrid fright—Fainall, I shall never say it—well—I think—I'll endure you.

MRS. FAIN. Fie, fie! have him, have him, and tell him so in plain terms: for I am sure you have a mind to him.

MILLA. Are you? I think I have—and the horrid man looks as if he thought so too.—— Well, you ridiculous thing you, I'll have you—I won't be kissed, nor I won't be thanked—here, kiss my hand though. So, hold your tongue now, and don't say a word.

MRS. FAIN. Mirabell, there's a necessity for your obedience; you have neither time to talk nor stay. My mother is co : ing; and in my conscience, if she should see you, would fall into fits, and maybe not recover time enough to return to Sir Rowland, who, as Foible tells me, is in a fair way to succeed. Therefore spare your ecstasies for another occasion, and slip down the back stairs, where Foible waits to consult you.

MILLA. Ay, go, go. In the meantime I suppose you have said something to please me.

MIRA. I am all obedience.   (*Exit* MIRABELL.)

MRS. FAIN. Yonder Sir Wilfull's drunk, and so noisy that my mother has been forced to leave Sir Rowland to appease him; but he answers her only with singing and drinking. What they have done by this time I know not; but Petulant and he were upon quarrelling as I came by.

MILLA. Well, if Mirabell should not make a good husband, I am a lost thing, for I find I love him violently.

MRS. FAIN. So it seems, when you mind not what's said to you. If you doubt him, you had best take up with Sir Wilfull.

MILLA. How can you name that superannuated lubber? foh!

Enter WITWOUD *from drinking*

MRS. FAIN. So, is the fray made up, that you have left 'em?

WIT. Left 'em? I could stay no longer—I have laughed like ten christenings—I am tipsy with laughing. If I had stayed any longer I should have burst—I must have been let out and pieced in the sides like an unsized camlet. Yes, yes, the fray is composed; my lady came in like a *nolle prosequi* and stopped their proceedings.

MILLA. What was the dispute?

WIT. That's the jest; there was no dispute. They could neither of 'em speak for rage; and so fell a sputtering at one another like two roasting apples.

Enter PETULANT *drunk*

Now, Petulant, all's over, all's well. Gad, my head begins to whim it about. Why dost thou not speak? Thou art both as drunk and as mute as a fish.

PET. Look you, Mrs. Millamant—if you can love me, dear nymph—say it—and that's the conclusion—pass on, or pass off —that's all.

WIT. Thou hast uttered volumes, folios, in less than *decimo sexto*, my dear Lacedemonian. Sirrah Petulant, thou art an epito-mizer of words.

PET. Witwoud—you are an annihilator of sense.

WIT. Thou art a retailer of phrases; and dost deal in remnants of remnants, like a maker of pincushions—thou art in truth (metaphorically speaking) a speaker of shorthand.

PET. Thou art (without a figure) just one half of an ass; and Baldwin yonder, thy half-brother, is the rest. A gemini of asses split, would make just four of you.

WIT. Thou dost bite, my dear mustard seed; kiss me for that.

PET. Stand off—I'll kiss no more males—I have kissed your twin yonder in a humour of reconciliation, till he (*hiccup*) rises upon my stomach like a radish.

MILLA. Eh! filthy creature!—what was the quarrel?

PET. There was no quarrel—there might have been a quarrel.

WIT. If there had been words enow between 'em to have ex-pressed provocation, they had gone together by the ears like a pair of castanets.

PET. You were the quarrel.

MILLA. Me!

PET. If I have a humour to quarrel, I can make less matters conclude premises. If you are not handsome, what then, if I have a humour to prove it? If I shall have my reward, say so; if not, fight for your face the next time yourself.—I'll go sleep.

WIT. Do, wrap thyself up like a woodlouse, and dream revenge —and hear me, if thou canst learn to write by to-morrow morn-ing, pen me a challenge—I'll carry it for thee.

PET. Carry your mistress's monkey a spider—go flea dogs and read romances!—I'll go to bed to my maid.   (*Exit.*)

MRS. FAIN. He's horridly drunk. How came you all in this pickle?

WIT. A plot, a plot, to get rid of the knight—your husband's advice; but he sneaked off.

Enter LADY WISHFORT, *and* SIR WILFULL, *drunk*

LADY WISH. Out upon't, out upon't, at years of discretion, and comport yourself at this rantipole rate!

SIR WIL. No offence, Aunt.

LADY WISH. Offence? As I'm a person, I'm ashamed of you. Fogh! how you stink of wine! D'ee think my niece will ever endure such a borachio! you're an absolute borachio.

SIR WIL. Borachio!

LADY WISH. At a time when you should commence an amour and put your best foot foremost——

SIR WIL. 'Sheart, an you grutch me your liquor, make a bill. Give me more drink, and take my purse.   (*sings*)

> Prithee fill me the glass
> Till it laugh in my face,
> With ale that is potent and mellow;
> He that whines for a lass,
> Is an ignorant ass,
> For a bumper has not its fellow.

But if you would have me marry my cousin, say the word, and I'll do't—Wilfull will do't, that's the word—Wilfull will do't, that's my crest—my motto I have forgot.

LADY WISH. My nephew's a little overtaken, Cousin—but 'tis with drinking your health. O' my word you are obliged to him——

SIR WIL. *In vino veritas*, Aunt.—— If I drunk your health to-day, Cousin—I am a borachio. But if you have a mind to be married, say the word, and send for the piper; Wilfull will do't. If not, dust it way, and let's have t'other round.—— Tony, 'odsheart, where's Tony? Tony's an honest fellow, but he spits after a bumper, and that's a fault.   (*sings*)

> We'll drink and we'll never ha' done, boys,
> Put the glass then around with the sun, boys,
> Let Apollo's example invite us;
> For he's drunk every night,
> And that makes him so bright,
> That he's able next morning to light us.

The sun's a good pimple, an honest soaker, he has a cellar at your Antipodes. If I travel, Aunt, I touch at your Antipodes. Your Antipodes are a good rascally sort of topsy-turvy fellows. If I had a bumper, I'd stand upon my head and drink a health to 'em.—— A match or no match, Cousin with the hard name? —— Aunt, Wilfull will do't. If she has her maidenhead, let her look to't; if she has not, let her keep her own counsel in the meantime, and cry out at the nine months' end.

MILLA. Your pardon, Madam, I can stay no longer—Sir Wilfull grows very powerful. Egh! how he smells! I shall be overcome if I stay. Come, Cousin.

(*Exeunt* MILLAMANT *and* MRS FAINALL.)

LADY WISH. Smells! he would poison a tallow-chandler and his family. Beastly creature, I know not what to do with him.—— Travel, quoth a; ay travel, travel, get thee gone, get thee but far enough, to the Saracens, or the Tartars, or the Turks—for thou art not fit to live in a Christian commonwealth, thou beastly pagan.

SIR WIL. Turks, no; no Turks, Aunt: your Turks are infidels, and believe not in the grape. Your Mahometan, your Mussulman, is a dry stinkard—no offence, Aunt. My map says that your Turk is not so honest a man as your Christian—I cannot find by the map that your Mufti is orthodox—whereby it is a plain case, that orthodox is a hard word, Aunt, and (*hiccup*) Greek for claret. (*sings*)

> To drink is a Christian diversion,
> Unknown to the Turk and the Persian:
>   Let Mahometan fools
>   Live by heathenish rules,
> And be damn'd over tea-cups and coffee.
>   But let British lads sing,
>   Crown a health to the king,
> And a fig for your Sultan and Sophy.

Ah, Tony!

Enter FOIBLE *and whispers* LADY WISHFORT

LADY WISH. Sir Rowland impatient? Good lack! what shall I do with this beastly tumbril?—— Go lie down and sleep, you sot—or as I'm a person, I'll have you bastinadoed with broomsticks.—— Call up the wenches. (*Exit* FOIBLE.)

SIR WIL. Ahey! Wenches, where are the wenches?

LADY WISH. Dear Cousin Witwoud, get him away, and you will bind me to you inviolably. I have an affair of moment that invades me with some precipitation. You will oblige me to all futurity.

WIT. Come, Knight.—— Pox on him, I don't know what to say to him.—— Will you go to a cock-match?

SIR WIL. With a wench, Tony? Is she a shake-bag, Sirrah? Let me bite your cheek for that.

WIT. Horrible! He has a breath like a bagpipe.—— Ay, ay; come, will you march, my Salopian?

SIR WIL. Lead on, little Tony—I'll follow thee, my Anthony, my Tantony. Sirrah, thou shalt be my Tantony; and I'll be thy pig.

—And a fig for your Sultan and Sophy.

(*Exit singing with* WITWOUD.)

LADY WISH. This will never do. It will never make a match— at least before he has been abroad.

Enter WAITWELL, *disguised as for* SIR ROWLAND

Dear Sir Rowland, I am confounded with confusion at the retrospection of my own rudeness—I have more pardons to ask than the pope distributes in the year of jubilee. But I hope where there is likely to be so near an alliance, we may unbend the severity of decorum, and dispense with a little ceremony.

WAIT. My impatience, Madam, is the effect of my transport, and till I have the possession of your adorable person, I am tantalized on a rack, and do but hang, Madam, on the tenter of expectation.

LADY WISH. You have excess of gallantry, Sir Rowland; and press things to a conclusion with a most prevailing vehemence. But a day or two for decency of marriage——

WAIT. For decency of funeral, Madam. The delay will break my heart—or if that should fail, I shall be poisoned. My nephew will get an inkling of my designs, and poison me—and I would willingly starve him before I die—I would gladly go out of the world with that satisfaction. That would be some comfort to me, if I could but live so long as to be revenged on that unnatural viper.

LADY WISH. Is he so unnatural, say you? Truly I would con-

tribute much both to the saving of your life and the accomplishment of your revenge. Not that I respect myself, though he has
been a perfidious wretch to me.

WAIT. Perfidious to you!

LADY WISH. O Sir Rowland, the hours that he has died away
at my feet, the tears that he has shed, the oaths that he has
sworn, the palpitations that he has felt, the trances, and the
tremblings, the ardours and the ecstasies, the kneelings and the
risings, the heart-heavings, and the hand-gripings, the pangs and
the pathetic regards of his protesting eyes! Oh, no memory can
register!

WAIT. What, my rival! is the rebel my rival? a' dies.

LADY WISH. No, don't kill him at once, Sir Rowland; starve
him gradually inch by inch.

WAIT. I'll do't. In three weeks he shall be barefoot; in a month
out at knees with begging an alms; he shall starve upward and
upward, till he has nothing living but his head, and then go out
in a stink like a candle's end upon a save-all.

LADY WISH. Well, Sir Rowland, you have the way—you are no
novice in the labyrinth of love—you have the clue. But as I am
a person, Sir Rowland, you must not attribute my yielding to
any sinister appetite, or indigestion of widowhood; nor impute
my complacency to any lethargy of continence. I hope you do
not think me prone to any iteration of nuptials.

WAIT. Far be it from me——

LADY WISH. If you do, I protest I must recede—or think that
I have made a prostitution of decorums, but in the vehemence
of compassion, and to save the life of a person of so much importance——

WAIT. I esteem it so——

LADY WISH. Or else you wrong my condescension——

WAIT. I do not, I do not——

LADY WISH. Indeed you do.

WAIT. I do not, fair shrine of virtue.

LADY WISH. If you think the least scruple of carnality was an
ingredient——

WAIT. Dear Madam, no. You are all camphire and frankin-
cense, all chastity and odor.

LADY WISH. Or that——

Enter FOIBLE

FOIB. Madam, the dancers are ready, and there's one with a letter, who must deliver it into your own hands.

LADY WISH. Sir Rowland, will you give me leave? Think favourably, judge candidly, and conclude you have found a person who would suffer racks in honour's cause, dear Sir Rowland, and will wait on you incessantly. (*Exit.*)

WAIT. Fie, fie! What a slavery have I undergone! Spouse, hast thou any cordial?—I want spirits.

FOIB. What a washy rogue art thou, to pant thus for a quarter of an hour's lying and swearing to a fine lady!

WAIT. Oh, she is the antidote to desire. Spouse, thou wilt fare the worse for't—I shall have no appetite to iteration of nuptials —this eight and forty hours: by this hand I'd rather be a chairman in the dog-days—than act Sir Rowland till this time tomorrow.

Enter LADY WISHFORT *with a letter*

LADY WISH. Call in the dancers.—— Sir Rowland, we'll sit, if you please, and see the entertainment. (*dance*)

Now with your permission, Sir Rowland, I will peruse my letter—I would open it in your presence, because I would not make you uneasy. If it should make you uneasy I would burn it—speak if it does—but you may see by the superscription it is like a woman's hand.

FOIB. (*to him*) By heaven! Mrs. Marwood's, I know it—my heart aches—get it from her——

WAIT. A woman's hand? No, Madam, that's no woman's hand, I see that already. That's somebody whose throat must be cut.

LADY WISH. Nay, Sir Rowland, since you give me a proof of your passion by your jealousy, I promise you I'll make you a return, by a frank communication. You shall see it—we'll open it together—look you here.

(*reads*) "Madam, though unknown to you,"—Look you there, 'tis from nobody that I know—"I have that honour for your character, that I think myself obliged to let you know you are abused. He who pretends to be Sir Rowland is a cheat and a rascal——" Oh heavens! what's this?

FOIB. Unfortunate, all's ruined.

WAIT. How, how, let me see, let me see! (*reading*) "A rascal, and disguised and suborned for that imposture,"—O villainy! O villainy!—"by the contrivance of——"

LADY WISH. I shall faint, I shall die, I shall die, oh!

FOIB. (*to him*) Say 'tis your nephew's hand. Quickly, his plot, swear, swear it.

WAIT. Here's a villain! Madam, don't you perceive it, don't you see it?

LADY WISH. Too well, too well. I have seen too much.

WAIT. I told you at first I knew the hand. A woman's hand? The rascal writes a sort of a large hand, your Roman hand. I saw there was a throat to be cut presently. If he were my son, as he is my nephew, I'd pistol him——

FOIB. O treachery! But you are sure, Sir Rowland, it is his writing?

WAIT. Sure? am I here? do I live? do I love this pearl of India? I have twenty letters in my pocket from him, in the same character.

LADY WISH. How!

FOIB. Oh, what luck it is, Sir Rowland, that you were present at this juncture! This was the business that brought Mr. Mirabell disguised to Madam Millamant this afternoon. I thought something was contriving when he stole by me and would have hid his face.

LADY WISH. How, how! I heard the villain was in the house indeed, and now I remember, my niece went away abruptly, when Sir Wilfull was to have made his addresses.

FOIB. Then, then, Madam, Mr. Mirabell waited for her in her chamber, but I would not tell your Ladyship to discompose you when you were to receive Sir Rowland.

WAIT. Enough, his date is short.

FOIB. No, good Sir Rowland, don't incur the law.

WAIT. Law! I care not for law. I can but die, and 'tis in a good cause—my lady shall be satisfied of my truth and innocence, though it cost me my life.

LADY WISH. No, dear Sir Rowland, don't fight; if you should be killed I must never show my face; or hanged—oh, consider my reputation, Sir Rowland! No, you shan't fight. I'll go in and examine my niece, I'll make her confess. I conjure you, Sir Rowland, by all your love, not to fight.

WAIT. I am charmed, Madam, I obey. But some proof you must let me give you; I'll go for a black box, which contains the writings of my whole estate, and deliver that into your hands.

LADY WISH. Ay, dear Sir Rowland, that will be some comfort; bring the black box.

WAIT. And may I presume to bring a contract to be signed this night? May I hope so far?

LADY WISH. Bring what you will; but come alive, pray come alive. Oh, this is a happy discovery!

WAIT. Dead or alive I'll come—and married we will be in spite of treachery; ay, and get an heir that shall defeat the last remaining glimpse of hope in my abandoned nephew. Come, my buxom widow:

> Ere long you shall substantial proof receive
> That I'm an arrant knight——

FOIB.   Or arrant knave. (*Exeunt.*)

ACT V

Scene continues

LADY WISHFORT *and* FOIBLE

LADY WISH. Out of my house, out of my house, thou viper, thou serpent, that I have fostered! thou bosom traitress, that I raised from nothing!—begone, begone, begone, go, go!—that I took from washing of old gauze and weaving of dead hair, with a bleak blue nose, over a chafing-dish of starved embers, and dining behind a traverse rag, in a shop no bigger than a bird-cage,—go, go, starve again, do, do!

FOIB. Dear Madam, I'll beg pardon on my knees.

LADY WISH. Away, out, out, go set up for yourself again!—do, drive a trade, do, with your three-pennyworth of small ware, flaunting upon a pack-thread, under a brandy-seller's bulk, or against a dead wall by a ballad-monger! Go, hang out an old Frisoneer gorget, with a yard of yellow colberteen again! do! an old gnawed mask, two rows of pins, and a child's fiddle; a glass necklace with the beads broken, and a quilted nightcap with one ear! Go, go, drive a trade! These were your commodities, you treacherous trull, this was your merchandise you dealt in, when I took you into my house, placed you next myself, and made you governante of my whole family! You have forgot this, have you, now you have feathered your nest?

FOIB. No, no, dear Madam. Do but hear me; have but a moment's patience—I'll confess all. Mr. Mirabell seduced me; I am not the first that he has wheedled with his dissembling tongue; your Ladyship's own wisdom has been deluded by him—then how should I, a poor ignorant, defend myself? O Madam, if you knew but what he promised me, and how he assured me your Ladyship should come to no damage!—Or else the wealth of the Indies should not have bribed me to conspire against so good, so sweet, so kind a lady as you have been to me.

LADY WISH. No damage? What, to betray me, to marry me to a cast servingman; to make me a receptacle, an hospital for a decayed pimp? No damage? O thou frontless impudence, more than a big-bellied actress!

FOIB. Pray, do but hear me, Madam; he could not marry your Ladyship, Madam.—No indeed, his marriage was to have been void in law; for he was married to me first, to secure your Ladyship. He could not have bedded your Ladyship; for if he had consummated with your Ladyship, he must have run the risk of the law, and been put upon his clergy.—Yes indeed, I enquired of the law in that case before I would meddle or make.

LADY WISH. What, then I have been your property, have I? I have been convenient to you, it seems—while you were catering for Mirabell, I have been broker for you? What, have you made a passive bawd of me? This exceeds all precedent; I am brought to fine uses, to become a botcher of second-hand marriages between Abigails and Andrews! I'll couple you! Yes, I'll baste you together, you and your Philander! I'll Duke's Place you, as I'm a person. Your turtle is in custody already; you shall coo in the same cage, if there be constable or warrant in the parish.   (*Exit.*)

FOIB. Oh, that ever I was born! Oh, that I was ever married! —A bride, ay, I shall be a Bridewell-bride. Oh!

Enter MRS. FAINALL

MRS. FAIN. Poor Foible, what's the matter?

FOIB. O Madam, my lady's gone for a constable; I shall be had to a justice, and put to Bridewell to beat hemp! Poor Waitwell's gone to prison already.

MRS. FAIN. Have a good heart, Foible; Mirabell's gone to give security for him. This is all Marwood's and my husband's doing.

FOIB. Yes, yes; I know it, Madam; she was in my lady's closet and overheard all that you said to me before dinner. She sent the letter to my lady; and that missing effect, Mr. Fainall laid this plot to arrest Waitwell, when he pretended to go for the papers; and in the meantime Mrs. Marwood declared all to my lady.

MRS. FAIN. Was there no mention made of me in the letter? My mother does not suspect my being in the confederacy? I fancy Marwood has not told her, though she has told my husband.

FOIB. Yes, Madam; but my lady did not see that part; we stifled the letter before she read so far. Has that mischievous devil told Mr. Fainall of your Ladyship then?

MRS. FAIN. Ay, all's out, my affair with Mirabell, everything discovered. This is the last day of our living together, that's my comfort.

FOIB. Indeed, Madam, and so 'tis a comfort if you knew all; he has been even with your Ladyship, which I could have told you long enough since, but I love to keep peace and quietness, by my good will: I had rather bring friends together than set 'em at distance. But Mrs. Marwood and he are nearer related than ever their parents thought for.

MRS. FAIN. Say'st thou so, Foible? Canst thou prove this?

FOIB. I can take my oath of it, Madam, so can Mrs. Mincing; we have had many a fair word from Madam Marwood, to conceal something that passed in our chamber one evening when you were at Hyde Park; and we were thought to have gone a-walking, but we went up unawares—though we were sworn to secrecy too. Madam Marwood took a book and swore us upon it; but it was but a book of verses and poems. So as long as it was not a Bible oath, we may break it with a safe conscience.

MRS. FAIN. This discovery is the most opportune thing I could wish.—— Now, Mincing?

Enter MINCING

MINC. My lady would speak with Mrs. Foible, Mem. Mr. Mirabell is with her; he has set your spouse at liberty, Mrs. Foible, and would have you hide yourself in my lady's closet, till my old lady's anger is abated. Oh, my old lady is in a perilous passion at something Mr. Fainall has said; he swears, and my old lady cries. There's a fearful hurricane, I vow. He says, Mem, how that he'll have my lady's fortune made over to him or he'll be divorced.

MRS. FAIN. Does your lady and Mirabell know that?

MINC. Yes, Mem, they have sent me to see if Sir Wilfull be sober, and to bring him to them. My lady is resolved to have him, I think, rather than lose such a vast sum as six thousand pound. Oh, come, Mrs. Foible, I hear my old lady.

MRS. FAIN. Foible, you must tell Mincing that she must prepare to vouch when I call her.

FOIB. Yes, yes, Madam.

MINC. Oh, yes, Mem, I'll vouch anything for your Ladyship's service, be what it will.   (*Exeunt* MINCING *and* FOIBLE.)

Enter LADY WISHFORT *and* MRS. MARWOOD

LADY WISH. Oh, my dear friend, how can I enumerate the benefits that I have received from your goodness? To you I owe the timely discovery of the false vows of Mirabell; to you the detection of the impostor Sir Rowland. And now you are become an intercessor with my son-in-law, to save the honour of my house, and compound for the frailties of my daughter. Well, friend, you are enough to reconcile me to the bad world, or else I would retire to deserts and solitudes; and feed harmless sheep by groves and purling streams. Dear Marwood, let us leave the world, and retire by ourselves and be shepherdesses.

MRS. MAR. Let us first dispatch the affair in hand, Madam. We shall have leisure to think of retirement afterwards.—Here is one who is concerned in the treaty.

LADY WISH. O Daughter, Daughter, is it possible thou shouldst be my child, bone of my bone, and flesh of my flesh, and as I may say, another me, and yet transgress the most minute particle of severe virtue? Is it possible you should lean aside to iniquity, who have been cast in the direct mould of virtue? I have not only been a mould but a pattern for you, and a model for you, after you were brought into the world.

MRS. FAIN. I don't understand your Ladyship.

LADY WISH. Not understand? Why, have you not been naught? Have you not been sophisticated? Not understand? Here I am ruined to compound for your caprices and your cuckoldoms. I must pawn my plate and my jewels, and ruin my niece, and all little enough——

MRS. FAIN. I am wronged and abused, and so are you. 'Tis a false accusation, as false as hell, as false as your friend there, ay, or your friend's friend, my false husband.

MRS. MAR. My friend, Mrs. Fainall? Your husband my friend! what do you mean?

MRS. FAIN. I know what I mean, Madam, and so do you; and so shall the world at a time convenient.

MRS. MAR. I am sorry to see you so passionate, Madam. More temper would look more like innocence. But I have done. I am sorry my zeal to serve your Ladyship and family should admit of misconstruction, or make me liable to affronts. You will pardon me, Madam, if I meddle no more with an affair in which I am not personally concerned.

LADY WISH. O dear friend, I am so ashamed that you should meet with such returns!—— You ought to ask pardon on your knees, ungrateful creature! she deserves more from you than all your life can accomplish.—— Oh, don't leave me destitute in this perplexity!—no, stick to me, my good genius.

MRS. FAIN. I tell you, Madam, you're abused.—Stick to you? ay, like a leech, to suck your best blood—she'll drop off when she's full. Madam, you sha' not pawn a bodkin, nor part with a brass counter in composition for me. I defy 'em all. Let 'em prove their aspersions: I know my own innocence, and dare stand by a trial.   (*Exit.*)

LADY WISH. Why, if she should be innocent, if she should be wronged after all, ha? I don't know what to think—and I promise you, her education has been unexceptionable—I may say it; for I chiefly made it my own care to initiate her very infancy in the rudiments of virtue, and to impress upon her tender years a young odium and aversion to the very sight of men; ay, friend, she would ha' shrieked if she had but seen a man, till she was in her teens. As I'm a person, 'tis true. She was never suffered to play with a male-child, though but in coats; nay, her very babies were of the feminine gender. Oh, she never looked a man in the face but her own father, or the chaplain, and him we made a shift to put upon her for a woman, by the help of his long garments, and his sleek face, till she was going in her fifteen.

MRS. MAR. 'Twas much she should be deceived so long.

LADY WISH. I warrant you, or she would never have borne to have been catechised by him; and have heard his long lectures against singing and dancing, and such debaucheries; and going to filthy plays, and profane music-meetings, where the lewd trebles squeak nothing but bawdy, and the basses roar blasphemy. Oh, she would have swooned at the sight or name of an obscene play-book—and can I think, after all this, that my daughter can be naught? What, a whore? And thought it excommunication to set her foot within the door of a play-house! O my dear friend, I can't believe it, no, no! As she says, let him prove it, let him prove it!

MRS. MAR. Prove it, Madam? What, and have your name prostituted in a public court! yours and your daughter's reputation worried at the bar by a pack of bawling lawyers? To be ushered in with an "Oyez" of scandal; and have your case opened by an old fumbling lecher in a quoif like a man midwife, to bring your daughter's infamy to light; to be a theme for legal punsters, and quibblers by the statute; and become a jest, against a rule of court, where there is no precedent for a jest in any record, not even in Doomsday Book; to discompose the gravity of the bench, and provoke naughty interrogatories in more naughty law Latin; while the good judge, tickled with the proceeding, simpers under a grey beard, and fidges off and on his cushion as if he had swallowed cantharides, or sat upon cowitch!

LADY WISH. Oh, 'tis very hard!

MRS. MAR. And then to have my young revellers of the Temple take notes, like prentices at a conventicle, and after, talk it all over again in Commons, or before drawers in an eating-house.

LADY WISH. Worse and worse!

MRS. MAR. Nay, this is nothing; if it would end here, 'twere well. But it must after this be consigned by the shorthand writers to the public press; and from thence be transferred to the hands, nay, into the throats and lungs of hawkers, with voices more licentious than the loud flounder-man's, or the woman that cries grey-pease; and this you must hear till you are stunned; nay, you must hear nothing else for some days.

LADY WISH. Oh, 'tis insupportable. No, no, dear friend, make it up, make it up; ay, ay, I'll compound. I'll give up all, myself and my all, my niece and her all—anything, everything for composition.

MRS. MAR. Nay, Madam, I advise nothing; I only lay before you, as a friend, the inconveniencies which perhaps you have overseen. Here comes Mr. Fainall. If he will be satisfied to huddle up all in silence, I shall be glad. You must think I would rather congratulate than condole with you.

Enter FAINALL

LADY WISH. Ay, ay, I do not doubt it, dear Marwood; no, no, I do not doubt it.

FAIN. Well, Madam; I have suffered myself to be overcome by the importunity of this lady your friend; and am content you shall enjoy your own proper estate during life, on condition you oblige yourself never to marry, under such penalty as I think convenient.

LADY WISH. Never to marry?

FAIN. No more Sir Rowlands; the next imposture may not be so timely detected.

MRS. MAR. That condition, I dare answer, my lady will consent to without difficulty; she has already but too much experienced the perfidiousness of men. Besides, Madam, when we retire to our pastoral solitude we shall bid adieu to all other thoughts.

LADY WISH. Ay, that's true; but in case of necessity, as of health, or some such emergency——

FAIN. Oh, if you are prescribed marriage, you shall be considered; I will only reserve to myself the power to choose for you. If your physic be wholesome, it matters not who is your apothecary. Next, my wife shall settle on me the remainder of her fortune, not made over already, and for her maintenance depend entirely on my discretion.

LADY WISH. This is most inhumanly savage; exceeding the barbarity of a Muscovite husband.

FAIN. I learned it from his Czarish majesty's retinue, in a winter evening's conference over brandy and pepper, amongst other secrets of matrimony and policy, as they are at present practised in the northern hemisphere. But this must be agreed unto, and that positively. Lastly, I will be endowed, in right of my wife, with that six thousand pound, which is the moiety of Mrs. Millamant's fortune in your possession; and which she has forfeited (as will appear by the last will and testament of your deceased husband, Sir Jonathan Wishfort) by her disobedience in contracting herself against your consent or knowledge; and by refusing the offered match with Sir Wilfull Witwoud, which you, like a careful aunt, had provided for her.

LADY WISH. My nephew was *non compos,* and could not make his addresses.

FAIN. I come to make demands—I'll hear no objections.

LADY WISH. You will grant me time to consider?

FAIN. Yes, while the instrument is drawing, to which you must set your hand till more sufficient deeds can be perfected: which I will take care shall be done with all possible speed. In the meanwhile, I will go for the said instrument, and till my return you may balance this matter in your own discretion.

(*Exit* FAINALL.)

LADY WISH. This insolence is beyond all precedent, all parallel; must I be subject to this merciless villain?

MRS. MAR. 'Tis severe indeed, Madam, that you should smart for your daughter's wantonness.

LADY WISH. 'Twas against my consent that she married this barbarian, but she would have him, though her year was not out. Ah! her first husband, my son Languish, would not have carried it thus. Well, that was my choice, this is hers; she is matched now with a witness. I shall be mad, dear friend—is there no comfort for me? Must I live to be confiscated at this rebel-rate?—— Here come two more of my Egyptian plagues, too.

Enter MILLAMANT *and* SIR WILFULL

SIR WIL. Aunt, your servant.

LADY WISH. Out, caterpillar, call not me aunt! I know thee not!

SIR WIL. I confess I have been a little in disguise, as they say— 'sheart! and I'm sorry for't. What would you have? I hope I committed no offence, Aunt—and if I did I am willing to make satisfaction; and what can a man say fairer? If I have broke any thing, I'll pay for't, an it cost a pound. And so let that content for what's past, and make no more words. For what's to come, to pleasure you I'm willing to marry my cousin. So pray let's all be friends; she and I are agreed upon the matter before a witness.

LADY WISH. How's this, dear niece? Have I any comfort? Can this be true?

MILLA. I am content to be a sacrifice to your repose, Madam; and to convince you that I had no hand in the plot, as you were misinformed, I have laid my commands on Mirabell to come in person, and be a witness that I give my hand to this flower of knighthood; and for the contract that passed between Mirabell and me, I have obliged him to make a resignation of it in your Ladyship's presence; he is without, and waits your leave for admittance.

LADY WISH. Well, I'll swear I am something revived at this testimony of your obedience; but I cannot admit that traitor; I fear I cannot fortify myself to support his appearance. He is as terrible to me as a Gorgon; if I see him, I fear I shall turn to stone, petrify incessantly.

MILLA. If you disoblige him, he may resent your refusal, and insist upon the contract still. Then, 'tis the last time he will be offensive to you.

LADY WISH. Are you sure it will be the last time? If I were sure of that—shall I never see him again?

MILLA. Sir Wilfull, you and he are to travel together, are you not?

SIR WIL. 'Sheart, the gentleman's a civil gentleman, Aunt, let him come in; why, we are sworn brothers and fellow-travellers. We are to be Pylades and Orestes, he and I. He is to be my interpreter in foreign parts. He has been overseas once already; and with *proviso* that I marry my cousin, will cross 'em once again, only to bear me company. 'Sheart, I'll call him in; an I set on't once, he shall come in; and see who'll hinder him.

(*Exit.*)

MRS. MAR. This is precious fooling, if it would pass; but I'll know the bottom of it.

LADY WISH. O dear Marwood, you are not going?

MAR. Not far, Madam; I'll return immediately. (*Exit.*)

Re-enter SIR WILFULL *and* MIRABELL

SIR WIL. Look up, man, I'll stand by you; 'sbud, an she do frown, she can't kill you; besides—hark'ee, she dare not frown desperately, because her face is none of her own; 'sheart, an she should, her forehead would wrinkle like the coat of a cream-cheese; but mum for that, fellow-traveller.

MIRA. If a deep sense of the many injuries I have offered to so good a lady, with a sincere remorse, and a hearty contrition, can but obtain the least glance of compassion, I am too happy. Ah, Madam, there was a time—but let it be forgotten—I confess I have deservedly forfeited the high place I once held, of sighing at your feet; nay, kill me not, by turning from me in disdain—I come not to plead for favour—nay, not for pardon; I am a suppliant only for your pity—I am going where I never shall behold you more——

SIR WIL. How, fellow-traveller! You shall go by yourself then.

MIRA. Let me be pitied first; and afterwards forgotten—I ask no more.

SIR WIL. By'r Lady, a very reasonable request, and will cost you nothing, Aunt. Come, come, forgive and forget, Aunt; why you must, an you are a Christian.

MIRA. Consider, Madam, in reality you could not receive much prejudice; it was an innocent device; though I confess it had a face of guiltiness, it was at most an artifice which love contrived —and errors which love produces have ever been accounted venial. At least think it is punishment enough that I have lost what in my heart I hold most dear, that to your cruel indignation I have offered up this beauty, and with her my peace and quiet; nay, all my hopes of future comfort.

SIR WIL. An he does not move me, would I might never be o' the quorum!—an it were not as good a deed as to drink, to give her to him again, I would I might never take shipping!—— Aunt, if you don't forgive quickly, I shall melt, I can tell you that. My contract went no further than a little mouth glue, and that's hardly dry—one doleful sigh more from my fellow-traveller and 'tis dissolved.

LADY WISH. Well, nephew, upon your account.—Ah, he has a false insinuating tongue!—— Well, Sir, I will stifle my just resentment at my nephew's request. I will endeavour what I can to forget—but on *proviso* that you resign the contract with my niece immediately.

MIRA. It is in writing and with papers of concern; but I have sent my servant for it, and will deliver it to you, with all acknowledgments for your transcendent goodness.

LADY WISH. (*apart*) Oh, he has witchcraft in his eyes and tongue! When I did not see him, I could have bribed a villain to his assassination; but his appearance rakes the embers which have so long lain smothered in my breast.

Enter FAINALL *and* MRS. MARWOOD

FAIN. Your date of deliberation, Madam, is expired. Here is the instrument; are you prepared to sign?

LADY WISH. If I were prepared, I am not impowered. My niece exerts a lawful claim, having matched herself by my direction to Sir Wilfull.

FAIN. That sham is too gross to pass on me, though 'tis imposed on you, Madam.

MILLA. Sir, I have given my consent.

MIRA. And, Sir, I have resigned my pretensions.

SIR WIL. And, Sir, I assert my right; and will maintain it in defiance of you, Sir, and of your instrument. 'Sheart, an you talk of an instrument, Sir, I have an old fox by my thigh shall hack your instrument of ram vellum to shreds, Sir! It shall not be sufficient for a *mittimus* or a tailor's measure; therefore, withdraw your instrument, Sir, or by'r Lady I shall draw mine.

LADY WISH. Hold, Nephew, hold!

MILLA. Good Sir Wilfull, respite your valour!

FAIN. Indeed? Are you provided of a guard, with your single beefeater there? But I'm prepared for you; and insist upon my first proposal. You shall submit your own estate to my management, and absolutely make over my wife's to my sole use, as pursuant to the purport and tenor of this other covenant. I suppose, Madam, your consent is not requisite in this case; nor, Mr. Mirabell, your resignation; nor, Sir Wilfull, your right. You may draw your fox if you please, Sir, and make a bear-garden flourish somewhere else; for here it will not avail. This, my Lady Wishfort, must be subscribed, or your darling daughter's turned adrift, like a leaky hulk to sink or swim, as she and the current of this lewd town can agree.

LADY WISH. Is there no means, no remedy, to stop my ruin? Ungrateful wretch! dost thou not owe thy being, thy subsistence, to my daughter's fortune?

FAIN. I'll answer you when I have the rest of it in my possession.

MIRA. But that you would not accept of a remedy from my hands—I own I have not deserved you should owe any obligation to me; or else perhaps I could advise——

LADY WISH. Oh, what? what? to save me and my child from ruin, from want, I'll forgive all that's past; nay, I'll consent to anything to come, to be delivered from this tyranny.

MIRA. Ay, Madam; but that is too late, my reward is intercepted. You have disposed of her, who only could have made me a compensation for all my services. But be it as it may, I am resolved I'll serve you—you shall not be wronged in this savage manner!

LADY WISH. How! Dear Mr. Mirabell, can you be so generous at last! But it is not possible. Hark'ee, I'll break my nephew's match, you shall have my niece yet, and all her fortune, if you can but save me from this imminent danger.

MIRA. Will you? I take you at your word. I ask no more. I must have leave for two criminals to appear.

LADY WISH. Ay, ay, anybody, anybody!

MIRA. Foible is one, and a penitent.

Enter MRS. FAINALL, FOIBLE, *and* MINCING

MRS. MAR. (*to* FAINALL) Oh, my shame! these corrupt things are bought and brought hither to expose me.

(MIRABELL *and* LADY WISHFORT *go to* MRS. FAINALL *and* FOIBLE.)

FAIN. If it must all come out, why let 'em know it; 'tis but the *way of the world*. That shall not urge me to relinquish or abate one tittle of my terms; no, I will insist the more.

FOIB. Yes, indeed, Madam, I'll take my Bible oath of it.

MINC. And so will I, Mem.

LADY WISH. O Marwood, Marwood, art thou false? my friend deceive me? Hast thou been a wicked accomplice with that profligate man?

MRS. MAR. Have you so much ingratitude and injustice to give credit against your friend, to the aspersions of two such mercenary trulls?

MINC. Mercenary, Mem? I scorn your words. 'Tis true we found you and Mr. Fainall in the blue garret; by the same token, you swore us to secrecy upon Messalina's poems. Mercenary? No, if we would have been mercenary, we should have held our tongues; you would have bribed us sufficiently.

FAIN. Go, you are an insignificant thing!—— Well, what are you the better for this! Is this Mr. Mirabell's expedient? I'll be put off no longer.—— You thing that was a wife, shall smart for this! I will not leave thee wherewithal to hide thy shame; your body shall be naked as your reputation.

MRS. FAIN. I despise you, and defy your malice! You have aspersed me wrongfully—I have proved your falsehood. Go you and your treacherous—I will not name it—but starve together—perish!

FAIN. Not while you are worth a groat, indeed, my dear. Madam, I'll be fooled no longer.

LADY WISH. Ah, Mr. Mirabell, this is small comfort, the detection of this affair.

MIRA. Oh, in good time. Your leave for the other offender and penitent to appear, Madam.

Enter WAITWELL *with a box of writings*

LADY WISH. O Sir Rowland!—Well, rascal!

WAIT. What your Ladyship pleases. I have brought the black box at last, Madam.

MIRA. Give it me. Madam, you remember your promise.

LADY WISH. Ay, dear Sir.

MIRA. Where are the gentlemen?

WAIT. At hand, Sir, rubbing their eyes—just risen from sleep.

FAIN. 'Sdeath, what's this to me? I'll not wait your private concerns.

Enter PETULANT *and* WITWOUD

PET. How now? what's the matter? whose hand's out?

WIT. Hey day! what, are you all got together, like players at the end of the last act?

MIRA. You may remember, gentlemen, I once requested your hands as witnesses to a certain parchment.

WIT. Ay, I do, my hand I remember—Petulant set his mark.

MIRA. You wrong him, his name is fairly written, as shall

appear. You do not remember, gentlemen, anything of what that
parchment contained?   (*undoing the box*)

WIT. No.

PET. Not I. I writ, I read nothing.

MIRA. Very well, now you shall know.—— Madam, your
promise.

LADY WISH. Ay, ay, Sir, upon my honour.

MIRA. Mr. Fainall, it is now time that you should know that
your lady, while she was at her own disposal, and before you
had by your insinuations wheedled her out of a pretended settlement of the greatest part of her fortune——

FAIN. Sir! pretended!

MIRA. Yes, Sir. I say that this lady while a widow, having, it
seems, received some cautions respecting your inconstancy and
tyranny of temper, which from her own partial opinion and
fondness of you she could never have suspected—she did, I say,
by the wholesome advice of friends and of sages learned in the
laws of this land, deliver this same as her act and deed to me in
trust, and to the uses within mentioned. You may read if you
please (*holding out the parchment*)—though perhaps what is
inscribed on the back may serve your occasions.

FAIN. Very likely, Sir. What's here? Damnation! (*reads*) "A
deed of conveyance of the whole estate real of Arabella Languish,
widow, in trust to Edward Mirabell."

Confusion!

MIRA. Even so, Sir; 'tis the *way of the world*, Sir—of the
widows of the world. I suppose this deed may bear an elder
date than what you have obtained from your lady.

FAIN. Perfidious fiend! then thus I'll be revenged——

(*offers to run at* MRS. FAINALL)

SIR WIL. Hold, Sir! now you may make your bear-garden flourish somewhere else, Sir.

FAIN. Mirabell, you shall hear of this, Sir, be sure you shall.
—— Let me pass, oaf.   (*Exit.*)

MRS. FAIN. Madam, you seem to stifle your resentment. You
had better give it vent.

MRS. MAR. Yes, it shall have vent—and to your confusion, or
I'll perish in the attempt.   (*Exit.*)

LADY WISH. O Daughter, Daughter! 'tis plain thou hast inherited thy mother's prudence.

MRS. FAIN. Thank Mr. Mirabell, a cautious friend, to whose advice all is owing.

LADY WISH. Well, Mr. Mirabell, you have kept your promise—and I must perform mine. First, I pardon for your sake Sir Rowland there and Foible. The next thing is to break the matter to my nephew—and how to do that——

MIRA. For that, Madam, give yourself no trouble; let me have your consent. Sir Wilfull is my friend; he has had compassion upon lovers, and generously engaged a volunteer in this action for our service, and now designs to prosecute his travels.

SIR WIL. 'Sheart, Aunt, I have no mind to marry. My cousin's a fine lady, and the gentleman loves her and she loves him, and they deserve one another; my resolution is to see foreign parts—I have set on't—and when I'm set on't, I must do't. And if these two gentlemen would travel too, I think they may be spared.

PET. For my part, I say little—I think things are best off or on.

WIT. I'gad, I understand nothing of the matter; I'm in a maze yet, like a dog in a dancing-school.

LADY WISH. Well, Sir, take her, and with her all the joy I can give you.

MILLA. Why does not the man take me? Would you have me give myself to you over again?

MIRA. Ay, and over and over again; for I would have you as often as possibly I can. (*kisses her hand*) Well, heaven grant I love you not too well, that's all my fear.

SIR WIL. 'Sheart, you'll have him time enough to toy after you're married; or if you will toy now, let us have a dance in the meantime, that we who are not lovers may have some other employment besides looking on.

MIRA. With all my heart, dear Sir Wilfull. What shall we do for music?

FOIB. O Sir, some that were provided for Sir Rowland's entertainment are yet within call.   (*a dance*)

LADY WISH. As I am a person, I can hold out no longer; I have wasted my spirits so to-day already, that I am ready to sink under the fatigue; and I cannot but have some fears upon me yet that my son Fainall will pursue some desperate course.

MIRA. Madam, disquiet not yourself on that account; to my knowledge his circumstances are such he must of force comply. For my part, I will contribute all that in me lies to a reunion;

in the meantime, Madam (*to* MRS. FAINALL), let me before these witnesses restore to you this deed of trust. It may be a means, well managed, to make you live easily together.

From hence let those be warn'd, who mean to wed;
Lest mutual falsehood stain the bridal-bed:
For each deceiver to his cost may find,
That marriage frauds too oft are paid in kind. (*Exeunt omnes.*)

EPILOGUE

Spoken by MILLAMANT

After our epilogue this crowd dismisses,
In thinking how this play'll be pull'd to pieces.
But pray consider, ere you doom its fall,
How hard a thing 'twould be to please you all.
There are some critics so with spleen diseas'd,
They scarcely come inclining to be pleas'd:
And sure he must have more than mortal skill,
Who pleases anyone against his will.
Then, all bad poets we are sure are foes,
And how their number's swell'd the town well knows:
In shoals, I've mark'd 'em judging in the pit; ⎫
Though they're on no pretence for judgment fit, ⎬
But that they have been damn'd for want of wit. ⎭
Since when, they by their own offences taught,
Set up for spies on plays and finding fault.
Others there are whose malice we'd prevent; ⎫
Such who watch plays with scurrilous intent ⎬
To mark out who by characters are meant. ⎭
And though no perfect likeness they can trace;
Yet each pretends to know the copy'd face.
These with false glosses feed their own ill-nature,
And turn to libel what was meant a satire.
May such malicious fops this fortune find,
To think themselves alone the fools design'd:
If any are so arrogantly vain, ⎫
To think they singly can support a scene, ⎬
And furnish fool enough to entertain. ⎭

For well the learn'd and the judicious know,⎫
That satire scorns to stoop so meanly low, ⎬
As any one abstracted fop to show.   ⎭
For, as when painters form a matchless face,
They from each fair one catch some different grace,
And shining features in one portrait blend,
To which no single beauty must pretend;
So poets oft do in one piece expose
Whole *belles assemblées* of coquettes and beaux.

The Beaux' Stratagem

A COMEDY

By GEORGE FARQUHAR

PROLOGUE

Spoken by ARCHER

When strife disturbs, or sloth corrupts an age,
Keen satire is the business of the stage.
When the Plain Dealer writ, he lash'd those crimes
Which then infested most—the modish times:
But now, when faction sleeps and sloth is fled,
And all our youth in active fields are bred;
When through Great Britain's fair extensive round,
The trumps of fame the notes of Union sound;
When Anna's sceptre points the laws their course,
And her example gives her precepts force:
There scarce is room for satire; all our lays
Must be, or songs of triumph, or of praise.
But as in grounds best cultivated, tares
And poppies rise among the golden ears;
Our products so, fit for the field or school,
Must mix with nature's favourite plant—a fool:
A weed that has to twenty summers ran,
Shoots up in stalk, and vegetates to man.
Simpling our author goes from field to field,
And culls such fools as may diversion yield;

And, thanks to Nature, there's no want of those,
For, rain or shine, the thriving coxcomb grows.
Follies to-night we show ne'er lash'd before,
Yet such as Nature shows you every hour;
Nor can the pictures give a just offence,
For fools are made for jests to men of sense.

PERSONS REPRESENTED

MEN

AIMWELL,⎱ two gentlemen of broken fortunes, the first as
ARCHER, ⎰ master, and the second as servant
COUNT BELLAIR, a French officer, prisoner at Lichfield
SULLEN, a country blockhead, brutal to his wife
FREEMAN, a gentleman from London
FOIGARD, a priest, chaplain to the French officers
GIBBET, a highwayman
HOUNSLOW,⎱ his companions
BAGSHOT, ⎰
BONNIFACE, landlord of the inn
SCRUB, servant to Mr. Sullen

WOMEN

LADY BOUNTIFUL, an old, civil country gentlewoman, that cures
    all her neighbours of all distempers, and foolishly fond of
    her son, Sullen
DORINDA, Lady Bountiful's daughter
MRS. SULLEN, her daughter-in-law
GIPSEY, maid to the ladies
CHERRY, the landlord's daughter in the inn

SCENE: *Lichfield*

THE BEAUX' STRATAGEM

ACT I

SCENE: *An inn*

Enter BONNIFACE, *running*

BON. Chamberlain! maid! Cherry! daughter Cherry! all asleep? all dead?

Enter CHERRY, *running*

CHER. Here, here! Why d'ye bawl so, Father? d'ye think we have no ears?

BON. You deserve to have none, you young minx! The company of the Warrington coach has stood in the hall this hour, and nobody to show them to their chambers.

CHER. And let 'em wait farther; there's neither red-coat in the coach, nor footman behind it.

BON. But they threaten to go to another inn to-night.

CHER. That they dare not, for fear the coachman should over-turn them to-morrow.—— Coming! coming!—— Here's the London coach arrived.

Enter several people with trunks, bandboxes,
and other luggage, and cross the stage

BON. Welcome, Ladies!

CHER. Very welcome, gentlemen!—— Chamberlain, show the *Lion* and the *Rose*. (*Exit with the company.*)

Enter AIMWELL *in riding-habit,* ARCHER *as*
footman carrying a portmantle

BON. This way, this way, gentlemen!

AIM. Set down the things; go to the stable, and see my horses well rubbed.

ARCH. I shall, Sir. (*Exit.*)

AIM. You're my landlord, I suppose?

599

BON. Yes, Sir, I'm old Will Bonniface, pretty well known upon this road, as the saying is.

AIM. O Mr. Bonniface, your servant!

BON. O Sir! What will your honour please to drink, as the saying is?

AIM. I have heard your town of Lichfield much famed for ale; I think I'll taste that.

BON. Sir, I have now in my cellar ten tun of the best ale in Staffordshire; 'tis smooth as oil, sweet as milk, clear as amber, and strong as brandy, and will be just fourteen year old the fifth day of next March, old style.

AIM. You're very exact, I find, in the age of your ale.

BON. As punctual, Sir, as I am in the age of my children. I'll show you such ale!—— Here, tapster, broach number 1706, as the saying is.—— Sir, you shall taste my *Anno Domini*. I have lived in Lichfield, man and boy, above eight-and-fifty years, and, I believe, have not consumed eight-and-fifty ounces of meat.

AIM. At a meal, you mean, if one may guess your sense by your bulk.

BON. Not in my life, Sir. I have fed purely upon ale; I have eat my ale, drank my ale, and I always sleep upon ale.

Enter Tapster with a bottle and glass

Now, Sir, you shall see!—(*filling it out*) Your Worship's health. —Ha! delicious, delicious!—fancy it burgundy, only fancy it, and 'tis worth ten shillings a quart.

AIM. (*drinks*) 'Tis confounded strong!

BON. Strong! It must be so, or how should we be strong that drink it?

AIM. And have you lived so long upon this ale, Landlord?

BON. Eight-and-fifty years, upon my credit, Sir; but it killed my wife, poor woman, as the saying is.

AIM. How came that to pass?

BON. I don't know how, Sir; she would not let the ale take its natural course, Sir; she was for qualifying it every now and then with a dram, as the saying is; and an honest gentleman that came this way from Ireland made her a present of a dozen bottles of usquebaugh—but the poor woman was never well after. But, howe'er, I was obliged to the gentleman, you know.

AIM. Why, was it the usquebaugh that killed her?

BON. My Lady Bountiful said so. She, good lady, did what could be done; she cured her of three tympanies, but the fourth carried her off. But she's happy, and I'm contented, as the saying is.

AIM. Who's that Lady Bountiful you mentioned?

BON. Ods my life, Sir, we'll drink her health.—(*drinks*) My Lady Bountiful is one of the best of women. Her last husband, Sir Charles Bountiful, left her worth a thousand pound a year; and, I believe, she lays out one-half on't in charitable uses for the good of her neighbours; she cures rheumatisms, ruptures, and broken shins in men; green-sickness, obstructions, and fits of the mother in women; the king's evil, chincough, and chilblains in children: in short, she has cured more people in and about Lichfield within ten years than the doctors have killed in twenty; and that's a bold word.

AIM. Has the lady been any other way useful in her generation?

BON. Yes, Sir; she has a daughter by Sir Charles, the finest woman in all our country, and the greatest fortune. She has a son too, by her first husband, Squire Sullen, who married a fine lady from London t'other day; if you please, Sir, we'll drink his health.

AIM. What sort of a man is he?

BON. Why, Sir, the man's well enough; says little, thinks less, and does—nothing at all, faith. But he's a man of a great estate, and values nobody.

AIM. A sportsman, I suppose?

BON. Yes, Sir, he's a man of pleasure; he plays at whisk and smokes his pipe eight and forty hours together sometimes.

AIM. And married, you say?

BON. Ay, and to a curious woman, Sir.—But he's a—he wants it here, Sir. (*pointing to his forehead*)

AIM. He has it there, you mean.

BON. That's none of my business; he's my landlord, and so a man, you know, would not—But—icod, he's no better than—Sir, my humble service to you.—(*drinks*) Though I value not a farthing what he can do to me; I pay him his rent at quarter-day; I have a good running-trade; I have but one daughter, and I can give her—but no matter for that.

AIM. You're very happy, Mr. Bonniface; pray, what other company have you in town?

BON. A power of fine ladies; and then we have the French officers.

AIM. Oh, that's right, you have a good many of those gentlemen. Pray, how do you like their company?

BON. So well, as the saying is, that I could wish we had as many more of 'em; they're full of money, and pay double for everything they have: they know, Sir, that we paid good round taxes for the taking of 'em, and so they are willing to reimburse us a little. One of 'em lodges in my house.

Enter ARCHER

ARCH. Landlord, there are some French gentlemen below that ask for you.

BON. I'll wait on 'em——(*to* ARCHER) Does your master stay long in town, as the saying is?

ARCH. I can't tell, as the saying is.

BON. Come from London?

ARCH. No.

BON. Going to London, mayhap?

ARCH. No.

BON. An odd fellow this.—— I beg your Worship's pardon, I'll wait on you in half a minute.   (*Exit.*)

AIM. The coast's clear, I see. Now, my dear Archer, welcome to Lichfield!

ARCH. I thank thee, my dear brother in iniquity.

AIM. Iniquity! prithee, leave canting; you need not change your style with your dress.

ARCH. Don't mistake me, Aimwell, for 'tis still my maxim that there is no scandal like rags, nor any crime so shameful as poverty.

AIM. The world confesses it every day in its practice, though men won't own it for their opinion. Who did that worthy lord, my brother, single out of the side-box to sup with him t'other night?

ARCH. Jack Handicraft, a handsome, well-dressed, mannerly, sharping rogue, who keeps the best company in town.

AIM. Right! And, pray, who married my lady Manslaughter t'other day, the great fortune?

ARCH. Why, Nick Marrabone, a professed pickpocket, and a

good bowler; but he makes a handsome figure, and rides in his
coach, that he formerly used to ride behind.

AIM. But did you observe poor Jack Generous in the Park last
week?

ARCH. Yes, with his autumnal periwig shading his melancholy
face, his coat older than anything but its fashion, with one hand
idle in his pocket, and with the other picking his useless teeth;
and though the Mall was crowded with company, yet was poor
Jack as single and solitary as a lion in a desert.

AIM. And as much avoided, for no crime upon earth but the
want of money.

ARCH. And that's enough. Men must not be poor; idleness is
the root of all evil; the world's wide enough, let 'em bustle.
Fortune has taken the weak under her protection, but men of
sense are left to their industry.

AIM. Upon which topic we proceed, and, I think, luckily
hitherto. Would not any man swear now that I am a man of
quality, and you my servant, when if our intrinsic value were
known——

ARCH. Come, come, we are the men of intrinsic value who can
strike our fortunes out of ourselves, whose worth is independent
of accidents in life or revolutions in government; we have heads
to get money, and hearts to spend it.

AIM. As to our hearts, I grant ye, they are as willing tits as any
within twenty degrees; but I can have no great opinion of our
heads from the service they have done us hitherto, unless it be
that they have brought us from London hither to Lichfield, made
me a lord, and you my servant.

ARCH. That's more than you could expect already. But what
money have we left?

AIM. But two hundred pound.

ARCH. And our horses, clothes, rings, etc. Why, we have very
good fortunes now for moderate people; and let me tell you, besides, that this two hundred pound, with the experience that
we are now masters of, is a better estate than the ten thousand
we have spent. Our friends, indeed, began to suspect that our
pockets were low; but we came off with flying colours, showed no
signs of want either in word or deed.

AIM. Ay, and our going to Brussels was a good pretence

enough for our sudden disappearing; and, I warrant you, our friends imagine that we are gone a-volunteering.

ARCH. Why, faith, if this prospect fails, it must e'en come to that. I am for venturing one of the hundreds, if you will, upon this knight-errantry; but, in case it should fail, we'll reserve the t'other to carry us to some counterscarp, where we may die, as we lived, in a blaze.

AIM. With all my heart; and we have lived justly, Archer; we can't say that we have spent our fortunes, but that we have enjoyed 'em.

ARCH. Right! So much pleasure for so much money; we have had our pennyworths, and, had I millions, I would go to the same market again. O London! London! Well, we have had our share, and let us be thankful; past pleasures, for aught I know, are best, such as we are sure of: those to come may disappoint us.

AIM. It has often grieved the heart of me to see how some inhuman wretches murther their kind fortunes; those that, by sacrificing all to one appetite, shall starve all the rest. You shall have some that live only in their palates, and in their sense of tasting shall drown the other four. Others are only epicures in appearances, such who shall starve their nights to make a figure a-days, and famish their own to feed the eyes of others: a contrary sort confine their pleasures to the dark, and contract their specious acres to the circuit of a muff-string.

ARCH. Right! But they find the Indies in that spot where they consume 'em, and I think your kind keepers have much the best on't; for they indulge the most senses by one expense: there's the seeing, hearing, and feeling, amply gratified; and, some philosophers will tell you that from such a commerce there arises a sixth sense, that gives infinitely more pleasure than the other five put together.

AIM. And to pass to the other extremity, of all keepers I think those the worst that keep their money.

ARCH. Those are the most miserable wights in being; they destroy the rights of nature, and disappoint the blessings of Providence. Give me a man that keeps his five senses keen and bright as his sword, that has 'em always drawn out in their just order and strength, with his reason as commander at the head

of 'em; that detaches 'em by turns upon whatever party of
pleasure agreeably offers, and commands 'em to retreat upon the
least appearance of disadvantage or danger. For my part, I can
stick to my bottle while my wine, my company, and my reason
holds good; I can be charmed with Sappho's singing without
falling in love with her face; I love hunting, but would not, like
Actæon, be eaten up by my own dogs; I love a fine house, but let
another keep it; and just so I love a fine woman.

AIM. In that last particular you have the better of me.

ARCH. Ay, you're such an amorous puppy that I'm afraid you'll
spoil our sport; you can't counterfeit the passion without feeling
it.

AIM. Though the whining part be out of doors in town, 'tis
still in force with the country ladies; and let me tell you, Frank,
the fool in that passion shall outdo the knave at any time.

ARCH. Well, I won't dispute it now; you command for the day,
and so I submit. At Nottingham, you know, I am to be master.

AIM. And at Lincoln, I again.

ARCH. Then, at Norwich I mount, which, I think, shall be our
last stage; for, if we fail there, we'll embark for Holland, bid
adieu to Venus, and welcome Mars.

AIM. A match!

Enter BONNIFACE

Mum!

BON. What will your Worship please to have for supper?

AIM. What have you got?

BON. Sir, we have a delicate piece of beef in the pot, and a pig
at the fire.

AIM. Good supper-meat, I must confess. I can't eat beef, Landlord.

ARCH. And I hate pig.

AIM. Hold your prating, Sirrah! do you know who you are?

BON. Please to bespeak something else: I have everything in
the house.

AIM. Have you any veal?

BON. Veal! Sir, we had a delicate loin of veal on Wednesday
last.

AIM. Have you got any fish or wildfowl?

BON. As for fish, truly, Sir, we are an inland town, and indifferently provided with fish, that's the truth on't; and then for wildfowl—we have a delicate couple of rabbits.

AIM. Get me the rabbits fricasseed.

BON. Fricasseed! Lard, Sir, they'll eat much better smothered with onions.

ARCH. Pshaw! Damn your onions!

AIM. Again, Sirrah!—Well, Landlord, what you please. But hold, I have a small charge of money, and your house is so full of strangers that I believe it may be safer in your custody than mine; for when this fellow of mine gets drunk, he minds nothing.—— Here, Sirrah, reach me the strong-box.

ARCH. Yes, Sir. (*aside*) This will give us a reputation.

(*brings the box*)

AIM. Here, Landlord; the locks are sealed down both for your security and mine; it holds somewhat above two hundred pound; if you doubt it, I'll count it to you after supper; but be sure you lay it where I may have it at a minute's warning; for my affairs are a little dubious at present; perhaps I may be gone in half an hour, perhaps I may be your guest till the best part of that be spent; and pray order your ostler to keep my horses always saddled. But one thing above the rest I must beg, that you would let this fellow have none of your *Anno Domini*, as you call it; for he's the most insufferable sot.—— Here, Sirrah, light me to my chamber.   (*Exit, lighted by* ARCHER.)

BON. Cherry! Daughter Cherry!

Enter CHERRY

CHER. D'ye call, Father?

BON. Ay, child, you must lay by this box for the gentleman; 'tis full of money.

CHER. Money! all that money! Why sure, Father, the gentleman comes to be chosen parliament-man. Who is he?

BON. I don't know what to make of him; he talks of keeping his horses ready saddled, and of going perhaps at a minute's warning, or of staying perhaps till the best part of this be spent.

CHER. Ay, ten to one, Father, he's a highwayman.

BON. A highwayman! Upon my life, girl, you have hit it, and this box is some new-purchased booty.—Now, could we find him out, the money were ours.

CHER. He don't belong to our gang?

BON. What horses have they?

CHER. The master rides upon a black.

BON. A black! ten to one the man upon the black mare; and since he don't belong to our fraternity, we may betray him with a safe conscience. I don't think it lawful to harbour any rogues but my own. Look ye, child, as the saying is, we must go cunningly to work; proofs we must have. The gentleman's servant loves drink—I'll ply him that way; and ten to one loves a wench —you must work him t'other way.

CHER. Father, would you have me give my secret for his?

BON. Consider, child, there's two hundred pound to boot.— (*ringing without*) Coming! coming!——— Child, mind your business.   (*Exit.*)

CHER. What a rogue is my father! My father! I deny it. My mother was a good, generous, free-hearted woman, and I can't tell how far her good nature might have extended for the good of her children. This landlord of mine, for I think I can call him no more, would betray his guest, and debauch his daughter into the bargain—by a footman, too!

Enter ARCHER

ARCH. What footman, pray, Mistress, is so happy as to be the subject of your contemplation?

CHER. Whoever he is, friend, he'll be but little the better for't.

ARCH. I hope so, for I'm sure you did not think of me.

CHER. Suppose I had?

ARCH. Why, then you're but even with me; for the minute I came in I was a-considering in what manner I should make love to you.

CHER. Love to me, friend!

ARCH. Yes, child.

CHER. Child! manners! If you kept a little more distance, friend, it would become you much better.

ARCH. Distance! Good-night, saucebox.   (*going*)

CHER. A pretty fellow! I like his pride.——— Sir, pray, Sir, you see, Sir, (ARCHER *returns*) I have the credit to be intrusted with your master's fortune here, which sets me a degree above his footman; I hope, Sir, you an't affronted?

ARCH. Let me look you full in the face and I'll tell you whether you can affront me or no.—'Sdeath, child, you have a pair of delicate eyes, and you don't know what to do with 'em!

CHER. Why, Sir, don't I see everybody?

ARCH. Ay, but if some women had 'em, they would kill everybody. Prithee, instruct me, I would fain make love to you, but I don't know what to say.

CHER. Why, did you never make love to anybody before?

ARCH. Never to a person of your figure, I can assure you, Madam; my addresses have been always confined to people within my own sphere; I never aspired so high before. (*a song*)

> But you look so bright,
> And are dress'd so tight, etc.

CHER. (*aside*) What can I think of this man?—— Will you give me that song, Sir?

ARCH. Ay, my dear, take it while 'tis warm.—(*kisses her*) Death and fire! her lips are honeycombs.

CHER. And I wish there had been bees too, to have stung you for your impudence.

ARCH. There's a swarm of Cupids, my little Venus, that has done the business much better.

CHER. (*aside*) This fellow is misbegotten as well as I.—— What's your name, Sir?

ARCH. (*aside*) Name! i'gad, I have forgot it.—— Oh! Martin.

CHER. Where were you born?

ARCH. In St. Martin's parish.

CHER. What was your father?

ARCH. St. Martin's parish.

CHER. Then, friend, good-night.

ARCH. I hope not.

CHER. You may depend upon't.

ARCH. Upon what?

CHER. That you're very impudent.

ARCH. That you're very handsome.

CHER. That you're a footman.

ARCH. That you're an angel.

CHER. I shall be rude.

ARCH. So shall I.

CHER. Let go my hand.

ARCH. Give me a kiss. (*kisses her*)

(Call without.) Cherry! Cherry!

CHER. I'm–m—my father calls; you plaguy devil, how durst you stop my breath so? Offer to follow me one step, if you dare. *(Exit.)*

ARCH. A fair challenge, by this light! This is a pretty fair opening of an adventure; but we are knight-errants, and so Fortune be our guide. *(Exit.)*

ACT II

SCENE I

SCENE: *A gallery in* LADY BOUNTIFUL's *house*

MRS. SULLEN *and* DORINDA, *meeting*

DOR. Morrow, my dear Sister; are you for church this morning?

MRS. SUL. Anywhere to pray; for heaven alone can help me. But I think, Dorinda, there's no form of prayer in the liturgy against bad husbands.

DOR. But there's a form of law in Doctors Commons; and I swear, Sister Sullen, rather than see you thus continually discontented, I would advise you to apply to that: for besides the part that I bear in your vexatious broils, as being sister to the husband, and friend to the wife, your example gives me such an impression of matrimony that I shall be apt to condemn my person to a long vacation all its life. But supposing, Madam, that you brought it to a case of separation, what can you urge against your husband? My brother is, first, the most constant man alive.

MRS. SUL. The most constant husband, I grant ye.

DOR. He never sleeps from you.

MRS. SUL. No, he always sleeps with me.

DOR. He allows you a maintenance suitable to your quality.

MRS. SUL. A maintenance! Do you take me, Madam, for an hospital child, that I must sit down and bless my benefactors for meat, drink, and clothes? As I take it, Madam, I brought your brother ten thousand pounds, out of which I might expect some pretty things, called pleasures.

DOR. You share in all the pleasures that the country affords.

MRS. SUL. Country pleasures! Racks and torments! Dost think, child, that my limbs were made for leaping of ditches, and clambering over stiles? or that my parents, wisely foreseeing my future happiness in country pleasures, had early instructed me in the rural accomplishments of drinking fat ale, playing at whisk, and smoking tobacco with my husband? or of spreading of plasters, brewing of diet-drinks, and stilling rosemary-water, with the good old gentlewoman, my mother-in-law?

DOR. I'm sorry, Madam, that it is not more in our power to divert you; I could wish, indeed, that our entertainments were a little more polite, or your taste a little less refined. But, pray, Madam, how came the poets and philosophers, that laboured so much in hunting after pleasure, to place it at last in a country life?

MRS. SUL. Because they wanted money, child, to find out the pleasures of the town. Did you ever see a poet or philosopher worth ten thousand pound? If you can show me such a man, I'll lay you fifty pound you'll find him somewhere within the weekly bills. Not that I disapprove rural pleasures, as the poets have painted them; in their landscape, every Phyllis has her Corydon, every murmuring stream, and every flow'ry mead, gives fresh alarms to love. Besides, you'll find that their couples were never married.—— But yonder I see my Corydon, and a sweet swain it is, heaven knows! Come, Dorinda, don't be angry, he's my husband, and your brother; and, between both, is he not a sad brute?

DOR. I have nothing to say to your part of him—you're the best judge.

MRS. SUL. O Sister, Sister! if ever you marry, beware of a sullen, silent sot, one that's always musing, but never thinks. There's some diversion in a talking blockhead; and since a woman must wear chains, I would have the pleasure of hearing 'em rattle a little. Now you shall see, but take this by the way. He came home this morning at his usual hour of four, wakened me out of a sweet dream of something else by tumbling over the tea-table, which he broke all to pieces; after his man and he had rolled about the room, like sick passengers in a storm, he comes flounce into bed, dead as a salmon into a fishmonger's basket; his feet cold as ice, his breath hot as a furnace, and his hands and his face as greasy as his flannel night-cap. O matrimony! He tosses up the clothes with a barbarous swing over his shoulders, disorders the whole economy of my bed, leaves me half naked, and

my whole night's comfort is the tuneable serenade of that wakeful nightingale, his nose! Oh, the pleasure of counting the melancholy clock by a snoring husband!—But now, Sister, you shall
see how handsomely, being a well-bred man, he will beg my
pardon.

Enter SULLEN

SUL. My head aches consumedly.

MRS. SUL. Will you be pleased, my dear, to drink tea with us
this morning? It may do your head good.

SUL. No.

DOR. Coffee, Brother?

SUL. Pshaw!

MRS. SUL. Will you please to dress, and go to church with me?
The air may help you.

SUL. Scrub!

Enter SCRUB

SCRUB. Sir.

SUL. What day o' th' week is this?

SCRUB. Sunday, an't please your Worship.

SUL. Sunday! Bring me a dram; and d'ye hear, set out the
venison-pasty, and a tankard of strong beer upon the hall-table;
I'll go to breakfast.   (*going*)

DOR. Stay, stay, Brother, you shan't get off so; you were very
naught last night, and must make your wife reparation; come,
come, Brother, won't you ask pardon?

SUL. For what?

DOR. For being drunk last night.

SUL. I can afford it, can't I?

MRS. SUL. But I can't, Sir.

SUL. Then you may let it alone.

MRS. SUL. But I must tell you, Sir, that this is not to be borne.

SUL. I'm glad on't.

MRS. SUL. What is the reason, Sir, that you use me thus in-
humanely?

SUL. Scrub!

SCRUB. Sir.

SUL. Get things ready to shave my head.   (*Exit.*)

MRS. SUL. Have a care of coming near his temples, Scrub, for fear you meet something there that may turn the edge of your razor. (*Exit* SCRUB.)—Inveterate stupidity! did you ever know so hard, so obstinate a spleen as his? O Sister, Sister! I shall never ha' good of the beast till I get him to town: London, dear London, is the place for managing and breaking a husband.

DOR. And has not a husband the same opportunities there for humbling a wife?

MRS. SUL. No, no, child, 'tis a standing maxim in conjugal discipline, that when a man would enslave his wife he hurries her into the country; and when a lady would be arbitrary with her husband, she wheedles her booby up to town. A man dare not play the tyrant in London, because there are so many examples to encourage the subject to rebel. O Dorinda, Dorinda! a fine woman may do anything in London: o' my conscience, she may raise an army of forty thousand men.

DOR. I fancy, Sister, you have a mind to be trying your power that way here in Lichfield; you have drawn the French count to your colours already.

MRS. SUL. The French are a people that can't live without their gallantries.

DOR. And some English that I know, Sister, are not averse to such amusements.

MRS. SUL. Well, Sister, since the truth must out, it may do as well now as hereafter; I think one way to rouse my lethargic, sottish husband is to give him a rival. Security begets negligence in all people, and men must be alarmed to make 'em alert in their duty: women are like pictures, of no value in the hands of a fool, till he hears men of sense bid high for the purchase.

DOR. This might do, Sister, if my brother's understanding were to be convinced into a passion for you; but I fancy there's a natural aversion of his side; and I fancy, Sister, that you don't come much behind him, if you dealt fairly.

MRS. SUL. I own it; we are united contradictions, fire and water. But I could be contented, with a great many other wives, to humour the censorious mob, and give the world an appearance of living well with my husband, could I bring him but to dissemble a little kindness to keep me in countenance.

DOR. But how do you know, Sister, but that, instead of rousing your husband by this artifice to a counterfeit kindness, he should awake in a real fury?

MRS. SUL. Let him: if I can't entice him to the one, I would provoke him to the other.

DOR. But how must I behave myself between ye?

MRS. SUL. You must assist me.

DOR. What, against my own brother!

MRS. SUL. He's but half a brother, and I'm your entire friend. If I go a step beyond the bounds of honour, leave me; till then, I expect you should go along with me in everything; while I trust my honour in your hands, you may trust your brother's in mine. The count is to dine here to-day.

DOR. 'Tis a strange thing, Sister, that I can't like that man.

MRS. SUL. You like nothing; your time is not come: love and death have their fatalities, and strike home one time or other. You'll pay for all one day, I warrant ye. But come, my lady's tea is ready, and 'tis almost church time.　　　　(*Exeunt.*)

SCENE II

SCENE: *The inn*

Enter AIMWELL *dressed, and* ARCHER

AIM. And was she the daughter of the house?

ARCH. The landlord is so blind as to think so; but I dare swear she has better blood in her veins.

AIM. Why dost think so?

ARCH. Because the baggage has a pert *je ne sais quoi;* she reads plays, keeps a monkey, and is troubled with vapours.

AIM. By which discoveries I guess that you know more of her.

ARCH. Not yet, faith; the lady gives herself airs, forsooth, nothing under a gentleman!

AIM. Let me take her in hand.

ARCH. Say one word more o' that, and I'll declare myself, spoil your sport there, and everywhere else; look ye, Aimwell, every man in his own sphere.

AIM. Right; and therefore you must pimp for your master.

ARCH. In the usual forms, good Sir, after I have served myself. —But to our business. You are so well dressed, Tom, and make so handsome a figure, that I fancy you may do execution in a country church; the exterior part strikes first, and you're in the right to make that impression favourable.

AIM. There's something in that which may turn to advantage. The appearance of a stranger in a country church draws as many gazers as a blazing star; no sooner he comes into the cathedral, but a train of whispers runs buzzing round the congregation in a moment: "Who is he? Whence comes he? Do you know him?" Then I, Sir, tips me the verger with half a crown; he pockets the simony, and inducts me into the best pew in the church. I pull out my snuff-box, turn myself round, bow to the bishop, or the dean, if he be the commanding officer; single out a beauty, rivet both my eyes to hers, set my nose a-bleeding by the strength of imagination, and show the whole church my concern by my endeavouring to hide it; after the sermon, the whole town gives me to her for a lover, and by persuading the lady that I am a-dying for her, the tables are turned, and she in good earnest falls in love with me.

ARCH. There's nothing in this, Tom, without a precedent; but instead of riveting your eyes to a beauty, try to fix 'em upon a fortune; that's our business at present.

AIM. Pshaw! no woman can be a beauty without a fortune. Let me alone, for I am a marksman.

ARCH. Tom!

AIM. Ay.

ARCH. When were you at church before, pray?

AIM. Um—I was there at the coronation.

ARCH. And how can you expect a blessing by going to church now?

AIM. Blessing! nay, Frank, I ask but for a wife.   (*Exit.*)

ARCH. Truly, the man is not very unreasonable in his demands.
          (*Exit at the opposite door.*)

Enter BONNIFACE *and* CHERRY

BON. Well, Daughter, as the saying is, have you brought Martin to confess?

CHER. Pray, Father, don't put me upon getting anything out of a man; I'm but young, you know, Father, and I don't understand wheedling.

BON. Young! why, you jade, as the saying is, can any woman wheedle that is not young? Your mother was useless at five and twenty. Not wheedle! would you make your mother a whore, and me a cuckold, as the saying is? I tell you his silence confesses it, and his master spends his money so freely, and is so much a gentleman every manner of way, that he must be a highwayman.

Enter GIBBET, *in a cloak*

GIB. Landlord, Landlord, is the coast clear?

BON. O Mr. Gibbet, what's the news?

GIB. No matter, ask no questions, all fair and honourable.——Here, my dear Cherry. (*gives her a bag*) Two hundred sterling pounds, as good as any that ever hanged or saved a rogue; lay 'em by with the rest; and here—three wedding or mourning rings, 'tis much the same, you know.—Here, two silver-hilted swords; I took those from fellows that never show any part of their swords but the hilts. Here is a diamond necklace which the lady hid in the privatest place in the coach, but I found it out. This gold watch I took from a pawnbroker's wife; it was left in her hands by a person of quality—there's the arms upon the case.

CHER. But who had you the money from?

GIB. Ah! poor woman! I pitied her; from a poor lady just eloped from her husband. She had made up her cargo, and was bound for Ireland, as hard as she could drive; she told me of her husband's barbarous usage, and so I left her half a crown. But I had almost forgot, my dear Cherry, I have a present for you.

CHER. What is't?

GIB. A pot of ceruse, my child, that I took out of a lady's under-pocket.

CHER. What! Mr. Gibbet, do you think that I paint?

GIB. Why, you jade, your betters do; I'm sure the lady that I took it from had a coronet upon her handkerchief. Here, take my cloak, and go, secure the premises.

CHER. I will secure 'em.   (*Exit.*)

BON. But, hark ye, where's Hounslow and Bagshot?

GIB. They'll be here to-night.

BON. D'ye know of any other gentlemen o' the pad on this road?

GIB. No.

BON. I fancy that I have two that lodge in the house just now.

GIB. The devil! How d'ye smoke 'em?

BON. Why, the one is gone to church.

GIB. That's suspicious, I must confess.

BON. And the other is now in his master's chamber; he pretends to be servant to the other. We'll call him out and pump him a little.

GIB. With all my heart.

BON. Mr. Martin! Mr. Martin!

Enter MARTIN, *combing a periwig and singing*

GIB. The roads are consumed deep; I'm as dirty as Old Brentford at Christmas.—— A good pretty fellow that.—— Whose servant are you, friend?

ARCH. My master's.

GIB. Really?

ARCH. Really.

GIB. That's much.—— The fellow has been at the bar by his evasions.—— But pray, Sir, what is your master's name?

ARCH. *Tall, all dall!* (*sings and combs the periwig*) This is the most obstinate curl——

GIB. I ask you his name.

ARCH. Name, Sir—*tall, all dall!*—I never asked him his name in my life. *Tall, all dall!*

BON. What think you now?

GIB. Plain, plain; he talks now as if he were before a judge.—— But pray, friend, which way does your master travel?

ARCH. A-horseback.

GIB. Very well again, an old offender, right.—— But I mean, does he go upwards or downwards?

ARCH. Downwards, I fear, Sir.—*Tall, all!*

GIB. I'm afraid my fate will be a contrary way.

BON. Ha, ha, ha! Mr. Martin, you're very arch. This gentleman is only travelling towards Chester, and would be glad of your company, that's all.—— Come, Captain, you'll stay tonight, I suppose? I'll show you a chamber. Come, Captain.

GIB. Farewell, friend!

ARCH. Captain, your servant. (*Exeunt* BONNIFACE *and* CIBBET.) —Captain! a pretty fellow! 'Sdeath, I wonder that the officers of the army don't conspire to beat all scoundrels in red but their own.

Enter CHERRY

CHER. (*aside*) Gone! and Martin here! I hope he did not listen; I would have the merit of the discovery all my own, because I would oblige him to love me.—— Mr. Martin, who was that man with my father?

ARCH. Some recruiting sergeant, or whipped-out trooper, I suppose.

CHER. All's safe, I find.

ARCH. Come, my dear, have you conned over the catechise I taught you last night?

CHER. Come, question me.

ARCH. What is love?

CHER. Love is I know not what, it comes I know not how, and goes I know not when.

ARCH. Very well, an apt scholar.—(*chucks her under the chin*) Where does love enter?

CHER. Into the eyes.

ARCH. And where go out?

CHER. I won't tell ye.

ARCH. What are the objects of that passion?

CHER. Youth, beauty, and clean linen.

ARCH. The reason?

CHER. The two first are fashionable in nature, and the third at court.

ARCH. That's my dear. What are the signs and tokens of that passion?

CHER. A stealing look, a stammering tongue, words improbable, designs impossible, and actions impracticable.

ARCH. That's my good child, kiss me.—What must a lover do to obtain his mistress?

CHER. He must adore the person that disdains him, he must bribe the chambermaid that betrays him, and court the footman that laughs at him.—He must, he must——

ARCH. Nay, child, I must whip you if you don't mind your lesson; he must treat his——

CHER. Oh, ay! he must treat his enemies with respect, his friends with indifference, and all the world with contempt; he must suffer much, and fear more; he must desire much, and hope little; in short, he must embrace his ruin, and throw him-self away.

ARCH. Had ever man so hopeful a pupil as mine? Come, my dear, why is Love called a riddle?

CHER. Because, being blind, he leads those that see, and, though a child, he governs a man.

ARCH. Mighty well!—And why is Love pictured blind?

CHER. Because the painters out of the weakness or privilege of their art chose to hide those eyes that they could not draw.

ARCH. That's my dear little scholar, kiss me again.—And why should Love, that's a child, govern a man?

CHER. Because that a child is the end of love.

ARCH. And so ends love's catechism.—And now, my dear, we'll go in and make my master's bed.

CHER. Hold, hold, Mr. Martin! You have taken a great deal of pains to instruct me, and what d'ye think I have learnt by it?

ARCH. What?

CHER. That your discourse and your habit are contradictions, and it would be nonsense in me to believe you a footman any longer.

ARCH. 'Oons, what a witch it is!

CHER. Depend upon this, Sir, nothing in this garb shall ever tempt me; for, though I was born to servitude, I hate it. Own your condition, swear you love me, and then——

ARCH. And then we shall go make the bed?

CHER. Yes.

ARCH. You must know, then, that I am born a gentleman, my education was liberal; but I went to London a younger brother, fell into the hands of sharpers, who stripped me of my money; my friends disowned me, and now my necessity brings me to what·you see.

CHER. Then take my hand—promise to marry me before you sleep, and I'll make you master of two thousand pound.

ARCH. How!

CHER. Two thousand pound that I have this minute in my own custody; so, throw off your livery this instant, and I'll go find a parson.

ARCH. What said you? A parson!

CHER. What! do you scruple?

ARCH. Scruple! no, no, but—two thousand pound, you say?

CHER. And better.

ARCH. 'Sdeath, what shall I do?—— But hark'ee child, what need you make me master of yourself and money, when you may have the same pleasure out of me, and still keep your fortune in your hands?

CHER. Then you won't marry me?

ARCH. I would marry you, but——

CHER. O sweet Sir, I'm your humble servant! you're fairly caught: would you persuade me that any gentleman who could bear the scandal of wearing a livery would refuse two thousand pound, let the condition be what it would? No, no, Sir. But I hope you'll pardon the freedom I have taken, since it was only to inform myself of the respect that I ought to pay you. (*going*)

ARCH. Fairly bit, by Jupiter!—— Hold! hold! And have you actually two thousand pound?

CHER. Sir, I have my secrets as well as you; when you please to be more open, I shall be more free, and be assured that I have discoveries that will match yours, be what they will—in the meanwhile, be satisfied that no discovery I make shall ever hurt you; but beware of my father! (*Exit.*)

ARCH. So! we're like to have as many adventures in our inn as Don Quixote had in his. Let me see—two thousand pound! If the wench would promise to die when the money were spent, i'gad, one would marry her; but the fortune may go off in a year or two, and the wife may live—Lord knows how long. Then an innkeeper's daughter! ay, that's the devil—there my pride brings me off.

For whatsoe'er the sages charge on pride,
The angels' fall, and twenty faults beside,
On earth, I'm sure, 'mong us of mortal calling,
Pride saves man oft, and woman too, from falling. (*Exit.*)

ACT III

SCENE I

Enter MRS. SULLEN, DORINDA

MRS. SUL. Ha, ha, ha! my dear Sister, let me embrace thee—now we are friends indeed; for I shall have a secret of yours as a pledge for mine—now you'll be good for something; I shall have you conversable in the subjects of the sex.

DOR. But do you think that I am so weak as to fall in love with a fellow at first sight?

MRS. SUL. Pshaw! now you spoil all; why should not we be as free in our friendships as the men? I warrant you the gentleman has got to his confidant already, has avowed his passion, toasted your health, called you ten thousand angels, has run over your lips, eyes, neck, shape, air, and everything, in a description that warms their mirth to a second enjoyment.

DOR. Your hand, Sister, I an't well.

MRS. SUL. So—she's breeding already! Come, child, úp with it —hem a little—so—now tell me, don't you like the gentleman that we saw at church just now?

DOR. The man's well enough.

MRS. SUL. Well enough! is he not a demigod, a Narcissus, a star, the man i' the moon?

DOR. O Sister, I'm extremely ill!

MRS. SUL. Shall I send to your mother, child, for a little of her cephalic plaster to put to the soles of your feet, or shall I send to the gentleman for something for you? Come, unlace your stays, unbosom yourself—the man is perfectly a pretty fellow; I saw him when he first came into church.

DOR. I saw him too, Sister, and with an air that shone, me-thought, like rays about his person.

MRS. SUL. Well said, up with it!

DOR. No forward coquette behaviour, no airs to set him off, no studied looks nor artful posture—but Nature did it all——

MRS. SUL. Better and better! One touch more—come!

DOR. But then his looks—did you observe his eyes?

MRS. SUL. Yes, yes, I did. His eyes, well, what of his eyes?

DOR. Sprightly, but not wandering; they seemed to view, but never gazed on anything but me. And then his looks so humble were, and yet so noble, that they aimed to tell me that he could with pride die at my feet, though he scorned slavery anywhere else.

MRS. SUL. The physic works purely!—— How d'ye find your-self now, my dear?

DOR. Hem! much better, my dear.—— Oh, here comes our Mercury!

Enter SCRUB

Well, Scrub, what news of the gentleman?

SCRUB. Madam, I have brought you a packet of news.

DOR. Open it quickly, come.

SCRUB. In the first place I enquired who the gentleman was; they told me he was a stranger. Secondly, I asked what the gentleman was; they answered and said, that they never saw him before. Thirdly, I enquired what countryman he was; they replied, 'twas more than they knew. Fourthly, I demanded whence he came; their answer was, they could not tell. And, fifthly, I asked whither he went; and they replied, they knew nothing of the matter—and this is all I could learn.

MRS. SUL. But what do the people say? Can't they guess?

SCRUB. Why, some think he's a spy, some guess he's a mountebank, some say one thing, some another; but for my own part, I believe he's a Jesuit.

DOR. A Jesuit. Why a Jesuit?

SCRUB. Because he keeps his horses always ready saddled, and his footman talks French.

MRS. SUL. His footman!

SCRUB. Ay, he and the count's footman were gabbering French like two intriguing ducks in a mill-pond; and I believe they talked of me, for they laughed consumedly.

DOR. What sort of livery has the footman?

SCRUB. Livery! Lord, Madam, I took him for a captain, he's so bedizened with lace! And then he has tops to his shoes, up to his mid leg, a silver-headed cane dangling at his knuckles; he carries his hands in his pockets just so—(*walks in the French air*) —and has a fine long periwig tied up in a bag. Lord, Madam, he's clear another sort of man than I!

MRS. SUL. That may easily be.—— But what shall we do now, Sister?

DOR. I have it. This fellow has a world of simplicity, and some cunning; the first hides the latter by abundance.—— Scrub!

SCRUB. Madam!

DOR. We have a great mind to know who this gentleman is, only for our satisfaction.

SCRUB. Yes, Madam, it would be a satisfaction, no doubt.

DOR. You must go and get acquainted with his footman, and

invite him hither to drink a bottle of your ale, because you're
butler today.

SCRUB. Yes, Madam, I am butler every Sunday.

MRS. SUL. O brave, Sister! O' my conscience, you understand
the mathematics already—'tis the best plot in the world: your
mother, you know, will be gone to church, my spouse will be got
to the ale-house with his scoundrels, and the house will be our
own—so we drop in by accident, and ask the fellow some questions ourselves. In the country, you know, any stranger is company, and we're glad to take up with the butler in a country-
dance, and happy if he'll do us the favour.

SCRUB. Oh! Madam, you wrong me! I never refused your
Ladyship the favour in my life.

Enter GIPSEY

GIP. Ladies, dinner's upon table.

DOR. Scrub, we'll excuse your waiting. Go where we ordered
you.

SCRUB. I shall.   (*Exeunt.*)

SCENE II

Scene changes to the inn

Enter AIMWELL and ARCHER

ARCH. Well, Tom, I find you're a marksman.

AIM. A marksman! who so blind could be, as not discern a
swan among the ravens?

ARCH. Well, but hark'ee, Aimwell——

AIM. Aimwell! Call me Oroondates, Cesario, Amadis, all that
romance can in a lover paint, and then I'll answer. O Archer! I
read her thousands in her looks; she looked like Ceres in her
harvest: corn, wine and oil, milk and honey, gardens, groves, and
purling streams played on her plenteous face.

ARCH. Her face! her pocket, you mean; the corn, wine, and oil
lies there. In short, she has ten thousand pound, that's the English on't.

AIM. Her eyes——

ARCH. Are demi-cannons, to be sure; so I won't stand their battery.   (*going*)

AIM. Pray excuse me; my passion must have vent.

ARCH. Passion! what a plague, d'ee think these romantic airs will do our business? Were my temper as extravagant as yours, my adventures have something more romantic by half.

AIM. Your adventures!

ARCH. Yes,

> The nymph that with her twice ten hundred pounds,
> With brazen engine hot, and quoif clear starch'd,
> Can fire the guest in warming of the bed——

There's a touch of sublime Milton for you, and the subject but an innkeeper's daughter! I can play with a girl as an angler does with his fish; he keeps it at the end of his line, runs it up the stream and down the stream, till at last he brings it to hand, tickles the trout, and so whips it into his basket.

Enter BONNIFACE

BON. Mr. Martin, as the saying is—yonder's an honest fellow below, my Lady Bountiful's butler, who begs the honour that you would go home with him and see his cellar.

ARCH. Do my *baise-mains* to the gentleman, and tell him I will do myself the honour to wait on him immediately.

(*Exit* BONNIFACE.)

AIM. What do I hear?

> Soft Orpheus play, and fair Toftida sing!

ARCH. Pshaw! damn your raptures! I tell you, here's a pump going to be put into the vessel, and the ship will get into harbour, my life on't. You say there's another lady very handsome there?

AIM. Yes, faith.

ARCH. I am in love with her already.

AIM. Can't you give me a bill upon Cherry in the meantime?

ARCH. No, no friend, all her corn, wine, and oil is ingrossed to my market.—And once more I warn you to keep your anchorage clear of mine; for if you fall foul of me, by this light you shall go to the bottom! What! make prize of my little frigate, while I am upon the cruise for you!

AIM. Well, well, I won't.   (*Exit* ARCHER.)

Enter BONNIFACE

Landlord, have you any tolerable company in the house? I don't care for dining alone.

BON. Yes, Sir, there's a captain below, as the saying is, that arrived about an hour ago.

AIM. Gentlemen of his coat are welcome everywhere; will you make him a compliment from me, and tell him I should be glad of his company?

BON. Who shall I tell him, Sir, would——

AIM. Ha! that stroke was well thrown in!—— I'm only a traveller like himself, and would be glad of his company, that's all.

BON. I obey your commands, as the saying is. (*Exit.*)

Enter ARCHER

ARCH. 'Sdeath! I had forgot; what title will you give yourself?

AIM. My brother's, to be sure; he would never give me anything else, so I'll make bold with his honour this bout—you know the rest of your cue.

ARCH. Ay, ay. (*Exit.*)

Enter GIBBET

GIB. Sir, I'm yours.

AIM. 'Tis more than I deserve, Sir, for I don't know you.

GIB. I don't wonder at that, Sir, for you never saw me before —(*aside*) I hope.

AIM. And pray, Sir, how came I by the honour of seeing you now?

GIB. Sir, I scorn to intrude upon any gentleman—but my landlord——

AIM. O Sir, I ask your pardon! You're the captain he told me of.

GIB. At your service, Sir.

AIM. What regiment, may I be so bold?

GIB. A marching regiment, Sir, an old corps.

AIM. (*aside*) Very old, if your coat be regimental.—— You have served abroad, Sir?

GIB. Yes, Sir, in the plantations; 'twas my lot to be sent into the worst service. I would have quitted it indeed, but a man of honour, you know—Besides, 'twas for the good of my country that I should be abroad. Anything for the good of one's country —I'm a Roman for that.

AIM. (*aside*) One of the first, I'll lay my life.—— You found the West Indies very hot, Sir?

GIB. Ay, Sir, too hot for me.

AIM. Pray, Sir, han't I seen your face at Will's coffee-house?

GIB. Yes, Sir, and at White's too.

AIM. And where is your company now, Captain?

GIB. They an't come yet.

AIM. Why, d'ye expect 'em here?

GIB. They'll be here to-night, Sir.

AIM. Which way do they march?

GIB. Across the country.—— The devil's in't, if I han't said enough to encourage him to declare; but I'm afraid he's not right; I must tack about.

AIM. Is your company to quarter in Lichfield?

GIB. In this house, Sir.

AIM. What! all?

GIB. My company's but thin, ha, ha, ha! we are but three, ha, ha, ha!

AIM. You're merry, Sir.

GIB. Ay, Sir, you must excuse me, Sir; I understand the world, especially the art of travelling; I don't care, Sir, for answering questions directly upon the road—for I generally ride with a charge about me.

AIM. (*aside*) Three or four, I believe.

GIB. I am credibly informed that there are highwaymen upon this quarter; not, Sir, that I could suspect a gentleman of your figure. But truly, Sir, I have got such a way of evasion upon the road, that I don't care for speaking truth to any man.

AIM. Your caution may be necessary. Then I presume you're no captain?

GIB. Not I, Sir; captain is a good travelling name, and so I take it; it stops a great many foolish inquiries that are generally made about gentlemen that travel; it gives a man an air of something, and makes the drawers obedient—and thus far I am a captain, and no farther.

AIM. And pray, Sir, what is your true profession?

GIB. O Sir, you must excuse me! Upon my word, Sir, I don't think it safe to tell you.

AIM. Ha, ha, ha! upon my word, I commend you.

Enter BONNIFACE

Well, Mr. Bonniface, what's the news?

BON. There's another gentleman below, as the saying is, that hearing you were but two, would be glad to make the third man, if you would give him leave.

AIM. What is he?

BON. A clergyman, as the saying is.

AIM. A clergyman! Is he really a clergyman? or is it only his travelling name, as my friend the captain has it?

BON. O Sir, he's a priest, and chaplain to the French officers in town.

AIM. Is he a Frenchman?

BON. Yes, Sir, born at Brussels.

GIB. A Frenchman, and a priest! I won't be seen in his company, Sir; I have a value for my reputation, Sir.

AIM. Nay, but, Captain, since we are by ourselves—— Can he speak English, Landlord?

BON. Very well, Sir; you may know him, as the saying is, to be a foreigner by his accent, and that's all.

AIM. Then he has been in England before?

BON. Never, Sir; but he's a master of languages, as the saying is—he talks Latin—it does me good to hear him talk Latin.

AIM. Then you understand Latin, Mr. Bonniface?

BON. Not I, Sir, as the saying is; but he talks it so very fast that I'm sure it must be good.

AIM. Pray, desire him to walk up.

BON. Here he is, as the saying is.

Enter FOIGARD

FOI. Save you, gentlemens, both.

AIM. A Frenchman!—— Sir, your most humble servant.

FOI. Och, dear joy, I am your most faithful shervant, and yours alsho.

GIB. Doctor, you talk very good English, but you have a mighty twang of the foreigner.

FOI. My English is very vel for the vords, but we foreigners, you know, cannot bring our tongues about the pronunciation so soon.

AIM. (*aside*) A foreigner! a downright Teague, by this light! —— Were you born in France, Doctor?

FOI. I was educated in France, but I was borned at Brussels; I am a subject of the King of Spain, joy.

GIB. What King of Spain, Sir? speak!

FOI. Upon my shoul, joy, I cannot tell you as yet.

AIM. Nay, Captain, that was too hard upon the doctor; he's a stranger.

FOI. Oh, let him alone, dear joy; I am of a nation that is not easily put out of countenance.

AIM. Come, gentlemen, I'll end the dispute.—— Here, Landlord, is dinner ready?

BON. Upon the table, as the saying is.

AIM. Gentlemen—pray—that door——

FOI. No, no, fait, the captain must lead.

AIM. No, Doctor, the church is our guide.

GIB. Ay, ay, so it is.   (*Exit foremost, they follow.*)

SCENE III

Scene changes to a gallery in LADY BOUNTIFUL's *house*

Enter ARCHER *and* SCRUB *singing and hugging one another,* SCRUB *with a tankard in his hand,* GIPSEY *listening at a distance*

SCRUB. *Tall, all dall!*—— Come, my dear boy, let's have that song once more.

ARCH. No, no, we shall disturb the family. But will you be sure to keep the secret?

SCRUB. Pho! upon my honour, as I'm a gentleman.

ARCH. 'Tis enough.—You must know, then, that my master is the Lord Viscount Aimwell; he fought a duel t'other day in London, wounded his man so dangerously that he thinks fit to withdraw till he hears whether the gentleman's wounds be mortal or not. He never was in this part of England before, so he chose to retire to this place, that's all.

GIP. And that's enough for me.   (*Exit.*)

SCRUB. And where were you when your master fought?

ARCH. We never know of our masters' quarrels.

SCRUB. No? If our masters in the country here receive a challenge, the first thing they do is to tell their wives; the wife tells the servants, the servants alarm the tenants, and in half an hour you shall have the whole county in arms.

ARCH. To hinder two men from doing what they have no mind for.—But if you should chance to talk now of my business?

SCRUB. Talk! ay, Sir, had I not learnt the knack of holding my tongue, I had never lived so long in a great family.

ARCH. Ay, ay, to be sure there are secrets in all families.

SCRUB. Secrets! ay—but I'll say no more. Come, sit down; we'll make an end of our tankard: here——

ARCH. With all my heart; who knows but you and I may come to be better acquainted, eh?—Here's your ladies' healths; you have three, I think, and to be sure there must be secrets among 'em.

SCRUB. Secrets! ay, friend. I wish I had a friend——

ARCH. Am not I your friend? Come, you and I will be sworn brothers.

SCRUB. Shall we?

ARCH. From this minute.—Give me a kiss. And now, Brother Scrub——

SCRUB. And now, Brother Martin, I will tell you a secret that will make your hair stand on end. You must know that I am consumedly in love.

ARCH. That's a terrible secret, that's the truth on't.

SCRUB. That jade, Gipsey, that was with us just now in the cellar, is the arrantest whore that ever wore a petticoat; and I'm dying for love of her.

ARCH. Ha, ha, ha! Are you in love with her person or her virtue, Brother Scrub?

SCRUB. I should like virtue best, because it is more durable than beauty; for virtue holds good with some women long and many a day after they have lost it.

ARCH. In the country, I grant ye, where no woman's virtue is lost till a bastard be found.

SCRUB. Ay, could I bring her to a bastard, I should have her all to myself; but I dare not put it upon that lay, for fear of being sent for a soldier.—Pray, Brother, how do you gentlemen in London like that same Pressing Act?

ARCH. Very ill, Brother Scrub; 'tis the worst that ever was made for us. Formerly I remember the good days, when we could dun our masters for our wages, and if they refused to pay us, we could have a warrant to carry 'em before a justice; but now if we talk of eating, they have a warrant for us, and carry us before three justices.

SCRUB. And to be sure we go, if we talk of eating; for the justices won't give their own servants a bad example. Now this is my misfortune—I dare not speak in the house, while that jade Gipsey dings about like a fury. Once I had the better end of the staff.

ARCH. And how comes the change now?

SCRUB. Why, the mother of all this mischief is a priest.

ARCH. A priest!

SCRUB. Ay, a damned son of a whore of Babylon, that came over hither to say grace to the French officers, and eat up our provisions. There's not a day goes over his head without dinner or supper in this house.

ARCH. How came he so familiar in the family?

SCRUB. Because he speaks English as if he had lived here all his life; and tells lies as if he had been a traveller from his cradle.

ARCH. And this priest, I'm afraid, has converted the affections of your Gipsey.

SCRUB. Converted! ay, and perverted, my dear friend: for I'm afraid he has made her a whore and a papist! But this is not all; there's the French count and Mrs. Sullen, they're in the confederacy, and for some private ends of their own, to be sure.

ARCH. A very hopeful family yours, Brother Scrub! I suppose the maiden lady has her lover too.

SCRUB. Not that I know. She's the best on 'em, that's the truth on't. But they take care to prevent my curiosity by giving me so much business, that I'm a perfect slave. What d'ye think is my place in this family?

ARCH. Butler, I suppose.

SCRUB. Ah, Lord help you!—I'll tell you. Of a Monday I drive the coach; of a Tuesday I drive the plough; on Wednesday I follow the hounds; a-Thursday I dun the tenants; on Friday I go to market; on Saturday I draw warrants; and a-Sunday I draw beer.

ARCH. Ha, ha, ha! if variety be a pleasure in life, you have enough on't, my dear Brother.—— But what ladies are those?

SCRUB. Ours, ours; that upon the right hand is Mrs. Sullen, and the other is Mrs. Dorinda. Don't mind 'em; sit still, man.

Enter MRS. SULLEN *and* DORINDA

MRS. SUL. I have heard my brother talk of my Lord Aimwell; but they say that his brother is the finer gentleman.

DOR. That's impossible, Sister.

MRS. SUL. He's vastly rich, but very close, they say.

DOR. No matter for that; if I can creep into his heart, I'll open his breast, I warrant him. I have heard say, that people may be guessed at by the behaviour of their servants; I could wish we might talk to that fellow.

MRS. SUL. So do I; for I think he's a very pretty fellow. Come this way, I'll throw out a lure for him presently.

> (*They walk a turn towards the opposite side of the stage.* MRS. SULLEN *drops her glove,* ARCHER *runs, takes it up and gives it to her.*)

ARCH. Corn, wine, and oil indeed! But, I think, the wife has the greatest plenty of flesh and blood; she should be my choice. —— Ah, a, say you so!—Madam—your Ladyship's glove.

MRS. SUL. O Sir, I thank you!—— What a handsome bow the fellow has!

DOR. Bow! why, I have known several footmen come down from London set up here for dancing-masters, and carry off the best fortunes in the country.

ARCH. (*aside*) That project, for aught I know, had been better than ours.—— Brother Scrub, why don't you introduce me?

SCRUB. Ladies, this is the strange gentleman's servant that you see at church to-day; I understood he came from London, and so I invited him to the cellar, that he might show me the newest flourish in whetting my knives.

DOR. And I hope you have made much of him?

ARCH. Oh yes, Madam, but the strength of your Ladyship's liquor is a little too potent for the constitution of your humble servant.

MRS. SUL. What, then you don't usually drink ale?

ARCH. No Madam; my constant drink is tea, or a little wine

and water. 'Tis prescribed me by the physician for a remedy against the spleen.

SCRUB. O la! O la! a footman have the spleen!

MRS. SUL. I thought that distemper had been only proper to people of quality.

ARCH. Madam, like all other fashions it wears out, and so descends to their servants; though in a great many of us I believe it proceeds from some melancholy particles in the blood, occasioned by the stagnation of wages.

DOR. How affectedly the fellow talks!—— How long, pray, have you served your present master?

ARCH. Not long; my life has been mostly spent in the service of the ladies.

MRS. SUL. And pray, which service do you like best?

ARCH. Madam, the ladies pay best; the honour of serving them is sufficient wages; there is a charm in their looks that delivers a pleasure with their commands, and gives our duty the wings of inclination.

MRS. SUL. That flight was above the pitch of a livery.—— And, Sir, would not you be satisfied to serve a lady again?

ARCH. As a groom of the chamber, Madam, but not as a footman.

MRS. SUL. I suppose you served as footman before.

ARCH. For that reason I would not serve in that post again; for my memory is too weak for the load of messages that the ladies lay upon their servants in London. My Lady Howd'ye, the last mistress I served, called me up one morning, and told me, "Martin, go to my Lady Allnight with my humble service; tell her I was to wait on her ladyship yesterday, and left word with Mrs. Rebecca, that the preliminaries of the affair she knows of are stopped till we know the concurrence of the person that I know of, for which there are circumstances wanting which we shall accommodate at the old place; but that in the meantime there is a person about her ladyship that, from several hints and surmises, was accessary at a certain time to the disappointments that naturally attend things, that to her knowledge are of more importance——"

MRS. SUL., DOR. Ha, ha, ha! Where are you going, Sir?

ARCH. Why, I han't half done!—The whole howd'ye was about

half an hour long; so I happened to misplace two syllables, and was turned off, and rendered incapable.

DOR. The pleasantest fellow, Sister, I ever saw!—— But, friend, if your master be married, I presume you still serve a lady.

ARCH. No, Madam, I take care never to come into a married family; the commands of the master and mistress are always so contrary, that 'tis impossible to please both.

DOR. (*aside*) There's a main point gained.—— My lord is not married, I find.

MRS. SUL. But I wonder, friend, that in so many good services you had not a better provision made for you.

ARCH. I don't know how, Madam. I had a lieutenancy offered me three or four times; but that is not bread, Madam—I live much better as I do.

SCRUB. Madam, he sings rarely.—I was thought to do pretty well here in the country till he came; but alack-a-day, I'm nothing to my brother Martin!

DOR. Does he?—— Pray, Sir, will you oblige us with a song?

ARCH. Are you for passion or humour?

SCRUB. Oh la! he has the purest ballad about a trifle——

MRS. SUL. A trifle! pray, Sir, let's have it.

ARCH. I'm ashamed to offer you a trifle, Madam; but since you command me——

(*sings to the tune of Sir Simon the King*)

A trifling song you shall hear,
Begun with a trifle and ended, etc.

MRS. SUL. Very well, Sir, we're obliged to you.—Something for a pair of gloves.   (*offering him money*)

ARCH. I humbly beg leave to be excused: my master, Madam, pays me; nor dare I take money from any other hand without injuring his honour, and disobeying his commands.

(*Exit* ARCHER *and* SCRUB.)

DOR. This is surprising! Did you ever see so pretty a well-bred fellow?

MRS. SUL. The devil take him for wearing that livery!

DOR. I fancy, Sister, he may be some gentleman, a friend of my lord's, that his lordship has pitched upon for his courage, fidelity, and discretion, to bear him company in this dress, and who, ten to one, was his second too.

MRS. SUL. It is so, it must be so, and it shall be so—for I like him.

DOR. What! better than the count?

MRS. SUL. The count happened to be the most agreeable man upon the place; and so I chose him to serve me in my design upon my husband. But I should like this fellow better in a design upon myself.

DOR. But now, Sister, for an interview with this lord and this gentleman; how shall we bring that about?

MRS. SUL. Patience! You country ladies give no quarter if once you be entered.—Would you prevent their desires, and give the fellows no wishing-time?—Look ye, Dorinda, if my Lord Aimwell loves you or deserves you, he'll find a way to see you, and there we must leave it. My business comes now upon the tapis. Have you prepared your brother?

DOR. Yes, yes.

MRS. SUL. And how did he relish it?

DOR. He said little, mumbled something to himself, promised to be guided by me——but here he comes.

Enter SULLEN

SUL. What singing was that I heard just now?

MRS. SUL. The singing in your head, my dear; you complained of it all day.

SUL. You're impertinent.

MRS. SUL. I was ever so, since I became one flesh with you.

SUL. One flesh! rather two carcasses joined unnaturally together.

MRS. SUL. Or rather a living soul coupled to a dead body.

DOR. So, this is fine encouragement for me!

SUL. Yes, my wife shows you what you must do.

MRS. SUL. And my husband shows you what you must suffer.

SUL. 'Sdeath, why can't you be silent?

MRS. SUL. 'Sdeath, why can't you talk?

SUL. Do you talk to any purpose?

MRS. SUL. Do you think to any purpose?

SUL. Sister, hark ye! (*whispers*)—— I shan't be home till it be late.   (*Exit.*)

MRS. SUL. What did he whisper to ye?

DOR. That he would go round the back way, come into the

closet, and listen as I directed him. But let me beg you once more, dear Sister, to drop this project; for as I told you before, instead of awakening him to kindness, you may provoke him to a rage; and then who knows how far his brutality may carry him?

MRS. SUL. I'm provided to receive him, I warrant you. But here comes the count——vanish! (*Exit* DORINDA.)

Enter COUNT BELLAIR

Don't you wonder, Monsieur le Count, that I was not at church this afternoon?

COUNT BEL. I more wonder, Madam, that you go dere at all, or how you dare to lift those eyes to heaven that are guilty of so much killing.

MRS. SUL. If heaven, Sir, has given to my eyes, with the power of killing, the virtue of making a cure, I hope the one may atone for the other.

COUNT BEL. Oh, largely, Madam. Would your Ladyship be as ready to apply the remedy as to give the wound? Consider, Madam, I am doubly a prisoner—first to the arms of your general, then to your more conquering eyes. My first chains are easy—there a ransom may redeem me; but from your fetters I never shall get free.

MRS. SUL. Alas, Sir! why should you complain to me of your captivity, who am in chains myself? You know, Sir, that I am bound, nay, most be-tied up in that particular that might give you ease: I am like you, a prisoner of war—of war, indeed! I have given my parole of honour; would you break yours to gain your liberty?

COUNT BEL. Most certainly I would, were I a prisoner among the Turks; dis is your case: you're a slave, Madam, slave to the worst of Turks, a husband.

MRS. SUL. There lies my foible, I confess; no fortifications, no courage, conduct, nor vigilancy can pretend to defend a place where the cruelty of the governor forces the garrison to mutiny.

COUNT BEL. And where de besieger is resolved to die before de place. Here will I fix (*kneels*)—with tears, vows, and prayers assault your heart, and never rise till you surrender; or if I must storm—Love and St. Michael! And so I begin the attack.

MRS. SUL. Stand off!—(*aside*) Sure he hears me not! And I could almost wish he—did not! The fellow makes love very prettily.—— But, Sir, why should you put such a value upon my person, when you see it despised by one that knows it so much better?

COUNT BEL. He knows it not, though he possesses it; if he but knew the value of the jewel he is master of, he would always wear it next his heart, and sleep with it in his arms.

MRS. SUL. But since he throws me unregarded from him——

COUNT BEL. And one that knows your value well comes by and takes you up, is it not justice?   (*goes to lay hold on her*)

Enter SULLEN *with his sword drawn*

SUL. Hold, villain, hold!

MRS. SUL. (*presenting a pistol*) Do you hold!

SUL. What! murther your husband to defend your bully!

MRS. SUL. Bully! for shame, Mr. Sullen. Bullies wear long swords, the gentleman has none; he's a prisoner, you know. I was aware of your outrage, and prepared this to receive your violence, and, if occasion were, to preserve myself against the force of this other gentleman.

COUNT BEL. O Madam, your eyes be bettre fire-arms than your pistol; they nevre miss.

SUL. What! court my wife to my face!

MRS. SUL. Pray, Mr. Sullen, put up; suspend your fury for a minute.

SUL. To give you time to invent an excuse!

MRS. SUL. I need none.

SUL. No, for I heard every syllable of your discourse.

COUNT BEL. Ay! and begar, I tink de dialogue was vera pretty.

MRS. SUL. Then I suppose, Sir, you heard something of your own barbarity?

SUL. Barbarity! 'Oons, what does the woman call barbarity? do I ever meddle with you?

MRS. SUL. No.

SUL. As for you, Sir, I shall take another time.

COUNT BEL. Ah, begar, and so must I.

SUL. Look'ee, Madam, don't think that my anger proceeds from any concern I have for your honour, but for my own, and if you can contrive any way of being a whore without making me a cuckold, do it and welcome.

MRS. SUL. Sir, I thank you kindly; you would allow me the sin but rob me of the pleasure. No, no, I'm resolved never to venture upon the crime without the satisfaction of seeing you punished for't.

sul. Then will you grant me this, my dear? Let anybody else do you the favour but that Frenchman, for I mortally hate his whole generation. *(Exit.)*

count bel. Ah, Sir, that be ungrateful, for begar, I love some of yours.—— Madam—— *(approaching her)*

mrs. sul. No, Sir.——

count bel. No, Sir!—Garzoon, Madam, I am not your husband!

mrs. sul. 'Tis time to undeceive you, Sir. I believed your addresses to me were no more than an amusement, and I hope you will think the same of my complaisance; and to convince you that you ought, you must know that I brought you hither only to make you instrumental in setting me right with my husband, for he was planted to listen by my appointment.

count bel. By your appointment?

mrs. sul. Certainly.

count bel. And so, Madam, while I was telling twenty stories to part you from your husband, begar, I was bringing you together all the while?

mrs. sul. I ask your pardon, Sir, but I hope this will give you a taste of the virtue of the English ladies.

count bel. Begar, Madam, your virtue be vera great, but garzoon, your honeste be vera little.

Enter DORINDA

mrs. sul. Nay, now, you're angry, Sir.

count bel. Angry!—*Fair Dorinda. (sings 'Dorinda,' the opera tune, and addresses to* DORINDA*)* Madam, when your Ladyship want a fool, send for me. *Fair Dorinda, Revenge, etc.* *(Exit.)*

mrs. sul. There goes the true humour of his nation—resentment with good manners, and the height of anger in a song!—— Well, Sister, you must be judge, for you have heard the trial.

dor. And I bring in my brother guilty.

mrs. sul. But I must bear the punishment. 'Tis hard, Sister.

dor. I own it; but you must have patience.

mrs. sul. Patience! the cant of custom—Providence sends no evil without a remedy—should I lie groaning under a yoke I can shake off, I were accessary to my ruin, and my patience were no better than self-murder.

DOR. But how can you shake off the yoke? Your divisions don't come within the reach of the law for a divorce.

MRS. SUL. Law! what law can search into the remote abyss of nature? what evidence can prove the unaccountable disaffections of wedlock? Can a jury sum up the endless aversions that are rooted in our souls, or can a bench give judgment upon antipathies?

DOR. They never pretended, Sister; they never meddle, but in case of uncleanness.

MRS. SUL. Uncleanness! O Sister! casual violation is a transient injury, and may possibly be repaired, but can radical hatreds be ever reconciled?—No, no, Sister, Nature is the first lawgiver, and when she has set tempers opposite, not all the golden links of wedlock nor iron manacles of law can keep 'um fast.

Wedlock we own ordain'd by heaven's decree,
But such as heaven ordain'd it first to be,
Concurring tempers in the man and wife
As mutual helps to draw the load of life.
View all the works of Providence above,
The stars with harmony and concord move;
View all the works of Providence below,
The fire, the water, earth, and air, we know,
All in one plant agree to make it grow.
Must man, the chiefest work of art divine,
Be doom'd in endless discord to repine?
No, we should injure heaven by that surmise;
Omnipotence is just, were man but wise.

ACT IV

SCENE I

Scene continues

Enter MRS. SULLEN

MRS. SUL. Were I born an humble Turk, where women have no soul nor property, there I must sit contented. But in England, a country whose women are its glory, must women be abused? where women rule, must women be enslaved? nay, cheated into slavery, mocked by a promise of comfortable society into a wilderness of solitude? I dare not keep the thought about me. —— Oh, here comes something to divert me.

Enter a Country Woman

WOM. I come, an't please your Ladyships—you're my Lady Bountiful, an't ye?

MRS. SUL. Well, good woman, go on.

WOM. I have come seventeen long mail to have a cure for my husband's sore leg.

MRS. SUL. Your husband! what, woman, cure your husband!

WOM. Ay, poor man, for his sore leg won't let him stir from home.

MRS. SUL. There, I confess, you have given me a reason. Well, good woman, I'll tell you what you must do. You must lay your husband's leg upon a table, and with a chopping-knife you must lay it open as broad as you can; then you must take out the bone, and beat the flesh soundly with a rolling-pin; then take salt, pepper, cloves, mace, and ginger, some sweet herbs, and season it very well; then roll it up like brawn, and put it into the oven for two hours.

WOM. Heavens reward your Ladyship! I have two little babies too that are piteous bad with the graips, an't please ye.

MRS. SUL. Put a little pepper and salt in their bellies, good woman.

Enter LADY BOUNTIFUL

I beg your Ladyship's pardon for taking your business out of your hands; I have been a-tampering here a little with one of your patients.

LADY BOUN. Come, good woman, don't mind this mad creature; I am the person that you want, I suppose. What would you have, woman?

MRS. SUL. She wants something for her husband's sore leg.

LADY BOUN. What's the matter with his leg, goody?

WOM. It come first, as one might say, with a sort of dizziness in his foot, then he had a kind of a laziness in his joints, and then his leg broke out, and then it swelled, and then it closed again, and then it broke out again, and then it festered, and then it grew better, and then it grew worse again.

MRS. SUL. Ha, ha, ha!

LADY BOUN. How can you be merry with the misfortunes of other people?

MRS. SUL. Because my own make me sad, Madam.

LADY BOUN. The worst reason in the world, Daughter; your own misfortunes should teach you to pity others'.

MRS. SUL. But the woman's misfortunes and mine are nothing alike: her husband is sick, and mine, alas! is in health.

LADY BOUN. What! would you wish your husband sick?

MRS. SUL. Not of a sore leg, of all things.

LADY BOUN. Well, good woman, go to the pantry, get your bellyful of victuals, then I'll give you a receipt of diet-drink for your husband. But d'ye hear, goody, you must not let your husband move too much.

WOM. No, no, Madam, the poor man's inclinable enough to lie still.   (*Exit.*)

LADY BOUN. Well, Daughter Sullen, though you laugh, I have done miracles about the country here with my receipts.

MRS. SUL. Miracles indeed, if they have cured anybody; but I believe, Madam, the patient's faith goes farther toward the miracle than your prescription.

LADY BOUN. Fancy helps in some cases; but there's your husband, who has as little fancy as anybody; I brought him from death's door.

MRS. SUL. I suppose, Madam, you made him drink plentifully of ass's milk.

Enter DORINDA, *runs to* MRS. SULLEN

DOR. News, dear Sister! news! news!

Enter ARCHER, *running*

ARCH. Where, where is my Lady Bountiful? Pray, which is the old lady of you three?

LADY BOUN. I am.

ARCH. O Madam, the fame of your Ladyship's charity, good-ness, benevolence, skill, and ability, have drawn me hither to implore your Ladyship's help in behalf of my unfortunate master, who is this moment breathing his last.

LADY BOUN. Your master! where is he?

ARCH. At your gate, Madam. Drawn by the appearance of your handsome house to view it nearer, and walking up the avenue within five paces of the courtyard, he was taken ill of a sudden with a sort of I know not what, but down he fell, and there he lies.

LADY BOUN. Here, Scrub! Gipsey! all run, get my easy chair downstairs, put the gentleman in it, and bring him in quickly, quickly!

ARCH. Heaven will reward your Ladyship for this charitable act.

LADY BOUN. Is your master used to these fits?

ARCH. Oh yes, Madam, frequently—I have known him have five or six of a night.

LADY BOUN. What's his name?

ARCH. Lord, Madam, he's a-dying! a minute's care or neglect may save or destroy his life!

LADY BOUN. Ah, poor gentleman! Come, friend, show me the way; I'll see him brought in myself.   (*Exit with* ARCHER.)

DOR. O, Sister, my heart flutters about strangely! I can hardly forbear running to his assistance.

MRS. SUL. And I'll lay my life he deserves your assistance more than he wants it; did not I tell you that my lord would find a way to come at you? Love's his distemper, and you must be the physician; put on all your charms, summon all your fire into your eyes, plant the whole artillery of your looks against his breast, and down with him.

DOR. O Sister! I'm but a young gunner; I shall be afraid to shoot, for fear the piece should recoil and hurt myself.

MRS. SUL. Never fear, you shall see me shoot before you, if you will.

DOR. No, no, dear Sister; you have missed your mark so unfortunately that I shan't care for being instructed by you.

Enter AIMWELL *in a chair carried by* ARCHER *and* SCRUB; LADY
   BOUNTIFUL, GIPSEY. AIMWELL *counterfeiting a swoon*

LADY BOUN. Here, here, let's see the hartshorn drops.——
Gipsey, a glass of fair water! His fit's very strong. Bless me, how his hands are clinched!

ARCH. For shame, ladies, what d'ye do? why don't you help us?—(*to* DORINDA) Pray, Madam, take his hand and open it, if you can, whilst I hold his head.   (DORINDA *takes his hand.*)

DOR. Poor gentleman! Oh! he has got my hand within his, and squeezes it unmercifully——

LADY BOUN. 'Tis the violence of his convulsion, child.

ARCH. Oh, Madam, he's perfectly possessed in these cases— he'll bite if you don't have a care.

DOR. Oh, my hand! my hand!

LADY BOUN. What's the matter with the foolish girl? I have got this hand open, you see, with a great deal of ease.

ARCH. Ay, but, Madam, your daughter's hand is somewhat warmer than your Ladyship's, and the heat of it draws the force of the spirits that way.

MRS. SUL. I find, friend, you're very learned in these sorts of fits.

ARCH. 'Tis no wonder, Madam, for I'm often troubled with them myself; I find myself extremely ill at this minute.

(*looking hard at* MRS. SULLEN)

MRS. SUL. (*aside*) I fancy I could find a way to cure you.

LADY BOUN. His fit holds him very long.

ARCH. Longer than usual, Madam.—— Pray, young lady, open his breast, and give him air.

LADY BOUN. Where did his illness take him first, pray?

ARCH. To-day at church, Madam.

LADY BOUN. In what manner was he taken?

ARCH. Very strangely, my Lady. He was of a sudden touched with something in his eyes, which, at the first, he only felt, but could not tell whether 'twas pain or pleasure.

LADY BOUN. Wind, nothing but wind!

ARCH. By soft degrees it grew and mounted to his brain; there his fancy caught it, there formed it so beautiful, and dressed it up in such gay, pleasing colours, that his transported appetite seized the fair idea, and straight conveyed it to his heart. That hospitable seat of life sent all its sanguine spirits forth to meet, and opened all its sluicy gates to take the stranger in.

LADY BOUN. Your master should never go without a bottle to smell to.—— Oh—he recovers! The lavender-water—some feathers to burn under his nose—Hungary-water to rub his temples.—— Oh, he comes to himself!—— Hem a little, Sir, hem.—— Gipsey bring the cordial-water.

(AIMWELL *seems to awake in amaze.*)

DOR. How d'ye, Sir?

AIM. Where am I?   (*rising*)

Sure I have pass'd the gulf of silent death,
And now I land on the Elysian shore!
Behold the goddess of those happy plains,
Fair Proserpine. Let me adore thy bright divinity.

(*kneels to* DORINDA, *and kisses her hand*)

MRS. SUL. So, so, so! I knew where the fit would end!

AIM. Eurydice perhaps—

How could thy Orpheus keep his word,
And not look back upon thee?
No treasure but thyself could sure have brib'd him
To look one minute off thee.

LADY BOUN. Delirious, poor gentleman!

ARCH. Very delirious, Madam, very delirious.

AIM. Martin's voice, I think.

ARCH. Yes, my Lord. How does your Lordship?

LADY BOUN. Lord! did you mind that, girls?

AIM. Where am I?

ARCH. In very good hands, Sir. You were taken just now with one of your old fits, under the trees, just by this good lady's house; her ladyship had you taken in, and has miraculously brought you to yourself, as you see.

AIM. I am so confounded with shame, Madam, that I can now only beg pardon—and refer my acknowledgments for your Ladyship's care till an opportunity offers of making some amends. I dare be no longer troublesome.—— Martin! give two guineas to the servants.   (*going*)

DOR. Sir, you may catch cold by going so soon into the air; you don't look, Sir, as if you were perfectly recovered.

(*Here* ARCHER *talks to* LADY BOUNTIFUL *in dumb show.*)

AIM. That I shall never be, Madam; my present illness is so rooted that I must expect to carry it to my grave.

MRS. SUL. Don't despair, Sir; I have known several in your distemper shake it off with a fortnight's physic.

LADY BOUN. Come, Sir, your servant has been telling me that you're apt to relapse if you go into the air. Your good manners shan't get the better of ours. You shall sit down again, Sir. Come, Sir, we don't mind ceremonies in the country. Here, Sir, my service t'ye. You shall taste my water; 'tis a cordial I can assure you, and of my own making—drink it off, Sir.—(AIMWELL *drinks.*) And how d'ye find yourself now, Sir?

AIM. Somewhat better—though very faint still.

LADY BOUN. Ay, ay, people are always faint after these fits. —— Come, girls, you shall show the gentleman the house.—— 'Tis but an old family building, Sir; but you had better walk about and cool by degrees, than venture immediately into the air. You'll find some tolerable pictures.—— Dorinda, show the gentleman the way. I must go to the poor woman below.

(*Exit.*)

DOR. This way, Sir.

AIM. Ladies, shall I beg leave for my servant to wait on you? for he understands pictures very well.

MRS. SUL. Sir, we understand originals as well as he does pictures, so he may come along.

(*Exeunt* DORINDA, MRS. SULLEN, AIMWELL, ARCHER. AIMWELL *leads* DORINDA.)

Enter FOIGARD *and* SCRUB, *meeting*

FOI. Save you, Master Scrub!

SCRUB. Sir, I won't be saved your way—I hate a priest, I abhor the French, and I defy the devil. Sir, I'm a bold Briton, and will spill the last drop of my blood to keep out popery and slavery.

FOI. Master Scrub, you would put me down in politics, and so I would be speaking with Mrs. Shipsey.

SCRUB. Good Mr. Priest, you can't speak with her; she's sick, Sir, she's gone abroad, Sir, she's—dead two months ago, Sir.

Enter GIPSEY

GIP. How now, impudence! how dare you talk so saucily to the Doctor?—— Pray, Sir, don't take it ill; for the common people of England are not so civil to strangers, as——

SCRUB. You lie! you lie! 'Tis the common people that are civilest to strangers.

GIP. Sirrah, I have a good mind to— Get you out, I say!

SCRUB. I won't.

GIP. You won't, sauce-box!—— Pray, Doctor, what is the captain's name that came to your inn last night?

SCRUB. The captain! Ah, the devil, there she hampers me again—the captain has me on one side, and the priest on t'other —so between the gown and the sword, I have a fine time on't. But *cedunt arma togæ.** (going)

GIP. What, Sirrah, won't you march?

SCRUB. No, my dear, I won't march—but I'll walk.—— And I'll make bold to listen a little too. (*goes behind the side-scene and listens*)

GIP. Indeed, Doctor, the count has been barbarously treated, that's the truth on't.

FOI. Ah, Mrs. Gipsey, upon my shoul, now, gra, his complainings would mollify the marrow in your bones, and move the bowels of your commiseration! He veeps, and he dances, and he fistles, and he swears, and he laughs, and he stamps, and he sings: in conclusion, joy, he's afflicted *à la française,* and a stranger would not know whider to cry or to laugh with him.

GIP. What would you have me do, Doctor?

FOI. Noting, joy, but only hide the count in Mrs. Sullen's closet when it is dark.

GIP. Nothing! is that nothing? It would be both a sin and a shame, Doctor.

FOI. Here is twenty louis d'ors, joy, for your shame; and I will give you an absolution for the shin.

GIP. But won't that money look like a bribe?

FOI. Dat is according as you shall tauk it. If you receive the money beforehand, 'twill be *logice* a bribe; but if you stay till afterwards, 'twill be only a gratification.

GIP. Well, Doctor, I'll take it *logice*. But what must I do with my conscience, Sir?

FOI. Leave dat wid me, joy; I am your priest, gra; and your conscience is under my hands.

GIP. But should I put the count into the closet——

FOI. Vel, is dere any shin for a man's being in a closhet? One may go to prayers in a closhet.

GIP. But if the lady should come into her chamber, and go to bed?

FOI. Vel, and is dere any shin in going to bed, joy?

* Arms should yield to the gown.

GIP. Ay, but if the parties should meet, Doctor?

FOI. Vel den—the parties must be responsible. Do you be after putting the count in the closet; and leave the shins wid themselves. I will come with the count to instruct you in your chamber.

GIP. Well, Doctor, your religion is so pure! Methinks I'm so easy after an absolution, and can sin afresh with so much security, that I'm resolved to die a martyr to't. Here's the key of the garden door, come in the back way when 'tis late; I'll be ready to receive you; but don't so much as whisper, only take hold of my hand; I'll lead you, and do you lead the count, and follow me.   (*Exeunt.*)

Enter SCRUB

SCRUB. What witchcraft now have these two imps of the devil been a-hatching here? There's twenty louis d'ors; I heard that, and saw the purse. But I must give room to my betters.   (*Exit.*)

Enter AIMWELL, *leading* DORINDA, *and making love in dumb show;* MRS. SULLEN *and* ARCHER

MRS. SUL. (*to* ARCHER) Pray, Sir, how d'ye like that piece?

ARCH. Oh, 'tis Leda! You find, Madam, how Jupiter comes disguised to make love——

MRS. SUL. But what think you there of Alexander's battles?

ARCH. We only want a Le Brun, Madam, to draw greater battles, and a greater general of our own. The Danube, Madam, would make a greater figure in a picture than the Granicus; and we have our Ramillies to match their Arbela.

MRS. SUL. Pray, Sir, what head is that in the corner there?

ARCH. O Madam, 'tis poor Ovid in his exile.

MRS. SUL. What was he banished for?

ARCH. His ambitious love, Madam. (*bowing*) His misfortune touches me.

MRS. SUL. Was he successful in his amours?

ARCH. There he has left us in the dark. He was too much a gentleman to tell.

MRS. SUL. If he were secret, I pity him.

ARCH. And if he were successful, I envy him.

MRS. SUL. How d'ye like that Venus over the chimney?

ARCH. Venus! I protest, Madam, I took it for your picture; but now I look again, 'tis not handsome enough.

MRS. SUL. Oh, what a charm is flattery! If you would see my picture, there it is, over that cabinet.—How d'ye like it?

ARCH. I must admire anything, Madam, that has the least resemblance of you. But, methinks, Madam—(*He looks at the picture and* MRS. SULLEN *three or four times, by turns.*) Pray, Madam, who drew it?

MRS. SUL. A famous hand, Sir.

(*Here* AIMWELL *and* DORINDA *go off.*)

ARCH. A famous hand, Madam!—Your eyes, indeed, are featured there; but where's the sparkling moisture, shining fluid, in which they swim? The picture, indeed, has your dimples; but where's the swarm of killing Cupids that should ambush there? the lips too are figured out; but where's the carnation dew, the pouting ripeness, that tempts the taste in the original?

MRS. SUL. ——Had it been my lot to have matched with such a man!

ARCH. Your breasts too—presumptuous man!—what, paint heaven!—Apropos, Madam, in the very next picture is Salmoneus, that was struck dead with lightning for offering to imitate Jove's thunder; I hope you served the painter so, Madam?

MRS. SUL. Had my eyes the power of thunder, they should employ their lightning better.

ARCH. There's the finest bed in that room, Madam! I suppose 'tis your Ladyship's bedchamber.

MRS. SUL. And what then, Sir?

ARCH. I think the quilt is the richest that ever I saw. I can't at this distance, Madam, distinguish the figures of the embroidery; will you give me leave, Madam——?

MRS. SUL. The devil take his impudence! Sure, if I gave him an opportunity, he durst not offer it?—I have a great mind to try.—(*going*) 'Sdeath, what am I doing?—And alone, too!—(*returns*) Sister! Sister! (*runs out*)

ARCH. I'll follow her close—

For where a Frenchman durst attempt to storm,

A Briton sure may well the work perform. (*going*)

Enter SCRUB

SCRUB. Martin! Brother Martin!

ARCH. O Brother Scrub, I beg your pardon, I was not a-going; here's a guinea my master ordered you.

SCRUB. A guinea! hi, hi, hi! a guinea! eh—by this light it is a guinea! But I suppose you expect one and twenty shillings in change.

ARCH. Not at all; I have another for Gipsey.

SCRUB. A guinea for her! Faggot and fire for the witch! Sir, give me that guinea, and I'll discover a plot.

ARCH. A plot!

SCRUB. Ay, Sir, a plot, and a horrid plot! First, it must be a plot, because there's a woman in't; secondly, it must be a plot, because there's a priest in't; thirdly, it must be a plot, because there's French gold in't; and fourthly, it must be a plot, because I don't know what to make on't.

ARCH. Nor anybody else, I'm afraid, Brother Scrub.

SCRUB. Truly, I'm afraid so too; for where there's a priest and a woman there's always a mystery and a riddle. This I know, that here has been the doctor with a temptation in one hand and an absolution in the other; and Gipsey has sold herself to the devil; I saw the price paid down, my eyes shall take their oath on't.

ARCH. And is all this bustle about Gipsey?

SCRUB. That's not all; I could hear but a word here and there; but I remember they mentioned a count, a closet, a back door, and a key.

ARCH. The count!—Did you hear nothing of Mrs. Sullen?

SCRUB. I did hear some word that sounded that way; but whether it was Sullen or Dorinda, I could not distinguish.

ARCH. You have told this matter to nobody, Brother?

SCRUB. Told! No, Sir, I thank you for that; I'm resolved never to speak one word *pro* nor *con*, till we have a peace.

ARCH. You're i' the right, Brother Scrub; here's a treaty afoot between the count and the lady: the priest and the chambermaid are the plenipotentiaries.—— It shall go hard but I find a way to ɔɔ 'ncluded in the treaty.—— Where's the doctor now?

scᴿᵁB. He and Gipsey are this moment devouring my lady's nᵒ malade in the closet.

AIM. (*from without*) Martin! Martin!

ARCH. I come, Sir, I come.

SCRUB. But you forget the other guinea, Brother Martin.

ARCH. Here, I give it with all my heart.

SCRUB. And I take it with all my soul.—— Icod, I'll spoil your plotting, Mrs. Gipsey! and if you should set the captain upon me, these two guineas will buy me off.   (*Exeunt severally.*)

Enter MRS. SULLEN *and* DORINDA, *meeting*

MRS. SUL. Well, Sister!

DOR. And well, Sister!

MRS. SUL. What's become of my lord?

DOR. What's become of his servant?

MRS. SUL. Servant! he's a prettier fellow, and a finer gentleman by fifty degrees than his master.

DOR. O' my conscience, I fancy you could beg that fellow at the gallows-foot!

MRS. SUL. O' my conscience I could, provided I could put a friend of yours in his room.

DOR. You desired me, Sister, to leave you, when you transgressed the bounds of honour.

MRS. SUL. Thou dear censorious country girl! what dost mean? You can't think of the man without the bedfellow, I find.

DOR. I don't find anything unnatural in that thought; while the mind is conversant with flesh and blood, it must conform to the humours of the company.

MRS. SUL. How a little love and good company improves a woman! Why, child, you begin to live—you never spoke before.

DOR. Because I was never spoke to. My lord has told me that I have more wit and beauty than any of my sex; and truly I begin to think the man is sincere.

MRS. SUL. You're in the right, Dorinda; pride is the life of a woman, and flattery is our daily bread; and she's a fool that won't believe a man there, as much as she that believes him in anything else. But I'll lay you a guinea that I had finer things said to me than you had.

DOR. Done! What did your fellow say to ye?

MRS. SUL. My fellow took the picture of Venus for mine.

DOR. But my lover took me for Venus herself.

MRS. SUL. Common cant! Had my spark called me a Venus directly, I should have believed him a footman in good earnest.

DOR. But my lover was upon his knees to me.

MRS. SUL. And mine was upon his tiptoes to me.

DOR. Mine vowed to die for me.

MRS. SUL. Mine swore to die with me.

DOR. Mine spoke the softest moving things.

MRS. SUL. Mine had his moving things too.

DOR. Mine kissed my hand ten thousand times.

MRS. SUL. Mine has all that pleasure to come.

DOR. Mine offered marriage.

MRS. SUL. O Lard! D'ye call that a moving thing?

DOR. The sharpest arrow in his quiver, my dear Sister! Why, my ten thousand pounds may lie brooding here this seven years, and hatch nothing at last but some ill-natured clown like yours. Whereas, if I marry my Lord Aimwell, there will be title, place, and precedence, the Park, the play, and the drawing-room, splendour, equipage, noise, and flambeaux.—"Hey, my Lady Aimwell's servants there!—Lights, lights to the stairs!—My Lady Aimwell's coach put forward!—Stand by, make room for her Ladyship!"—Are not these things moving?——What! melancholy of a sudden?

MRS. SUL. Happy, happy Sister! your angel has been watchful for your happiness, whilst mine has slept regardless of his charge. Long smiling years of circling joys for you, but not one hour for me!   (weeps)

DOR. Come, my dear, we'll talk of something else.

MRS. SUL. O Dorinda! I own myself a woman, full of my sex, a gentle, generous soul—easy and yielding to soft desires; a spacious heart, where Love and all his train might lodge. And must the fair apartment of my breast be made a stable for a brute to lie in?

DOR. Meaning your husband, I suppose?

MRS. SUL. Husband! no—even husband is too soft a name for him.——But, come, I expect my brother here to-night or to-morrow; he was abroad when my father married me; perhaps he'll find a way to make me easy.

DOR. Will you promise not to make yourself easy in the meantime with my lord's friend?

MRS. SUL. You mistake me, Sister. It happens with us as among the men, the greatest talkers are the greatest cowards; and there's a reason for it; those spirits evaporate in prattle, which might do more mischief if they took another course. Though, to confess the truth, I do love that fellow; and if I met him dressed as he should be, and I undressed as I should be—look ye, Sister, I have no supernatural gifts—I can't swear I could resist the temptation; though I can safely promise to avoid it; and that's as much as the best of us can do. (*Exeunt* MRS. SULLEN *and* DORINDA.)

SCENE II

Enter AIMWELL *and* ARCHER, *laughing*

ARCH. And the awkward kindness of the good motherly old gentlewoman——

AIM. And the coming easiness of the young one—'Sdeath, 'tis pity to deceive her!

ARCH. Nay, if you adhere to those principles, stop where you are.

AIM. I can't stop; for I love her to distraction.

ARCH. 'Sdeath, if you love her a hair's breadth beyond discretion, you must go no farther.

AIM. Well, well, anything to deliver us from sauntering away our idle evenings at White's, Tom's, or Will's, and be stinted to bear looking at our old acquaintance, the cards, because our impotent pockets can't afford us a guinea for the mercenary drabs.

ARCH. Or be obliged to some purse-proud coxcomb for a scandalous bottle, where we must not pretend to our share of the discourse, because we can't pay our club o' th' reckoning. Damn it, I had rather sponge upon Morris, and sup upon a dish of bohea scored behind the door!

AIM. And there expose our want of sense by talking criticisms, as we should our want of money by railing at the government.

ARCH. Or be obliged to sneak into the side-box, and between both houses steal two acts of a play, and because we han't money to see the other three, we come away discontented, and damn the whole five.

AIM. And ten thousand such rascally tricks—had we outlived our fortunes among our acquaintance. But now——

ARCH. Ay, now is the time to prevent all this. Strike while the iron is hot. This priest is the luckiest part of our adventure; he shall marry you, and pimp for me.

AIM. But I should not like a woman that can be so fond of a Frenchman.

ARCH. Alas, Sir! necessity has no law. The lady may be in distress; perhaps she has a confounded husband, and her revenge may carry her farther than her love. Igad, I have so good an opinion of her, and of myself, that I begin to fancy strange things; and we must say this for the honour of our women, and indeed of ourselves, that they do stick to their men as they do to their *Magna Charta*. If the plot lies as I suspect, I must put on the gentleman.——But here comes the doctor. I shall be ready.

(*Exit.*)

Enter FOIGARD

FOI. Sauve you, noble friend.

AIM. O Sir, your servant! Pray, Doctor, may I crave your name?

FOI. Fat naam is upon me? My naam is Foigard, joy.

AIM. Foigard! a very good name for a clergyman. Pray, Doctor Foigard, were you ever in Ireland?

FOI. Ireland! No, joy. Fat sort of plaace is dat saam Ireland? Dey say de people are catched dere when dey are young.

AIM. And some of 'em when they're old—as for example.—— (*takes* FOIGARD *by the shoulder*) Sir, I arrest you as a traitor against the government; you're a subject of England, and this morning showed me a commission by which you served as chaplain in the French army. This is death by our law, and your reverence must hang for't.

FOI. Upon my shoul, noble friend, dis is strange news you tell me! Fader Foigard a subject of England! de son of a burgomaster of Brussels a subject of England! ubooboo——

AIM. The son of a bog-trotter in Ireland! Sir, your tongue will condemn you before any bench in the kingdom.

FOI. And is my tongue all your evidensh, joy?

AIM. That's enough.

FOI. No, no, joy, for I vil never spake English no more.

AIM. Sir, I have other evidence.—— Here, Martin!

Enter ARCHER

You know this fellow?

ARCH. (*in a brogue*) Saave you, my dear Cussen, how does your health?

FOI. (*aside*) Ah! upon my shoul dere is my countryman, and his brogue will hang mine.—— *Mynheer, Ick wet neat watt hey zacht.*—— *Ick universton ewe neat, sacrament!*

AIM. Altering your language won't do, Sir; this fellow knows your person, and will swear to your face.

FOI. Faace! fey, is dear a brogue upon my faash too?

ARCH. Upon my soulvation dere ish, joy! But Cussen Mackshane, vil you not put a remembrance upon me?

FOI. (*aside*) Mackshane! by St. Paatrick, dat is my naame, shure enough!

AIM. I fancy, Archer, you have it.

FOI. The devil hang you, joy! By fat acquaintance are you my cussen?

ARCH. Oh, de devil hang yourshelf, joy! You know we were little boys togeder upon de school, and your foster-moder's son was married upon my nurse's chister, joy, and so we are Irish cussens.

FOI. De devil taak the relation! Vel, joy, and fat school was it?

ARCH. I tinks it vas—aay—'twas Tipperary.

FOI. No, no, joy; it vas Kilkenny.

AIM. That's enough for us—self-confession. Come, Sir, we must deliver you into the hands of the next magistrate.

ARCH. He sends you to gaol, you're tried next assizes, and away you go swing into purgatory.

FOI. And is it so wid you, cussen?

ARCH. It vil be sho wid you, cussen, if you don't immediately confess the secret between you and Mrs. Gipsey. Look'ee, Sir, the gallows or the secret, take your choice.

FOI. The gallows! Upon my shoul I hate that saam gallow, for it is a diseash dat is fatal to our family.—— Vel, den, dere is nothing, shentlemens, but Mrs. Shullen would spaak wid the count in her chamber at midnight, and dere is no haarm, joy, for I am to conduct the count to the plash, myshelf.

ARCH. As I guessed.—— Have you communicated the matter to the count?

FOI. I have not sheen him since.

ARCH. Right again! Why then, Doctor—you shall conduct me to the lady instead of the count.

FOI. Fat, my cussen to the lady! Upon my shoul, gra, dat is too much upon the brogue.

ARCH. Come, come, Doctor; consider we have got a rope about your neck, and if you offer to squeak, we'll stop your windpipe,

most certainly. We shall have another job for you in a day or
two, I hope.

AIM. Here's company coming this way; let's into my chamber,
and there concert our affair farther.

ARCH. Come, my dear cussen, come along.   (*Exeunt.*)

Enter BONNIFACE, HOUNSLOW, *and* BAGSHOT *at one door,*
GIBBET *at the opposite*

GIB. Well, gentlemen, 'tis a fine night for our enterprise.

HOUN. Dark as hell.

BAG. And blows like the devil; our landlord here has showed
us the window where we must break in, and tells us the plate
stands in the wainscot cupboard in the parlour.

BON. Ay, ay, Mr. Bagshot, as the saying is, knives and forks,
and cups and cans, and tumblers and tankards. There's one tankard, as the saying is, that's near upon as big as me; it was a
present to the squire from his godmother, and smells of nutmeg
and toast like an East India ship.

HOUN. Then you say we must divide at the stairhead?

BON. Yes, Mr. Hounslow, as the saying is. At one end of that
gallery lies my Lady Bountiful and her daughter, and at the
other Mrs. Sullen. As for the squire——

GIB. He's safe enough, I have fairly entered him, and he's
more than half-seas over already. But such a parcel of scoundrels are got about him now, that, igad, I was ashamed to be
seen in their company.

BON. 'Tis now twelve, as the saying is. Gentlemen, you must
set out at one.

GIB. Hounslow, do you and Bagshot see our arms fixed, and
I'll come to you presently.

HOUN., BAG. We will.   (*Exeunt.*)

GIB. Well, my dear Bonny, you assure me that Scrub is a
coward.

BON. A chicken, as the saying is. You'll have no creature to
deal with but the ladies.

GIB. And I can assure you, friend, there's a great deal of address and good manners in robbing a lady; I am the most a
gentleman that way that ever travelled the road. But, my dear
Bonny, this prize will be a galleon, a Vigo business. I warrant
you we shall bring off three or four thousand pound.

BON. In plate, jewels, and money, as the saying is, you may.

GIB. Why then, Tyburn, I defy thee! I'll get up to town, sell off my horse and arms, buy myself some pretty employment in the Household, and be as snug and as honest as any courtier of 'um all.

BON. And what think you then of my daughter Cherry for a wife?

GIB. Look'ee, my dear Bonny—Cherry "is the goddess I adore," as the song goes; but it is a maxim that man and wife should never have it in their power to hang one another; for if they should, the Lord have mercy on 'um both!   (*Exeunt.*)

ACT V

SCENE I

Scene continues

Knocking without

Enter BONNIFACE

BON. Coming! Coming!——A coach and six foaming horses at this time o' night! Some great man, as the saying is, for he scorns to travel with other people.

Enter SIR CHARLES FREEMAN

SIR CHAS. What, fellow! a public house, and abed when other people sleep?

BON. Sir, I an't abed, as the saying is.

SIR CHAS. Is Mr. Sullen's family abed, think'ee?

BON. All but the squire himself, Sir, as the saying is; he's in the house.

SIR CHAS. What company has he?

BON. Why, Sir, there's the constable, Mr. Gage the exciseman, the hunchbacked barber, and two or three other gentlemen.

SIR CHAS. I find my sister's letters gave me the true picture of her spouse.

Enter SULLEN, *drunk*

BON. Sir, here's the squire.

SUL. The puppies left me asleep.—— Sir!

SIR CHAS. Well, Sir.

SUL. Sir, I'm an unfortunate man—I have three thousand pound a year, and I can't get a man to drink a cup of ale with me.

SIR CHAS. That's very hard.

SUL. Ay, Sir; and unless you have pity upon me, and smoke one pipe with me, I must e'en go home to my wife, and I had rather go to the devil by half.

SIR CHAS. But I presume, Sir, you won't see your wife to-night; she'll be gone to bed—you don't use to lie with your wife in that pickle?

SUL. What! not lie with my wife! Why, Sir, do you take me for an atheist or a rake?

SIR CHAS. If you hate her, Sir, I think you had better lie from her.

SUL. I think so too, friend. But I'm a justice of peace, and must do nothing against the law.

SIR CHAS. Law! As I take it, Mr. Justice, nobody observes law for law's sake, only for the good of those for whom it was made.

SUL. But if the law orders me to send you to gaol, you must lie there, my friend.

SIR CHAS. Not unless I commit a crime to deserve it.

SUL. A crime? 'Oons, an't I married?

SIR CHAS. Nay, Sir, if you call marriage a crime, you must disown it for a law.

SUL. Eh!—I must be acquainted with you, Sir. But, Sir, I should be very glad to know the truth of this matter.

SIR CHAS. Truth, Sir, is a profound sea, and few there be that dare wade deep enough to find out the bottom on't. Besides, Sir, I'm afraid the line of your understanding mayn't be long enough.

SUL. Look'ee, Sir, I have nothing to say to your sea of truth, but if a good parcel of land can intitle a man to a little truth, I have as much as any he in the country.

BON. I never heard your Worship, as the saying is, talk so much before.

SUL. Because I never met with a man that I liked before.

BON. Pray, Sir, as the saying is, let me ask you one question: are not man and wife one flesh?

SIR CHAS. You and your wife, Mr. Guts, may be one flesh, because ye are nothing else; but rational creatures have minds that must be united.

SUL. Minds!

SIR CHAS. Ay, minds, Sir; don't you think that the mind takes place of the body?

SUL. In some people.

SIR CHAS. Then the interest of the master must be consulted before that of his servant.

SUL. Sir, you shall dine with me to-morrow!——'Oons, I always thought that we were naturally one.

SIR CHAS. Sir, I know that my two hands are naturally one, because they love one another, kiss one another, help one another in all the actions of life; but I could not say so much if they were always at cuffs.

SUL. Then 'tis plain that we are two.

SIR CHAS. Why don't you part with her, Sir?

SUL. Will you take her, Sir?

SIR CHAS. With all my heart.

SUL. You shall have her to-morrow morning, and a venison-pasty into the bargain.

SIR CHAS. You'll let me have her fortune too?

SUL. Fortune! Why, Sir, I have no quarrel at her fortune. I only hate the woman, Sir, and none but the woman shall go.

SIR CHAS. But her fortune, Sir——

SUL. Can you play at whisk, Sir?

SIR CHAS. No, truly, Sir.

SUL. Nor at all-fours?

SIR CHAS. Neither!

SUL. (aside) 'Oons! where was this man bred?—— Burn me, Sir! I can't go home; 'tis but two o'clock.

SIR CHAS. For half an hour, Sir, if you please. But you must consider 'tis late.

SUL. Late! that's the reason I can't go to bed. Come, Sir!

(*Exeunt.*)

Enter CHERRY, *runs across the stage and knocks at*
AIMWELL'S *chamber door. Enter* AIMWELL *in his
nightcap and gown.*

AIM. What's the matter? You tremble, child; you're frighted.

CHER. No wonder, Sir. But, in short, Sir, this very minute a gang of rogues are gone to rob my Lady Bountiful's house.

AIM. How!

CHER. I dogged 'em to the very door, and left 'em breaking in.

AIM. Have you alarmed anybody else with the news?

CHER. No, no, Sir, I wanted to have discovered the whole plot, and twenty other things, to your man Martin; but I have searched the whole house, and can't find him. Where is he?

AIM. No matter, child; will you guide me immediately to the house?

CHER. With all my heart, Sir; my Lady Bountiful is my god-mother, and I love Mrs. Dorinda so well——

AIM. Dorinda! The name inspires me, the glory and the danger shall be all my own.—— Come, my life, let me but get my sword.   (*Exeunt.*)

SCENE II

Scene changes to a bedchamber in LADY
BOUNTIFUL'S *house*

Enter MRS. SULLEN, DORINDA *undressed; a table and lights*

DOR. 'Tis very late, Sister. No news of your spouse yet?

MRS. SUL. No, I'm condemned to be alone till towards four, and then perhaps I may be executed with his company.

DOR. Well, my dear, I'll leave you to your rest; you'll go directly to bed, I suppose?

MRS. SUL. I don't know what to do. Heigh-ho!

DOR. That's a desiring sigh, Sister.

MRS. SUL. This is a languishing hour, Sister.

DOR. And might prove a critical minute, if the pretty fellow were here.

MRS. SUL. Here! What, in my bedchamber at two o'clock o' th' morning, I undressed, the family asleep, my hated husband abroad, and my lovely fellow at my feet!——O 'gad, Sister!

DOR. Thoughts are free, Sister, and them I allow you. So, my dear, good night.

MRS. SUL. A good rest to my dear Dorinda!—(*Exit* DORINDA.) Thoughts free! are they so? Why, then suppose him here, dressed like a youthful, gay, and burning bridegroom, (*here* ARCHER *steals out of the closet*) with tongue enchanting, eyes bewitching, knees imploring.—(*turns a little o' one side and sees* ARCHER *in the posture she describes*)—Ah!—(*shrieks, and runs to the other side of the stage*) Have my thoughts raised a spirit?—— What are you, Sir, a man or a devil?

ARCH. (*rising*) A man, a man, Madam.

MRS. SUL. How shall I be sure of it?

ARCH. Madam, I'll give you demonstration this minute.

(*takes her hand*)

MRS. SUL. What, Sir! do you intend to be rude?

ARCH. Yes, Madam, if you please.

MRS. SUL. In the name of wonder, whence came ye?

ARCH. From the skies, Madam—I'm a Jupiter in love, and you shall be my Alcmena.

MRS. SUL. How came you in?

ARCH. I flew in at the window, Madam; your cousin Cupid lent me his wings, and your sister Venus opened the casement.

MRS. SUL. I'm struck dumb with admiration!

ARCH. And I—with wonder!   (*looks passionately at her*)

MRS. SUL. What will become of me?

ARCH. How beautiful she looks! The teeming, jolly spring smiles in her blooming face, and when she was conceived, her mother smelt to roses, looked on lilies—

> Lilies unfold their white, their fragrant charms,
> When the warm sun thus darts into their arms.

(*runs to her*)

MRS. SUL. (*shrieks*) Ah!

ARCH. 'Oons, Madam, what d'ye mean? you'll raise the house.

MRS. SUL. Sir, I'll wake the dead before I bear this! What! approach me with the freedoms of a keeper! I'm glad on't, your impudence has cured me.

ARCH. If this be impudence—(*kneels*) I leave to your partial self; no panting pilgrim, after a tedious, painful voyage, e'er bowed before his saint with more devotion.

MRS. SUL. (*aside*) Now, now, I'm ruined if he kneels!——

Rise, thou prostrate engineer, not all thy undermining skill shall
reach my heart. Rise, and know I am a woman without my sex;
I can love to all the tenderness of wishes, sighs, and tears—but
go no farther. Still, to convince you that I'm more than woman,
I can speak my frailty, confess my weakness even for you—
but——

ARCH. (*going to lay hold on her*) For me!

MRS. SUL. Hold, Sir! build not upon that; for my most mortal
hatred follows if you disobey what I command you now. Leave
me this minute.—(*aside*) If he denies, I'm lost.

ARCH. Then you'll promise——

MRS. SUL. Anything another time.

ARCH. When shall I come?

MRS. SUL. To-morrow when you will.

ARCH. Your lips must seal the promise.

MRS. SUL. Pshaw!

ARCH. They must! they must!—(*kisses her*) Raptures and
paradise!——And why not now, my angel? the time, the place,
silence, and secrecy, all conspire. And the now conscious stars
have preordained this moment for my happiness.

(*takes her in his arms*)

MRS. SUL. You will not, cannot, sure!

ARCH. If the sun rides fast, and disappoints not mortals of to-
morrow's dawn, this night shall crown my joys.

MRS. SUL. My sex's pride assist me!

ARCH. My sex's strength help me!

MRS. SUL. You shall kill me first!

ARCH. I'll die with you.   (*carrying her off*)

MRS. SUL. Thieves! thieves! murther!——

Enter SCRUB *in his breeches, and one shoe*

SCRUB. Thieves! thieves! murther! popery!

ARCH. Ha! the very timorous stag will kill in rutting time.

(*draws, and offers to stab* SCRUB)

SCRUB. (*kneeling*) Oh pray, Sir, spare all I have, and take my
life!

MRS. SUL. (*holding* ARCHER's *hand*) What does the fellow
mean?

SCRUB. O Madam, down upon your knees, your marrow-bones!
He's one of 'um.

ARCH. Of whom?

SCRUB. One of the rogues—— I beg your pardon, Sir, one of the honest gentlemen that just now are broke into the house.

ARCH. How!

MRS. SUL. I hope you did not come to rob me?

ARCH. Indeed I did, Madam, but I would have taken nothing but what you might ha' spared; but your crying "Thieves" has waked this dreaming fool, and so he takes 'em for granted.

SCRUB. Granted! 'tis granted, Sir; take all we have.

MRS. SUL. The fellow looks as if he were broke out of Bedlam.

SCRUB. 'Oons, Madam, they're broke into the house with fire and sword; I saw them, heard them; they'll be here this minute.

ARCH. What, thieves?

SCRUB. Under favour, Sir, I think so.

MRS. SUL. What shall we do, Sir?

ARCH. Madam, I wish your Ladyship a good night.

MRS. SUL. Will you leave me?

ARCH. Leave you! Lord, Madam, did not you command me to be gone just now, upon pain of your immortal hatred?

MRS. SUL. Nay, but pray, Sir——   (takes hold of him)

ARCH. Ha, ha, ha! now comes my turn to be ravished. You see now, Madam, you must use men one way or other; but take this by the way, good Madam, that none but a fool will give you the benefit of his courage, unless you'll take his love along with it. —— How are they armed, friend?

SCRUB. With sword and pistol, Sir.

ARCH. Hush!—I see a dark lanthorn coming through the gallery.—— Madam, be assured I will protect you, or lose my life.

MRS. SUL. Your life! No, Sir, they can rob me of nothing that I value half so much; therefore, now, Sir, let me intreat you to be gone.

ARCH. No, Madam, I'll consult my own safety for the sake of yours; I'll work by stratagem. Have you courage enough to stand the appearance of 'em?

MRS. SUL. Yes, yes, since I have 'scaped your hands, I can face anything.

ARCH. Come hither, Brother Scrub! don't you know me?

SCRUB. Eh! my dear Brother, let me kiss thee.

                                                 (kisses ARCHER)

ARCH. This way—here——

> (ARCHER *and* SCRUB *hide behind the bed.*)

Enter GIBBET, *with a dark lanthorn in one hand, and*
a pistol in t'other

GIB. Ay, ay, this is the chamber, and the lady alone.

MRS. SUL. Who are you, Sir? what would you have? d'ye come
to rob me?

GIB. Rob you! Alack-a-day, Madam, I'm only a younger
brother, Madam; and so, Madam, if you make a noise, I'll shoot
you through the head; but don't be afraid, Madam.—(*laying his*
lanthorn and pistol upon the table) These rings, Madam—don't
be concerned, Madam, I have a profound respect for you,
Madam; your keys, Madam—don't be frighted, Madam, I'm the
most of a gentleman.—(*searching her pockets*) This necklace,
Madam—I never was rude to a lady;—I have a veneration—for
this necklace——

> (*Here* ARCHER, *having come round and seized the*
> *pistol, takes* GIBBET *by the collar, trips up his heels,*
> *and claps the pistol to his breast.*)

ARCH. Hold, profane villain, and take the reward of thy sacrilege!

GIB. Oh! pray, Sir, don't kill me; I an't prepared.

ARCH. How many is there of 'em, Scrub?

SCRUB. Five-and-forty, Sir.

ARCH. Then I must kill the villain, to have him out of the way.

GIB. Hold, hold, Sir, we are but three, upon my honour.

ARCH. Scrub, will you undertake to secure him?

SCRUB. Not I, Sir; kill him, kill him!

ARCH. Run to Gipsey's chamber, there you'll find the doctor; bring him hither presently.—(*Exit* SCRUB, *running.*) Come,
rogue, if you have a short prayer, say it.

GIB. Sir, I have no prayer at all; the government has provided
a chaplain to say prayers for us on these occasions.

MRS. SUL. Pray, Sir, don't kill him. You fright me as much as
him.

ARCH. The dog shall die, Madam, for being the occasion of my
disappointment.—— Sirrah, this moment is your last.

GIB. Sir, I'll give you two hundred pound to spare my life.

ARCH. Have you no more, rascal?

GIB. Yes, Sir, I can command four hundred, but I must reserve two of 'em to save my life at the sessions.

Enter SCRUB *and* FOIGARD

ARCH. Here, Doctor, I suppose Scrub and you between you may manage him. Lay hold of him, Doctor.

(FOIGARD *lays hold of* GIBBET.)

GIB. What! turned over to the priest already!—— Look ye, Doctor, you come before your time; I an't condemned yet, I thank ye.

FOI. Come, my dear joy, I vill secure your body and your shoul too; I vill make you a good Catholic, and give you an absolution.

GIB. Absolution! can vou procure me a pardon, Doctor?

FOI. No, joy

GIB. Then you and your absolution may go to the devil!

ARCH. Convey him into the cellar; there bind him. Take the pistol, and if he offers to resist, shoot him through the head— and come back to us with all the speed you can.

SCRUB. Ay, ay; come, Doctor, do you hold him fast, and I'll guard him.   (*Exit* FOIGARD *and* SCRUB *with* GIBBET.)

MRS. SUL. But how came the doctor——

ARCH. In short, Madam—(*shrieking without*) 'Sdeath! the rogues are at work with the other ladies. I'm vexed I parted with the pistol; but I must fly to their assistance. Will you stay here, Madam, or venture yourself with me?

MRS SUL. Oh, with you, dear Sir, with you.

(*Takes him by the arm and exeunt.*)

SCENE III

Scene changes to another apartment in the same house

Enter HOUNSLOW *dragging in* LADY BOUNTIFUL, *and* BAGSHOT *hauling in* DORINDA; *the rogues with swords drawn*

BAG. Come, come, your jewels, Mistress!

HOUN. Your keys, your keys, old gentlewoman!

Enter AIMWELL *and* CHERRY

AIM. Turn this way, villains! I durst engage an army in such a cause.   (*He engages 'em both.*)

DOR. O Madam, had I but a sword to help the brave man!

LADY BOUN. There's three or four hanging up in the hall; but they won't draw. I'll go fetch one, however.   (*Exit.*)

Enter ARCHER *and* MRS. SULLEN

ARCH. Hold, hold, my Lord! every man his bird, pray.
          (*They engage man to man; the rogues are thrown and disarmed.*)

CHER. What! the rogues taken! then they'll impeach my father; I must give him timely notice.   (*runs out*)

ARCH. Shall we kill the rogues?

AIM. No, no, we'll bind them.

ARCH. Ay, ay.—(*To* MRS. SULLEN, *who stands by him.*) Here, Madam, lend me your garter.

MRS. SUL. (*aside*) The devil's in this fellow! he fights, loves, and banters, all in a breath.—— Here's a cord that the rogues brought with 'em, I suppose.

ARCH. Right, right, the rogue's destiny, a rope to hang himself.—— Come, my Lord.—— This is but a scandalous sort of an office (*binding the rogues together*) if our adventures should end in this sort of hangman-work; but I hope there is something in prospect that——

Enter SCRUB

Well, Scrub, have you secured your Tartar?

SCRUB. Yes, Sir; I left the priest and him disputing about religion.

AIM. And pray carry these gentlemen to reap the benefit of the controversy.
          (*delivers the prisoners to* SCRUB, *who leads 'em out*)

MRS. SUL. Pray, Sister, how came my lord here?

DOR. And pray, how came the gentleman here?

MRS. SUL. I'll tell you the greatest piece of villainy—
                              (*They talk in dumb show.*)

AIM. I fancy, Archer, you have been more successful in your adventures than the housebreakers.

ARCH. No matter for my adventure, yours is the principal. Press her this minute to marry you—now while she's hurried between the palpitation of her fear and the joy of her deliverance, now while the tide of her spirits are at high-flood. Throw yourself at her feet, speak some romantic nonsense or other—address her like Alexander in the height of his victory, confound her senses, bear down her reason, and away with her. The priest is now in the cellar and dare not refuse to do the work.

Enter LADY BOUNTIFUL

AIM. But how shall I get off without being observed?

ARCH. You a lover, and not find a way to get off!—Let me see——

AIM. You bleed, Archer.

ARCH. 'Sdeath, I'm glad on't; this wound will do the business. I'll amuse the old lady and Mrs. Sullen about dressing my wound, while you carry off Dorinda.

LADY BOUN. Gentlemen, could we understand how you would be gratified for the services——

ARCH. Come, come, my Lady, this is no time for compliments; I'm wounded, Madam.

LADY BOUN., MRS. SUL. How! wounded!

DOR. I hope, Sir, you have received no hurt?

AIM. None but what you may cure——

(*makes love in dumb show*)

LADY BOUN. Let me see your arm, Sir.—I must have some powder-sugar to stop the blood.—O me! an ugly gash, upon my word, Sir! You must go into bed.

ARCH. Ay, my Lady, a bed would do very well.—(*To* MRS. SULLEN.) Madam, will you do me the favour to conduct me to a chamber.

LADY BOUN. Do, do, Daughter—while I get the lint and the probe and the plaster ready.

(*Runs out one way;* AIMWELL *carries off* DORINDA *another.*)

ARCH. Come, Madam, why don't you obey your mother's commands?

MRS. SUL. How can you, after what is passed, have the confidence to ask me?

ARCH. And if you go to that, how can you, after what is passed, have the confidence to deny me? Was not this blood shed in your defence, and my life exposed for your protection? Look ye, Madam, I'm none of your romantic fools, that fight giants and monsters for nothing; my valour is downright Swiss; I'm a soldier of fortune, and must be paid.

MRS. SUL. 'Tis ungenerous in you, Sir, to upbraid me with your services!

ARCH. 'Tis ungenerous in you, Madam, not to reward 'em.

MRS. SUL. How! at the expense of my honour?

ARCH. Honour! can honour consist with ingratitude? If you would deal like a woman of honour, do like a man of honour. D'ye think I would deny you in such a case?

Enter a Servant

SERV. Madam, my lady ordered me to tell you that your brother is below at the gate.   (*Exit.*)

MRS. SUL. My brother! Heavens be praised!—— Sir, he shall thank you for your services; he has it in his power.

ARCH. Who is your brother, Madam?

MRS. SUL. Sir Charles Freeman. You'll excuse me, Sir; I must go and receive him.   (*Exit.*)

ARCH. Sir Charles Freeman! 'Sdeath and hell! my old acquaintance. Now unless Aimwell has made good use of his time, all our fair machine goes souse into the sea like the Eddystone. (*Exit.*)

SCENE IV

Scene changes to the gallery in the same house

Enter AIMWELL *and* DORINDA

DOR. Well, well, my Lord, you have conquered; your late generous action will, I hope, plead for my easy yielding; though I must own your Lordship had a friend in the fort before.

AIM. The sweets of Hybla dwell upon her tongue!—— Here, Doctor——

Enter FOIGARD, *with a book*

FOI. Are you prepared, boat?

DOR. I'm ready. But first, my Lord, one word. I have a frightful example of a hasty marriage in my own family; when I reflect upon't, it shocks me. Pray, my Lord, consider a little——

AIM. Consider! Do you doubt my honour or my love?

DOR. Neither. I do believe you equally just as brave;, and were your whole sex drawn out for me to choose, I should not cast a look upon the multitude if you were absent. But, my Lord, I'm a woman; colours, concealments may hide a thousand faults in me—therefore know me better first. I hardly dare affirm I know myself in anything except my love.

AIM. (*aside*) Such goodness who could injure! I find myself unequal to the task of villain; she has gained my soul, and made it honest like her own. I cannot, cannot hurt her.—— Doctor, retire.—(*Exit* FOIGARD.) Madam, behold your lover and your proselyte, and judge of my passion by my conversion! I'm all a lie, nor dare I give a fiction to your arms; I'm all counterfeit, except my passion.

DOR. Forbid it, heaven! a counterfeit!

AIM. I am no lord, but a poor needy man, come with a mean, a scandalous design to prey upon your fortune. But the beauties of your mind and person have so won me from myself that, like a trusty servant, I prefer the interest of my mistress to my own.

DOR. Sure I have had the dream of some poor mariner, a sleepy image of a welcome port, and wake involved in storms! Pray, Sir, who are you?

AIM. Brother to the man whose title I usurped, but stranger to his honour or his fortune.

DOR. Matchless honesty! Once I was proud, Sir, of your wealth and title, but now am prouder that you want it; now I can show my love was justly levelled, and had no aim but love.—— Doctor, come in.

Enter FOIGARD *at one door,* GIPSEY *at another,*
who whispers DORINDA

——Your pardon, Sir, we sha'not want you now.—— Sir, you must excuse me. I'll wait on you presently. (*Exit with* GIPSEY.)

FOI. Upon my shoul, now, dis is foolish. (*Exit.*)

AIM. Gone! and bid the priest depart!—It has an ominous look.

Enter ARCHER

ARCH. Courage, Tom! Shall I wish you joy?

AIM. No.

ARCH. 'Oons, man, what ha' you been doing?

AIM. O Archer! my honesty, I fear, has ruined me.

ARCH. How?

AIM. I have discovered myself.

ARCH. Discovered! and without my consent? What! have I embarked my small remains in the same bottom with yours, and you dispose of all without my partnership?

AIM. O Archer! I own my fault.

ARCH. After conviction—'tis then too late for pardon. You may remember, Mr. Aimwell, that you proposed this folly. As you begun, so end it. Henceforth I'll hunt my fortune single. So, farewell!

AIM. Stay, my dear Archer, but a minute.

ARCH. Stay! what, to be despised, exposed, and laughed at? No, I would sooner change conditions with the worst of the rogues we just now bound than bear one scornful smile from the proud knight that once I treated as my equal.

AIM. What knight?

ARCH. Sir Charles Freeman, brother to the lady that I had almost—but no matter for that; 'tis a cursed night's work, and so I leave you to make your best on't.   (*going*)

AIM. Freeman!—One word, Archer. Still I have hopes; methought she received my confession with pleasure.

ARCH. 'Sdeath! who doubts it?

AIM. She consented after to the match; and still I dare believe she will be just.

ARCH. To herself, I warrant her, as you should have been.

AIM. By all my hopes, she comes, and smiling comes!

Enter DORINDA, *mighty gay*

DOR. Come, my dear Lord—I fly with impatience to your arms. The minutes of my absence was a tedious year. Where's this tedious priest?

Enter FOIGARD

ARCH. 'Oons, a brave girl!

DOR. I suppose, my Lord, this gentleman is privy to our affairs?

ARCH. Yes, yes, Madam, I'm to be your father.

DOR. Come, priest, do your offic,

ARCH. Make haste, make haste, couple 'em any way.—(*takes*
AIMWELL's *hand*) Come, Madam, I'm to give you——

DOR. My mind's altered; I won't.

ARCH. Eh!——

AIM. I'm confounded!

FOI. Upon my shoul, and sho is myshelf.

ARCH. What's the matter now, Madam?

DOR. Look ye, Sir, one generous action deserves another. This
gentleman's honour obliged him to hide nothing from me; my
justice engages me to conceal nothing from him. In short, Sir, you
are the person that you thought you counterfeited; you are the
true Lord Viscount Aimwell, and I wish your Lordship joy.——
Now, priest, you may be gone; if my Lord is pleased now with
the match, let his Lordship marry me in the face of the world.

AIM., ARCH. What does she mean?

DOR. Here's a witness for my truth.

Enter SIR CHARLES FREEMAN *and* MRS. SULLEN

SIR CHAS. My dear Lord Aimwell, I wish you joy.

AIM. Of what?

SIR CHAS. Of your honour and estate. Your brother died the day
before I left London; and all your friends have writ after you
to Brussels; among the rest I did myself the honour.

ARCH. Hark ye, Sir Knight, don't you banter now?

SIR CHAS. 'Tis truth, upon my honour.

AIM. Thanks to the pregnant stars that formed this accident!

ARCH. Thanks to the womb of time that brought it forth!—
away with it!

AIM. Thanks to my guardian angel that led me to the prize!
                                        (*taking* DORINDA's *hand*)

ARCH. And double thanks to the noble Sir Charles Freeman.
—— My Lord, I wish you joy.—— My Lady, I wish you joy.
—— Igad, Sir Freeman, you're the honestest fellow living!——
'Sdeath, I'm grown strange airy upon this matter!—— My Lord,
how d'ye? A word, my Lord; don't you remember something of a
previous agreement, that entitles me to the moiety of this lady's
fortune, which, I think, will amount to five thousand pound?

AIM. Not a penny, Archer; you would ha' cut my throat just
now, because I would not deceive this lady.

ARCH. Ay, and I'll cut your throat again, if you should deceive her now.

AIM. That's what I expected; and to end the dispute, the lady's fortune is ten thousand pound; we'll divide stakes: take the ten thousand pound or the lady.

DOR. How! is your Lordship so indifferent?

ARCH. No, no, no, Madam; his Lordship knows very well that I'll take the money; I leave you to his Lordship, and so we're both provided for.

Enter COUNT BELLAIR

COUNT BEL. *Mesdames et messieurs,* I am your servant trice humble! I hear you be rob here.

AIM. The ladies have been in some danger, Sir.

COUNT BEL. And, begar, our inn be rob too!

AIM. Our inn! by whom?

COUNT BEL. By the landlord, begar! Garzoon, he has rob himself and run away!

ARCH. Robbed himself!

COUNT BEL. Ay, begar, and me too of a hundre pound.

ARCH. A hundred pound?

COUNT. BEL. Yes, that I owed him.

AIM. Our money's gone, Frank.

ARCH. Rot the money! my wench is gone.—*Savez-vous quelque chose de Mademoiselle Cherry?*

Enter a Fellow with a strong-box and a letter

FELL. Is there one Martin here?

ARCH. Ay, ay—who wants him?

FELL. I have a box here and letter for him.

ARCH. (*taking the box*) Ha, ha, ha! what's here? Legerder-main!—— By this light, my Lord, our money again!—But this unfolds the riddle.—(*opening the letter, reads*) Hum, hum, hum!—Oh, 'tis for the public good, and must be communicated to the company.

MR. MARTIN,

My father being afraid of an impeachment by the rogues that are taken to-night, is gone off; but if you can procure him

a pardon, he will make great discoveries that may be useful
to the country. Could I have met you instead of your master
to-night, I would have delivered myself into your hands, with
a sum that much exceeds that in your strong-box, which I
have sent you, with an assurance to my dear Martin that I
shall ever be his most faithful friend till death.

CHERRY BONNIFACE.

There's a billet-doux for you! As for the father, I think he ought
to be encouraged; and for the daughter—pray, my Lord, persuade your bride to take her into her service instead of Gipsey.

AIM. I can assure you, Madam, your deliverance was owing
to her discovery.

DOR. Your command, my Lord, will do without the obligation.
I'll take care of her.

SIR CHAS. This good company meets opportunely in favour of
a design I have in behalf of my unfortunate sister. I intend to
part her from her husband. Gentlemen, will you assist me?

ARCH. Assist you! 'Sdeath, who would not?

COUNT BEL. Assist! Garzoon, we all assest!

Enter SULLEN

SUL. What's all this?—— They tell me, spouse, that you had
like to have been robbed.

MRS. SUL. Truly, spouse, I was pretty near it—had not these
two gentlemen interposed.

SUL. How came these gentlemen here?

MRS. SUL. That's his way of returning thanks, you must know.

COUNT BEL. Garzoon, the question be apropos for all dat.

SIR CHAS. You promised last night, Sir, that you would deliver
your lady to me this morning.

SUL. Humph!

ARCH. Humph! what do you mean by humph? Sir, you shall
deliver her! In short, Sir, we have saved you and your family;
and if you are not civil, we'll unbind the rogues, join with 'um,
and set fire to your house.—— What does the man mean? not
part with his wife!

COUNT BEL. Ay, garzoon, de man no understan common justice.

MRS. SUL. Hold, gentlemen, all things here must move by

consent; compulsion would spoil us. Let my dear and I talk the matter over, and you shall judge it between us.

SUL. Let me know first who are to be our judges.—— Pray, Sir, who are you?

SIR CHAS. I am Sir Charles Freeman, come to take away your wife.

SUL. And you, good Sir?

AIM. Thomas, Viscount Aimwell, come to take away your sister.

SUL. And you, pray, Sir?

ARCH. Francis Archer, esquire, come——

SUL. To take away my mother, I hope.—— Gentlemen, you're heartily welcome; I never met with three more obliging people since I was born!—— And now, my dear, if you please, you shall have the first word.

ARCH. And the last, for five pound!

MRS. SUL. Spouse!

SUL. Rib!

MRS. SUL. How long have we been married?

SUL. By the almanac, fourteen months—but by my account, fourteen years.

MRS. SUL. 'Tis thereabout by my reckoning.

COUNT BEL. Garzoon, their account will agree.

MRS. SUL. Pray, spouse, what did you marry for?

SUL. To get an heir to my estate.

SIR CHAS. And have you succeeded?

SUL. No.

ARCH. The condition fails of his side.—— Pray, Madam, what did you marry for?

MRS. SUL. To support the weakness of my sex by the strength of his, and to enjoy the pleasures of an agreeable society.

SIR CHAS. Are your expectations answered?

MRS. SUL. No.

COUNT BEL. A clear case! a clear case!

SIR CHAS. What are the bars to your mutual contentment?

MRS. SUL. In the first place, I can't drink ale with him.

SUL. Nor can I drink tea with her.

MRS. SUL. I can't hunt with you.

SUL. Nor can I dance with you.

MRS. SUL. I hate cocking and racing.

SUL. And I abhor ombre and piquet.

MRS. SUL. Your silence is intolerable.

SUL. Your prating is worse.

MRS. SUL. Have we not been a perpetual offence to each other? a gnawing vulture at the heart?

SUL. A frightful goblin to the sight?

MRS. SUL. A porcupine to the feeling?

SUL. Perpetual wormwood to the taste?

MRS. SUL. Is there on earth a thing we could agree in?

SUL. Yes—to part.

MRS. SUL. With all my heart.

SUL. Your hand.

MRS. SUL. Here.

SUL. These hands joined us, these shall part us. Away!

MRS. SUL. North.

SUL. South.

MRS. SUL. East.

SUL. West—far as the poles asunder.

COUNT BEL. Begar, the ceremony be vera pretty!

SIR CHAS. Now, Mr. Sullen, there wants only my sister's fortune to make us easy.

SUL. Sir Charles, you love your sister, and I love her fortune; every one to his fancy.

ARCH. Then you won't refund——

SUL. Not a stiver.

ARCH. Then I find, Madam, you must e'en go to your prison again.

COUNT BEL. What is the portion?

SIR CHAS. Ten thousand pound, Sir.

COUNT BEL. Garzoon, I'll pay it, and she shall go home wid me

ARCH. Ha, ha, ha! French all over.—— Do you know, Sir what ten thousand pound English is?

COUNT BEL. No, begar, not *justement*.

ARCH. Why, Sir, 'tis a hundred thousand livres.

COUNT BEL. A hundre tousand livres! Ah, garzoon! me canno do't; your beauties and their fortunes are both too much for me

ARCH. Then I will. This night's adventure has proved strangely lucky to us all—for Captain Gibbet in his walk had made bold, Mr. Sullen, with your study and escritoire, and had taken out all the writings of your estate, all the articles of marriage with his lady, bills, bonds, leases, receipts to an infinite value. I took 'em from him, and I deliver them to Sir Charles.

(*gives him a parcel of papers and parchments*)

SUL. How, my writings!—my head aches consumedly.—— Well, gentlemen, you shall have her fortune, but I can't talk. If you have a mind, Sir Charles, to be merry, and celebrate my sister's wedding and my divorce, you may command my house— but my head aches consumedly.—— Scrub, bring me a dram.

ARCH. (*to* MRS. SULLEN) Madam, there's a country-dance to the trifle that I sung to-day; your hand, and we'll lead it up.

(*here a dance*)

ARCH. 'Twould be hard to guess which of these parties is the better pleased, the couple joined or the couple parted; the one rejoicing in hopes of an untasted happiness, and the other in their deliverance from an experienced misery.

Both happy in their several states we find,
Those parted by consent, and those conjoin'd.
Consent, if mutual, saves the lawyer's fee,
Consent is law enough to set you free.

AN EPILOGUE

Designed to be Spoke in THE BEAUX' STRATAGEM

If to our play your judgment can't be kind,
Let its expiring author pity find.
Survey his mournful case with melting eyes,
Nor let the bard be damn'd before he dies.
Forbear, you fair, on his last scene to frown,
But his true exit with a plaudit crown;
Then shall the dying poet cease to fear
The dreadful knell, while your applause he hears.
At Leuctra so the conqu'ring Theban dy'd,
Claim'd his friends' praises, but their tears deny'd:
Pleas'd in the pangs of death he greatly thought
Conquest with loss of life but cheaply bought.

The difference this, the Greek was one would fight, ⎫
As brave, though not so gay, as Sergeant Kite; ⎬
Ye sons of Will's, what's that to those who write? ⎭
To Thebes alone the Grecian ow'd his bays, ⎫
You may the bard above the hero raise, ⎬
Since yours is greater than Athenian praise. ⎭

The Best of the World's Best Books
COMPLETE LIST OF TITLES IN
THE MODERN LIBRARY

A series of handsome, cloth-bound books, formerly available only in expensive editions.

MODERN LIBRARY

MISCELLANEOUS